DK

TOP 10 WORLD

Colosseum, Rome, Italy

Craft Museum, Delhi, India

Isla Mujeres, the Yucatán, Mexico

Long-tail boat on a *khlong* (canal), Bangkok, Thailand

LONDON, NEW YORK,
MELBOURNE, MUNICH AND DELHI
www.dk.com

Produced by Coppermill Books
55 Salop Road London E17 7HS

Printed in China by South China
Printing Co. Ltd., China

First published in Great Britain in 2012
by Dorling Kindersley Limited
80 Strand, London WC2R 0RL
A Penguin Company

Also available in eBook formats.

Based on content previously published across our Eyewitness Top 10 and Eyewitness Travel Guide titles.

A CIP catalogue record is available from the British Library.

ISBN 978 1 40938 249 2

Within each Top 10 list in this book, no hierarchy of quality or popularity is implied. All 10 are, in the editor's opinion, of roughly equal merit.

Contents

Europe's Top 10

The information in this DK Eyewitness Top 10 Travel Guide is checked regularly.

Every effort has been made to ensure that this book is as up-to-date as possible at the time of going to press. Some details, however, such as telephone numbers and websites are liable to change. The publishers cannot accept responsibility for any consequences arising from the use of this book, nor for any material on third-party websites, and cannot guarantee that any website address in this book will be a suitable source of travel information. We value the views and suggestions of our readers very highly.

Please write to:
Publisher, DK Eyewitness Travel Guides,
Dorling Kindersley, 80 Strand, London WC2R 0RL.

Sydney Opera House, Australia

Stained glass, Santa Maria del Popolo, Rome

The Venetian and The Mirage, Las Vegas, USA

Beach at Piha, North Island, New Zealand

The Americas' Top 10

Asia's Top 10

The Rest of the World's Top 10

Ticino, Lake Maggiore, Switzerland

Copacabana Beach, Rio de Janeiro, Brazil

Nine Dragon Screen, Beijing Beihai Park, China

Tomb of Senneferi, Luxor, Egypt

Switzerland
The town of Ascona, on Lake Maggiore

ALBERGO CASTELLO HOTEL

Algarve

The Moors called their al-Gharb the Sunset Land, and visitors have been waxing lyrical ever since. Blessed with a mild winter climate and a sunny disposition, Portugal's playground province remains one of the most popular year-round holiday destinations in southern Europe. Lively coastal resorts spill over ribbons of golden sand in sharp contrast to the quiet villages of the hinterland, where history and tradition go hand in hand.

1 Monchique

The Serra da Monchique *(above)* rises 458 m (1,500 ft), enveloping the hillside town of Monchique and its neighbouring spa centre.

3 Faro

The biggest city in southern Portugal, Faro *(left)* is the capital of the Algarve and an important centre of tourism, trade and commerce. Its historic quarter overlooks a pretty marina and the Ria Formosa.

4 Tavira

Nearly 40 churches endow this elegant riverside town with a romantic and disarmingly timeless air. The Gilão river glides effortlessly through the centre – a Roman bridge connects the two sides of one of the prettiest towns in the Algarve.

Silves 2

Once the grandiose capital of the Moorish province of al-Gharb, Silves today is dominated by the ochre ramparts of its huge castle *(right)*. Lush orange groves blanket the countryside around the town.

TOP 10 Moments in History

1 3000 BC: Early Peoples and Trade
Stone burial chambers (dolmens) and *menhirs* are characteristic of this period. By 1000 BC, the Phoenicians had established sizeable trading stations. The Greeks also came, but their trade links were severed by the Carthaginians, who blockaded the Straits of Gibraltar and in 550 BC founded the city of Portus Hannibalis (Portimão).

2 218–202 BC: Second Punic War
The Romans defeated the Carthaginians, then swept through the Iberian peninsula. Over the next 400 years, grand Roman cities sprang up.

3 AD 415: Visigoths
After the fall of the Roman Empire, power was seized by the Visigoths, a formidable warrior caste from eastern France and Germany.

4 711: The Moors
Internal strife and persecution among the Visigoths ultimately led to one faction appealing for aid from Muslim North Africa. An enormous army of Berbers and Arabs conquered huge swathes of the Iberian peninsula. The Moors would dominate the Algarve for well over 500 years, giving the region its name, al-Gharb, and transforming Silves into an intellectual hub of staggering opulence.

5 Christian Crusades
Christians reconquered central Portugal in the 12th century, but the Algarve was still firmly under Moorish rule. Dom Sancho (1185–1211) briefly took Silves in 1189, but the city was recaptured by Yaqub Al-Mansur in 1191. Dom Sancho II (1223–48) later launched a campaign to invade southern Portugal with the help of northern European Crusaders.

6 Birth of a Nation
Faro was the last Moorish stronghold to fall, in 1249. Portuguese sovereignty over the Algarve was confirmed in a treaty with the kingdom of Castile in 1297.

7 Era of the Great Discoveries
Henry "the Navigator" was made governor of the Algarve in 1418 and initiated voyages that led to the discovery of Madeira, the Azores and Cape Verde, as well as the mapping of much of the west coast of Africa. In 1488 Bartolomeu Dias rounded the Cape of Good Hope, and in 1498 Vasco da Gama opened the trade route to India.

8 Artistic Extravagance
The discovery of gold and diamonds in Brazil during the reign of Pedro II (1683–1706) financed a period of great artistic extravagance under João V, who ruled until 1750.

9 Great Earthquake of 1755
An earthquake devastated Lisbon and much of southern Portugal, plunging the nation into crisis. Napoleon's troops invaded in 1807.

10 Republicanism and Integration with Europe
The late 19th century witnessed political strife, with Republicanism taking root. António de Oliveira Salazar became prime minister in 1932, turning round a stagnating economy at the expense of democracy. In 1974 a near-bloodless military coup overthrew the government. In 2002 Portugal adopted the euro.

5 Parque Natural da Ria Formosa

One of the most important wetland zones in Europe, the park's expansive lagoon *(above)*, sand dunes and marshland are a sanctuary for a wealth of wildlife.

Lagos 6

A young, vibrant and carefree spirit imbues this resort. The nearby beaches, pocked with outcrops of sandstone rock, are spectacular *(right)*.

7 Sagres

The supposed location of Henry the Navigator's lauded school of navigation, Sagres sits on an isolated promontory pounded by the Atlantic. Dramatic views along the coast include the Cabo de São Vicente.

8 Loulé

Loulé hosts a colourful weekly market *(above)* and is a thriving centre for local handicrafts. It is also the gateway to the central hinterland and the Caldeirão mountain range.

9 Vila Real and Castro Marim

These two frontier towns are within earshot of each other but have little in common. Sedate Castro Marim glories in its twin castles, while Vila Real de Santo António *(above)* enjoys a livelier culture.

10 Albufeira

This top holiday spot is the Algarve's largest resort, boasting some of the most effervescent nightlife in Portugal. Generous beaches *(above)* flank bustling esplanades brimming with cafés and trendy clubs.

TOP 10 Inland Villages

1 Alte
The town's pretty cobbled streets, full of white houses with bright window frames, give it a special charm. Alte's church is situated near a leafy square, and the spring that flows along its flank tumbles under an old mill, making a perfect picnic spot.

2 Caldas de Monchique
The warm spa waters here have brought visitors since at least Roman times. Pine and eucalyptus woods offer a lush, cooling canopy in the heat of the summer.

3 Alcoutim
The town's 14th-century castle keeps a timeworn eye on its old adversary, Sanlúcar, on the Spanish side of the Guadiana river. The peace here is interrupted only by the chiming of the hour and the rattle of stork bills as they chatter from church towers and chimney stacks.

4 Estói
The Palácio do Visconde de Estói is a 19th-century palace (now a beautiful *pousada*), with gardens fanned by giant palms and cooled by fountains. A 20-minute walk leads to the Roman complex of Milreu.

5 Salir
The walls of Salir's Moorish castle are eerily lit up at night, but the views from it are more benign, stretching seaward across the valley.

6 Paderne
This little village, clustered around its church, is today a sleepy place of faded charm and modest means, but its architecture retains a certain grandeur, and a Moorish castle stands close by.

7 Querença
Each January Querença hosts its *festa das chouriças* (sausage festival). For the rest of the year it is comparatively quiet – an isolated but attractive settlement surrounded by the Caldeirão mountain range.

8 Guerreiros do Rio
The road that leads south here from Alcoutim follows the Guadiana river part of the way, passing through a landscape lush with olive, fig and carob trees. The former schoolhouse houses a modest museum tracing the history of the river.

9 Martin Longo
The storks that nest in the belfry of the parish church are as appealing as their home is unusual. Also worth a look is "A Flor da Agulha", where traditional, hand-crafted jute dolls depicting country characters are made.

10 Barão de São João
Set in classic hill-walking country and pleasantly lost in time, Barão de São João is best visited during its antiques fair, on the last Sunday of every month.

Amsterdam

Amsterdam has an appeal that is absolutely unique. It's a vibrant place, a treasure-trove of extraordinary artistic riches, and the living embodiment of 900 years of history, during which it rose to become the centre of a huge global empire. After a period of decline, it matured into today's relaxed and tolerant modern metropolis. Elegant and serene, Amsterdam also has its seamy side, and this too is part of its character, as much as its famous network of canals. Whatever you are looking for, this small city packs a big punch.

Groningen
North Sea
AMSTERDAM
Den Haag
NETHERLANDS
Rotterdam
GERMANY
Eindhoven
BELGIUM

1 Begijnhof
A haven of peace, the Begijnhof *(left)* was built as a refuge for the Beguines, a lay Catholic sisterhood. Amsterdam's oldest house is here.

2 Amsterdam Museum
Housed in the old city orphanage, this vibrant collection traces the history of Amsterdam from the 12th century.

3 Van Gogh Museum
The Van Gogh Museum houses the most comprehensive collection of the artist's work to be seen anywhere in the world – including some of his most famous paintings *(right)*. The collection also features works by other 19th-century artists, such as his friend Paul Gauguin.

Top 10 Moments in History

1 c.1125: First Settlers
Fishermen settled at the mouth of the Amstel river, building huts on man-made mounds called *terps* for flood protection.

2 1275: Freedom from Tolls
In the earliest document to refer to Amsterdam, Count Floris V of Holland granted its citizens exemption from tolls when transporting their goods by river across his territory at The Hague.

3 1345: Miracle of Amsterdam
A dying man, given the last sacraments, was unable to eat the communion wafer, so it was thrown on the fire. Next day, it was found intact in the embers. News of this miracle made Amsterdam into a place of pilgrimage.

4 1566 and 1578: Iconoclasm and Alteration
As Protestantism swept northern Europe, Dutch Calvinists rebelled against their Spanish Catholic ruler, Philip II, storming Catholic churches and destroying religious artifacts. The city finally became Protestant in a peaceful revolution – the *Alteratie* or Alteration.

5 1609: Plans for the Grachtengordel
The Golden Age, when the arts flourished in Amsterdam, introduced ambitious plans for a triple canal ring to be built around the city.

6 1634–7: Tulipmania
Tulip bulbs were introduced from Asia in the 16th century. In 1634, the tulip was quoted on the Stock Exchange, and speculation began. Fortunes were made overnight, but the inevitable crash caused scores of bankruptcies.

7 1806: Kingdom of the Netherlands
After the formation of the Batavian Republic in 1795, rule was shared between the invading French and the Dutch Patriots. In 1806, Napoleon Bonaparte took control, created the Kingdom of the Netherlands and installed his brother, Louis Napoleon, as head of state.

8 1940–45: German Occupation
Germany invaded Holland in May 1940. The deportation of Jews to concentration camps began in 1942 and the Dutch Resistance became active. Canadian troops liberated Amsterdam on 5 May 1945.

9 Mid-1960s: Provo Demonstrations
The radical counterculture Provo movement took off in the 1960s. Peaceful street demonstrations turned into full-scale rioting on 10 March 1966, the day of Princess Beatrix's wedding. Provo was disbanded in 1967.

10 2002: Wedding of the Crown Prince
On 2 February 2002, Crown Prince Willem-Alexander married Máxima Zorreguieta in the Nieuwe Kerk.

4 Rijksmuseum
The country's largest national museum houses an unrivalled collection of 17th-century Dutch art, and much besides. Star sights include Rembrandt's *Night Watch* and *The Jewish Bride (above)*.

5 Oude Kerk
This great Gothic basilica *(above)* preserves a number of its treasures, despite being stripped of its paintings and statuary during the Iconoclasm.

6 Anne Frank House
The hiding place of Anne Frank and her family, before they were discovered, arrested and sent to their deaths, is today a deeply moving museum *(below)*.

7 Museum Van Loon
Visitors to the Van Loon family residence on the Keizersgracht, lovingly restored in the style of the mid-18th century, have a rare opportunity to see behind the façade of a grand canal house – and to wander freely about it *(above)*.

8 Canals and Waterways
Amsterdam's canals, in particular the elegant ring of three 17th-century canals known as the Grachtengordel, are its defining feature *(above)*.

9 Museum Ons' Lieve Heer op Solder
Things are not always what they seem, and that is certainly true of this gem of a 17th-century house in the Red Light District; tucked away on its upper floors is a rare example of a perfectly preserved hidden Catholic church. The rest of the museum is fascinating, too – the interior has changed little since the Golden Age.

10 Dam Square
Where it all started; Amsterdam's main square *(left)* is on the site of the dam on the Amstel around which the city grew. Now it hosts concerts, events and all shades of city life.

Top 10 Canals and Waterways

1 Herengracht
Stateliest canal of the Grachtengordel, the Herengracht is famous for its Golden Bend – a grand but rather lifeless stretch of mansions built for the richest merchants. An even more beautiful stretch lies between Huidenstraat and Leidsestraat, best viewed from the east side.

2 Keizersgracht
This, the central canal of the Grachtengordel, has some particularly fine stretches between Brouwersgracht and Raadhuisstraat, and again between Runstraat and Leidsestraat.

3 Prinsengracht
The outermost canal of the Grachtengordel, designed for warehouses and artisans' housing, has a breezy, laidback air. It is peppered with cafés, art galleries and house-boats. Cycle its 3-km (2-mile) length, or explore short stretches on foot.

4 Entrepotdok
An imposing stretch of former dockland has been superbly restored to provide offices and apartments, with outdoor cafés overlooking the colourful houseboats.

5 Reguliersgracht
Much loved for its pretty houses and hump-backed bridges, Reguliersgracht was cut in 1664. Look out for Nos 57, 59 and 63.

6 Amstel River
Until the construction of the Grachtengordel, the river Amstel was the city's *raison d'être*. It is still used by barges to transport goods to the city's port.

7 Brouwersgracht
The happy-go-lucky feel of the "brewers" canal makes a pleasant contrast to the sophisticated elegance of the Grachtengordel.

8 Bloemgracht
A charming canal crossed by pretty cast-iron bridges, Bloemgracht is known as "the Herengracht of the Jordaan", because of its elaborately gabled houses.

9 Leidsegracht
This lovely – and exclusive – canal was cut in 1664, when it was the main barge route from Amsterdam to Leiden.

10 Singel
Once a fortified moat, the Singel is now home to Bloemenmarkt, the domed Ronde Lutherse Kerk and the soaring Neo-Gothic Krijtberg church.

Andalucía and the Costa del Sol

Córdoba 6
Baeza 9
9 Úbeda
Seville 3 4
ANDALUCIA
Granada 1
10 Sierra Nevada
Parque Nacional del Coto Doñana 2
Ronda 7
Cádiz 5
8 Costa del Sol
Mediterranean Sea

The diverse and politically semi-autonomous region of Andalucía has a population of some 8 million and embodies what is usually thought of as typically Spanish – an accurate portrait of the place and its people must include the bullfight, flamenco, gypsies, remote white villages, high sierras and mass tourism on endless stretches of beach. The memories you take with you after a visit here will be colourful, joyous, intense and deeply stirring.

1 Moorish Granada

Andalucía's 1,300-year-old Moorish heritage evokes pure Romanticism that is hard to equal. The delicate art and architecture is among the most splendid to be found on European soil *(above)*.

2 Parque Nacional del Coto Doñana

The immense delta of the Guadalquivir river constitutes one of the world's most important nature reserves, without which birdlife throughout Europe would be seriously compromised. The zone has a fascinating mix of terrains, but can be visited on guided tours only.

3 Real Alcázar, Seville

A mix of styles is evident in this vast and luxurious pleasure palace, built almost entirely by Moorish artisans on behalf of their Christian overlords, including the lush gardens.

4 Seville Cathedral and La Giralda

These two chief wonders of Seville *(above)* beautifully embody the juxtaposition of the Moors and the triumphalism of their Christian conquerors.

TOP 10 Moments in History

1 Bronze Age Developments
Bronze began to be smelted and worked in Andalucía around 2500 BC. Some of the early tribes here built the oldest megalithic tombs *(dolmens)* in western Europe.

2 Phoenician and Greek Colonies
Lured by the area's mineral wealth, the Phoenicians founded a trading post at what is now Cádiz in 1100 BC, while the Greeks established a toehold near Málaga in 636 BC. The two maintained a mercantile rivalry until Carthage, a former Phoenician colony, dominated the region.

3 Roman Spain
The first Roman town in Spain, Itálica, was founded in 206 BC; Rome finally wrested the entire region from the Carthaginians in 201 BC. Andalucía became one of the empire's wealthiest outposts.

4 Arab Domination
Some 700 years later, when the Roman Empire began to come apart, tribes from northern Europe laid claim to the peninsula. The Vandals and then the Visigoths ruled for three centuries. An issue of rightful succession in AD 710 led to the enlistment of Muslim armies from North Africa. Within 10 years the Moors had taken over.

5 Moorish Sophistication
The Moors were custodians of the best features of Roman civilization: religious tolerance, scientific and philosophical thought, and engineering and cultural refinements. In the 10th century, under the Caliphate of Abd ar-Rahman III, Córdoba became the largest and wealthiest city in Europe.

6 Reconquista
The dissolution of the Caliphate in 1031 marked the beginning of the end for Moorish Spain. Some 30 *taifas* (principalities), jostling for political power, proved no contest for the Christians. The eight-month siege and *reconquista* of magnificent Moorish Granada in 1492 was the most poignant loss.

7 Discovery of America
That same year the New World was discovered for Spain by Christopher Columbus. The result was a wealth of gold and silver from the new empire.

8 Imperial Collapse
Colonial losses that began in 1713, following the War of Spanish Succession, reached their *dénouement* with Spain's defeat in the Spanish-American War of 1898. In Andalucía, this long decline meant grinding poverty and mass emigration.

9 Civil War and Franco
The Spanish Civil War (1936–9) was ignited by a military coup led by General Francisco Franco, who was against Spain's continuance as a Republic. On 18 July 1936 the war began when his troops took Cádiz, Seville and Granada. Then followed the grim years (1939–75) of Franco's dictatorship.

10 Seville Expo '92
The world fair in 1992 celebrated the quincentenary of Columbus's discovery of the New World. It brought a sprucing-up of Seville and 42.5 million visitors to Andalucía, but it left bankruptcy in its wake.

5 Cádiz
Said to be Europe's oldest city, Cádiz *(above)* still retains an aura of age-old mystery. The golden-domed cathedral on the waterfront is a spectacular sight.

6 Córdoba City and La Mezquita
In the 10th century, Córdoba was the most important city in Europe, a fact illustrated by the architectural masterpiece of La Mezquita, the Great Mosque *(above)*, began in AD 786.

8 Costa del Sol
From the wealthiest of the yachting-set enclaves to all-inclusive package deals for young families, this famous expanse of sand and former fishing villages has something for everyone *(above)*.

7 Ronda
The largest of several white villages *(pueblos blancos)* scattered throughout the region, Ronda is built on a table of rock that is spectacularly split by the Tajo gorge *(above)*. It is also reputed to be the birthplace of the modern style of bullfighting.

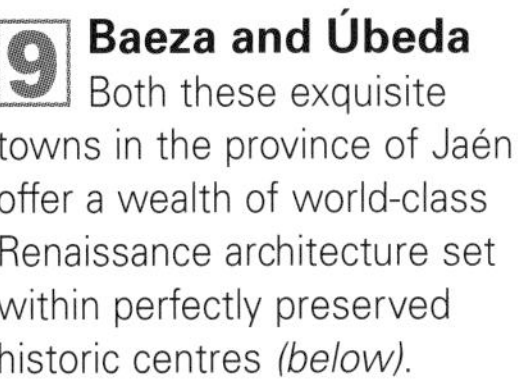

9 Baeza and Úbeda
Both these exquisite towns in the province of Jaén offer a wealth of world-class Renaissance architecture set within perfectly preserved historic centres *(below)*.

10 Sierra Nevada
Europe's second highest mountain range after the Alps offers the continent's southernmost ski resort, a wealth of wildlife for trekkers to wonder at, and dozens of remote villages along its southern slopes that preserve ancient cultural traditions and unique forms of vernacular architecture *(above)*.

TOP 10 Costa del Sol

1 Estepona
The first major resort on this coast is an excellent family choice, with 19 km (12 miles) of sandy beach. Plaza Las Flores, in the *casco antiguo* (old town), retains great charm. The early-morning fish market on the harbour is well worth a visit.

2 Marbella
The 15th-century Plaza de los Naranjos is the heart of the old town of Marbella, Spain's most expensive resort. Nearby Puerto Banús is the town's glittering marina, where mere mortals can admire the fabulous yachts and breathe the same air as the super-rich.

3 Mijas
Come here for the views of the coast, as well as the maze of old Moorish streets and numerous tiny squares filled with charming shops.

4 Fuengirola
This large resort is the most family-orientated of all, with a Blue Flag beach and a seafront promenade. There is a restored 10th-century Moorish castle perched high above the town.

5 Benalmádena
This resort comes in three parts: the old town inland; the beach and port area; and Arroyo de la Miel, a lively suburb.

6 Torremolinos
Torre de los Molinos (Tower of the Windmills) refers to a Moorish watchtower that was at one time surrounded by 19 flourmills. The ancient Torre Vigia is still here, but surrounding it now is a big, brash, modern resort that's all about inexpensive fun.

7 Málaga
Málaga is usually just a transit point for the average visitor, and thus remains very Spanish in character. Andalucía's second largest city has an interesting historic district dominated by a massive 8th-century fortress and the ruins of the 14th-century Castillo de Gibralfaro.

8 Torre del Mar
This resort is favoured by Spanish families, so is less tawdry than others to the west. The tree-lined seafront promenade is part of an attempt to prettify facilities.

9 Vélez-Málaga
The old quarter of this market town has beautiful Mudéjar features. An annual flamenco guitar competition is held here every July.

10 Nerja
No high-rises here; Nerja is all white-washed good taste, surmounting attractive, verdant cliffs with quiet pebble beach coves below.

Athens

The capital of Greece is simultaneously known as the Classical, marble-pillared cradle of Western civilization and as a modern urban sprawl of concrete and traffic. Between the extremes lies a kaleidoscopic city, where the influences of East and West entwine in the markets, cafés and tavernas, built upon ancient ruins and rubbing shoulders with gold-leafed Byzantine churches.

1 Museum of Cycladic Art
The world's largest collection of Cycladic art *(left)* showcases a matriarchal island culture whose 5,000-year-old icons still inspire artists of the modern world.

2 Temple of Olympian Zeus
Ancient Greece's most colossal temple *(right)* stands alongside the monumental arch that divided the old Athens – city of the Greek hero Theseus – from the new – that of the formidable Roman emperor Hadrian.

TOP 10 Moments in History

1 Birth of Athens
The Acropolis was first inhabited in Neolithic times (around 3000 BC). It began to take on the form of a city when it was fortified by the Mycenaeans about 1400 BC.

2 Golden Age
The 6th and 5th centuries BC saw the city-state grow into a colonial power. Under Perikles (495–429 BC), the Parthenon, Erechtheion and Temple of Nike were built. Cultural and intellectual life flourished until defeat by Sparta in the Peloponnesian War (431–404 BC).

3 Roman Athens
Roman rule began in 146 BC and lasted five centuries. In 86 BC a movement towards Athenian independence was brutally crushed. Emperor Hadrian (AD 76–138) was an admirer of Greek culture, however, and, with Greek scholar Herodes Atticus, he set up various building schemes, including the great theatre.

4 Byzantine Period
When Roman territory was divided in AD 395, Greece became part of the Byzantine Empire. Pagan philosophical schools were closed and many temples were rebuilt as churches.

5 Athens Under Ottoman Rule
Under the Ottoman Turks from 1458, the city became a provincial backwater. In the 18th century, English and French artists and writers visited Athens on the Grand Tour, sparking its revival but also walking off with many ancient artworks.

6 War of Independence
In 1821 the Greeks rose up against Ottoman rule. The war ended in 1829, but the Ottomans held the Acropolis until 1834, when the new king, Otto I, entered the city. Athens became capital of the new Greek state and was rebuilt, largely in Neo-Classical style.

7 World War II
Mussolini declared war on Greece in October 1940, and the German army entered Athens in April 1941, raising the swastika over the Acropolis.

8 Post-World War II
At the close of WWII Greece fell into civil war. The US gave economic and military aid on the proviso that the Communist Left would not gain power. In the 1950s and '60s, Athens saw rapid industrialization and mass migration from rural areas.

9 Military Dictatorship
In April 1967, a coup led by Georgios Papadopoulos signalled the beginning of a seven-year military junta.

10 Modern-Day Athens
Hosting the 2004 Olympic Games left Athens with improved transport, sports and cultural facilities. In the 2010s it is the focal point for fierce anti-austerity protests.

3 Roman Forum and Tower of the Winds
The Romans abandoned the ancient Agora and created this orderly new commercial centre. Its showpiece was the magnificent Tower of the Winds, which housed an ingenious water clock *(below)*.

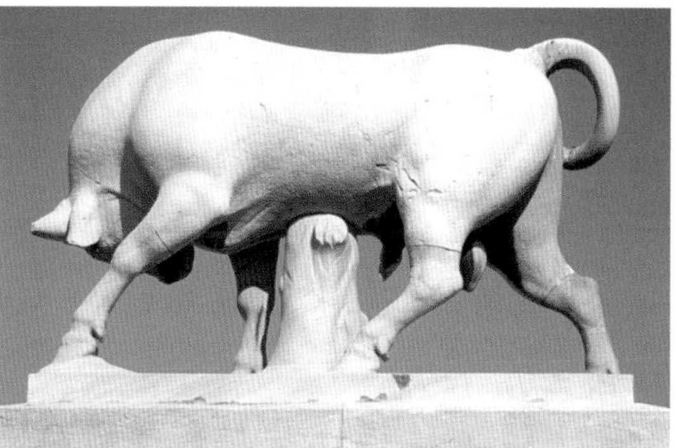

5 Kerameikos

Classical Athens' cemetery provides a fascinating cross-section of life, and death, at the city's edge, with elaborate tombs *(above)*, temples, sacred roads – and even an ancient brothel.

4 Acropolis

The crown jewel of Greece, if not all of Europe, the temples of the Acropolis are the most influential buildings in Western architecture *(above)*.

6 The Agora

Socrates, Aristotle and St Paul all held forth in the marketplace below the Acropolis. This was the heart of the ancient city *(above)*.

7 National Archaeological Museum

The greatest collection of finds from some of the world's greatest cultures is housed here. Exhibits include the gold treasure of Mycenae *(above)* and the first sculptures to depict the complexity of the human form.

10 Filopappos Hill

A green-gladed respite in the city centre *(above)*, Filopappos Hill has a wonderful view and a mix of monuments that encompass ancient, Byzantine and modern Greek culture.

8 Byzantine Museum

The rich, complex history of the great Byzantine Empire is told through the greatest of its works, from the intricacy of precious metalwork to the solemnity of the many icons.

9 Benaki Museum

A first-rate collection of Greek art, from Neolithic to present times, is housed in a beautifully renovated Neo-Classical mansion with an intriguing history and famed rooftop view.

Top 10 Philosophers and Writers

1 Homer c.700 BC
Next to nothing is known about the man who compiled the tales of *The Iliad* and *The Odyssey*. These poems are arguably the greatest and most influential in history.

2 Aeschylus 535–456 BC
When the "Father of Tragedy" began writing, theatre was in its infancy. His was a sweeping vision of humans working out a plan of cosmic justice, in works such as *Prometheus Unbound* and the *Oresteia*.

3 Sophocles 496–406 BC
Only seven of Sophocles' plays survive today, but his reputation rests securely on three: *Antigone*, *Oedipus at Colonus* and *Oedipus Rex*. The last, the story of a king bound by fate to murder his father and marry his mother, is the greatest masterpiece of Greek tragedy.

4 Euripides 484–407 BC
Euripides reinterpreted myths of human suffering by recasting the heroes as ordinary people. His most famous plays, *The Bacchae* and *Medea*, are about mothers murdering their children.

5 Socrates 470–399 BC
Although Socrates himself wrote nothing, his teachings, recorded in the writings of historians and especially his pupil Plato, have earned him the status of forefather of Western philosophy.

6 Aristophanes 447–385 BC
Greece's greatest comic playwright was a breath of fresh air after the age of the great tragedians. *Lysistrata*, in which the women of warring Sparta and Athens refuse to sleep with their husbands until they stop fighting, is one of the greatest anti-war messages of all time.

7 Plato 428–348 BC
Plato's works, from his early dialogues reprising Socrates' teachings, to later masterworks such as *Republic*, comprised the backbone of every major intellectual movement to follow.

8 Aristotle 384–322 BC
After studying with Plato, Aristotle tutored Alexander the Great. His *Poetics* is one of the most important works of literary criticism, and his *Nichomachean Ethics* among the greatest on ethics.

9 Nikos Kazantzakis 1883–1957
Kazantzakis' most famous work is *Zorba the Greek*. Darker in mood is the *Last Temptation of Christ* and best of all is his audacious *The Odyssey: A Modern Sequel*.

10 George Seferis 1900–71
Greece's first Nobel Laureate was born in Smyrna, which was later claimed by Turkey, and his lyrical poetry is inspired by history and feelings of exile.

Barcelona

With warm, crystal-clear waters lapping its sandy shores, and mountains nuzzling up to its northern edge, this glittering jewel on the Mediterranean is blessed with desirable geographical genes. From the buoyant, bustling revamped port area to the atmospheric medieval streets of the Barri Gòtic and the beautiful *Modernista* buildings of the Eixample, Barcelona has it all. A host of treasure-filled museums, architectural wonders, lively beaches and enchanting squares provide the icing on the cake.

Atlantic Ocean
A Coruña
Bilbao
FRANCE
BARCELONA
SPAIN
PORTUGAL
Madrid
Valencia
Seville
Mediterranean Sea

1 Sagrada Família

The enduring symbol of the city and its *Modernista* legacy is this basilica, Gaudí's other-worldly *pièce de résistance*. Piercing the Barcelona skyline are eight of the twelve planned spires *(right)* that have so far been built.

2 La Rambla

Barcelona's centrepiece, this 1-km (0.6-mile) thriving pedestrian thoroughfare *(below)* cuts a wide swathe through the old town, from the lively Plaça de Catalunya to the glistening Mediterranean sea.

3 Barcelona Cathedral

Dominating the heart of the old town is this magnificent Gothic Cathedral *(right)*, with a soaring, elaborate façade, immense nave, dazzling stained glass and a graceful, sun-dappled cloister containing palm trees and white geese.

TOP 10 Moments in History

1 BC: Founding of a City
Barcino, as it was first known, was founded in the 3rd century BC by Carthaginian Hamilcar Barca. It was taken by the Romans in 218 BC.

2 4th–11th Centuries AD: Early Invasions
As the Roman Empire began to fall in the 5th century, the Visigoths took over the city, followed by the Moors in the 8th century. Around AD 800, Charlemagne conquered the area with the help of the Pyrenean counts.

3 12th–16th Centuries: The Middle Ages
Barcelona was capital of an empire that included much of modern Spain and parts of the Mediterranean. As Castile expanded into the New World, trading patterns shifted and Barcelona came under Castilian domination.

4 1638–1652: Catalan Revolt
In reaction to the oppressive policies set out in Madrid, local factions revolted. Fighting began in 1640 and dragged on until 1652, when the Catalans and their French allies were defeated.

5 19th Century: Industry and Prosperity
Booming industry and trade with the Americas brought prosperity. The old city walls gave way to broad avenues.

6 1888–1929: The Renaixença
This new wealth sparked a renaissance of Catalan culture, and splendid *Modernista* mansions sprouted up.

7 1909–31: The Revolutionary Years
In 1909, protests against the Moroccan war sparked a brutal riot, the *Setmana Tràgica* (Tragic Week). Catalonia passed under a dictatorship before being declared a Republic in 1931.

8 1936–75: Civil War
At the outbreak of war in 1936, Barcelona's workers and militants fended off Franco's troops, but the city was taken in 1939 and harsh Catalan repression followed.

9 1975–80s: Transition to Democracy
Franco's death in 1975 paved the way for full democracy. Catalonia was given regional autonomy, and 1980 saw the first Catalan government.

10 1992: The Olympics & Beyond
Barcelona was catapulted onto the world stage by the 1992 Olympics and enjoyed a period of urban renewal. In the 2010s, like other Spanish cities, it has witnessed its share of anti-austerity riots.

4 Parc de la Ciutadella

A verdant oasis in the city centre, Barcelona's largest park is criss-crossed with pleasant paths. It boasts a zoo, two museums and a lavish fountain *(above)*.

5 La Pedrera

Unmistakably Gaudí, this *Modernista* marvel of a building seems to grow from the very pavement itself. Fluid and eerily alive, its curving façade sprouts sinuously writhing wrought-iron balconies. A cluster of mosaic chimneys keeps watch over the rooftop like shrewd-eyed knights.

6 Museu Picasso

Housed in a medieval palace complex, this museum charts Picasso's rise to fame with an extensive collection of his early works, including numerous masterful portraits painted at the age of just 13.

7 Museu Nacional d'Art de Catalunya

The stately Palau Nacional *(above)* is home to the Museu Nacional d'Art de Catalunya (MNAC), which holds one of the most extensive collections of Romanesque art in the world. The works were rescued from churches around Catalonia in the 1920s.

8 Fundació Joan Miró

An incomparable blend of art and architecture, this spacious museum, awash with natural light, showcases the work of Joan Miró, one of Catalonia's greatest 20th-century artists. Paintings, sculptures, drawings and textiles represent 60 prolific years *(above)*.

9 Palau de la Música Catalana

No mere concert hall, the aptly named Palace of Catalan Music *(left)* is one of the finest, and most exemplary, *Modernista* buildings in Barcelona.

10 Museu d'Art Contemporani and Centre de Cultura Contemporània

The city's gleaming white contemporary art museum *(above)* and its cutting-edge cultural centre, known as the CCCB, have sparked an urban revival in the once down-at-heel El Raval area.

TOP 10 Markets

1 Mercat de La Boqueria
At Barcelona's most famous and mouthwatering food market, hundreds of stalls sell the very finest produce. The many fish stalls reflect the city's seaside status.

2 Els Encants
Barcelona's best flea market, this is the place to find everything from electrical goods and toys to hand-made pottery. Bargain-hunters arrive early.

3 Fira de Santa Llúcia
During the Christmas season, artisans set up shop outside the Cathedral. Look out for row upon row of *caganers*, tiny pottery figures squatting to *fer caca* (take a poop).

4 Mercat de Sant Antoni
Spend Sunday morning browsing stalls laden with tattered paperbacks, ancient tomes, stacks of magazines, comics, postcards and lots more, from coins to videos.

5 Fira Artesana
The speciality at this monthly organic food market on Plaça del Pi is honey, from the clear clover nectar of the Pyrenees to nutty concoctions from Morella.

6 Fira de Filatelia i Numismàtica
Set out in the elegant Plaça Reial, this popular Sunday stamp and coin market draws avid collectors. The latest must-haves are phone cards and old *xapes de cava* (cava bottle cork foils).

7 Mercat de Barceloneta
At this striking covered market, as well as produce stalls, there are several fine restaurants including the Michelin-starred Lluçanès.

8 Mercat de Santa Caterina
Each *barri* has its own food market, but this one boasts a spectacular building too, by Catalan architect Enric Miralles (1955–2000).

9 Mercat del Art
At weekends, local artists set up their easels and sell their work in the Barri Gòtic's Plaça de Sant Josep Oriol.

10 Mercat dels Antiquaris
Every Thursday, antiques aficionados rummage contentedly through the assorted trinkets and bric-a-brac at this long-running antiques market in front of the Cathedral.

Italy
Dome of St Peter's
Basilica, Rome

ES PETRVS ET SVPER HANC

Berlin

Berlin is Germany's liveliest city and one of the most fascinating capitals in the world. You'll find no other place where art and culture, museums and theatres, entertainment and nightlife are more diverse and exciting than on the banks of the Spree river. Once reunited, Berlin quickly developed into a cosmopolitan city, and today there is an air of energy and vibrancy about it.

1 Brandenburger Tor and Pariser Platz
The Brandenburg Gate *(above)*, Berlin's most famous sight, is located in Pariser Platz, where the famous Hotel Adlon and the embassies exude a modern, stylish elegance.

Potsdamer Platz 2
The new heart of the old metropolis beats on Potsdamer Platz, where exciting modern structures such as the Sony Center *(right)* have been erected. With its many restaurants, shops, film museum and cinemas, it is a self-contained world of entertainment.

TOP 10 Moments in History

1 1685: Edict of Potsdam
Berlin's history as a cultural capital began in 1685, when the Edict of Potsdam decreed that around 20,000 Huguenots would be taken in by Berlin. Many were excellent craftsmen and scientists, who, having fled Catholic France because of their Protestant beliefs, brought a new age of cultural ascendancy to this provincial town.

2 1744: Frederick the Great
In 1740 Frederick the Great began to transform the city into a new metropolis. The "Forum Fridericianum" in Unter den Linden brought new splendours to the town, and masterpieces such as the national opera house helped turn Berlin into one of Europe's most important cities.

3 1928: Golden Twenties
Between 1919 and 1933, film, theatre, cabaret shows and thousands of restaurants and bars transformed Berlin into an international centre of entertainment. In the realms of fine art and architecture, too, Berlin set new standards.

4 1945: Surrender
Signed in Berlin-Karlshorst on 8 May 1945, Germany's unconditional surrender marked more than the end of World War II. The previous Jewish population of 161,000 had virtually disappeared and Berliners called their city "the empire's fields of rubble".

5 1953: Workers' Uprising in East Germany
On 17 June 1953, construction workers in Frankfurter Allee demonstrated against an increase in the average rate of production. Soviet tanks suppressed the rebellion while, in West Berlin, the uprising was interpreted as a demonstration in favour of German unification.

6 1961: Building the Wall
The building of the Berlin Wall, which commenced during the night of 12 August 1961, was a traumatic event for Berliners. Families were torn apart by the concrete wall and over 100 people would be killed in the following 30 years at the border dividing East and West.

7 1963: "I am a Berliner"
No other politician was as enthusiastically received in Berlin as the US President John F. Kennedy. On 17 July 1963, on the steps of Rathaus Schöneberg, he declared to a cheering crowd: "I am a Berliner." Berliners had forgiven the US for staying silent when the Wall was built. Kennedy confirmed once more that the Western Allies would stand by Berlin and support the town, just as they had done during the blockade of 1948–9, when the US and Britain airlifted food to the "island" of West Berlin.

8 1968: The Late Sixties
During the late 1960s, West Berlin students transformed Germany. Rudi Dutschke and others proposed political change and a reappraisal of Germany's Nazi past. The movement came to an untimely end when Dutschke was hurt in an assassination attempt in April 1968.

9 1989: Fall of the Wall
The fall of the Berlin Wall in November 1989 heralded a new dawn. For the first time in 30 years, Berliners from both halves of the divided city were able to visit each other. The town celebrated all along Ku'damm and in front of the Brandenburg Gate. When the Wall was built, Willy Brandt, then governing mayor of West Berlin, had promised: "Berlin will survive!" He was right.

10 1991: Capital City
In 1991, Berlin was declared capital of a reunified Federal Republic of Germany. Allied Forces left the city in 1994, but it was only when the Bundestag, the German parliament, moved here from Bonn in April 1999 that Berlin became the "real" capital.

3 Reichstag

No other building is a more potent symbol of Germany's history than the Reichstag *(above)*. Since its redesign by Sir Norman Foster in 1997–9, the structure has become one of the most popular sights in Berlin. Visitors are especially attracted by its vast, egg-shaped dome, affording fantastic views across the city.

4 Unter den Linden

This magnificent, tree-lined boulevard in the eastern part of the city has always been a central axis. Berlin's most important historic buildings are assembled here.

8 Museumsinsel

Among the museums in the complex known as "Museum Island" is the Pergamonmuseum *(above)*, which houses the colossal Pergamon Altar from ancient Greece.

5 Schloss Charlottenburg

The historic rooms of the former Hohenzollern summer residence *(above)* invite visitors to experience a slice of Prussian history, while the Baroque-style gardens, among the most beautiful in Germany, are perfect for strolling and sunbathing.

7 Kulturforum

This spectacular complex of museums includes the famous Gemäldegalerie (gallery of paintings), the Kunstgewerbemuseum (museum of arts and crafts) and the Neue Nationalgalerie, as well as concert halls such as the Philharmonie. It guarantees a unique cultural experience for visitors to Berlin.

Zoologischer Garten 9

Germany's oldest and most famous zoo and aquarium *(right)*, in the centre of the city, boasts some 17,000 animals and over 1,500 different species.

10 Kurfürstendamm

Berlin's much-visited strolling and shopping avenue is the main thoroughfare in the heart of the western city. Restaurants and stylish boutiques have increased the hustle and bustle along this grand boulevard.

Top 10 Art Galleries

1 Gemäldegalerie
Berlin's best art museum, the Gemäldegalerie focuses on European art of the 13th to 19th centuries, including works by Dürer, Rembrandt and Rubens.

2 Neue Nationalgalerie
The National Gallery's collection includes modern German art and classics of the 20th century. It is also known for its spectacular temporary exhibitions.

3 Alte Nationalgalerie
The Old National Gallery, on the Museumsinsel, holds a collection of 19th-century, mainly German, paintings and sculpture.

4 Hamburger Bahnhof
The historic Hamburg Station houses modern paintings, installations and multimedia art, with works by Joseph Beuys, Andy Warhol, Jeff Koons, Robert Rauschenberg, Anselm Kiefer and many others.

5 Museum Berggruen
Berlin-born art dealer Heinz Berggruen (1914–2007), left his priceless collection to the city. Including works from Picasso's "blue period", it is based in a historic Charlottenburg building.

6 Bauhaus-Archiv
Few schools have exercised as much influence on 20th-century architecture and design as the Bauhaus, founded in 1919 by Walter Gropius. Its archive displays furniture, sketches, everyday objects and paintings.

7 Deutsche Guggenheim
Sponsored by Deutsche Bank, this branch of the Guggenheim is one of the most popular art venues in the city, hosting temporary exhibitions of modern art, often from the US.

8 Berlinische Galerie
This striking museum shows works mostly by German, east European and Russian painters, photographers, graphic designers and architects of the 20th century.

9 Bröhan-Museum
A unique collection of Art Nouveau and Art Deco objects from around Europe is displayed here, along with paintings by Berlin artists.

10 Kupferstichkabinett
Five centuries of prints and calligraphy on show here include works by Botticelli, Dürer, Rembrandt, Goya and the Dutch Old Masters.

6 Kaiser-Wilhelm-Gedächtnis-Kirche

The ruined tower of the memorial church *(below)*, built to commemorate Kaiser Wilhelm I and damaged by bombing raids of 1943, stands today as a reminder of the horrors of war.

Bruges

It is hard to describe the capital of the West Flanders province of Belgium without using the phrase "fairy tale". The medieval city is encircled by a tranquil canal and filled with quaint, step-gabled houses and glorious Gothic buildings, many of them now treasure-filled museums. Although the main squares are usually busy with tourists, it is easy to find quiet corners where time seems to have stood still.

1 Belfort
For a breathtaking view over Bruges' medieval streets, climb the 366 steps to the top of the Belfort (belfry) *(above)*. The set of bells at the top includes 47 carillon bells that are still rung by a mechanism installed in 1748.

The Burg 2
This intimate, charming square is a glittering confection made up of fine historic architecture, sculpture and gilding. It was the focal point of old Bruges and the spectacular Gothic Town Hall *(right)*, dating from 1376, is to be found here.

3 Memling in Sint-Jan-Hospitaalmuseum
The medieval St John's Hospital *(left)* hold a priceless collection of the works of Hans Memling (1435–94), one of the leading artists of Burgundian Flanders.

4 Arentshuis (Brangwynmuseum)
Bruges-born Frank Brangwyn (1867–1956) was one of several British artists and architects who helped restore the city to its Gothic glory. The 18th-century Arentshuis has a gallery of his works.

TOP 10 Eastern Bruges: Sint-Anna

1 Onze-Lieve-Vrouw ter Potterie
Set in a 13th-century hospital complex, this delightful small museum combines a fine collection of treasures with an extraordinarily elaborate Baroque chapel.

2 Duinenbrug
In the days when barges brought goods into the centre of Bruges, its canals were spanned by little drawbridges that could be raised to allow boats to pass. This one was reconstructed in 1976.

3 Museum voor Volkskunde
Occupying a group of alms-houses, Bruges' folk museum has a fascinating and copious collection of historic artifacts that shed light on everyday life in Bruges in the 19th and early 20th centuries.

4 Sint-Annakerk
The interior of this pretty parish church looks like a snapshot of the 17th century – a tranquil place of worship enlivened by harmonious Baroque flourishes.

5 Guido Gezelle-museum
Set in the part of Sint-Anna called the Verloren Hoek (Lost Corner), this rustic house and garden was the birthplace and childhood home of one of the best-loved poets of the Dutch (and Flemish) language, the priest Guido Gezelle (1830–99).

6 Schuttersgilde Sint-Sebastiaan
St Sebastian's guild of long-bowmen still functions as an archery club in its atmospheric 16th-century home, which also has a museum of treasures and mementos.

7 Muur der Doodgeschotenen
A bullet-marked wall stands as a memorial to a dozen men executed here by the German occupying army during World War I.

8 Jeruzalemkerk and the Kantcentrum
The Jerusalem Church is a 15th-century chapel inspired by pilgrimages, with fanciful replicas of holy sites. Next door is a small lace museum, where visitors can see lace being made and buy samples.

9 Kruisvest Windmills
In the past, the earth ramparts around Bruges were lined with windmills. Here, four have been restored, of which two are open to the public.

10 Kruispoort
Huge walls were built around Bruges after 1297. Of these, only four city gates survive, including the Kruispoort (1403).

5 Gruuthusemuseum

This museum presents a rich collection of everyday artifacts from the homes of the merchant classes, from kitchenware to musical instruments, furniture, textiles and weapons. The 15th-century building *(left)* was once the palace of the Lords of Gruuthuse; it has a gallery overlooking the choir of the Onze-Lieve-Vrouwekerk next door.

6 Steenhouwersdijk and Groenerei

One of the prettiest stretches of canal is where the Steenhouwersdijk (stonemason's embankment) becomes the Groenerei (green canal). The 1714 almshouse, De Pelikaan, is named after the symbol of Christian charity, the pelican.

7 Begijnhof

This beautiful enclave *(above)* was home to a community of *béguines* (a lay Catholic sisterhood) from 1245 until 1928. Around the tree-shaded park are the 17th- and 18th-century whitewashed homes of the *béguines*. Visitors can explore the grounds and see inside the *béguinage* church and one of the houses *(Begijnhuisje)*.

8 Markt

The central marketplace of Bruges *(above)* still retains much of its original outline, flanked by old, step-gabled guildhouses, but the Provinciaal Hof, the provincial government building on the eastern side, is actually a late-19th-century creation. The Markt remains the focal point of Bruges, and is the site of a large market on Wednesday mornings, as well as a small Christmas market.

9 Onze-Lieve-Vrouwekerk

The towering spire of the Church of Our Lady *(below)* is a landmark of Bruges' skyline. The church is the setting for one of the great treasures of Europe: Michelangelo's *Madonna and Child* (1504–5). Its museum displays the beautiful gilt-brass tombs of Charles the Bold (1433–77), Duke of Burgundy, and his daughter.

10 Groeningemuseum

Not only is this one of the great north European collections, with star roles played by the late medieval masters of Flemish painting, such as Jan van Eyck and Hans Memling; it is also refreshingly small *(above)*.

Top 10 Belgian Beers

1 Trappist Beer
Trappist beer is made by five breweries with close ties to the Cistercian monasteries: Chimay, Westmalle, Orval, Rochefort and Westvleteren. Yeast is added at bottling to start a second fermentation, so pour carefully.

2 Abbey Beer
Other abbeys also produced beer, but many have licensed them to commercial brewers. Still, many abbey beers are excellent, and there are good abbey styles, such as Ename, Floreffe and St Feuillien.

3 Witbier/Bière Blanche
Wheat, rather than barley, makes a distinctive "white beer" to which flavours such as coriander and orange peel may be added. The result is light and refreshing, often served cloudy with sediment.

4 Christmas Beers
Many breweries produce ales for the festive season. These may just be prettily labelled versions of their usual brew, but may also be enriched, powerful ales.

5 Lambic
The valley of the Senne has a natural air-borne yeast. For centuries, brewers here have left their "wort" uncovered to allow this yeast in. The distinctive, winey result is called *lambic* – the quintessential beer of Brussels.

6 Gueuze
Lambic is blended and then fermented a second time in the bottle to make *gueuze*. Fizzy like Champagne, it is matured again to accentuate its winey qualities.

7 Kriek
Lambic can be flavoured with cherries during fermentation to create *kriek*; with raspberries to make *framboise*; or with candy sugar for *faro*.

8 Double/Triple
Traditionally, beers were graded by strength. Some breweries (notably the abbeys) still label their beers double *(dubbel)* and triple *(tripel)*. Double is usually a dark and sweetish brew, triple often golden-blond.

9 Lager-Style Beers
Lager, or *pils*, is a light beer often sniffed at by real ale enthusiasts, but in Belgium it is brewed to a high standard.

10 Strong Ales
Some breweries pride themselves on sheer strength. Duvel ("Devil"), at 8.5%, is a famous example.

Brussels

Northern Belgium has a rich cultural heritage dating back to medieval times, when this was one of the most vibrant trading regions in the world. Today, Brussels is often called the "Capital of Europe". Home to Tintin, Magritte, over 80 museums and a cosmopolitan population, it is a richly rewarding city for visitors, not only in cultural sights, but also in delightful places to stay, eat and drink.

1 Sablon

The name of this district refers to the sandy marshland that made up the site until it was reclaimed in the 17th century. The Place du Grand Sablon *(left)* is a centre for antiques and home to two of Brussels' leading chocolatiers: Wittamer and Pierre Marcolini.

2 Musées Royaux des Beaux-Arts

Brueghel, Rubens, Van Dyck, Magritte – this splendid collection takes the visitor on a tour of some of the greatest names in the history of art *(above)*.

3 Église Saint-Jacques-sur-Coudenberg

This charming 18th-century church *(below)*, with its Roman-style façade and lantern bell tower, sits on the top of the Coudenberg, the aristocratic enclave of the Upper Town.

TOP 10 Moments in History

1 50s BC: Julius Caesar
The Roman army suffered repeated setbacks in its struggle to conquer the courageous "Belgae", but in the end Rome won out, and Belgium flourished under the Pax Romana for 400 years.

2 AD 843: Treaty of Verdun
After the Romans came the Franks, whose empire reached its apogee under Charlemagne. On his death, his homeland was split into what would later become Flanders and Wallonia.

3 1302: Battle of the Golden Spurs
France dominated Flanders for much of the medieval period. At the Battle of the Golden Spurs, a Flemish rebel force humiliated the cream of the French army.

4 1384: Burgundy Rules
When the Count of Flanders died in 1384, his title was inherited by his son-in-law Philip the Bold, Duke of Burgundy. Burgundian rule reached a Golden Age under Philip the Good, who reigned from 1419 to 1467.

5 1568: Religious Strife
Charles V, Holy Roman Emperor and King of Spain, inherited the Burgundian territories, but faced violent revolt there as Protestantism gathered pace. Eventually the territory was divided into the Protestant north (the Netherlands) and Catholic south (now Belgium).

6 1815: Battle of Waterloo
A growing movement for Belgian independence was swept aside in 1794 when Napoleon Bonaparte's French revolutionary armies invaded. He was finally defeated by the Allies at Waterloo.

7 1830: The Belgian Revolution
After Waterloo, the Congress of Vienna placed Belgium under Dutch rule, a deeply unpopular solution. Anger finally boiled over in 1830, independence was declared, and the Dutch army was forced out of Brussels.

8 1914–18: World War I
At the outbreak of World War I, the German army swept into neutral Belgium. The front settled near the medieval town of Ypres. Over the next four years, half a million people from both sides died there.

9 1940–44: World War II
History was repeated in May 1940, when the German army launched a *Blitzkrieg* against neutral Belgium to outflank the Maginot Line, which blocked their entry into France. Brussels was liberated in September 1944.

10 1957: Treaty of Rome
The Belgians were strong supporters of the Treaty of Rome, which laid the foundations for the European Union. Over time, Brussels has effectively become the "Capital of Europe".

4 Grand Place
For sheer architectural theatre, the historic centrepiece of Brussels *(above)* is hard to beat – just as it must have been three centuries ago.

Musée des Instruments de Musique 5
The magnificent Art Nouveau former Old England department store building *(right)* houses the "MIM". The museum contains thousands of musical instruments – ancient, modern, ethnic and just plain wacky.

6 Centre Belge de la Bande Dessinée
The "Comic Strip Centre" *(below)* reveals all about this very Belgian art form – Tintin and beyond.

7 Cathédrale des Saints Michel et Gudule
Brussels' largest church *(left)*, built over three centuries from 1225 onward, is a splendid example of the light and flowery style known as Brabantine Gothic.

8 Musée Magritte
A handsome building on Place Royale is a fitting home for this unrivalled collection of the works of a Belgian national treasure – the Surrealist artist René Magritte. Over 200 of his distinctive works are beautifully displayed on a chronological and themed "trail".

9 Musée Charlier
Brussels is a city of grand 19th-century mansions, or *maisons de maître*. This museum provides a rare opportunity to see inside one. On display are works by leading artists of the time, plus an impressive collection of antique furniture.

Horta Museum 10
Victor Horta was a founding father of Art Nouveau, and his house *(right)* was the perfect expression of his art, designed by him down to the last doorknob. It is now a magnificent museum.

TOP 10 Sights of Outer Brussels

1 Parc du Cinquantenaire
In 1880 a grand international fair was held to celebrate the 50th anniversary of Belgian independence. The exhibition halls, set in a glorious park, now house major museums including the Musées Royaux d'Art et d'Histoire, magnificent collections of treasures from around the world.

2 Musées d'Extrême-Orient
The Chinese Pavilion and Japanese Tower house porcelain, samurai armour and Art Nouveau glass.

3 Musée David et Alice van Buuren
This beautifully preserved Art Deco home has superb furniture and stained glass, plus contemporary paintings.

4 The Atomium
This giant model of an iron crystal was built as Belgium's exhibit at Brussels' 1958 Universal Exposition.

5 Musée du Tram Bruxellois
Visitors cannot fail to be won over by this collection of over 60 Brussels trams, from the horse-drawn "hippomobiles" of the 1860s to sleek models of 1960s modernity, housed in an old tram depot. Historic tram rides add to the fun.

6 Koninklijk Museum voor Midden-Afrika (KMMA)
The Royal Museum of Central Africa is a huge and elegant Neo-Classical palace opened in 1910 to promote the then Belgian colony of the Congo. Exhibits include a massive canoe hewn from a single tree trunk, plus items from the history of exploration, such as Henry Stanley's cap.

7 Musée Communal d'Ixelles
This small but exceptional art collection just south of the city has a number of minor works by great masters, as well as a fine collection of posters by Toulouse-Lautrec and works by the much-loved Belgian Fauvist Rik Wouters.

8 Musée Constantin Meunier
Constantin Meunier (1831–1905) was internationally famous for his bronzes of working people, especially forge workers. The museum is based in his former home.

9 Musée Antoine Wiertz
Antoine Wiertz (1806–65) was an artist whose self-esteem far outstripped his talent. This grand studio was built so he could paint on a scale to rival Michelangelo. The grandiose canvases are interesting, but so too are the smaller works, many so macabre and moralistic they inspire more hilarity than awe.

10 Parlement Européen
The Quartier Léopold is dominated by the huge glass-and-steel European Parliament building. Visitors must be over 14.

History and Culture

From the rugged Viking heritage of the northlands to the refined Mediterranean cultures of ancient Greece and Rome; from medieval and Renaissance splendours to the most daring innovations of modern architecture; from stately piles once lived in to ancient towns and villages still lived in and loved – Europe's historic and cultural sites offer every visitor a unique experience.

1 Visby, Gotland *SWEDEN*

A former Viking trading post and member of the Hanseatic League of trading cities, set against the rugged coastline and picturesque countryside of the island of Gotland, Visby is a fascinating place to visit. With the remains of several medieval churches, a harbour, towered boundary wall and beautiful botanical gardens, this charming town – now a UNESCO World Heritage Site – deserves the nickname "the City of Roses and Ruins". Its lively Medieval Week celebrations in summer draw costumed revellers from far and wide.

2 Sir John Soane's Museum, London *ENGLAND*

One of joys of the Sir John Soane's Museum is seeing visitors' faces as they enter each room. Their eyes widen, their jaws drop, and they invariably smile at cornucopia of treasures within. On the outside, this straight-laced Georgian terraced building gives no hint of what is in store. Sir John Soane was one of the founders of the British Museum, and his London home is like the Tardis – it seems to contain more art and antiquities than such a house could possibly hold, much of it in specially made cabinets and display cases.

3 Bratislava Old Town *SLOVAKIA*

It seems natural to compare Bratislava with Prague: from the end of World War I until the "Velvet Divorce" of the Czech Republic and Slovakia in 1993, the two cities were yoked together as part of Czechoslovakia. Historically, though, Bratislava, once part of the Austro-Hungarian Empire, has more in common with Vienna or Budapest. Modern parts of the city will earn few devotees, but the medieval Old Town is a treat. At its heart are two lovely pedestrianized squares, Františkánska námestie and Hlavné námestie, with the distinctive Old Town Hall on the latter. The City Gallery of Bratislava is housed in three of the city's impressive palaces and in the rebuilt castle overlooking all.

4 Arènes de Nîmes *FRANCE*

This is the most complete surviving Roman amphitheatre in the world. It still entertains the crowds today, regarded as one of France's best music venues as well as playing host to a season of bullfights. It is easy, on a balmy night, in this incredible atmosphere, to forget that the building is 2,000 years old. Its 34 rows of seats are arranged in three tiers, originally socially graded – from the good front seats for dignitaries to the distant, high rows allocated to slaves. Every sporting stadium since has been modelled on this ideal design.

5 Akrotiri, Santorini *GREECE*

The Bronze Age settlement of Akrotiri, once the largest Minoan city outside Crete, suffered a Pompeii-like end when it was buried in ash following the explosion of the volcanic island of Thera (modern-day Santorini) around 1500 BC. This eruption was one of the most devastating in recorded history, and is thought to have inspired Plato's legend of Atlantis, which told of an island that vanished without trace. The ash preserved much of Akrotiri in a near-perfect condition, and today you'll find three-storey houses complete with pottery and furniture and a remarkable array of frescoes.

Visby, Gotland Heralds on horseback lead the Medieval Week celebrations *(above)*

Akrotiri, Santorini Amphoras, damaged but preserved in the volcanic ash *(below)*

Arènes de Nîmes Statue of a matador outside the amphitheatre *(above)*

Sintra Palácio Nacional, towering regally above the town *(below)*

6 Galla Placidia Mausoleum, Ravenna *ITALY*

Most visitors go to Ravenna to see the beautiful mosaics of the Basilica di San Vitale, unaware that, just a few steps away, actually within the grounds of the church, lies this splendid cruciform mausoleum. Dating from AD 425–30, it is decorated with some of the earliest and most fabulous mosaics in Western art. Heavenly, starry blue covers the ceiling, and the Apostles are all represented, while over the door a Christ-figure sits in a country setting guarding his flock. The windowpanes are made of stone panels so thin the light seeps through them.

7 Sintra *PORTUGAL*

This charming town is where the nobility of Portugal used to come to escape Lisbon's summer heat. Hidden among wooded hills above the Atlantic Ocean are a scattering of palatial retreats, their fanciful turrets peeking out. At their centre is the Palácio Nacional de Sintra. Begun by the Moors, it was the summer residence for some of Portugal's royal family for several centuries. To explore Sintra by foot involves lots of walking, but take heart – you can always hop aboard a horse-drawn carriage if you tire of climbing the town's steep hills.

8 Guggenheim Bilbao *SPAIN*

On its completion in 1997, Frank Gehry's Guggenheim Bilbao transformed this once drab industrial city overnight. Visitors come from all over the globe to see the soaring curves and funky angles, formed of glass, titanium and limestone, and reflecting light off its many faces. They are greeted at the main entrance by *Puppy*, a 13-m (43-ft) topiary terrier by Jeff Koons, which has become another symbol of the city.

9 Musée Jacquemart-André, Paris *FRANCE*

The splendid 19th-century town-house of banker Edouard André and his society-painter wife, Nélie Jacquemart, positively drips with art and atmosphere. Dutch paintings in the library include portraits by Van Dyck and Rembrandt, while the upstairs "Italian Museum" boasts an Uccello *St George and the Dragon*, Botticelli's *Virgin and Child*, Mantegna's *Ecce Homo* and sculptures by Donatello and Della Robbia. Other rooms house works by French artists, and the double spiral staircase is presided over by Tiepolo frescoes depicting the arrival of Henri III in Venice.

10 Galleria Borghese, Rome *ITALY*

Cardinal Scipione Borghese began collecting art for his villa in the (then) outskirts of Rome in 1605. Over the course of a lifetime he amassed an awe-inspiring collection. Each one of the Galleria Borghese's rooms contains treasures. On the ground floor, the sculptures include some of Bernini's finest work, and the paintings include a Titian, a Raphael and six Caravaggios.

Budapest

The finest of the Habsburg triumvirate of Budapest, Vienna and Prague, the Hungarian capital is much grander in scale than the Austrian and Czech capitals. Comprising three separate towns – hilly Buda and Óbuda on the Danube's western bank, and flat Pest on the eastern bank – this is a city rich in historical sights, including the Roman ruins of Aquincum, the Turkish baths and the Neo-Gothic Parliament. At night it buzzes with lively bars and clubs, and offers some top-quality options for eating out.

1 Hungarian Parliament Viewed from the opposite bank of the Danube *(left)*, the façade of the Hungarian Parliament is one of Budapest's defining sights. Its rooms contain boundless treasures.

Váci utca 2 For centuries, Váci Street *(right)* has been the centre of the Hungarian commercial world. Traders, swindlers, prostitutes and gentlemen all mingled in the street's packed hostelries and shops.

3 Gellért Hotel and Baths Budapest is famous for its numerous thermal baths, of which the best are the indoor and outdoor pools at the legendary Gellért Hotel *(above)*.

TOP 10 Moments in History

1 AD 409: The Huns Conquer Aquincum
Aquincum, as Budapest was first known, was an important garrison town in the Roman province of Pannonia. It was conquered by the Huns in 409, and subsequently ruled by the Goths, the Longobards and the Avars.

2 896: Árpád Leads the Magyars into Pannonia
Prince Árpád led the nomadic Magyars into Pannonia in 896. He settled first on Csepel Island, in the middle of the Danube in southern Budapest, and later in Óbuda (Ancient Buda in Hungarian).

3 1000: King Stephen I
Stephen (István) was the first Magyar to accept Christianity, and the pope crowned him king. The Árpád dynasty lasted a further 300 years.

4 1687: The Habsburgs
In 1687, Hungarians gave up their right to elect their king, and ceded the crown to the Habsburg Empire, which ruled Hungary until 1918.

5 1849: Chain Bridge Links Buda and Pest
The first permanent bridge over the Danube, the Chain Bridge, was completed in 1849, allowed the unification of Buda, Óbuda and Pest some 20 years later.

6 1916: Charles IV, Last King of Hungary
On the death of Emperor Franz Joseph in 1916, Charles IV was crowned king. He abdicated in November 1918. In 1919 he was exiled to Madeira, and died in 1922.

7 1944: The Budapest Ghetto
In 1944 the Nazis herded over 70,000 Jews into the area around the Great Synagogue. Over 20,000 died. Survivors were liberated by the Soviet army in February 1945.

8 1956: Uprising
In response to mass anti-Soviet protests in October 1956, on 4 November the Soviet army invaded Hungary. Popular Prime Minister Imre Nagy was arrested, and in 1958 he was executed.

9 1989: The Fall of Communism
In October 1989, as part of the change sweeping Eastern Europe, the People's Republic became the Republic of Hungary. In January 1990, free elections were held for the first time since 1919.

10 2004: Hungary Joins the European Union
Hungary became a full member of the EU in June 2004, an occasion marked with days of celebrations throughout the country.

4 Hungarian National Gallery

The six permanent exhibitions, spread throughout much of Budapest's Royal Palace *(right)*, constitute the most valuable collection of Hungarian art in the world.

5 Statue Park & Memento Park

Almost all of Hungary's Communist-era statues, which once stood in the public squares, are now displayed at this bizarre but fascinating open-air museum on the outskirts of Budapest *(below)*.

6 St Stephen's Basilica

Vith its 96-m- (315-ft-) igh dome visible om all over Budapest, t Stephen's Basilica ouses the city's most izarre relic – the nummified forearm f King István.

7 State Opera House

Built to rival the grand opera houses of Vienna and Dresden, Budapest's sublime State Opera House *(left)* is best viewed while taking in one of its world-class performances.

9 Mátyás Church

The coronation church of the Hungarian kings, with its Gothic spire towering above much of Upper Buda, is as impressive close up as it is from afar *(above)*.

8 Hungarian National Museum

The Hungarian National Museum is a treasure-trove f exhibits and artifacts from every period of Hungary's urbulent history.

10 Margaret Island

Isolated until the 19th century and long a retreat for religious contemplation, the lush and still-secluded Margaret Island is an ideal place for a peaceful stroll *(left)*.

Top 10 Danube Sights

1 Chain Bridge
On either side of the Bridge are two huge towers that support the mammoth chains from which it takes its name. It is one of the city's most-photographed sights.

2 River Cruises
A number of companies run cruises along the Danube during the summer, starting from Vigadó tér.

3 Elizabeth Bridge
The longest suspension bridge in the world when it was completed in 1903, Elizabeth Bridge (Erzsébet híd) had to be completely rebuilt after World War II, and did not reopen until 1963.

4 Inner City Parish Church
Almost destroyed to make way for Elizabeth Bridge when it was being rebuilt, the Inner City Parish Church, dating from the 14th century, with a vaulted Gothic chapel, is the oldest building in Pest. Damaged by fire in 1723, it was rebuilt in 1725–39.

5 Queen Elizabeth Monument
Although the wife of the Habsburg emperor Franz Joseph was not Hungarian, she adored her subjects. This 1932 monument to her overlooks the Danube from the Gellért embankment.

6 Margaret Bridge
The gateway to Margaret Island, Margit híd was built from 1872 to 1876, and is distinguished by its unusual chevron shape.

7 Academy of Sciences
The 1864 Academy stands in Széchenyi István tér facing the square, but its superb Neo-Classical façade can be admired when travelling upstream. The aspect that faces the Danube is no less impressive.

8 Liberty Bridge
Legendary Hungarian *tural* birds sit atop the Modernist girders of the Szabadság híd. The bridge is an exact replica of the 1899 original destroyed by the Nazis.

9 Embankment Walk
This walk runs along most of the Pest embankment. Several boats moored on the quays have cafés aboard.

10 Buda Castle Funicular
Kids of all ages love to ride this archaic funicular. The journey is short, the cabins tiny, but the views of the Danube below are superb.

Copenhagen

A kaleidoscope of history, culture and contemporary entertainment, Copenhagen is Denmark's vibrant capital city and offers an incredible array of experiences. Walk through the cobbled streets of an ancient city, explore world-class museums, experience the finest restaurants and hippest nightlife, or simply unwind beside the gorgeous waters of a peaceful seaside town. Copenhagen has a compact centre that can easily be seen on foot and is also a great city for cycling. This charming destination has something for everyone.

North Sea
Aalborg
Kattegat
SWEDEN
Herning
Aarhus
DENMARK
COPENHAGEN
Esbjerg
Odense
Svendborg
GERMANY

1 Harbour Sights

The best way to soak in the city's plentiful and beautiful harbour sights – including the iconic Little Mermaid statue *(above)* – is to take a harbour trip along the canals of Slotsholmen and Christianshavn. It is also a fantastic way to understand Copenhagen's development over the years.

2 Tivoli

This pleasure garden *(below)* and fun fair attracts kids and adults alike. At night, it turns especially magical with sparkling fairy lights and Chinese lanterns. The rides are brilliant for an adrenaline rush and if you feel peckish, head to one of the many restaurants.

3 Rosenborg Slot and Kongens Have

Set amid one of Copenhagen's prettiest parks, this 17th-century Renaissance castle *(above)* houses the royal collection, including the spectacular Crown Jewels in the basement.

TOP 10 Moments in History

1 Founding of Copenhagen
Copenhagen was founded around AD 1000 on the island of Slotsholmen by Sweyn I. He subjugated Denmark, Norway and England, which he ruled for five weeks before his death in 1014.

2 Growth of Trade
Given by Valdemar I to his adviser, Bishop Absalon, in the 1160s, the village of Havn prospered from fishing. Havn's prosperity threatened the Hanseatic league, an alliance that monopolized trade in Northern Europe. They repeatedly attacked Havn's castle, finally destroying it in 1367.

3 Capital of Denmark
Erik VII took up residence in Havn, now Kjøbmande-havn (Merchants' Harbour), in 1416. Now a major economic centre, it was proclaimed as the capital in 1443.

4 Civil War and the Reformation
Between 1534 and 1536, the Protestant king, Christian III successfully withstood an uprising in favour of his Catholic cousin, Christian II. Christian III brought about the Reformation in Denmark.

5 Absolute Monarchy
Frederik III introduced Absolute Monarchy in 1660, enhancing the powers of the middle classes. Frederik VII later abolished it in favour of an elected Parliament.

6 Wars with Sweden
Sharing the Sound meant constant conflict between Swedes and Danes. An attack on Copenhagen in 1657 led to Denmark ceding its Swedish territories in the Treaty of Roskilde.

7 The Great Plague
Between June 1711 and March 1712, Copenhagen was hit by bubonic plague, wiping out 20,000 of its 60,000 inhabitants.

8 The Fire of 1728
In October, within four days, fire wiped out almost all of northern Copenhagen. Five churches, the university library, and 1,600 houses were destroyed.

9 The Battles of Copenhagen
The city suffered more lasting damage when the British attacked in 1801, and again in 1807 to discourage Danes from supporting France in the Napoleonic wars.

10 Rescue of the Jews
The Nazis occupied Denmark from 1940–45. In 1943, when Jews were ordered to be deported to Germany, almost the entire Jewish population was secretly evacuated to safety in Sweden.

Slotsholmen 5

This is where it all began in the 12th century, when Bishop Absalon built a castle here (you can still see its remains). The present Neo-Baroque castle *(right)* was built in 1907–28, but was never inhabited by the monarch. It is now shared between the Royal family and the Parliament.

4 The Latin Quarter

One of the oldest areas in :openhagen, the Latin Quarter is just off ne main pedestrianized street, Strøget. : is home to the university and the few nedieval buildings in the city.

6 Nationalmuseet

Here is a perfect example of how brilliantly the Danes design their museums. Formerly a palace, the museum houses collections devoted to Danish history. You will also find fabulous ethnographic artifacts from around the world, as well as an excellent children's museum.

7 Kongens Nytorv and Nyhavn

Kongens Nytorv (King's New Square) is a splendid 3aroque square that leads down to Nyhavn. Previously a eedy haunt for sailors, complete with drinking dens and rothels, it has transformed radically in recent times. oday, this scenic area is a popular waterside attraction vith plenty of restaurants and bars *(above)*.

8 Statens Museum for Kunst

You will find a wonderful collection of Danish and European sculpture and paintings at the national gallery. It is set inside a 19th-century building, connected by a glass bridge to a modern wing. There is also a large green park behind the museum.

9 Amalienborg

Home to the royal family since 1794, this complex of palaces represents some of the best Rococo architecture in Denmark. The museum housed in Christian VIII's palace has some fascinating displays.

10 Ny Carlsberg Glyptotek

This fabulous, renovated and extended museum is a definite must-see. It includes wonderful ancient Egyptian, Roman and Mediterranean works of art *(left)*. The new wing boasts an impressive collection of French Impressionist and Post-Impressionist art.

TOP 10 Hans Christian Andersen Sights

1 Det Kongelige Teater
Hans Christian Andersen arrived in Copenhagen, aged 14, on 6 September 1819. Determined to become an actor, he went straight to the Royal Theatre in search of a job.

2 Bakkehusmuseet
Andersen met Knud Rahbek and his wife in the early 1820s. Bakkehus, their home, soon became a meeting place for authors. The museum houses Andersen mementoes.

3 Vingårdsstræde 6
Andersen lived here for a year in 1827, preparing for his university exams. It is where he wrote his sad poem, *The Student*.

4 Nyhavn 20, 67 & 18
Andersen lodged at 20 Nyhavn in 1834, 67 in 1848 and 18 in 1871–5, when he fell terminally ill and moved in with the Melchior family, who nursed him.

5 Magasin du Nord
In 1838, Andersen lived in Hotel du Nord, now the Magasin du Nord store. Mini's Café (now Café à Porta), a regular haunt for the writer, was next door.

6 Rundetårn
The exhibition hall here was once the university library used by Andersen. His tale *The Tinderbox* (1835) talks of a dog with eyes "as big as a tower", a possible reference to the Rundetårn.

7 Hotel d'Angleterre
Andersen stayed here in November 1860, between August 1869 and March 1870, and finally during April–May 1871.

8 Lille Kongensgade 1
In October 1866, Andersen rented a suite of rooms on the third floor from a photographer, Thora Hallager. Here, he bought furniture for the first time in his life (at the age of 61), as this was an unfurnished apartment.

9 Vor Frue Kirke
Andersen died on 4 August 1875 of liver cancer. His funeral, a national event attended by the king and crown prince, was held at Vor Frue Kirke in the Old Town.

10 Assistens Kirkegård
This is the cemetery where Andersen was buried. The gravestone is inscribed with lines from his poem *The Old Man* (1874).

Corsica

Corsica encapsulates the best the Mediterranean has to offer. Protected by strict environmental laws, its coastline has escaped the kind of development that has subsumed the French Rivieras, while the forests, gorges and crumbling villages of the interior have altered little in centuries. The island also preserves a wealth of historic monuments, ranging from the Bronze Age menhirs of the Torréen people to spectacular Genoese citadels.

1 Ajaccio

Beneath the Mediterranean chic of its high-rise outskirts, the capital of Corsica *(left)* has retained a strong historic accent, underlined by the presence of the remarkable Musée Fesch – a storehouse of priceless Renaissance art.

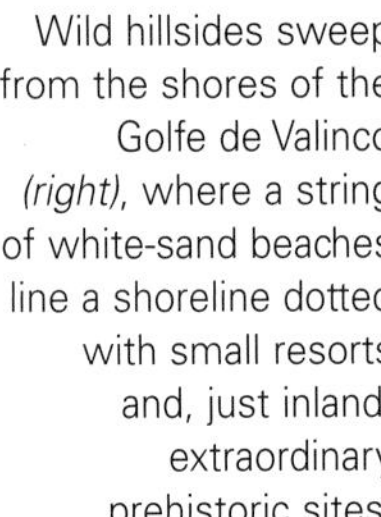

Golfe de Valinco 2

Wild hillsides sweep from the shores of the Golfe de Valinco *(right)*, where a string of white-sand beaches line a shoreline dotted with small resorts and, just inland, extraordinary prehistoric sites.

3 Bonifacio

The striated chalk cliffs of Bonifacio *(above)* are southern Corsica's iconic sight. A perfectly preserved Genoese *haute ville* (upper town) perches on the cliffs above the translucent turquoise water.

Top 10 Moments in History

1 1077: Corsica Becomes a Pisan Protectorate
To rein in feuding local warlords who refused to swear allegiance to the Church, the Pope placed Corsica under Pisan "protection". Some 300 Romanesque chapels survive from the Pisan occupation.

2 1284: The Battle of Meloria
Genoa's naval victory over Pisa at the Battle of Meloria saw it wrest control of Corsica from its long-time adversaries.

3 1564: Sampiero Corso's Rebellion
The Corsican-born mercenary led a succession of uprisings against the Genoese. He died three years later in a vendetta killing at the hands of his wife's brothers.

4 1736: Theodore von Neuhof Uprising
The brief interlude during which this German adventurer set himself up as "King of Corsica" ended after a couple of ineffectual sieges exposed his incompetence.

5 1754: Paoli Returns to Corsica
Son of an exiled nationalist hero, Pascal Paoli made a triumphant return to Corsica to spearhead a full-scale rebellion, as Genoa ceded its territorial rights to France.

6 1769: The Battle of Ponte Nuovo
French forces slaughtered Paoli's ragtag army of patriots and Corsica became a fully integrated part of the French Republic – which it has remained ever since.

7 1918: The End of World War I
Corsica suffered terribly in the aftermath of World War I. Its work force decimated, the rural economy lapsed into a decline from which it has never recovered.

8 1943: Liberation of Corsica
The Allied invasion of southern Italy triggered the withdrawal of German forces from Corsica. The Corsican resistance fought the retreating Germans with great spirit.

9 1975: The Siege of Aléria
In protest against fraudulent wine-making practices by Algerian immigrants, a cell of Corsican nationalists took over the Depeille wine cellar near Aléria. The event marked the start of armed resistance against French rule.

10 1998: Murder of Claude Erignac
The assassination of Corsica's most senior French official galvanized attempts to resolve the armed conflict.

4 Bastia

Facing Tuscany across the Tyrrhenian Sea, Bastia *(left)* has a more chaotic, Italian feel than its southern rival Ajaccio, at its most pervasive in the picturesque Vieux Port.

5 Le Sartenais

Head here if you are searching for wilderness. Prehistorica standing stones are strewn over a landscape of pristine Mediterranean scrub, edged by a succession of remote beaches.

6 Cap Corse

Lovely views of the distant Tuscan Islands lend this peninsula *(above)*, due north of Bastia, a special atmosphere – best savoured with a glass of the local muscat wine.

7 St-Florent and the Nebbio

The attractive port of St-Florent *(right)* is a world away from the bustle of Bastia. Travel across its gulf to swim in some of the Mediterranean's most dazzlingly turquoise coves.

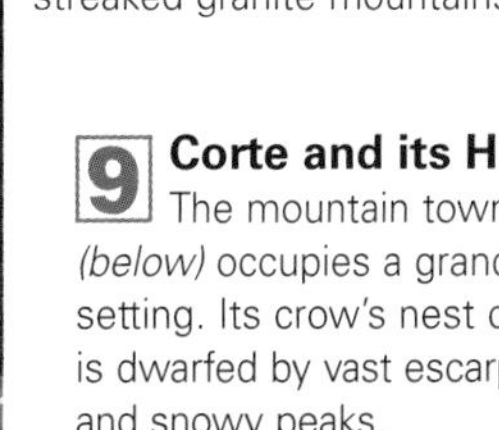

8 Calvi

Calvi's weathered Genoese citadel *(left)* presides over a lovely sweep of white sand, sparkling sea water and snow-streaked granite mountains.

9 Corte and its Hinterland

The mountain town of Corte *(below)* occupies a grandiose setting. Its crow's nest citadel is dwarfed by vast escarpments and snowy peaks.

10 Golfe de Porto

Admire the breathtaking scenery of the northwest, where cliffs of red porphyry plunge into a deep blue gulf. Hop on a boat from Porto's marina to see the Calanches rock formations *(above)*.

Top 10 Prehistoric Sites

1 Castellu d'Araggio
Set high in the hills north of Porto-Vecchio and well worth a detour for the views alone, this marvellous Torréen site retains traces of prehistoric cooking fires.

2 Musée de Préhistoire Corse et d'Archéologie, Sartène
Neolithic pottery fragments, obsidian arrowheads and polished stone axes hold centre stage in this collection of prehistoric artifacts drawn from all over Corsica.

3 Filitosa
This privately owned site in southwest Corsica has earned UNESCO World Heritage status for its statue-menhirs, many of which sport skilfully carved faces and daggers. There's a fascinating small museum.

4 Alignement de Stantari
Two of the carved menhirs here have clearly sculpted features, diagonal swords and sockets in their heads into which horns must once have been fitted.

5 Dolmen de Fontanaccia
This striking granite structure, which dates from the late-megalithic period, ranks among the best-preserved in southern Europe. Its former contents now reside in the museum at Sartène.

6 Alignement de Palaggiu
Most of the 258 menhirs at this extraordinary site date from 1800 BC. Sited near the coast, they may have been a deterrent to would-be invaders. Whatever their origins, the stones still cast an undeniably eerie spell.

7 Pianu di Levie (Cucuruzzu)
A fairytale woodland of twisted oaks and mossy boulders enfolds the magical Pianu di Levie, whose *pièce de résistance*, Cucuruzzu, is a well-preserved Torréen castle dating from around 1400 BC.

8 Musée de l'Alta Rocca, Levie
This otherwise unremarkable village museum has a single prize exhibit: "La Dame de Bonifacio" – a female human skeleton dating from 6570 BC.

9 U Nativu, Patrimonio
This superb statue-menhir dating from 900–800 BC bears distinct if somewhat sombre facial features and a T-shaped breastbone.

10 The Pieve Menhirs
This village in the hills overlooking St-Florent has three statue-menhirs. The family group, chiselled some 3,500 years ago from local granite, appear to be gazing wistfully over the valley.

Costa Blanca

Sun, sea and sand are excellent reasons to visit Spain's Costa Blanca, but its attractions don't stop there. Inland, you can explore magnificent natural parks, wild sierras and remote hill villages, or visit historic towns with fascinating museums and a wealth of fabulous architecture. The engaging capital cities of Alicante (Alacant) and Murcia are crammed with great shops and tapas bars, and a string of lively resorts along the coast offers splendid beaches, fantastic nightlife and plenty of opportunities for fun. Best of all, there's always a secret cove or rugged cape to be discovered if the crowds get too much.

1 Parque Regional de Calblanque

This gorgeous stretch of unspoilt coastline *(left)* is one of the region's best-kept secrets. The golden beaches and quiet coves are peaceful even in the height of the tourist season.

2 Castillo de Santa Bárbara, Alicante

Visible for miles around, Alicante's dramatic castle *(above)* looms high on a dusty pinnacle. Its sturdy ramparts and watchtowers offer spectacular views over the endless blue of the Mediterranean.

3 Guadalest

The enchanting hilltop village of Guadalest *(above)* sits under the romantic ruins of a battered castle, and overlooks a beautiful valley with a deep turquoise lake.

Top 10 Moments in History

1 c. 50000 BC–c.1000 BC: Prehistory
Cave dwellers lived in the inland hills from around 50000 BC. Iberian settlements began to appear around 3000 BC.

2 c.1000 BC–c. 200BC: Phoenicians, Greeks and Carthaginians
By 1000 BC, the Phoenicians and the Greeks had trading settlements along the coast. The Carthaginians founded Cartago Nova (Cartagena) in the 3rd century BC.

3 c. 200 BC–c. AD 400: Roman Rule
Rome's defeat of Carthage began their domination of the Iberian Peninsula. They established settlements at Denia (Dénia), Alicante (Alacant) and Cartagena.

4 c. 400–711: Visigoths
By the mid-4th century AD, the Roman Empire had splintered, and the Peninsula was invaded by successive northern tribes. The Visigoths arrived in 411 and eventually took control of most of Spain.

5 711–c.1200: Arabs
In 711, the first Berber armies invaded the Iberian Peninsula, conquering most of it within a decade and renaming it Al-Andalus.

6 c.1200–c.1300: The Reconquista
Pockets of northern Spain remained resistant to the Arabs, and from here the Christian Reconquest began. Battles raged through much of the 13th century.

7 1244–c.1700: The Kingdom of Valencia
After the Reconquest, Jaime I re-established the Kingdom of Valencia, with privileges including its own court and currency. These rights were stripped after it backed the losing side in the War of the Succession (1700–14).

8 1244–c.1700: Murcia on the Frontier
In 1244, Murcia, strategically located on the border with Arabic Granada, became a vassal of the Kingdom of Castile, which annexed it in 1266. Granada fell in 1492, and Muslim converts flooded into Murcia. Their expulsion in the early 17th century caused economic crisis.

9 The Lost Years (1700–1939)
Spain endured wars and political upheavals throughout the 18th and 19th centuries. Then simmering unrest in the early 20th century erupted into the Civil War (1936–9), won by General Franco.

10 Since 1939
The 1960s advent of mass tourism brought jobs, money and new development to popular coastal regions like the Costa Blanca. After Franco died in 1975, democracy was peacefully restored.

4 Penyal d'Ifac (Peñón de Ifach)

A designated Natural Park, this extraordinary rock *(left)* erupts spectacularly from the sea. The views from the summit are breathtaking.

5 Casa-Museo Modernista, Novelda

Every detail of this Art Nouveau-style town house *(below)* is exquisite, from the sinuous staircase with its vine-leaf motif to the rainbow-coloured skylights.

6 Sierra de Espuña

A beautiful stretch of forest and craggy peaks, the Natural Park of Sierra de Espuña *(above)* offers excellent hiking, a wealth of wildlife and complete peace.

7 Hort del Cura, Elx (Elche)

This luxuriant garden, the most beautiful corner of the famous palm groves of Elx, is a tranquil enclave of tropical flowers and cactuses shaded by palm trees.

8 Isla Tabarca

The tiny island of Tabarca *(above)* is rimmed with rocky coves and sandy beaches, and the surrounding marine reserve is a paradise for snorkellers and divers.

9 Catedral de Santa María, Murcia

Several centuries in the making, Murcia Cathedral *(above)* is one of the finest Baroque buildings in Spain, with a frilly bell tower, a sumptuous façade and lavishly decorated chapels.

10 Palau Ducal, Gandia

This sumptuous Gothic palace *(left)*, towering over the river Serpis and magnificently embellished over the centuries, was home to St Francis of Borja.

Top 10 Wine Towns

1 Jumilla
Jumilla tumbles down a hillside, overlooked by a 15th-century castle. The local *bodegas* make a robust red from Monastrell and a rosé from Garnacha grapes.

2 Yecla
Yecla is the prettiest of all the wine towns in the Costa Blanca. It's best known for its light, fruity red wines. Many of Yecla's *bodegas* offer tastings and tours.

3 Bullas
This medieval village sits in a valley lush with endless rows of vines. Wine has been made here since Roman times; the Museo del Vino tells the story. Good for rosés and red table wines.

4 Abanilla
Albanilla produces much of its wine under the Alicante D.O. Robust reds and some whites, they are usually drunk young, and are well suited to the local cuisine.

5 Monóvar
One of the Alicante region's major wine towns. At its many *bodegas* you can pick up a potent local red, fresh rosé, or the celebrated El Fondillón, a dessert wine that takes 20 years to mature.

6 Alguenya (Algueña)
This small village is known for its hearty traditional cuisine, particularly cured sausages. The local wine, a strong, earthy red, is the perfect accompaniment.

7 Hondón
Two hamlets in the midst of a vine-covered plain, Hondón de las Nieves and Hondón de los Frailes, sell their wines in the *bodegas* lining the Monóvar–Jumilla road.

8 El Pinós (Pinoso)
Sitting on a low hill above a sea of vines, El Pinós is an affluent little town with a rambling old centre around a pretty clock tower. Sample its vigorous young reds at one of the many *bodegas*.

9 Teulada
The smart, upmarket resort of Teulada has long been famous for its moscatel grapes, which are used to make its refreshing but sweet white *mistela* wine.

10 Xaló (Jalón)
The formerly sleepy village of Xaló is now surrounded by holiday homes, but some traditions, including wine-making, continue, with reds, whites, rosés and a sweet white *mistela* produced.

Cracow

The Polish city of Cracow is one of the most beautiful cities in Europe. Over the centuries, many important artists and architects came to work here, among them Veit Stoss from Germany, Bartolomeo Berrecci and Giovanni Maria Padovano from Italy, and Tylman van Gameren from Holland. Because it escaped significant damage in the two World Wars, Cracow preserves the largest assemblage of historic buildings and monuments in Poland. In 1978 UNESCO declared it a World Heritage Site.

Baltic Sea
RUSSIA
Gdańsk
Szczecin
BELARUS
Poznan
Warsaw
POLAND
Wrocław
Katowice
CRACOW
CZECH REPUBLIC
UKRAINE
SLOVAKIA

1 Barbican

This late-15th-century moated cylindrical structure *(left)* with 3-m- (10-ft-) thick walls is one of the few elements of Cracow's medieval fortifications to remain intact.

2 Main Market Square

Laid out in 1257, this huge market square *(above)* – one of the largest in Europe – seethes with life all year round, as visitors flock to its cafés, bars, restaurants, shops, museums, galleries and historic sights.

3 Czartoryski Museum

This museum may be on a relatively modest scale but it has one of the most interesting art collections in Poland. Its star exhibits are Leonardo da Vinci's *Lady with an Ermine* *(left)* and Rembrandt's *Landscape with Good Samaritan.*

TOP 10 Moments in History

1 Prehistoric Cracow
Traces of settlements from the Paleolithic and Neolithic periods have been found, as well as from the Bronze and Iron Ages.

2 Celts, Romans and Moravians
From the 1st to the 4th century AD, Celts, Scythians and Huns living the area traded with the Roman Empire. In the 9th century, the area came under the rule of the Great Moravian Empire.

3 Medieval Cracow
Cracow became the capital of Poland in 1038, and developed rapidly. Although destroyed by Mongol invaders during the 13th century, it was rebuilt and became celebrated as a centre for culture and learning.

4 Cracow's Golden Age
During the 15th and 16th centuries, Cracow flourished. The art and culture of the Italian Renaissance was adopted by the royal courts. In 1572 King Sigismund II died childless, precipitating a succession crisis. In 1596 the capital moved to Warsaw.

5 The Partitions
A series of invasions weakened Poland in the 17th and 18th centuries. During the 1790s Poland's powerful neighbours, Prussia, Russia and Austria, divided Poland up between themselves.

6 Cracow in the Austro-Hungarian Empire
After a period of Austrian occupation, Cracow was briefly incorporated into the Duchy of Warsaw. Russian occupation followed. In 1815 the Republic of Cracow was established, but by 1846 it was under Austrian rule again.

7 The "Polish Athens"
During the 19th century Cracow was the only Polish territory to enjoy relative freedom. It embarked upon a mission of safeguarding traditions, becoming the spiritual capital of Poland.

8 World Wars I and II
Poland regained its independence in 1918 at the end of World War I. It was occupied by the Nazis in World War II, and control ceded to the Soviets in 1945. Cracow was spared destruction, and its historical centre preserved.

9 Soviet Rule
The city expanded under the Soviets, who built the new industrial suburb of Nowa Huta. In 1978 the Old Town became a UNESCO World Heritage Site. Poland was under Soviet rule until 1989 and the fall of Communism.

10 Modern Cracow
Poland's first free elections were held in 1991. In 2004 the country joined the EU. Cracow preserved its role as the nation's cultural capital.

4 Wawel Royal Castle

Once the hub of Polish cultural and political life, this imposing Renaissance castle *(right)* set on a Jurassic limestone rock remains a potent symbol of national identity.

5 National Museum

The huge main building of Cracow's National Museum is home to three main collections: decorative arts, militaria and 20th-century painting and sculpture.

6 Ulica Floriańska

This charming street in the old town *(left)*, now full of restaurants, cafés and shops, was once part of the Royal Route, along which rulers would ride on their way from Warsaw to their coronation in Cracow.

7 Former Jewish Quarter

Founded in the 14th century by Kazimierz the Great, the district of Kazimierz was home to Cracow's Jewish population for more than 500 years. Steven Spielberg's film *Schindler's List* was largely shot here.

8 Plac Szczepański

Recently restored to its former splendour, this historic square lined with magnificent town houses is also home to the oldest theatrical building in Poland, as well as some interesting art galleries.

9 Cloth Hall

This beautiful Renaissance building *(below)* in the centre of Main Market Square replaced an earlier Gothic market hall. Today it is home to a selection of cafés and souvenir shops, and, on the upper floor, the Gallery of Polish Painting.

10 Royal Cathedral

The site of coronations and royal burials through the ages, this Gothic cathedral *(above)* is still regarded as Poland's national sanctuary. Its 18 chapels are full of artistic treasures.

TOP 10 Churches and Abbeys

1 Church of St Mary
Designed to rival the Royal Cathedral, building began in 1355 and was not completed until the 16th century. The great Basilica, with its rows of side chapels, contains an exceptional number of great works of art. A trumpet call is sounded hourly from the Henjal tower.

2 Dominican Church
This is a magnificent Gothic building, with mortuary chapels that are works of Renaissance and Baroque art in their own right. Those of the Zbaraski and the Myszkowski families are particularly lovely.

3 Piarist Church
The exceptionally beautiful Rococo façade of Piarist church conceals that of an older, Baroque church. The interior has fine stucco work.

4 Church of St Anne
It is impossible to miss this imposing, twin-towered church, set on a narrow street. There are fine murals, Baroque choir stalls and a lavish reliquary.

5 Franciscan Church
The most notable features of this church are the gorgeous Art Nouveau murals and stained-glass windows, by Stanislaw Wyspianski and dating from around 1900.

6 Church of Saints Peter and Paul
One of the most beautiful early Baroque churches in Poland, it was built for the Jesuits soon after their arrival in Cracow.

7 Pauline Church on the Rock
This impressive Baroque church, with its adjoining monastery complex, has a crypt which has been converted into something of a Pantheon to Polish writers and artists.

8 Church of Corpus Christi
This mighty Gothic church was built in the 14th and 15th centuries. It has some fine works of art, including *The Birth of Christ* by Thomasso Dolabella.

9 Benedictine Abbey in Tyniec
On the site of a Romanesque basilica, this handsome abbey is set on a chalky outcrop overlooking the Vistula river. Elements of the original building can be seen underground in the adjacent abbey.

10 Cistercian Abbey in Mogila
Behind the Baroque façade is concealed the interior of an early Gothic interior and a remarkable collection of Renaissance paintings.

Croatia

Croatia is a fascinating country with great ethnic, historical and architectural diversity as well as varied topography. The north had close ties with the former Austrian empire, and the bell towers alongside 19th-century Baroque churches and buildings have a Viennese look. The eastern side marks the start of the Hungarian plain, with broad rivers and houses with overhanging roofs. The Adriatic coast is quite different, with its indented coastline fringed with lovely islands. The coastal cities reflect the centuries-old Venetian culture, with churches, monasteries, palaces and forts testifying to the brilliance of the late Middle Ages and the greatness of the Renaissance period.

1 St Mark's Square, Zagreb

Zagreb's oldest square, with its fine Gothic church *(left)* of the same name, is the heart of the Gornji Grad district.

3 Plitvice Lakes National Park

One of nature's wonders, this area of 300 sq km (115 sq miles) encompasses 16 lakes surrounded by forest, with a rich variety of flora and bird life. The park is particularly known for its spectacular waterfalls.

2 Basiclica of Euphrasius, Poreč

The splendid mosaics that decorate this stunning 6th-century church *(right)* are among the best-preserved examples of Byzantine art in Croatia.

4 Kornati National Park

Surrounded by clear seas, this archipelago of more than 150 wooded, rocky islands *(above)*, with underwater caves and sheltered coves, presents an unforgettable sight.

TOP 10 Moments in History

1 Prehistoric Croatia
Human remains dating from the Neanderthal period have been found in Croatia. From about 1200 BC, several Indo-European tribes settled in an area which came to be known as Ilyria.

2 Roman Conquest
The Romans subdued the entire region by 9AD. They built an impressive road network, established new settlements, and erected grand monuments such as those in Pula and Split.

3 The Kingdom of the Croats
After the fall of the Roman Empire, waves of invaders – Avars, Slavs, Bulgars and Byzantines – poured into the country. The Croats began to settle in the 7th century.

4 Union with Hungary
The Hungarian king Ladislaus conquered Croatia in the 12th century. He was crowned king of Croatia and Dalmatia. Fortresses were built to defend against the threat of the Tartars and the Turks.

5 Venice and the Republic of Ragusa
Venice conquered Istria and the city of Dubrovnik in 1205, and ruled for 150 years. In the 14th century, Dubrovnik (Ragusa in Italian) became a thriving republic.

6 Ottoman Domination
In 1463 the Ottomans invaded Croatia and conquered much of Hungary over the following century. In 1527 Habsburg ruler Ferdinand I became king and Croatia became part of the Austro-Hungarian Empire.

7 The Austro-Hungarian Empire
After the Ottoman retreat, Croatia stayed under Austrian control until the assassination of Archduke Franz Ferdinand in Sarajevo in 1914, which triggered World War I.

8 World War I
The Habsburg Empire waned during World War I and Croatia was granted independence in 1918. It became part of a state formed by Slovenes and Serbs, later replaced by the Kingdom of Yugoslavia.

9 World War II
Yugoslavia was occupied by Germany and Italy during World War II, but the invaders met heavy resistance from anti-Fascists led by Tito.

10 Post-World War II
At the end of World War II, Croatia became part of the Socialist Federal Rupublic of Yugoslavia. After the collapse of Communism, Croatia declared independence in 1991, sparking a war which ended in 1995. In 2013 Croatia joined the European Union.

5 The Palace of Diocletian, Split

The largest Roman building in the Adriatic *(above)* was built by Emperor Diocletian at the end of the 3rd century as his retirement home. The city of Split grew up in and around it.

Zagorje 6

This fascinating area near the border with Slovenia is somewhat off the beaten tourist track, despite its lovely scenery of vine-covered hills *(right)*, spa towns, forests and medieval castles.

7 Kopački Rit Park

Once a year in this park *(above)*, the Danube overflows and creates an immense wetland marsh that gives sanctuary to hundreds of bird species.

8 The Tvrđa, Osijek

A magnificent series of fortified Baroque buildings in the centre of Osijek, the Tvrđa was commenced after the defeat of Ottoman forces in 1687. More like a city than a fort, it houses the Town Hall, the university faculties and the Museum of Slavonia.

9 Dubrovnik

Set in the limpid waters of the Adriatic, Dubrovnik *(above)* is one of the top international tourist destinations of Dalmatia, renowned for the beauty of its monuments, its magnificent city walls and also its welcoming atmosphere *(see also pp48–9)*.

10 Pula Amphitheatre

The huge arena in Pula *(left)* remained intact until the 15th century when its stone was used in the castle and other buildings. It has been restored and is now a venue for opera, rock concerts and an annual film festival.

TOP 10 Outdoor Activities

1 Sailing
The Croatian coastline is a paradise for sailors. In fact, the best way to explore the rugged beauty of its Adriatic coast is by boat. Conditions are perfect for learning to sail, too, and there are plenty of courses for beginners.

2 Windsurfing
Most coastal resorts hire boards and run courses, but serious windsurfers should head for Bol on the island of Brač, or Viganj or the Pelješac peninsula. The season runs from April to October.

3 Diving
Corals, underwater caves, sea walls, wrecks and an abundance of fish in crystal-clear waters make for great diving. Lošinj Island has a combination of all these.

4 Fishing
The Adriatic Sea has some of the richest fish stocks in Europe and draws all kinds of fishermen. Licences are not expensive but there are strict regulations on what and where you may fish.

5 Mountain Hiking
Croatia is criss-crossed by hiking paths and trekking trails, all clearly marked. Don't stray off the trails, though, as the removal of unexploded mines from the 1991–5 war is still ongoing.

6 Climbing
Croatia's rugged limstone karst peaks offer challenges to experienced and novice climbers alike. The Palenica National Park has over 400 climbing routes.

7 Cycling
Regional tourist boards have worked hard to establish designated bike routes, and national parks and nature reserves offer clearly marked circuits. A bike is often the best way to get around an island – expect to pay around €10–15 a day for bike hire.

8 Tennis
The country that gave the world Goran Ivanišević is very proud of its tennis facilities, and almost every town, holiday hotel and campsite will offer clay courts of a high standard.

9 Whitewater Rafting
The most accessible of the extreme sports took off in Croatia in the late 1980s, opening up canyons and rivers known only before to kayakers and fishermen. The rivers of Dalmatia and central Croatia offer plenty of thrills.

10 Thermal Spas
For some outdoor inactivity, few things can beat the fabulous open-air thermal spas in northern Croatia, certain to cure every ache.

Cyprus

Cyprus packs a remarkable array of sights and attractions into such a small space: museums and archaeological sites that span more than five millennia of history, throbbing beach resorts, medieval fortresses, age-old temples standing on empty hillsides, cool mountain forests and pretty valleys chequered with vineyards, grain fields and olive groves all complete the landscape. On an island where one can swim and ski all in the same day, this is truly a holiday paradise with something for everyone.

1 Troodos Painted Churches

The plain stone walls of these old Orthodox sanctuaries, hidden in remote valleys and glens of the Troodos mountains, conceal a unique treasury of vividly coloured frescoes *(left)* depicting scenes from both the Old and New Testaments.

Agia Napa 2

This resort has a reputation as the liveliest spot in Cyprus *(right)*, with great beaches, watersports and a huge number of bars, cafés and restaurants catering to every taste.

3 Akamas Peninsula

The hillsides and headlands of the Akamas form the island's last undeveloped frontier. Here, on Cyprus's only uncrowded beaches *(above)*, turtles come each year to nest.

TOP 10 Moments in History

1 Prehistoric Cyprus
Neolithic people settled Cyprus more than 10,000 years ago. By 2500 BC Cyprus was part of a Bronze Age civilization with links to Egypt, Asia Minor and the Aegean. In the 12th century BC Achaean Greeks began to oust the original inhabitants.

2 Geometric, Archaic and Classical Periods
By 1050 BC there were ten city-states and a flourishing cult of Aphrodite. The wealth of Cyprus lured Phoenicians, who settled at Kition, as well as Assyrian, Egyptian and Persian invaders. In 325 BC Alexander the Great added Cyprus to his empire.

3 Hellenistic Era
After Alexander's death Cyprus fell to the Ptolemy dynasty of Alexandria until 58 BC, when the island was conquered by Rome. The saints Paul and Barnabas brought Christianity in AD 45.

4 Byzantine Era
From AD 330 Cyprus was ruled by Constantinople. For three centuries the island was plagued by Arab pirates who were not defeated until 965.

5 The Lusignans
Richard the Lionheart seized Cyprus in 1191 and sold it to the Knights Templar, who sold it on to Guy de Lusignan. Roman Catholicism supplanted the Greek Orthodox faith.

6 The Venetians
Venice acquired Cyprus in 1489, and fortified Nicosia and Famagusta against the Ottomans, but in 1571 the island finally fell to the Turks.

7 The Ottomans
The Turks restored the Greek Orthodox faith whilst also encouraging conversion to Islam. In 1878, Britain took over in return for supporting Turkey against Russia and, in 1914, annexed Cyprus.

8 Independent Cyprus
Cyprus won independence from Britain in August 1960 after a violent liberation struggle by Greek Cypriots. Friction between Greek and Turkish Cypriot communities continued and, in 1974, Athens engineered a coup against the Cypriot government, aimed at uniting Cyprus with Greece. Turkey invaded to protect Turkish Cypriots. Since then, the "Green Line", patrolled by UN troops, divides the Turkish-occupied north from the south.

9 Divided Cyprus
In 1983 the northern part of the island declared itself independent as the Turkish Republic of Northern Cyprus, still recognized only by Turkey.

10 Rapprochement
In April 2003 the Turkish Cypriot authorities approved free movement by Greek Cypriots and visitors to the north of the island. Members of both communities now regularly visit the "other side".

4 Historic Limassol (Lemesos)

Narrow market streets full of produce stalls and craft workshops surround the sturdy medieval castle in the heart of the old quarter. Mosques and minarets are reminders of the island's multicultural history.

5 Cyprus Museum, Nicosia (Lefkosia)

This superb museum *(below)* has a collection of finds from ancient and medieval sites all over the island. The display of clay figurines is just one of its fascinating exhibits.

6 Pierides-Marfin Laiki Bank Museum, Larnaka

Founded by a 19th-century philanthropist to rescue Cyprus's vanishing heritage, this collection includes remarkable ancient idols and early 20th-century traditional costumes.

7 Kourion

The multi-tiered stone theatre of ancient Kourion *(above)* is often the summer setting for concerts; when not in use it offers views over the peninsula.

8 Ancient Amathous

It takes a little imagination to conjure up an image of Amathous in ancient times, from the fragments of walls that still remain, but this hillside temple site *(above)*, just a short distance from the busy coastal highway, is proof of the city's glorious past.

9 Nicosia Walled City

The divided city, within medieval ramparts, is full of interest. With a clutch of museums, monuments *(above)*, historic buildings, a lively morning market and authentic cafés and restaurants, it merits a leisurely visit.

10 Kato Pafos Archaeological Park

The superb mosaics *(right)* that adorned the floors of lavish villas built at Pafos in its Roman Imperial heyday are now part of a UNESCO World Heritage Site. Today they are one of the island's top historical attractions.

Top 10 Monasteries and Convents

1 Stavrovouni Monastery
This monastery, founded in the 4th century by St Helena, mother of Constantine the Great, is said to house a fragment of the Holy Cross. Its monks, who keep strict vows, are renowned icon painters. No women are allowed to enter.

2 Agios Irakleidos Convent
Founded in AD 400, this monastery (now a convent) honours Irakleidos, who welcomed saints Paul and Barnabas to Cyprus. His bones are displayed in an ornate silver reliquary.

3 Agios Minas Convent
Graceful white cloisters surround a 15th-century church. The fine icons painted by the nuns are sought-after by collectors.

4 Machairas Monastery
Picturesquely located and sensitively restored, Machairas was founded in 1148. The centuries-old monks' cells are fascinating, and there is a fine collection of superbly executed icons.

5 Agios Georgios Alamanos Convent
Lovingly tended flower and herb gardens surround this little convent, which was founded almost 900 years ago. They are cultivated by a small community of nuns, who also make their own honey, for sale here.

6 Panagia tis Amasgou
Wonderful but unrestored frescoes, dating from the 12th to the 16th centuries, are the must-see feature of this nunnery church.

7 Kykkos Monastery
This 900-year-old shrine guards a miracle-working icon of the Virgin Mary. It has been hidden from profane eyes for centuries and remains so to this day. Kykkos is a centre for Greek Orthodoxy, attracting pilgrims from all over the world.

8 Chrysorrogiatissa Monastery
A treasury of icons and religious ornaments has been hoarded here since the monastery's foundation in the 12th century. The monks also make some of Cyprus's finest wines.

9 Panagia tou Sinti Monastery
Standing on the banks of the river Xeros, 16th-century Panagia tou Sinti is one of the island's most important Venetian buildings.

10 Agios Neofytos Monastery
The elaborate iron crowns and silken vestments of Orthodox bishops are among the highlights of this 12th-century monastery's museum. Equally fascinating are the frescoes in its cave-like chapel, a grotto dug by Neofytos, the hermit who founded it.

Devon and Cornwall

The southwest peninsula holds some of Britain's most forbidding moorland, dramatic coastline and enticing beaches. Its history, dating from Celtic times, is strikingly illustrated in its castles and stately homes, while year-round, a range of outdoor activities and all-weather attractions provide entertainment and instruction for the whole family. Equally renowned for old-fashioned tranquillity and soul-stirring views, Devon and Cornwall provide the ideal canvas for the perfect holiday.

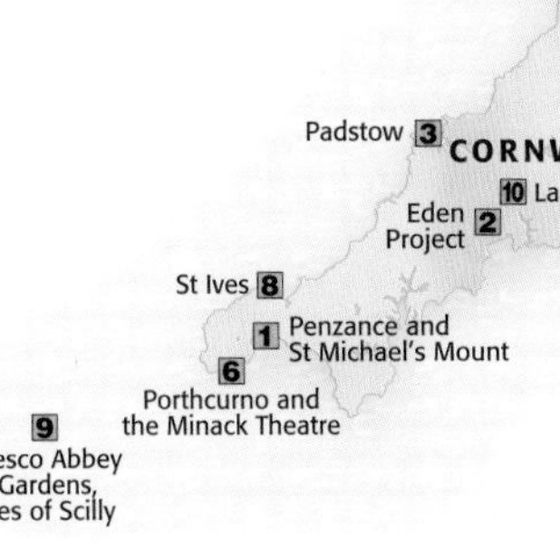

1 Penzance and St Michael's Mount

Penzance sits at the northern end of Mount Bay. Art-lovers will appreciate the two excellent galleries here. Across the bay is St Michael's Mount *(left)*, known locally as The Mount – a fortified house crowning an island which is linked to the mainland by a causeway.

2 Eden Project

Conservation is made fun at this wide-ranging exploration of the plant world, dominated by two giant greenhouses *(right)*. Summer concerts, winter ice-skating and several cafés and restaurants serving great food enhance its appeal.

3 Padstow

This North Cornwall fishing port *(above)* is famous for its gourmet restaurants, beaches, historic houses and a cycling and walking trail.

TOP 10 Moments in History

1 AD 50–55: The Romans Invade
The Romans occupied Exeter and established a strong garrison without penetrating further west, where Celts held sway. Few vestiges of Roman occupation remain.

2 6th and 7th Centuries: Anglo-Saxons Settle
As the Romans withdrew, Anglo-Saxon tribes began to settle in the region, but they made little headway against the hardy Celts, whose strongholds were largely concentrated in Cornwall.

3 11th to 16th Centuries: Wool
Devon's wool industry flourished under the Normans. Owners of fertile inland pastures built mansions, and merchants exported produce to Europe from the southern ports, which grew rich.

4 1530s: Dissolution of the Monasteries
The great monastic houses were suppressed by order of Henry VIII. Some were destroyed; others, like Buckfast Abbey, became grand residences.

5 1558–1603: The Elizabethan Era
During the Spanish conflict, there were strategic military and naval bases at Exeter and Plymouth. The first English colonists of the New World set sail from here.

6 1642–51: The Civil War
During the Civil War the region was largely Royalist. Charles I defeated the Earl of Essex's army in 1644 but Royalists were checked by Thomas Fairfax's forces, leading to the fall of Pendennis Castle and Exeter in 1646.

7 18th Century: Tin and Copper Mining
Scientific advances in the 18th century allowed the tin and copper mining industry to become highly profitable. Copper mining, based around Redruth and Camborne, peaked in the 1840s.

8 1743–86: Wesleyism
The impoverished conditions of the region's miners led to widespread acceptance of the Methodist preaching of John Wesley. Methodist chapels are still visible in the region today.

9 1884 Onwards: Artists' Colonies Established
Drawn by intense light, dramatic seascapes and the life of fishing communities, painter Stanhope Forbes settled in Newlyn, near Penzance, in 1884 and became the leading figure in the artists' colony.

10 1939–45: World War II
Plymouth suffered the worst bombing of any British seaport during World War II. Exeter was also targeted in the "Baedeker raids", aimed at cultural centres mentioned in Baedeker guidebooks.

4 Dartmoor

A range of activities is possible on this bleak expanse of moorland *(above)*, which is complemented by grand houses and cosy villages sheltering thatched pubs.

5 Plymouth

Enjoying a superb location, this seafaring city was the home port of the intrepid sailor Sir Francis Drake. It still preserves traces of the Elizabethan era. Within a short distance are palatial houses and country parks.

6 Porthcurno and the Minack Theatre

Porthcurno has a range of outdoor attractions, including a sandy beach between high cliffs and the open-air Minack Theatre, hewn out of the rock.

7 Exeter

Rising from the River Exe, the capital of Devon has a strong historical flavour, not least in its cathedral *(above)* and other ancient monuments. It also has a buzzing and vibrant contemporary cultural life.

8 St Ives

Home to the Tate St Ives gallery, this quirky seaside town *(above)* has a thriving arts scene. Sandy beaches and excellent restaurants are further attractions here.

9 Tresco Abbey Gardens

Out in the Atlantic, on the wind-blasted island of Tresco in the Isles of Scilly, this gracious garden of semi-tropical plants has been created within the walls of a ruined abbey.

10 Lanhydrock

This impressive mansion with a 17th-century gatehouse *(right)* is filled with Jacobean art and Victorian furnishings. Immaculate gardens and sweeping parkland surround the house.

TOP 10 Beaches

1 Porthcurno
This wedge of white sand mixed with tiny shells fringes one of the finest bays of the Penwith Peninsula. Close by are pubs, cafés, the rock-hewn Minack Theatre and a small museum of telegraphy.

2 Par Beach, Isles of Scilly
Majestic, bare and wild, the beaches of St Martin's are the best on Scilly. This long, empty strand on the island's southern shore is probably the most impressive.

3 Whitesand Bay
This expanse of fine sand near Land's End is favoured by surfers and families alike. It has a good beachside café and, at the southern end, the Old Success Inn.

4 Kynance Cove
Beaches are scarce on the Lizard Peninsula. This is one of the best, with fine white sands, rocky spires and surrounding grassy areas, though swimming is limited by the tides.

5 Woolacombe Bay
This famous surfing beach is also popular with families. Crowds gather at the northern end; the southern end is quieter. The small resort of Woolacombe has shops and cafés.

6 Fistral Bay
Surf aficionados flock here. Most of the sand is covered by water at high tide and strong currents mean that kids need to be careful.

7 Watergate Bay
This arc of golden sand north of Newquay is home to the Extreme Academy, which offers adventurous pursuits like kite-surfing and land-boarding. Close by are Jamie Oliver's famous restaurant Fifteen, as well as the more casual Beach Hut.

8 Tunnels Beach, Ilfracombe
This private beach is named after the tunnels that have provided access to it since 1823. There is a tidal bathing pool and lifeguards make the beach safe for kids.

9 Croyde Bay
Sandwiched between the extensive west-facing Saunton Sands and Woolacombe, this compact bay has fine sand. There are campsites nearby.

10 Blackpool Sands
This family-friendly beach, one of South Devon's best swimming spots, makes an enticing sight as it swings into view on the road from Dartmouth, as does the renowned Venus Café.

Dublin

One of the most popular capitals in Europe, Dublin (from the Irish Gaelic *dubh linn*, meaning "black pool") is a city steeped in history. Huddled together within a small vicinity you'll find Viking remains, medieval cathedrals and churches, Georgian squares and excellent museums. But it's not just about buildings – music, theatre, literature and pubs play just as strong a part in the atmosphere of this diverse, creative and vibrant city.

1 Trinity College
The elder statesman of Ireland's universities, Trinity *(above)* is also one of the oldest in Europe. Its buildings and grounds are a landmark in the heart of the city.

2 Guinness Storehouse
A pint of Guinness could be the country's national symbol *(below)*. This fascinating exhibition at the Guinness Brewery ends with a welcome free pint of the famous black stuff in the sampling bar.

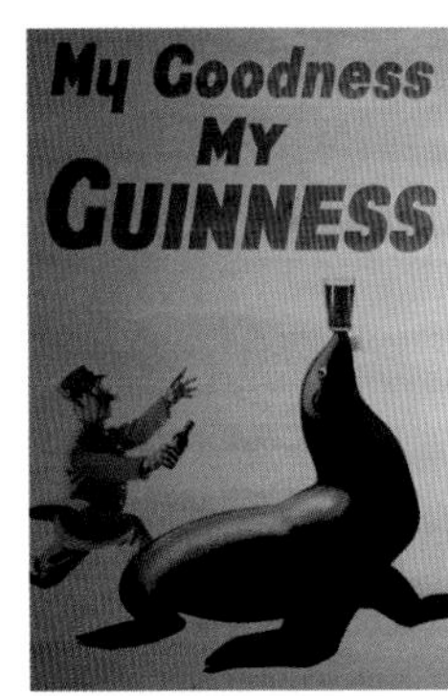

3 Dublin Castle
A surprisingly peaceful area, the castle *(above)* was built into the medieval walls of the city and originally protected by the River Liffey to the north and the now underground River Poddle.

TOP 10 Moments in History

1 Newgrange
The first Neolithic settlers arrived in Ireland from the Continent around 4500 BC, bringing with them farming skills and rudimentary tools. The stone tomb at Newgrange is thought to date from around 3000 BC. and is one of the most important passage graves in Europe.

2 Celts Arrive
Tribes of powerful Celtic warriors became established in Central Europe around 600 BC. They were able to progress across the Continent to Ireland, imposing their authority, culture and language on earlier inhabitants.

3 Christianity Comes to Ireland
The Romans never settled in Ireland, but helped bring Christianity to its shores. The first bishop was appointed in AD 431, although it is St Patrick who established the Church between 432 and 461.

4 Viking Ireland
The Vikings established their own communities in Ireland in the 10th century. In 1030, a wooden church was built where Christ Church Cathedral now stands.

5 First Irish Parliament
By the 1350s the Normans had settled in Ireland and introduced the feudal system of government, led by a justiciar. He was assisted by a council of officials, and would occasionally summon a parliament consisting of his council, bishops, abbots and feudal lords. By the end of the 14th century, county and town representatives formed a Lower House, or Commons.

6 Battle of the Boyne
After his defeat by William of Orange at the Battle of the Boyne in 1690, James II fled to France, leaving Ireland in the hands of the Protestant Ascendancy (descendants of English settlers). The native Irish suffered for more than a century from stringent penal measures inflicted on them.

7 Georgian High Culture
Many of the most important sights in the city, such as Custom House, were built during the Georgian era. Artists and musicians flocked to Dublin from all parts of Europe – one of the highlights was the premiere of Handel's oratorio, *The Messiah*, in Dublin in 1741.

8 The Great Famine
The potato famine dominated 19th-century Ireland. The crop failed first in 1845, then again in 1846–7. Over a million people died of starvation or emigrated in desperation. By 1849 the population had decreased by about two million.

9 The Easter Rising
On Easter Monday 1916, Patrick Pearse and others who were opposed to British rule proclaimed the Declaration of Independence from the General Post Office in O'Connell Street. An uprising ensued and 15 insurgents were executed. In May 1921, the Anglo-Irish treaty was signed, creating the Irish Free State.

10 Pope John Paul II
In 1979, Pope John Paul II visited Ireland. The high point of his visit was his mass in Phoenix Park, which was attended by more than a million people. The Papal Cross marks the spot.

4 National Gallery of Ireland

Wonderful Italian, French, Dutch and panish works are exhibited here, alongside great collection of Irish art *(above)*.

5 National Museum of Ireland

Three collections in three locations nake up this outstanding museum. They ange from dinosaurs to military history.

6 Phoenix Park

The great pride and play area of Dubliners, this is the largest city park in Europe. Historic monuments and Dublin Zoo *(below)* are only a few of its delights.

7 St Patrick's Cathedral

Known colloquially as the "People's Cathedral", this is one of the earliest Christian sites in the city and is the Protestant community's main place of worship in the capital *(right)*.

8 Temple Bar

This ancient part of the city has been revamped into one of its busiest areas, day and night *(above)*. There is no shortage of places to eat and drink.

9 Christ Church Cathedral

Striking Norman, Gothic, Romanesque and Victorian features jostle for attention in this former Viking church, rebuilt in 1172.

10 Kilmainham Gaol and Kilmainham Hospital

After a sobering tour of the one-time prison *(left)*, lighten the mood at the former hospital, which now houses the Irish Museum of Modern Art.

TOP 10 Dublin Writers

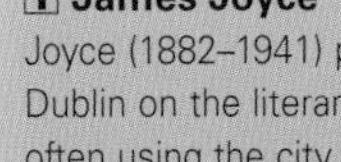

1 James Joyce
Joyce (1882–1941) put Dublin on the literary map, often using the city as the setting for his novels. His works include *Dubliners* (1914), *Portrait of the Artist as a Young Man* (1916), *Ulysses* (1922) and *Finnegan's Wake* (1938).

2 William Butler Yeats
Yeats (1865–1939) was born in Dublin. *The Wanderings of Oisin and Other Poems* (1889) established his reputation as a major poet. His play *On Baile's Strand* was chosen for the Abbey Theatre's opening in 1904.

3 George Bernard Shaw
Born in Dublin, Shaw (1856–1950) moved to England in 1876. A prolific playwright; *The Devil's Disciple* (1897) and *Pygmalion* (1914) are just two of his works. In 1925, he was awarded the Nobel Prize for Literature.

4 Jonathan Swift
Swift (1667–1745) was born and educated in Dublin. A noted satirist, in *A Modest Proposal* (1729) he suggests feeding poor children to the rich. It is ironic that his best-known work, *Gulliver's Travels* (1726), is a children's classic.

5 Oscar Wilde
Dublin-born Wilde (1854–1900) studied classics at Trinity College and later at Oxford. His highly popular plays include *An Ideal Husband* (1895) and *The Importance of Being Earnest* (1895).

6 Sean O'Casey
O'Casey (1880–1964) achieved instant success with his 1923 play *The Shadow of a Gunman*, followed by *Juno and the Paycock* in 1924 and his best-known work *The Plough and the Stars* in 1926. Later plays failed to have the same appeal.

7 Samuel Beckett
After a distinguished career at Trinity College, Beckett (1906–89) spent much of his life in France. The play *Waiting for Godot* (1952) brought him international acclaim. He won the Nobel Prize for Literature in 1969.

8 John McGahern
Celebrated for his honest exploration of Irish rural life, McGahern (1934–2006) left the country after his early novel, *The Dark* (1965), was banned. He returned in 1970 and lived on a farm in County Leitrim until he died.

9 Elizabeth Bowen
Although born in Dublin, Elizabeth Bowen (1899–1973) spent much of her childhood in Cork. Her London years are evoked in her novels, including *The Heat of the Day* (1949).

10 Patrick Kavanagh
Kavanagh (1904–67), born in Monaghan, moved to London in 1939 and began a career as a journalist and poet. His reputation was established with a bitter poem on rural life, *The Great Hunger* (1942).

Natural Wonders

You are never far from water, and its effects, in Europe. The landscape has been carved, shaped, smoothed and hollowed by ice ages, rivers and seas since the world cooled. Fire has played a part as well, bubbling up from the core of the planet into strange formations and pushing mountains into shape. Many of Europe's greatest natural wonders are the result.

1 Norway's Coastline

Norway's dramatic coastline is one of the world's natural wonders. Forest-coated mountains sit with their feet in the water and their snowy peaks raked with cloud. Waterfalls plunge into pristine fjords and glaciers crown cols between mountains. Sea eagles soar, cormorants dive from lichen-covered rocks, kittiwakes swoop and gulls skim dark waters that glisten with silver light. Inland, the scenery is just as captivating. Russet barns dot the farmland. In brightly coloured hamlets, neat wooden houses are painted in spice shades of mustard and cinnamon, and bells ring out from traditional wooden churches, calling people to Sunday prayer.

2 Haute Route, Mont Blanc

FRANCE AND SWITZERLAND

With a backdrop comprising 10 of the 12 highest mountains in the Alps, including mighty Mont Blanc and the Matterhorn, the Haute Route is absolutely breathtaking. The trail leaves Chamonix and crosses forested valleys, ascends passes and traverses glittering ice-slopes to arrive in Switzerland at the picturesque village of Zermatt. Nights are spent in mountain huts. There is also a more challenging Haute Route, which takes in glaciers and requires more technical experience – an option that should never be attempted without an experienced guide.

3 Holy Island, Northumberland

ENGLAND

Holy Island, also known as Lindisfarne, lies off the coast of northeast England and is accessible only via a paved causeway at low tide. It's a wild, remote place, fringed by miles of golden beaches with fascinating rock pools and rolling dunes. The main beach is lined with upturned fishing vessels, which were once part of a 19th-century herring fleet and now serve as work sheds. Also on the island are the ruins of a 7th-century Benedictine priory and a 16th-century castle, built in defence of England against the Scots. Only 160 people live here, and the pace of life is slow.

4 Aurora Borealis, Lapland *FINLAND*

Forget Father Christmas – Lapland's real draw is its awesome scenery and tangible sense of remoteness. Summers are short and magnificent, winters long and dark, and the sky seems impossibly vast. During late autumn and winter you can witness nature's amazing light show, the aurora borealis. Much mystery still surrounds this extraordinary natural phenomenon; scientists do not know, for example, why the geomagnetic storms behind it are strongest during the equinoxes. But you don't have to understand the science to appreciate the most spectacular show on earth.

5 Blue Caves, Zákynthos *GREECE*

A rock formation of arches and caverns, the Blue Caves are foremost among the natural wonders of Zákynthos. The sea appears bright blue due to the reflection of the sun between the arches, and contrasts sharply with the white cliffs. Take a boat from Cape Skinári lighthouse for the best views.

Aurora Borealis Lapland is one of the best places to view this amazing natural pheno

Plitvice Lakes Visitors crossing multiple waterfalls on wooden footbridges *(below)*

Norway's Coastline View of the Aurlandsfjord, Sogn og Fjordane *(above)*

ant's Causeway Columnar basalt, formed by quick-cooling lava *(below)*

6 Giant's Causeway *NORTHERN IRELAND*

The Causeway, designated a World Heritage Site in 1986, is a truly remarkable natural spectacle, its thousands of hexagonal basalt rock pillars clustered like a gigantic piece of honeycomb. The rocks descend from seafront cliffs and disappear into the water. In folklore, the Causeway is said to have been created by legendary warrior Finn MacCool as his stepping stones to Scotland; in reality, it is the result of a volcanic eruption some 60 million years ago.

7 Gorges du Cians, Provence *FRANCE*

The deep gorge carved through the mountains by the River Cians is made all the more spectacular by the deep red of the exposed rock. The river descends 1,600 m (5,250 ft) in just 25 km (15 miles) between the eyrie village of Beuil and Touet-sur-Var, where the Cians meets the larger river Var. The canyon is at its narrowest and most spectacular at Pra d'Astier, around midway between the two villages.

8 Playa de Cabo de Gata, Almería *SPAIN*

In contrast to much of Spain's overcrowded coastline, the southeast coast of Almería remains relatively neglected by tourists. The region has volcanic terrain, and many undiscovered beaches lie tucked beneath its craggy cliffs. Most impressive is Playa de Cabo de Gata, a 5-km (3-mile) beach that is buffeted by open sea.

9 Plitvice Lakes *CROATIA*

Nature's own champagne pyramid, Croatia's Plitvice Lakes are arranged on stepped limestone terraces linked to one another by a series of rapids and waterfalls. The views across these overflowing pools and sparkling white cascades to an Eden-like emerald forest are mesmerizing. The lakes change hue constantly, from deep blue to azure, green and grey, according to sunlight and changing mineral content. These tumbling pools lie in Plitvice Lakes National Park, a UNESCO World Heritage Site, which is also home to threatened fauna, including bears, wolves and lynxes.

10 Dettifoss Falls, Jökulsárgljúfur National Park *ICELAND*

Situated in a remote area of northeast Iceland, Dettifoss Falls is nature at its wildest and most elemental. A great sheet of foaming water plummets dramatically into an enormous canyon, surrounded by a volcanic landscape of bleak basalt plains, where eruptions continued until as recently as 1984. This majestic waterfall sits on the Jökulsá á Fjöllum river, which is fed by water from Iceland's largest glacier, the Vatnajökull icefield, and boasts a staggering average flow of 200 cubic m (7,060 cubic ft) per second.

Dubrovnik and the Dalmatian Coast

Whether you visit for the sun, the sailing, the scenery, or the freshest seafood imaginable, the Dalmatian coast is quite simply one of Europe's most stunning escapes. Long stretches of glorious beach are lapped by the azure waters of the Adriatic. The coastline is punctuated by a series of lively towns and cities in which the region's long and eclectic history comes alive in wonderfully preserved "old cores" – nowhere more so than Dubrovnik, a UNESCO World Heritage Site returned to its former splendour after the siege of the early 1990s.

1 Old City Walls, Dubrovnik For centuries, the remarkable old city walls *(left)* have afforded Dubrovnik protection. Today they allow visitors a bird's-eye view of one of Europe's most impressive cities.

2 Rector's Palace, Dubrovnik Under the Republic of Ragusa, the city's figurehead presided here, amidst a flurry of Gothic and Renaissance architecture. This impressive palace has now been reinvented as a museum and cultural venue *(below)*.

3 Cathedral of St James, Šibenik Now fully restored since its shelling in 1991, this splendid cathedral *(above)* is one of Europe's finest – and another UNESCO-World-Heritage-listed gem.

4 Kornati National Park This necklace of largely uninhabited islands strung out in the Adriatic has become a paradise for sailors, and for those looking to escape the strains and stresses of modern life.

TOP 10 Moments in History

1 4th Century BC: Greeks and Illyrians
Greek settlers began to cross the seas and join the Illyrian tribes who had already been eking out a living on the Dalmatian coastline. As the population expanded, proto-settlements flourished.

2 1st Century AD: Romans in Dalmatia
The Roman Empire surged eastwards, engulfing whole swathes of Croatia. Wine production flourished as the conquerors applied their skills to a soil and climate perfect for wine-production.

3 6th Century: Arrival of Slavic Tribes
During this great period of Slavic expansion, tribes from the north began to arrive on the Dalmatian coast.

4 925: Alleged First Croatian King Crowned
Croatia first became a nation under King Tomislav, the "Father of the Croats". The country's independence, however, was soon quashed by the superior power of the Huns and the mighty Venetian doges, who soon started to wield greater influence over Dalmatia.

5 1202: City of Zadar Sacked by the Crusaders
Zadar was attacked and looted by Christian Crusaders as the Balkans became a battleground for Christian Europe to the west and the increasingly powerful Ottoman Empire to the east.

6 1593: Battle of Sisak
The Austrian Habsburgs had developed the Vojna Krajina, a "military frontier" intended to prevent further Turkish advances into Europe. The Ottomans were finally halted at the landmark Battle of Sisak, just south of Zagreb.

7 1699: Dalmatia Under Venetian Control
Large swathes of Dalmatia fell under the control of Venice, although the Republic of Ragusa, centred on Dubrovnik, retained its independence from both Venice and Constantinople.

8 1808: Napoleon Annexes Ragusa
In 1806, French troops saved Dubrovnik from a month-long siege by Russian and Montenegrin forces. Two years later, Napoleon claimed Ragusa for France and established the Illyrian Provinces.

9 1945: Marshal Tito
In the aftermath of war the Croatian-born Tito established a socialist republic where ethnic differences were suppressed in favour of allegiance to the "mother country".

10 1991: Independence
A landslide referendum saw Croatia declare independence from Yugoslavia. Irregular Serbian units, backed by the Yugoslav military, attacked the fledgling republic and besieged Dubrovnik. Hostilities ceased in 1995, and all captured Croatian territory was returned by 1998.

5 Krka National Park

Established to protect the middle and lower reaches of the River Krka, this idyllic natural playground of lakes, waterfalls and waterways *(right)* near Šibenik attracts small kids and big kids alike.

6 Trogir

Set on its own island, this perfectly preserved old city shimmers with churches, palaces and one of Europe's most striking cathedrals, whose beauty is recognized by UNESCO.

8 Stradun, Dubrovnik

Along its polished expanse, Dubrovnik's elegant pedestrianized main thoroughfare *(above)* boasts a wealth of churches, palaces, shops, fountains and pavement cafés.

9 Zadar Old Town

This proud survivor is now back to its lively best, with Slavic culture meeting Roman remnants on a striking Adriatic peninsula.

10 Korčula Town

It may or may not be the birthplace of Marco Polo, but Korčula Town *(left)* is simply sublime, set on its own peninsula, framed by sea and mountains. Its cathedral is one of the most charming ecclesiastical buildings in the Adriatic.

7 Diocletian's Palace, Split

The palatial, UNESCO-World-Heritage-listed retirement home of Emperor Diocletian *(above)* forms the frenetic heart of the dashing Mediterranean city of Split.

TOP 10 More Old Towns

1 Nin
Once the political heart of Croatia, this small, unassuming town, long ignored by tourists, is becoming more popular – not just for its relaxed ambience, but for its lovely ecclesiastical buildings and excellent beaches.

2 Novigrad
It comes as a pleasant surprise to discover that Novigrad – "New Town" – has a delightful old core, which meanders off up the hillside towards the ruined medieval fortress above.

3 Cavtat
First settled in the 3rd century BC, this resort still bears the marks of the Illyrians, Greeks, Romans and Slavs who occupied it at one time or another.

4 Ston
The Republic of Ragusa left an enduring reminder of its presence in Ston, whose 14th-century fortifications resemble a miniature Great Wall of China.

5 Vid
Inhabited by both Greeks and Romans, Vid thrived as a trading post between the islands and the hinterland until the 7th century AD.

6 Hvar Town
Hvar Town is the favourite summer getaway of Croatia's cognoscenti. High above its charming old core, a rambling fort watches over the summer scene of pavement cafés, fish restaurants and bobbing tour boats.

7 Kut (Vis Town)
Vis Town's Kut district offers an outstanding Renaissance triple-naved church, a swathe of old Venetian merchant dwellings, and a trio of first-rate restaurants.

8 Šibenik
Šibenik's charming old town rambles up in search of the city's fort through a tangle of narrow streets that have not yet been air-brushed for the needs of mass tourism.

9 Pag Town
Pag's old town – largely the work of Dalmatian architect Juraj Dalmatinac – is a web of streets expertly crafted to afford inhabitants protection against the biting bora winds.

10 Lastovo Town
Lastovo Town turns its back on the Adriatic and tumbles in the opposite direction. Its most striking buildings are a group of 20 or so Renaissance stone houses.

England's Lake District

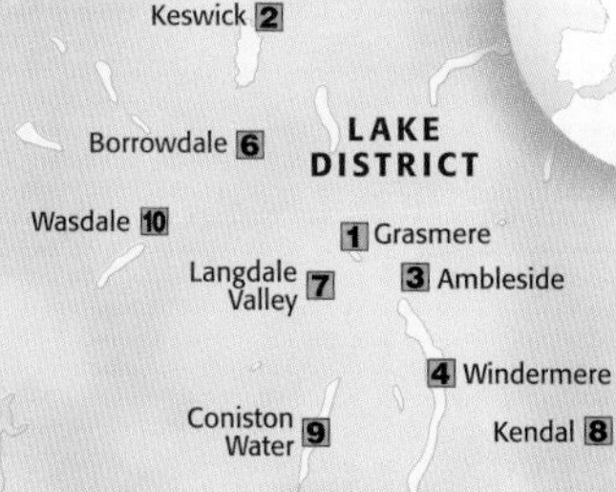

The Lake District is one of the most beautiful and romantic parts of Britain, with spectacular mountains, verdant valleys and, of course, plenty of lakes. It is a terrific place for outdoor activities – by evening every country pub is playing host to recuperating hikers. The district was put on the tourist map by the poet William Wordsworth, and it has long been accustomed to providing hearty food, real ale and a comfortable bed for visitors. Wild it may be, but domestic pleasures are always reassuringly close at hand in the Lakes.

1 Grasmere

Pretty Grasmere *(above)* is an enchanting destination, circled by high fells and isolated tarns, and replete with teashops and handsome stone cottages. William Wordsworth's famous Dove Cottage is just a short walk away.

2 Keswick

This busy market town in the northern Lake District offers full amenities plus intriguing museums and a celebrated theatre. Keswick also has some iconic walks, as well as Derwent Water *(left)*, nearby.

3 Ambleside

Centrally located and with a bustling air, this little town makes an excellent base for a holiday in the Lakes.

Top 10 Moments in History

1 3000 BC: Neolithic People
The first farmers in the Lakes area created the stone circle at Castlerigg. Stone axes have been found at Scafell and bronze tools at Ambleside.

2 AD 69: The Romans
The Roman presence in the Lakes is still tangible. The most impressive remnant is the lonely hilltop fort on the Hardknott Pass.

3 800–900: The Vikings
The Vikings arrived with less of a vengeance here than in other areas. These Norse invaders were part of a wave of settlement, as opposed to one of rape and pillage.

4 The Medieval Period: Lakeland Industries
The Middle Ages saw the establishment of sheep-farming. Graphite was extracted for pencil-making and glazing. Slate and copper mining became integral to the local economy.

5 1400–1700: Border Raids
In the 15th–16th century, Border Reivers launched raids from the border between Scotland and England, rustling livestock and kidnapping. "Pele" towers were built as defences. Many still stand, and formed the basis for later country houses.

6 The 18th Century: The Romantic Period
Wordsworth, Coleridge, Turner, Gainsborough and Constable were the poets and artists who immortalized the Lake District. They were also the reluctant inspiration of the Lakes' tourism industry.

7 1847: The Railways
The first passenger railway line between Kendal and Windermere was completed in 1847, transforming the latter into a boom town. It brought large numbers of tourists and walkers, cementing for ever the popularity of the Lakes.

8 1895 and 1951: Conservation
These dates mark milestones in protecting the area from overdevelopment. In 1895 the National Trust was founded; its land ownership in the Lakes owes much to Beatrix Potter, who made large bequests to the Trust. The Lake District National Park was established in 1951 in order to prevent insensitive development.

9 2001: Farming Crisis
The Foot and Mouth crisis of 2001 was a body blow to the farmers in the Lakes – many had to destroy their livestock. Tourists were banned, so farm B&Bs also suffered. Today's emphasis on local produce is a new source of optimism for the region's hill farmers.

10 2009: Flooding
In November 2009 the Lakes were hit by the most severe floods in a millenium. The western areas, especially Cockermouth, were worst affected. Bridges were swept away and the army had to be brought in to help.

4 Windermere
Taking a cruise on England's largest lake (*left*) is a must. The surrounding area is rich in historic homes, such as Blackwell and Townend.

5 Wordsworth's Lake District
The area is scattered with walks, houses and views associated with the poet Wordsworth and his sister Dorothy, whose journals inspired some of his best poems, including *Daffodils*.

6 Borrowdale
Lush and thickly wooded, Borrowdale (*above*) is scattered with wonderful stone farmhouses and pretty villages, many in the shadow of high fells.

7 The Langdale Valley
With high mountains, tumbling waterfalls, country pubs and hiking opportunities galore, Langdale (*above*) should not be missed.

8 Kendal
The gateway town to the Lake District, Kendal features an exceptional art gallery, a fine museum, some good restaurants and a lively arts centre.

9 Coniston Water
Elongated Coniston Water was the inspiration behind Arthur Ransome's much loved *Swallows and Amazons* children's books; as a child, he spent his holidays at Nibthwaite, which sits at the lake's southern end.

10 Wasdale
One of the most remote and scenic parts of the area, Wasdale is perfect for hikes or even more energetic pursuits. Wasdale Head Inn (*right*) is the home of British rock climbing.

Top 10 Walks

1 Helvellyn
Helvellyn should not be approached lightly. The narrow Striding Edge route makes for a challenging though exhilarating scramble, and is only for experienced and well-equipped hikers.

2 Ambleside to Skelwith Bridge
This lovely route is suitable for everyone. It winds via Loughrigg Tarn to Skelwith Bridge, which is a good place for a pint. As you walk, the Langdale Pikes provide a magnificent backdrop.

3 The Coffin Trail
This is the route taken by coffin bearers shouldering their load to St Oswald's in Grasmere for burial. The wooded paths link Grasmere with Rydal and Ambleside, and are not too demanding.

4 Aira Force
A steep, lovely and fairly short walk from the shores of Ullswater leads up to the magnificent 20-m (65-ft) drop of Aira Force (waterfall). You may spot red squirrels.

5 Grizedale Forest
Grizedale Forest, on the eastern shores of Coniston, is 6,000 acres (2,400 ha) of larch, oak, spruce and pine. A haven for red deer and roe deer, it also features a sculpture trail with works by British artists such as Andy Goldsworthy and David Nash.

6 Scafell Pike
At 978 m (3,210 ft), this is the highest mountain in England, and a challenge even for experienced fell walkers and climbers.

7 Great Gable
One of the Lake District's iconic climbs, Great Gable has a distinctive pyramidical peak. The summit offers stunning views of Wasdale, Scafell and Scafell Pike.

8 Easedale Tarn
Hike from Grasmere up the fellsides to Easedale Tarn, a lake set among forbidding peaks. A round trip takes about 3 hours, and the ascent is pretty steep.

9 The Old Man of Coniston
Visitors can still see the remnants of slate mining works here. The mountain has epic views over Coniston, and its well-worn trails make it a favourite with hikers.

10 Crinkle Crags
The five "crinkles" make for a strenuous hike, best done on a clear day, both for the views and for safety.

Florence

Florence was a medieval seat of power under the Medicis, and the cradle of the Renaissance. Great art, splendid architecture and a wealth of culture of all kinds are everywhere you look. Any visit will include at least some of these treasures, but take time as well to enjoy the simpler pleasures of this charming Tuscan city, famed for its cuisine and its style as well as its art.

1 The Uffizi This veritable "who's who" of the greatest of the Renaissance masters is installed in the former *uffizi* – offices *(left)* – of the ruling Medici family.

3 Galleria dell'Accademia The original of Michelangelo's proud *David* (1501–4) *(above)* stands pensively at the end of a corridor lined by the artist's *Slaves*.

Piazza della Signoria 2 Set around Ammannati's *Neptune* fountain *(right)*, this is Florence's public living room and outdoor sculpture gallery. Outside the Palazzo Vecchio are copies of Donatello's *Marzocco* and *Judith*, and Michelangelo's *David*. The Loggia dei Lanzi shelters Cellini's masterpiece *Perseus* (1545) as well as Giambologna's *Rape of the Sabine Women* (1583).

TOP 10 Medici Rulers

1 Giovanni di Bicci (1360–1429)
The founder of the Medici fortune also served in the Florentine government and was a sponsor of Ghiberti's Baptistry commission.

2 Cosimo il Vecchio (1389–1464)
Cosimo managed his family fortune, political clout and personal image to become ruler of Florence. Each time he was exiled or imprisoned by rivals, popular sentiment brought him back to power.

3 Lorenzo the Magnificent (1449–92)
The best-loved of the Medici rulers was a devout humanist and patron of the arts who sponsored Michelangelo's early career.

4 Pope Leo X (Giovanni: 1475–1521)
Lorenzo's second son, Leo famously said, "Since God has given us the papacy, let us enjoy it" The brother and nephews he groomed to take over Florence all died, so his cousin Giulio took the reins.

5 Pope Clement VII (Giulio: 1478–1534)
Cardinal Giulio fared well at running Florence but, as Pope, spent his energies fighting Emperor Charles V, leaving Florence in the hands of his incompetent young relatives Alessandro and Ippolito.

6 Alessandro (1511–37)
Clement VII's bastard son inherited the ducal mantle at 19, and became a despot, carousing with his cousin Lorenzino, who grew jealous and murdered him.

7 Cosimo I (1519–74)
The first Medici to gain the title Grand Duke was created duke at the age of 17, when the primary Medici line died out. He conquered Siena and ruled judiciously but with something of an iron fist.

8 Ferdinando I (1549–1609)
This popular, hands-on Grand Duke founded hospitals, promoted agriculture and gave poor girls dowries. His wife's noble Lorraine family were to inherit the grand ducal title.

9 Anna Maria (1667–1743)
The last of the main Medici line, she willed all the family possessions to the Lorraine grand dukes on condition that they would never be removed from Florence.

10 Gian Gastone (1671–1737)
The last Medici ruler was an obese sensualist who rarely stirred from bed except to prove he was still alive, when he leaned out of his carriage only to vomit on his subjects.

4 Ponte Vecchio
The shops hanging from both sides of Taddeo Gaddi's 1354 "old bridge" *(above)* have housed gold- and silversmiths since Ferdinando I evicted the butchers in the 16th century; his private corridor from the Uffizi to the Pitti passed overhead, and he couldn't stand the smell.

5 Il Bargello
Florence's sculpture gallery contains early Michelangelos, Mannerist Giambologna's *Flying Mercury* (1564) and the city's best Donatello collection.

6 Santa Croce
This magnificent church *(above)* holds the tombs of such Tuscan greats as Michelangelo, Machiavelli and Galileo. There are Giotto frescoes, a chapel designed by Brunelleschi, and a museum with a *Last Supper* by Taddeo Gaddi.

7 The Duomo Group
Brunelleschi's noble dome *(above)* towers over an ensemble including the magnificent Baptistry, adorned by Ghiberti's monumental bronze doors; Giotto's slender belltower; Michelangelo's tortured *Pietà*; and two panoramic terraces.

8 Pitti Palace
This massive Medici palace has a painting collection to rival the Uffizi, museums of porcelain, carriages and modern art, and formal gardens.

9 Palazzo Vecchio
Arnolfo di Cambio's mighty town hall (1299–1302) is still Florence's seat of government. Cosimo I hired Vasari to redecorate in the 1540s – among the results is the fresco of a grand Medici marriage around the courtyard.

10 San Marco
This monastery of 1437 was Fra Angelico's home. He frescoed his brothers' cells with devotional images *(above)*. His portrait of Savonarola hangs in the "Mad Monk's" room, beside a scene of the religious zealot's fiery death.

TOP 10 Uffizi Collections

1 Pre-Renaissance
A trio of *Maestàs* runs from Byzantine Cimabue, through Duccio's Sienese Gothic, to Giotto's version. Gentile da Fabriano and Lorenzo Monaco show the International Gothic style of the early 1400s.

2 Early Renaissance
The earthiness of Masaccio, the delicacy of Fra Angelico and the flowing lines of Filippo Lippi lead up to the languid grace of Lippi's protégé, Botticelli.

3 Botticelli
The famed *Birth of Venus* and *Primavera* hang alongside other masterpieces such as *Pallas and the Centaur* and *Adoration of the Magi* (with a self-portrait in yellow robes on the right).

4 Leonardo da Vinci
As an apprentice, Leonardo painted the angel on the left of Verrocchio's *Baptism of Christ*. Also on show are his unfinished *Adoration of the Magi* and the *Annunciation*.

5 Northern Italian and European Masters
Bellini, Giorgione, Mantegna and Correggio are joined by their German and Flemish contemporaries Cranach, Holbein and Dürer.

6 High Renaissance and Mannerism
Here are the Renaissance big guns, Michelangelo and Raphael; High Renaissance Venetians Titian, Veronese and Tintoretto; plus Andrea del Sarto and his students representing Mannerism.

7 Baroque
The best examples in the Uffizi are by Caravaggio, along with self-portraits by Rembrandt and Rubens.

8 The Tribune
The Uffizi's original display space is a chamber with a mother-of-pearl tiled dome and inlaid stone floor and table. It was built to show off the *Medici Venus* and other Classical statues.

9 The U-Shaped Corridor
The main corridor linking the galleries is lined with statues – mostly Roman copies of Greek originals. Its ceiling vaults are frescoed with scenes of Florence's history, thinkers, leaders and artists.

10 The Vasari Corridor
The long corridor from the Pitti Palace to the Uffizi was damaged in a terrorist bombing in 1993. It is lined with 17th- to 20th-century art.

Gran Canaria

Gran Canaria has been described as "a continent in miniature", and with good reason. Within its 1,500 sq km (590 sq miles) you can travel from the rugged northern coast through verdant laurel forests and extinct volcanoes to the emblematic central peaks, reaching almost 2,000 m (6,562 ft) above sea level, before descending through ancient pine woods into the deep ravines of the south and west, which peter out as the arid landscape gives way to golden beaches. The fine sand and perfect climate ensure that the island is no stranger to tourists, but it is still easy to escape the crowds in this magical Atlantic haven.

2 Puerto de las Nieves

Scores of visitors pass through Puerto de las Nieves daily en route to Tenerife, but this pretty fishing village *(left)* is a destination in its own right. Watch the boats, enjoy a seafood lunch, and unwind.

1 Jardín Botánico Canario

Spain's largest botanical garden *(right)* is a mixed bouquet of endemic and tropical plants. Giant lizards bask in the sun while songbirds chirrup in the laurel and pine plantations.

3 La Cumbre

Wherever you are in the island's central mountains *(above)*, there are awe-inspiring views of La Cumbre's high ridges and strange rock formations.

Top 10 Moments in History

1 Volcanic Origins
Like all of the Canary Islands, Gran Canaria is volcanic in origin and first emerged from the ocean 15 million years ago. Further volcanic activity created the northeast of the island 11 million years later.

2 Arrival of the First Inhabitants
Many argue that the Guanches arrived from North Africa around 2,000 BC. Others believe they were Vikings, or even Atlanteans! Discovery of Cro-Magnon skulls suggests that Cro-Magnon and Mediterranean man may have co-existed on the island.

3 Early Exploration
Portuguese and Mallorcans had sailed past, but it wasn't until 1405 that Jean de Bethencourt landed, though he failed to conquer the tough Canarios. Juan Rejón had better luck in 1478, founding Real de Las Palmas, the island's future capital.

4 Baptism and Defeat
The natives proved no match for Spanish invaders. Tenesor Semidan, the Northern chief, was captured and baptized. Final defeat came in 1483, when many remaining fighters jumped into a deep ravine rather than live as slaves.

5 Pirates Attack
Being on major trade routes brought fortune, but also attracted pirates. Sir Francis Drake attacked Las Palmas in 1595, though failed to defeat the locals. A more successful assault by Dutch corsair Pieter Van Der Does ravaged the capital in 1599, leaving scores of buildings in ruins.

6 Mass Emigration
After the discovery of the New World, thousands of islanders crossed the ocean. Most made for the Caribbean and Venezuela, often known as the "eighth island" due to its links with the archipelago.

7 Boom and Bust
Contact with Latin America led to competition, ruining Gran Canaria's sugar cane industry. The cochineal and wine trades went the same way and, by the end of the 19th century, things were looking desperate, rekindling the exodus to Latin America.

8 Getting Connected
Development of Puerto de la Luz in 1881 changed the island's fortunes for ever. It became the main port, and today is one of Europe's largest. The Canary Islands' first airport was built south of Las Palmas in 1930.

9 Franco's Military Coup
In July 1936, General Franco and his followers launched an uprising from their base in Las Palmas, triggering the Spanish Civil War. In 1939, Franco came to power and Fascist rule began in Spain.

10 Tourism Takes Hold
After the failed industries of earlier centuries, salvation arrived in the 1960s as tomato plantations gave way to high-rise hotels. Tourism is now key to the archipelago's economy. Rather than being a place to escape from, Gran Canaria is now a desirable destination for immigrants.

4 Barranco de Guayadeque

Step back in time in this breathtaking ravine, once populated by Guanches but now home to a handful of cave dwellers.

5 Museo Canario, Las Palmas

Since they died out soon after the Spanish Conquest, there is little information on how the Guanches (early Canarios) lived. Gain insight at the Museo Canario, a one-stop exploration of the mysteries of ancient Canarian culture *(right)*.

6 Teror

Set in an area of out-standing natural beauty, this quiet, architecturally exquisite Canarian town *(above)* has deep historical roots. It's also home to a tasty local variety of *chorizo* sausage.

7 Catedral de Santa Ana, Las Palmas

Standing proud in Las Palmas's historic centre *(above)*, the cathedral has been an emblem of the city since the Spanish conquered the island. Its intermittent construction over 400 years explains the magnificent potpourri of styles that singles it out as one of the most important artistic monuments in Gran Canaria.

8 Casa Museo de Colón, Las Palmas

Trace Columbus's epic journeys in this atmospheric museum, based in the 15th-century governor's house where the Atlantic explorer stayed en route to the New World.

9 Caldera de Bandama

A reminder of the island's volcanic origins, this deep crater *(below)* is an easy visit from Las Palmas. Enjoy the fabulous views, or hike down to the crater floor.

10 Maspalomas

Maspalomas, with its golden dunes *(above)*, is both a tourist resort and an area of stunning natural beauty, visited by holidaymakers and migrating birds alike.

TOP 10 Guanche Sights

1 Cueva Pintada
In 1860, a local farmer stumbled across this painted cave, uncovering probably the most important archeological find in the whole archipelago. Only a limited number of visitors are allowed in at a time.

2 Tufia
This settlement contains examples of both types of aboriginal home common to the island: cave dwellings, and the low stone houses unique to Gran Canaria.

3 Cuatro Puertas
This is probably the most remarkable man-made cave on Gran Canaria. The large room with four "doors" was a sacred place.

4 Túmulo de La Guancha
This Guanche cemetery outshines the others scattered around the island. It is thought that the central sepulchre contained the *guanarteme* (king), while the aristocracy were laid to rest around him.

5 Cenobio de Valerón
This cluster of miniature artificial caves represents an awe-inspiring feat of early engineering. Once believed to be a convent, it is now widely agreed that the caves were used to store grain.

6 Maipés de Arriba
With around 500 tombs, the Maipés de Arriba may have been the Guanches' main burial ground. Look out for the circular towers, almost certainly the graves of aboriginal aristocracy.

7 Letreros de Balos
Cave drawings have been found across the islands, but the variety at this site is remarkable. Some seem to depict fertility symbols and there are even alphabetical inscriptions, linked to North African peoples.

8 Arteara
The island's most important burial site boasts a stunning location, nestled in a palm grove in the Fataga ravine. Information panels explain the piles of rocks before you.

9 La Fortaleza de Ansite
The Guanches' last stronghold is pock-marked with caves overlooking the Tirajana ravine. Imagine the islanders' plight as they tried in vain to repel the Spaniards, then threw themselves into the void.

10 Roque Bentayga
Numerous dwellings and grain stores have been unearthed around this huge monolith, which was considered sacred by the Guanches.

Greek Islands

Comprising over 6,000 islands and islets, spread across several archipelagos, the Greek Islands offer a fabulous choice of holiday destinations. Some host bustling holiday resorts, while others consist solely of rural communities, and ancient temples sit alongside cosmopolitan towns. Add beaches, pine forests, olive groves and coastlines indented with spectacular coves and bays, and the result is a collection of islands just begging to be explored.

1 Delos

According to Greek mythology, this tiny uninhabited island *(left)* was the birthplace of Apollo and Artemis, and an important place of worship. It is home to remains of civilizations dating back to the 3rd century BC.

Rhodes Old Town 2

This city *(right)* was occupied by the Knights Hospitallers (1309–1522), who left such magnificent treasures as the Palace of the Grand Masters and the Street of the Knights.

3 Corfu Old Town

The arcaded terraces of the Listón *(above)*, the ancient fortresses of Palaió Froúrio and Néo Froúrio, and Plateía Spianáda, with its Venetian architecture, all combine to give Corfu Old Town its infinite charm. Museums include the Antivouniótissa Museum.

Top 10 Moments in History

1 3000–1000 BC: Cycladic Civilization
An early-Bronze Age colony existed in the Cyclades. Possibly the oldest civilisation in the islands, its people were expert fishermen.

2 700 BC: Creation of the Dorian Hexapolis
The Dorians, who feature in the *Odyssey*, formed the Dorian Hexapolis, a coalition of six cities – Camirus, Lindus and Lalysos on Rhodes, Cnidus and Halicarnassus in Caria (west Anatolia) and Kos.

3 431–405 BC: Peloponnesian War
The Peloponnesian War was fought between the empires of Athens and Sparta. Sparta eventually triumphed at the naval battle of Aegospotami.

4 197–146 BC: Roman Invasion
Subjugation by Rome started in 197 BC, and the Roman period began when Corinth was defeated in 146 BC. It was a period of change, with Greece becoming the cultural centre of the Roman Empire.

5 AD 1204–1797: Venetian Occupation
The Republic of Venice took control of the Ionians in 1204. Strong Venetian fortifications helped save the islands from occupation during the Ottoman invasion of Greece.

6 1309–1522: Knights Hospitallers
In the 14th century, Knights Hospitallers invaded many islands. Their architectural legacy is most notable in Rhodes. They were driven out by the Ottomans in 1522.

7 Ottoman Rule
The 14th, 16th, 17th and 19th centuries saw periods of Ottoman rule. In the 1500s, for example, Suleiman the Magnificent captured the Cyclades and Dodecanese, and Crete fell in 1646.

8 1814–64: British Protectorate
In 1814 the islands became a British protectorate. The Greek War of Independence (1821–9) ended Ottoman rule and the islands acquired union with Greece in 1864.

9 1941: Axis Occupation
During World War II, the Axis alliance, including Germany and Italy, took over Greece and, in 1941, many islands were ruled by Italy. In 1943, the Germans evicted the Italians, sending the local Jews to their death.

10 1953: Major Earthquake
An earthquake, measuring 7.1 on the Richter scale, hit the Ionian islands in 1953. It caused massive damage, destroying many towns.

4 Néa Moní, Híos

Containing one of Greece's finest collections of mosaics, this 11th-century monastery *(left)* was built by Emperor Constantine IX Monomachos.

5 Monastery of St John, Pátmos

Dedicated to St John, who reputedly wrote the *Book of Revelation* nearby, this 11th-century monastery is a protected UNESCO site.

6 Phaestos Palace, Crete

The remains of this palace *(left)*, one of two from the Minoan period, were found at one of the most important archaeological sites on the island.

7 Évvia

This long, narrow, largely mountainous island lies off the coast of mainland Greece. Évvia has been ruled in turn by Macedonians, Romans, Venetians and Ottoman Turks. Their influence gives the island its inimitable character and distinct architecture *(above)*.

8 Palace of Knossos, Crete

The largest Bronze Age archaeological site on Crete, the remains of the Minoan Palace of Knossos give an incomparable insight into this ancient civilization.

9 Temple of Aphaia, Égina

A well-preserved Doric temple dedicated to Aphaia, the ancient Greek goddess of fertility, this structure *(above)* dates from around 480 BC. It stands on a hilltop covered with pine trees on the island of Égina.

TOP 10 Natural Wonders

1 Islets
Thousands of islets dot the sea around Greece's islands. Some, such as Néa Kaméni off Santoríni, are uninhabited and volcanic. Others, such as the Diapontian islands off Corfu, have great beaches and small communities.

2 Samariá Gorge, Crete
The gorge stretches for about 16 km (10 miles). Towering rock walls have been created over millennia, and at a spot called Iron Gates (Sideróportes) are only 3 m (10 ft) apart.

3 Blue Caves, Zákynthos
The caves are foremost among Zákynthos' natural wonders. The bright blue of the sea contrasts sharply with the white cliffs. For the best view, take a boat from Cape Skinári lighthouse.

4 Korissíon Lagoon, Corfu
This magical freshwater lagoon, enclosed by a forest and separated from the sea by a narrow stretch of sand dunes, is a haven for wildlife, including many bird species.

5 Caves of Sámi, Kefalloniá
Melissáni cave and lake are the highlights of an extraordinary network of subterranean waterways and caverns. It is said to have been the sanctuary of the god Pan.

6 Extinct Volcano Polyvótis, Níssyros
This extinct volcano is around 260 m (860 ft) in diameter and 30 m (100 ft) deep. Steps lead down to its core.

7 Mýrtos Bay, Kefalloniá
This bay is famous for its dazzling white-pebble beach and vivid turquoise waters. Mýrtos beach is considered one of the best in the world.

8 Nydrí Waterfalls, Lefkáda
These are the most spectacular of the many falls on the island. Cascades of water fall into crystal-clear pools, which are popular with swimmers.

9 Caldera, Santoríni
A huge volcanic eruption created this water-filled cauldron in 1450 BC. The Néa Kaméni and Palaia Kaméni islands later emerged from the water.

10 Thérmes Hot Springs, Kos
Thérmes beach is known for this naturally warm pool in the rocks, which is fed by hot springs and is said to have curative powers.

10 Pythagóreio and Heraion, Sámos

The remains of Pythagóreio, an ancient Greek and Roman fortified port, and Heraion, a Neolithic temple, have put Sámos on the heritage map *(above)*.

Greece
The coastline of Santorini, in the Cycladees Islands

Hamburg

With almost 1.8 million inhabitants, the Free and Hanseatic City of Hamburg, as it is officially known, is Germany's second-largest city. As befits one of Europe's most important ports and trading centres, Hamburg has always welcomed the world, and there is something for every visitor among the variety of cultural sights and attractions on offer here, which include a zoo, an opera house, two symphony orchestras, some 40 theatres and more than 60 museums and galleries – not to mention, on the seamier side of things, the Reeperbahn, at several of whose clubs The Beatles had residencies early in their career.

1 St Pauli Fish Market

Night-owls and early-risers, business people and punks, bargain-hunters and shoppers in search of a unique experience – they all flock to this vibrant fish market in the wee hours of the morning *(left)*. It's all over by 9:30am.

2 Planten un Blomen

Located within the former walls of the city, this park, whose name means "plants and flowers" in Low German dialect, certainly lives up to its name. Features include a Rose Garden, with more than 300 kinds of rose, and a pair of Japanese gardens. In summer, concerts are held in the music pavilion and water–light concerts take place on the lake.

3 Rickmer Rickmers

This 97-m- (318-ft-) long sailing ship *(right)*, built in 1896, once carried its cargoes as far afield as Hong Kong and Chile, but now it's going nowhere – as a finely restored museum ship moored at the Landungsbrücken.

TOP 10 Moments in History

1 Early Settlements
Small settlements existed in prehistoric times, and the area was settled by Saxons from the 7th century AD. In 808 Charlemagne ordered the construction of a castle here, called the Hammaburg.

2 Medieval Hamburg
In 1189 Hamburg was declared an Imperial Free City by the Holy Roman Emperor. The city was briefly ruled by the Danish and then by the Counts of Holstein, but retained much autonomy.

3 The Hanseatic League
Hamburg grew increasingly important as a trade centre. A pact with Lübeck in 1241 led to an alliance that would go on to become known as the Hanseatic League. This powerful league of trading cities and merchants' guilds eventually stretched from the North Sea to the Baltic.

4 The Reformation
In the early 16th century, the city became Lutheran and, subsequently, a refuge for other Protestants and Jews.

5 17th- and 18th-Century Hamburg
With the Age of Exploration in the 16th century, Hamburg grew into one of Europe's largest trading hubs. However, the new trading routes that developed cause a decline in the power of the League.

6 19th-Century Hamburg
Hamburg was occupied by the French from 1810 until 1814, and joined the German Confederation in 1815. In the late 19th century, it became Europe's largest port.

7 World War I
A trade blockade in World War I badly affected Hamburg, which also lost 40,000 men to the fighting, but the city recovered rapidly during the post-war period.

8 World War II
Hamburg lost its free city status under the Third Reich and was heavily bombed by the Allies. More than half the city was destroyed, and thousands died in air raids. The city was occupied by the British from 1945 until 1949.

9 Post-War Hamburg
The proximity of the Iron Curtain contributed to the city's demise as a trading centre. However, after German Reunification in 1990, Hamburg began to rebuild trade, becoming an important container port and shipping centre.

10 Hamburg Today
Hamburg today is one of Germany's most affluent cities, with a booming shipping trade and an important tourist industry.

4 Speicherstadt

Work on the world's largest warehouse district founded on mber piles began in 1885. Today this elegant "city" of red-brick uildings set on canals *(above)* is part business, part residential, art cultural – several museums are based here.

Museum für Kunst und Gewerbe 5

One of Europe's leading applied arts museums *(right)*, the MKG's wide-ranging collection includes photography, antiquities, contemporary design, fashion and textiles, porcelain and faience ware, Art Nouveau poster art and historical musical instruments.

6 Hamburger Kunsthalle

Set in three connected city-centre buildings, the Hamburger Kunsthalle is one of the most stimulating art galleries in northern Germany. It covers European art from the 14th century to the present day, including an important collection of 19th-century German Romantics.

7 Rathaus

Hamburg is both city and state, and both are un from this august edifice – one of Germany's randest *(above)*. Built from 1886–97 in Neo-Renaissance style, its façade is richly adorned with sculptures. Its huge dimensions and 12-m (367-ft) tower cannot fail to impress.

8 St Michaelis

The city's skyline would not be the same without the presence of the 132-m- (433-ft-) high tower of the Baroque church that Hamburgers affectionately referred to as "Michel".

9 Landungsbrücken

Hamburg would not be Hamburg without the Landungsbrücken – ten oating pontoons amounting to 700 m 2,300 ft) in length. Round trips of the arbour begin and end here, passenger erries depart from here and numerous estaurants, bars and food stalls have prung up along the way.

Reeperbahn 10

This street in Hamburg's St Pauli district is notorious as the epicentre of the city's red-light district *(right)*. It is also home to other forms of nightlife, centred on bars, nightclubs, cafés, restaurants and a number of theatres.

TOP 10 Reeperbahn Sights

1 TUI Operettenhaus
This venue is one of the largest and most important music theatres in Hamburg. Top shows such as *Cats* and *Mama Mia!* have pulled in millions of visitors for years.

2 Panoptikum
The oldest (founded in 1879) and largest wax museum in Germany features over 120 figures of personalities from the worlds of showbusiness, sport, politics and history, ranging from Napoleon to Madonna, Albert Einstein to Michael Schumacher.

3 Schmidt Theater
Vaudeville is alive and well here, along with comedy, musical theatre and live music. Next door, Schmidts Tivoli is one of the most beautiful theatres in the city, with a reputation for developing its own musicals entirely in-house.

4 St Pauli Theater
The performances of modern and classical plays staged is this theatre cleverly take their cue from New York's Broadway shows.

5 Davidwache
The smallest police station in Germany is also the most famous, appearing in many movies and TV shows. It has a big role to play in real life too, policing the red light district around Reeperbahn.

6 Hans-Albers-Statue
The bronze likeness of this beloved Hamburg actor and singer was created in 1986 by Jörg Immendorff.

7 Herzblut St Pauli
The "Heartblood" of the Reeperbahn by name and nature, this lively bar and restaurant, decked out in maritime and football memorabilia, is a great place to people-watch.

8 Café Keese
Café Keese is a hub of Hamburg's nightlife and music scene. The hotel above it is convenient for night owls, but not if you like a quiet night's sleep.

9 Spielbudenplatz
This square runs down the centre of the Reeperbahn. Two moveable stages, one at either end, can be illuminated spectacularly at night.

10 Tanzende Türme
These two glass and steel towers, completed in 2012, are architectural landmarks curiously reminiscent of a tango-dancing couple.

Iceland

Iceland sits on an active volcanic ridge at the edge of the Arctic Circle, its interior a wilderness of looming icecaps, solidified lava flows and black-sand deserts. Only birds and foxes inhabited the land when Scandinavian Vikings arrived in the 8th century to found the egalitarian Commonwealth of the heroic Saga Age. After 1262, when Norway and then Denmark ruled the country, Iceland fell into poverty and it was not until the 18th century that towns were established. Today, Iceland enjoys a hi-tech infrastructure and most of its 300,000 population lives around the capital, Reykjavík.

1 Geysir Hot Springs Area

Just an hour from the comforts of downtown Reykjavík, this hillside of violently bubbling pools *(left)* and erupting water spouts has given its name to similar formations worldwide.

Þingvellir National Park 2

A broad rift valley where the European and American tectonic plates are visibly tearing apart in a riot of geology, Þingvellir National Park *(right)* was the site of Iceland's Viking parliament.

3 The Blue Lagoon

Take a sauna or soak in the warm, pale blue waters of Iceland's most sublime outdoor spa *(above)*, all set among a dramatic landscape of black lava boulders.

TOP 10 Moments in History

1 AD 860: Viking Exploration
Around AD 860, a Viking named Naddoður discovered uninhabited coastline north of the Faroe Islands. Later, Norseman Flóki Vilgerðarson, after a harsh winter there, named it "Ísland" (Iceland).

2 870: Reykjavík Settled
Norwegian Ingólfur Arnarson became Iceland's first permanent settler. He built his homestead at a place he called Reykjavík (Smoky Bay).

3 930: Alþing Established at Þingvellir
By AD 930, regional chieftains decided to form a national government. A Parliament (Alþing) met annually at Þingvellir to make laws and settle disputes.

4 1000: Iceland Becomes Catholic
After Norway's king Ólafur Tryggvason threatened to invade if Iceland did not become Christian, the Alþing of AD 1000 made Catholicism Iceland's official religion.

5 1262: The Old Treaty with Norway
Civil war broke out in the 13th century. Norway acted as peacemaker and in 1262 Iceland became a semi-independent state under Norwegian sovereignty.

6 1397: Danish Rule
Denmark's "Lady King" Margrete, absorbed the Norwegian throne under the Kalmar Union. Later on, Denmark rejected Iceland's autonomy, and in 1661 imposed absolute rule.

7 1550: Lutheran Iceland
In 1542, the Danish ruler appointed Iceland's first Lutheran bishop. Jón Arason, the last Catholic bishop took up arms, but was defeated and executed in 1550.

8 1783: Lakagígar Eruption
A eruption on the Laki craters flooded southeastern Iceland with lava. Poisonous fallout then wiped out agriculture, leading to a famine that killed one in three Icelanders over the next three years.

9 1874: The Nationalist Movement
The mid-19th century saw a growth of nationalism. This led to the Danish king finally restoring legislative power to the Alþing in 1874.

10 1944: Independence
Denmark's invasion by Nazi Germany in 1940 nullified its rule over Iceland. On 17 June 1944, the country's first president, Sveinn Björnsson, proclaimed Iceland an independent nation, ending 700 years of foreign rule.

4 Gullfoss
Huge and powerful, this two-tier waterfall *(above)* on the Hvítá river has been a national ymbol since it was saved from oblivion during the 1920s by the first environmental activist Iceland, Sigríður Tómasdóttir.

5 Vatnajökull National Park
This colossal reserve *(above)* protects not only the central Vatnajökull icecap and its score of out-running glaciers, but also a handful of exceptionally beautiful rivers, gorges and mountain formations.

6 Landmannalaugar Area
Landmannalaugar's bridgeless rivers, shattered grey mountains and hot springs *(right)* make you feel like an explorer in the wilds. Summer buses make this part of the Interior easily accessible.

7 Látrabjarg Bird Cliffs
Fantastically remote even by elandic standards, northwesterly átrabjarg supports one of the largest eabird colonies in Europe, and is ome to millions of gulls, guillemots nd puffins *(below)*.

8 Snæfellsjökull National Park
Western Iceland's long, snoutlike peninsula peaks with the snowy cone of Snæfellsjökull, a slumbering volcano crossed by hiking trails. It is tall enough to be visible from Reykjavík.

9 Lake Mývatn Area
Lake Mývatn collects the best of Iceland in one place: abundant wildfowl, volcano cones, mud pits, thermal pools and steaming lava flows.

10 Jökulsárlón
Make an easy tour along the Ringroad to this southeastern lagoon *(left)* between the Atlantic Ocean and the end of the Breiðamerkurjökull glacier, crammed full of powder-blue icebergs and seals.

TOP 10 Volcanoes

1 Hekla
This volcano has erupted over a dozen times since Settlement, most famously burying nearby Viking farms under ash in 1104.

2 Eyjafjallajökull
In April 2010, eruption of this volcano sent a vast cloud of volcanic ash across Europe. Many countries closed their airspace.

3 Snæfell
This stratovolcano – one whose cone has built up gradually over successive eruptions – is believed to have last erupted around AD 250. Today it is covered by the Snæfellsjökull icecap.

4 Öræfajökull
Iceland's tallest volcano, it erupted in 1362, burying almost a third of the country under gravel. An eruption in 1727 caused less damage.

5 Lakagígar
In 1783, land outside Kirkjubæjarklaustur split open. For seven months, fire and poisonous fumes belched out. Local pastor, Jón Steingrímsson, bundled citizens into the church and is said to have prayed they be spared – the lava halted right at the church boundary.

6 Eldfell
A 1973 eruption at Eldfell buried a third of the town under lava and the rest under ash. Spraying seawater on encroaching lava saved the harbour.

7 Katla
Sited under the Mýrdalsjökull icecap, this volcano erupts at about 70-year intervals. The last eruption, in 1918, sent meltwater and gravel flooding down nearby valleys.

8 Grímsvötn
Iceland's most active volcano smoulders below the Vatnajökull icecap. A volcanically induced flash flood tore out from under the Skeiðarárjökull in 1995. There was another eruption in 2011.

9 Krafla
The Krafla Fires of 1975–84 delayed the completion of Leirbotn Geothermal Power Station. However, this new source of natural heat might help increase the station's projected 60 MW output.

10 Askja
In winter 1875, a vent in the Askja caldera exploded, vaporizing two cubic kilometres of rock that fell as a thick layer of pumice over northeastern Iceland.

Istanbul

Istanbul is one of the greatest cities the world has ever known. Inhabited for at least 5,000 years, it was capital of two of the world's most powerful empires – those of the Byzantines and the Ottomans – and its every stone is steeped in history. The highlights are easy; you can cover the major attractions in the first couple of days. But after that, the choice can be overwhelming, especially as this ancient city is reinventing itself once more as a modern centre for nightlife, food and shopping. The only answer is to come back again – and again. If you do, this endlessly fascinating city will certainly reward you.

1 Topkapı Palace

A palace fit for a sultan, several wives, hundreds of concubines and thousands of retainers, the Topkapı *(left)* was not only a royal residence, but also the Ottoman Empire's centre of government.

TOP 10 Moments in History

1 AD 330–95: Division of the Roman Empire
In 330, Emperor Constantine moved his capital to the city of Byzantium, later renamed Constantinople. In 395, Theodosius divided the Empire, wiith the eastern half run from Constantinople.

2 1071: Battle of Manzikert
The Seljuk Turks from Persia defeated Byzantine forces at Manzikert in 1071, seizing most of Anatolia.

3 1204: Sacking of Constantinople
In 1204, the armies of the Fourth Crusade sacked Constantinople. Crusaders held Constantinople until 1261, when Byzantine Emperor Michael VIII Palaeologus retook the city.

4 1453: Birth of Istanbul
In 1453, Ottoman Sultan Mehmet II captured Constantinople, renaming it İslambol ("the City of Islam"). The last Byzantine emperor, Constantine IX, died defending the city walls.

5 1529: Siege of Vienna
In spring 1529, Süleyman I mustered a huge army with the aim of extending his lands in Hungary and moving on to Vienna. But a spirited defence of the city sent the Turks packing and ended Ottoman expansion into Western Europe.

6 1777: Turkish Delight
Ali Muhiddin Hacı Bekir, confectioner to the imperial court, invented a chewy, rosewater-flavoured sweet: *rahat lokum* ("morsel of contentment"), better known as Turkish delight.

7 1853–6: Crimean War
When Russia encroached on Ottoman territory, Britain and France weighed in on the side of the Turks. A hospital set up by Florence Nightingale in Istanbul helped to define modern nursing practice.

8 1919–23: Birth of the Republic
Mustafa Kemal Paşa – or Atatürk – led a bloodless revolution that abolished the sultanate, and fought a fierce war of independence. In 1923, as first president of the Republic of Turkey, he moved the capital to Ankara.

9 1973: Bosphorus Bridge
The Bosphorus Bridge, linking European Turkey to Asian Anatolia, was opened in 1973, between Ortaköy and Beylerbeyi.

10 2010: Istanbul European Capital of Culture
Istanbul was one of 2010's European Capitals of Culture. A programme of events showcased Istanbul's rich cultural heritage.

2 Dolmabahçe Palace

This 19th-century Occidental fantasy was a key component in the downfall of the Ottoman Empire. Sultan Abdül Mecit's decision to build a lavishly opulent European-style palace *(above)* almost bankrupted the Treasury, and in the end could be financed only by foreign loans.

3 Blue Mosque

Sultan Ahmet I's great mosque *(above)* is one of the world's most famous religious buildings – "blue" on accoun of the delicately patterned İznik tiles which adorn the interic

Archaeological Museum 4

urkey's world-class national ollection, which remarkably was begun only in the mid-19th century, contains ancient treasures from oss the length and breadth of the Ottoman Empire and nd, including artifacts from ylon, Syria, Egypt, Greece, Rome and Persia *(right)*.

6 Grand Bazaar

More mall than market since its last restoration, the Grand Bazaar *(above)* remains a true Turkish delight, a shopaholic's colourful fantasy that is also a photographer's dream. Whether you are after a Hereke carpet or a pair of silk slippers, you will be satisfied here – in the bazaar at the western end of the Silk Road.

5 Haghia Sophia

One of the greatest icons of the Christian church, Haghia Sophia *(left)* has stood for 1,500 years – a miraculous feat of design and engineering that has survived fire, war and earthquake, and outlived two great empires. A mosque from 1453 to 1931, it is now a museum.

7 Süleymaniye Mosque

Sultan Süleyman I, the Ottomans' greatest emperor, and Sinan, the empire's most talented architect, created more than 400 buildings together. This imposing mosque is their masterwork.

Çemberlitaş Baths 8

The perfect way to recuperate from an overdose of sightseeing is to steam gently beneath the marble domes of a traditional Turkish bath *(right)* before allowing an attendant to massage those aching feet. The experience is cleansing, cultural and reviving.

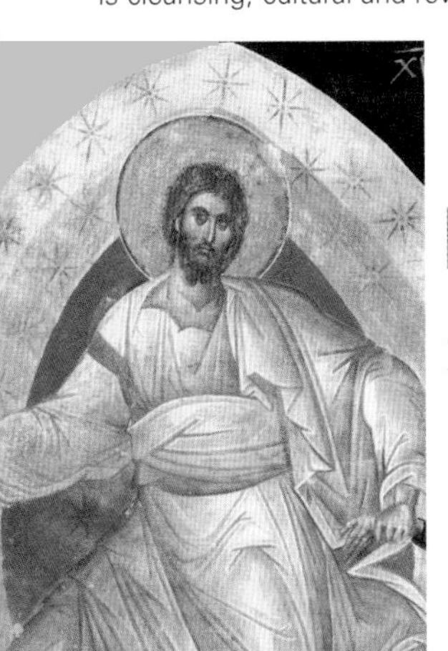

9 Church of St Saviour in Chora

With more than 100 profoundly beautiful early-14th-century mosaics and frescoes of biblical scenes *(left)*, this church is one of the greatest of Istanbul's many Byzantine treasures.

10 Bosphorus Cruise

Take to the water on a ferry trip up the Bosphorus, and enjoy a fabulously lazy day off. The air is clean, the pace unhurried and, best of all, sightseeing can be done from the deck, with the promise of a great lunch ahead.

Top 10 Facts About Turkish Carpets

1 Origins
Turkish rug-weaving skills originate from techniques used by Central Asian nomads. They wove goats' hair into carpets, tents and clothes that were warm and virtually waterproof.

2 Flat-Weaves
Kilims are the most basic form, with the design or horizontal (weft) threads woven into the vertical (warp) threads. In *cicims*, a third thread is woven in to create the what looks like an embroidered design.

3 The Oldest Carpets
Kilims have been made in Turkey for about 8,000 years. Fragments of 2,000-year-old knotted pile carpets survive, but the oldest intact pile carpets date from the 13th-century.

4 Weaving Materials
The basic materials used for Turkish carpets are wool, cotton and silk. Most finer carpets have a cotton warp and wool or silk weft; flat-weaves are generally made entirely from cotton.

5 Natural Dyes
The finest carpets use natural, such as madder root for shades from pink to red, orange and purple, and woad or indigo for blues.

6 Hereke Imperial Carpet Factory
A factory at Hereke, 60 km (38 miles) east of Istanbul, was set up in 1843 to provide carpets for the Ottoman court. Its carpets, made from Bursa silk, were larger and more finely woven than any known before.

7 Prayer Rugs
Prayer rugs (*namazlık*) usually contain an image of a *mihrab* (prayer niche). They were designed to be carried around and laid down for prayers five times a day.

8 Symbolism
Women wove their lives and longings into their carpets. Look for motifs, such as those symbolizing fate (an eight-pointed star) or heroism (rams' horns).

9 Number of Knots
The more knots in a carpet, the denser the weave and the clearer the design on the reverse side. The finest Hereke carpet could have an astonishing 324 knots per sq cm (2,090 per sq inch).

10 Regional Styles
Carpets used to be made in a profusion of distinctive regional styles, but now makers often simplify designs to appeal to the growing export market.

Italian Lakes

The spectacular natural beauty of the Italian Lakes region, sheltering under the Alps at the top of Italy, is matched by its historical legacy. Attractive lake villages, laid-back resorts and pretty towns offer a variety of fine art, architecture and cuisine, as well as unlimited opportunities for walking, cycling and watersports activities. The climate is special too, with the larger lakes acting as "solar batteries", producing a temperate climate.

1 Lake Idro and the Valvestino

The villages and hamlets in this forgotten corner of Lombardy tucked between Lake Garda and Lake Iseo enjoy clean waters, pristine countryside and a pace of life rarely found in 21st-century Europe *(left)*.

Northern Lake Maggiore 2

Italy melts into Switzerland at the northern end of Lake Maggiore and the Alps loom larger. Stunning displays of flora flourish in the lake's peculiar microclimate in the small, attractive resorts dotted around here *(right)*.

3 Bellagio

At the centre of Lake Como – the Centro Lago, where the three branches of the lake meet – stands Bellagio, with its pretty village centre of stepped streets *(above)*.

TOP 10 Moments in History

1 1st Century AD: Lake Como Flourishes
Peace and security having been established by the emperor Augustus and his successors, large agricultural estates began to spring up, and lakeside holiday villas were built by residents of Bergamo, Brescia and Milan.

2 313: Edict of Milan
Emperor Constantine's edict granted Christians freedom of worship. Under its charismatic bishop Ambrogio (St Ambrose), Milan became a centre of Christianity.

3 773: Charlemagne Declared King of the Franks and Lombards
With the fall of Rome, tribes from Northern Europe swept in. The Lombards took control of Pavia, but were ousted by Charlemagne, whose rule brought peace to Europe.

4 1176: The Defeat of "Barbarossa"
After numerous attempts to conquer northern Italy, Emperor Frederick I was defeated by an alliance of city states including Milan, Como, Cremona and Mantua.

5 11th–15th Centuries: Renaissance City States
From the 11th century the power of the city-states in northern Italy was unrivalled. After the Treaty of Lodi (1454), northern Italy was dominated by the Sforzas in Milan and the Venetian Republic.

6 1559: Spain controls the Duchy of Milan
Marking the beginning of over 300 years of foreign rule, Milan fell into the hands of the Spanish, who did little to solve the economic and social problems of this period.

7 1805: Napoleon Crowned King of Italy
Once he had invaded Austrian-ruled northern Italy in 1796, Napoleon took Milan and swept down the peninsula. His 20-year reign prepared the ground for independence.

8 1861: The Crowning of Vittorio Emanuele I
Lombards paid a high price for a united Italy. The Battle of Solferino, near Lake Garda, ended Austrian occupation, and Garibaldi's army of Red Shirts secured southern territories for the new kingdom.

9 1919: Italy Gains South Tyrol from Austria
The border region with Austria had been in dispute since 1866. The modern-day areas of Alto-Adige and Trentino were ceded to Italy for their part in World War I.

10 1945: The Capture of Mussolini
In April 1945, Mussolini and his mistress, Claretta Petacci, were executed in the village of Mezzegra on Lake Como. Their bodies were taken to Milan, where they were strung up in Piazza Loreto.

4 Bergamo
Venetian walls surround Bergamo's upper town *(right)*, while orchards and vineyards tumble down the hillside to the 19th-century avenues of the lower town.

5 Verona
Just east of Lake Garda, romantic Verona *(left)* is the perfect blend of ancient streets, historical buildings and fine food and wine.

7 Como
Wrapped around a bay at the southern end of Lake Como, the silk-producing town of Como is a historical place with a grand cathedral *(right)* and cobbled streets within a medieval wall.

6 Certosa di Pavia, Pavia
This charterhouse complex, founded in 1396 as a mausoleum for the Visconti family, is worth visiting not just for its splendid architecture but also for the insight into the daily lives of successive meditative orders of monks.

8 Orta San Giulio
Lake Orta's honey-coloured village, Orta San Giulio *(left)*, is nestled between the quiet woods of its Sacro Monte, or Holy Mountain, and the lake with Isola San Giulio opposite.

9 Sirmione and Southern Lake Garda
The very popular resort of Sirmione, with its Roman ruins *(below)* and remarkably intact medieval castle, juts out into the sapphire waters of Southern Lake Garda. Nearby, there is a host of attractive lakeside villages that boast ancient centres, grand hotels and excellent beaches.

10 Isola Bella
The sumptuous rooms of the palace of Isola Bella on Lake Maggiore only begin to prepare you for the extravagant terraced gardens *(above)* and their grottoes.

TOP 10 Swimming Spots

1 Lido Giardino, Menaggio, Lake Como
This complex on the northern outskirts of Menaggio offers a lake beach, some grassy patches, two pools, a children's playground and lovely sunbathing areas.

2 Belvedere, Iseo, Lake Iseo
This low-key lido with great views has grassy sections, a shady picnic area and a swimming pool with slides and a beach. Watersports are offered, as well as equipment hire for windsurfing.

3 Punta San Vigilio, Lake Garda
In a charming little corner of the lake, the Parco Baia delle Sirene, a clean, stony pay beach, is backed by grassy olive groves. There's a picnic spot, activities for kids and refreshment kiosks.

4 Lido delle Bionde, Sirmione, Lake Garda
Sirmione's lido is a good spot for swimming and sunbathing, and refreshments are available.

5 Manerba, Lake Garda
At the southern end of Lake Garda, Manerba boasts 11 km (7 miles) of fine beaches with fabulous views across the lake to the distant mountains.

6 Torri del Benaco Beach, Lake Garda
The north-facing, white shingle beach at the end of the promenade to the north of town is a good spot for cooling down. On the corner is a leafy public park with a children's playground.

7 Bellagio, Lake Como
Bellagio does not have the best swimming on the lake, but if you cannot bear the heat, head towards the waters off the Punta Spartivento for a dip.

8 Aqua Paradise Park, Lake Garda
Europe's largest water park has something for everyone: slides, rapids, a relaxed beach, a sunbathing area and an exciting medley of children's theme sections.

9 Gravedona Beach and Lido, Lake Como
Just by the entrance into Gravedona, the town's beach has a small lido with two pools, a bar and great views over the lake and mountains. Watersports are offered.

10 Cannobio, Lake Maggiore
This clean and spacious beach backed by shady trees offers windsurfing and sailing, although it can get crowded in peak season.

Lisbon

These days, fewer visitors approach Portugal's capital from the sea than once they used to, but the wide turn many passenger jets make over the beach at Caparica – before crossing the river above the red suspension bridge and sweeping over the city's roofs to the airport – is a pretty good introduction too. Lisbon is a city of immediate charms, and of a deeper beauty that must be sought out. The light loves it, painting it in warm pink hues and bright blues. It is an old place, steeped in history, but not closed in on itself as it once was. Lisbon's youthful, modern side includes a nightlife which is among Europe's liveliest, latest and most diverse.

1 Castelo de São Jorge
Crowning the hill where Lisbon's original settlers lived, the city's medieval castle *(above)* is a successful and evocative reconstruction. Best of all are the views from the esplanade.

2 Sé Catedral
Lisbon's cathedral was built in the middle of the 12th century, just after the Christian reconquest. It is a fortress-like structure whose stone glows amber as the sun sets.

3 Museu Nacional de Arte Antiga
Housed in a grand 17th-century palace, Portugal's national gallery displays art that places Portugal in a historical context – as well as other treasures.

4 Parque das Nações
Flanked by the Vasco da Gama Bridge, the site of Lisbon's sea-themed Expo 98 has been transformed into a dynamic leisure, business and residential area *(above)*.

TOP 10 Moments in History

1 138 BC: Roman Occupation
Although they had reached the Iberian peninsula in the second century BC, the Romans did not conquer its westernmost parts until nearly a century later. The trading post Olisipo, Lisbon's Greek name (often associated with Ulysses), was occupied in 138 BC.

2 AD 714: Moorish Occupation
Roman Lisbon was invaded by Alan tribes from the north, and then by the Visigoths, who ruled from Toledo. The Visigoths were later swept from power by Moorish armies crossing into Iberia at the Straits of Gibraltar. Lisbon fell to the Moors in 714.

3 1147: Reconquest
The Christian reconquest of the Iberian peninsula began in the north, where Afonso Henriques founded the Portuguese kingdom in 1140. His armies reached Lisbon in 1147 and took the city after a three-month seige.

4 1497: Vasco da Gama Sails from Belém
The crowning achievement of Portugal's era of discovery and expansion was Vasco da Gama's well-documented, nearly year-long voyage to India. Rounding the Cape of Good Hope, he proved Columbus wrong and gave the Portuguese an important competitive edge in the lucrative spice trade.

5 1640: Independence from Spain
Spain usurped the Portuguese throne in 1581, after the death of Dom Sebastião and much of the Portuguese nobility in an ill-conceived military adventure in north Africa. The 1640 coup at Lisbon's royal palace reinstated self-rule and proclaimed the Duke of Bragança king of Portugal.

6 1755: The Great Earthquake
On 1 November 1755, a massive earthquake hit southern Portugal and laid waste to central Lisbon. Three shocks were followed by fires and tidal waves. The scale of the destruction shocked the world.

7 1910: Portugal Becomes a Republic
In 1908 Dom Carlos and his heir were assassinated by republican activists in Terreiro do Paço. The king's surviving son became Dom Manuel II, but abdicated in October 1910 in the face of a republican revolution. The Republic was formalized on 5 October.

8 1933: The New State
António de Oliveira Salazar, who had been appointed finance minister in the hope that he could solve the country's financial crisis, was asked to form a government in 1932. The following year his new constitution was passed by parliament, in effect making him an authoritarian dictator.

9 1974: The Carnation Revolution
Salazar's successor Marcelo Caetano was overthrown in a virtually bloodless coup by a group of army captains on 25 April 1974. Crowds outside headquarters of the PIDE, the political police, cheered the end of its reign of fear.

10 1986: European Union Membership
After a few tumultuous years following the 1974 revolution, stable democracy returned. Independence was restored to most of the colonies and Portugal was now ready to turn to Europe. Membership brought an economic boost, in the form of both subsidies and foreign investment.

5 Mosteiro dos Jerónimos

The Manueline is Portugal's own architectural style. Its beginnings, and some of its greatest expressions, can be seen in the glorious national monument that is the Jerónimos Monastery *(above)*.

6 Museu Calouste Gulbenkian

A museum of the highest international calibre, the Gulbenkian is a small, coolly pleasant universe of art history, where visitors can drift around oblivious of any other.

7 Museu Nacional do Azulejo

This beautiful museum displays and explains the essential Portuguese decorative element – the tile *(above)*. It also has some of the city's most stunning convent and church interiors.

8 Torre de Belém

The boot-shaped defensive tower at Belém *(above)* is one of Lisbon's emblems, but it is also one of the most perfect examples of the Manueline style, with proportions that please, rather than inspire awe.

9 Palácio de Queluz

A Rococo feast, ripe with culture and aspiration, this summer palace *(right)* just outside Lisbon was, for a brief period, the royal family's permanent residence.

10 Sintra

Sintra *(above)* is a powerful magnet for most visitors to Lisbon, but it is wise to do as Lord Byron did, and absorb the city first before moving on to Sintra – the better to appreciate the contrast.

TOP 10 City Views

1 Castelo
The fine views from under the umbrella pines on the Castle's esplanade take in Alfama, the Baixa, Bairro Alto on the hill opposite, and the river.

2 Santa Luzia
Most tourists head for the Largo das Portas do Sol viewpoint, on the far side of the Santa Luzia church. But this one has a pergola with tiled pillars, walls and seats as a veranda for the view.

3 São Pedro de Alcântara
This small garden is one of Lisbon's best known viewpoints. The sweeping view extends over Restauradores and the Baixa to the Sé and the Castle.

4 Miradouro de Santa Catarina
Not just a vantage point, this is also a place to meet and hang out. Adamastor, the mythical creature from Camões' epic poem *The Lusiads*, presides over events from a stone plinth.

5 Igreja da Graça
The pine-shaded esplanade by the Graça church has a café with a classic view of the lower city, the river and the bridge. It is best visited in the late afternoon.

6 Senhora do Monte
One of the highest vantage points in the city, Our Lady of the Mount (there is a chapel behind the viewpoint) affords a grand vista.

7 Elevador de Santa Justa
The best close-up overview of the Baixa and Rossio, with the Castle above, is from the terrace at the top of the Elevador de Santa Justa. It is reached via an extremely tight spiral staircase.

8 Cristo Rei
From his tall perch on the south side of the river, the huge 1959 statue of Christ the King is a great vantage point for taking in all of Lisbon and the Tejo estuary. Lifts ascend to the platform beneath the statue.

9 Jardim do Torel
The Jardim do Torel is a less well-known viewpoint in a small garden overlooking Restauradores and the Avenida da Liberdade – providing not just a fine view but a great place for quiet contemplation too.

10 Parque Eduardo VII
Climb to the top of this unprepossessing park and Lisbon stretches away in an unbroken perspective right down to the river.

London

A city of infinite colour and variety, London is both richly historic, tracing its roots back over 2,000 years, and unceasingly modern, being at the forefront of fashion, music and the arts. There is a fantastic wealth of architecture, cultural events and places of interest to entertain the visitor is this truly cosmopolitan city.

Atlantic Ocean
Glasgow
Edinburgh
North Sea
REPUBLIC OF IRELAND
Manchester
Leeds
UNITED KINGDOM
Cardiff
LONDON
FRANCE

1 British Museum
The oldest museum in the world *(left)* contains a rich collection of treasures and artifacts from every corner of the globe.

3 London Eye
The world's tallest cantilevered observation wheel *(above)* sits on the South Bank of the River Thames, opposite the Houses of Parliament, and offers great views of the city.

2 National Gallery and National Portrait Gallery
The nation's most important art collections are on display at the National Gallery *(right)*. Next door, the National Portrait Gallery features images of illustrious British men and women.

TOP 10 Moments in History

1 AD 43: Roman Invasion
Roman settlers constructed a bridge over the Thames and encircled Londinium with a wall, part of which is still visible. Their forum was in Cornhill and an amphitheatre lies beneath the Guildhall.

2 1066: Norman Conquest
William, Duke of Normandy, led the next conquest. He was crowned King of England in Westminster Abbey on Christmas Day 1066.

3 1240: First Parliament
The first parliament sat in Westminster and became a seat of government separate from the mercantile City, which continued to expand on the former Roman site.

4 1534: The Reformation
A quarrel between Henry VIII and Pope Clement VII over the king's divorce led to Henry breaking with Rome and declaring himself head of the church in England. The sovereign remains the head of the Church of England.

5 1649: Charles I Executed
Charles I's belief in the divine right of kings led to civil war. The royalist cause lost and the king was beheaded in 1649. After 11 years of Puritan rule, the British monarchy was restored.

6 1666: Great Fire of London
Five days of fire destroyed much of the city, including the medieval St Paul's, which was replaced by Christopher Wren's masterpiece.

7 1863: First Underground
Built to link London's main stations, the Metropolitan Line was the world's first underground railway. The original carriages were little more than trucks.

8 1875: Embankments Constructed
Embankments on either side of the Thames were designed by Sir Joseph Bazalgette to house a new sewage system, taking waste to pumping stations outside London.

9 1940–41: The Blitz
Between September 1940 and May 1941, German air raids destroyed large areas of London, leaving 30,000 dead. Many sought shelter at night in Underground stations.

10 1992 to the Present
Regeneration of Docklands from 1992 saw the building of Canary Wharf. In July 2005, the city transport system was rocked by four terrorist bombs, with tragic loss of life. In 2012 London hosted the Olympics.

4 Tate Modern and Tate Britain

London's two Tate galleries house a superb collection of international art. Tate Modern *(left)* focuses entirely on work created after 1900, and Tate Britain on art from 1500 to the present.

5 Science Museum

This huge museum has fascinating exhibits *(right)* that demonstrate and explain the wonders of science.

6 Westminster Abbey and Parliament Square

This royal abbey has, since 1066, been the place where all Britain's monarchs have been crowned.

7 Tower of London

Steeped in bloody history, the Tower *(below)* has been a royal palace, fortress and prison, and is the home of the spectacular Crown Jewels.

8 St Paul's Cathedral

Sir Christopher Wren's Baroque masterpiece *(above)*, St Paul's still dominates the City skyline and has been the setting of many great ceremonial events.

9 Buckingham Palace

The official home of the Queen, Buckingham Palace is one of the city's most recognizable landmarks, where the changing of the Queen's guard *(left)* usually happens every day.

10 Natural History Museum

The enormous and varied collection here explores the origin and structure of the Earth, as well as the incredible range of life that the planet supports *(right)*.

Top 10 Performing Arts Venues

1 Royal Opera House
One of the greatest opera houses in the world, major opera and ballet productions are staged in its sumptuous main auditorium. The Linbury and Clore theatres offer a more intimate setting for smaller-scale performances.

2 The National Theatre
Within the walls of this innovative building, designed by Denys Lasdun in 1976, you can see a musical, a classic or a new play in one of three theatres: the Olivier, the Lyttelton or the Cottesloe. Free shows and exhibitions are held in the foyer.

3 Barbican Centre
Home of the London Symphony Orchestra, the Barbican is the City's most important arts complex. Theatre, cinema, concerts, dance and exhibitions all feature here, along with restaurants, cafés and bars.

4 London Coliseum
London's other principal opera house presents productions sung in English by the English National Opera. The building is a superb example of Edwardian architecture.

5 Southbank Centre
This riverside complex includes three major music venues, the Royal Festival Hall, the Queen Elizabeth Hall and the Purcell Room.

6 Sadler's Wells
After winning a reputation as one of the best dance theatres in London in the 1950s, Sadler's Wells now also hosts music and opera. The stunning glass building is worth a visit in itself.

7 Royal Albert Hall
This distinctive, circular building was designed to resemble a Roman amphitheatre. The excellent acoustics make it a great venue for all kinds of concert.

8 Royal Court Theatre
The cream of new drama can be seen at this charming small theatre. Both the main and the tiny upstairs theatre are important London venues. You can play "actor spotting" in the restaurant and bar.

9 Riverside Studios
This fascinating arts and media centre presents an eclectic mix of cinema, theatre, comedy, dance, music and the visual arts. The café and river terrace are a draw in themselves.

10 ICA
A stately, colonnaded, Nash terrace houses the Institute of Contemporary Arts, one of London's hippest galleries. The ICA's cutting-edge policy on the visual arts includes the development of challenging digitally produced works.

Madeira

Madeira is an island of astonishing contrasts. From the sophistication of the capital, Funchal, it is a short step to the primeval woodland that cloaks the dramatic cliffs and canyons of the island's interior. The fertility of Madeira's flower-filled gardens is in marked contrast to the aridity of the island's volcanic peaks. And nothing could be more different than the gentle rippling of the *levadas* (canals), which carry water into Madeira's deepest valleys, and the crash of the waves that dash the island's rocky shores. Madeira has been called a place where all the continents meet. It has something of them all – including snow.

1 Museu da Quinta das Cruzes, Funchal
Explore a gracious Madeiran mansion and its sculpture-filled gardens *(above)*, built where the island's first ruler, João Gonçalves Zarco, had his home.

2 Meu de Arte Sacra, Funchal
Trade contacts with Antwerp in the 15th century enabled Madeira's merchants to sell their sugar – so valuable that it was known as "white gold" – and buy the superb Flemish paintings and sculptures that fill this art museum.

3 The Old Blandy Wine Lodge, Funchal
Madeira is renowned for its wines, famous for their complexity and depth of flavour. At this historic wine lodge you can learn to be a Madeira connoisseur.

4 Funchal Cathedral (Sé)
Hewn out of the island's volcanic rock and using its abundant timber supplies, Madeira's cathedral *(above)* is a monument to the faith and piety of the island's first settlers.

TOP 10 Moments in History

1 Island Formation
Twenty million years ago the islands of the Madeiran group began to emerge from the sea. Pockets of fertile soil were created as storms eroded the softer layers of volcanic ash. Slowly the island came to life, as seeds took root and spread.

2 Early Visitors
Sailors visited Madeira to gather sap from dragon trees, for use in dying clothes. Mentioned in the *Natural History* of Pliny the Elder (AD 23–79), Madeira first appears on the Medici Map of 1351, as Isola de Lolegname (meaning "Wooded Isle").

3 Zarco Arrives
Prince Henry "the Navigator" (1394–1460) saw how useful Madeira was to explorers in the Atlantic. He sent João Gonçalves Zarco (1387–1467) to the islands. In 1420 Zarco claimed Madeira for Portugal.

4 Colonization
Portuguese colonization began in 1425. Machico was their first capital, but Funchal had a better harbour and gained city status in 1508.

5 Prosperity
By 1470, Madeira's early settlers were busy exporting wheat, dyes, wine and timber, but sugar made the biggest profits. For around 150 years the island was Europe's most important sugar producer.

6 Wine
Caribbean and Brazilian sugar hit European markets in the mid-16th century. *Malvazia* (Malmsey), a sweet fortified wine, took over as Madeira's main export – the favourite drink of Shakespeare's roistering character Falstaff.

7 The British Arrive
British merchants dominated the wine trade after Charles II married Portuguese princess Catherine of Braganza in 1662. British (and American) taxes on Madeira wine were reduced as part of the marriage settlement. So valuable was Madeira to the British that an armed force was sent in 1801 to prevent Napoleon from capturing it.

8 Reid's Hotel
Madeira became a popular winter holiday destination for wealthy Europeans. Symbolic of the era is Reid's Hotel, founded by William Reid. He arrived a poor sailor in 1836 and made his fortune renting houses to aristocratic visitors.

9 Autonomy
Madeira escaped the worst effects of the two World Wars but by 1974 it had become Europe's poorest region. In that year, Portugal's dictatorship was toppled in a coup by army officers. In 1976 Madeira became largely autonomous, except for tax, foreign policy and defence.

10 Catastrophe
In 2008 Funchal celebrated its 500th anniversary as the capital of an increasingly prosperous island, but in February 2010 a devastating storm caused widespread floods. Lives were lost, and homes, roads and bridges destroyed. Funchal was badly affected, but was functioning again within weeks thanks to the resolve of the islanders.

5 Mercado dos Lavradores, Funchal

Funchal's historic farmers' market *(left)* is a bustling medley of colourful stalls positively bursting with exotic fruits, ocean-fresh fish, scented flowers and local crafts.

6 Jardim Botânico, Funchal

The Botanical Gardens *(above)* are a showcase for all the plants that thrive in the island's warm and humid climate, from jungle orchids to bristling cacti.

Quinta do Palheiro Ferreiro 7

Two centuries of cultivation have produced this magnificent all-seasons garden *(right)* in which the flowers of the world combine with the English flair for garden design.

9 Curral das Freiras

During pirate attacks, the nuns of Santa Clara took refuge in this hidden green valley encircled by sheer cliffs *(above)*, a place of breathtaking scenic beauty.

Monte 8

Escape to a romantic world of gardens, teahouses and cobbled walks, home to Emperor Charles I in exile. Afterwards, return to the capital on the exhilarating Monte toboggan run *(right)*.

Pico do Arieiro 10

Feel on top of the world as you view the ridges and ravines of the island's mountainous interior from the summit *(right)* of Madeira's third highest peak (1,818 m/5,965 ft).

Top 10 Facts About Levada-Walking

1 What Are Levadas?
The word *levada* means "to take". A *levada* is an irrigation channel, designed to take water from places where it is plentiful to those where it is not, and is needed.

2 Why Levadas?
Water is abundant in the mountains to the north of the island, but scarce in the fertile and sunny south, where most crops are grown. The island's earliest settlers began the buiding of irrigation channels that form the basis of today's network.

3 Water and Power
Water was key to the growth of Madeira. It irrigated the crops, powered the sawmills for timber used in construction and ship-building, and turned the wheels of the mills that crushed sugar.

4 Construction
Constructing *levadas* was a feat of engineering, involving cutting channels into a sheer rockface, or building aqueducts over deep ravines. To reach inaccessible spots, the *levada* builders were lowered down cliffs in baskets.

5 Contour Lines
To prevent the water from running too fast, causing soil erosion, most *levadas* follow the contours of the landscape, winding in and out of valleys, descending gradually from north to south.

6 Levada Maintenance
Levadas require constant maintenance to clear anything that might block the flow of water. Paths were built alongside to allow the *levadeiros*, or maintenance men, access to do the work.

7 Levadas as Footpaths
On a visit to Madeira in 1974, Pat and John Underwood realized that maintenance paths offered easy walking routes with stunning views. Their book, *Landscapes of Madeira*, brings walkers by the thousand to the island.

8 Guided Tours
Levada walking is easiest if you join a guided tour. both Madeira Explorers and Nature Meetings are good companies; the tourist board will have details of others.

9 Levada dos Tornos
Combine a *levada* walk with a visit to the Quinta do Palheiro Ferreiro. Turn right out of the garden and walk to the village. Follow signs to the Levada dos Tornos and Jasmin Tea House – an ideal spot for lunch.

10 Rabaçal
A popular walk starts from Rabaçal. Walk down to the Foresters' House, and turn right along the *levada* signposted "Risco". After a 20- or 30-minute walk through primeval woodland, you will reach a pretty waterfall.

Madrid

Madrid's three world-class art museums and two royal palaces alone would set the pulses racing, but there is more to Spain's exciting and diverse capital than its tourist sights. The fashion boutiques of the Salamanca district showcase Europe's top designers and are just the tip of a shopping iceberg, perfectly complementing the informality of the fascinating El Rastro market, while Madrid's world-famous tapas bars vie for attention with gourmet restaurants and humble *tabernas* in a city that never sleeps. Simply to watch the world go by, head for the supremely elegant Plaza Mayor.

1 Palacio Real

The former residence of Spain's Bourbon rulers *(left)* boasts more rooms than any other palace in Europe. With priceless collections of tapestries, clocks, paintings, furniture, even Stradivarius violins, there is something here for everyone.

2 Museo de América

Spain's fascination with America began with the voyages of Columbus in the 15th century, but this museum casts its net wider than the former Spanish colonies to embrace artifacts *(left)* from the whole continent.

3 Plaza Mayor

This magnificent square *(right)*, now lined with shops, has been the focal point of the city ever since Madrid became the capital of Spain's world empire in the 16th century.

TOP 10 Moments in History

1 Birth of a City
The founding of the city is usually dated to AD 852 when Muhammed I built a fortress on the escarpment now home to the Palacio Real.

2 Christian Conquest
In 1083 the important city of Toledo fell to northern Christian armies and the *alcázar* of Madrid was surrendered without a fight. The new settlers lived harmoniously with their Arab neighbours, although mosques were converted into churches.

3 A New Capital
In 1561 Felipe II moved his capital from Valladolid to Madrid, then a small, squalid town of 9,000 inhabitants. He transformed the market-place outside the walls into a public square, Plaza Mayor.

4 Growth of the City
By the time the Plaza Mayor was completed in1619, Madrid's population had swollen to around 85,000. The overcrowding led Felipe IV to order the building of a new perimeter wall.

5 Mayor-King
Carlos III (1759–88) gave the city imposing thoroughfares, such as the Paseo del Prado. Streets were paved and lit, and sewers were dug. He became known as *El Rey-Alcalde* (the Mayor-King).

6 Insurrection
On 2 May 1808, two months after a French army occupied the city, the people of Madrid rose in revolt. But within a few hours, the insurrection had been crushed and the leaders were executed.

7 Re-Awakening
In 1919 Alfonso XIII opened Madrid's first metro line. Streets were demolished to make way for the Gran Vía, and around Calle de Alcalá grew a new financial district.

8 Madrid Under Siege
Three months into the Spanish Civil War, General Franco's Nationalist army surrounded Madrid. Republican resistance was fierce and the siege dragged on for two-and-a-half years, the city finally falling to the rebels in March 1939.

9 Death of Franco
After ruling Spain with an iron fist for 36 years, Franco died in 1975. His successor was Prince (later King) Juan Carlos. The first democratic elections were held in 1977.

10 Tejero's Coup
On 23 February 1981, Franco loyalists under Colonel Tejero attempted a coup. Tejero forced his way into the parliament building, firing shots. The coup collapsed when the king confirmed that the army had remained loyal.

4 Museo del Prado

This world-famous art gallery *(above)* is Madrid's most obvious must-see. The outstanding collections of Spanish and European painting reflect the taste of royal connoisseurs.

5 El Escorial

Set in the town of San Lorenzo de El Escorial, about 45 km (28 miles) northwest of Madrid, against the stunning backdrop of the Sierra de Guadarrama mountains, Felipe II's awe-inspiring palace and monastery *(above)* was founded as a mausoleum for Spain's Habsburg rulers.

6 El Rastro

The roots of Madrid's famous flea market go back over 400 years. The location in Lavapiés, one of Madrid's most colourful working-class neighbourhoods, is another plus.

7 Museo Reina Sofía

No visitor should miss the chance to see Picasso's *Guernica*, perhaps the most famous 20th-century painting in the world. This fabulous museum also showcases other modern Spanish greats including Salvador Dalí, Joan Miró and Juan Gris.

8 Parque del Retiro

Once the preserve of royalty, this beautiful park *(above)* in the heart of the city is now enjoyed by visitors and *Madrileños* alike.

9 Museo Thyssen-Bornemisza

Madrid was the envy of the world when it outbid the Getty Foundation and other front runners for this priceless collection of great European art, which attracts around three quarters of a million visitors every year.

10 Monasterio de las Descalzas Reales

When the daughters of Spain's aristocratic families withdrew from the outside world in the 17th century to live a life of devotion, they donated their wealth to this royal convent *(left)* in the form of fabulous works of art.

TOP 10 Spanish Paintings in the Prado

1 St Dominic Presiding over an Auto-de-Fé
In this painting by the Italian-influenced Pedro Berruguete (c.1445–1503), St Dominic is shown in judgement with members of the Inquisition.

2 The Adoration of the Shepherds
Born in Crete, El Greco (1541–1614) was given his nickname ("The Greek") after settling in Toledo. This masterpiece was intended for his tomb.

3 Still Life with Pottery Jars
Francisco Zurbarán (1598–1664) is best-known for his religious paintings. This still life reveals his great technical skills, in details such as the gleam of light on pewter.

4 Maja Naked
This famous portrait by Francisco de Goya (1746–1828) is one of the rare nudes in Spanish painting of the time. *Maja Clothed* is in the same room for comparison.

5 Holy Family with Little Bird
Bartolomé Esteban Murillo (1617–82) worked mainly in the decoration of convents and monasteries. This work, painted with fluent brush-strokes, is typical of him.

6 Las Meninas
This virtuoso exercise in perspective is by Diego Velázquez (1599–1660). Flanking the Infanta Margarita are her two ladies-in-waiting (*las Meninas*). The scene also includes the artist, paint-brush and palette in hand.

7 The Tapestry Weavers
Velázquez's depiction of Madrid upholsterers is also a complex allegory based on the legend of Arachne.

8 The Meadow of St Isidore
This Goya landscape evokes the atmosphere of the San Isidro celebrations and the clear light of spring.

9 St Jerome
José de Ribera (1591–1652) painted this expressive portrait of St Jerome. Like many Spanish artists of the period, Ribera was much influenced by Caravaggio.

10 The Third of May 1808
In this dramatic painting, Goya captures the execution on Principe Pio hill of the leaders of the ill-fated insurrection against the French. The illuminated, Christ-like figure represents freedom being mowed down by the forces of oppression.

Mallorca

Known variously as the "Golden Isle", the "Wooded Isle" and the "Tranquil Isle", Mallorca is all of these, despite its decades-long dependence on mass tourism. The island is laden with history and sights, from its castles and enchanted gardens to spectacular caves and mountains. The eastern and southern coasts still sport some of the cleanest, most beautiful beaches in the Mediterranean, and the city of Palma is more attractive, culturally alive and fun than ever.

1 La Seu: Mallorca Cathedral

Looming over Palma Bay, the Gothic cathedral's immensity is beautifully counterpoised by its soft golden colour and delicate filigree-like carvings *(left)*. Among the treasures within are the tombs of Mallorca's first kings.

2 Castell de Bellver, Palma

Standing sentinel on a hilltop, the castle of Bellver is immaculately preserved *(right)*. Its walls have held queens and scholars, and they now contain an intriguing museum that evokes the island's past.

3 Jardins d'Alfàbia

Created by an Arab *wali* (viceroy) 1,000 years ago, these gardens *(above)* include parterres, arbours and dells surrounding an all but derelict house. It's a great place for exploring and relaxing.

Top 10 Moments in History

1 Prehistory
Neolithic pastoral societies formed by at least 4000 BC. They lived in caves and kept domesticated animals. The bronze-working Talayot period began around 1400 BC.

2 Carthaginian Conquest
Various peoples, including the Greeks, used the island as a trading post. However, the absence of metal ores deterred colonization until the Carthaginian Empire spread to this part of the Mediterranean in the 7th century BC.

3 Roman Conquest
In the third century BC, Carthage came into conflict with the expanding Roman Empire. Rome prevailed in 146 BC and established order for the next 500 years. In AD 404 Mallorca and its neighbouring islands were established as the province of Balearica.

4 Vandal Invasion
Barely had the new province gained official recognition than the Vandals – in about AD 425 – swept across the Balearics, bringing a swift end to Roman rule. So destructive was their takeover that few traces of the Romans are left.

5 Byzantine Conquest
In 533 the Byzantines defeated the Vandals. Under their rule, prosperity returned and Christianity arrived. At the end of the 7th century, the island became more or less independent, with close ties to Catalonia.

6 Moorish Conquest
In 902 the Moors occupied the Balearics as a fiefdom of the Emirate of Córdoba. They held on for the next 327 years, forcibly converting all the inhabitants to Islam.

7 The Reconquista
In 1229 the forces of King Jaume I of Aragón landed on the west coast of Mallorca and laid siege to Medina Mayurqa (the Moorish name for Palma). The city fell to him on 31 December.

8 Upheaval
On the death of King Jaume in 1276 the kingdom spiralled into ungoverned turmoil as it was contested by his sons.

9 Unification with Spain
In 1344 the Balearics were united with Aragón. In 1479 the marriage of Fernando V of Aragón to Isabella I of Castile created a Spanish superstate, of which the islands were an outpost of little importance.

10 Since 1945
General Franco instigated the development of mass tourism, which brought a much-needed influx of foreign money, transforming the Balearics from a backwater to one of the 21st century's choicest venues of international celebrity.

4 Valldemossa

Arguably Mallorca's most beautiful town, Valldemossa (above) is where Polish pianist and composer Frédéric Chopin and his lover, French writer George Sand, spent a miserable but creative winter in 1838–9.

5 Fundació Pilar i Joan Miró, Palma

The creative genius and visionary power of the consummate Catalan artist are concentrated here, allowing you to experience the full range of Joan Miró's work and immerse yourself in the atmosphere of his studio.

6 La Granja

This mountain estate of gracious architecture and bucolic surrounds is a charming haven *(left)* – yet it is also home to a horrific collection of torture devices used by the dreaded Inquisition.

7 Península de Formentor

A dramatic extension of the Serra de Tramuntana mountain range, this is the site of Mallorca's very first luxury resort, where kings, presidents and movie stars have come to play *(above)*.

8 Alcúdia

This popular resort is home to the island's only remaining medieval walled city. It was built on the site of a Roman outpost, the theatre and ruins of which can still be seen *(right)*.

9 Monestir de Nostra Senyora de Lluc

Mallorca's most ancient holy site is the spiritual epicentre of island life. The monastery houses a sacred statue of the Virgin and Child; each year, thousands of pilgrims come to pay homage.

10 Coves del Drac

The island is peppered with fantastic *coves* (caves), of which these are the biggest and best. Spectacularly lit, the chambers echo with lilting classical music, played live from boats on one of the world's largest underground lakes.

Top 10 Ports and Resorts

1 Cala Fornells
A pleasant resort of coves with turquoise water, sandy beaches and large, flat rocks on which to bask. Families flock here, and it's good for snorkelling. Nearby Peguera has the nightlife.

2 Port d'Andratx
One of the island's choicest resort ports, frequented by the Spanish king and other stellar visitors. Most shops and restaurants are on the south side, with a smart sailing club on the north.

3 Port de Valldemossa
More a cove than a port, the beach here is rocky, houses are made of rock, and rocky villas dot the hill. Getting here involves hair-raising hairpin bends down a cliff that's subject to rockslides, especially after rain. The one restaurant, Es Port, is a treat.

4 Cala Deià
A narrow, winding road from Deià leads to a picturesque cove surrounded by steep cliffs. Getting down to the car park is the usual routine of narrow switchbacks.

5 Port de Sóller
The lovely bay offers calm waters for swimming. The resort hotels and nightlife venues cater to both young and old. Be sure to take a ride on the antique tram that shuttles to and from downtown Sóller.

6 Port de Pollença
The family-friendly resort, situated 6 km (4 miles) to the east of Pollença town, beside a pleasant bay, is an attractive place with a long, sandy beach. Many retired ex-pats live here.

7 Port d'Alcúdia
Big and a bit brash, this resort has it all, including what most visitors might prefer to do without – tacky fast food joints and too many fluorescent lights. Still, the beaches are good, and some of the restaurants excellent.

8 Cala Rajada
Ideal for watersports of all kinds, this is still a fully operational fishing port. Fine coves and beaches nearby include popular Cala Guyá, Cala Mezquida and Cala Torta, which allows nudists.

9 Platja de Canyamel
If a tranquil resort is what you're after, then this is the place. Even in high season, it remains quiet and family-oriented – just a long, curving sandy beach backed by pine forests, with a few tasteful hotels here and there.

10 Portopetro
Although on the verge of being swallowed whole by Cala d'Or, this little fishing village has so far managed to retain its original flavour – possibly because there is no beach and only one hotel.

Family Attractions

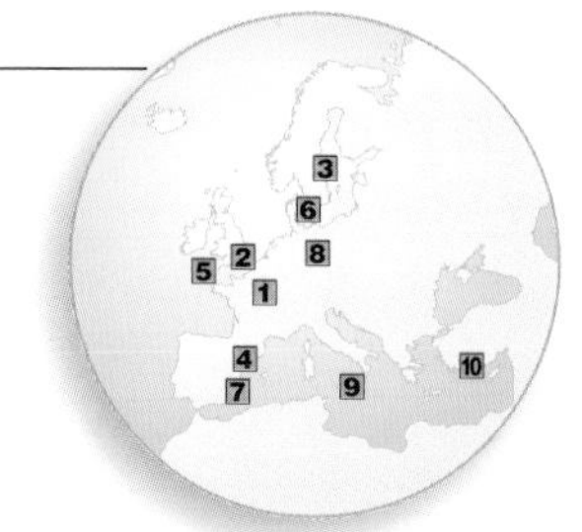

If anyone ever tells you that Europe is all about culture and history, and that you'll be dragging bored kids around museums and galleries for the entire visit – tell them to think again. From theme parks at their most fun to nature at its wildest, there is plenty to keep the brood in awe, and everywhere you go has clever ways to captivate young imaginations.

1 Disneyland® Resort, Paris *FRANCE*

Anyone visiting Paris with young children will probably feel compelled to visit the Paris branch of Disneyland®. The French offspring of America's favourite theme park is a clone of its parent, and has now been joined by the Walt Disney Studios® Park, which involves visitors in the world of film making. Both have big queues, so arrive early. There are rides for children of all ages and most adults are equally enchanted by the hi-tech workings and imagination behind such attractions as "Pirates of the Caribbean" and "The Haunted House".

2 London Zoo *ENGLAND*

There's a full day out to be had in this zoo on the north side of Regent's Park. Home to around 600 different animal species, the zoo emphasizes its important international role in research and conservation work, and you can see the breeding programmes of endangered animals, such as the western lowland gorillas and Sumatran tigers. The Meet the Monkeys enclosure provides a rainforest habitat for free-roaming monkeys and other wildlife.

3 Skansen, Stockholm *SWEDEN*

Located in the beautiful hilly parkland on Djurgården, this amazing open-air museum – a journey through historic Sweden – is deservedly one of the city's most enduring attractions. It features over 150 traditional buildings from around the country, including a bakery, manor houses and an 18th-century wooden church; all were dismantled, transported and rebuilt on site. It is also home to animals native to Scandinavia, such as elks, bears, lynxes and wolves, as well as trees and plants from all over Sweden. Skansen changes naturally with the seasons – bustling and lively in summer, calm and serene in winter – but it is so vast that it is easy to find a quiet spot.

4 L'Aquàrium, Barcelona *SPAIN*

Come face to face with the Mediterranean's marine world at the largest aquarium in Europe – an underwater kingdom of 21 enormous tanks brimming with nearly 400 marine species. The highlight of a visit is the Oceanari, where an 80-m (262-ft) underwater glass tunnel brings you face to face with three huge grey sharks – named Drake, Morgan and Maverick – lurking in 4.5 million litres (990,000 gallons) of water. A huge hit with the kids is the Explora! floor, which has interactive exhibits that allow you to explore the ecosystems of the Mediterranean Sea.

5 Eden Project, Cornwall *ENGLAND*

Since opening in a former clay pit in 2000, the Eden Project has become one of Cornwall's biggest success stories. With its giant greenhouses and imaginative scope, Eden is a visitor attraction with a difference. It describes itself as a "living theatre of plants and people" – a fantastic illustration of the diversity of the earth's plant life. Above all, the striking beauty of these plants make this an essential stop and one worth visiting at different times of the year in order to capture its seasonal changes.

Eden Project, Cornwall Visitors inside a tropical biome *(above)*

Disneyland® Resort, Paris Grand entrance to the theme park *(below)*

Tivoli Gardens, Copenhagen Thrill-seekers riding the carousel swings *(above)*

Mount Etna, Sicily Hikers on the trail to the summit *(below)*

6 Tivoli Gardens, Copenhagen *DENMARK*

Famous for its fairy-tale ambience, exotic buildings, gorgeous landscaped gardens and upmarket entertainment and restaurants, the Tivoli Gardens are more than an amusement park.

The atmosphere is magical enough to merit a visit even if you are not interested in the excellent rides on offer. The best time to take kids to Tivoli is during the day, when the atmosphere is more family-oriented. The many fun rides include cars on tracks, dragon boats on the lake, the pantomime theatre and the trolley bus. There are changing facilities, and plenty of child-friendly places to eat.

7 Terra Mítica, Benidorm *SPAIN*

The biggest, most exciting theme park on the Costa Blanca, Terra Mítica has it all, from thrilling roller-coasters to enormous waterslides. Each section of the park is dedicated to one of the great Mediterranean civilizations of the past, and so there are Roman, Greek, Egyptian and Iberian regions. With hundreds of shows (both day and night), as well as restaurants, bars and shops, the park has everything required for a full day out.

8 Deutsches Technikmuseum, Berlin *GERMANY*

This fascinating technology museum, located in the grounds of a former station, is a giant playground for children, and an excellent place for learning through play. For younger children there are locomotives to clamber over and windmills to play with, while the exhibition "Spektrum" allows older children to conduct their own physics and chemistry experiments. Visitors can also learn about developments in aviation and admire 40 different planes, including a Junkers Ju 52 commercial airliner and a "raisin bomber".

9 Mount Etna, Sicily *ITALY*

Sicily's nature reserves are good places to spot wildlife, climb about, picnic and go swimming. Hiking trails are graded for various levels of expertise. Mount Etna is probably the most fascinating – the volcano is always at least smoking, if not throwing red sparks into the air. Guides give a lively account of lava flowing underfoot and the gift shops screen spectacular footage from past eruptions.

10 Antalya Beach Park *TURKEY*

Antalya's Beach Park stretches out alongside Konyaaltı beach – a Blue-Flag-Award-winning beach that extends for 7 km (4 miles) southwest of the city. The main attractions are the AquaLand water park and DolphinLand, whose shows feature sea otters, dolphins and a white whale. There's also a paintballing area, beach bars, cafés and open-air restaurants aplenty.

Malta and Gozo

The tiny Maltese archipelago, floating on the cusp of Europe and Africa, has been coveted and invaded throughout its history. The Knights of St John (later of Malta) bequeathed palaces, fortresses and the glorious golden capital Valletta, while the British left red telephone boxes, iced buns and a predilection for tea. It was the islands' earliest settlers who left the most spectacular legacy: the extraordinary megalithic temples, unparalleled elsewhere in the world. Malta, the largest island, has the most cosmopolitan resorts and the edge in cultural treasures, while sleepy Gozo and tiny Comino offer unspoilt countryside and a gentler pace.

1 Grand Master's Palace, Valletta
This is a fittingly splendid home for the supreme head of the Knights *(above)*. The opulent apartments are filled with treasures ranging from paintings and armour to elaborate friezes.

2 Ħaġar Qim and Mnajdra
These hauntingly beautiful temples *(above)* made of creamy limestone are set on a wild and rugged clifftop overlooking the sea. Ħaġar Qim is fascinatingly complex, while Mnajdra's South Temple is the best preserved of all Malta's ancient sites.

3 St John's Co-Cathedral, Valletta
This, one of the world's finest Baroque churches *(left)*, still belongs to the Knights of Malta. The Oratory contains Caravaggio's masterpiece, *The Beheading of John the Baptist*.

Top 10 Moments in History

1 Prehistoric Malta (5000 BC–2500 BC)
Human settlement in Malta dates back at least to 5200 BC, although there is evidence to suggest that it may have begun as early as 7200 BC. The first of the islands' great temples were built around 3600 BC – a thousand years before the first pyramid in Egypt.

2 Phoenicians, Romans and Carthaginians (800 BC–AD 4th century)
Little is known of the civilization that occupied the islands from the end of the temple period until the arrival of the Phoenicians in around 800 BC. The Carthaginians used the islands as a military base from the 6th century BC until their defeat by the Romans in 218 BC. According to legend, St Paul was shipwrecked on Malta in AD 60, initiating the country's long history of religious devotion.

3 Byzantine and Muslim Eras (4th century–1090)
After the division of the Roman Empire in 395, Malta came under the control of the Byzantines until their defeat by the Arab caliphs. The islands fell to Count Roger the Norman in 1090.

4 Medieval Malta (1090–1282)
The Maltese enjoyed relative independence under Norman rule, and most continued to practise Islam. In 1194, control of the islands passed to the Swabian kings, who expelled the Muslims for ever. After a brief period of French rule, Malta was acquired by Spain in 1282.

5 Spanish Rule (1282–1530)
Under the Aragonese and later the Castilians, the first local governing body, the Università, was created and the first Maltese nobles were appointed. Charles V gave the islands to the Knights of St John in 1530.

6 Knights of Malta (1530–1798)
The Knights built Valletta, along with many palaces, fortifications and engineering works like the Wignacourt Aqueduct. They defeated the Turks in the Great Siege of 1565, a fatal blow to Muslim aims in the Mediterranean.

7 French Rule (1798–1800)
In 1798, Napoleon took Malta from the Knights without a struggle. He stayed just six days, but stripped the islands bare of all valuables. The outraged Maltese revolted and sought British help. The French were defeated and the British took control.

8 British Rule (1814–1939)
After defeating the French, the British declared Malta a colony in 1814 at the Treaty of Paris. It grew wealthy as an important refuelling station for British steamships en route to India. In World War I, Malta was used as a vast hospital.

9 World War II (1939–1945)
During World War II, Malta became the most bombed place on earth. The brave Maltese were awarded the George Cross in 1942 "to bear witness to a heroism and devotion that will long be famous in history".

10 Post-War Malta (1945–present)
After the devastation of the war, Maltese yearning for independence grew stronger and was finally granted in 1964. In 1979, the last British forces left the islands. Malta joined the EU in 2004.

4 Mdina and Rabat

Mdina, Malta's ancient capital, is a magical little city girdled by sturdy walls *(left)* and filled with medieval palaces and fine churches. Next-door Rabat boasts some of the most important Christian sites in Malta.

5 Palazzo Parisio, Naxxar

This splendid private palace *(left)* was utterly transformed by the 2nd Marquis of Scicluna in the early years of the 20th century. Its opulent salons and glorious gardens were embellished by the finest craftsman from Malta and Italy.

6 Marsaxlokk

In this enchanting little fishing illage *(above)*, traditional, brightly ainted *luzzus* (fishing boats) bob n the blue bay. Maltese families our in on Sundays to visit the amous fish market on the quays, nd then to linger in one of the xcellent seafront restaurants.

7 Ħal Saflieni Hypogeum, Paola

More than 55 centuries ago, men hewed this extraordinary necropolis out of solid rock. The chambers are spread over three levels and are magnificently carved and decorated.

8 Citadel, Rabat/Victoria

The tiny walled Citadel *(above)* sits high on a lofty promontory right in the centre of Gozo; from this vantage point, views unfold across the entire island and beyond to Malta. Within its walls is a clutch of fascinating museums.

9 Dwejra, Gozo

Gozo's wild, dramatic vestern coastline is spectacularly eautiful around Dwejra, where he huge Azure Window frames tunning views of the receding liffs *(above)*. It's perfect hiking erritory, and the diving is among he best in the Mediterranean.

10 Comino

The smallest inhabited island in the Maltese archipelago, tiny Comino is an unspoilt wilderness where the air is still spicily scented with the cumin that gives it its name. You can swim in the Blue Lagoon or hike to spectacular cliffs.

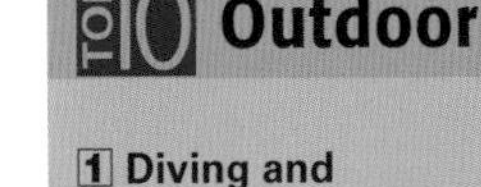

Top 10 Outdoor Activities

1 Diving and Snorkelling
Maltese waters are famous for diving and snorkelling. Natural harbours, bays, wrecks, reefs and caves offer endless opportunities for experienced and novice divers alike. The water is warm and clear, and there is a wealth of marine life.

2 Sailing
Malta has a long-established maritime tradition. Yachting is very popular. The biggest marinas are to be found in Marsamxett Harbour.

3 Other Watersports
Most hotels can arrange jet-skis, water-skiing, para-sailing, windsurfing and so on. The best windsurfing areas are Mellieħa and Baħar iċ-Cagħaq. Water polo is a national obsession.

4 Hiking
Both Malta and Gozo boast excellent hiking trails; Gozo has the edge because it is much less crowded. Comino is also great for a hike (albeit a short one), if only because few visitors venture beyond the bays.

5 Bird-Watching
Hunters and trappers have done their best to wipe out the bird population, but they haven't succeeded yet. They eliminated the Mediterranean peregrine falcon from the beautiful Ta' Ċenċ cliffs, but the area is still home to all kinds of bird life, including the largest colony of breeding Cory's Shearwaters in the Maltese islands.

6 Golf
Malta has just one golf course, the Royal Malta Golf Club. It is open to visitors, but advance booking is essential. Facilities include changing rooms, bar, restaurant, pro shop, practice putting green and driving range. "Proper golf attire" (polo shirt, tailored trousers or shorts) is compulsory.

7 Boat Excursions
Numerous boat excursions are available, from a tour of the Grand Harbour to jaunts taking in all three main islands. In Malta, most trips start from Sliema; in Gozo, from Xlendi Bay.

8 Rock-Climbing
There are no mountains, but the cliffs offer exciting challenges for climbers. Over 1,200 established routes include climbs for people of all abilities.

9 Horse-Riding
Malta has a long tradition of horse-riding, and boasts Europe's oldest polo club. There are numerous stables where you can arrange children's pony rides or longer treks for experienced riders. Malta's Tourism Authority can supply a list of approved centres.

10 Cycling
The volume of traffic, poor roads and appalling driving make cycling a bad idea on the Malta. On Gozo, the surfaces and drivers are just as bad, but the roads are generally very quiet. Be prepared for steep hills.

Milan

Set in the north of Italy, just 50 km (31 miles) from the border with Switzerland, Milan has long been a city of influence, as attested to by its impressive cultural heritage of important art galleries and ancient churches. Today it is Italy's economic powerhouse, a bustling city of finance, industry and commerce, whose media empires and fashion houses are among the most influential in Europe.

1 Leonardo's Last Supper

One of the largest and most ingenious works created by the ultimate Renaissance man, it is now in an advanced state of deterioration, but even the shadow that remains of this great work can teach us volumes about Renaissance ideals *(above)*.

2 Castello Sforzesco

This sprawling 15th-century castle is home to collections of tapestries, archaeological artifacts, paintings by Bellini and Mantegna, and sculptures that include Michelangelo's final work, the *Rondanini Pietà*.

3 Sant'Ambrog

One of the oldes churches in Milan *(left* it was founded by the city's bishop and patron saint Ambrose in 379, and is filled with mosaics and carvings dating back to the 4th century.

4 I Navigli

Milan's historic canal *(navigli)* district *(above)* is its liveliest, most bohemian neighbourhood. Old warehouses now house fashionable apartments, and the towpaths are lined with restaurants, clubs, bars and shops. This part of the city even stays open during the dog days of August.

TOP 10 Moments in History

1 283 BC: Conquest by Rome
The Po Valley and land to the north was a Celtic province often at war with Rome. An alliance with the Samnites failed, and Rome pushed its boundary north of the Po.

2 AD 313: Edict of Milan
During Rome's decline Milan was capital of the Western Empire. Constantine, holding court here, made Christianity the official religion.

3 569–72: Fall to the Lombards
Germanic Lombards took Milan in 569 and Pavia in 572, settling in the Po Valley, and across the north. The region gradually dissolved into a network of city-states.

4 1176: Defeat of Barbarossa
Swabian Emperor Frederick I (Barbarossa) levelled Milan and set up his own puppet mayors. The region's city-states formed the Lombard League to forced him out.

5 1277: Ottone Visconti Defeats the Torriani
Archbishop Visconti overthrew the leading Torriani family in 1277. In 160 years of Visconti rule, Milan's power spread over much of the north.

6 1450: Francesco Sforza Comes to Power
The last Visconti died in 1447. His only child, an illegitimate daughter, could not inherit the title. Her husband, Francesco Sforza, hired to protect the city from Venice, cut a deal instead to split the territory and made himself duke.

7 1499: French Milan
Lodovico Sforza brought the Renaissance to Milan but, in 1499, ceded control to Louis XII of France. The city changed hands repeatedly until Austria seized power in 1706.

8 1848: Cinque Giornate Revolt
Fired up by the Risorgimento (unification movement) a five-day revolt in Milan brought the end of Austrian rule.

9 1945: Mussolini Executed
As World War II drew to a close, the ousted Fascist leader Mussolini fled from the approaching Allies with his mistress. Shot by the partisans, their bodies were strung up and stoned on Milan's Piazzale Loreto.

10 1990: A New Lombard League
Northern resentment over sharing wealth with the poor south led to the founding of the Lombard League, which came to prominence in 1990. As the Northern League, it gained power as part of the Forza Italia coalition (now the Popolo della Libertà) led by Silvio Berlusconi.

5 Il Duomo di Milano

The world's largest Gothic cathedral *(above)* took more than 400 years to complete, a forest of stone pinnacles, flying buttresses, more than 3,500 statues and fantastic panoramas from its roof.

6 Pinacoteca di Brera

Northern Italy's greatest painting gallery displays masterpieces by Mantegna, Giovanni Bellini, Piero della Francesca, Raphael and Caravaggio.

7 Museo Bagatti Valsecchi

Two brothers created this palazzo in 1883–94. They acquired what they could by way of furnishings; and what they could not they hired master craftsmen to create. The overall effect is a glorious mixture of Renaissance craftsmanship and Romantic sensibilities.

8 Cimitero Monumentale

Milan's vast 19th-century cemetery has a pantheonic monument housing the remains of the city's great and good, and the grounds are filled with Art Nouveau tombs of Milan's top families. There is also a monument to the Milan Jews deported by the Nazis.

9 La Scala

The world's greatest opera house was built in 1776–8 under the Austrians. It boasts a sumptuous interior *(left)*, excellent acoustics and a staggering list of premieres.

10 Pinacoteca Ambrosiana

This library and art gallery complex *(right)*, founded in the 17th century, contains works by Leonardo, Botticelli, Raphael and Caravaggio.

Top 10 Notable Buildings

1 Triennale (Palazzo dell'Arte)
The Triennale is Italy's first Design Museum, housed in a dramatic 1930s palazzo on the edge of Parco Sirmione.

2 Palazzo della Ragione
The arcade at ground level of this Lombard Romanesque palace once hosted the city's market. The relief on the façade shows 13th-century mayor Oldrado da Tresseno on horseback.

3 Torre Velasca
This red 106-m (348-ft) tower block of 1956–8 has its top nine floors extended beyond the lower ones on struts, like an oversized medieval tower. Maintenance costs have proved horrendous.

4 Ca' Granda
One of Francesco Sforza's greatest public works, this huge hospital had separate wings for men and women, set around beautiful arcaded courtyards. It is now part of the University of Milan.

5 Galleria Vittorio Emanuele II
This four-storey shopping arcade, roofed with a steel-and-glass canopy, was built in 1864–8 by Giuseppe Mengoni, who fell to his death from its scaffolding just days before the King arrived to open the galleria and lend it his name.

6 Palazzo Marino
Milan's *comune* (city hall) has two distinct façades: a 1558 Mannerist one, and an 1860 Neo-Classical one facing La Scala. The former was built by Galeazzo Alessi, who also designed the lovely main courtyard.

7 Casa degli Omenoni
Renaissance sculptor Leone Leoni, whose works also grace the Duomo, built this palace in 1565. The lower level of the façade has eight giant telamones – columns in the form of a male figure.

8 Villa Necchi Campiglio
This perfectly preserved and restored 1930s villa has technology far ahead of its time, including a heated pool and internal phones. It also houses two galleries of art.

9 Pirelli Tower
Milan once had a rule that no building could rise higher than the golden Madonnina atop the Duomo. In 1960 the 127.1-m (417-ft) Pirelli Tower broke that tradition, but placed a replica of the Madonnina on its own roof.

10 Stazione Centrale
Milan's vast railway station, completed in 1931, is seen as an example of Fascist-era architecture, though its design of 1912 pre-dates this period and owes more to the Liberty style.

Moscow

Despite Stalin's destruction of much of Moscow's architectural heritage, what remains is enough to convey the impression of a medieval capital that collided with a Soviet juggernaut. It is a city where petite onion-domed churches and 19th-century mansions compete with epic neo-Gothic skyscrapers and ten-lane ring roads. Communism's greatest contribution to the city, though, is the magnificent metro system, deep underground. In recent years, bold modern structures have been added to Moscow's progressive skyline and Muscovites have recovered pride in their city.

1 St Basil's Cathedral

Built in the 16th century, during the uncertain times of Ivan the Terrible, Moscow's magnificent centrepiece *(left)* continues to be as enthralling as ever.

2 Pushkin Museum of Fine Arts

This superb collection takes in some 600,000 masterly artworks from across the globe, including ancient artifacts, sculptures and paintings.

3 Red Square

The historic square *(above)* – Krasnaya Ploshchad in Russian – is home to two of Moscow's most famous sights: St Basil's Cathedral and the Lenin Mausoleum.

TOP 10 Moments in History

1 First Recorded Reference
Moscow was first mentioned in the *Ipatievskaya Chronicles* of 1147. Then, Kiev was the capital of Russia and Moscow a minor outpost.

2 Mongol Invasion
In 1237–8 the fledgling town was razed and its denizens massacred by Mongol armies. Under the Mongols, Russian principalities were left to govern themselves and Moscow grew into a powerful city.

3 Ivan the Great's Reign
When Ivan the Great became Grand Prince of Moscow in 1462, the city gained in power and Russian territory was expanded. This enabled him to wrest Russia from Mongol control. To celebrate, he invited Italian architects to remodel the Kremlin in 1472.

4 Polish-Muscovite War
During this war (1605–18), Polish and Lithuanian troops succeeded in occupying Moscow in 1610. In 1612, however, they were routed.

5 Capital Relocated
Peter the Great loathed Moscow and in 1713 moved Russia's capital to the new city of St Petersburg. Moscow remained culturally and commercially active, however.

6 Moscow Burns
In 1812 Napoleon conquered Moscow, but Muscovites had already set the city ablaze as he advanced and his troops were left without shelter or supplies. As winter set in, Napoleon's army was forced to retreat.

7 Capital Returns
As German forces advanced on St Petersburg in 1918, Lenin feared the collapse of the Bolshevik Revolution and moved Russia's government to Moscow, which became the official capital in 1922.

8 German Invasion
Hitler's surprise invasion of Russia in 1941 took German troops to within 20 km (12 miles) of Moscow. The city was saved by a severe winter for which the invading troops were unprepared.

9 USSR Dissolved
Following a failed coup to oust Mikhail Gorbachev in 1991, Boris Yeltsin orchestrated the dissolution of the USSR; Gorbachev resigned as President on 24 December and the Soviet Union ceased to exist.

10 Dubrovka Theatre Siege, 2002
In a poorly managed attempt to rescue a theatre audience taken hostage by Chechen separatists, 39 terrorists and 129 hostages were killed.

4 Cathedral of the Assumption
The cathedral's stunning gilt frescoed interior *(above)* has osted coronation ceremonies since the 16th century.

5 State Armoury
With its array of gleaming weaponry and priceless treasures, including exquisite diamonds and Fabergé eggs, the Armoury offers a fascinating insight into the life of Russia's nobility.

6 Tretyakov Gallery
From its humble beginnings in the family home of the art enthusiast Pavel Tretyakov, this gallery *(above)* has evolved into one of the world's greatest collections of Russian art.

Bolshoi Theatre 7
Home to one of the oldest ballet companies in the world, the Bolshoi *(right)* is Europe's second-largest opera house, after Milan's La Scala. Large-scale renovations have successfully restored the theatre's original acoustics and grandeur.

Metro Stations 8
Moscow's palatial metro stations are artistic monuments in their own right. Some are filled with striking sculptures, while others feature stained-glass panels or, as in the evocation of the Great Patriotic War at Park Pobedy metro station *(right)*, mosaics.

9 Novodevichiy Convent
This UNESCO-listed convent *(left)* is a wonderfully preserved example of 17th-century Moscow Baroque architecture; it also boasts the city's most famous graveyard.

10 Kolomenskoe Estate
A favourite summer home of the tsars, Kolomenskoe enjoys an idyllic location beside the Moskva River and makes for a lovely day out.

TOP 10 Soviet Buildings

1 Ukraina Hotel (1950–56)
One of Stalin's Seven Sisters, this 206-m- (676-ft-) high, 1,600-room building is Europe's tallest hotel.

2 Ministry of Foreign Affairs (1948–53)
This astounding structure, one of the Seven Sisters, was supposedly modelled on Manhattan's skyscrapers.

3 Moscow State University (1949–53)
The main university building is the largest of Stalin's Seven Sisters. The design is perfectly symmetrical, with four wings converging on the central tower.

4 Lenin Library (1928–60)
The Neo-Classical finish of this stately building reflects a compromise between its Constructivist and Classicist architects, who fought over its design in the 1920s. The library holds a copy of every book published in Russia since 1922 and now has over 43 million volumes.

5 Lermontov Tower (1949–53)
Another of the Seven Sisters, this building has motifs inspired by historic Russian architecture. Its name honours the poet Lermontov, on whose birthplace the building stands.

6 Vosstaniya Apartment Building (1950–54)
Two of the Seven Sisters were designed as apartment blocks for the Soviet elite. The Vostaniya was reserved for scientists, cosmonauts and pilots.

7 Northern River Terminal (1932–7)
Topped by a bold red star, this elegant building was designed to resemble a 19th-century steamboat with fountains at either end.

8 Druzhba Arena (1979)
Nicknamed "The Spider" for its 28 concrete legs, the Druzhba Arena was built for the 1980 Olympics; it was then the world's largest concrete dome. The arena is now used for tennis.

9 Monument to the Conquerors of Space (1964)
This monument captures the dynamism of a rocket launch. Its dark granite base features reliefs of scientists, engineers and cosmonauts preparing for lift-off.

10 Begovaya Apartment Building (1965–78)
Multiple concrete legs and overlapping wall panels have earned this building the nickname "Centipede". It epitomizes the Soviet Brutalist architectural style.

Munich

Of the city he lived in for many years, 20th-century German writer Thomas Mann said "Munich glows". And indeed, the sky is often a brilliant blue dotted with puffy white clouds in "Italy's northernmost city", where the relaxed lifestyle gives it a southern flair. The Englischer Garten and the Isar meadows are green spaces in the heart of the city; Starnberger See and the mountains are virtually on the doorstep. But Munich is also a city of art and culture with an abundance of historic buildings, museum treasures and a lively cultural scene.

1 Deutsches Museum
Renowned as the oldest and largest museum of science and technology in the world, the museum *(above)* attracts more than 1.3 million visitors every year.

2 Museum District
Three Pinakotheken (picture galleries) now lie side by side in the Museum District. The oldest, the Alte Pinakothek in a reconstructed building from 1836, is devoted to historic European painting – its collection boasts priceless treasures including panels by Albrecht Dürer.

Schloss Nymphenburg 3
The grand Steinerner Saal (Stone Hall) *(right)* is decorated in resplendent Rococo style with lavish gilding, glittering chandeliers and fine ceiling frescoes of the gods at play.

TOP 10 Moments in History

1 1158: Foundation of the City
Welf Henry the Lion, Duke of Bavaria, built a new crossing over the Isar River. There, the small town of Munichen grew into the royal residence city of Munich.

2 1240–1918: The Wittelsbach Dynasty
From 1240 the Wittelsbach family was elevated from dukes to electors to kings, and even Holy Roman Emperors, before the dynasty fell from power after World War I.

3 1328: Ludwig the Emperor
In 1314 Duke Ludwig IV (known as the Bavarian) was elected king of Germany; in 1328 he was made Holy Roman Emperor.

4 1442: Expulsion of the Jews from Munich
Following pogroms against the Jews in the 13th and 14th centuries, Duke Albrecht III gave the order to expel all Jews from Upper Bavaria in 1442. Jewish culture did not return to Munich for 300 years.

5 1806: Capital of the Kingdom of Bavaria
In the wake of the Napoleon's redrafting of Europe, the Electorate of Bavaria was elevated to a kingdom, with Munich as the capital.

6 1848: March Revolution
Revolutionary uprisings led to the storming of the Zeughaus (the arsenal, currently the Stadtmuseum). Having lost the confidence of the court and the bourgeoisie, Ludwig I was forced to abdicate.

7 1918: November Revolution
On the night of 8 November 1918 the socialist Kurt Eisner proclaimed the Free State of Bavaria. After his assassination in February 1919 *Räterepubliken* (Soviet republics) grew in Munich and other Bavarian cities but were swiftly crushed by government troops.

8 1935–45: "Capital of the Movement"
Hitler's party, the NSDAP, grew out of a cell that began in Munich. The city was given the honorary title "Capital of the Movement" in 1935, after the Nazis seized power.

9 1962: Summer Riots
In the summer of 1962 violent clashes between youths and the Munich police forces lasted for several days.

10 1972: Olympic Games
Munich hosted the 20th Olympic Games in 1972. On 5 September a terror attack against the Israeli team, with the deaths of nine athletes, overshadowed the Games.

4 Olympia-park
In 1972 a large park, including an artificial hill, was created from World War II rubble for the Summer Olympics. At the time, the distinctive tent roof *(left)* was an architectural innovation.

Residenz 5
Dating back to 1385, the Residenz *(right)* has been expanded by various wings and courtyards over the centuries.

6 Beer Gardens
Locals are passionate about their eer garden tradition – bring your own ood and pay only for a cool pint.

Oktoberfest 7
Some six million visitors flock to Munich every year between late September and the first week of October to celebrate this folk festival – the world's biggest – first held to celebrate the wedding of Ludwig I (1810).

8 Around Marienplatz
Site of the Neues Rathaus (New Town Hall) *(above)*, Marienplatz is Munich's main square. The historic carved figures of the Glockenspiel in the town hall tower come alive in a coopers' dance three times a day.

9 Schloss Neu-schwanstein
Ludwig II's most famous castle *(left)* was inspired by his admiration for Wagner's operas.

10 Starnberger See
This lovely scenic lake on Munich's doorstep is surrounded by picturesque towns, royal summer palaces and the popular Buchheim Museum.

TOP 10 Markets and Fairs

1 Viktualienmarkt
This farmers' market has evolved into a gourmet shopping destination. From Monday to Saturday you will find the finest, fresh local produce as well as exotic and speciality foods. There's also a small beer garden.

2 Markt am Elisabethplatz
Located in Schwabing, this market has been here since 1903 and is the second-largest in Munich. Many of the stalls sell home-made specialities. The small market café is especially attractive.

3 Markt am Wiener Platz
Movies shot in Munich often use the market stalls on Wiener Platz in Haidhausen as a backdrop. Local workers drop by on their coffee breaks for a quick snack at one of the kiosks.

4 Großmarkthalle
Opened in 1912, Munich's indoor *Großmarkt* (wholesale market) has a vibrant atmosphere. Several excellent restaurants and pubs can be found in and around the market.

5 Auer Dulten
Church festivals, held here from the 14th century, evolved into annual fairs *(Dulten)*, and eventually into three nine-day fairs: Maidult, in late April; Jakobidult, starting on 25 July; and Herbstdult, in late October.

6 Antikmärkte
For antique furniture, head to Antikpalast. The flea and antique market in Daglfing has a large selection of glass, silver, porcelain, paintings, rustic furniture, and more. Treasures can also be found at the flea and antiques market in Munich-Freimann.

7 Second-Hand & Flea Markets
Perfect for rummaging and strolling are the giant flea market on the Theresienwiese in April and the largest open-air flea market in Bavaria, on the grounds of the Neue Messe.

8 Second-Hand Stores
Perhaps a sign of the times, second-hand has gone mainstream, and "vintage" stores are springing up overnight, examples being Städtisches Gebrauchtwarenhaus and Diakonia Gebraucht-Warenhaus.

9 Weihnachtsmärkte
Christmas markets run throughout December and are a long-standing and charming tradition here. The largest is on Marienplatz, while the ones located in Schwabing and Haidhausen offer the best atmosphere.

10 Magdalenenfest
Held in Hirschgarten, this huge funfair and market takes place around the feast of St Mary Magdalene in July, and is Munich's oldest fair, dating back to 1728.

Naples and the Amalfi Coast

From one perspective, this area is an anomaly, at once one of the earth's most beautiful and yet most accursed places. It has been the choice of the great and wealthy as their playground, while also being the scene of some of the greatest natural disasters and the grittiest human misery. Perhaps these irreconcilable twists of fate are at the root of the Neapolitans' famously optimistic cynicism. The city of Naples itself is a vibrant urban setting, almost non-European in its intensity, while the beauty of the surrounding coast has been known to make grown men weep.

1 Palazzo Reale
With its commanding position near the bay, the Royal Palace *(above)* dominates the grandest part of the city.

Castel Nuovo 2
Despite its bulky towers of volcanic stone, this Renaissance castle *(right)* also features one of the most graceful archway entrances of the period, delicately carved in the purest white marble.

3 Duomo
In effect, Naples' cathedral is at least three churches in one, including a treasure-laden Palaeo-Christian basilica from the 4th century. The side chapel dedicated to the city's adored patron saint, San Gennaro, is so large and resplendent that it is really a church in its own right *(above)*.

Top 10 Moments in History

1 Greek Colonization
From the 8th to 5th centuries BC Greek city-states set up trading posts in the region. In 470 BC Neapolis (New City) was founded, which became modern Naples.

2 Vesuvius Erupts
By the 1st century AD Naples – now in the Roman empire – was a renowned centre of learning. But in August AD 79 Mount Vesuvius – dormant for centuries – erupted. Within a few hours, the city was buried in boiling volcanic mud.

3 Byzantine Siege
After the fall of Rome in the 5th century, the area was overrun by northern tribes – particularly Goths. In 553 the Byzantine general Belisarius conquered the region.

4 Norman Conquest
In 1140 the Norman king Roger II made his triumphant entry into Naples. The Normans had already gained possession of Sicily and most of southern Italy, and Naples now had to take a back seat to Palermo.

5 Angevin Capital
In the mid-13th century, the French Anjou dynasty shifted its capital from Palermo to Naples. Many new buildings were constructed, including, in 1279, the Castel Nuovo.

6 Sicilian Vespers
With the removal of the capital to the mainland, Sicilian resentment came to a head on Easter Monday 1282. A riot, known as the Sicilian Vespers, left 2,000 Frenchmen dead and initiated a 20-year war.

7 Plague of 1656
In the early 17th century Naples was Europe's largest city, with a population of some 300,000, but an outbreak of plague in 1656 killed three-quarters of the population.

8 King Charles III Enters in Triumph
In 1734 the Spanish king arrived in Naples. He was heir to the Farnese clan, who were Italian by birth, and transformed his new home town into a city of the Enlightenment.

9 Naples Joins a Unified Italy
On 21 October 1860 Naples voted to join a united Italy, under the rule of King Vittorio Emanuele II.

10 Le Quattro Giornate Napoletane
Neapolitans showed their true character in September 1943 when the occupying Nazis threatened to deport the city's young males. Four days of popular rioting allowed the Allies to get a toehold and rout the enemy.

4 Museo Archeologico Nazionale

his fascinating museum *(above)* is the epository of ancient art that has been nearthed from Pompeii and other rchaeological digs around Vesuvius. These mazing finds evoke a Classical civilization f great refinement and grandeur.

5 Pompeii and Herculaneum

Taken together, two of the world's most famous archaeological sites *(above)* capture an entire culture frozen at the moment nearly 2,000 years ago when Vesuvius erupted.

6 Capodimonte

What started out as an unassuming hunting lodge soon grew to become a vast royal palace. It is now a museum housing one of Italy's finest collections of art.

7 Certosa di San Martino

If there is one museum that manages to capture the true Naples, this is it *(right)*. Come for the unparalleled views from the gardens, for the masterpieces of the Neapolitan Baroque and for the world's finest collection of nativity figures.

8 Capri

This small island *(above)* has had a fabled ıistory of glamour and decadence yet it still emains essentially a simple place.

9 Ravello

High above the gorgeous Amalfi Coast :his serenely elegant town *(above)* offers ınforgettable views, gorgeous gardens, aristocratic architecture and poetic inspiration.

10 Paestum

Some of the best-preserved Greek temples in the world *(above)* stand in timeless splendour on this evocative plain south of Naples.

TOP 10 Naples Sights

1 Santa Chiara
The façade of this church resembles a huge cliff of buff-coloured tufa. Inside, the decor has been returned to its Gothic origins; its Baroque ornament was destroyed in wartime bombings.

2 Sansevero Chapel
This family chapel designed by the 18th-century eccentric Prince Raimondo di Sangro contains some of Naples' most famous statuary, particularly the "veiled" figures of Christ and Modesty.

3 Piazza Bellini
This square is one of the most appealing places in Naples, lined with inviting cafés, bookshops and the façades of palaces.

4 Santi Apostoli
Rebuilt in the 17th century, with decoration added over the next 100 years, this church is a treasury of 17th- and 18th-century art by local artists and some of the greatest masters of the day.

5 Orto Botanico
This botanical garden of 1807 is still one of the most important in Italy, housing examples of nearly all of the world's plants and flowers.

6 Palazzo dello Spagnol
This palace of 1728 offers a fine example of a characteristically Neapolitan feature, the so-called staircase *"ad ali di falco"* (with falcon wings) – double flights of steps with tiered archways.

7 San Giovanni a Carbonara
Within this 14th-century church are a circular chapel with 15th-century frescoes and bas-reliefs by Spanish masters Bartolomé Ordoñez and Diego de Siloe.

8 Teatro San Carlo
Officially opened on 4 November 1737, this opera house, which predates the famous La Scala in Milan by some 40 years, is one of the most important in the world. There's also a museum charting its history.

9 Galleria Umberto I
Part of the Urban Renewal Plan following the cholera epidemic of 1884, this light-filled mall with elegant buildings overarched by a roof of iron and glass evokes an air of bygone charm.

10 Museo Nazionale della Ceramica Duca di Martina
This former villa is home to a prestigious collection of European and Oriental decorative art donated by the Duke of Martina. Highlights are Hispano-Moorish lustreware, Italian majolica tiles, Limoges porcelain and 18th-century Oriental porcelain.

Normandy

Normandy brings a dozen different images to mind: William the Conqueror, the D-Day landings, Mont-St-Michel; the bleak landscape of the Cotentin coast, the sparkling summertime playground of the Côte Fleurie; sumptuous châteaux, historic abbeys, famous gardens; the orchards of the Auge, the picture-postcard scenery of the Suisse Normande; Monet's home at Giverny, the Cabourg immortalized by Proust – or perhaps it's cider, calvados and camembert. Whatever your list, it will barely scratch the surface of this rich and rewarding region.

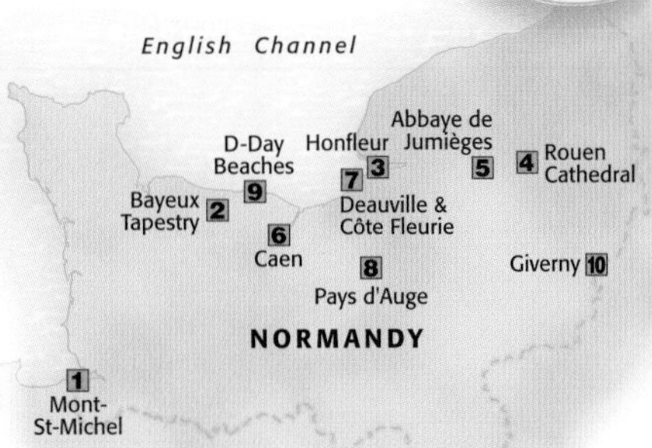

1 Mont-St-Michel
Now iconic in its fame, this solitary rock *(above)* dominated by its monumental abbey became a place of pilgrimage when St Aubert built an oratory here over 1,000 years ago.

2 Bayeux Tapestry
Unique historical document, astonishing work of art, the tapestry tells the story of the Norman Conquest of England in 1066.

Honfleur 3
A magnet for artists today as it has been since the 19th century, this picturesque maritime town *(right)* was also an important centre of trade.

TOP 10 Moments in History

1 58–51 BC: Roman Invasion
By 56 BC the Romans had swept through the region, conquering the Celtic-Gallic settlers. They built roads, amphitheatres, viaducts and fortified settlements, including Augustodurum (Bayeux), Rotomagus (Rouen), and Mediolanum (Evreux).

2 AD 911: Treaty of St-Clair-sur-Epte
By the early 10th century, the Carolingian king, Charles the Simple, realized that the Vikings, who had invaded in 800, would not go away quietly, so he ceded Rouen, making their leader Rollo the first duke of Normandy.

3 1066: Norman Conquest
When Edward the Confessor died without an heir, his cousin William saw his chance to claim the English throne. He sailed for England on 27 September 1066, triumphed at Hastings on 14 October, and was crowned King of England on Christmas Day.

4 1204: Union of Normandy and France
Since the accession of Henry II, King of England and Duke of Normandy, the French had tried to wrest control of the duchy from England. They succeeded in 1204, when King John lost Normandy to Philippe Auguste.

5 1315: Normandy Charter
Signed by Louis X, this charter gave the region provincial autonomy, a sovereign court of justice in Rouen, and control over taxes. In return, local taxes were increased dramatically – amounting to a quarter of the entire country's tax bill.

6 1450: French Recovery of Normandy
In the final phase of the Hundred Years' War, the decisive Battle of Formigny saw the French under the Comte de Clermont using guns and heavy cavalry to inflict a major defeat on English archers. This battle marked the end of fighting in Normandy and led to its recovery by France.

7 1789: Caen Revolt
During the French Revolution, there were royalist pockets throughout Normandy, but Caen became a centre for the republican Girondin movement (many of whose members were from the Gironde). Like the republicans who stormed the Bastille, their Norman counterparts demolished the château prison in Rouen.

8 1940: German Occupation
On 7 June 1940 the German army marched into Forges-les-Eaux and, two days later, into Rouen – the prelude to four years of occupation, during which local people were imprisoned, tortured, deported and executed.

9 1944: D-Day
In June 1944 Norman beaches became the target for Operation Overlord. By 20 August, the Allied forces were advancing towards Paris, which was liberated on 25 August.

10 2004: 60th Anniversary of D-Day
Every 10 years, surviving D-Day veterans gather to commemorate the dead; the 2004 gathering may have been one of the last.

Rouen Cathedral 4

It took nearly 400 years to build this splendid monument to the Gothic style *(right)*, from the beautifully harmonious nave to the ornately carved west front.

5 Abbaye de Jumièges

These magnificent, eerie ruins *(left)* – a subtle blend of Romanesque and Gothic architecture – are the remains of the Benedictine abbey founded by St Philibert in the 7th century.

6 Caen

Old and new cohabit in this lively, cultured regional capital, still dominated by William the Conqueror's Château Ducal and his two great abbeys – the Abbaye aux Dames and the Abbaye aux Hommes *(above)*.

7 Deauville and La Côte Fleurie

The string of resorts on this lovely stretch of Normandy's oastline *(above)* creates a summer paradise. Racy and omantic, Deauville is a magnet for glamorous visitors.

8 Pays d'Auge

This is quintessential Normandy, amous for its cider, its cheese, its ently rolling landscape, its orchards nd its half-timbered manor houses.

9 D-Day Beaches

The Allied landings of June 1944 nd the Battle of Normandy that followed re movingly commemorated in nuseums, memorials and cemeteries hroughout the area *(above)*.

10 Giverny

The house where Monet lived and worked for more than 40 years, and the stunning garden he created using flowers as his palette, are a tribute to the great painter *(above)*.

Top 10 Unspoilt Villages

1 Barfleur
Brightly painted fishing boats jostle in the harbour of this charming port, with beaches for shell gathering and a lighthouse you can climb.

2 St-Fraimbaul
Each spring, 100,000 flowers swamp this *village fleuri* in colour as villagers try to outdo each other's displays. It all culminates in a mid-August festival.

3 St-Céneri-le-Gérei
Crowned by a fine Romanesque church, this ravishing village overlooks the gentle River Sarthe as it flows around a rocky promontory on the edge of the Alpes Mancelles.

4 Beuvron-en-Auge
All the charms of the Pays d'Auge are summed up in Beuvron. Its flower-decked houses are prettily striped and patterned with timber, and there's a delightful 15th-century manor house.

5 Putot-en-Auge
This sleepy village has little more than a church (with a fine Romanesque portal, and a cemetery for Allied soldiers), manor house and little brick-built *mairie* (town hall), but it somehow encapsulates the rural delights of the Auge region.

6 Lyons-la-Forêt
A captivating medley of 16th- to 18th-century half-timbered buildings, Lyons-la-Forêt stands in a sylvan setting deep in the lovely Forêt de Lyons.

7 Montville
This *village fleuri* has an attractive lake, a park with a superb 300-year-old purple beech, and the Musée des Sapeurs-Pompiers, full of old hand pumps and gleaming red fire engines.

8 Allouville-Bellefosse
An extraordinary oak tree, thought to be at least 1,300 years old, has put this little village on the map. Inside its trunk are a sanctuary and a hermit's cell fashioned by a local priest in 1696.

9 Le Bec-Hellouin
This quintessential Norman village set among fields and apple orchards is named after the stream that runs beside it and the Norman knight Herluin, founder of the impressive 11th-century Benedictine abbey.

10 St-Valéry-en-Caux
This fishing village and seaside resort in a charming spot on the Côte d'Albâtre is where tranquil Pays de Caux countryside meets beach, boats and bikinis.

Paris

From Notre-Dame to the Eiffel Tower, France's capital holds some of the world's most famous sights and these ten attractions should be top of the list for any first-time visitor. With the exception of the overtly modern Pompidou Centre, they have been landmarks of this elegant and romantic city for centuries and remain awe-inspiring sights, no matter how often you visit.

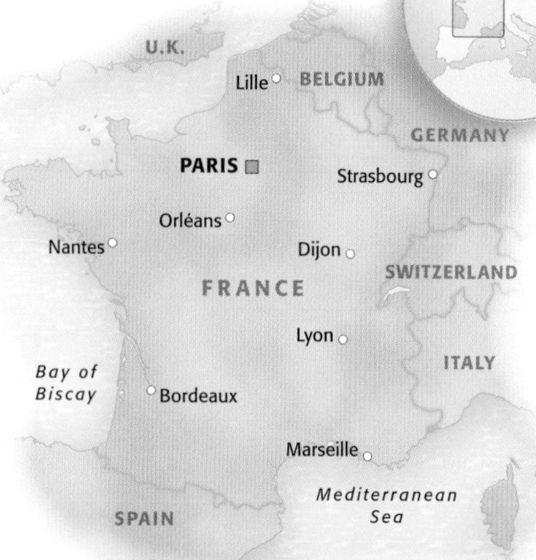

1 Musée du Louvre

The world's largest museum *(left)* also contains one of the world's finest collections of art and antiquities (up to 1848). To complete the superlatives, the building was once France's largest royal palace.

2 Panthéon

The great and the good of France are buried in the Panthéon, including Voltaire, Emil Zola, Victor Hugo, and Marie and Pierre Curie.

3 Hôtel des Invalides

The shining golden dome of the Hôtel des Invalides church *(right)* is unmistakable across the rooftops of Paris.

4 Centre Georges Pompidou

Home to France's National Museum of Moder Art, the building itself *(above)* is a work of contemporary art. There are also extensive research facilitie

TOP 10 Moments in History

1 Arrival of the Parisii
Despite Neolithic remains dating back to 4500 BC, the first settlers were a Celtic tribe called the Parisii, who lived on the Ile de la Cité in the 3rd century BC. They named their village Lutetia, or "boatyard on a river".

2 Roman Settlement
The Romans defeated the Parisii in 52 BC, founding their own city on the Left Bank. In AD 360 Lutetia was renamed Paris, after its original inhabitants.

3 Founding of France
In 476 the Franks captured Paris, and made it the capital of their new kingdom, France.

4 Charlemagne
Charlemagne was crowned Holy Roman Emperor in 800 and moved his capital to Aix-La-Chapelle (Aachen). Hugues Capet became king in 987, and Paris was capital once more.

5 St Bartholomew's Day
Marguerite, daughter of Catherine de' Medici, married Protestant Henri of Navarre in 1572. Many Protestants came to Paris for the wedding and religious tensions erupted into massacre. The killings began on 23 August and thousands died. Henri survived and later became Henri IV, the first Bourbon king.

6 French Revolution
Following decades of royal excess and the growing gulf between rich and poor, Paris erupted with the storming of the Bastille prison in 1789. Louis XVI and Marie-Antoinette were guillotined in 1793.

7 Napoleon Bonaparte
In 1795 a young Corsican general, Napoleon Bonaparte, saved the city from a royalist revolt. After military victories in Italy and Egypt, he crowned himself Emperor of France in Notre-Dame in 1804.

8 The Second Empire
In 1851 Napoleon's nephew siezed power as Emperor Napoleon III. He appointed Baron Haussmann to oversee massive building works that transformed Paris into the most glorious city in Europe.

9 The Paris Commune
After France's defeat in the Franco-Prussian War in 1871, many Parisians revolted at the harsh surrender terms, forming the Paris Commune. Government troops attacked, much of the city burned and thousands were killed.

10 Liberation of Paris
Allied forces liberated Paris from Nazi occupation on 25 August 1944; two days earlier, German commander Von Choltitz had disobeyed Hitler's order to burn the city.

5 Arc de Triomphe
Napoleon's triumphal arch *(left)*,celebrating battle victories, stands proudly at the top of the Champs-Elysées and, along with the Eiffel Tower, is one of the city's most enduring icons.

6 Sainte-Chapelle
Called "a gateway to heaven", this splendid medieval church was built to house the relics collected by King Louis IX on his many Crusades. Its stained-glass windows are breathtaking.

7 Eiffel Tower
Some six million visitors a year ascend to the top of this most famous Paris landmark *(above)* for the spectacular views. It was erected for the Universal Exhibition of 1889.

8 Sacré-Coeur
The terrace in front of this monumental white-domed basilica *(above)*, perched magnificently at the top of Montmartre, affords one of the finest free views over Paris.

9 Musée d'Orsay
This former railway station is one of the world's leading art galleries *(left)* and, for many, reason alone to visit Paris.

10 Notre-Dame
This great Gothic cathedral *(above)*, built on the site of a Gallo-Roman temple, is a veritable repository of French art and history. It is also the geographical "heart" of France.

TOP 10 Novels Set in Paris

1 Les Misérables
This 1862 novel by Victor Hugo (1802–85) paints a vivid picture of poverty in early 19th-century Paris. The character of Marius is based on Hugo's own experiences.

2 The Hunchback of Notre-Dame
Better known by its English title, Victor Hugo's Gothic novel was published in 1831 as *Notre-Dame de Paris.*

3 A Tale of Two Cities
Charles Dickens (1812–70) set his 1859 tale of mistaken identity in London and Paris, against the background of the French Revolution.

4 Le Père Goriot
Honoré de Balzac (1799–1850) chronicled Paris life in his 80-volume *La comédie humaine.* This 1853 novel is certainly among the finest.

5 A Sentimental Education
This work of 1870, *L'Education sentimentale* in French, by Gustave Flaubert (1821–80), stands alongside his greatest novel, *Madame Bovary* (1857).

6 Bel-Ami
Guy de Maupassant (1850–93) published this, one of his best novels, in 1885, mocking the get-rich-quick Parisian business world of the *belle époque* (Beautiful Age).

7 A la Recherche du Temps Perdu
The master work of Marcel Proust (1871–1922) was written in 13 volumes, the first appearing in 1913. His epic tale is the fictionalized story of his own life.

8 Nana
Emile Zola (1840–1902), perhaps the greatest Parisian chronicler of all, was born, lived and died in the city. *Nana*, published in 1880, tells a shocking tale through the eyes of a courtesan.

9 L'Assommoir
Published in 1877, Zola's *L'Assommoir* (The Drunkard) shows a side of Paris that many at the time would have preferred to ignore – the alcoholism of the working classes.

10 Thérèse Raquin
Zola focuses on the secret passions that lurk behind a single Paris shopfront, in a tale of obsessive lust that leads to a brutal murder. Published in 1867, and only his second novel, it shows his astonishing maturity and unflinching gaze.

BEBOB

Netherlands
Bridges over the Prinsengracht canal, Amsterdam

Prague

At the geographical heart of Europe, Prague's beautiful cityscape has been carved and sustained by a variety of emperors, artists and religious communities, from the Gothic exuberance of its cathedral and castle, to the dignity of the medieval Jewish Cemetery, and the 19th-century opulence of the "new" town. Under Communist rule, Prague was off the tourist map, but since 1989 it has seen a surge of visitors eager to take in this spectacular city.

1 Charles Bridge

Linking the city across the the Vltava river *(left)*, it can be difficult to appreciate the beautiful carved statues of former citizens, due to the incessant crowds and trinket stalls. But it's worth the effort.

2 Petřín Hill

Perched above the Lower Town, the forested Petřín Hill *(right)* is criss-crossed with footpaths, giving visitors some of the finest views in the city. The old Ukrainian church is wonderfully romantic.

3 St Vitus's Cathedral

The glory of the castle complex, St Vitus's took more than 600 years to build. Visit the beautiful chapels adjoining the cathedral, or its crypt to see the tombs of Bohemia's Holy Roman Emperors.

4 Old Town Square

Prague's central square has been a market since the Middle Ages, and was witness to the rise and fall of numerous regimes and no shortage of bloodshed. The city has few charms finer than watching the moon rise between the towers of the Church of Our Lady Before Týn *(above)*.

TOP 10 Moments in History

1 Wenceslas Assassinated
The "Good King" solidified Bohemia's ties with Rome and with German merchants. Murdered by his brother in 935, he was later canonized.

2 Charles IV Becomes Holy Roman Emperor
Charles acceded to both the Roman and Bohemian thrones in 1333. Prague became the seat of imperial power under his reign, as well as an archbishopric and home to central Europe's first university.

3 Hussite Wars
After the Church Council at Constance burned Catholic reformer Jan Hus at the stake in 1415, his followers rose up against both church and crown. Fierce animosity between Protestant Czechs and German Catholics would rage for centuries.

4 Reign of Rudolph II
This melancholy emperor was a benefactor of the arts and sciences, and supported Johannes Kepler's studies of planetary motion.

5 Battle of White Mountain
In 1620, in the first battle of the Thirty Years' War, Imperial forces devastated the Czechs. Czech lands were forcibly re-Catholicized as a result.

6 Independence
During World War I, National Revival leaders such as Tomáš Masaryk turned to the United States for support for an independent Czechoslovakia. As the war drew to a close in 1918, the new republic of Czechoslovakia was born.

7 World War II
Under the Munich Agreement of 1938 the First Republic was forced to cede Czech lands to Nazi Germany. Nearly 80,000 Czechs died in the Holocaust. After the war, the nation exacted revenge by expelling its German citizens.

8 Rise of Communism
Grateful to the Red Army for liberating Prague in 1945, Czechoslovakia gave Soviet Communism the benefit of the doubt in the February 1948 elections.

9 Prague Spring
In 1968 First Secretary Alexandr Dubček introduced economic and social reforms that did not please Moscow. Warsaw-Pact tanks rolled through Prague streets killing more than 100 protestors.

10 Velvet Revolution
After 10 days of mass protests in 1989, the Communist government bowed to the population's indignation. Czechs proudly recall that not a window was broken during the revolt.

The Loreto 5

Pilgrims have visited this Baroque shrine to the Virgin Mary *(right)* since the 17th century. Visitors can see priceless ornaments in its treasury.

6 National Gallery

One of the first Functionalist buildings in Europe (1928), the Trade Fair Palace now houses the National Gallery's collection of modern and contemporary art, including 14 Picassos.

7 Old Jewish Cemetery

The jumble of tombstones in this tiny graveyard *(above)* give some indication of the number of bodies buried here. Prague's Jewish community, once one of the largest in Europe, lived and worshipped in the surrounding ghetto.

8 Prague Castle

The hilltop fortress of the Přemyslids *(above)* is home to the head of the Czech Republic. Spend a day exploring the castle's many impressive palaces, churches, galleries and gardens.

9 Wenceslas Square

From its origins as a humble horse market, Wenceslas Square has grown into a modern business centre. Monuments on the square *(left)* remind visitors of its role in the nation's tumultuous history.

10 St Agnes's Convent

Founded in 1231, Prague's oldest Gothic building is home to the National Gallery's collection of medieval art *(above)* and remains a monument to its founder, a Přemyslid princess who gave up a life at court to pursue her faith.

TOP 10 House Signs

1 The White Swan (Nerudova 49)
Originally, many of the house signs seen all over Prague had alchemical significance, but much of their meaning has been lost. The White Swan is one such; probably it began as a golden goose.

2 The Two Suns (Nerudova 47)
This house was the birthplace of the much-loved poet and author Jan Neruda (1834–91), after whom this street in the writers' and artists' quarter is named.

3 The Golden Key (Nerudova 27)
Goldsmiths, such as the ones who worked here in the 17th century, paid fees to the city entitling them to advertise their wares, as seen on this building's façade.

4 The Red Lamb (Nerudova 11)
The scarlet sheep on this façade has an alchemical significance so arcane that not even the current owner of the house can explain it.

5 St Wenceslas's Horse (Staroměstské náměsté)
Clearly seen in Old Town Square, on the façade of Štorch House, this is a tribute both to the patron saint of Bohemia and the blacksmiths who shod horses bound for the castle.

6 The Three Lillies (Nerudova 15)
Although their image no longer adorns the façade, the three flowers remain atop the house.

7 The Golden Wheel (Nerudova 28)
Another alchemical symbol, the wheel represents a stage in the *magnum opus*, the process by which lead was purportedly turned into gold.

8 The Three Fiddles (Nerudova 12)
It's said that a demonic trio screeches on their violins here on moonlit nights.

9 The Devil
Lucifer pops up as a cuddly character on houses all over town, more a folksy trickster than a prince of darkness.

10 The Green Lobster (Nerudova 43)
Who can imagine what they were thinking when they hung the crustacean above their door. Perhaps they were just trying to keep up with the neighbours at the Pendant Parsnip (No. 39).

Provence & the Côte d'Azur

The top sights of Provence span the region's rich and varied history, from Roman arenas, isolated abbeys and the palace of the medieval popes, to the more recent opulence of the *belle époque* era and the glamorous resorts beloved of the jet set. Sunsoaked beaches, pretty villages nestled among lavender fields and a mountainous hinterland have inspired generations of artists, and continue to enchant every visitor to the south of France.

3 Vaison-la-Romaine
Palais des Papes 7
9 Notre-Dame de Sénanque
Grand Canyon du Verdon 10
Casino Monte C
4 Arles
PROVENCE
Vieux Nice 2 6
5 The Camargue
1 Aix-en-Provence
Marseille
8 St-Tropez
Mediterranean Sea

1 Aix-en-Provence

Cosmopolitan Aix *(left)* is packed with fascinating museums and historic buildings. Nearby Mont Ste-Victoire inspired one of the greatest Provençal painters, Paul Cézanne.

2 Vieux Nice

Nice *(above)* is lively and sophisticated; its Old Town retains a quiet authenticity.

3 Vaison-la-Romaine

A treasury of archaeological finds *(left)* has been unearthed in this small town, once one of Provence's most important Roman sites.

TOP 10 Moments in History

1 Early Settlers

Carvings and tools discovered in the Grotte d'Observatoire in Monaco, and cave paintings found in the Grotte Cosquer near Marseille, date from as far back as 1 million BC. Between 2500 and 2000 BC, dwellers in the Vallée des Merveilles left behind carvings of beasts and human figures that justify the term "marvels".

2 Foundation of Aix

In 123 BC the Phoenician Greeks, settled in Marseille since 600 BC, asked for Roman help against the invading Celtic tribes inland. After defeating the Celts, the Romans founded Aquae Sextia (Aix) in the area.

3 Advent of Christianity

In AD 40 St Honorat brought Christianity to Provence, founding the first monastery on Ile de Lérins. Camarguais legend, however, claims Christianity was brought here by Mary Magdalene herself.

4 Franks and Saracens

With the fall of the Roman Empire in AD 476, Provence was pillaged by barbarians, eventually coming under the rule of the Franks. From the 8th century the coasts were harried by Moorish pirates who gave their name to the Massif des Maures. They were finally defeated in 974 by Guillaume le Libérateur, Count of Arles.

5 Dawn of a Dynasty

In 1297 François Grimaldi, a supporter of the papacy in the Guelph-Ghibelline feuds which beset 13th-century Italy, seized Monaco and its castle to found the dynasty which still rules there today.

6 The Avignon Papacy

Pope Clement V relocated to Avignon in 1309 to escape strife-torn Rome, the first of a succession of nine French pontiffs who were to reside in the Provençal town. Their magnificent Papal Palace was begun in 1335, taking 20 years to complete. In 1348 Clement VI bought the city and Avignon remained the seat of the papacy until 1377.

7 Union with France

In 1486 King René of Naples, the last of the Anjou dynasty who ruled Provence from 1246, died without leaving an heir, and most of the region became part of France. Nice and the Alpes Maritimes, however, remained a part of the Kingdom of Savoy, before finally passing to France in 1860.

8 Plague and War

In the second half of the 16th century, religious strife erupted in the Luberon between reforming Vaudois (Huguenot) factions and conservative Catholic forces. The plague of 1580 added to the region's woes.

9 The Marseillaise

When the French Revolution erupted in 1789, the people of Marseille were among its staunchest supporters, marching to a stirring tune that became known as *La Marseillaise*, now France's national anthem.

10 Resistance and Liberation

After the Nazi invasion of 1940, Provence was ruled by the collaborationist Vichy government, until it was occupied by Germany in 1942. Guerrilla fighters in the *maquis* (scrubland) resisted. On 15 August 1944, Allied troops landed, liberating the region within two weeks.

4 Roman Arles
Arles was one of the Roman Empire's
ost important cities, and its splendid arena
ill evokes the age of the Caesars.

5 The Camargue
Vast lagoons inhabited
 wading flamingoes and
ains dotted with black bulls
d white horses are just part
 the protected landscape of
e Camargue.

6 Casino de Monte Carlo
Walk in the footsteps of princes, courtesans and film stars at the Riviera's most dazzling example of 19th-century grandeur.

7 Palais des Papes
The honey-coloured walls and towers of this medieval palace *(above)*, the seat of 14th-century pontiffs, dominate the delightful town of Avignon.

8 St-Tropez
Pretty and chic St-Tropez *(above)*, with its yacht-filled
arbour and gorgeous beaches, is the place to see and be
een on the Provençal coast.

9 Notre-Dame de Sénanque
The great Cistercian abbey is a wonderful example of Romanesque religious architecture, set in a sea of lavender fields.

10 Grand Canyon du Verdon
The Verdon river flows through deep limestone gorges into the turquoise waters of the Lac de Ste-Croix *(left)*, creating one of Provence's most stunning natural landscapes

TOP 10 Marseille Sights

1 Vieux Port
The old port remains the heart of city life. Bobbing with pleasure boats and fringed with *bouillabaisse* restaurants, it's where the locals gather for festivities.

2 Notre-Dame-de-la-Garde
This Romanesque-Byzantine church is the symbol of Marseille. Perched on the city's highest hill and topped by a great, gold statue of the Virgin, it can be seen from everywhere in the city.

3 Le Panier
This ancient district is where the city's immigrants began their new lives, and the tiny streets are alive with different accents and cultures. The main feature is La Vieille Charité, the 17th-century workhouse now a wonderful cultural and museum centre.

4 Palais Longchamp
Longchamp is the greatest expression of Marseille's 19th-century "golden age". Its two ornate wings are home to the Fine Arts and Natural History museums.

5 Musée Grobet-Labadié
In the former home of a 19th-century rich, art-loving family, rooms are hung with Gobelin and Aubusson tapestries and are filled with sculpture, paintings and furniture from the 13th to 19th centuries.

6 Les Calanques
Within 15 minutes' drive of the city centre, white rocks plunge into the blue sea and the road snakes into inlets *(calanques)* of great beauty.

7 Prado Beaches
Around the corniche from the Vieux Port lie Marseille's resolutely modern beaches. At night, the Escale Borély beach area offers some of the town's hottest nightspots.

8 Fort St-Nicholas
On the south side of the Vieux Port is this fort, built in 1680 by Louis XIV to impose authority on the truculent city – its cannons pointed inland. Star-shaped and built in pink-tinged limestone, it stares across at the much older Fort St-Jean.

9 Château d'If
This offshore island fortress was built in the 16th century to protect the city's port, and became a prison in 1634. Among its inmates were the real Comte de Mirabeau, and the fictional Count of Monte Cristo, the antihero of Dumas' novel of the same name.

10 Musée de la Faïence
The lovely Second Empire Château Pastre contains a fabulous assembly of 1,500 items of pottery, ceramics and earthenware from across Europe and dating from the Neolithic period to the present day.

Rome

Although functioning as a vibrant, modern capital akin to any in Europe, the unique appeal of Rome is that the entire city is a vast, 3,000-year-old, indoor-outdoor museum. In every quarter you'll find ancient monuments, art treasures and timeless architecture in churches, galleries and protected ruins. Home to the world's smallest country, the Vatican, Rome has religion at its heart and history in its soul – a city that dazzles and inspires visitors time and time again.

1 Vatican City This tiny city-state is home to the Pope, the world's greatest museum, largest church and the most astounding work of art ever created – Michelangelo's Sistine Chapel ceiling *(left)*.

St Peter's Basilica 2 The principal church of the Vatican is packed with artworks, including pieces by Bernini and Michelangelo, while the dome *(right)* affords panoramic city views.

3 The Pantheon The most perfectly preserved of all ancient temples, this marvel of architectural engineering fron around AD 126 has, at the centre of its dome, a gian oculus forever open to the sky *(above)*.

TOP 10 Moments in History

1 Romulus and Remus
Twins Romulus and Remus are said to have founded rival villages on the Palatine in 753 BC. When Romulus killed Remus during an argument, it was his "Rome" that went on to greatness.

2 Rape of the Sabine Women
To boost the female population, Romulus's men kidnapped women from the Sabine kingdom. As Rome began to expand, however, the kingdoms were united.

3 Assassination of Caesar
A series of military victories, adding Gaul (France) to Rome, increased General Julius Caesar's popularity. He declared himself Dictator for Life, then on 15 March 44 BC was assassinated.

4 Rome Burns
In AD 64 fire destroyed much of Rome. Emperor Nero then appropriated land to build his Golden House. Hounded from office, he committed suicide in AD 68.

5 Battle at Milvian Bridge
In 312 Emperor Constantine had a vision of victory under the sign of the Cross and defeated co-emperor Maxentius at Milvian Bridge. He then declared Christianity the state religion.

6 Fall of the Empire
By the late 4th century Rome was in decline, as Barbarians from across the Rhine and Danube conquered outlying provinces. In 476 the Empire fell.

7 Papacy moves to Avignon
Following the departure of the papacy to France in 1309, the city became a backwater. When the papacy returned in 1377, the city was reborn.

8 Sack of Rome
Rome was conquered for the first time in more than a millennium in 1527. Emperor Charles V's Germanic troops held the city until Pope Clement VII promised to address concerns of the new Protestant movement.

9 Unification of Italy
Piemontese King Vittorio Emanuele II and his general, Garibaldi, conquered many separate kingdoms to create Italy. The process was completed in 1870, when Garibaldi took Rome.

10 Mussolini Takes Power
Benito "Il Duce" Mussolini, leader of the Fascist Party, marched on Rome in 1922 and was declared prime minister. When the tides turned against Fascism in WWII, he was deposed.

4 Roman Forum

At the once-bustling heart of ancient political, judicial and commercial power there's now an evocative emptiness, punctuated by grandiose arches, sporadic columns and carved rubble *(left)*.

5 Galleria Borghese

A stunningly beautiful pleasure-palace *(above)*, this was the vision of an immensely rich, hedonistic papal nephew, who filled it with Graeco-Roman, Renaissance and Baroque works by the greatest masters.

6 Colosseum

Imperial Rome constructed many npressive monuments, including this pectacular amphitheatre *(above)*.

7 Musei Capitolini

At the ancient entre of religious Rome re found some of the vorld's greatest nasterpieces, from th-century BC Greek culptures to Caravaggio's evolutionary – even candalous – paintings.

8 Museo Nazionale Romano

These collections, housed at two sites, feature some of the world's finest ancient art, including Classical sculpture *(right)* and stunning mosaics.

9 Santa Maria del Popolo

Built over emperors' tombs, this church offers one of Rome's richest displays of Renaissance and Baroque art *(left)*, including masterpieces by Pinturicchio, Raphael, Caravaggio and Bernini.

10 San Clemente

With its mysterious passages and legends, this fascinating church provides first-hand experience of the layers that comprise Rome; here you can descend to a depth of 18 m (60 ft) and go back over 2,000 years.

TOP 10 Palatine Hill Features

1 Domus Flavia
Marked today mainly by the remains of two fountains, this imposing edifice was the official wing of a vast emperors' palace, built by Domitian in AD 81.

2 Livia's House
Now below ground level, this 1st-century BC structure formed part of the residence of Augustus. Here you can see a number of frescoes and mosaic pavements.

3 Palatine Museum and Antiquarium
This former convent houses a wealth of artifacts unearthed here, including pottery, statuary, ancient graffiti and fine mosaics. You can also study a model of the Iron Age Palatine.

4 Romulus's Iron-Age Huts
Traces of these three 9th-century BC huts were uncovered in the 1940s. Legend says that this tiny village was founded by Romulus, son of Mars, who gave Rome its name.

5 Stadium
Possibly a racetrack, or just a large garden, this sunken rectangle formed part of Domitian's palatial 1st-century abode.

6 Domus Augustana
All that remains of the private wing of Domitian's imperial extravaganza are the massive vaults.

7 Temple of Cybele
The orgiastic Cult of the Great Mother was the first of the Oriental religions to come to Rome, in 191 BC. Still here is a decapitated statue of the goddess. Priests worshipping Cybele ritually castrated themselves at this temple.

8 Farnese Gardens
Plants and elegant pavilions grace part of what was once an extensive pleasure-garden, designed by Vignola and built in the 16th century over the ruins of Emperor Tiberius's palace.

9 Cryptoporticus
This series of underground corridors, their vaults decorated with delicate stucco reliefs, stretches 130 m (425 ft). It connected the Palatine to Nero's fabulous Golden House.

10 Domus Septimius Severus
Huge arches and broken walls are all that remain of this emperor's 2nd-century AD extension to Domitian's Domus Augustana.

Festivals and Parties

When it comes to festivals and parties, Europe has plenty to celebrate, with centuries of art, music and theatre; millennia of history, culture and tradition; a bountiful harvest of food and drink; and (in summer, at least) long, warm days and balmy evenings in which to make merry. From big city events to simple local festivities, you're never far away from the fun.

1 Mimosa Festival, Herceg Novi *MONTENEGRO*

The gentle fragrance of mimosa blossom wafts over Herceg Novi's sunny streets during this annual festival every February. Floral floats fill the promenade and local horticulturists strive to outdo one another with imaginative displays. There is local theatre, music and dance, and the chance to go mimosa-picking along the lush banks of the riviera.

2 Carnival, Binche *BELGIUM*

Dressed in the Belgian national colours of red, yellow and black, the character of Gilles de Binche dominates this carnival. Wearing masks with spectacles and moustaches, and hats bursting with ostrich feathers, festival-goers known as "Gilles" stomp away the winter gloom in wooden clogs at the town's Grand Place, and toss Seville oranges into an excitable crowd. This three-day festival, which takes place at the end of February, dates back to the 16th century. Today it attracts thousands of revellers who, come nightfall, dance in the streets beneath a firework-filled sky to the sound of local brass bands.

3 Easter, Kalymnos *GREECE*

Easter celebrations here are varied and elaborate, starting on Holy Friday with a candlelit procession that follows flower-decked "epitaphs", symbolizing Christ's tomb, to the cathedral for a celebratory Mass. On Saturday a feast of lamb stuffed with rice and liver is prepared and, at midnight, the church bells ring out and dynamite is lit on the mountains behind the port, the explosions booming out into the night.

4 White Nights Festival, St Petersburg *RUSSIA*

A three-month international cultural event, the White Nights Festival is a series of classical ballet, opera and music performances staged during a season when the sun hardly sets – hence the "White Nights" name. The festival draws high-profile Russian performers and international guest stars, and you can expect renowned conductors and soloists at The Stars of the White Nights Festival, the event's opening celebration, held at the famous Mariinskiy Theatre and new Mariinskiy Concert Hall. Watch out for other star appearances at Palace Square, where Paul McCartney and the Rolling Stones have done turns, and the spectacular fireworks at the popular closing Scarlet Sails party.

5 Las Hogueras de San Juan *SPAIN*

The fabulous fiery festival of Las Hogueras (Fogueres in Valenciano), the biggest on the Alicante calendar, culminates on midsummer day, 24 June, the feast day of St John the Baptist. It begins with a bang – literally – on 20 June, with "La Mascletà", an ear-splitting barrage of firecrackers. Each neighbourhood vies to create the best *hoguera*, an enormous figure of wax or papier mâché. At midnight on the 24th, after a spectacular fireworks display from the top of San Juan's castle, all the *hogueras* are set on fire – even the winning entry. The festival also encompasses folk parades, bullfights, medieval markets and firecracker competitions throughout the week.

Avignon Festival Lively street performers *(above)*

Latitude festival, Southwold Festival-goers at this alternative event *(below)*

Asti Palio Jockeys ride their horses in the Piazza Alfieri *(above)*

ival, Binche Parade of the Gilles de Binche with their wax masks *(below)*

6 Avignon Festival *FRANCE*

Founded in 1947 by theatre director Jean Vilar, the Festival d'Avignon is an enormous celebration of the arts. With its handsome medieval architecture and massive ramparts, the pretty town of Avignon provides an ideal setting for the event, which represents all aspects of culture, from theatre and ballet to the latest in dance, music, cinema and opera. Many venues are involved around the town; best of all is the floodlit inner courtyard of the Palais des Papes, one of the most important Gothic buildings in Europe, which plays host to many productions during the three-week period in July.

7 Latitude, Southwold *ENGLAND*

Once described as "the festival for people who don't like festivals", Latitude, held in July, is environmentally conscious and attracts a rather well-heeled crowd. It features literature and comedy as well as music, and the small, scenic site makes it pleasant simply to wander and lap up the laid-back atmosphere.

8 Mozart Festival, Salzburg *AUSTRIA*

Over 4,000 cultural events take place in Mozart's home city of Salzburg throughout the year, but the most coveted tickets are for the five-week Summer Festival, when packed concert halls, palaces and churches resound to thrilling performances by some of the world's greatest musicians. Crowned and uncrowned heads of Europe descend on this most elegant and sophisticated of festivals; ball gowns are, of course, *de rigueur* for premieres.

9 Asti Palio *ITALY*

Siena's *palio*, staged each July and August, is perhaps the most celebrated festival in Italy – but why not wait until September, out of high season, and enjoy the *palio* in Asti? Each of the 21 neighbourhoods and villages in and around Asti enters a horse and jockey dressed in its own colours, and all 21 of them run in four races during a single day, thundering round the tight corners of the track again and again. And as night falls, the fun really hots up. Join in the exuberant street parties or enjoy the celebrations in one of the town's local trattorias.

10 Galway Oyster Festival *IRELAND*

The main attraction at this long-running four-day festival, which hits the charming city of Galway at the end of September, is, naturally enough, the oysters, which are carefully selected from beds within Galway Bay, where the native oyster still grows wild. A particular highlight of the festivities is the Guinness World Oyster Opening Championships, after which the oysters are served in the festival marquee, washed down with plenty of Guinness (the national drink of Ireland).

St Petersburg

From the pre-revolutionary grandeur of the Hermitage and the Mariinskiy Theatre to the ubiquitous reminders of the country's Soviet period, St Petersburg is a city where eras, and architectural styles, collide. Blessed with some of the world's most magnificent skylines, the city has been the inspiration for many of Russia's greatest writers, from Gogol to Dostoevsky. Known throughout the country as "The Venice of the North", Russia's second city is a place of wonder and enigma, of "White Nights" and long, freezing winters.

RUSSIA
FINLAND
Yekaterinburg
ST PETERSBURG
Nizhny Novgorod
Samara
Moscow
BELARUS
KAZAKHSTAN
Volgograd
UKRAINE
Rostov-on-Don

1 St Isaac's Cathedral
The largest church in Russia *(left)*, the construction of the cathedral took 40 years to complete. Its interiors, such as the detailed ceiling paintings, survived shelling during World War II.

2 Mariinskiy Theatre
Russia is famed for its ballet and opera, and the splendid auditorium of this theatre is the perfect setting in which to see a performance.

3 Russian Museum
Housed in the fine Neo-Classical Mikhailovsky Palace *(right)*, the museum features a wide range of Russian art.

4 The Hermitage
This opulent former residence of the tsars *(above)* contains one of the world's largest art collections, boasting masterpieces by Leonardo da Vinci and Michelangelo.

TOP 10 Moments in History

1 Founding of the City
St Petersburg was founded by Peter the Great in 1703 as Russia's "Window to Europe". Constructed on swampland, it was built by thousands of serfs, many of whom died, their bones laying the city's foundations. It became the capital of Russia in 1712, and remained so until 1918.

2 "Bloody Sunday"
On 9 January 1905, peaceful demonstrators carrying a petition to Nicholas II were gunned down by the army as they marched towards the Winter Palace. Around 1,000 perished. This horrifying event led to the 1905 Revolution.

3 1917 Revolution
Following a series of strikes in 1917, the tsar was forced to abdicate, and a provisional government assumed power. This was the signal for exiled revolutionaries, led by Lenin, to return to Russia, where they overthrew the fledgling government in October, heralding the start of more than 70 years of Soviet rule.

4 Siege of 1941–4
The Nazi's Siege of Leningrad plunged its inhabitants into a living hell. By the time it was broken, after 900 days, around two million had lost their lives.

5 1991 Coup
When hardliners opposed to Gorbachev's reforms seized power, his supporters gathered in Palace Square to protest.

6 Name Changes
The city's name was changed to the more Russian sounding Petrograd in 1914, then to Leningrad in 1924, after the death of Lenin. Its original name was restored after the collapse of the USSR in 1991.

7 "Criminal" 1990s
Immediately after the era of *perestroika* (restructuring), a criminal class sprang up and St Petersburg earned the title of "Crime Capital of Russia".

8 Reburial of Nicholas II
In 1998 the remains of Nicholas II and his family were reburied in the Cathedral of SS Peter and Paul.

9 300th Anniversary
The 300th anniversary of St Petersburg's founding saw a long-needed renovation of the city. Over ten days of celebrations were attended by heads of state from more than 45 countries.

10 Election of Vladimir Putin
A St Petersburg native, Putin came to power on New Year's Eve, 1999. A former KGB man, he has overseen a period of economic growth as well as a crackdown on press freedom.

5 Nevskiy Prospekt

The cultural heart of the city, this area is home to many of the top sights, including the Cathedral of Our Lady of Kazan *(left)*.

6 Peter and Paul Fortress

The history of the city dates from the founding of the fortress in 1703. It was originally intended to defend the city against Swedish invaders.

7 Peterhof

This extraordinary collection of palaces, fountains and magnificently landscaped gardens is set on the shore of the Gulf of Finland, 30 km (19 miles) west of St Petersburg. It perfectly encapsulates the extravagance of tsarist Russia.

8 Tsarskoe Selo

This fine example of tsarist architectural grandeur, with its lavish imperial palace *(above)* and beautiful parks, located 24 km (15 miles) south of St Petersburg.

9 Church on Spilled Blood

The striking church *(left)* is one of the city's most famous landmarks.

10 Pavlovsk

Set in a substantial park dotted with romantic ruins and statuary *(right)*, this palace, a short distance from her residence at Tsarskoe Selo, was a gift of Catherine the Great to her son, the future tsar Paul I.

Top 10 Bridges and Waterways

1 Trinity Bridge
Opened in 1903 on the 200th anniversary of the founding of St Petersburg, Trinity Bridge is one of the most beautiful of the city's 800 bridges.

2 Griboedov Canal
This canal, stretching 5 km (3 miles) through the very heart of the city, is crossed by 21 bridges.

3 Bridge Passage
Linking the Griboedov Canal and the Moyka river, Bridge Passage (1829–31) consists of the Malo-Konyushenny and Theatre bridges, cleverly designed to create the impression of a single bridge.

4 Anichkov Bridge
The Anichkov Bridge (1839–41) is noteworthy for its evocative bronze statues of men taming wild horses. When viewed in an anti-clockwise direction, the wild horses seem steadily to become domesticated.

5 Lomonosov Bridge
Notable for its curious stone turrets, this bridge was built between 1785 and 1787. Its granite towers originally housed its opening mechanism. When the bridge was rebuilt in 1912, the landmark towers were left in place.

6 Bank Bridge
This pedestrian bridge is less than 2 m (7 ft) wide. It is famed for its four gold-winged griffins, which also hold up the bridge's cables.

7 Egyptian Bridge
A 19th-century bridge here collapsed into the Fontanka in 1905 when a large cavalry squadron was passing. The magnificent sphinxes on this 1955 replacement were salvaged from the original.

8 Lion Bridge
The two pairs of proud lions on this bridge date from 1825–6. One of the earliest pedestrian suspension bridges in the city, it is today a popular place for romantic meetings.

9 Blagoveshchenskiy Bridge
Built in 1850, this was the first permanent crossing over the Neva river. It retains its original, intricate cast-iron sea horse and trident railings.

10 Winter Canal
The narrowest waterway in the city, the Winter Canal is one of its most picturesque. Crossed by three bridges, and by the Hermitage's Theatre Foyer, it is another favourite for romantic trysts.

Scotland

Scotland has an overwhelming abundance of natural beauty, hundreds of castles stand proud from its long and turbulent past, and an innate flair for enterprise and travel has endowed the nation with artistic treasures from around the world. Its gift in return has been scientific, medical and industrial innovation. The culture remains vibrant today, and there's much to celebrate.

1 Loch Ness and the Great Glen

Ancient geology scarred Scotland, and the Great Glen is its deepest cut, a swath that splits the land in two. A course of water runs through this great valley, forming charismatic lochs, such as Loch Ness *(above)*, famous for its mythical monster, Nessie.

2 The Cairngorms

This region *(left)* offers truly spectacular views. Bird watchers, walkers and winter sports enthusiasts praying for snow all head to the woodlands, rivers, lochs, mountains and plateaux of the Cairngorms, the highest landmass in Britain. From ospreys to reindeer to Arctic flowers, it's all here to discover.

3 National Gallery of Scotland

An internationally significant collection of paintings *(above)*, spanning from early Renaissance masterpieces to works by Rembrandt, Velazquez and Monet, to Scottish artists such as Ramsay and Raeburn.

TOP 10 Moments in History

1 St Columba Founds a Monastery on Iona
In 563 a fiery Irish missionary founded a monastery on Iona. Columban monks travelled widely, consolidating the Christian faith and unifying Scottish tribes into a nation.

2 Battle of Bannockburn
Facing an English onslaught in 1314, the Scots, led by Robert the Bruce, achieved a great victory. Their independence was ratified by Papal Bull in 1329, but war with England continued for 300 years.

3 Battle of Flodden
James IV invaded England in 1513 and met the enemy just over the border at Flodden. A massacre ensued, and 10,000 Scots died, James included.

4 John Knox Leads the Reformation
Scotland was Catholic when Mary Queen of Scots came to the throne. But in 1559 a revolutionary preacher, John Knox, brought Protestantism to Scotland. For the next 150 years, religious intolerance was rife in the country.

5 Union of the Crowns
Elizabeth I of England died without an heir, so James VI of Scotland was crowned James I of England in 1603.

6 Union of Parliaments
A trading misadventure in Panama almost bankrupted Scotland, and union with England in 1707 was need for economic survival.

7 Battle of Culloden
In 1745 James VII's grandson "Bonnie Prince Charlie" sailed from France to Scotland to raise an army of "Jacobites" and reclaim the British throne. The Hanoverian army, augmented by royalist Scots, slaughtered the rebels at Culloden, the last battle fought on British soil.

8 Industrial Revolution
James Watt's transformation of the steam engine heralded the advent of the Industrial Revolution, which had a profound effect on Scotland, and Glasgow in particular, which became known as "the workshop of the Empire".

9 Dwindling Numbers
World War I claimed 74,000 Scottish soldiers and almost as many civilians. In addition, between 1901 and 1961, 1.4 million Scots emigrated.

10 Re-establishment of a Scottish Parliament
In a 1997 referendum, the Scots emphatically voted for the re-establishment of a Scottish Parliament. It opened in 1999, returning the political forum to the heart of Scotland after an absence of 292 years.

4 Kelvingrove Art Gallery and Museum
Inside its grand Spanish-Baroque shell in Glasgow, cotland's premier museum and art gallery *(above)* ouses one of Europe's great civic art collections.

5 The Royal Mile
The main thoroughfare of Edinburgh's old town treads a fairly straight but nonetheless diverting path from the world-famous Castle to Holyroodhouse, the Queen's official residence in Scotland.

6 Museum of Scotland and Royal Museum
Now merged as the National Museum of Scotland, these two neighbouring collections bring together the best of Scotland's antiquities.

7 Culzean Castle
The castle *(above)* stands proud on a windswept cliff-top, but Culzean is a velvet hand in an iron glove, and inside all is given over to Robert Adam's dexterous play with the rules of Classicism. The result is a little splash of Regency gentility and fashion in a land prized for its wildness.

8 Edinburgh Castle
Presiding over the nation's capital, the castle *(above)* is Scotland's re-eminent sight, a truly inspirational historical and cultural landmark.

9 Glencoe
To Dickens this was a burial ground of a race f giants", and, indeed, there something ominous in the aw terrain of this region. is a magnificent, sublime ndscape, chilled by the istory of a bloody nassacre of 1692.

Isle of Skye 10
An island of romantic tales and the pursuit of royalty, of strange landscapes and mighty mountain ranges, of castle strongholds and religious communities – Skye *(right)* is a beautiful, wild and magical isle.

Top 10 Whisky Distillery Tours

1 Laphroaig
With their heavy smoked-peat flavour, the Islay malts are in a class of their own. This malt is pronounced "la-froyg". A delightfully informal and intimate tour in a fine sea-edge location.

2 Lagavulin
Like its rival Laphroaig, this is a very distinctive malt. It's made in a traditional distillery with unusual pear-shaped stills. A highly personal tour.

3 Glenkinchie
A rare Lowland distillery, founded in 1837. It is a popular place, just 15 miles (24 km) from Edinburgh, and rather crowded, but it's up to the task, with a state-of-the-art visitor centre.

4 Edradour
Established in 1825, this is Scotland's smallest distillery, virtually unchanged for 150 years. Only 12 casks a week are produced, making it "a rare treat for a few". Friendly and knowledgeable guides.

5 Glenlivet
ne of the first distilleries to be legalized, in 1824. The best bit of a comprehensive tour is the musty warehouse where the whisky "sleeps" for 12–18 years.

6 Glenfarclas
Established in 1836, owned and managed by the fifth generation of the Grant family, this is one of the few independent companies and justly proud of it. The tour ends with a dram in the splendid Ships Room.

7 Macallan
A famous Speyside brand, and one of the most modern visitor centres in the valley. For a small fee you can book an individually tutored nosing and tasting tour.

8 Cardow
The only distillery to have been pioneered by a woman and, aside from producing a distinguished single malt, it provides the heart of the Johnnie Walker blend. A range of tours and tastings.

9 Talisker
The only distillery on Skye has been producing a highly respected malt since 1830. Tours last 40 minutes and are bright and informative.

10 Highland Park
Not the most famous whisky (though among the greats), but definitely the best tour. Prepare to be taken through deep piles of malt drying in a delicious reek of peat.

Sicily

The island of Sicily is Italy's largest region and also its most varied. In terms of geography, there are offshore islands, endless coastline, rugged mountains, rolling wheatfields and volcanos, but its history and architecture are also of note. Sicily formed a significant portion of the Greek Empire, was strategically vital to Rome, and was invaded in succession by the Byzantines, Arabs, Normans, French, Spanish and Bourbons, before unifying with Italy. Each conquest left its distinctive cultural imprint on the island.

1 Norman Palermo

The Normans ruled Sicily for only a century, but they left a rich legacy of law, culture and architecture. Some of their most impressive monuments, including the cathedral, are grouped around a fortified site in the heart of Palermo.

2 Noto

Destroyed by an earthquake in 1693, Noto was rebuilt during the 1700s when the Baroque style was at its height *(right)*. A unified building programme creates harmony between landscape and village.

3 Aeolian Islands

Volcanic activity lent to each of these seven islands its own land and seascape. Evidence of 6,000 years of history, a live volcano, black lava beaches, the magnificently limpid sea, and food and wines intensely flavoured by the sun are well worth the trip out *(above)*.

Top 10 Moments in History

1 Ducetius
In the last resistance effort against the Greeks, Ducetius unified his people, the Sicels of eastern Sicily, in 452 BC, before suffering final defeat at the hands of Syracuse.

2 Supremacy of Syracuse
The Syracusan tyrants Heiron, Gelon and Dionysus assured the ascendancy of Greek Sicily. The Greek colonies fought amongst themselves, but united to defeat the Carthaginians at Himera in 480 BC, ending 50 years of Carthaginian aggression.

3 Roman Rule
Rome's successful siege of Syracuse in 212 BC quashed Greek power on the island. *Praetors* were sent to Sicily to govern, including Verres, later prosecuted by Cicero for his misdeeds. He looted everything from Sicilian wheat to works of art.

4 Arab Invasion
The Moors invaded in 827 AD at Mazara del Vallo, after three centuries of Byzantine rule. Four years later they took Palermo, made it their capital and transformed it into the cosmopolitan city it remains today. They improved irrigation and introduced new ways of farming and fishing.

5 Count Roger
Norman crusader Roger de Hautville took Sicily at the end of the 11th century. Over a century of Norman rule, Sicily slowly changed from an Eastern to a Western society.

6 The Sicilian Vespers
On Easter Monday 1282, on the excuse that a French soldier had insulted a local woman, Sicilians killed every Frenchman on the island. They invited Peter of Aragón to become their king, and Spanish domination of the island lasted for 500 years.

7 Unification
Popular revolts against foreign feudal misrule began in 1820. In May 1860, Italian socialist Garibaldi took the island and convinced the peasant class to vote for Italian Unification.

8 Emigration
After Unification, Sicily found itself highly taxed and ignored. Poverty and near-starvation prompted mass emigration to the Americas in the late 1800s and early 1900s.

9 Earthquakes
In 1908 an earthquake killed over 70,000 people. Another devastating quake, in 1968, destroyed scores of villages. Thousands were housed in shelters for 15 years, waiting for government help.

10 Mafia Crackdown
More than 350 *mafiosi* were convicted during the late 1980s, as a result of which the judges Giovanni Falcone and Paolo Borsellino were murdered in 1992. "Boss of Bosses" Salvatore "Totò" Riina was finally convicted of arranging their murders.

4 Agrigento

The famed Valle dei Templi is home to ruined Greek temples *(above)* set against a backdrop of the distant sea – as awe-inspiring today as they must have been to the peoples who constructed them 2,500 years ago.

5 Monreale

Despite its rather austere exterior, Monreale Cathedral's mosaic cycle *(left)*, which dates from the 12th and 13th centuries, is one of the wonders of the medieval world.

6 Mount Etna

The largest and most active volcano in Europe has been threatening the island since before records began. Its awesome presence dominates eastern Sicily *(above)*.

7 Taormina

As Sicily's first resort and an obligatory top on the Grand Tour, Taormina has been welcoming visitors for centuries. The town, draped with bougainvillea, offers breathtaking views, an ancient theatre *(above)*, and cafés and terraces overlooking the sea.

8 Villa Romana del Casale

The extensive mosaic decorations of this luxurious Roman hunting villa are considered to be the best preserved of their kind in the world.

9 Syracuse

This once mighty Greek colony and rival to Athens is today a thriving modern city endowed with vestiges of its former glory.

Selinunte 10

The romantic remains of Greek Selinus rise spectacularly from a promontory high above the sea *(right)*. Comprising the largest archaeological park in Europe, Selinunte offers the chance for a solitary ramble among the ruins, walking in the footsteps of history.

TOP 10 Wines and Wine Producers

1 Nero d'Avola
The classic Sicilian red, made from at least 80 per cent of grapes of the same name with added Perricone, is characterized by its intense ruby colour and a flavour of aromatic herbs.

2 Bianco d'Alcamo
Eighty per cent Catarratto plus a dash of Damaschino, Grecanico and Trebbiano make this dry and fruity wine the classic Sicilian white.

3 Marsala
A fortified wine produced in Marsala since the 18th century, Marsala is available as Fine, Superiore (aged at least two years), Riserva (aged at least four years) or Vergine and Soleras (aged at least 10 years). The wine is amber with a rich perfume of citrus flowers and almonds.

4 Cerasuolo di Vittoria
This cherry-red, dry and fruity wine is made from a blend of Frappato, Calabrese and Nerello grapes grown near Vittoria in the province of Ragusa.

5 Malvasia and Passito
Producers on Salina leave their Malvasia delle Lipari grapes to dry out on the vine or on mats to make a rich dessert wine. Pantelleria's Zibibbo grapes are treated in a similar way, left on the vine until the flavours have condensed to make a wine with intense flavours of dried fruits and vanilla.

6 Etna Bianco and Etna Rosso
In the southern and eastern zone of Mount Etna, the white grapes Cataratto and Carricante flourish. Reds, mostly Nerello Mascalese, grow around the base. The wines were awarded Sicily's first DOC in 1968.

7 Regaleali
The estate near Valledolmo has been in the same family since 1830. Their reds, based on Nero d'Avola, include Regaleali Rosso and Rosso del Conte; whites, primarily of Inzolia and their own Varietà Tasca, include Villa Tasca and Nozze d'Oro.

8 Marco de Bartoli
Marco de Bartoli and his sons cultivate indigenous grapes and remain faithful to the traditions of the area. Their wines includes classic Marsalas and the unfortified Vecchio Samperi, aged for 20 or 30 years.

9 Planeta
At his estate near Sambuca di Sicilia, Diego Planeta grows indigenous and international grapes. For La Segreta Rosso he blends Nero d'Avola with Merlot and Syrah.

10 Artisan Producers
Many artisan producers are making excellent wines. Look out for Fondo Antico, Occhipinti, COS, Graci, Frank Cornelissen, Palari, Girolamo Russo, La Moresca and Terra delle Sirene.

Turkey
Travertine terraces,
Pamukkale

Stockholm

A city of contrasts dictated by the weather, Stockholm can offer Christmas card scenes in winter and sun-drenched quaysides and waterways in summer. Unique museums and cool nightlife make it a year-round destination, but wrap up for Sweden's harsh winter months. No one would ever pretend that Stockholm is cheap to visit, but there are bargains for those in the know and museums, attractions and transport are all very reasonably priced.

1 Stockholm Archipelago
An entire summer would not be enough to explore the archipelago's gems – beaches and forests, seaside restaurants and camp sites. Hop aboard a steam ship *(left)* for a relaxing tour of the islands.

Gröna Lund 2
Merging the best traditions of fairgrounds with the latest hair-raising rides, Gröna Lund has something for all ages and tastes *(right)*, from 19th-century-style merry-go-rounds and sideshows to free-fall towers.

3 Stadshuset (City Hall)
The City Hall belies its stark and imposing exterior with magnificently decorated halls *(above)*. Climb up its tower for views across the city.

TOP 10 Moments in History

1 1252: Foundations
Stockholm is first mentioned in the 13th century, its name probably coming from "stock" (log) and "holm" (islet) – the logs used for building in the Gamla Stan area.

2 1520: Stockholm Bloodbath
The culmination of a long Danish campaign to take control of Sweden, the Stockholm Bloodbath saw around 80–90 Swedes being executed at Stortorget, outside the Tre Kronor palace.

3 1523: King Gustav Vasa
Gustav Vasa led a rebellion against Danish rule that ended with him being crowned king on 6 June 1523, Sweden's National Day.

4 1792: Murder of Gustav III
Gustav III was a big patron of culture and initiated reform programmes. But opposition to his absolute powers and costly foreign policy cost him his life, when he was shot at a masked ball in 1792.

5 1871: Industrialization
Stockholm began its late but rapid industrial progress in the 1870s, and in 1876 Lars Magnus Ericsson founded the Ericsson phone company in the capital.

6 1912: Summer Olympics
The Stockholm Olympic Stadium, built for the 1912 Olympics, is still used today. The games were known as the "Swedish masterpiece" and included the first use of electronic timing.

7 1936: Rise of the Social Democrats
Dominating Swedish politics from 1936 until the 1980s, the Social Democrats established the modern welfare state and shaped the development of Stockholm.

8 1965: Housing Programme
An immense project of apartment construction from 1965 to 1974 succeeded in building over a million new homes, even if many of the blocks were uninspiring.

9 1986: Olof Palme's Assassination
The killing of popular Prime Minister Olof Palme in central Stockholm in 1986 shook Sweden; his murder has never been solved.

10 The 21st Century
Present-day Sweden has a robust economy and is a leader in design and many technological fields. A strong promoter of equal rights, Sweden was ranked third in the 2011 Quality of Life index and joint first for democracy.

4 Vasamuseet

The *Vasa* warship *(left)* sank in Stockholm harbour on its maiden voyage in 1628. Lifted from the sea bed in 1961, it emerged in remarkably good condition and can be seen up close in this fascinating museum.

5 The Royal Palace

Built over 63 years, after its predecessor burned down in 1697, the Royal Palace is an extravagant combination of Italian, French and Swedish influences. Although no longer a royal residence, it still hosts many state functions *(above)*.

6 Drottningholm

Home to the Swedish royal family, this [U]NESCO World Heritage Site takes visitors back [to] 17th- and 18th-century grandeur *(above)*. The [ex]tensive, free-to-visit gardens are a delight.

7 Historiska Museet

Opened in 1943, this museum is known for its Viking-era exhibits but also has exceptionally good collections from the early Middle Ages. The Goldrummet (Gold Room) is one of Stockholm's most remarkable sights.

8 Hagaparken

A green oasis on the city's northern [e]dge, this "English park" reveals its secrets [al]ong winding, wooded paths.

9 Nordiska Museet

Experience the Swedish way of life from [th]e 16th to the 21st century in this museum *(right)*, [h]ome to over one and a half million exhibits – from jewellery and Strindberg's [p]aintings to everyday items from typical homes.

10 Skansen

Part re-creation of [S]wedish traditional life, [p]art zoo, part children's [fa]ir, there are surprises [ar]ound every corner at [Sk]ansen's hilly park. Put [a]side at least half a day [t]o make the most of it.

TOP 10 Specialist Museums

1 Fotografiska Museet
Housed in an Art Nouveau-style former industrial building on Stockholm's waterfront, the photography museum presents a mix of large and small exhibitions.

2 Millesgården
A sculpture park with works by Carl Milles (1875–1955) set amid terraces and fountains, Millesgården offers a beautiful view over the harbour and has an outdoor restaurant.

3 Moderna Museet
This museum has one of the world's finest collections of 20th-century art, including works by Picasso, Matisse and Dali, as well as ongoing acquisitions of contemporary art.

4 Arkitekturmuseet
This fascinating museum explores Swedish architecture and construction from a thousand years ago to the present day.

5 Naturhistoriska Riksmuseet
The natural sciences are shown in a lively and interactive manner – everything from dinosours to outer space is covered, with forays into the polar regions and the earth's interior.

6 Spårvägsmuseet
The history of transport in Stockholm is told, focusing especially on the expansion of the public transport network in the 20th century.

7 Stockholms Stadsmuseum
This delightful museum tells the story of Stockholm through the ages. Children love the City Square, where they can load carts, wrap fish up in newspaper and play at market stalls.

8 Östasiatiska Museet
This museum houses collections of art from the Far East, India and Southeast Asia.

9 Medelhavsmuseet
Dedicated to Mediterranean and Near East antiquities, the museum has Egyptian exhibits and collections showing Islamic art from the 7th century onwards.

10 Leksaksmuseet
This toy museum has a large and fascinating collection of steam engines from the 19th century to the present day, vintage Disney figures, dolls, dolls' houses (some from as far back as the 16th century) and cuddly teddy bears – not to mention cars, boats, planes and motorbikes.

Switzerland

A landlocked nation in the cultural and geographical heart of Europe, Switzerland is admired for the beauty of its Alpine environment and the excellence of its skiing, while its people are respected for their social responsibility, their centuries-old tradition of neutrality, their industry and their technical ingenuity. Picturesque mountain villages and atmospheric medieval towns contast with the cosmopolitan cities of Bern, Geneva, Zürich, Lausanne, Luzern and Basel.

1 Lausanne On the north side of Lake Geneva *(left)*, Lausanne is a vibrant cultural centre. In the medieval core, the cathedral is undoubtedly one of Switzerland's most important Gothic buildings.

2 The Matterhorn The most distinctive and dramatic peak in the Swiss Al *(above)* – though at 4,478 m (14,692 ft) not the highest – t Matterhorn has become one of Switzerland's national sym

3 Val Bregaglia One of Graubünden's Italian-speaking valleys *(above)*, Val Bregaglia is dotted with small churches, ruined castles and picturesque villages. It is also a mountaineers' paradis with scenic hiking trails and extraordinary rock formations.

TOP 10 Moments in History

1 Early Peoples
From about 500 BC the lands that now make up Switzerland were settled by two peoples, the Rhaetians, possibly an Etruscan people, and the Helveti, a Celtic tribe.

2 Romans and Franks
By 58 BC Helvetia and Rhaetia had become part of the Roman Empire. The region was attacked by Germani tribes in AD 260, and the Romans abandoned the province in 401. The lands were later taken by the Franks and became part of the Holy Roman Empire.

3 Alliance of the Cantons
During the 11th century feudal dynasties came to prominence. In 1291 three cantons formed an alliance against the Habsburgs; in the 14th century they were joined by five more. By 1513 13 cantons had joined the confederation.

4 Territorial Expansion
The Swiss Confederation won independence in 1499 and began to consolidate and expand its territories. After a defeat by Venice, it reverted to a policy of neutrality.

5 The Reformation
The Reformation originated in Germany in the early 16th century and quickly spread. The urban cantons embraced it, while the poorer cantons of central Switzerland stayed faithful to Catholicism.

6 Time to Expand
The Swiss Confederation remained neutral during the 17th-century Wars of Religion and boomed economically. A flood of refugees, particularly Huguenots, brought with them clock-making skills.

7 World War I
Switzerland maintained its neutrality during World War I, and embarked on a wide-ranging aid programme for prisoners-of-war and refugees. Russian revolutionaries were among the asylum-seekers, and their ideas fomented unrest among Swiss workers.

8 Inter-War Years
In 1920 Switzerland voted to join the new League of Nations and Geneva was chosen as the organization's headquarters. The country fell into depression in the 1930s.

9 World War II
The economy picked up with the onset of war, due to the burgeoning arms industry and the importance of Swiss banks. Despite the threat of invasion, Switzerland again remained neutral.

10 Post-War Switzerland
Post-war Switzerland was relatively untouched by the upheaval of war. The Swiss are not members of the European Union, although the country voted to join NATO in 2002.

4 Bern

Bern is one of the most beautiful historic towns in Switzerland. With a picturesque setting on the River Aare *(left)* and fine buildings lining the cobbled streets of its medieval centre, it's a capital city on a provincial scale.

5 Schaffhausen

Set on the north bank of the Rhine *(above)*, the capital of Switzerland's northernmost canton has an atmospheric old town (Altstadt), whose cobbled streets are lined with Gothic, Renaissance, Baroque and Rococo buildings.

6 Geneva

This cosmopolitan, cultured city – the headquarters of over 250 international organizations and NGOs – enjoys a magnificent setting on the largest lake in Western Europe.

7 Zürich

Zürich is Switzerland's capital of finance and its richest ity; its exuberant popular culture and arts scene also make one of Europe's liveliest cities. It is lovely, too, with a lakeide setting, elegant quays *(above)* and a fine historic core.

8 Bellinzona

Its location on the route over the great Alpine passes ave this historic town great strategic importance from oman times onwards. Its three castles, Castelgrande, Aontebello and Sasso Corbaro, are jointly a UNESCO Vorld Heritage Site.

Luzern 9

This charming city *(right)*, set on Lake Luzern and ringed by mountains, is the cultural capital of central Switzerland. Highlights include the grand Renaissance Hofkirche and the Wagner Museum, dedicated to the great 19th-century composer.

10 Basel

Located at the point vhere the Rhine becomes avigable, Basel is this landocked country's only port. t hosts Art Basel, the world's argest contemporary art fair, nd is famous for its festivals, specially Fasnacht, an xuberant masked carnival.

TOP 10 Bern Sights

1 Barenplatz
Named "Bear Square" for the bear pits that used to be here, Bern's main square is laid out, along with northern neighbour Waisenhausplatz, on the course of a former moat. It's for this reason that they seem more like wide avenues than squares.

2 Marktgasse
This is the centre of Bern's shopping district, the arcades that line it filled with shops, restaurants and cafés. Laid out in the 13th century, it runs east to west from Bern's original town gate.

3 Zytglogge
This tower is Bern's central landmark, the first town gate and famed for its splendid astronomical clock. Dating from 1527–30, the clock's mechanical figures parade on its east face four minutes before each hour is struck.

4 Rathaus
The seat of Bern's legislative assemblies since it was built in 1406, the Rathaus is an attractive building with a fine Gothic façade.

5 Kunstmuseum
Bern's fabulous Museum of Fine Arts holds a collection of over 3,000 paintings of international importance. Spanning the 14th to the 20th centuries, it includes early Renaissance works, 16th- and 17th-century Old Masters, and 19th- and 20th-century French paintings by artists such as Monet, Klee, Picasso and Cézanne. Swiss art is also well represented.

6 Munster St Vinzenz
Completed in 1893, this is technically the most recent of Switzerland's great Gothic cathedrals, yet it was begun in 1421. The medieval stained-glass windows are superb.

7 Bear Park
What was once the site of bear pits is now a forested park, providing a wonderful natural environment for the brown bears, the symbol of the city, to live in.

8 Gerechtigkeitsgasse
Some of the oldest and most beautiful buildings in Bern line this street. Many are guild houses, decorated with motifs of their trade.

9 Kunsthalle
This Modernist building is an important showcase for modern art, though it has no permanent collection.

10 Naturhistorisches Museum
One of Switzerland's oldest museums features dioramas of stuffed animals, including Barry, a heroic St Bernard rescue dog, as well as many Alpine minerals and fossils.

Tallinn

Estonia's capital city is one of northern Europe's historical gems, with a well-preserved Old Town encircled by surviving city walls. Gothic houses and slender-spired churches add character to the narrow streets. However, there is much more to Tallinn than this, and it is well worth branching out to destinations such as Kadriorg Park to the east and the Estonian Open-Air Museum further west for a refreshing mix of woodland beauty and rural culture.

1 Town Hall Square
Swarming with locals and visitors both day and night, Town Hall Square *(above)* is the focal point of Tallinn's Old Town. Looming above the square is one of the city's defining monuments, the starkly beautiful Town Hall.

2 Pikk Street
There are few better ways of getting to grips with Tallinn's history than taking a stroll along Pikk Street, a cobbled alleyway lined with architectural wonders from every age.

3 Niguliste Church
Few places offer a more sumptuous feast of medieval art than Niguliste Church *(below)*. Home to a fine collection of statues, altarpieces and church silverware, the church also house Tallinn's single most valuable artistic treasure – Bernt Notke's *Danse Macabre*.

TOP 10 Moments in History

1 1219: Tallinn is Founded by the Danes
Although an Estonian trading post aready existed here, the history of Tallinn really began with the arrival of Danish King Valdemar II, who used Tallinn as his base for the conquest of the rest of the country.

2 1345: Tallinn is Sold to the Livonian Order
Denmark's empire-building proved too expensive, and its Estonian possessions were sold to the Livonian Order of German knights.

3 1561: Tallinn Passes to Sweden
The Livonian Order eventually crumbled and Tallinn was absorbed by Sweden. This period is known as the "Good Old Swedish Times".

4 1710: Peter the Great Takes Tallinn
Russia and Sweden fought for control over the Baltic region for almost 200 years. The Russians, under Peter the Great, finally won in 1710 and Tallinn became a major port city of the Russian Empire.

5 1918: An Independent Republic
Estonia's independence was declared on 24 February 1918, but the new country spent years fighting off Bolsheviks and German Freikorps before securing its freedom.

6 1939: The Molotov-Ribbentrop Pact
In August 1939 Soviet foreign minister Molotov and German Ribbentrop agreed to divide up Eastern Europe. Estonia fell into the Soviet half, and was occupied in June 1940.

7 1945: Reoccupation by the Soviet Union
The Nazis entered Estonia in 1941 but, by 1945, the Soviets were back in control again. Thousands of Estonians were deported to Siberia in 1949.

8 1988: The Singing Revolution
A relaxation of censorship in the 1980s allowed Estonians to discuss the injustices they had suffered. Folk festivals became an arena for public protest, giving the freedom movement its musical title.

9 1991: Estonia Regains Independence
The Kremlin was fatally weakened by an unsuccessful coup in August 1991. Estonia used the power vaccuum to declare independence.

10 2004: Estonia Joins the European Union
Estonia introduced economic reforms in the 1990s and embraced new technology with a speed that far out-stripped its Eastern European neighbours. It became part of the EU in May 2004.

4 The City Walls

The limestone walls and pinnacled towers of Tallinn's medieval fortifications *(left)* remain one of the city's most unforgettable sights. They were built to save Tallinn from successive sieges in the 16th century.

6 Museum of Occupations

A compelling account of Estonia's 20th-century misfortunes, this is one museum display *(above)* that will linger in the memory for a long time.

7 Dome Church

Filled with grave memorials honouring the great and the good, Tallinn's main Lutheran cathedral is both a sculpture gallery and a place of worship.

8 City Museum

The lives and times of Tallinners through the ages are thrown into sharp relief by this absorbing collection of artifacts and artworks *(left)*. The Gothic museum building is an attraction in itself.

9 KUMU

Estonia's National ‹rt Museum *(above)* is oth a thrilling piece of ontemporary architecture nd an engrossing gallery ollection, with master- ieces by 20th-century stonian artists.

10 The Estonian Open-Air Museum

Ranged across a partly forested seaside park, west of the town centre, is this collection of traditional farm buildings *(above)*. They were brought to Tallinn timber-by-timber from various Estonian provinces.

5 Kadriorg Park

Peter the Great's 18th-century pleasure gardens have survived to become Tallinn's best-loved park *(above)*, boasting tree-shaded pathways, a huge children's playground and the city's most fascinating art museums.

TOP 10 Sights Along Pikk Street

1 Maritime Museum
Model ships, antique telescopes and other seafaring memorabilia are gathered together in the Old Town branch of the Maritime Museum. The museum is housed in the interior of a drum-shaped tower known as Fat Margaret.

2 The Three Sisters
This trio of 15th-century houses represents Gothic Tallinn at its picturesque best. The southernmost of the sisters has a façade with arched and circular niches.

3 Oleviste Church
Towering above the Old Town's northern end, the Oleviste Church is famous for its soaring steeple, which was the highest in the world when first built in 1500.

4 Former KGB Building
This 19th-century apartment block was once the HQ of the Soviet security department. Little sign of its sinister role remains.

5 Roheline Turg
One of the smallest green spaces in Tallinn, this park overlooks the junction of Pikk and Olevimägi. Once the site of a vegetable market, its name means "Green Square". The dainty Orthodox chapel at the end of the park dates from 1909.

6 House of the Blackheads
At No.26, Tallinn's most famous façade is studded with reliefs by the Dutch stonemason Arent Passer. Particularly exquisite are the plaques portraying duelling knights, just above the first-floor windows.

7 The Canute Guild
This striking 19th-century mansion in English neo-Tudor style was once home to the Canute Guild, an association of artisans who took their name from King Canute IV. The building now serves as a dance theatre.

8 Draakoni House
Built in 1911, this fine Art Nouveau building (now an art gallery) owes its name to the flamboyant façade decorations – a pair of black-winged dragons sprawling above the first-floor windows.

9 The Great Guild
Built in 1407 when the guild of Tallinn's merchants wielded considerable power, this building is an outstanding example of Tallinn Gothic.

10 Maiasmokk
Site of a café for 200 years, Maiasmokk (Sweet Tooth) is a Tallinn institution. Sweet-makers can be observed at work behind the counter of the café's sweet shop.

Turkey's Southwest Coast

With fascinating ruins, top-class tourist facilities and superb weather virtually guaranteed, this glorious stretch of coastline has something for everyone. Resorts, ranging from compact and exclusive to large and bustling, offer all-inclusive packages, while independent visitors can opt for comfortable hotels or self-catering accommodation in tranquil seaside locations. The broad variety of activities and excursions available in high season means there needn't be a dull moment.

Ephesus 3
4 Pamukkale and Hierapolis
TURKEY
Marmaris 9
Termessos 2
1 Antalya
8 Fethiye
6 Side
Alanya
Lycian Way 5
Kaş 10
Mediterranean Sea

1 Antalya

The main point of arrival for most visitors to the coast, Antalya *(below)* is a busy modern city with an ancient heart. Close to several major sites, it's an ideal base for day trips.

2 Termessos

This remarkable hilltop site *(above)* is partially overgrown and often lost in the clouds. Once a powerful and independent city protected by great stone walls, Termessos' monumental ruins include a stunningly situated theatre and some striking rock tombs.

Ephesus 3

As the ancient capital of the Roman province of Asia, Ephesus was a grand city second only to Rome. Many splendid buildings have been unearthed; some, like the Celsus Library *(right)*, have been partially restored to their former glory.

TOP 10 Moments in History

1 546 BC: Persian Invasion
The Persians, under King Cyrus II (576–530 BC), added Pamphylia and Lycia to their vast empire, remaining in control for over 200 years.

2 334 BC: Alexander the Great
The legendary commander Alexander crushed the Persian empire in a fierce campaign. After his death in 323 BC the region was divided between his generals, and a period of Greek influence began.

3 133 BC: Anatolia Under Roman Rule
Attalus III of Pergamon (170–133 BC), knowing he would die without an heir, left his kingdom to the Romans, who established the province of Asia. Its capital moved from Pergamon to Ephesus.

4 AD 330: Founding of the Byzantine Empire
Emperor Constantine founded the Byzantine Empire when he consecrated its new capital, Constantinople, on the site of former Byzantium.

5 1068: Invasion of the Selçuk Muslims
Expanding westwards from Persia, the Selçuk muslims invaded the Byzantine Empire, establishing principalities on the south and west coasts.

6 1453: The Ottomans take Constantinople
Following gradual territorial incursions by the Ottomans over the previous century, Mehmed II (1432–81) captured Constantinople, making it his new capital and renaming it Istanbul.

7 1919: Treaty of Sèvres
On the defeat of the Ottoman Empire in World War I, Greece was given control of much of the western Turkish coast. This sparked the Turkish War of Independence (1919–23).

8 1923: Formation of the Turkish Republic
The Treaty of Lausanne led to the recognition of the new Republic of Turkey. President Mustafa Kemal Atatürk began sweeping reforms intended to transform Turkey into a modern, democratic nation.

9 1980s: Tourism Boom
The Tourism Encouragement Law of 1982 saw the number of tourists visiting annually rise from one million in 1974 to over 25 million in 2008.

10 2005: Invitation to Join the EU
Despite major reservations from within the European Union, in 2005 Turkey was invited to begin negotiations to join, having first applied in 1987. Observers consider it unlikely to gain accession much before 2020.

4 Pamukkale and Hierapolis

Pamukkale's glistening white travertine pools *(left)* have drawn visitors since Roman times, when the spa town of Hierapolis grew up around them.

5 The Lycian Way

Tracking the coastline for over 500 km (313 miles), this well-marked hiking trail *(above)* takes in unspoiled villages, mountain ranges, desolate ruins and isolated bays.

6 Side

Before the Romans, Side *(above)* was home to pirates and slave-traders. These days it's a bustling tourist centre where shops, restaurants and *pensions* are intermingled with the ruins.

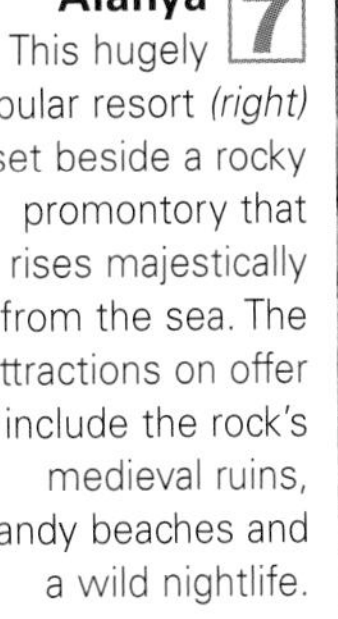

Alanya 7

This hugely opular resort *(right)* set beside a rocky promontory that rises majestically from the sea. The attractions on offer include the rock's medieval ruins, sandy beaches and a wild nightlife.

8 Fethiye

Particularly popular with British tourists, Fethiye a pleasant seaside town surrounded by wooded lls. Ancient highlights include majestic Lycian tombs elow) and a theatre facing the harbour.

9 Marmaris

With some of the coast's best nightlife, a superb marina, myriad shopping opportunities and a seafront jammed with mile after mile of lively bars and restaurants, Marmaris is a perennial favourite for package tourists from all over Europe and beyond.

10 Kaş

This small coastal town with a relaxed ambience, laid-back cafés and quirky craft shops has retained a distinct Turkish flavour despite the large number of foreign tourists.

TOP 10 Boat Trips

1 Üçağiz and Kaş to Kekova
The quickest way to reach the sunken ruins at Kekova is by fishing boat from Üçağiz. Alternatively, larger boats depart from Kaş for day trips that include Kekova. There are also kayaking trips to Kekova from Kaş.

2 Dalyan River Trips
Small boats chug up and down the Dalyan Strait in high season, ferrying day-trippers between the mud baths at Köyceğiz Lake, past the rock tombs cut into the cliffs, and on to İztuzu beach and the coastal ruins of Kaunos.

3 Alanya's Caves
Fishing boats run hour-long trips around Alanya's rocky promontory, stopping at the ancient shipyard, Tersane, Pirate's Cave, Phosphorous Cave and Cleopatra Beach. Larger *gulets* offer day trips.

4 Twelve Islands
Double-decker wooden *gulets* leave Fethiye each morning. There are plenty of places for a swim, including one at Tersane Island, as well as at several smaller islands with idyllic bays. Lunch is included.

5 Kaş to Meis
The large island just a short distance from Kaş is Greek territory. Known as Meis or Kastellorizo, it is the smallest of the Dodecanese islands and, like many others, it has a scattering of Ottoman-era ruins. The trip from Kaş harbour takes 45 minutes.

6 Datça to Knidos
Day trips from Datça, via fishing boat or *gulet*, follow the peninsula to the ruins at Knidos. There are swimming spots at secluded bays and dinner is provided.

7 Kemer to Phaselis
The picturesque coastal ruins of Phaselis can be visited by *gulet* on a day trip that also stops at isolated bays for swimming breaks, with lunch on board included.

8 Gemiler Beach to Aya Nikola Island
Aya Nikola lies in a sheltered bay, a short boat trip away from Gemiler Beach. Local fishermen drop tourists at the island for picnics and to explore the ruins of a chapel and Lycian tombs.

9 Manavgat Falls
Boats from Manavgat ferry tourists upriver to the Falls. Despite their lack of height, the volume of water gushing down is quite a spectacle, and the trip itself is pleasant.

10 Marmaris to Rhodes
For a change of scene, board a catamaran (1 hour) or car ferry (2 hours) from Marmaris to Rhodes; both depart daily at 9am, returning at 4pm, giving you plenty of time to explore historic Rhodes Town.

Tuscany

Limiting the choice of prime sights to ten is not an easy task in a region as rich and varied as Tuscany in Italy. Its sundrenched, rolling landscape, redolent of history and dotted with slender cypresses, offers medieval hill towns, fabled wines, mouthwatering food and an unrivalled collection of Renaissance artistic masterpieces. Here, however, is the best of the Tuscan best *(for Florence, see pp52–3)*.

1 Campo dei Miracoli, Pisa

A grassy "Field of Miracles", the Campo is studded with masterpieces of Romanesque architecture: a Baptistry and Cathedral containing Gothic pulpits by Pisano and, of course, that ridiculously leaning, famous belltower *(above)*.

San Gimignano 2

This medieval fairy-tale town *(right)* has stone towers and churches garlanded with frescoes, all surrounded by patchwork fields and terraced vineyards.

3 Arezzo

Steeped in 2,500 years of history, Arezzo is perhaps best known today for the splendid sequence of frescoes by Piero della Francesca, *Legend of the True Cross (left)*.

4 Cortona

Cortona is Tuscany in miniature: sweeping views, a medieval atmosphere, first-class art, handcrafted ceramics and fine wines.

TOP 10 Tuscan Artists

1 Giotto (1266–1337)
A humble shepherd boy, who dragged painting from its static, Byzantine methodology and set it on the road to the Renaissance, he imbued his work with earthy reality, giving his figures bulk and life.

2 Simone Martini (1284–1344)
Martini took a medieval eye for narrative and iconography and matched it with a vibrant Gothic palette, richly patterned fabrics and intense drama in his courtly, graceful figures.

3 Donatello (1386–1466)
This Renaissance sculptor cast the first freestanding nude and first equestrian statue since antiquity, and developed *schiacciato*, using etched perspective lines to create the illusion of great depth in a shallow relief.

4 Fra Angelico (1395–1455)
His origins as a manuscript illuminator informed his art. But his work is grounded in the Renaissance precepts of naturalism and perspective.

5 Masaccio (1401–28)
Not only did Masaccio imbue Renaissance painting with an unflinching naturalism, he also perfected single point perspective (Florence's Santa Maria Novella's *Trinità*).

6 Piero della Francesca (1416–92)
A visionary early Renaissance master whose paintings have an ethereal spirituality, and his well-modelled figures great humanity. His complex compositions show his early mastery of perspective.

7 Botticelli (1444–1510)
The master of languid figures and grand mythological scenes is said to have tossed his own "blasphemous" canvases onto Savonarola's "Bonfires of the Vanities".

8 Leonardo da Vinci (1452–1519)
The ultimate Renaissance Man: a genius painter, draftsman, inventor and scientist. His *sfumato* technique of blurring outlines and hazy backgrounds lent his works great depth and realism.

9 Michelangelo (1475–1564)
A sculptor of genius by his early 20s, who painted the Sistine Chapel only under protest, he also found time to design Florence's defences, write sonnets and become a significant architect.

10 Pontormo (1494–1556)
Mixing Andrea del Sarto's experimentation with twisting figures and Michelangelo's use of non-primary colours, Pontormo took these concepts to vivid, complex extremes.

5 Campo and Palazzo Pubblico, Sienna

This sloping brick scallop shell is Siena's living room, its public palace a museum celebrating the maestros of Gothic art *(left).*

6 Carrara

Carrara is a quarry town, its snowy-white marble the source of grandiose sculpture from ancient Rome to Michelangelo to Henry Moore.

7 Duomo, Siena

This striped giant of a cathedral *(above)* is stuffed with carvings, frescoes, Michelangelo's sculptures and Bernini's chapel.

8 Chianti

The ultimate Tuscan idyll *(above)*, this is a landscape of hills clad in grape vines, topped y castles, and scattered with countryside *trattorie* serving Italy's most famous wine.

Lucca 9

In this elegant city of opera and arcaded Romanesque façades, the medieval towers and 16th-century ramparts are now domesticated as pretty little parks *(right).*

10 Impruneta

This attractive, erracotta-producing own has a miracle- eavy Renaissance Collegiata church nd a lively festival each October.

TOP 10 Tuscan Culinary Highlights

1 Bistecca Fiorentina
Super-thick T-bone steak is best from the famous white Chiana cattle, brushed with olive oil and cracked pepper and grilled over a wood fire.

2 Crostini
These rounds of toasted bread are garnished with toppings such as *fegatini* – a blend of chicken livers, capers, onions and anchovy.

3 Ribollita
The king of Tuscan soups is a rich vegetable and bean mix, thickened by soaking stale bread in it overnight and re-boiling the next day (hence the name, *ri-bollita*). Serve over fresh slices of bread, drizzled with olive oil.

4 Pappardelle al Cinghiale
Pappardelle are Tuscany's very wide, yellow ribbons of pasta usually folded around a sauce made from *cinghiale* (wild boar) stewed so long that it falls apart in shreds.

5 Fagioli all'Uccelleto
Tuscans are nicknamed *mangiafagioli*, bean-eaters, because of their love of cannellini beans. Try them *all'uccelleto*, beans stewed with fresh tomatoes, sage, garlic cloves and olive oil.

6 Trippa alla Fiorentina
Florence serves tripe diced and stewed with tomatoes, sage and *parmigiano* cheese. You will also see carts here serving tripe sandwiches.

7 Cacciucco
Livorno's *bouillabaisse* is a rich, *pepperoncino*-spiked tomato and seafood stew, poured over stale bread. The recipe varies with the day's catch, but usually includes some tentacles.

8 Pici (or Pinci)
Appicicare means to roll between the hands. These fat, chewy, misshapen home-made spaghetti are made only from flour and water, and are usually served in a simple tomato sauce.

9 Pecorino
Italy's finest sheep's milk cheese comes in various forms, from soft (*non-stagionato* and *marzolino*) to harder and sharper (*semistagionato* and the full *stagionato*). The latter can be grated over pasta.

10 Panzanella
Panzanella is a summertime salad of stale bread soaked in water and vinegar, topped with diced tomatoes, onions, basil and olive oil.

Venice

The uniquely romantic Italian city of Venice was built entirely on water and has managed to survive into the 21st century without cars. Narrow alleyways and canals pass between sumptuous palaces and magnificent churches, colourful neighbourhood markets and quiet backwaters, unchanged for centuries. Few cities possess such an awesome line-up of sights for visitors.

1 Grand Canal The city's majestic main watercourse *(left)* swarms with all manner of floating craft, while its embankments boast a dazzling succession of palaces from as early as the 13th century.

Rialto Market 2 This fresh produce market *(right)* has enlivened the quayside since medieval times and is arguably still the best market in the world.

3 Campo Santa Margherita This is a wonderful square, bustling with life day and night thanks to its market stalls and outdoor cafés. An added bonus is its many architectural styles.

4 Piazza San Marco Elegance and opulence sit side by side in what Napoleon named "the most elegant drawing room in Europe". This magnificent square *(above)* is adorned with monuments that give testimony to Venice's glorious past.

TOP 10 Venice Architects

1 Jacopo Sansovino
Trained in Florence under Andrea Sansovino, whose name he adopted, Jacopo (1486–1570) fled to Venice to escape the sacking of Rome. The Libreria and the Zecca are fine examples of his work.

2 Andrea Palladio
One of the most influential architects of the western world, Palladio (1508– 80) designed many Classical villas, along with the churches of Redentore and San Giorgio Maggiore in Venice.

3 Baldassare Longhena
The majestic Santa Maria della Salute, designed by him at the age of 26, is Longhena's (1598–1682) masterpiece, but his flamboyant style can be seen in other churches and palaces, notably Ca' Rezzonico.

4 Pietro Lombardo
A native of Lombardy, sculptor Pietro (1435–1515) took over at the Doge's Palace when director of works Antonio Rizzo fled, accused of embezzlement. His trademark is a leafy *bas-relief* pattern, which is also found on his Renaissance masterpiece, Santa Maria dei Miracoli.

5 Mauro Coducci
The designs of Lombardy-born Coducci (c.1440–1504) can be seen in the shape of Palazzo Vendramin-Calergi and the churches of San Zaccaria and San Michele.

6 Bartolomeo Bon
Gothic sculptor and architect Bon's (1374–1464) designs were the basis for the church and Scuola di San Rocco. With his son Giovanni, he was also responsible for the Ca' d'Oro ("Golden House").

7 Michele Sanmicheli
Military fortifications by this Mannerist architect (1484–1559) are to be found on the former Venetian islands of Crete and Cyprus.

8 Antonio Da Ponte
Renowned for his landmark Rialto bridge, this engineer and architect (1512–95) also made many contributions to the Doge's Palace.

9 Giannantonio Selva
In Venice, French-inspired Selva (1757–1819) is best remembered for designing the elegant Fenice theatre, though he also had a hand in works of the Napoleonic era including restructuring the Accademia Galleries.

10 Carlo Scarpa
The Venice-born Modernist Scarpa (1906–78) admirably reorganized the Accademia collection and the Querini Stampalia along Japanese-inspired lines.

5 Island of Torcello

Escape the crowds in the city with a ferry ride over the vast expanse of the lagoon to this peaceful, lush island *(left)*, the site of Venice's original settlement.

6 Gallerie dell' Accademia

This unsurpassed collection of Venetian paintings, with masterpieces by Titian, Bellini and Giorgione, is a must, not only for art lovers.

7 Basilica San Marco

Venice's fairytale cathedral *(above)* is pure Byzantine in essence, while its façade and interior have been embellished with resplendent mosaics and exquisite works of art through the ages.

8 Doge's Palace

This was the powerhouse of the city's ılers for nearly 900 years *(above)*. Passing ırough its maze of rooms gives visitors an ısight into the sumptuous lifestyle that so ften accompanied state affairs.

9 Peggy Guggenheim Collection

Italy's leading museum for 20th-century uropean and American art is housed in a one-oor palace on the Grand Canal *(below)*.

10 Santa Maria Gloriosa dei Frari

A Gothic interior with grandiose works of art lies in store behind this church's brick façade *(above)*.

TOP 10 Venice Bridges

1 Bridge of Sighs
This evocatively named bridge once led convicts from the Doge's Palace to the adjacent prisons.

2 Rialto Bridge
Michelangelo, Sansovino and Palladio all entered the 1578 contest to design this now-iconic bridge. There had been two previous bridges on the site, including a timber one which collapsed in 1444 under the weight of a crowd.

3 Ponte degli Scalzi
One of the city's greatest viewpoints, this 1934 bridge in Istrian stone was named after the nearby monastery of barefoot monks.

4 Ponte della Libertà
This 3.6-km (2-mile) "Bridge of Freedom", the first road link with the mainland, was opened in 1933, while Italy was under Fascist rule. An Austrian-built railway bridge preceded it by 86 years. Before that, the city relied entirely on boats.

5 Ponte dei Tre Archi
A favourite subject for artists, this unusual three-arched high bridge, dating from 1688, crosses the Cannaregio canal close to where it joins the lagoon.

6 Ponte dei Pugni
Fistfights *(pugni)* between rival clans took place here until 1705 when they were outlawed for their violence. Stone footprints marked the starting point of the combat, but contestants usually ended up in the canal.

7 Ponte delle Tette
In the 1400s the city's prostitutes were permitted to display their feminine wares at the windows over the "Bridge of Breasts".

8 Bridge with No Parapet
One of only two remaining bridges with no side guards, this one spans a quiet side canal in Cannaregio. The other is the Ponte del Diavolo on Torcello.

9 Tre Ponti
Not three but five interlocking bridges span the Rio Nuovo canal near Piazzale Roma. The timber and stone structures afford views taking in 13 other bridges.

10 Ponte Lungo
Marvellous views of Piazza San Marco can be had from this iron bridge. Halfway along the Giudecca, from 1340 it served as a link with newly reclaimed tidal flats.

Vienna

Splendid edifices, magnificent palaces and imposing churches spanning the centuries all make Vienna a wonderful city to visit; it oozes charm and atmosphere. Although its imperial grandeur can still be felt, this city of music has more to offer than just a glorious past; contemporary architecture, a brimming cultural scene and a vibrant nightlife add to its appeal. The following sights are a must for any first-time visitor, but no matter how many times you return, you'll always discover something new.

1 Schloss Schönbrunn

The former summer residence *(above)* of the imperial Habsburg family remains today as a magnificent palace with splendid Baroque gardens and the world's oldest zoo. It attracts some 110,000 visitors a year.

2 Karlskirche

Built in the early 18th century, this magnificent Baroque church with an impressive elongated dome dominates the south side of Karlsplatz. It is framed by two Roman-style columns decorated with bas-reliefs *(left)*.

3 Secession Building

The white Secession building is a magnificent Art Nouveau edifice *(left)* that reflects the ideals of the Secessionist movement – purity and functionalism.

4 Staatsoper

The Vienna State Opera attracts music lovers from all over the world. Its grand entrance hall with majestic staircase is a fine introduction to an evening of classical music.

TOP 10 Moments in History

1 Early Vienna
Early settlements date back to the late Stone Age (5000 BC). The Celts established the kingdom of Noricum in 200 BC. This was conquered by the Romans in 15 BC, who later set up a garrison, Vindobona, in AD 100.

2 Babenberg Rule
In AD 976 the Babenberg ruler Leopold was appointed Duke of the Eastern March. In 1156 Vienna became the residence of the Babenbergs and a centre of trade.

3 Habsburg Rule
On the death of the last Babenberg, the Habsburg Rudolf I was elected king in 1273. Vienna became centre of the Holy Roman Empire and remained the Habsburg imperial city until 1918.

4 Turkish Siege
The Ottoman Turks failed to conquer Vienna in 1529, but a 200,000 strong army under Kara Mustafa returned in 1683. The city was besieged for three months, but was liberated in September 1683.

5 Vienna Congress
After Napoleon had been defeated at Leipzig (1813), the European powers met in Vienna in 1814–15 to come to territorial agreements and create a balance of power.

6 1848 Revolution
Under Chancellor Metternich there was a period of calm and rich cultural life (1815–48), but renewed social discontent led to the revolution of 1848. Metternich was ousted from power and a monarchy under Franz Joseph I was installed.

7 End of the Austro-Hungarian Empire
On the death of Franz Joseph in 1916, the Austro-Hungarian monarchy lost its one uniting figure. The empire's defeat in World War I resulted in the Habsburgs losing both their lands and their crown.

8 First Republic
When a new European map was drawn in 1918, the small Republic of Austria emerged. But social unrest led to a civil war in February 1934, and then authoritarian rule.

9 Anschluss
In March 1938 Adolf Hitler took Vienna and declared Austria part of the Third Reich. Vienna was badly bombed in World War II, and lost many of its famous landmarks.

10 Second Republic
In 1945 Vienna was divided into four zones occupied by the four Allied powers (Great Britain, France, Russia and the USA). Ten years later the last Allied soldiers left the country, and Austria regained full sovereignty in May 1955.

5 The Belvedere
The former summer residence of the th-century war hero Prince Eugen is a lendid Baroque palace with vast French rdens, and is now home to the Austrian ational Gallery. It houses world-famous intings by Austrian artists, including Gustav imt's Art Nouveau work *The Kiss*.

Hundertwasserhaus 6
Designed by Austrian artist Friedensreich Hundertwasser, this unconventional, colourful building *(right)* is characterized by uneven floors, rooftop gardens and unique windows.

7 Hofburg Palace
The former imperial palace *(above)*, with its many ings and courtyards, has always been of historic nportance. The interior reflects Austria's glorious ast and is the setting for grand balls.

8 Museumsquartier
The former imperial stables have been converted into a museum complex, exhibiting, amongst other things, collections of modern and contemporary art.

9 Kunsthistorisches Museum
This remarkable museum contains a stunning array of paintings, including one of the world's largest collections of Old Masters.

10 Stephansdom
The Gothic cathedral *(left)* is one of Vienna's most prominent landmarks, dominating the city centre. From its spire you can enjoy a spectacular view over the rooftops to the Vienna Woods.

TOP 10 Composers

1 Wolfgang Amadeus Mozart
Although born in Salzburg, Mozart's life is inextricably intertwined with Vienna. It was here that he wrote his greatest works, celebrated all his triumphs and misfortunes, and died, aged 35.

2 Ludwig van Beethoven
When Beethoven (1770–1827) gave his first concert in Vienna in 1795 he already had a reputation as an great pianist. Born in Bonn, he moved to Vienna aged 22 to receive tuition from Joseph Haydn and, possibly, Mozart.

3 Joseph Haydn
Haydn (1732–1809) is the third important composer of the Viennese Classical period. He composed some of his greatest works in his house at Haydngasse 19.

4 Franz Schubert
Schubert (1797–1828) was the twelfth child born in the family home at Nussdorfer Strasse 54. It is perhaps for his songs that he is best remembered.

5 Johann Strauss
Vienna's "Waltz King" (1825–99) was one of a dynasty of composers and musicians. He wrote the *Blue Danube Waltz* (1876), Austria's unofficial national anthem.

6 Johannes Brahms
Brahms (1833–97) became musical director of the Vienna Singakademie and the Vienna Philharmonic Orchestra before devoting all his time to composition in 1878.

7 Anton Bruckner
Bruckner (1824–96) moved to Vienna in 1868 to teach at the musical academy. His contemporaries were critical of his work and not all of it was performed in his lifetime.

8 Gustav Mahler
Gustav Mahler (1860–1911) composed 10 symphonies and song cycles, yet during his lifetime he was better known as a conductor.

9 Arnold Schönberg
Schönberg (1874–1951),one of the most distinguished composers of the 20th century, left Vienna in 1933 during the rise of National Socialism and died in the US.

10 Alban Berg
Berg (1885–1935) is known for his operas *Wozzeck* and *Lulu*. During the Nazi era, his music was considered indecent and was banned.

Wales

Wales is a country of outstanding natural beauty with varied landscapes. Visitors come to climb dramatic mountain peaks, go walking in the forests, fish in the broad rivers and enjoy the miles of unspoilt coastline. The country's many seaside resorts have long been popular with English holidaymakers. As well as outdoor pursuits there is the vibrancy of Welsh culture, with its strong Celtic roots, to be experienced. Finally there are many fine castles, ruined abbeys, mansions and cities full of magnificent architecture.

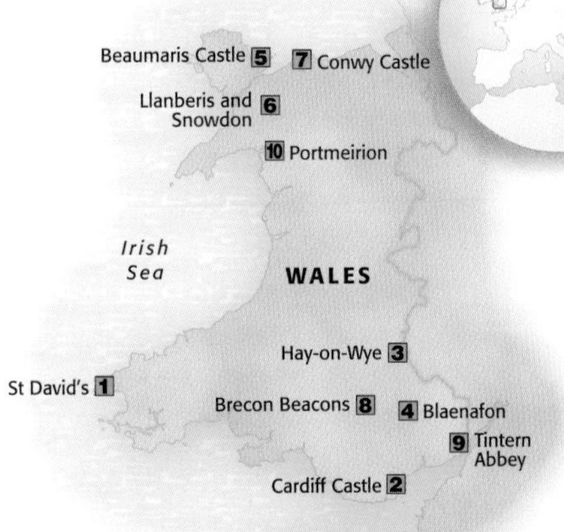

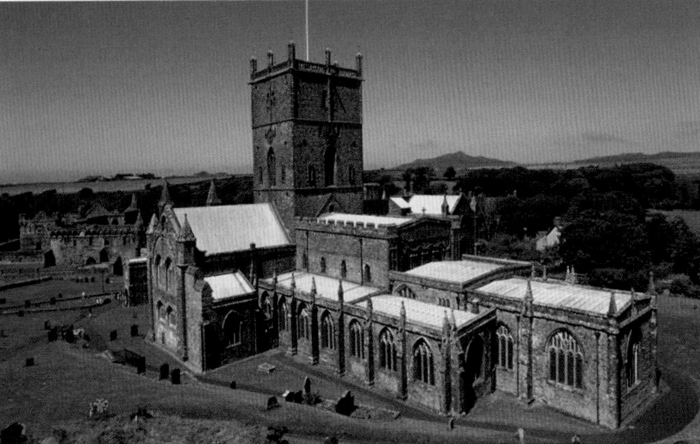

1 St David's
The smallest city in Britain is home to the largest cathedral in Wales *(left)*, whose nave is noted for its carved oak roof and beautiful rood screen. Next to the cathedral is the medieval Bishop's Palace, now a ruin.

Cardiff Castle 2
This ornate Victorian-Gothic mansion *(right)* started out as a Roman fort. Centuries later a Norman keep was built within its ruins. After further accretions, the castle eventually passed to John Crichton-Stuart, 3rd Marquess of Bute, who engaged the eccentric but gifted architect William Burges to rebuild it as a fantasy castle.

3 Hay-on-Wye
Book-lovers from all over the world come to this quiet border town *(above)* in the Black Mountains, home to more than 30 bookshops stocking millions of titles. Every summer Hay hosts a prestigious Festival of Literature.

Top 10 Moments in History

1 Prehistoric Wales
Wales was inhabited some 230,000 years ago. By the Iron Age, Celtic farmers had established hill forts and their own religion, Druidism.

2 Roman Settlements
The Romans conquered Wales in AD 78, and built fortresses and roads, and mined lead, silver and gold. From the 4th century AD, Wales was converted to Christianity by missionaries from Europe. The legions withdrew around AD 400.

3 Celtic Nation
By AD 500 a number of kingdoms had emerged in Wales, with strong links between them. In 770 the Saxon King Offa built a defensive earthwork, Offa's Dyke, along the border.

4 Marcher Lords
The Norman invasion of 1066 did not reach Wales, but the border territory, the Marches, was given to favoured barons by William the Conqueror The Marcher Lords made many incursions into Wales and controlled most of the lowlands. Edward I completed the conquest of Wales in 1283.

5 Owain Glyndŵr's Rebellion
In 1400 Owain Glyndŵr, a descendant of Welsh princes, led a dramatic but futile revolt with the aid of Celtic allies.

6 Union with England
In 1485 Welshman Henry Tudor became Henry VII. The Act of Union in 1535 gave Wales parliamentary representation in London.

7 Industrialization
The industrialization of Wales began in the 1760s with the development of open-cast coal mining, followed in the the 19th century by deep pits in the Rhondda Valley. Poor living and working conditions led to forcibly quashed riots.

8 Welsh Nationalism
In 1916 David Lloyd George became the first British Prime Minister from a Welsh family. In 1926 Plaid Cymru, the Welsh Nationalist Party, was formed.

9 Home Rule
In 1955 Cardiff was recognized as the capital of Wales. A referendum in 1998 resulted in limited home rule, and in 1999 the National Assembly for Wales was established.

10 Wales Today
Mass unemployment has declined, thanks to the emergence of high tech industries, and through a growth in tourism. Cardiff is home to many major tourist attractions including the Millennium Stadium.

4 Blaenafon

Coal is no longer produced at Big Pit in laenafon, but the mining museum *(above)* ovides a vivid reminder of this tough industry. sitors follow a marked-out route around the ine's surface, then descend 90 m (300 ft) for tour of the underground workings.

5 Beaumaris Castle

Begun in 1295, Beaumaris, on the island of Anglesey, was planned as part of Edward I's "iron ring" to contain the rebellious Welsh, but it was never completed. Nonetheless it has a sophisticated defence structure unparalleled in Wales.

6 Llanberis and Snowdon

Famous for dangerous, high peaks, this area has long been popular with climbers. Mount Snowdon's summit is most easily reached from Llanberis. Its Welsh name, Yr Wyddfa Fawr, means "great tomb" and it is the legendary burial place of a giant slain by King Arthur.

7 Conwy Castle

Built by Edward I, Conwy Castle *(above)* guards one of the best-preserved medieval fortified towns in Britain. The castle was besieged and came close to surrender in 1294. It was taken by Owain Glyndŵr's supporters in 1401.

8 Brecon Beacons

This national park *(above)*, a lovely area of mountains, forest and ıoorland in South Wales, is a favourite with walkers, climbers, cavers nd nature-lovers. Pen-y-Fan is one of the principal summits.

9 Tintern Abbey

Once the richest abbey in Vales, Tintern's skeletal ruins, et in the steep and wooded Vye Valley, are now roofless and xposed, the soaring arches and vindows giving them a poignant race and beauty. They have nchanted travellers since the 8th century.

Portmeirion 10

Created by architect Sir Clough Williams-Ellis, this Italian-style private village, some of whose buildings are assembled from architectural remnants taken from sites around the country *(right)*, seems rather incongruous in the Welsh landscape.

Top 10 Brecon Beacons Sights

1 Llyn y Fan Fach
This remote, myth-laden glacial lake is a splendid 6.5-km (4-mile) walk from Llanddeusant, home to a red kite feeding centre where you can observe these magnificent raptors from a specially built hide.

2 The Black Mountain
A largely unexplored wilderness of knife-edged ridges and high, empty moorland, the Black Mountain fills the western part of the national park that bears it name.

3 Carreg Cennen
Spectacularly sited on a sheer limestone cliff near the village of Trapp, Carreg Cennen is a ruined medieval fortress typical of Wales.

4 Dan-yr-Ogof Caves
A labyrinth of caves runs below the Brecon Beacons. Guided tours of two of the largest accessible caves are offered here, at the National Showcaves Centre for Wales.

5 Pen y Fan
At 886 m (2,907 ft) Pen y Fan is the highest point in South Wales. Its distinctive flat-topped summit, once a Bronze Age burial ground, can be reached by footpath and affords stunning views.

6 Monmouthshire and Brecon Canal
Completed in 1812, this peaceful waterway was once used to transport raw materials between Brecon and industrial Newport. One of the most scenic canals, it is perfect for boating holidays.

7 Llanthony Priory
This 12th-century ruin has simply carved but elegant stonework, in marked contrast to its wild and rugged setting. In the 19th century a small hotel (still open) was built in part of it.

8 Hay Bluff
At 677 m (2,221 ft), Hay Bluff looks out across border country. A narrow mountain road climbs from Hay-on-Wye to the dramatic Gospel Pass before it drops down to Llanthony.

9 Fforest Fawr
The "Great Forest" was a royal hunting ground in the Middle Ages. It is as much open upland as it is forest.

10 Brecon
Brecon itself is a charming historic cathedral and market town whose quaint, narrow streets are lined with handsome Jacobean and Georgian buildings.

Warsaw

The capital of Poland – a vibrant modern metropolis of around 1.7 million inhabitants – is both old and young. Old because its origins lie in the 13th century; young because some 80 per cent of its buildings were destroyed in World War II and much of the Old City has since been painstakingly reconstructed. For the visitor there is a wide range of attractions to sample: museums and galleries, parks and palaces, churches, monuments, great shopping, wonderful cafés and restaurants, and a cornucopia of cultural events, whose highlight is perhaps the International Chopin Piano Competition, held once every five years since 1927.

1 Royal Castle
Devasted by the Nazis during the Warsaw Uprising, this magnificent example of Baroque architecture took 17 years to reconstruct. Today it is a museum *(above)* housing furniture, paintings and numerous *objets d'art*.

2 Wilanów Palace and Park
Set in magnificent grounds, this remarkable relic of Poland's royal past *(above)*, with interiors decorated by some of Europe's finest craftsmen, survived the Partitions and two World Wars intact.

3 St Anna's Church
This imposing Gothic building with a magnificent interior has been University Church since 1864, and remains the most popular wedding venue for Warsaw's students. It is said that any marriage celebrated at St Anna's will be a happy one.

TOP 10 Moments in History

1 Early Settlements
Prince Bolesław II established a castle in a former fishing village called Warszowa In the late 1200s. It soon grew into a sizeable settlement.

2 Medieval Warsaw
Warsaw became the capital of Masovia in 1413 and the town developed rapidly. Even though Cracow was capital of Poland, Warsaw remained the seat of the Mazovian dukes until the dynasty died out in 1526 and the king took control of the duchy.

3 The Golden Years
Warsaw became capital of Poland in 1596. The devastating Swedish invasion of 1655 severely damaged the city, which was then substantially rebuilt in the Baroque style.

4 Saxon Warsaw
In the first half of the 18th century, the Saxon kings of Poland August II and August III brought the finest Saxon craftsmen to Warsaw, where they created lavish buildings. But the kings also dragged the country into futile wars.

5 The Last Polish King
Stanisław August Poniatowski (reigned 1764–95) made Warsaw into a major European cultural centre, but the country was weakened by a rebellious aristocracy and lack of military strength, and was invaded by Prussia, Russia and Austria.

6 Warsaw During the Partitions
Prussia, Russia and Austria divided Poland in a series of treaties which culminated in the Third Partition of 1795; Poland would not officially exist for another 123 years. Warsaw's importance declined as Russian control tightened.

7 World War I
After three years of German occupation, Poland regained its independence in 1918. Border disputes with the Bolsheviks ended with the defeat of the Red Army at the Battle of Warsaw in 1920.

8 World War II
Warsaw fell to the Nazis in 1939. Less than half of the city's population survived the war, and Warsaw lay in ruins. In 1945 control over Poland was ceded to the Soviets.

9 Soviet Rule
The Soviets rebuilt the city. Warsaw's Old Town was painstakingly restored and became a UNESCO World Heritage Site. 1989 marked the end of Communist rule.

10 Modern Warsaw
Post-Communist Warsaw boomed and expanded rapidly. Poland joined the European Union in 2004.

4 Monument to the Ghetto Heroes

Created from labradorite, the stone that the Nazis ordered or a victory arch, this powerful monument *(above)* symbolizes he heroic defiance of the Ghetto Uprising in 1943. Reliefs depict nen, women and children struggling to flee the burning ghetto.

5 St John's Cathedral

This 15th-century church in Mazovian Gothic style became a cathedral in 1798. Much of the building had to be reconstructed after damage inflicted by the Nazis during World War II

6 National Museum

Established in 1862, the museum's vast holdings span three millenia, from ancient artifacts and medieval paintings to contemporary works, including important collections of Polish art. There is also a gallery devoted to archaeological finds from Faras in present-day Sudan.

7 Palace of Culture and Science

The city's most visible landmark, this vast, monolithic building *(above)* was a "gift" from Soviet Russia to the people of Warsaw. Nowadays it houses theatres, a cinema, an excellent bookshop and office space.

8 Old Town Market Square

Formerly the site of fairs, municipal festivities and the odd execution, this storic square *(above)* gets its unique character from the grand 17th-century ouses that frame it. Today, it is lined by café tables and stalls, and horse-drawn arriages stand ready to offer tours of the Old Town to visitors.

9 Grand Theatre

Built in 1825–33 and greatly nlarged after World War II, the Grand heatre is currently home to Poland's ational Opera and Ballet. Its striking odern interiors were designed by chitect Bohdan Pniewski.

10 Łazienki Park and Palaces

One of Warsaw's most popular attractions, this romantic landscaped park is the setting for several palaces – including the fine Palace on the Water – pavilions, an amphitheatre, a Neo-Classical temple and two orangeries.

TOP 10 Royal Castle Sights

1 Exterior
What looks like an imposing Baroque palace is in fact a lovingly recreated replica of the original building that was completely destroyed by the Nazis in World War II. There are some original details, however, that were rescued from the ruins and kept safe until needed.

2 Ballroom
Decorated with 17 pairs of golden columns, mirrors and glittering chandeliers, the ballroom is one of the castle's most elaborate interiors.

3 Marble Room
The interior of the Marble Room dates from the time of Wladyslaw IV. Only the magnificent portraits of Polish rulers by Marcello Bacciarelli are later additions.

4 Lanckoroński Gallery
On the second floor of the castle, this gallery contains, amongst it exhibits, two paintings by Rembrandt: *Portrait of a Young Woman* and *Scholar at his Desk*.

5 Senator's Room
In this room, the Constitution of 3 May was formally adopted in 1791, a radical but short-lived step towards democracy and reform. The coats of arms of all the regions and territories of the Republic are on the walls, and a reconstructed royal throne is also on display.

6 Knights' Hall
The finest piece in this beautiful interior is the Neo-Classical sculpture of a world-weary *Chronos* by Jakub Monaldi.

7 Canaletto Room
The walls of this room are decorated with scenes of Warsaw by the famous Venetian painter.

8 Apartment of Prince Stansław Poniatowski
The Rococo panelling, thought to be by the French cabinet-maker Juste-Aurèle Meissonier, was taken from the former Tarnowski Palace.

9 Zygmunt Tower
This tower, 60 m (197 ft) high, was built in 1619. It is crowned by a cupola with a spire. It is also known as the Clock Tower (Zegarowa) since a clock was installed in 1622.

10 Royal Princes' Rooms
A collection of fine historical paintings by Polish master Jan Matejko (1838–93) is on display here.

Best of the Rest: City Sights

Historic Buildings

1 Hampton Court, London, England
The finest piece of Tudor architecture in Britain, this was the home of Henry VIII – fine galleries, royal apartments, courtyards and gardens.

2 Château de Versailles, Versailles, France
Louis XIV created the largest and most opulent palace in Europe when he moved his court here in 1678.

3 Villa Farnesina, Rome, Italy
A little gem of gracious living, decorated by some of the greatest artists of the Renaissance.

4 Custom House, Dublin, Ireland
Built in 1791, the elegant Classicism of the Custom House graces the north bank of Dublin's River Liffey.

5 Mozarthaus, Vienna, Austria
Mozart composed some of his masterworks here – the Haydn quartets, a handful of piano concerti and *The Marriage of Figaro.*

6 Royal Yacht Britannia, Edinburgh, Scotland
From 1953 to 1997, this was the Queen's floating home.

7 Landnámssýningin, Reykjavík, Iceland
The "Settlement Exhibition" centres upon a Viking-age longhouse, perhaps the home of Iceland's first settler, who sailed from Norway in around AD 870.

8 Arsenale, Venice, Italy
The Corderie building in the historic Arsenale shipyards is the perfect setting for the Biennale Arts show.

9 Hôtel de Ville, Brussels, Belgium
The 15th-century Town Hall was the first major building on the Grand Place. It retains its original spire, topped by a statue of St Michael killing the devil.

10 Hôtel-Dieu, Beaune, France
This building was founded as a hospice in 1443, after the Hundred Years' War. With its multicoloured Burgundian roof tiles, it is a medieval gem.

Architectural Gems

1 Círculo de Bellas Artes, Madrid, Spain
A building from the golden age of the Arts Club in the 1920s and 1930s, the Círculo promotes all manner of culture.

2 Moscow State University, Moscow, Russia
With four wings converging on a central tower, the university is the largest of Stalin's "Seven Sisters".

3 The Metro, St Petersburg, Russia
The city's metro stations are socialist palaces, complete with chandeliers, marble columns, mosaics and murals.

4 Hackesche Höfe, Berlin, Germany
This complex of 19th-century buildings consists of nine interlinked courtyards, some decorated in Art-Nouveau style.

5 House for an Art Lover, Glasgow, Scotland
Designed in 1901 by Charles Rennie Mackintosh, this innovative house wasn't actually built until 1989.

6 Ca' d'Oro, Venice, Italy
The breathtaking Gothic delicacy of this "golden palace" was crafted by 15th-century stonemasons.

7 Stadsbiblioteket, Stockholm, Sweden
The City Library by Eric Gunnar Asplund is Stockholm's best example of the 1920s Neo-Classicist style.

8 Villa Majorelle, Nancy, France
A combined effort of outstanding Art Nouveau craftmanship, the villa has delightful details throughout.

9 Giotto's Bell Tower, Pisa, Italy
This exquisite masterpiece of the Florentine Renaissance was designed by Giotto to look as if it were painted.

10 Fred and Ginger Building, Prague, Czech Republic
Frank Gehry's building beside the Vltava river, finished in 1996, really does resemble a man and woman dancing together – "Ginger", leaning against her more upright partner, is more evident than "Fred".

Museums and Galleries

1 Musée Rodin, Paris, France
This extensive collection of Rodin's works includes sculptures such as *The Thinker* and *The Burghers of Calais,* which are grouped in the gardens.

2 Villa Giulia, Rome, Italy
The state collection of pre-Roman art, including Etruscan artifacts, is housed in a 16th-century country retreat.

3 V&A Museum, London, England
With 145 astonishingly eclectic galleries, this decorative arts museum is one of London's great pleasures.

4 Louisiana Museum, Copenhagen, Denmark
The museum houses art by modern masters, including Picasso, Giacometti, Francis Bacon and Per Kirkeby.

5 Gorky House Museum, Moscow, Russia
Moscow's finest example of Art Nouveau architecture was presented by Stalin to Maxim Gorky in 1931. It now serves as a museum to the writer.

6 Museum Het Rembrandthuis, Amsterdam, Netherlands
Completely restored to look as it did in Rembrandt's day, the house includes a recreation of the painter's studio and a room devoted to his etchings.

7 Museu del FC Barcelona, Barcelona, Spain
Trophies and other memorabilia celebrate the club's 100-year history.

8 Museo de Bellas Artes, Seville, Spain
Paintings here include early works by Velázquez, Zurbarán, Ribera, El Greco, Murillo and Valdés Leal.

9 Museo Internazionale delle Marionette Antonio Pasqualino, Palermo, Sicily, Italy
Here you'll find examples of puppet traditions from all over the world.

10 Museum of Applied Arts, Budapest, Hungary
Don't miss the Oriental rugs, nor the Zsolnay ceramics or Secessionist furniture in this outstanding museum.

Religious Buildings

1 Igreja de Santa Engrácia, Lisbon, Portugal
One of Lisbon's most uplifting churches, this Baroque beauty is most famous for having taken 284 years to build.

2 Frauenkirche, Munich, Germany
Built in record time (1468–88), the church is the largest Gothic basilica in southern Germany.

3 Church of the Pammakaristos (Fethiye Camii), Istanbul, Turkey
This 12th-century Byzantine church was the centre of the Greek Orthodox faith in the 15th and 16th centuries.

4 Great Synagogue, Budapest, Hungary
Built in Byzantine style in 1854–9, the largest synagogue in Europe is also home to a Jewish Museum.

5 La Mezquita, Córdoba, Spain
Although officially a Christian site for almost nine centuries, La Mezquita's identity as a mosque is inescapable – albeit with a cathedral in its midst.

6 Smolnyy Convent, St Petersburg, Russia
A stunning 19th-century cathedral wit a dome and cupolas topped by gold orbs is the convent's crowning glory.

7 Mosquée de Paris, Paris, France
The city's Grand Mosque was built in the 1920s, its Moorish architecture executed by North African craftsmen.

8 Sa Seu Cathedral, Palma, Mallorca
Dominating the entire port, La Seu Cathedral is the second largest Gothi church in the world.

9 Aachen Cathedral, Germany
Dating from 805, Aachen is the oldes cathedral in Northern Europe, and a worthy celebration of Charlemagne's coronation as Roman Emperor.

10 Reims Cathedral, France
The magnificent early 13th-century Gothic Cathédrale Notre-Dame at Reims is noted for its balance of harmony and monumentality.

âteau de Versailles, France

Art Deco, Prague, Czech Republic

Parc Güell, Barcelona, Spain

Piazza Santa Maria in Trastevere, Rome, Italy

TOP 10 Performing Arts Venues

Musikverein, Vienna, Austria
is grand concert hall was commis-
oned by the Society of Friends of
usic in 1869 as the concerts they
omoted grew in popularity.

Teatro Nacional e la Zarzuela, Madrid, Spain
is beautiful theatre dates from 1856
d was built to stage *zarzuela,* a form
light opera unique to Spain.

Bayerische Staatsoper, unich, Germany
uilt in 1811, the Neo-Classical
tional theatre is famous for
emiering Wagner's operas.

Santa Maria dello Spasimo, cily, Italy
is bombed-out church acts as an
nazing venue for concerts, roman-
ally staged in the roofless nave.

La Scala, Milan, Italy
is glorious 18th-century theatre is
mous throughout the world. It is
here Verdi was house composer and
allas formerly graced the stage.

6 Sadler's Wells, London, England
Arguably the best dance theatre in London, Sadler's Wells also hosts music and opera.

7 Philharmonie, Berlin, Germany
Built in 1963, the seat of the Berlin Philharmonic Orchestra is one of the best concert halls in the world.

8 Hellenic Festival, Epidauros, Greece
The 4th-century BC Theatre of Epidauros is marvellously preserved, with astounding acoustics.

9 Clube de Fado, Lisbon, Portugal
This essential Alfama *fado* venue is owned by *guitarrista* Mário Pacheco, who showcases new stars.

10 Arena di Verona, Italy
A summer night watching the opera here is unforgettable. For these events, the building is transformed into an auditorium for 15,000.

TOP 10 Beaches and Green Spaces

1 Parc Güell, Barcelona, Spain
The esplanade, with its stunning, curved, mosaic bench, is the park's centrepiece. From here there are spectacular views of the entire city.

2 Parc des Buttes Chaumont, Paris, France
This wonderful retreat was created in 1867, with artificial cliffs, waterfalls, streams and a lake island crowned by a Roman-style temple.

3 Hampstead Heath, London, England
This green grandstand overlooking the city is a rural mix of meadows, woods, lakes and ponds for swimming.

4 Englischer Garten, Munich, Germany
The largest urban park in Germany, this garden, meadow and lake haven is a complete leisure paradise in summer.

5 National Gardens, Athens, Greece
The winding paths of the lush National Gardens are a great place to stroll.

6 Pirita Beach, Tallinn, Estonia
Stretching east from the Pirita river is this lovely ribbon of silver sand.

7 Jardin de la Villa Ephrussi de Rothschild, St-Jean-Cap-Ferrat, France
This sumptuous garden with seven geographically themed areas is rich with plants, sculptures and fountains.

8 Koločep Island, Dubrovnik, Croatia
One of the Elafiti Islands, Koločep's main attractions are a sandy beach, two small villages and dense woods.

9 Villa Borghese, Rome, Italy
Extensive, elegant and full of shady glades and beautiful fountains, this is a great park for a stroll, a picnic or a jog.

10 Långholmen, Stockholm, Sweden
This hilly island is a locals' favourite for walking, picnics, swimming and recreation. The island has beaches and open-air stages, and there are fine views from its eastern shores.

TOP 10 Special Spots

Pfaueninsel, Berlin, Germany
eacock Island, in the middle of
Vannsee, was a love nest for Friedrich
Vilhelm II in the 19th century.

Ile St-Louis, Paris, France
nis tiny island in the Seine has
uperb little art galleries, boutiques,
nd a village-like atmosphere.

Castelo, Lisbon, Portugal
he view from under the umbrella
ines on the castle's esplanade takes
Alfama, the Baixa, Bairro Alto on the
ll opposite, and the river.

Piazza Santa Maria in rastevere, Rome, Italy
perfect neighbourhood square:
afés, shops, a fine restaurant and
17th-century palazzo abutting a
edieval church, its mosaics
omantically floodlit at night.

Plaça Comercial, arcelona, Spain
he buzzy Passeig del Born culminates
Plaça Comercial, an inviting square
otted with cafés and bars.

6 Bloemenmarkt, Amsterdam, Netherlands
One of Amsterdam's most picturesque sights, the floating flower market is a magnet for visitors and locals alike.

7 Campiello del Remer, Venice, Italy
This delightful square faces the Grand Canal and boasts Byzantine features such as the wellhead of Verona stone.

8 Piazza Bellini, Naples, Italy
With café tables lined up on the sunny side and elegant architecture all around, this is Naples' most inviting square.

9 Thames Path, South Bank, London, England
From the London Eye, walk along the riverside to London Bridge and the Design Museum at Butler's Wharf.

10 Çukurcuma, Galatasaray, Istanbul, Turkey
Many travellers fall in love with this charming old quarter of Beyoğlu, with its stalls of antiques and second-hand wares spilling onto the streets.

TOP 10 Shopping

1 Kaufhaus des Westens (KaDeWe), Berlin, Germany
On eight floors, KaDeWe offers more than three million products in Europe's largest temple of consumption.

2 Liberty, London, England
Long associated with the Arts and Crafts movement, Liberty is great for floral fabrics, furnishings and fashion.

3 Via dei Condotti, Rome, Italy
Here, all the biggest names in *haute couture* have staked out their turf, from Gucci to Bulgari, Prada to Armani, and Hermès to Ferragamo.

4 Patrimonio Comunal Olivarero, Madrid, Spain
Spain is the world's largest producer of olive oil; this grower's cooperative shop is the place to get the best of it.

5 Art Deco, Prague, Czech Republic
Attire yourself in Jazz-Age style, right down to the spats and cigarette holder, or dress up your parlour with an Art Nouveau clock or cordial set.

6 Quadrilatero d'Oro, Milan, Italy
Via Montenapoleone, Via Borgospesso and Via della Spiga are the streets where you'll find the hometown boutiques of fashion labels such as Prada, Armani, Versace and all the rest.

7 Le Bon Marché, Paris, France
Paris's first department store was founded in 1852. Its in-store boutique has wonderful avant-garde fashions.

8 El Born, Barcelona, Spain
Amid El Born's web of streets are all sorts of art and design shops, plus clothing and shoe boutiques.

9 Napul'é (nativity figures), Naples, Italy
This little workshop is a place to see craftsmen at work, refining the lifelike details of wonderful nativity figures.

10 Nørrebro, Copenhagen, Denmark
Check out the shops located around Sankt Hans Torv for the best second-hand stores and chic boutiques.

Best of the Rest: Out of Town

Top 10 Towns and Villages

1 Galway, Ireland
The pleasant, bustling regional capital has a great atmosphere, with plenty of music and traditional shops.

2 Fontaine-de-Vaucluse, Provence, France
The "*fontaine*" is actually Europe's most powerful natural spring, which gives birth to the River Sorgue. It's a spectacular setting for a lovely village.

3 Pélekas, Corfu, Greece
Pélekas is a picturesque village of bougainvillea-covered stone houses, olive groves and vineyards, with traditional tavernas and small hotels.

4 Girona, Spain
The old town's atmospheric Jewish quarter (El Call) is one of the best-preserved medieval enclaves in Europe. Girona's cathedral is a must.

5 Almonaster La Real, Andalucía, Spain
This lovely *pueblo blanco* looks like a sprinkling of snow amid the green of the surrounding forests.

6 Alcalá de Henares, Spain
Designated a UNESCO World Heritage Site for its splendid Renaissance and Baroque architecture, the town is also the birthplace of Miguel de Cervantes.

7 Petralia Soprana, Sicily, Italy
Narrow alleyways are filled with the aroma of traditional cinnamon biscuits being baked, while the vistas of the rolling mountains are breathtaking.

8 Marechiaro, Italy
This fishing village is ever popular, with its ancient ruins, restaurants and a celebrated panoramic vista of Vesuvius.

9 Tittmoning, Germany
Two city gates lead to a trapezoidal town square with stuccoed houses – one of the most beautiful small towns in bucolic eastern Bavaria.

10 Haarlem, Amsterdam, Netherlands
Centred around the Grote Markt, with its buzzing pavement cafés and lovely buildings, the historic centre of this lively, well-heeled city is a delight.

Top 10 Castles and Museums

1 Musée International de la Parfumerie, Grasse, France
One of the star exhibits in this 3,000-year history of perfume is Marie-Antoinette's travelling kit.

2 Musée du Mobilier Miniature, Vendeuvre, France
This collection of meticulously crafted miniature furniture is housed in the orangery of Château de Vendeuvre.

3 Glamis Castle, Scotland
This 17th-century fairytale castle is best known for Duncan's Hall, which provided the setting for the King's murder in Shakespeare's *Macbeth*.

4 Archaeological Museum Pythagóreio, Sámos, Greece
The main attraction here is an impressive collection of pottery dating from the 9th to the 2nd century BC.

5 Museu do Trajo, São Brás de Alportel, Portugal
This delightful ensemble brings together local costumes, papier-mâché dolls and other traditional handicraft.

6 Aranjuez, Spain
The sumptuously decorated Palacio Real, summer residence of Spain's Bourbon rulers, is the highlight here, but the whole town is a gem.

7 Reggia di Caserta, Naples, Italy
This 18th-century palace was built by the Bourbons and is Neapolitan Baroque at its most refined.

8 Burghausen, Germany
Burghausen experienced its heyday in the Middle Ages, when it was a centre of the salt trade. Its enormous castle, dating to 1255, dominates the town.

9 Gödöllő Palace, Hungary
The 18th-century Royal Palace at Gödöllő today hosts a museum and a theatre for open-air concerts.

10 Design Museum Gent, Ghent, Belgium
Charted here are the changing styles of decorative arts, from the domestic elegance of the 17th century to irreverence in Milanese Post-Modernism.

Top 10 Religious Buildings

1 Chapelle du Rosaire de Vence, Provence, France
The white interior walls of this chapel are adorned with line drawings of the Stations of the Cross by Henri Matisse, who designed this building in 1949.

2 La Trinité, Fécamp, France
This austerely beautiful church owes its vast scale to a casket containing the Holy Blood of Christ, which has drawn pilgrims for centuries.

3 Monestir de Montserrat, Spain
The dramatic mount of Montserrat, with its remote monastery of 1025, is a place of pilgrimage for Catalans.

4 Santa Iglesia Catedral del Salvador, Orihuela, Spain
Orihuela's Gothic cathedral of pale stone was begun in the 14th century.

5 Cappella degli Scrovegni, Padua, Italy
Beneath a sky-blue vault studded with gold stars are Giotto's vibrant frescoes narrating the lives of Mary and Jesus.

6 Cathedral, Cefalù, Sicily, Italy
Famous for its Byzantine mosaic decoration, the church was founded in thanks for safe voyage by the Norman King Roger II in the mid-12th century.

7 Kloster Andechs, Germany
Situated on a hill above the eastern shore of the Ammersee, this monastery is an important pilgrimage site – it also brews very good beer.

8 Osios Loukas, Greece
Looking across a valley to the soaring Elikonas mountains, and with superb Byzantine frescoes within, this is perhaps the finest monastery in Greece.

9 St Andrew's, Dacre, England
This 12th-century church has a Viking monument and four bear statues to guard each corner of the churchyard.

10 San Galgano, Montesiepi, Italy
This roofless 13th-century abbey honours a 12th-century soldier who plunged his sword into a stone to mark the end of his warrior ways.

Top 10 Gardens and Forests

1 Jardins de Bellevue, Normandy, France
Two national collections of Himalayan blue poppies and Lenten roses are included in these lovely gardens.

2 Domaine du Rayol, Rayol-Canadel, Provence, France
On one of the most magnificent sites on the coast, Rayol offers an overview of Mediterranean-style plant life.

3 Inverewe Gardens, Loch Ewe, Scotland
These world-famous gardens were nurtured into astonishing fertility in 1862 on the shores of on Loch Ewe.

4 Villa Carlotta, Lake Como, Italy
These romantic lakeside gardens are a delightful mix of terraces, statues, fountains, staircases and splendid views.

5 Monti dell'Uccellina, Tuscany, Italy
Tuscany's greatest protected parkland is a large area of pine forests, teeming with wild boar and other animals.

6 Lahemaa National Park, Estonia
Estonia's archetypal dense forests, boggy heaths and boulder-strewn coastline all meet in this national park

7 Keukenhof, Netherlands
Climaxing in mid-April when the tulips flower, a coastal strip between Leiden and Haarlem bursts into spring colour

8 Holker Hall, Lake District, England
These gardens combine structured and informal elements, such as stepped water cascades mixed with patches of ancient woodland.

9 Avondale Forest Park, Ireland
The beautiful forest park is criss-crossed with trails, some of them along the banks of the River Avonmor

10 Monserrate, Portugal
These gardens blend natural and artificial elements, and the exotic and the familiar. Just look at the artificial "ruin in the lower garden or at the rolling lawns flanked by tropical trees.

la Carlotta, Lake Como, Italy

Hydra Town, Island of Hydra, Greece

Glamis Castle, Scotland

Girona, Spain

TOP 10 Lakes, Rivers and Mountains

Parc Naturel Régional des oucles de la Seine Normande, ormandy, France
ıllowing the snaking loops of the eine, this park embraces forests chards, pastures and wetlands.

Mont Ventoux, rovence, France
ıe barren peak of Mont Ventoux, 1,910 m (6,260 ft), often features amatically in the Tour de France.

Aiguilles de Bavella, Corsica, rance
phalanx of seven mighty pinnacles, e needle-shaped peaks of Bavella ok like a fantastical vision.

Parc Natural de la Zona 'olcànica de la Garrotxa, Spain
is magical here in spring when ıousands of butterflies emerge om this volcanic landscape.

Loch Skeen, Scotland
ıe hidden treasure at the end of an tterly magical walk, Loch Skeen is a ny loch high up in moorland hills.

6 Eibsee, Germany
Embedded in the rocky landscape of the Zugspitz massif, the deep blue waters of Eibsee lie nearly 1,000 m (3,300 ft) above sea level.

7 Tejo Estuary, Portugal
This marshland area is one of Europe's 10 most important staging sites for migrating water birds.

8 Corinth Canal, Greece
The isthmus connecting mainland Greece to the Peloponnese frustrated sailors for thousands of years until 1893, when French engineers dynamited their way through the rock.

9 Racó del Duc, Costa Blanca, Spain
An old railway line has been converted into an excellent walking and cycling path which follows the River Serpis.

10 River Esk, Eskdale, Lake District, England
The course of River Esk, framed by stone bridges, is punctuated by natural pools that are perfect for a dip.

TOP 10 Islands

1 St Kilda, Scotland
Scotland's first World Heritage Site, this archipelago of monumental cliffs was, until 1930, inhabited by a highly individual community who lived off the islands' millions of seabirds.

2 Brač, Croatia
Marble from this mountainous island just off Split was used for Diocletian's Palace, the Hungarian Parliament and the White House in Washington DC.

3 Lampedusa, Sicily, Italy
The tiny islet Isola dei Conigli, off Lampedusa, and the bay in between are a nature reserve for sea turtles.

4 Porquerolles, Iles d'Hyères, Provence, France
The car-free idyll of Porquerolles is a paradise of vineyards, olive groves, scented forests and glorious beaches.

5 Grímsey, Iceland
At Iceland's northernmost point the sun really does not set here for a few days either side of 21 June; and it does not rise at all in late December.

6 Illa de Cabrera, Mallorca, Spain
Rocky, bare "Goat Island" served as a prison camp during the Napoleonic War and was used as a base by Barbary pirates.

7 Hydra, Greece
Lovely Hydra town, its cobbled paths and old mansions clustered around the clear-watered harbour, is one of Greece's most beautiful spots.

8 Ischia, Italy
The island of Ischia is surmounted by an extinct 788-m (2,585-ft) volcano, Monte Epomeo, and there are many hot mineral springs on the island.

9 Isla de Benidorm, Costa Blanca, Spain
The island is a marine reserve and home to a fabulous array of sea life.

10 Clare and Inishbofin Islands, Ireland
These islands were great hideaways and Clare was the stronghold of the infamous pirate Grace O'Malley.

TOP 10 Beaches

Calanque d'En-Vau, Cassis, France
Calanques" are inlets formed where ıe chalk cliffs plunge to the sea, and n-Vau is the prettiest of these.

2 Barneville-Plage, Normandy, France
t Barneville-Plage the coastline ecomes tame enough for a holiday each, full to bursting in summer, nd backed by lines of villas.

3 Plage du Loto, Corsica, France
Catch a boat from St-Florent to reach his splendid beach, with shining white sand and turquoise waters.

4 Psilí Ámmos Beach, Pátmos, Greece
Pretty Psilí Ámmos beach lives up to s name ("fine sand"), while the sea ere is shallow and crystal clear.

5 Praia de Odeceixe, Algarve, Portugal
One of the Algarve's best kept secrets, this crescent-shaped beach is sheltered and wonderfully uncrowded.

6 Cabo de Gata, Andalucía, Spain
Almería Province offers some of the finest beaches in the region, centred on Cabo de Gata Natural Park.

7 Vendicari, Sicily, Italy
This spectacular nature reserve offers sandy beaches set around a 15th-century Aragonese tower.

8 Pärnu, Estonia
The resort dubs itself "Estonia's summer capital", with visitors drawn to a glorious stretch of sandy beach.

9 Cala Sant Vicenç, Mallorca, Spain
The area consists of three coves – Cala Sant Vicenç, Cala Barques and Cala Molins – all of which are good, with an appealing aura of intimacy.

10 Dunas de Guardamar, Costa Blanca, Spain
These windswept dunes are rarely crowded, even in summer. They are part of a natural reserve backed by a pine forest with walking trails.

TOP 10 Food, Wine and Crafts

1 Distilleries and Domaines de Provence, France
Provence is the home of Bardouin *pastis*, which uses 50 herbs and spices in addition to the requisite star anise.

2 House of Waterford Crystal, Waterford, Ireland
This centre opened in 2010 to feature specialist glassblowing and cutting in a town with a glass-making pedigree.

3 Domaine Gentile, Corsica
Classic Corsican wines, including one of the island's top muscats, are produced according to strict organic principles in this region.

4 Porches Pottery, Algarve, Portugal
The blue and white façade of the building is unmistakable, and the pottery from here is equally striking.

5 Alt Penedès, Spain
Catalonia's most famous wine region is the *cava*-producing Penedès, and Cordoníu bodega is one of the most spectacular wineries to visit here.

6 Taracea Woodwork, Granada, Spain
Granada's Moorish-inspired marquetry uses bone, mother-of-pearl, amber and marble in the finest inlays.

7 Embutidos, Murcia, Spain
Murcia is celebrated for its cured pork sausages *(embutidos)*, including a dark blood sausage known as *morcilla*.

8 Sandalmakers, Capri, Italy
Cobblers jollier than these would be hard to find. Pick out a design and within a few hours you'll have your own made-to-measure sandals.

9 Lavender, Hvar Island, Croatia
This fragrant plant has been cultivated on Hvar for the past 75 years, and the myriad oils and balms that are produced provide an important source of revenue for the islanders.

10 Ribatejo Wine Route, Portugal
Some of the best wine producers in the Ribatejo region are on the bank of the Tejo, just north of Vila Franca de Xira, around Almeirim and Alpiarça.

Hotels and Restaurants

Top 10 Hotels: City Luxury

1 Eden, Rome, Italy
The celebrity choice for decades, every detail oozes refinement, and a superb rooftop restaurant/bar gazes down on entire city. *www.edenroma.com*

2 Hotel Arts, Barcelona, Spain
Barcelona's *grande dame* hotel is just steps away from the sea, with ample, sumptuous rooms and top-notch dining. *www.hotelartsbarcelona.com*

3 Ritz, Madrid, Spain
Madrid's oldest luxury hotel breathes refined comfort and impeccable service. The Belle Epoque decor is best viewed in the dining room. *www.ritz.es*

4 Hôtel de Crillon, Paris, France
With one of the best locations in Paris, one of the best restaurants and one of the best reputations, the Crillon is pure perfection. *www.crillon.com*

5 Hotel Sacher, Vienna, Austria
A Viennese institution since 1876, the Sacher still ranks among Vienna's most luxurious. All rooms are individually furnished. *www.sacher.com*

6 Savoy, London, England
Fortunate in its riverside setting, the Savoy is London's top traditional hotel, now restored to its original Art Deco splendour. *www.fairmont.com/savoy*

7 Hotel Palace, Berlin, Germany
The luxurious hotel in the Europa-Center is a real find. All rooms are exquisitely designed, and the staff is unobtrusive and very helpful. *www.palace.de*

8 Ritz Four Seasons, Lisbon, Portugal
Not the best location or the most character, but few hotels offer better service. *www.fourseasons.com/lisbon*

9 Miramare, Naples, Italy
This modernized hotel retains its Art Nouveau style, and has stunning views of the bay. *www.hotelmiramare.com*

10 The Dylan, Amsterdam, Netherlands
It's tucked behind the historical façades of Keizersgracht's canal houses, with a lovely courtyard and a Michelin-starred restaurant. *www.dylanamsterdam.com*

Top 10 Hotels: Beside the Seaside

1 Grecotel Corfu Imperial, Corfu, Greece
Set in gardens on its own private peninsula, this charming hotel has fabulous sea-view rooms and gourmet dining. *www.grecotel.com*

2 Hideaway Hotel, Kaş, Turkey
This appealing hotel has a great rooftop terrace where guests enjoy excellent local cuisine. *www.hotelhideaway.com*

3 Saunton Sands Hotel, Devon, England
The stunning location above the beach is the biggest draw of this clifftop hotel. *www.brend-hotels.co.uk*

4 Hotel Al Sur, Calabardina, Spain
Set in a quiet village, with a seductive Arabic feel. Beaches and restaurants are just steps away. *www.halsur.com*

5 Heliotrope Hotel, Lésvos, Greece
Standing in beachside gardens, this hotel has a seawater pool and offers hydro massage. *www.heliotrope.gr*

6 Hotel Petit, Cala Fornells, Mallorca, Spain
This hotel offers panoramic views, terraces with splashing fountains, four pools, a small secluded beach and its own cove. *www.petitcalafornells.com*

7 Villa Angelica, Ischia, Italy
Set on an island in the Bay of Naples, this hotel has its own spa, and the sea is on your doorstep. *www.villaangelica.it*

8 Hotel Playa de la Luz, Rota, Spain
This hotel is on an unspoiled beach nestled between pine forests and sand dunes. *www.hotelplayadelaluz.com*

9 Porto Loutro Hotel, Loutro, Crete, Greece
In two buildings set amongst palms, bougainvillea and tamarisk trees, this attractive hotel is accessible only by boat. *www.hotelportoloutro.com*

10 Lilium Maris, Corsica, France
This modern hotel on the water's edge overlooks the magnificent Tizzano beach. *www.lilium-maris.com*

Top 10 Hotels: Get Away From It All

1 Alquería de los Lentos, Niguelas, Spain
In the foothills of the Sierra Nevada surrounded by orchards, this 16th-century mill has its own organic restaurant. *www.alquerialoslentos.com*

2 Casa Musicale, Corsica, France
Wake to the tinkling of sheeps' bells in this gem of a small hotel, with lovely, bright rooms. *www.casa-musicale.org*

3 Hotel Rural Las Calas, San Mateo, Gran Canaria
This handsome traditional village building is well situated for exploring the mountains. *www.hotelrurallascalas.com*

4 Quinta das Barradas, Algarve, Spain
This charming group of converted barns is perfect for getting away from it all. *www.quintadasbarradas.com*

5 Moulin de la Camandoule, Fayence, France
Hidden away among vines and pines, this converted olive mill is an idyllic hotel. *www.camandoule.com*

6 Tenuta Gangivecchio, Sicily, Italy
The estate deep in the Madonie mountains was founded as an abbey in 1363. *www.gangivecchio.org*

7 Hótel Rangá, Hella, Iceland
A spendid countryside retreat with luxury pine cabins. Great for Northern Lights viewing. *www.hotelranga.is*

8 Castello Ripa d'Orcia, San Quirico d'Orcia, Italy
This converted 13th-century castle is nestled in the green hills of a nature reserve. *www.castelloripadorcia.com*

9 Flodigarry Country House, Skye, Scotland
Close to the sea, this 19th-century mansion retains many period features. Marvellous views from the sunny conservatory. *www.flodigarry.co.uk*

10 Swissotel Göcek Marina Resort, Göcek, Turkey
This secluded, country-mansion-style hotel has its own private beach and marina. *www.gocek.swissotel.com*

Top 10 Hotels: Unusual Places

1 Hotel Bloom!, Paris, France
All-white rooms in this hip, modern hotel near the Gard du Nord each have a fresco painted by a young European artist. *www.hotelbloom.com*

2 Struga Lighthouse, Lastovo, Croatia
Four apartments in this attractive 1839 lighthouse can sleep two to five people. On a remote island. *www.adriatica.net*

3 Castle Venlaw, Peebles, Scotland
A luxury boutique hotel in an 18th-century Scottish castle. One turret houses a bar. *www.venlaw.co.uk*

4 Amsterdam House, Netherlands
Treat the kids to a stay on a houseboat. Amsterdam House has eight of them available. *www.amsterdamhouse.com*

5 Botel Racek, Prague, Czech Republic
Floating on the Vltava's right bank, the Racek offers 86 rooms, a restaurant and a top-deck disco. *www.botelracek.eu*

6 1898, Barcelona, Spain
A 19th-century tobacco factory houses this chic hotel, which cleverly combines original fittings with 21st-century amenities. *www.barcelonahotel1898.com*

7 Accademia Villa Maravege, Venice, Italy
Book well ahead to stay in this lovely 17th-century villa near the Accademia. *www.pensioneaccademia.it*

8 The Rookery, London, England
A warren of rooms comprises this brilliant hotel that evokes Victorian London. *www.rookeryhotel.com*

9 York House, Lisbon, Portugal
This former 17th-century convent was turned into a boarding house by two Yorkshire women in the 19th century. *www.yorkhouselisboa.com*

10 Park Plaza Wallstreet, Berlin, Germany
The Wall Street theme manifests itself in dollar-bill carpets, stockbroker murals and business maxims on the walls. *www.parkplaza.com/berlinde_wallstrasse*

York House, Lisbon, Portugal

Savoy, London, England

Botín, Madrid, Spain

I Due Roccoli, Lake Iseo, Italy

TOP 10 Restaurants: Fine Dining

1 Primo al Pigneto, Rome, Italy
Italy's best gourmet guide lists this as one of the top ten restaurants serving gourmet Italian cuisine at a reasonable price. ✆ 06 701 3827

2 Rules, London, England
London's oldest restaurant (1798) is like a Victorian time capsule. Game is a speciality, and the English roast beef is the best in London. ✆ 020 7836 5314

3 Santceloni, Madrid, Spain
The sleek Madrid outpost of renowned Catalan chef Santi Santamaría. Booking is essential. ✆ 1 210 8840

4 Papagalos Restaurant, Santoríni, Greece
One of the best on the island and among the 50 best in Greece uses seafood straight from the sea and local organic produce. ✆ 22860 71469

5 Tantris, Munich, Germany
In what is arguably one of the best restaurants in the world, Hans Haas's philosophy of gastronomic pleasure is unequalled anywhere. ✆ www.tantris.de

6 Royal Yacht Britannia, Edinburgh, Scotland
The Queen's former floating home and Britain's roving royal court. Take tea and cucumber sandwiches on the Royal Deck. ✆ www.royalyachtbritannia.co.uk

7 L'Astrance, Paris, France
There is probably no more coveted table in Paris. Book a month ahead for lunch, two months for dinner. ✆ 01 40 50 84 40

8 Noma, Copenhagen, Denmark
René Redzepi's culinary wonderland has consistently been voted the world's best restaurant, serving extraordinary Nordic fare. ✆ www.noma.dk

9 Holbeck Ghyll Country House Hotel, Windermere, England
Perhaps the best restaurant in the region. Try the seven-course taster menu. ✆ 015394 32375

10 Louis XV, Monte Carlo, Monaco
France's leading chefs work Provençale cuisine into a sensual art form. If you have to think about the cost, you're in the wrong place. ✆ 003 77 98 06 88 64

TOP 10 Restaurants: Cheap and Cheerful

1 Da Bucatino, Rome, Italy
This old-school trattoria has wood-panelled walls and wooden tables. Service is loud and quick – the way the Romans like it. ✆ 06 574 6886

2 Bojo, Amsterdam, Netherlands
Inexpensive, informal and Indonesian – head here after most of the city's restaurants are shut. ✆ 020 622 7434

3 Osteria La Chiacchera, Florence, Italy
Remarkably cheap and no cover charge. The *cucina povera* ("poor people's cooking") and great desserts change daily. ✆ 0577 280 631

4 Thanassis, Athens, Greece
Athens' most famous *souvlaki* joint has been piling hot, juicy beef slathered with cool garlicky *tzatziki* into pittas since the 19th century. ✆ Mitropoleos 67

5 Botticelli, Dublin, Ireland
A genuine Italian, run by Italians. The simple menu has all the old favourites – a good, reasonably priced place for lunch or dinner. ✆ 01 672 7289

6 Rock and Sole Plaice, London, England
This is simply the best place in central London for traditional British fish and chips. ✆ 020 7836 3785

7 Le Petit Rétro, Paris, France
Cosy atmosphere in this 1900s bistro, and affordable prices. The *Blanquette de Veau* is delicious. ✆ 01 44 05 06 05

8 Leander, Berlin, Germany
This romantic bistro with an old-world feel is great at any time of day. The food is creative and cosmopolitan – and a bargain to boot. ✆ 030 29 00 48 03

9 Universal, Prague, Czech Republic
Serving substantial meals at small prices, it is especially recommended for its vegetarian dishes. ✆ 224 934416

10 Saffron, Truro, Cornwall, England
This friendly bistro serves local produce and organic beer. Express lunches and early-evening menus are good value. ✆ www.saffronrestauranttruro.co.uk

TOP 10 Restaurants: Local/Regional Cuisine

1 Botín, Madrid, Spain
In business since 1725, with original decor including *azulejo* tiles, Botín is famous for Castilian fare. ✆ 91 366 4217

2 Kouyiouka Watermill Restaurant, Paphos, Cyprus
Housed in a delightful 200-year-old former watermill, Kouyiouka serves traditional Cypriot meals. ✆ 26 632 847

3 A Pignata, Alta Rocca, Corsica, France
A restaurant-with-rooms serving great local cuisine in an idyllic rural setting. Try the perfect slow-roasted lamb with *cannelloni au brocciu*. ✆ 04957 84190

4 Plachutta, Vienna, Austria
For the ultimate *tafelspitz* (a spiced, simmered beef steak), go to one of the branches of Plachutta scattered across Vienna. ✆ 01 512 1577

5 Piperno, Rome, Italy
Roman Jewish cooking in the Ghetto since 1856. Quite pricy, and service can be a bit off-hand, but the artichokes can't be beaten. ✆ 06 6880 6629

6 Na Zdorovie! St Petersburg, Russia
Serving fresh, delicious Russian food at reasonable prices, Na Zdorovie! ("To your health!") needs no gimmicks to recommend it. ✆ 812 232 4039

7 Chez Madie, Marseille, France
Order your *bouillabaisse* 48 hours in advance, and dine on the terrace overlooking the port. ✆ 04 91 90 40 87

8 Alabárdos Étterem, Budapest, Hungary
From the goose-liver terrine to the delicious chicken paprika with curd strudel, everything on the menu is authentic. ✆ www.alabardos.hu

9 Patsouras, Kefalloniá, Greece
Dine in the courtyard on a delicious local dish, *krasáto* – pork cooked slowly in local wine with herbs. ✆ 26710 22779

10 Cantina Siciliana, Trapani, Sicily, Italy
Chef Pino Maggiore serves Trapani's classic *kus kus al pesce* (fish couscous). ✆ 0923 28 673

TOP 10 Restaurants: Food with a View

1 Portrait Restaurant, London, England
Enjoy fine British fare in the National Portait Gallery, with views over Trafalgar Square and Whitehall. ✆ 020 7312 2490

2 Grand Canal, Hotel Monaco, Venice, Italy
The traditional Venetian and Italian cuisine is of a very high standard. The setting, a terrace on the Grand Canal, is simply stunning. ✆ 041 520 02 11

3 I Due Roccoli, Iseo, Italy
Dine on the terracotta terrace high in the hills above Lake Iseo, with views across a rose-fringed lawn to forested mountains beyond. ✆ 030-982-2977

4 Mirador de Aixa, Granada, Spain
The food is a celebration of local dishes, and there are views of the Alhambra from the terrace. ✆ 958 22 36 16

5 Mirandus, Lagos, Portugal
This enchanting gourmet restaurant is perched on a clifftop, with fabulous views out to sea. ✆ 282 763 222

6 Mikla, Istanbul, Turkey
Reserve a terrace table at this stylish rooftop restaurant for the perfect view of the Golden Horn. ✆ 0212 293 56 56

7 Bens d'Avall, Deià-Sóller, Mallorca, Spain
Fresh fish is cooked in a wood-burning oven, and the terrace affords one of the island's best views. ✆ 971 632381

8 Zlatna Ribica, Brodarica, Croatia
Fresh fish is the speciality, with grilled platters and *brodet* (fish stew with polenta), plus a stunning view over the island of Krapanj. ✆ 020 3027 7154

9 Coast@Gironda, Kalkan, Turkey
Coast serves traditional Turkish cuisine and modern dishes fusing Turkish with Thai and European elements. There are lovely sea views. ✆ 0242 844 12 98

10 Kona, Ercolano, Italy
Dine on local seafood with a splendid view of the Gulf of Naples from the lovely terrace. ✆ 081 777 39 68

TOP 10 WORLD

THE AMERICAS

Brazil
Copacabana Beach, Rio de Janeiro

Boston

"The Hub", "Beantown" or "Baaahstin" – call it what you want, New England's largest city exists to be explored. Its colonial-era architecture, vibrant seafaring heritage and irrepressible Yankee character make it one of the country's most distinctive locales. Yet for all its big-city amenities – world-class restaurants, museums and shops – Boston remains surprisingly compact and eminently walkable.

1 The Freedom Trail

Boston's best walking tour is free, self-guided, chock-full of history and open all year round. Just follow the painted red stripe threading its way past historic buildings such as the Massachusetts State House *(left)*.

Top 10 Moments in History

1 1630: Boston Founded
Under the leadership of John Winthrop, English Puritans colonized the Shawmut Peninsula. Their city was named in honour of their leaders' home town.

2 1636: Harvard Created
Boston's leaders established a college at Newtowne (later Cambridge) to educate future generations of clergy. When young Charlestown minister John Harvard died two years later he left his books and half his money to the college, and it was renamed.

3 1775: Revolution
Over a decade of friction between colonists and the crown led to British troops marching on Lexington. Forewarned by Paul Revere, local militia, known as the Minute Men, fought back. In the second confrontation at Concord, the "shot heard round the world" marked the start of the Revolution.

4 1845: Irish Arrived
Irish fleeing the potato famine arrived in Boston in their tens of thousands. By 1900 they were the dominant ethnic group. The flexing of their political muscle led ultimately to the election of John F. Kennedy as president in 1960.

5 1848: Boston Public Library Founded
The Boston Public Library was established as the first publicly supported municipal library in the US.

6 1863: Black Boston Went to War
Following decades of agitation to abolish slavery, Boston sent the country's first African-American regiment to join Union forces in the Civil War. The regiment is honoured by the Shaw Memorial.

7 1897: Subway Opened
The Tremont Street subway, the first in the US, opened on 1 September 1897 to ease road congestion. It cost $4.4 million to construct and the initial fare was five cents.

8 1958: Freedom Trail Opened
This historical walking tour was based on a 1951 *Boston Herald Traveler* column by William Scofield, and was the first of its kind in the US.

9 2004: Sox Win
The Boston Red Sox overcame an alleged 86-year-old sporting curse to win baseball's World Series for the first time since 1918. The team thrilled fans of "Red Sox Nation" by winning again in 2007.

10 2008: The Big Dig
A $15 billion highway project to alleviate traffic congestion gave the city new parks and the soaring Zakim Bridge, the world's widest cable-stayed bridge. But sinkholes and other flaws may push the final bill over $22 billion.

2 Isabella Stewart Gardner Museum

The works of Rembrandt, Botticelli and Sargent appear all the more masterful in Isabella Stewart Gardner's Venetian-style palazzo. The courtyard's myriad treasures *(above)* includ an ancient Roman marble sarcophagus dating to AD 222.

3 New England Aquarium

Get personal with penguins, harbour seals and many other creatures of the deep. The 900,000-litre (200,000-gallo Giant Ocean Tank is the centrepiece of the aquarium, but there are plenty of specialized exhibits, including one devote to the many types of environment found in coral reefs *(above*

4 Harvard University

Boston may have its famous blue blood, but neighbouring Cambridge claims the Harvard Crimson. Pumping vigorously since 1636, the undisputed heart of American academia *(left)* has cultivated some of the world's greatest thinkers.

5 Charlestown Navy Yard

Boston's deep harbour made it ideal for one of the US Navy's first shipyards. USS *Constitution*, the most famous of the yard's progeny, is still docked here.

6 Trinity Church

This Neo-Romanesque church is regarded as the finest execution of architect H H Richardson's distinctive style. *David's Charge to Solomon (above)* is among the glorious works of stained glass here.

7 Museum of Fine Arts, Boston

The MFA, Boston's queen of the visual arts scene, boasts some of the most extensive collections of Japanese, ancient Egyptian and Impressionist works of art in the world. Van Gogh's *Houses at Auvers* is just one of many treasures in the European Art collection.

8 Around Newbury Street

This is where fashionistas share the sidewalk with punk rockers. Nowhere are the city's myriad fashions, faces and fortunes on more vibrant display than in the vicinity of Newbury Street *(above)*.

9 Boston Common and Public Garden

Swan boats drift beneath weeping willows, children lash in fountains and a bronzed General George Washington ersees the proceedings from his lofty steed *(above)*.

0 Faneuil Hall Marketplace

What was once a dilapidated, post-revolutionary ercantile area now sets the standard for urban-renewal ojects worldwide. It boasts an indoor food court in uincy Market *(above)*, shops and street performers.

TOP 10 Boston Harbor Islands

1 Georges Island
This is the gateway to Boston Harbor Islands National Park, an archipelago of 30 islands.

2 Grape and Bumpkin Islands
Both are naturalist's delights for wild flowers and bird life. On Bumpkin are the ruins of a 19th-century hospital that also held German prisoners captured in Boston Harbor during World War I.

3 Lovells Island
Known for its dunes, Lovells also has a swimming beach and hiking trails. The remains of Fort Standish, active in the Spanish American War and World War I, can be explored.

4 Peddocks Island
Hiking trails circle a pond, and cross salt marsh and coastal forest. Look out for black-crowned night herons.

5 Deer Island
Accessed by a causeway, part of this island is open for recreation – with dramatic views of the Boston skyline.

6 Spectacle Island
This has some of the highest peaks of the Harbor Islands and the best skyline view.

7 Little Brewster Island
Boston Light, the first US lighthouse, was built here in 1716. Tours visit the museum and the top of the Light.

8 Gallops Island
The island has an extensive sandy beach, a picnic area, hiking paths, and historic ruins of a former quarantine and immigration station.

9 Thompson Island
A learning centre since the 1830s, the island has a salt marsh and hardwood forest, deer, herons, and shorebirds.

10 World's End
This peninsula overlooking Hingham Bay is geographically very like the Harbor Islands. A 19th-century development planned by Frederick Law Olmsted was never built, but paths, formal plantings, and hedgerows remain.

Buenos Aires

Argentina's romantic, reinvigorated soul, Buenos Aires is La Capital, where tango combos keep time in crowded *milongas* (dance halls), young men cry out deliriously at gargantuan football stadiums and taxis swap lanes across some of the world's widest avenues. Porteños, as the residents of this sophisticated metropolis are called, move to a rhythm all of their own, while making time to dine, dress and even rest extraordinarily well. With spectacular museums, lovely open spaces and rich architecture brimming with history, the city is warm as well as energetic.

1 Plaza de Mayo

This square *(left)* has seen post-World Cup football victory dances as well as the deafening silence of the Mothers of the Plaza de Mayo's weekly marches.

2 Colonia del Sacramento, Uruguay

This picturesque town founded by Portuguese trader is a short hop across the River Plate from Buenos Aires. Its colourful colonial streets, Portuguese architecture and relaxed pace make it a popular weekend spot.

3 Teatro Colón

Having celebrated its centennial under scaffolding, the grandest of all Latin American opera houses *(above)* reopened in 2010 after an exhaustive restoration. El Colón is arguably the most beloved building in all of Argentina.

4 Cementerio de la Recoleta

As monument and metaphor for a country's fortunes, both gained and lost, la Recoleta *(above)* contrasts impeccable mausoleums with crumbling marble tombs.

TOP 10 Moments in History

1 1536: Pedro de Mendoza Arrives
Spanish explorer Mendoza sailed into the River Plate and founded the settlement of Nuestra Señora Santa María del Buen Ayre. In 1541, under attack from the native Querandí, it was abandoned.

2 1810: May Revolution
Buenos Aires led the region's push for freedom from Spain. In May 1810 the Viceroy was ousted by a revolutionary junta. The ensuing war ended in 1816 with the declaration of independence.

3 1877: Beef to Europe
The advent of frozen shipping made Argentina one of the world's wealthiest nations. Buenos Aires was remodelled along European lines as the "Paris of South America."

4 1917: Carlos Gardel records *Mi Noche Triste*
Since the 1890s tango had been the music of Buenos Aires' slum dwellers. In 1917 Gardel's recording of the first sung tango made him a world star and ushered tango into the salons of Paris.

5 1952: Death of Eva María Duarte de Perón
In 1946 Juan Domingo Perón revolutionized Argentina with the support of the country's urban poor. His wife Evita was key to his popularity and achieved saintlike status. Her death in 1952 provoked a huge wave of national grief.

6 1955: Bombing of Plaza de Mayo
After 1952 Perón's regime unravelled, and in 1955 he threatened civil war against his enemies. In the "Liberating Revolution" that followed, the Air Force bombed Plaza de Mayo before ousting Perón.

7 1983: Return of Democracy
The 1976–83 military dictatorship brutalized Argentina. Left-wing forces were crushed and suspected state enemies arrested, taken to secret torture camps and killed. The country's defeat in the Falklands War in 1983 saw civilian rule return.

8 1986: Football World Cup Victory
Argentina's 1986 World Cup victory brought glory to a nation struggling to heal the wounds of military dictatorship and produced a national icon in Diego Maradona.

9 1992: Israeli Embassy Bombing
The bombing of the Israeli Embassy in Buenos Aires left 29 dead. In another Jewish-targeted attack in 1994 the bombing of a cultural centre killed 87.

10 2001: December Riots
In the 1990s Argentina was crippled by foreign debt and a meltdown occurred in 2001. Government restrictions on bank withdrawals led to riots. President Fernando de la Rúa resigned after 27 died.

5 Museo de Arte Latinoamericano de Buenos Aires (MALBA)

The outstanding permanent collection of the museum of Latin American art *(right)*, including works by Diego Rivera and Xul Solar, is augmented by a schedule of temporary exhibitions, plus film screenings and a unique museum gift shop.

6 Museo Nacional de Bellas Artes

The modest scale of this national fine art museum belies a wonderfully curated permanent collection, which ranges from imposing Rodin bronzes to oils depicting the mythical Argentinian Pampas. The collection includes great works by many international artists.

7 San Telmo

Among the city's oldest *barrios*, cobblestoned San Telmo guards the lyrical spirit of the *bodegón* – the quintessentially *porteño* bar/café, where a vermouth or a croissant can be had at any time. Lanes lined with 19th-century homes fill with performers *(above)* on Sundays.

8 Avenida de Mayo

Buenos Aires' prized avenue *(above)* is a feast ›r architecture buffs – it contains the continent's best ›eserved *belle époque*, Art Nouveau and Art Deco ›ddresses. Old bookstores and cafés add to the charm.

9 Avenida 9 de Julio

The grandest of Latin American avenues , flanked by dozens of cultural highlights, the ›iggest of which is Teatro Colón. Take care ›hen crossing its 12-lane width, which takes few traffic-light cycles to accomplish.

10 Tango

Jaunty and humorous or dirge-like and mournful, tango, the capital's dance, musical and poetic art form, is still in full swoon, 120 years after its birth. With classes and performances galore, it is integral to the city's culture and captivates the people of Buenos Aires and the rest of the world *(left)*.

TOP 10 Tango Clubs and Milongas

1 Centro Cultural Torquato Tasso
At this intimate dinner-show venue, vocalists include Adriana Varela, contemporary tango's star. Also try the Sunday night *milonga*.

2 El Querandí
Dinner-tango shows, in a beautifully restored San Telmo building dating from 1867, tell the story of tango from its birth in the city's *bordellos* to its embracement by the world.

3 Tanguería El Beso
Belonging to the city's best tango school, this lovely little *milonga* welcomes dancers of all ages to classes and dances.

4 Niño Bien
At one of the city's most traditional *milongas*, invitations to dance are made by men only, via a series of nods (on the floor, dancers maintaining eye contact) – anything else is bad taste. Expect plenty of tourists.

5 Café de los Angelitos
Opened in 1890, this café hosts cabaret-style dinner-tango extravaganzas to a live six-piece orchestra. The bar has fine stained-glass murals and a mosaic floor.

6 Maldita Milonga
Bring your dancing shoes – this *milonga* holds open classes every Wednesday at 9pm. Performances, with an orchestra, begin at 11pm.

7 Salón Canning
This elegant salon is famed for its parquet floor, rated one of the best in the city. Classes and *milongas* pull in a mixed crowd. Thursday mixes tango with salsa.

8 Nuevo Salón La Argentina
The Nuevo Salon attracts an experienced crowd that dances *al suelo*, feet pegged to the floor in traditional style, with no fancy flicks.

9 El Viejo Almacén
Performances in a colonial house feature traditional and contemporary tangos to a six-piece orchestra. Dinner precedes the shows, and is eaten in a second historical building across the cobbled street.

10 Sin Rumbo
It is worth the trip to this outlying *barrio* of Buenos Aires to experience an authentic neighborhood *milonga*. Reserve ahead as the owners limit numbers to 150, closing the doors after that to guarantee plenty of dancing space.

California Wine Country

Alexander Valley 6 8
Francis Ford Coppola Winery
Calistoga 4
Russian River 7
Culinary Institute of America 9
Santa Rosa 3
The Silverado Tr
CALIFORNIA
The Hess Collection 2
Sonoma State Historic Park 10
1 Napa Wine

The warm, sheltered valleys north of San Francisco, popularly known as Wine Country, offer amazing diversity due to their varied terrain and microclimates. The wineries here produce excellent wines, and many of them even house art galleries and museums. Add to that historic towns with Victorian architecture; recreational activities such as hot-air ballooning and canoeing; plus excellent spas, world-class dining, and fabulous accommodations, and it is easy to understand why Wine Country is one of California's most popular regions.

1 Napa Valley Wine Train

A leisurely sightseeing tour with lunch or dinner aboard this restored historic train *(above)* is a relaxing and romantic way to see the Napa Valley end to end.

2 The Hess Collection

Tucked amid the slopes of Mount Veeder, this winery is renowned as much for its contemporary art collection as for its quality wines.

3 Santa Rosa

The largest city in Wine Country, Santa Rosa has museums, a restored historic district and children's attractions aplenty. Keen horticulturalists will not want to miss the Luther Burbank Home and Gardens *(below)*.

TOP 10 Moments in History

1 First Inhabitants
The region was originally populated by the Wappo and the Pomo. These sedentary hunter-gatherer cultures were almost wiped out by Mexican landlords, smallpox and, later, by gold-rush settlers.

2 Missions Founded
The first Spanish mission in California was established in 1769 at San Diego. Over the following 54 years, 20 more missions were founded along the 650 miles (1,040 km) of El Camino Real.

3 Bear Flag Revolt
On 14 June 1846 US settlers in Sonoma declared California an independent republic. Their flag featured a grizzly bear facing a red star. Nine days later, the US Army occupied the region.

4 First Vines Planted
The first vines were planted here in the late 18th century, grown from cuttings brought to Mexico in 1520 by Hernán Cortés. The "Mission grape" was the dominant variety until the 20th century.

5 First Winery
In 1857 Hungarian immigrant Agoston Haraszthy, known as the "Father of California Viticulture" for his *Report on the Grapes and Wines of California,* founded the Buena Vista Winery in Sonoma Valley.

6 Railroad Built
Initiated in 1864, the Napa Valley Railroad was financed by magnate Samuel Brannan to bring passengers to his spa resort at Calistoga, which it reached in 1868. Passenger services operated until 1928.

7 Phylloxera
The 1850s phylloxera epidemic that ravaged European vineyards originated in Californian vines. Native species were partially resistant, but their grafting with European vines led to their decimation by phylloxera in the 1980s.

8 Prohibition
On 16 January 1920 the 18th Amendment saw Prohibition introduced, banning the manufacture and sale of alcohol. Wineries made sacramental wines or grew table grapes. Of over 700 wineries, 140 were still in operation when the law was repealed in 1933.

9 Judgment of Paris
In 1976 French judges at a blind wine-tasting event gave top honors to California wines pitted against the best of Bordeaux and Burgundy.

10 Napa Valley Wine Train
In 1989 the old Napa Valley Railroad line became the Napa Valley Wine Train. It has carried more than 2 million passengers since its launch.

4 Calistoga

Full of historic charm, this town at the northern gateway to the Napa Valley is famous for a geyser *(left)* and its thermal springs and spas.

5 The Silverado Trail

This scenic highway runs along the tranquil east side of the Napa Valley and is a popular cycling route. It is lined with more than 40 wineries.

6 Francis Ford Coppola Winery

Decidedly diverse and family-friendly, the Francis Ford Coppola Winery has a movie gallery, amphitheatre, swimming pools and a gourmet restaurant.

7 Russian River

A centre for adventures, such as canoeing and fishing *(above)*, this region appeals for its redwood parks and riverside lodges. The Russian River Jazz and Blues Festival is world-renowned.

8 Alexander Valley

The valley's warm climate and alluvial soils *(above)* roduce voluptuous wines. It is home to some of the most ighly regarded wineries in Wine Country, as well as the elightful city of Healdsburg.

9 Culinary Institute of America

Housed in a landmark winery, the Culinary Institute hosts cooking and wine-tasting classes plus lectures, and has a superb restaurant, culinary marketplace and impressive gardens for guests to visit.

10 Sonoma State Historic Park

At the heart of Sonoma town, this park preserves many buildings from California's early capital city, laid out in traditional Mexican fashion, including Mission San Francisco Solano *(left)*.

Top 10 Grape Varieties

1 Chardonnay
This accounts for about a quarter of all wine produced in California. Many California Chardonnays are sweet and buttery due to heavy oaking.

2 Sauvignon Blanc
Crisp whites, with aromas of herbs or grass, are made from this grape. Warmer climates produce more robust wines, with flavours that hint of tropical fruits. In California it is often blended with Semillon.

3 Cabernet Sauvignon
The most important red wine varietal in California, Cabernet Sauvignon grapes produce full-bodied wines in hot climates. Blackberry and blackcurrant are key aromas.

4 Zinfandel
Overripe grapes with high sugar alcohol levels make deep, tannic wines, while cooler climes give subtle berry and cherry flavours, often found in rosés.

5 Petite Syrah
A red wine grape whose high skin-to-juice ratio makes for wines with intense fruit and pepper flavours, Petite Syrah is often blended with Zinfandel to tone down the latter's "jammy" qualities.

6 Syrah
This red wine varietal makes deep maroon wines with flavours of black pepper and chocolate. New World Syrah is often known as Shiraz.

7 Riesling
The German Riesling grape grows well in cooler climates. Lightness combines with fruity flavours, complex aromas, and high acidity, but the grape also produces delicious dessert wines.

8 Pinot Noir
Pinot Noir grows well in cooler areas of Wine Country. Its complex flavour reflects the region better than any other grape. Many of California's best sparkling wines use this grape.

9 Merlot
Second only to Cabernet Sauvignon in acreage planted in California, Merlot is often blended with that grape to achieve a well-balanced colour and bouquet.

10 Sangiovese
Sangiovese was introduced to California by 19th-century Italian immigrants. It makes slightly spicy young wines with hints of strawberry. Older wines can have a pronounced oaky quality.

USA
Broadway by night,
New York City

JERSEY BOYS
BEST MUSICAL
2006 TONY AWARD WINNER
AUGUST WILSON THEATRE, 245 WEST 52ND STREET
JERRY HERMAN
BOOK BY HARVEY FIERSTEIN
LACAGE.COM
SO MUCH HAPPENED BEFORE DOROTHY DROPPED IN.
WICKED
THE UNTOLD STORY OF THE WITCHES OF OZ
GERSHWIN THEATRE, 222 WEST 51st STREET
WickedtheMusical.com
Tonight belongs to...
PHANTOM
MAJESTIC THEATRE
city outdoor
TADS
CAPS T-SHIRTS
TADS STEAKS
sbarro
ONE WAY

Cancún and the Yucatán

Mexico's Yucatán Peninsula has a special atmosphere and an immense variety of attractions, including some of the world's best beaches and diving areas. The striking modern resorts of the east coast's "Mayan Riviera" lie alongside charming old Spanish Colonial towns, sleepy Mayan villages and the awesome remains of ancient civilizations.

Gulf of Mexico
Isla Mujeres 4
Cancún 1
Mérida 8
Chichén Itzá 7
Playa del Carmen 3
2 Cozumel
Uxmal 9
Tulum 5
YUCATAN PENINSULA
10 Campeche
Caribbean Sea
Sian Ka'an Reserve 6

1 Cancún

Mexico's biggest resort, with a stunning, "7"-shaped dune island, has 23 km (14 miles) of dazzling white sand beaches *(left)*, lavish hotels, restaurant of every kind and attractions from water parks to giant nightclubs for 24-hour fun.

2 Cozumel

The divers' favourite has over 20 coral reefs that can be enjoyed by first-time snorkellers and experienced divers alike *(above)*. Onshore there are fine beaches and glittering jewellery stores.

3 Playa del Carmen

The trendiest spot on the Riviera *(above)* has a more small-town scale than Cancún, superb swimming and snorkelling and an ever-buzzing nightlife.

Top 10 Moments in History

1 2000 BC–AD 100: Early Cultures
The Maya were in the Yucatán as early as 2000 BC, but it is not until 300 BC–AD 100 that characteristics of their culture appeared – a writing system, calendar, and city states.

2 250–900: Classic Era
For over 500 years, Mayan civilization flourished throughout the Yucatán, Chiapas, northern Guatemala, and Belize. From about 650, it blossomed in the northern Yucatán, reaching its peak at Chichén Itzá and Uxmal.

3 800–950: Collapse of Mayan Civilization
In just 150 years, Mayan civilization almost disappeared. Overpopulation, over-use of exhausted land, inter-Mayan wars, and drought all played their part. The southern city states were deserted, and the Mayan writing system virtually disappeared. In the north, however, cities were never entirely abandoned.

4 1150–1520: Post-Classic Revival
After a 200-year gap, Mayan culture revived on a modest scale in the northern Yucatán. Small coastal towns became links in a trade route between the Aztecs of Central Mexico and South America.

5 1517: Spaniards Arrive
Francisco Hernández de Córdoba made the first Spanish landfall in Mexico on Isla Mujeres. He continued to Campeche and Champotón, where he was attacked by the Maya and forced to turn back.

6 1526–42: Spanish Conquest
The Yucatán was conquered on the third attempt by the conquistadores. Besieged for months in the ruins of Ti'ho, they made this the site of their new city of Mérida.

7 1821: Independence
As Spain's American Empire failed, the Yucatán agreed reluctantly to become part of independent Mexico, but declared independence a few years later.

8 1847: Caste War
Mayans across the Yucatán rose against their white and *mestizo* (mixed-race) rulers – and they almost succeeded. Some continued to defy Mexican authority until 1930.

9 1860–1910: Henequen Boom
The Yucatán's economy was transformed by global demand for sisal rope, made from the *henequen* cactus. This vast new wealth was reflected in Mérida's lavish mansions, theatres and other attractions for *henequen* magnates and hacienda-owners. The boom even partially survived the Mexican Revolution, which began in 1910.

10 1971: Tourism Arrives
Another economic transformation began as the first hotel opened in Cancún, the dawn of the tourism era.

4 Isla Mujeres
This laid-back Caribbean island *(right)* has a beachcomber style. It is surrounded by rich diving reefs and fishing grounds.

5 Tulum
One of the most spectacular Mayan ruins [p]erches on a crag overlooking palm-lined sands [an]d relaxed *cabaña* hotels *(below)*.

6 Sian Ka'an Reserve
This almost uninhabited expanse of lakes, reefs, lagoon, mangroves and forest is home to jaguars, monkeys and millions of birds and rare plants.

7 Chichén Itzá
The most awe-inspiring of all Mayan cities *(above)*, Chichén's pyramids loom over huge plazas, intricately aligned with the movements of the sun and stars.

8 Mérida
Its charming squares, shady patios, whitewashed façades and wonderful markets make this one of the most romantic of all Mexico's historic Colonial cities.

9 Uxmal
The pyramids, palaces, and quadrangles of this dramatic ruined city have a special elegance and beauty, and are regarded by many as the pinnacle of ancient Mayan architecture *(left)*.

10 Campeche
The city is a [r]emarkable survivor [fr]om the Spanish [c]olonial era. It includes [a]n old section ringed [b]y ramparts and [b]astions and an [a]stonishing museum [o]f Mayan relics, [h]oused in an ancient [fo]rtress *(below)*.

Top 10 Cancún Sights

1 Night-Time Cancún
Cancún's pulsating nightlife is most concentrated in the Corazón, but extends all the way to Ciudad Cancún.

2 The Beaches
Cancún's fine white sand is soft and cool. The north side of the "7" is best for families; the more easterly beaches are great for surfing.

3 Laguna Nichupté
The placid lagoon enclosed by Cancún Island is a favourite place for water sports.

4 The Corazón
The heart of the action in the Hotel Zone strip is around the bend in the "7", with vast shopping malls, entertainment complexes and the biggest and hippest nightclubs.

5 Teatro de Cancún
This theatre is known for its lively, vibrant performances of traditional Mexican music and dance.

6 Shopping Areas
Cancún is a shopaholic's heaven with everything from international fashion in the malls to Mexican souvenirs in the markets of Downtown.

7 Avenida Tulum
The hub of the more Mexican town of Ciudad Cancún is the tree-lined Avenida Tulum, pleasant for a stroll and some souvenir-shopping, and with quieter restaurants and cafés than at the beach.

8 El Meco Ruins
The ruined city of El Meco dates back to AD 300. An impressive pyramid and the remains of an opulent Mayan palace can be seen.

9 El Rey Ruins
These ruins, situated in the Hotel Zone, are home to hundreds of friendly iguanas.

10 Wet'n Wild
This huge water park has a snorkelling pool with stingrays and (harmless) sharks; an interactive dolphin pool; and even bungee-jumping.

Chicago

Big-city sophistication combined with small-town hospitality create the perfect blend in this, the Midwest's largest city. Chicago's influential architecture, cuisine for every budget and taste, great shopping, diverse ethnic neighbourhoods and outstanding museums are reason enough for a visit. And the icing on the cake? The city boasts a lakefront and park system that are as beautiful as they are recreational.

1 Museum of Science and Industry

An enduring family favourite, this museum *(above)* is the only building left from the 1893 World's Columbian Exposition. Exhibits emphasizing interactivity cover everything from space exploration to coal-mining and include the Walk-Through Heart and Silver Streak train, which visitors can climb aboard.

TOP 10 Moments in History

1 1871: Great Chicago Fire
Over 250 people died and 17,000 buildings were destroyed in this fire, allegedly started by a cow kicking over a lantern.

2 1885: First Skyscraper
Though just nine storeys high, the Home Insurance Building (now demolished) was the tallest of its time. To build it, William LeBarron Jenney designed the first weight-bearing steel frame.

3 1886: Haymarket Riot
In May 1886, a labour protest ended in an explosion at Haymarket Square that killed eight policemen and two bystanders. A group of anarchists were charged and convicted of murder.

4 1892: First Elevated Train
The first elevated train tracks were built above city-owned alleys to avoid the need to negotiate with private property owners. By 1893, the line had been extended to Jackson Park for the World's Columbian Exposition.

5 1900: Reversal of the Chicago River
With sewage flowing into Lake Michigan, the source of the city's drinking water, contamination was a major problem. To solve it, engineers built a canal that forced the river away from the lake.

6 1919: Chicago Black Sox Scandal
After a group of White Sox players conspired to lose the 1919 World Series in a betting scandal, several were banned for life from baseball and nicknamed the "Black Sox."

7 1929: Valentine's Day Massacre
This brutal murder of seven of Al Capone's rivals is one of history's most notorious killings. Seven bushes mark the spot (at Clark Street and Dickens Avenue) where George "Bugsy" Moran's main men were shot.

8 1942: First Atom Split
Under the football stands on the campus of the University of Chicago, Enrico Fermi made history, when he supervised the creation of a primitive nuclear reactor.

9 1955: McDonald's First Franchise Opens
Salesman Ray Kroc pursuaded Dick and Mac McDonald to franchise their San Bernadino burger stand. That first franchise, west of Chicago in Des Plaines, has since become a museum.

10 1983: Washington Elected Mayor
Harold Washington was the city's first African-American mayor. He died in his second term, but his achievements included the creation of a new central library.

2 Willis Tower and its Views

The city's skyscraping superlative *(above)* is actually made up of nine tube-like sections. The views are absolutely awesome: on a clear day, you can see up to 64 km (40 miles) from the 103rd-floor Skydeck.

3 The University of Chicago

Opened in 1892, this private university is an important part of the southside Hyde Park neighbourhood. Its public attractions include museums and galleries *(left)*, and a Frank Lloyd Wright home.

4 Frank Lloyd Wright's Oak Park

Frank Lloyd Wright, creator of Prairie Style architecture, was based in this Chicago suburb for 20 years. His legacy is an "outdoor museum" of 25 buildings. Take a self-guided or guided tour of his creations and those of other Prairie Style architects.

5 Navy Pier

Once dilapidated, this Lake Michigan pier is now a ustling year-round playground for kids and adults alike, omplete with a Ferris Wheel *(above)* and carousel. In warm veather, take a boat tour or join the throngs that stroll along ne pier and get some amazing city views.

6 Lincoln Park Zoo

It might not be the biggest but it's one of the oldest zoos *(left)* in the country – and, after more than 100 years, is still free. Kids love the hands-on Pritzker Family Children's Zoo and Endangered Species Carousel.

7 The Art Institute of Chicago

This grande dame of Chicago's art scene features world-renowned collections. The ever-popular Impressionist section includes outstanding exhibits, such as Renoir's *Acrobats at the Cirque Fernando.*

8 Magnificent Mile

Chicago's premier shopping destination is a four-lane stretch of North Michigan Avenue *(above).* It has historic significance, as well, claiming two of only a handful of structures to survive the 1871 Great Chicago Fire.

9 John G. Shedd Aquarium

Chicago's amazing aquarium is located on the lakefront nd is home to thousands of marine animals from big beluga vhales to tiny seahorses. Get a fun, fish-eye view at the)ceanarium's underwater viewing galleries.

Field Museum 10

)elve into cultures and environments from ancient Egypt to modern Africa, via Midwestern wildlife and the underground life of bugs. The Field also offers a close-up of the world's largest and most complete *Tyrannosaurus rex* skeleton *(right)*, as well as many other fossils.

TOP 10 Frank Lloyd Wright & Prairie-Style Buildings

1 Unity Temple
This compact church (1908) wonderfully demonstrates Wright's use of poured concrete for both structural and decorative purposes.

2 Frank Lloyd Wright Home and Studio
Built when Wright moved to Oak Park (1889), this is where he designed more than 150 structures.

3 Pleasant Home
This 30-room Prairie-style 1897 home built by George Maher was Oak Park's first to have electricity. It holds a small history museum.

4 Arthur Heurtley House
Wright's 1902 house is absolute Prairie, with its low, broad chimney, dark band of windows and shallow roof with overhanging eaves.

5 Beachy House
This 1906 home contradicts many of Wright's trademarks. His range of materials is wider than usual and he has used a seven-gabled, rather than a hipped, roof.

6 Charles Matthews House
Architects Tallmadge and Watson designed this elegant 1909 residence for a wealthy druggist. Interior details include Prairie-inspired light fixtures and folding art-glass doors.

7 Edwin Cheney House
Now a B&B, this home sparked a tragic love affair between Wright and Mrs Cheney, leading him to abandon his family and practice. Cheney and her children were murdered at Wright's Wisconsin home by an insane servant in 1914.

8 The Bootleg Houses
Wright lost his job over these three private commissions, built while he was actually employed by Louis Sullivan. Though not typical of his style, they hint at the design elements that were to be his hallmarks.

9 Nathan Moore House
Wright built this charming Tudor-style home for his neighbour out of financial desperation. After a fire destroyed the top floors in 1922, Wright's modifications echoed his West Coast concrete block houses.

10 Harry Adams House
This 1913 home marks the last of Wright's Oak Park houses and features several of the elements that made him famous, such as exquisite stained glass and a low overhanging roof.

Chile

With its long, thin profile, quite unlike any other country, Chile is home to a huge geographical diversity. From its seemingly endless coastline the land rises rapidly eastwards to form the towering Andes. In between it has some of the world's driest desert; some of its most productive vineyards; a lushly forested Lake District studded with volcanoes; fjordlands; and ice fields. Far out into the Pacific lies the enigma that is Easter Island. The capital, Santiago, is a lively city where ancient and modern sit side-by-side. Chile really has something for everyone.

1 Plaza de Armas, Santiago

The symbolic heart of Santiago began life in 1547 under the Spanish as a parade ground *(left)*. It's now a vibrant social centre, drawing people who come to relax, play chess or enjoy the street performances.

2 Parque Nacional Lauca

Northern Chile's most scenic sanctuary *(above)* is an area of *altiplano* wilderness. Attractions include brilliantly coloured high-altitude lakes, snowy volcanoes, lava islands, tiny Aymara villages and an abundance of wildlife. Herds of vicuña graze on the lakeshores where flamingoes also feed and nest.

3 Parque Metropolitano de Santiago

This forested recreational park is the lungs of Santiago It features walking trails, a botanical garden, swimming pools and the city zoo. A cable car *(above)* ascends to the dramatic Statue of the Virgin atop Cerro San Cristobal for sweeping views of Santiago and the Andes.

Top 10 Moments in History

1 Early Peoples
The earliest human settlement probably dates from more than 13,000 years ago, while the first settlers arrived on Easter Island about 1,000 years ago from Polynesia.

2 The Incas
In the 15th century the Incas, who had conquered a huge swathe of South America, extended their empire south to modern-day Santiago.

3 Exploration and Colonization
Diego de Almagro made an unsuccessful attempt to conquer Chile for Spain with an expedition in 1535. Pedro de Valdiria was successful in 1541, founding the cities of Santiago and Valparaíso.

4 Struggle between Spain and Criollos
Tensions grew between Spain and the Criollos (Spaniards born in South America), and a military junta was formed in 1810 under Bernardo O'Higgins. This led to a struggle culminating in the Battle of Rancagua in 1814.

5 Independence
Independence from Spain was declared in 1818, and Bernardo O'Higgins was proclaimed head of state.

6 Expansion and Civil War
During the War of the Pacific (1879–84), Chile fought against Peru and Bolivia for control of strategic, mineral-rich lands. Chile won, and expanded into both neighbouring countries. Easter Island was annexed in 1888.

7 Early 20th Century
In 1907 more than 2,000 striking workers and their families were killed by the Chilean army in the Santa María School Massacre. In 1924 President Arturo Alessandri was outsted by a military junta, which was in turn overthrown by another coup in 1925 and power was returned to Alessandri.

8 Radical Allende
In 1970 the radical left-wing Salvador Allende Gosseus was made President. He promised to transform Chile by, amongst other means, nationalizing the copper industry and raising wages.

9 Pinochet Dictatorship
In September 1973 Augusto Pinochet, Commander-in-chief to Allende, overthrew him in a military coup, and went on to rule until 1990 in one of the continent's most brutal and bloody regimes.

10 Chile Today
In 2006 Michelle Bachelet was elected President, the country's first female leader. In 2010 Chile became the first nation in South America to join the Organisation for Economic Co-operation and Development (OECD).

Torres del Paine National Park

One of the most spectacular features of this dazzling tional park is the 4-km (2-mile) wide Glacier Grey, which scends from the Southern Ice Field. Boats cruise up to e glacier face *(above)* or you can kayak amid the icebergs.

5 Museo Chileno de Arte Precolumbino, Santiago

Housed in the Palacio Real de la Casa Aduana, this museum highlights the arts of pre-Columbian cultures *(left)*. Its collections of ceramics and textiles are unmissable.

Parque Nacional Villarrica

The smoking, snow-swathed cone of of Volcán llarica forms the centrepiece of the park. Treks to peak involve a hike over icy glaciers and a slide rough snow tunnels. Stupendous vistas include ews of the bubbling lava lake.

Valparaíso

A UNESCO World Heritage Site, much of the storic port of Valparaíso is beautifully preserved. Rising arply from the water's edge to cover over 45 steep lls, its winding streets are lined with colourful houses, st-Colonial architecture and fascinating museums.

TOP 10 Chilean Music and Dance

1 Cueca
The traditional *cueca*, which mimics the courtship of the rooster and hen, is danced primarily at Fiestas Patrias, and is much loved in rural areas. The *cueca choro* or *bravo* is the urban equivalent, with lyrics more associated with city life. The *cueca* in Chiloé is distinct in that the singer has a more important role than the musicians.

2 Rapa Nui Music
This comprises chanting and singing to instruments such as the *kauaha* (made from the jaw bone of a horse), drums and accordions. Polynesian rhythms blend with Latin sounds and cadences. Often, families form into a choir and compete in annual contests.

3 Mapuche Music
The Mapuche define rhythms as *kantun* (instrumental) or *öl* (ceremonial). Instruments include the *kultrun*, a drum made of wood and leather, and the *trutruka*, a trumpet made of bamboo and a cow's horn. Rich and melodious, the sounds reflects their close contact with nature.

4 Andean Music
Originating in the high plains areas, this music is instantly recognizable by the sound of *quena* flutes (bamboo, with six holes), pan pipes and 10-stringed charango lutes.

5 Tonada
The melodic *tonada* is similar to *cuenca* except that it is not danced. It arose in Spain and has Arab and Andalucian influences. Popular Chilean *tonada* groups include Huasos Quincheros.

6 Cumbia
A favourite of the working classes across Latin America, *cumbia*'s real-issue lyrics and tinny rhythm are popular to dance to at celebrations.

7 Nueva Canción Chilena
"New Chilean Music" arose in the 1960s and is based on Andean rhythms. Its original artists wrote lyrics focusing on social injustice for native cultures and those persecuted under the Pinochet regime.

8 Tango
Despite its Argentinian origins, the tango is becoming increasingly popular in urban areas.

9 Classical and Jazz
Both genres have a huge following in Chile, which has produced important artists and composers. Claudio Arrau is one of the world's foremost pianists.

10 La Armada Chileana
The children of exiled Chileans are making their mark internationally as DJs and hip-hop producers, and there's also a thriving rock and pop scene.

8 Colchagua Valley Wineries

The fertile floor and rolling hills of Chile's premier wine region are covered with vineyards and dotted with wineries, nearly all of which are open for tours and tastings. The historic Tren de Vino steam train is a lovely way to see the valley, with tastings and a vineyard lunch included.

9 San Pedro de Atacama

An oasis village of clay-coloured houses and dirt streets, San Pedro *(above)* is the gateway to a region of stunning natural highlights. As such, it's something of a tourist magnet, but retains a beguiling, authentic charm.

10 Easter Island

Four hours by jet from the mainland, and known to its inhabitants as Rapa Nui, Easter Island is most famous for its *Moai* statues *(left)*, enigmatic remnants of a vanished society.

Costa Rica

Brimming with natural wonders, Costa Rica's incredibly diverse terrain offers lush rain and cloud forests that host an array of colourful fauna; craggy mountains; smoke-spewing volcanoes; and stunning beaches in every shade from gold to taupe to black. Wildlife and adventure activities abound, ranging from canopy tours and turtle-watching to scuba diving and white-water rafting. The national parks and other natural attractions may be the highlights of Costa Rica, but its museums and historic buildings reveal another facet of this tropical jewel.

1 Parque Nacional Tortuergo

Created to protect the most important nesting site of the green turtle *(left)* in the Western Hemisphere, this park combines miles of Caribbean seaboard with pristine rainforest. Explore its canals, lagoons and deltas by boat.

2 Volcan Arenal

A National Park surrounds the country's most active volcano *(right)*. The home of the fire god to pre-Columbian tribes forms a dramatic backdrop for hiking, canopy tours, horseback riding and soaks in thermal hot springs.

Top 10 Moments in History

1 Indigenous Peoples
The indigenous peoples who inhabited the rugged terrain were relatively isolated from the more advanced imperial cultures north and south.

2 The Spanish Conquest
Columbus arrived in Costa Rica in 1502, and was soon followed by Spanish conquistadors. By 1543 most lowland areas had been charted and Spain's conquest assured. For the next 250 years Costa Rica was a somewhat neglected colony of Spain.

3 Spanish Colony
Most Spanish settlement was concentrated in the central valley of the interior highlands. However, on the northwestern coast, Spanish landowners established large cattle estates and exacted harsh tribute from Indians and mestizos. The Caribbean coast was the domain of pirates and smugglers.

4 Growing Fortunes
In the 18th century, exports of tobacco and hides boosted national fortunes and townships developed. Immigration from Europe increased, and in the 1740s the increased demand for labour led to the forced resettlement of natives.

5 Nascent Republic
Spain granted independence to the Central American nations in 1821. Costa Rica later became a sovereign state of the short-lived Federation of Central America.

6 The Coffee Era
Costa Rica's farmers benefited greatly from Europe's taste for coffee. By the end of the 19th century, Costa Rica had evolved into a modern nation.

7 The Second Republic
The inter-war years were beset with unrest and social problems. Despite attempts at reform, tensions continued to rise. In 1948 José "Don Pepe" Figueres, a radical utopian socialist, established the "Second Republic."

8 Years of Prosperity and Terror
The 1950s–70s saw growing prosperity, threatened when the Sandinistas took power in neighbouring Nicaragua, and Costa Rica's northern borders became a war zone. In 1987 there was a peaceful resolution of regional conflicts.

9 Environmental Era
The 1980s saw the start of a huge tourism boom, fuelled by Costa Rica's stewardship of its natural resources. After that, the government was plagued by scandals, protests and natural disasters, but nothing slowed the progress of Costa Rica's ecotourism.

10 Costa Rica Today
In 2010 Laura Chinchilla Miranda, became the first woman president.

3 Isla de Coco

Off the southwest coast of Costa Rica, the world's largest uninhabited island is a UNESCO World Heritage Site linked to the Galapagos chain, and the "Dinosaur Island" of *Jurassic Park*. Hundreds of hammerhead sharks *(above)* in its clear waters make for a thrilling scuba dive experience.

4 Parque Nacional Manuel Antonio

amed for a Spanish Conquisdor, this park *(above)* combines oral reefs, white-sand beaches nd lush forests full of wildlife. apuchin and squirrel monkeys, ucans and scarlet macaws are asily spotted from its many ell-maintained hiking trails.

5 Museo del Oro Precolombino, San José

Housed in a stark subterranean vault, San José's Gold Museum *(right)* boasts a dazzling display of over 1,600 ancient pieces ranging from amulets to early gold coins.

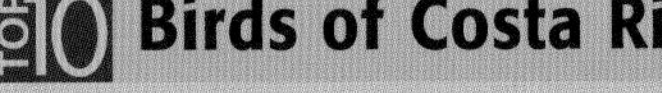

6 Volcán Poás

This volcano *(above)* is at the heart of the nation's most visited National Park. A viewing platform on the rim of one of the world's most active craters allows you to peer down into the heart of the hissing, steaming caldera.

7 Teatro Nacional, San José

This is San José's major architectural draw *(above)*. Completed in 1897, and paid for by a tax on coffee exports, it has a lavish Neo-Baroque interior, replete with statues, paintings, marble and gilt.

8 The Orosi Valley

Ringed by cloud-forested mountains, the valley is covered in coffee plantations and has some of the country's best colonial sites, as well as hot springs, whitewater rafting and horseback trails.

9 Monteverde

This world-famous cloud orest reserve is the best lace to see quetzals *(above)*. hese jewel-coloured birds re among 400 species found ere. Canopy walkways get ou close to the action.

10 Playa Grande

This is Costa Rica's most important nesting site for leatherback turtles. The long beach of coral-grey sand is also a famed surfing destination, luring hundreds of surfers a year to test its challenging Pacific breakers.

TOP 10 Birds of Costa Rica

1 Hummingbirds
Named for the bee-like hum of their tiny wings beating at a blurry 100 times per second, hummingbirds hover as they sip nectar through hollow, needle-like beaks.

2 Parrots and Macaws
Costa Rica is home to 16 species of parrot and two of macaws, including the scarlet – blood red with wings of yellow and blue.

3 Tanagers
Small, vibrant forest-dwellers, the summer tanager is flame red while the blue-grey is variegated in peacock hues. About 50 species of rare tanagers live in Costa Rica.

4 Toucans
Easily recognized, the toucan has a banana-yellow chest, a black body and a startling, rainbow-striped beak.

5 Trogons
Trogons have a black-and-white striped tail and usually a bicoloured body, such as blue and yellow. The rarest is the emerald-green quetzal.

6 Pelicans
Pelicans can be seen easily all year round on the Pacific coast as they dive for fish.

7 Raptors
Costa Rica has four species of vulture, and about 50 other types of raptor, including owls, osprey, the laughing falcon and the world's largest eagle, the endangered harpy.

8 Migratory Birds
Costa Rica's wetlands come alive with tens of thousands of teal, Muscovies, whistling ducks and countless others.

9 Seabirds
Coastal mangroves shelter blue herons and ibis; shores are stalked by oyster-catchers, whimbrel and sandpipers; and cliffs are nesting sites for boobies and storm petrels.

10 Yiquirros
Costa Rica's national bird is, in contrast to most, a small clay-brown type of thrush.

History and Culture

So much of the history of the Americas is the tale of a struggle against sometimes overwhelming odds – geography, weather, oppression, persecution. Its ancient peoples, its colonizers, even the eccentrics who came to its shores to fulfil a dream – all have left a rich culture in their wake, from the ancient rock dwellings of Mesa Verde to the Puritan settlement of Boston.

1 Rock Dwellings of Mesa Verde, Colorado *USA*

The well-preserved cliff dwellings of Mesa Verde National Park provide a rare and fascinating insight into the life and times of the "lost civilization" of the Ancient Puebloans, ancestors of today's Native American peoples of the Southwest. The park and its natural cliff alcoves were inhabited from as early as AD 500, but it is thought that the 600 cliff homes here were built in the 13th century. Though it must have been a mighty building project, the houses were inhabited for less than 100 years. The people and rock dwellings of Mesa Verde remain shrouded in mystery.

2 Great Pyramid of Cholula *MEXICO*

Cholula's pyramid is so enormous and overgrown that first-time visitors often mistake it for a hill. Although it is not as high as the Great Pyramid of Giza, it is larger, measuring a staggering 160,000 sq m (191,360 sq yd) at the base. Constructed over a period of 1,000 years, it was once topped with a temple dedicated to the Aztec god Quetzalcoatl, but this was replaced with a church by the conquistadors. Visitors explore some of the 8 km (5 miles) of tunnels that burrow into the heart of the massive structure.

3 Cueva de las Maravillas *DOMINICAN REPUBLIC*

Discovered in 1926, the Cueva de las Maravillas ("Cave of Miracles") is a veritable subterranean art gallery. The walls of the single huge grotto, over 800 m (2,625 ft) long, are decorated with almost 500 quaintly stylized and perfectly preserved pictographs and petroglyphs, created by the Taíno people around 1,000 years ago. The cave is also home to an impressive quantity of stalactites, stalagmites, columns and other unusual crystalline formations. It is well set up for visitors, offering guided tours, and is one of the few cave systems in the world accessible to wheelchairs.

4 National Museum of American History, Washington DC *USA*

Three huge floors filled with a whole range of fascinating objects make up this paean to American culture. The first floor focuses on science and technology, including hands-on experiments and exhibitions on transport, electricity, and machinery. The second floor is home to the famous Star-Spangled Banner, while the third floor features a stirring tribute to the American presidency and military history. The museum is undergoing major renovation work, which is ongoing in phases. Check its website for information on the latest exhibitions.

5 Habana Vieja, Havana *CUBA*

With almost 1,000 buildings of historic importance, this intimate quarter is perhaps the largest, most complete colonial complex in the Americas. Full of animated street life, Old Havana boasts an astonishing wealth of castles, churches, convents, palaces and other important buildings spanning five centuries. An ongoing restoration programme, now in its third decade, has transformed the finest structures into museums, hotels, cafés, restaurants, boutiques and trendy bars. Easily walkable, the cobbled plazas and the narrow, shaded streets exude colonial charm.

Rock Dwellings of Mesa Verde, Colorado Relics of an ancient building projec

Amazon Theatre, Manaus Opera in the rainforest *(below)*

Pisac Inca ruins along the Sacred Valley of the Incas *(above)*

Habana Vieja, Havana Musicians at Plaza de la Catedral *(below)*

6 Mission Dolores, San Francisco *USA*

The Misión San Francisco de Asís acquired its popular name, from a small stream that once flowed nearby. It is the oldest building in the city of San Francisco and the only intact mission chapel in the chain of 21 (of which it was the sixth) established under the direction of friar Father Junípero Serra. The site was consecrated in 1776, and the chapel was built in 1782–91, with the labour of Ohlone Indians. Its adobe walls are 1.2 m (4 ft) thick and its red-tile roofs are typical of the Mission Style which can be seen all over California in old and new buildings. It is said that 36,000 handmade and sun-dried adobe bricks were used in its construction.

7 Pisac *PERU*

The tranquil market town of Pisac takes little notice of the magnificent ruins in the hills behind it. In fact, you'd be hard-pressed to recognize its historic link to the Inca Trail at all. Which is good news for travellers who want to see near-intact remnants of a glorious Inca civilization. The hillside is lined with terraces built by the Inca and still in use. The ruins are divided into four areas, of which the Citadel and the Temple of the Sun are the best preserved. The views from the latter of the Sacred Valley below are nothing short of amazing. Pisac is a trekker's delight, with the area around ideal for spring and autumn hikes.

8 Amazon Theatre, Manaus *BRAZIL*

One might well ask how this preposterous pink *belle époque* opera house came to be built in a port city in the middle of the South American rainforest. Step inside and you could be in any opera house in Europe: its decorations and furniture hail from France, its marble come from Italy, its porcelain and glass from Venice and its cast-iron columns and banisters from Britain. Over 100 years on, the venue is thriving, with a repertoire of opera, dance, music and film.

9 Historic Boston *USA*

Founded in 1630 by Puritans who saw their settlement as a shining beacon to the world, Boston was among America's first great urban centres. Its patriots led the rebellion that grew into the American Revolution, and few places in the US evoke so vividly the birth of a new nation, with modern buildings nudging up against land-marks of the Colonial and Revolutionary eras.

10 Las Posas, Xilitla *MEXICO*

Rich, English, eccentric and a friend of the Surrealists, Edward James built his very own Garden of Eden. It was no small task. The garden is situated deep in the jungle, up in the mountains 7 hours north of Mexico City. Here, with his menagerie of pets and wild animals, he spent over 20 years nurturing exotic plants and creating houses, trails, bridges and dozens of ambitious concrete follies, many of which display a Surrealist twist.

Cuba

Cuba, the Caribbean's largest island, is a land of extraordinary beauty and amazing contrasts. From white-sand beaches and teal-blue seas to lush valleys and cloud-draped mountains, Cuba is kaleidoscopic in its terrains. Steeped in history, this Communist nation is in a time warp and brims with colonial buildings, pre-revolutionary 1950s cars and rural villages. The country's vivacious populace is a blend of Spanish, African and indigenous peoples.

Havana 1 2
8 Cordillera de Guaniguanico
10 Zapata Peninsula
Trinidad 9
Jardines del Rey 5
CUBA
7 Camagüey
Holguín 3
Baraco 4
Caribbean Sea
6 Santiago de Cuba

1 Habana Vieja, Havana

Colonial palaces, castles and cobbled plazas make Old Havana *(left)* the jewel in the crown of the island's capital, recalling days when it was the New World's wealthiest city.

TOP 10 Moments in History

1 c.500 BC: The Taíno
The Taíno people arrived from the Orinoco region of South America. Worshipping gods of nature, this peaceful society lived in villages led by *caciques* (chieftains).

2 AD 1492: Columbus Arrives
The Genoese explorer sighted Cuba during his first voyage and named it Juana. In 1509 his son Diego conquered the island and exterminated the Taínos. Conquistador Diego Velázquez founded the first town, Baracoa, in 1511.

3 1762: English Occupation
The English seized Havana, opening Cuba to free trade and expanding the slave trade. In 1763 they exchanged it with Spain for Florida.

4 1868: Ten Years War
Landowner Carlos Manuel de Céspedes freed his slaves and revolted against Spanish rule. A guerrilla war ensued; towns were razed and the economy was ruined. Later, US companies bought up Cuban sugar plantations.

5 1895: War of Independence
Exiled nationalist José Martí returned to lead the fight for independence. Though he was killed in battle, his forces gained the upper hand, but were sidelined after the USS *Maine* was bombed in Havana harbour. The US declared war on Spain, and invaded Cuba.

6 1902: Independence
After four years of military rule, the US granted Cuba independence. A period of mostly corrupt government followed and US corporations dominated the Cuban sugar-based economy.

7 1953: Castro Attacks
Castro launched the Cuban Revolution with an audacious attack during carnival in Santiago. The assault failed and 64 captured rebels were tortured to death.

8 1959: Revolution Triumphs
On New Year's Eve 1958, General Batista fled Cuba. A newly formed democratic government was usurped by Castro, who allied with the Soviet Union and initiated dramatic reforms.

9 1961: Bay of Pigs
CIA-trained Cuban exiles stormed ashore to assist counter-revolutionaries in toppling Castro. The attack was swiftly repelled.

10 1991: Período Especial Begins
Decades of economic support ended when the Soviet Union collapsed. Cubans faced extreme hardship, triggering a mass exodus to the US on flimsy rafts. But since 1994 a tourism boom has been helping to promote recovery.

2 The Modern City, Havana

This throbbing 20th-century metropolis encompasses interesting museums, spacious green parks, lovely white beaches, 1950s-era hotels and nightclubs, and stunning examples of latter-day architecture from Beaux Arts to *modernismo (above)*.

3 Holguín

This provincial capital has played a key role in Cuban history. Its plazas are lined with museums and cultural centres. Castro's birthplace and a beach resort *(above)* are two of its attractions.

Baracoa 4 Founded in 1511 as Cuba's first city, Baracoa enjoys a stupendous setting backed by rainforest-clad mountains. Buzzing street life, scenic mountain hikes, and Castillo de Seboruco *(right)*, a castle-turned-hotel, are this town's key attractions.

5 Jardines del Rey
Stretching 275 miles (442 km) along Cuba's northern coastline, this chain of offshore islands and cays is lined with stunning beaches. Three islands offer superb diving plus exciting watersports and deluxe hotels.

6 Santiago de Cuba
Santiago de Cuba exudes a mystique influenced by its French and Afro-Caribbean associations. Intriguing architecture includes Cuba's oldest building, a fine cathedral, plus numerous key sites and monuments relating to the Revolution.

7 Camagüey
The colonial buildings of Camagüey were made a World Heritage Site in 2008 and the city is slowly being restored. Rich in history, it is awash with grand, imposing churches looming over cobbled plazas.

8 Cordillera de Guaniguanico
A few hours west of Havana, these rugged mountains are a birder's and hiker's delight. The dramatic limestone formations rising over tobacco fields add surreal beauty to Valle de Viñales *(above)*.

9 Trinidad
Trinidad boasts a breeze-swept hillside setting *(above)*. This UNESCO World Heritage Site is Cuba's most complete colonial city, with great museums and an active *santería* tradition, plus a superb beach close by.

Zapata Peninsula 10
This vast swampland and park protects many of Cuba's crocodiles *(right)* and endemic bird species. It has great fishing flats and cave dive sites. Two museums recall the 1961 Bay of Pigs invasion.

TOP 10 Havana Sights

1 Catedral de La Habana
Havana's cathedral (1777) has an exquisite Baroque façade supported by pilasters and asymmetrical bell towers.

2 Plaza de Armas
This cobbled plaza, laid out in 1582 as the administrative centre of Cuba, is named for the military exercises that took place here.

3 Plaza Vieja
Dating from 1559, this plaza features columned arcades. Interesting buildings from four centuries rise on each side of the square, the finest of which is the Art Nouveau Palacio Cueto of 1906.

4 Basílica y Convento de San Francisco
The grandiose Basílica has not been used for worship since 1762. Today it hosts concerts. The adjoining convent's cloisters house a museum of religious art.

5 Calle Mercaderes
This cobbled street is lined with mansions housing tiny museums, boutiques and other fascinating places. Mesón de la Flota is a *bodega* that hosts live flamenco.

6 Museo Nacional de Bellas Artes
The 1927 Renaissance-style Centro Asturiano has treasures from the ancient world, plus works by the Old Masters. The Modernist Palace of Fine Arts, two blocks away, displays Cuban artworks.

7 Museo de la Revolución
Housed in the presidential palace of General Batista, this museum celebrates the Revolution, from the guerrilla war to today. The ornate, domed 1920 building is as fascinating as the collection.

8 Capitolio
Cuba's grandiose former congressional building was opened in 1929. Its Neo-Classical design closely resembles Washington DC's Capitol building.

9 Parque Central
An epicentre of social life in Havana, this palm-shaded square has a statue of José Martí and is surrounded by monumental 19th- and 20th-century buildings.

10 Plaza de la Revolución
The administrative and political centre of Cuba since the early 1950s, huge political rallies are held here. A visage of Che Guevara adorns the façade of the Interior Ministry.

Dominican Republic

The Dominican Republic is a country of surprising contrasts and extraordinary variety. From the chilly peak of the Caribbean's highest mountain to some of the region's most delightful beaches, the country boasts lush valleys, spectacular waterfalls and sun-baked deserts. The past and present also blend in a fascinating mix of colonial buildings and modern hotels, sleepy rural villages and lively tourist resorts. The people, too, reflect a kaleidoscope of influences – Spanish, African, indigenous – creating a culture that emphasizes both creativity and fun in the fields of music, sport and art.

1 Costa del Coco

The modern face of Dominican tourism is embodied by this idyllic 60-km (37-mile) coastline of white sand and swaying palms. Costa del Coco *(left)* is home to a cluster of all-inclusive resorts.

2 Santo Domingo: The Zona Colonia

The historic jewel in the capital's crown, this district of restored colonial buildings *(above* and shady plazas is filled with well-preserved reminders of a bygone age.

3 Santo Domingo: The Modern City

The modern metropolis encompasses crowded down-town streets, charming suburbs and relaxing parks, where art galleries rub shoulders with US-style shopping malls.

4 Santiago

The laid-back second city is very different in ambience to bustling Santo Domingo. A town of the tobacco boom, it streets are filled with monuments *(left)* to commemorate its past glories.

TOP 10 Moments in History

1 c. 500 BC: Taino Culture
The Taino people arrive on the island they call Quisqueya after a centuries-long migration up the Caribbean archipelago from the Orinoco Delta in South America.

2 AD 1492: Columbus Arrives
The Genoese explorer sets foot on Quisqueya and renames it Hispaniola. With Spanish colonialism comes the rapid extermination of the Tainos. The city of Santo Domingo is founded in 1498.

3 1586: Francis Drake Sacks Santo Domingo
The golden age of the Spanish colony ends when the English privateer loots and vandalizes his way through its main town.

4 1697: Ryswick Treaty
An agreement divides Hispaniola between French Saint Domingue and Spanish Santo Domingo. The French create a prosperous colony, based on slavery and sugar, while the underpopulated Spanish side languishes.

5 1804: Haitian Independence
An army of former slaves drives out Napoleon's troops from Saint Domingue and declare independence. The colony is returned to Spanish rule in 1809. Several Haitian invasions end with the occupation of Spanish Santo Domingo in February 1822.

6 1844: Independence
Led by Juan Pablo Duarte, a group of nationalists stage a revolt against the 22-year-old Haitian occupation, declaring an independent Dominican Republic.

7 1915–25: US Occupation
The Marines land in Santo Domingo to impose peace and "restore order". The US presence brings foreign investment in the sugar industry and throws peasants off their land.

8 1961: Assassination of Trujillo
Thirty years of brutal dictatorship come to an end when Trujillo is gunned down in Santo Domingo. His death signals a gradual move towards democracy.

9 1970s: Arrival of Tourism
The country begins to shrug off its reliance on sugar production as the first steps in creating a tourism industry take place with the building of hotels on the North Coast.

10 1996: First Fair Elections
A sorry record of voting fraud ends with the country's first free and fair elections, in which Leonel Fernández wins.

5 Lago Enriquillo

An inland saltwater sea surrounded by cactus-studded wilderness, this natural wonder involves a boat trip and close encounters with crocodiles and tame giant iguanas *(left)*.

6 Constanza and "The Dominican Alps"

Only 2 hours from the capital, the rugged interior is a walker's paradise of green meadows and clear rivers, surrounded by pine forests and mountains. Pico Duarte, the highest mountain in the Caribbean, stands here.

7 La Isabela Bay

The place where European colonization of the Americas really began, the beautiful bay *(above)* reveals the story of Columbus's first settlement. Other highlights include some wonderful beaches such as Playa Isabela and Punta Rucia Beach.

8 Las Terrenas

One of the coolest spots in the country, a once-tiny fishing village surrounded by idyllic beaches has become a magnet for independent travellers and sun-seekers.

9 Puerto Plata

Steeped in colonial history, the North Coast port *bove)* is also the hub for the area's thriving tourist omplexes, offering both sightseeing and entertainment. ourist attractions include the San Felipe Fortress, Parque entral with La Glorieta and Museo del Ambar.

0 La Romana

A town built on sugar now offers a different sweetness the form of one of the country's most luxurious resorts, asa de Campo, and an unforgettable transplant from Italy, tos de Chavón *(above)*.

TOP 10 Taino Indian Sites

1 El Pomier Caves
This network of bat-infested caves north of San Cristóbal contains the largest display of Taino wall paintings in the Caribbean. Spiritual symbols and pre-Columbian daily life are depicted.

2 Las Caritas La Descubierta
These expressive "little faces" are chiselled into the coral rock of the cave overlooking Lago Enriquillo.

3 Cueva El Puente
This long cave holding almost 70 figurative and abstract petroglyphs is in the Parque Nacional del Este.

4 Cueva de Panchito
Food and ceramic remains found in this cave in the Parque Nacional del Este indicate that it was actively used by the Tainos. A carving of a great *zemi* appears on the wall, along with about 30 other petroglyphs.

5 Sala de Arte Prehispánico
This museum displays delicately carved jewellery and decorated pottery. Clay *zemis*, depicting various gods, indicate the spiritual dimension of Taino society.

6 Cueva de las Maravillas
In this complex of grottoes and labyrinths are drawings and engravings depicting human figures and animals associated with death rituals.

7 Los Indios de Chacuey
A circle of rocks surrounds a stone slab in the middle of a huge open space. Nearby, religious petroglyphs suggest that this was an important ceremonial centre.

8 La Isabela
The museum at the Parque Nacional Histórico La Isabela highlights everyday life in a Taino village. Outside you can see an indigenous *bohío*, or thatched dwelling.

9 Parque Nacional Los Haitises
The Taino sites here can best be accessed through an organized boat trip. There are caves with drawings, including birds, whales and faces, and hunting scenes.

10 Cueva de Berna
This is one of the most spectacular caves in the Parque Nacional del Este, with more than 300 petroglyphs along the walls.

Honolulu and O'ahu

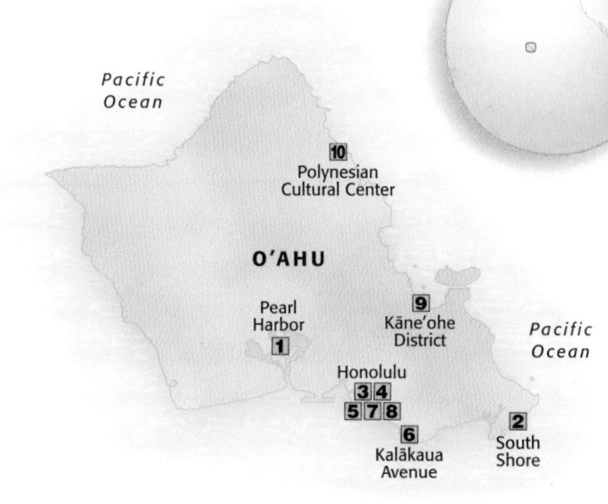

O'ahu is the most populous of the Hawai'ian islands, and its conjoined hubs are the city of Honolulu and the world-famous Waikīkī Beach. The vast majority of visitors make Waikīkī their base, venturing out on day trips to take in Honolulu's many cultural attractions, Pearl Harbor and other parts of the island. The family-friendly beaches and parks of the South Shore and Kāne'ohe District are in striking distance of Honolulu, while diehard surfers head for the North Coast. The Polynesian Cultural Center is also an easy day trip from the city.

1 Pearl Harbor

The World War II site draws 1.5 million visitors each year, including veterans and relatives of those who died. The warship *USS Arizona* is now a memorial *(left)*.

Top 10 Moments in History

1 Formation of the Islands
Each of the islands is the top of an underwater volcano. The oldest of the seven major islands (formed 70 million years ago) is Kaua'i; the youngest Hawai'i, where the active Kīlauea volcano adds more landmass daily.

2 Polynesian Migration
Marquesan voyagers came to Hawai'i as early as the 4th century, with Tahitians arriving in the 13th. These waves of migration by Polynesian seafarers populated the Hawaiian islands.

3 Western Contact
The landing of British explorer James Cook at Kealakekua Bay on Hawai'i in 1778 is thought to be the first time Hawai'ians had contact with westerners. Spanish ships sailed into island waters in the 16th century, but there are no records of any contact being made.

4 King Kamehameha I Unites the Islands
The Hawai'ian warrior chief Kamehameha I conquered O'ahu and Maui, then Kaua'i ceded to him, forming the Kingdom of Hawai'i in 1809.

5 Missionaries Arrive
In 1820 the first wave of Christian missionaries arrived in Hawai'i, a group of New England Congregationalists.

6 The Plantation Era
From the mid-1800s, sugar cane producers began to import contract workers. Chinese were followed by Portuguese, Japanese, Latin Americans and southeast Asians, resulting in the islands' diverse ethnic mix.

7 Overthrow of the Hawai'ian Monarchy
On 17 January 1893, Hawai'i's last Queen, Liliu'okalani, was forcibly removed from her throne and placed under house arrest in 'Iolani Palace. The coup was the work of American businessmen based in Hawai'i.

8 Pearl Harbor Attacked
On 7 December 1941 Japanese warplanes atttacked the U.S. fleet anchored at Pearl Harbor. This shocking and stunning attack marked the official entry of the United States into World War II.

9 Tourism
By the late 1950s, tourists were coming in increasing numbers to this tropical paradise within easy reach of the US. Today, more than seven million visit each year.

10 Statehood
Hawai'i became the 50th US state on 21 August 1959 (less than two years later, future US President Barack Obama would be born in Honolulu). The occasion is marked by a state holiday, Admission Day, celebrated on the third Friday in August.

2 South Shore

The South Shore of O'ahu has among its attractions several popular beaches, walking trails over Koko Head, and an underwater park at Hanauma Bay *(above)*.

3 Capitol District

Chinatown, the modern State Capitol and an old mansion that was once the home of Queen Lili'uokalani are just some of the attractions of this historic district in Honolulu *(right)*.

4 'Iolani Palace

The palace *(below)* was built for King Kalā-kaua and Queen Kapi'olani in the 19th century and was later the seat of government. It is now restored and open to the public.

5 Hawai'i Maritime Center

Down by Honolulu Harbor are a number of fascinating exhibits about Hawai'i's maritime history, including a four-masted, full-rigged ship *(left)*. There is a great viewing point from the top of nearby Aloha Tower.

6 Kalākaua Avenue

Kalākaua is Waikīkī's main thoroughfare, running along the ocean right up to the crater of Diamond Head. Halfway along the avenue are the "Pink Lady" and the "White Lady", two landmark oceanfront hotels with famous bars *(above)*.

7 Honolulu Academy of Arts

Arts of the Islamic and Oriental worlds are strong points of this museum, as well as 15,000 works by American and European artists. Polynesian works are displayed, too.

8 Bishop Museum and Planetarium

This state museum in Honolulu offers a fascinating insight into Hawai'ian culture. Its Science Garden represents the Hawai'ian land divisions called *ahupua'a*.

9 Kāne'ohe District

A stunning region northeast of Honolulu, Kāne'ohe as a scenic coastline, lush gardens, state parks and Japanese-style temple to explore *(above)*.

10 Polynesian Cultural Center

On the north shore of O'ahu, this centre is the lace to explore the rich traditions of Polynesia *(above)*, uch as the pageantry and cuisines of Hawai'i, Tahiti, onga and other Pacific islands.

Top 10 Music and Dance Styles

1 Hula Kahiko
In this famous art form, hula dancers are accompanied by percussive instruments made from natural materials and the intonations of one or more chanters. Ancient hula began, it is thought, as a religious ritual and a male preserve.

2 Hawai'ian Chant
As an oral tradition, Hawai'ian stories and family histories were related through chants *(oli)*. They are used for many reasons, from prayers and lamentations to requests for permission to gather flora.

3 Hula 'Auana
Hula was revived during the reign (1874–91) of the Merrie Monarch, David Kalākaua. *Hula 'auana* (modern hula), is accompanied by instruments and singing voices. It is more flowing than *hula kahiko*, and dancers generally wear western clothes.

4 Slack-Key Guitar
Slack-key refers to a style of playing the guitar in which the strings are loosened, producing a jangly sound.

5 Steel Guitar
The Hawai'ian steel guitar was born around the turn of the 20th century. It is held horizontally on the player's lap, and a sliding steel bar is used on the fret board.

6 The Sweet Leilani Era
From 1900 to the early 1940s, US composers were greatly influenced by Hawai'i, mostly due to the way the islands were portrayed by Hollywood. This time is called the *Hapa-Haole*, or Sweet Leilani, era.

7 Contemporary Hawai'ian Music
The modern renaissance of the Hawai'ian culture began in the late 1960s, with music playing a major role. The late Israel Kamakawiwo'ole is perhaps the best known international representative.

8 O-Bon
This traditional Japanese religious observance has evolved into a more secular event here. Dances honour deceased ancestors and are joyous occasions marked by music and festivities.

9 Lion Dance
During Chinese New Year celebrations, dancers don a lion costume and perform a ritual dance to ward off evil. Spectators fill red and gold envelopes with money and feed them to the lion for prosperity and good luck.

10 A World Beat
Jawaiian describes a blend of reggae and Hawai'ian music, and island rappers are now putting their own slant on hip-hop music.

Las Vegas

The Entertainment Capital of the World offers you just about everything: the world's largest hotels; the brightest stars in showbusiness; shops and restaurants that rival any on earth. It's true, too, that the lights are brighter in Las Vegas. Yet you don't have to go far from the glamour and glitter to find the natural beauty of lakes and the desert as well.

1 Bellagio The hotel *(left)* that upped the ante as far as Las Vegas luxury is concerned is well located, too.

TOP 10 Moments in History

1 1855: Mormons Establish a Trading Post
Inhabited first of all by Native Americans, and encountered by Spanish explorers in 1829, the Las Vegas area was only settled in 1855, when a group of Mormons established a trading post here.

2 1931: Gambling Legalized in Nevada
Relaxed gaming laws were passed in the Silver State in 1931. In reality, betting and gambling were already widespread and, sometimes, legal.

3 1935: Boulder Dam Dedicated by Roosevelt
The greatest hydroelectric project of the 20th century, the Boulder (later Hoover) Dam was begun in 1931 and completed four years later.

4 1940s: Air Con and Irrigation Arrive
These two innovations made the scorched Nevada desert suddenly more attractive to developers. In 1941 a Los Angeles hotelier bought land just south of downtown for $150 an acre and built the 100-room El Rancho motel.

5 1946: Bugsy Siegel Opens the Flamingo
When mobster Benjamin "Bugsy" Siegel opened his Flamingo Hotel, a Miami Beach style that was to be the hallmark of the Strip replaced the Wild West feel.

6 1960: The Rat Pack Comes to Town
Frank Sinatra performed at the Sands Hotel in 1960, with friends including John F Kennedy in the audience. Vegas became a playground of his so-called Rat Pack.

7 1966: Howard Hughes Arrives
Hughes played a dominant role in the Nevada hotel and casino industry. Increasingly eccentric, the billionaire lived as a recluse at the Desert Inn for 10 years until his death, emaciated and with uncut fingernails and hair.

8 1990s: The Era of the Theme Hotels Begins
In the 1970s and 1980s the hotels became larger and more flamboyant. In 1991 the groundbreaking MGM Grand, Treasure Island and pyramidal Luxor launched the theme hotel in earnest.

9 1998: Bellagio Opens
Hotelier Steve Wynn set a new standard for Las Vegas hotels with the luxurious Bellagio. He is acknowledged as the creative force behind the modern resort concept.

10 The Next Generation of Resorts
Las Vegas is a dynamic, ever-evolving city. The near future will see mega-resort "cities", with huge accommodation choice as well as countless restaurants, shops, and entertainment venues.

2 The Venetian
At this hotel, minstrels and nobility stroll among Venetian landmarks such as the Campanile and the Rialto bridge, while gondolas glide gently by *(above)*.

3 Grand Canyon
This is the ultimate excursion from Las Vegas. Whether their trip is by plane, bus or car, most visitors say the experience is unforgettable *(above)*.

ed Rock Canyon 4
Not far from the city lights, this escarpment *(right)* shimmers in the setting sun.

5 CityCenter
This "city-within-city" is the most pensive privately nded resort complex the United States.

6 **Glitter Gulch**
The heart of Las Vegas in its early days, and downtown's centrepiece, Glitter Gulch *(below)*, experienced a rebirth in the late 1990s.

7 **Wynn Las Vegas**
This opulent mega-resort is set in beautiful landscaped gardens.

8 **The Strip**
The neon artery of ambling *(above)* pulses with xcitement. Imaginatively iemed resorts make it a :reet that never sleeps.

9 **The Forum Shops at Caesars**
The glory that was Rome provides the backdrop for a choice of upmarket shops and restaurants.

10 **Hoover Dam**
An engineering marvel, the dam *(below)* not only amed the raging Colorado River but also created the normous Lake Mead, providing myriad aquatic pursuits, just ninutes from the Las Vegas city limits.

TOP 10 Wedding Chapels

1 Bellagio Wedding Chapels
Bellagio's two chapels offer among the most elegant and romantic wedding venues in Las Vegas. Each has a stained-glass window behind the altar and chandeliers of amethyst and Venetian glass.

2 Viva Las Vegas
Don't let the humble, rustic interior cramp your style: the chapel has a selection of fancy costumes at your disposal, covering such nuptial themes as Egyptian, Beach Party, Victorian, Gangster, Western and even Intergalactic.

3 Little Church of the West
Opened in 1942, this is one of the oldest wedding chapels in town. It is a favourite with the stars: Billy Bob Thornton and Angelia Jolie married (albeit briefly) here.

4 Jewish Weddings
Many chapels offer a Jewish wedding but, for requirements relating to a formal ceremony, contact Temple Beth Sholom or Temple Adat Ari El.

5 Christ Church Episcopal
This Episcopal church is the closest one to the Strip. Churches in the Episcopal Diocese of Nevada require pre-nuptial meetings with the rector before a wedding.

6 Guardian Angel Cathedral
Just steps away from the dazzling, bustling Strip, the Roman Catholic cathedral is refreshingly spartan.

7 Canterbury Wedding Chapels
Create your own Camelot by renting medieval costumes, even crowns, and tying the knot in one of Excalibur's two medieval-style, Gothic vaulted chapels.

8 Island Wedding Chapel
Located at the Tropicana, this chapel offers weddings in a tropical paradise – in the lush Polynesian Gardens Gazebo or the South Seas-style palm-thatched Chapel.

9 The Little White Chapel
For the bride and groom with only a few minutes to spare, here is the world's only Drive-Up Wedding Window. It never closes, and no appointment is necessary.

10 Hot-Air Balloon Ceremonies
In wintertime, you can hover peacefully above the Las Vegas noise and neon while the nuptial knot is tied.

Los Angeles

The myth, the velocity, the edginess in creative and technological fields – this is Los Angeles, where the multicultural future that awaits the rest of the country is already a firm reality. In just over 200 years, LA has grown from a dusty Spanish outpost into one of the world's largest and most complex cities, offering top venues for everything from archaeology and the arts to food. The birthplace of Mickey Mouse and Hollywood, LA has shaped the imaginations of millions.

1 The Getty Center

One of the best bargains in town, this striking hilltop complex *(left)* is a marvel of modern architecture and a mecca for fans of European art. There are stunning views from here too.

TOP 10 Moments in History

1 1781: The Founding of Los Angeles
Under orders of King Carlos III of Spain, Governor Felipe de Neve laid out a settlement along a river valley and called it El Pueblo de la Reina de Los Angeles (The Town of the Queen of the Angels).

2 1850: LA Becomes a City of the USA
Soon after the US-Mexican War ended in 1848, Los Angeles became part of the USA on 4 April 1850.

3 1876: The Arrival of the Railroad
Chinese immigrants built the Southern Pacific railroad from Los Angeles to San Francisco. The last spike – made of gold – was driven in on 5 September.

4 1911: The Movies Come to LA
British immigrants David and William Horsely founded Hollywood's first permanent movie studio, the Nestor Film Company, in an old tavern at the corner of Sunset Boulevard and Gower Street (now CBS Television). Within a decade, the district became the world's movie capital, reaching a "Golden Age" in the 1930s and 40s.

5 1913: The Opening of the LA Aqueduct
The world's longest aqueduct takes its water from the Owens Valley, some 400 km (250 miles) north of LA. The first drop arrived on 5 November, and the aqueduct continues to supply over 75 per cent of LA's water.

6 The 1920s: The Birth of the Aviation Industry
Driven by a dream, 28-year-old Donald Douglas began designing airplanes in the back of a barber shop. A year later, the first Cloudster cargo plane propelled his Douglas Aircraft Company into world prominence.

7 1965: The Watts Riots
The arrest of a young black motorist suspected of drunk driving by white policemen on 11 August sparked off six days of rioting.

8 1968: Assassination of Robert F. Kennedy
On 5 June, after wrapping up a speech to celebrate victory in the California primary, presidential candidate Robert F. Kennedy was gunned down by Sirhan Sirhan.

9 1992: The LA Riots
LA erupted into violence on 29 April after the acquittal of four white police officers on trial for beating up black motorist Rodney King.

10 1994: Northridge Earthquake
Millions were jolted awake on 17 January by a violent earthquake. It caused 57 deaths, 6,500 injuries and damaged many of the city's freeways and homes.

2 Griffith Park

The largest city park *(above)* in the nation offers a unique combination of rugged wilderness and such diversions as museums, a zoo and an observatory. The landmark Hollywood Sign is located here as well.

3 Disneyland® Resort

As timeless and ageless as Mickey Mouse himself, the original Disney park hasn't lost its magic over half a century since it first opened.

4 El Pueblo de Los Angeles

This historic district *(above)* preserves LA's oldest buildings and celebrates the city's Spanish-Mexican past with stores, eateries and festivals.

8 Sunset Strip
The heady mix of hip restaurants, nightclubs and bars along the city's entertainment mile *(above)* attracts legions of the young and the trendy.

9 Los Angeles County Museum of Art (LACMA)
One of the largest art museums in the US, LACMA offers a survey of artistic achievement in the world from prehistoric times to the latest art world trends.

10 Universal Studios Hollywood
A day at Universal *(right)* involves high-tech thrill rides, live action shows and special effects extravaganzas. The Studio Tour takes visitors to the backlot of this actual working movie studio.

5 Catalina Island
Catalina Island *(above)* is a quick and easy getaway, the considerable charms of which include crystal-clear waters, miles of undeveloped backcountry and a sense of being far away from the bustle of big city LA.

6 Huntington Library, Art Collections and Botanical Gardens
One of LA's great cultural treasures invites visitors to experience its fine paintings, rare manuscripts and gorgeous gardens.

7 Historic Hollywood Boulevard
The boulevard that gave birth to the movie industry is still associated with the stars, even if the only big names around today are those embedded in the sidewalk *(above)*.

Top 10 Movie Theatres

1 Pacific Theatres at The Grove
State-of-the-art meets Art Deco charm at this 14-screen complex that evokes the grand theatres of early Los Angeles. A great cinema for star sightings.

2 The Bridge
This cutting-edge theatre has been subtitled "cinema de lux" for good reason. Enjoy recently released movies sitting in large and luxurious leather chairs.

3 ArcLight Cinemas and Cinerama Dome
The exquisite 14-screen ArcLight is the shiny neighbour of the futuristic Cinerama Dome. The lobby, lorded over by a giant digital board, leads to a lively café-bar with terrace. A good place for star sightings.

4 El Capitan Theatre
Old-time Hollywood glamour has returned to Los Angeles courtesy of the Walt Disney Corporation, which restored this 1926 theatre. It functions as a first-run cinema, showing Disney flicks that are sometimes preceded by lavish live shows.

5 Grauman's Chinese Theatre
This flashy 1927 Chinese fantasy palace is still the site of movie premieres. Catch a blockbuster here – you never know which famous name might be sitting next to you.

6 The Egyptian Theatre
This oldest of Hollywood Boulevard's themed 1920s movie palaces houses the American Cinematheque. It presents art house fare and the documentary *Forever Hollywood* on weekends. Regular events feature famous directors and actors.

7 Silent Movie Theatre
The movies of Charlie Chaplin, Rudolph Valentino and other silent-era legends regularly reel off at the nation's only remaining silent-movie theatre. Live music from the 1920s and classic cartoons often precede screenings.

8 The Nuart Theatre
One of Los Angeles's finest independent theatres shows the kind of experimental and foreign fare that multiplexes tend to eschew. Cult classic *The Rocky Horror Picture Show* is shown on Saturdays.

9 Bing Theater at LACMA
LA's famous art museum presents high-brow retrospectives in its on-site theatre, which has a top-notch digital sound system. On Tuesdays at 1pm, catch classic films for a small fee.

10 California Science Center IMAX Theater
IMAX stands for "maximum image" and with a screen that is seven storeys tall and 27-m (90-ft) wide, it's a fitting name. The giant screen has a six-channel surround-sound system and ensures total sensorial immersion.

Maui, Moloka'i and Lana'i

Maui is known as the "valley isle," and most of its population nestles in the low-lying isthmus between the lush western mountains and the drier slopes of Haleakalā to the east. Skirting the coast are some of the world's finest beaches, from the popular resorts on the southwestern fringe to the wilder surfing beaches on the north and eastern shores. Maui's administrative group also includes the islands of Moloka'i and Lana'i, with more magnificent scenery and even greater remoteness.

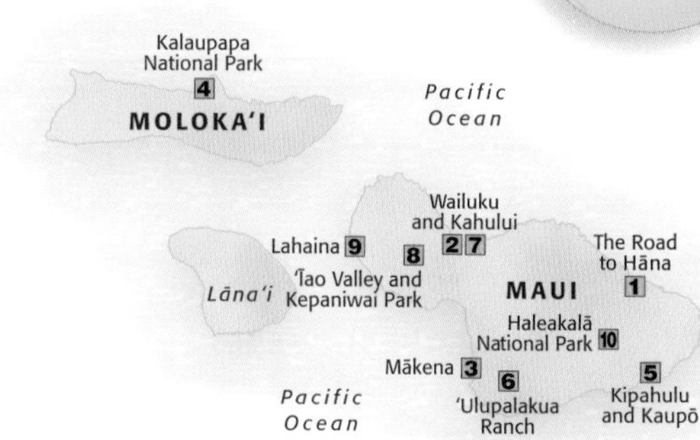

1 The Road to Hāna

This winding coastal road *(left)* runs for 56 miles (90 km), with jaw-dropping ocean views to the left and sparkling waterfalls amid shady woodlands to the right.

2 Wailuku and Kahului

These twin towns are where the majority of Maui's populace lives and works. The area also has fantastic sights from missionary churches *(above)* to ancient sites to lush, tropical plantations.

3 Mākena

Once the remotest spot on Maui's southern coast, Mākena *(above)* has become increasingly popular with divers and kayakers in recent years.

TOP 10 Beaches

1 Kā'anapali Beach
This beautiful white sand beach is clean and safe, and good for most water sports. It's also the best beach on Maui for "beautiful people watching" – the section in front of Whalers Village is popularly known as "Dig Me."

2 Nāpili Bay
A small, tranquil bay with a white sand beach that's good for swimming and safe for children; it's by the Nāpili Kai Beach Resort. There's no better place for a cocktail to accompany the sunset.

3 Kapalua Bay
This gorgeous crescent of a white sand beach perennially appears on lists of the world's best beaches. Even hump-back whales love it, and in winter often frolic offshore.

4 Baldwin
Just off the Hāna Highway between Kahului and Pā'ia, the sea can be a bit rough at times, and it tends to get windy by mid-morning. But, if you're an early morning person, Baldwin is lovely.

5 Keālia
One of the most serene of the south shore beaches, Keālia fronts a little beach plaza of shops. It's a good place for beginners to try out surfing or windsurfing, but if that's not your cup of tea, watch the fun and then duck into a nearby restaurant for a frosty cocktail instead.

6 Kama'ole I, II, III
If you're looking for all the amenities of a family beach park, these are the beaches for you. Although they are often referred to as Kam I, II, and III, Hawaiian language speakers prefer the use of their full and proper names.

7 Keawakapu
Keawakapu has it all: good for swimming and body boarding, a great view of Kaho'olawe, and there are lots of shallow spots, safe for even the youngest children.

8 Wailea Beach
A series of enticing white sand crescents, bordered by lava rock outcroppings, there are almost no waves at the edges of these beaches – excellent for swimming and very good for snorkelling too.

9 Malu'aka
The Mākena end of this wide beach is quite sheltered (*malu* means sheltered in Hawaiian) and safe for small children. Just above the beach at that end is a lovely picnic spot.

10 Hāmoa
Once described by Mark Twain as the most beautiful beach on earth, this is the Hawai'i of the travel posters. This is Maui's windward coast, so, if it looks a little wild, spread out your blanket and watch the local kids surf, bodysurf, and boogie board.

Kalaupapa National Park, Moloka'i 4

On the "get-away-from-it-all" island of Moloka'i, Kalaupapa *(right)* is an isolated peninsula, flat as a golf green and separated from the rest of the island by sheer cliffs. Formerly, it was used as a leper colony.

3 'Īao Valley and Kepaniwai Park Gardens

Up in the verdant 'Īao Valley, the Kepaniwai Park Gardens *(above)* celebrate the diverse cultures that make up modern Maui through a range of national gardens and structures.

5 Kīpahulu and Kaupō

On the wild, beautiful east coast of Maui, this area offers fantastic treks through forest paths to discover spectacular waterfalls *(above)* and idyllic, revitalising mountain pools.

6 'Ulupalakua Ranch

On the southern slopes of Haleakalā, this ranch is at the heart of the Tedeschi Vineyards. Before the introduction of vines, the winery experimented with a pineapple wine, Maui Blanc.

7 Bailey House Museum, Wailuku

A fascinating place that focuses on 19th-century missionary life and the earlier Hawaiian culture, which missionaries attempted to dispel.

9 Front Street, Lahaina

The well-preserved buildings along this street take you back to the early 1800s, when missionaries arrived to save the souls of bawdy sailors and bring Christianity to islanders.

10 Haleakalā National Park

The amazingly diverse terrain of this national park – from rainforest to desert – culminates in the moon-like landscape of Haleakalā's enormous crater *(above)*.

Top 10 Golf Courses

1 Kā'anapali Royal Course
The "grand dame" of Maui's courses, this 6,120-m (6,693-yd), par 71 course is designed to be played in the northeasterly tradewinds.

2 Kapalua Plantation Course
Players on this challenging 6,777-m (7,411-yd), par 73 course are rewarded with some of the most spectacular scenery on Maui.

3 Kapalua Bay Course
Among the many challenges of this 6,035-m (6,600-yd), par 72 course, are strategically placed trees, 68 bunkers and 8 water hazards.

4 The Dunes at Maui Lani
The Dunes course has been compared to classic British ones. Designer Robin Nelson visited Scotland to study the links courses and integrated some features into this par 72.

5 Waiehu Municipal
This 5,788-m (6,330-yd), par 72, set in Central Maui, offers stunning views of the ocean, Pu'u Kukui, and Haleakalā. The front nine run along the ocean, while the back nine negotiate an old sand dune.

6 Wailea Gold
This course rose to fame in 2001with the Champions Skin Game and the extraordinary foursome of Arnold Palmer, Jack Nicklaus, Gary Player and Hale Irwin; yet its 6,472-m (7,078-yd), par 72 layout is manageable even for weekend-only players.

7 Wailea Emerald
Everyone loves the pleasant, visually soft, almost laid-back style of this course. Some consider the 18th hole to be peerless, and the "19th" is the fine Gannon's restaurant.

8 Wailea Blue
Most of the hazards of this 6,185-m (6,765-yd), par 72 course are natural. Golfers must contend with the wonderful distraction of the spectacular surroundings.

9 Mākena Golf Course
Quick greens with lots of breaks are found at the Mākena course. There are natural features including rock walls and gullies.

10 Pukalani Country Club
This 6,366-m (6,962-yd), par 72 course is set high on the slopes of Mount Haleakalā, with views of the isthmus between East and West Maui, the 'Īao Needle, and both the north and south shores.

Natural Wonders

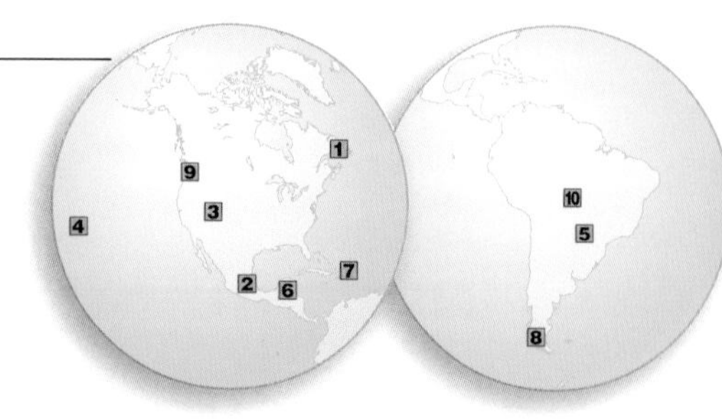

From its northernmost wastes to the glaciers of its southern tip, its highest, most dramatic peaks to the mysterious depths of its teeming ocean floors, the continent that encompasses the Americas is a vast tapestry of dazzling natural beauty. Some is right on the doorstep of civilization, some may take more effort to reach, every bit is spectacular in its rewards.

1 The Viking Trail, Newfoundland *CANADA*

If the idea of exploring wild tundra landscapes with few people and herds of roaming caribou appeals, make for Newfoundland's Viking Trail. This stunning route, which runs along a narrow sliver of highway that has been carved out of a spectacular landscape, is perfect for nature lovers. It runs northwards from the dramatic coastal mountains and fjords of Gros Morne National Park along an unforgettably wild coastline to the remote north tip of Newfoundland.

2 Peña de Bernal, San Sebastián Bernal *MEXICO*

When Peña de Bernal was formed, some 135 million years ago, it was three times the size of the eroded – but still impressive – mountain you see today. One of the tallest monoliths in the world, it's a popular attraction for walkers and pilgrims, who follow the trail to the chapel halfway up the mountain. The vertical route to the summit is the domain of expert rock climbers. The inhabitants of San Sebastián Bernal believe that the rock bestows a calming and life-enhancing energy to those living in its shadow. Each year at the spring equinox the villagers take part in an ancient ritual, dressing in white and forming a human chain around part of the monolith. There is also a Christian festival here every May, which culminates in a procession bearing a 45-kg (100-lb) cross to the mountain chapel, from where climbers carry it on to the summit.

3 Monument Valley, Utah *USA*

Heading down dead-straight Highway 161 towards the backdrop of Monument Valley's broken crags, you might well get the feeling that you have been this way before. And, in films, you have – this classic Western scene of unremitting desert scattered with the great, lonely fists of red rock known as "Mittens" has seen many a cowboy and stagecoach ride by. You can hire a horse or take a tour to reach places that are off-limits to those on foot. For an authentic touch, consider staying in a hogan – a traditional home of the Native American Navajo people.

4 Hulopo'e Beach, Lāna'i, Hawai'i *USA*

This beach is a gem – a gentle curve of soft sand fringed by low kiawe trees, and demarcated to the east by the russet Mānele Cone, an extinct volcanic relic. The whole bay forms part of a marine reserve – in winter, when humpback whales are frequently visible out to sea, snorkellers can hear their underwater songs.

5 Iguazú Falls *BRAZIL AND ARGENTINA*

Snaking westwards from southern Brazil for hundreds of miles, the Iguazú river grows in size as it is joined by over 30 tributaries on its way to the Argentine border. Here the ground falls away and the Iguazú plunges up to 60 m (200 ft) in over 250 separate churning waterfalls, forming the planet's widest span of falling water. This natural wonder, whose name comes from the native word for "big waters" – is shared between Argentina and Brazil, and faces a third country, Paraguay. The surrounding Iguazú National Park is an enchanted place of squalling toucans, screaming capuchin monkeys and kaleidoscopic-coloured butterflies, forming the perfect green frame for these spectacular waterfalls.

Torres del Paine, Patagonia Kayaking near floating icebergs *(above)*

Iguazú Falls The widest span of falling water in the world *(below)*

Monument Valley, Utah The iconic sandstone "Mittens" *(above)*

Lighthouse Reef, Belize The Blue Hole at the centre of the reef *(below)*

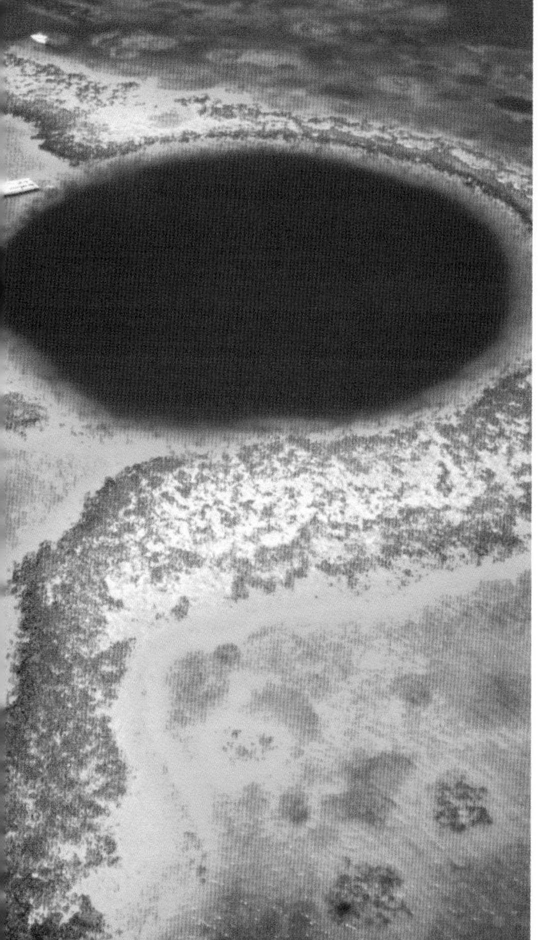

6 Lighthouse Reef *BELIZE*

This reef's famous Blue Hole, explored by Jacques Cousteau in 1972, is the jewel in Belize's diving crown. The barren circular tunnel, which drops to a depth of 450 m (1,475 ft), has stalactites hanging from a shelf at 40 m (130 ft), indicating that it was once dry land. The only fish you'll see here are reef sharks and groupers, but venture into other areas and you will find livelier spots, where bottom-feeding rays glide across sandy lagoons, pastel-toned sea plumes cover the raised barrier reef and pelagic species, including turtles, patrol the steep walls.

7 Dominica *CARIBBEAN*

This wild but fecund island with seven active volcanoes is famously captured on film in *Pirates of the Caribbean*. Most visitors explore the rainforests, where the air is alive with the sound of birds – 170 species in all, including two species of parrot found nowhere else. For divers, Dominica is an aquatic heaven, and sections of the coast are so remote that yours might be the first footprints on a black-sand beach.

8 Torres del Paine, Patagonia *CHILE*

The harsh, beautiful wilderness of Patagonia, shared by Argentina and Chile, rewards the few who make it this far south with truly breathtaking scenery. Torres del Paine National Park, encompassing mountains, fjords, glaciers, unbelievably blue lakes and perhaps the best fishing and big-game hunting on the continent, is the epicentre of this majestic place.

9 San Juan Island, Washington State *USA*

Visitors who arrive by ferry, gliding into the glorious San Juan archipelago for the first time, might feel that they are entering an enchanted land. Here, in a maze of inlets and channels, more than 450 islands – only 172 of them named – emerge from the bright blue waters of the northern Puget Sound. Hills carpeted in Douglas fir rise from the shores, while the soaring snow-capped peaks of the spectacular Olympic Peninsula tower in the distance. Find time to go whale-watching, either from a kayak or from Lime Kiln Point State Park on San Juan Island, where you might catch a glimpse of the resident population of orca whales as they feed.

10 Pantanal *BRAZIL*

The largest wetlands in the world, this vast, fertile region of central-west Brazil is home to some of the most exciting – and easily seen – creatures anywhere on the planet. In the wet season, from November to April, it rains for hours each afternoon and the aquatic flora rejoices; in the dry season, from May to October, a huge variety of birds flocks here. Giant otters, capybaras and marsh deer are among the animals to be seen all year. Stay on a cattle farm and explore by boat or on horseback.

Mexico City

Pulsating with life and culture, blessed with perpetually spring-like weather, and with a fascinating blend of history and modernity, Mexico City is endlessly surprising. With excellent museums, ornate churches, colonial palaces and urban parks, the city attracts a large number of visitors.

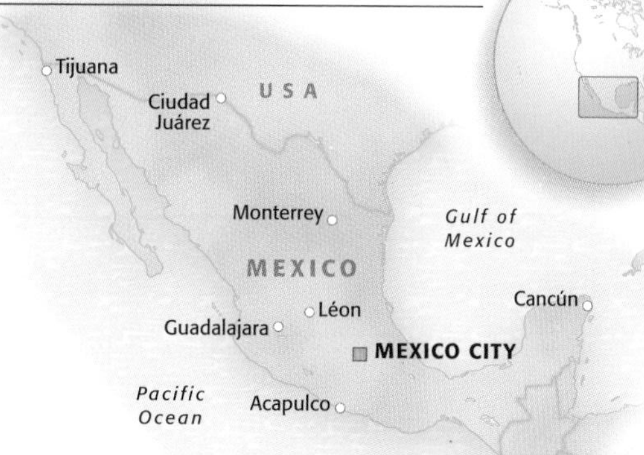

1 Museo Nacional de Antropología
One of the great museums of the world dramatically presents its pre-eminent collection of Mexican pre-Hispanic art by region *(above)*.

2 Palacio Nacional
This massive executive palace and government office stands along the east side of the Zócalo and showcases Diego Rivera's famous mural *Epic of the Mexican People.*

3 Catedral Metropolitana
The largest and most important colonial cathedral in the Western Hemisphere *(right)*, it took almost three centuries to build and majestically blends Baroque and Neo-Classical styles.

TOP 10 Moments in History

1 Early Inhabitants
Once the largest metropolis in the Western Hemisphere, Teotihuacan was a planned city of straight roads, plazas, government buildings and pyramids. It reached its height in AD 550 and was abandoned in AD 750.

2 Aztec Empire
The Aztecs arrived from the north in around 1325, initially as mercenaries and workers. Ruthless fighters with a firm hierarchy, the Aztecs gained control of this beautiful and extensive city by the 1420s. Their conquests then spread to the east and south.

3 Spanish Conquest
The Spanish conquistador Hernán Cortés landed with his troops near Veracruz in 1519. He joined forces with a strong tribe called the Tlaxcalans, and after a bloody siege in 1521 they jointly defeated the Aztecs.

4 Colonial Capital
The Spanish built Mexico City on Tenochtitlan's ruins. Silver mined all over Mexico fuelled the city's expansion and the building of huge palaces. When the silver industry declined, the city stagnated for much of the 17th and early 18th century.

5 Mexican Independence
In 1810 Padre Miguel Hidalgo famously called for independence from Spain, beginning the Mexican War of Independence. It raged on for more than a decade, culminating in the birth of a federal republic, the United States of Mexico, in 1824.

6 US Invasion
The USA invaded Mexico in 1847 and occupied Mexico City. During the battles in Bosque de Chapultepec, six young cadets, the Niños Héroes, leapt to their death rather than be captured.

7 War of Reform
Mexico's most loved leader, Benito Juárez, came to power in 1855. He enacted laws that restricted the power of the Church. A bitter war ensued, and finally, in 1861, the liberals won and Juárez was elected president.

8 The Maximilian Affair
In 1863 a French army invaded Mexico and the brief rule of Austrian Emperor Maximilian I began, before he was deposed and executed in 1867. After the Republic was restored, Juárez returned to power until his death in 1872.

9 Mexican Revolution
Dictator Porfirio Díaz came to power in 1872. Although he modernized the education and transport systems, the divide between rich and poor increased. When Díaz annulled the 1910 election victory by opponent Francisco I. Madero, the Mexican Revolution began.

10 20th-century Growth
The Revolution ended with Álvaro Obregón taking control in 1920. Under the ensuing stable government, Mexico flourished. Its capital grew exponentially, and continues to grow today.

7 Museo Nacional de Arte

This exquisite *palacio (above)* is home to the nation's extensive art collection, encompassing nearly five centuries of magnificent masterpieces by Mexico's finest artists, including Miguel Cabrera, José María Velasco and Diego Rivera.

4 Bosque de Chapultepec

Mexico City's lovely Bosque de Chapultepec is one of the largest urban parks in the world, and is home to many of the city's best museums and family attractions.

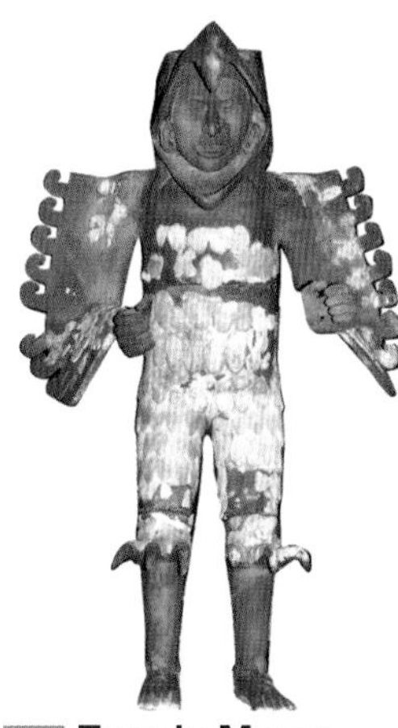

6 Templo Mayor

An accidental discovery led to a massive archeological effort that uncovered the ruins of this Aztec temple. A museum was built to house the recovered artifacts *(above)*.

5 Palacio de Bellas Artes

The spectacular performing arts *palacio (above)* is a city icon, combining an exquisite white marble exterior and an Art Deco interior with Mexican touches.

Xochimilco Floating Gardens 8

Colourfully decorated *trajineras*, or flat barges *(right)*, propelled by boatmen with long poles, carry merry-makers on floating parties along the shady, tree-lined Aztec canals of Xochimilco, "the place where flowers grow".

9 Villa de Guadalupe

One of the holiest Catholic shrines in the Americas honours the Virgin de Guadalupe, Mexico's patron saint, who appeared in a vision to Juan Diego, an indigenous Mexican peasant, in 1531.

10 Teotihuacan

The largest archaeological site in Mesoamerica *(left)*, and one of the most impressive in the world, this ancient city 48 km (30 miles) northeast of Mexico City reached its zenith in AD 550.

TOP 10 Mexican Markets

1 Mercado Jamaica
Beautiful and colourful, this is the city's wholesale flower market. Every imaginable type of seasonal flower grown in the country is here in abundance.

2 Mercado de la Merced
With crowded narrow paths between small booths offering towering piles of brilliantly coloured merchandise of every kind, a visit to the city's main wholesale and retail market is a must.

3 Mercado Sonora
Known as the "Witches' Market", locals come here to buy herbs, remedies and folk medicine – everything required to cast a spell, conjure up love, restore health or obtain wealth.

4 Mercado de Coyoacán
This friendly neighbourhood market has traditional Mexican wares, such as sombreros, brilliant rugs and papier-mâché *piñatas*.

5 Mercado Xochltl
Lively and colourful, this neighbourhood market offers meats, spices, fruits and flowers of exceptional quality that are grown along the Xochimilco canals.

6 Mercado Insurgentes
This indoor market is renowned for glittering displays of silver jewellery, pendants, earrings and bracelets. There are also silver bowls, platters, tableware and sculptures.

7 Mercado San Juan
The indoor booths of the market fill two floors with traditional handmade goods such as silver jewellery, painted ceramics and woven textiles.

8 Mercado de Artesanias de la Ciudadela
The largest gathering of souvenir and handicraft vendors in the Centro Histórico area.

9 Jardin de Arte
This weekly outdoor art market in Plaza del Carmen has artists lining the walkways with their vibrant works, the subjects ranging from historical scenes to contemporary themes.

10 Bazar de Sabado
A very popular weekly artisan and handicrafts market (Saturdays only), Bazar de Sabado also has a charming courtyard and an excellent restaurant.

Miami and the Keys

At its best, Miami is all pastel hues and warm, velvety zephyrs – a tropical reverie. The culture is sensuous and physical, often spiked with Caribbean rhythms and accents. Outdoor activities hold sway throughout the area, at the world-famous beaches and in the turquoise waters; the vibrant nightlife, too, attracts pleasure-seekers, while significant historical sights are around every corner.

1 SoBe Life
Ever since *Miami Vice* drew attention to this fun-zone *(left)*, hedonists have flocked to the beaches and nightlife in this part of the city.

Top 10 Snorkelling and Diving Sites

1 John Pennekamp Coral Reef State Park
Many say this park offers some of the best snorkelling in the world. Various boats can also be rented here.

2 Biscayne National Underwater Park
Closer to Miami than John Pennekamp, the Biscayne National Underwater Park has almost as many good snorkelling possibilities. Here you'll find vivid coral reefs to dive among.

3 Looe Key National Marine Sanctuary
A brilliant coral dive location, and the closest great snorkelling to Key West. Accessible from Bahia Honda State Park.

4 Dry Tortugas National Park
Located almost 110 km (70 miles) west of Key West, these seven islands and their surrounding waters comprise a fantastic park. The snorkelling sights are exceptional, due to shallow waters and the abundance of marine life. Snorkel directly off the beaches of Fort Jefferson or take one of the trips to the wreck of the *Windjammer*, which sank on Loggerhead Reef in 1907.

5 Key Biscayne Parks
Crandon and Bill Baggs Parks have excellent snorkelling areas in some of Miami's cleanest, clearest waters.

6 Fort Lauderdale Waters
Some of the best parts of the three-tiered natural reef system here are close to the shore, though most require a short boat ride. In addition, more than 80 artificial reefs have been built to enhance the growth of marine flora and fauna.

7 Red Reef Park
Boca Raton's Red Reef Park offers some of the best beaches and snorkelling in the area. An artificial reef can provide hours of delightful undersea viewing and is suitable for youngsters. The Gumbo Limbo Nature Center is just across the street.

8 Palm Beach
The Breakers and Four Seasons hotels both offer snorkelling options along the Palm Beach coast.

9 Bahia Honda State Park Waters
The beautiful, sandy beach of Bahia Honda in the Keys – often lauded as one of the best beaches in the US – has good waters for swimming and snorkelling.

10 Key West Waters
Take the plunge right off the beach at Fort Zachary Taylor State Park, or join an expedition out to the reefs that lie all around this island. Most trips offered by local companies take three to four hours, including at least an hour and a half of reef time.

2 Deco District
The whimsical architecture on South Beach traces its origin to 1920s Paris, but along the way the style underwent fruitful, exotic influences and blossomed into Florida's own Tropical Deco *(above)*.

3 Calle Ocho, Little Havana
The Cubanization of Miami changed it from sleepy resort to dynamic megalopolis. Little Havana fuels the impression that Miami is Latin American at heart *(above)*.

4 Vizcaya Museum and Gardens

One immensely rich man's aspiration to European andeur and appreciation of Western artistic heritage d to the creation of what is probably Miami's most autiful cultural treasure.

9 Gold Coast Highway A1A

Route A1A hugs the sands of the Gold Coast *(above)*, ending its way through the wealthiest and most beautiful eas in the state of Florida.

0 The Everglades

Taking up most of South Florida, the Everglades is a st sea of swamp and sawgrass, dotted with subtropical rests and populated with prolific wildlife *(above)*. It is also ome to Native American Seminoles and Miccosukees.

5 Merrick's Coral Gables Fantasies

The 1920s boom saw a need to build not only structures but also an identity. George Merrick rose to the challenge and created fantasy wonderlands *(right)* that continue to stir the imagination.

8 Key West

This mythic area *(above)* lives up to its reputation as the most outlandishly free spot in the US. A frothy mix of maritime traditions and laid-back style.

6 Lowe Art Museum

This major art museum, created by an endowment from George Merrick, has around 17,500 works of art, including masterpieces from cultures the world over and from every age.

7 The Wolfsonian–FIU

This superb museum (which began life as a storage company) owes much to its founder's passion for collecting 20th-century propaganda art and design artifacts of the 1885–1945 period.

TOP 10 Deco Buildings

1 Park Central
This 1937 favourite by Henry Hohauser, then the most famous architect in Miami, uses a nautical theme to great effect.

2 Beacon Hotel
The abstract decoration above the ground floor has been brightened by a vibrant colour scheme – an example of "Deco Dazzle", introduced by designer Leonard Horowitz in the 1980s.

3 Colony Hotel
This is perhaps the most famous of Miami's Deco hotels, primarily because its stunning blue neon sign has featured in so many movies and TV series.

4 Waldorf Towers
Here is one of the first examples (1937) of Nautical Moderne. The style is carried to one of its logical extremes with the famous ornamental rooftop lighthouse. Fantasy towers were the stock in trade for Deco architects.

5 Breakwater Hotel
This classic Streamline Moderne-style hotel was built in 1939. It features blue and white "racing stripes" and a striking central tower that seems to recall both a ship's funnel and Native-American totems.

6 The Tides
An Art Deco masterpiece, The Tides resembles a luxury ocean liner. All 45 spacious suites have expansive ocean views and the Goldeneye Suite has a hot tub at the centre of the room.

7 Essex House
Hohauser's Essex House is considered one of the best examples of maritime Art Deco. Erected in 1938, the building closely resembles a ship, with "porthole" windows and awnings that look like railings. It's topped by a neon-lit spire.

8 Leslie Hotel
The Leslie (1937) has a cockatoo colour scheme – white and yellow with grey accents. The interior has shades of turquoise and flamingo pink.

9 Cardozo Hotel
A late Hohauser work (1939), this is a Streamline Moderne masterpiece, with beautifully rounded sides, aerodynamic stripes and other expressions of the modern age.

10 Cavalier Hotel
While the Cardozo, next door, emphasizes the horizontal, the Cavalier's façade is starkly vertical and temple-like. The temple theme is enhanced by beautifully ornate vertical stucco friezes, which recall the geometric designs of the Aztecs.

Montréal

Situated on the mighty St Lawrence River, Montréal captivates with its history, culture and vibrancy. It shares much in common with Québec City *(see pp194–5)* – not only were they both major players in the foundation of Canada, but their portside locations have kept them at the heart of international commerce, resulting in a harmonious blend of heritage architecture and exciting modern venues that charm all those who visit.

1 Parc du Mont-Royal
Looming over Montréal's busy cityscape, this mountain park *(left)* is the most visited attraction in the city.

2 Parc Olympique
The Olympic Park's many attractions include botanical gardens, an insectarium and sports facilities *(above)*.

3 Place Jacques-Cartier and Place de la Dauversière
Two famous names in Canadian history have lovely squares across from one other *(above)*. Place Jacques-Cartier honours the discoverer of Canada; Place de la Dauversière celebrates Jérôme le Royer, whose idea it was to found a colony here.

TOP 10 Moments in the History of Québec

1 First Nations
Iroquoian and Algonquian peoples had lived in Québec for thousands of years when the first Europeans arrived. "Kebec" is an Algonquian word meaning "place where the river narrows."

2 Jacques Cartier
The French explorer sailed up the St Lawrence, claiming Canada for King François I of France in 1534. He got as far as the village of Hochelaga and named its mountain Mont-Royal, from which Montréal gets its name.

3 Samuel de Champlain
French colonization began in 1608 when this explorer, navigator and cartographer founded New France and Québec City. In 1611 he established a fur trading post on the Island of Montréal.

4 British Takeover
The struggle between the French and British in Europe continued in the New World. In 1759, after a lengthy siege and a brief battle during which he was mortally wounded, British General Wolfe took Québec City, and Montréal fell to the British the next year.

5 The Creation of Canada
The Union Act of 1841 created the Province of Canada under an English-speaking parliament but, by 1848, the British had to accept the use of French. On 1 July 1867, Québec and Ontario joined with Nova Scotia and New Brunswick as the Dominion of Canada.

6 The Dark Years
Well into the 20th century the Roman Catholic church held considerable political sway in Québec. The right-wing Union Nationale (1936–39 & 1944–59) used its influence to win votes.

7 A Brighter Future
In 1960 the Liberal Party was elected, bringing social reforms and economic development. Expo '67, held in Montréal, expressed the spirit of bright optimism in Canada's Centennial year.

8 The October Crisis
After increasing in popular support, the separatist movement suffered a major setback in October 1970, when the radical Front de Libération du Québec (FLQ) kidnapped two high-ranking politicians, murdering one.

9 Parti Québécois
The separatist Parti Québécois (PQ), in power from 1976 to 1985, ensured Francophone dominance in Québec with Bill 101, to the alarm of the English-speaking minority.

10 Oui ou Non?
In 1995 the PQ held the second referendum on whether Québec should split from Canada. The "no" side won with just 50.5 per cent of the vote. Despite this narrow defeat, support for separatism has dwindled.

6 **Basilique Notre-Dame**
North America's largest church when constructed in 1829 is the Gothic vival gem of Vieux-Montréal *(above)*, with exquisite stained-glass windows.

7 **Musée Pointe-à-Callière**
The true birthplace of Montréal represents a merging the city's past history and modern technology. Cutting-ge exhibitions and archaeological artifacts allow visitors experience six centuries of local life.

8 **Chinatown**
A stroll through the tern-lit streets around ulevard Saint-Laurent d rue de la Gauchetière ers a feast of authentic nic dining, cultural riosities and fascinating ops and stalls *(above)*.

9 **Little Italy**
Montréal's largest immigrant community traces its life in the city back to the early 19th century. Boulevard Saint-Laurent and its surrounds are full of places to wine, dine and shop in true Italian style.

10 **Les Laurentides**
This mountain range has long been the favourite year-und playground for week-enders and vacationers th its pristine lakes, hiking trails and ski slopes.

4 **Musée des Beaux-Arts de Montréal**
The oldest and largest Québec museum *(above)* contains works dating from antiquity to contemporary masters.

McGill University 5
A remarkable campus *(right)* spreads itself over a lush swathe of the Downtown district. Fine examples of Victorian architecture mix easily with the contemporary bustle of student life.

TOP 10 Children's Attractions

1 Insectarium
This astonishing exhibition was the brainchild of Georges Brossard, who traveled the world to collect the bugs. Although most are dead, there are live tarantulas and other creepy crawlies, safely ensconced behind glass.

2 Biodome
Here animals from the Arctic, Antarctic, Tropics, Laurentian and St Lawrence marine habitats are housed under one roof in settings resembling their natural habitats.

3 Planetarium
Under the Star Theatre's domed ceiling, visitors are whisked into the heavens on a high-tech virtual journey through time and space.

4 La Ronde Six Flags Amusement Park
The largest amusement park in Québec was opened for Expo '67, but new rides and attractions are added each year. Thrill-seekers will love Vertigo, which swings 18 m (60 ft) up in the air through a 360-degree rotation. Spinning tea cups and carousels will appeal to the little ones.

5 Laser Quest
This involves making your way around a dark labyrinth armed only with a laser gun. Score points by zapping other players, lose them by getting zapped. Rousing music adds to the atmosphere.

6 Centre des Sciences
The aim of iSci, as it's known, is to demystify science, such as how technology affects our daily lives. Entertaining and innovative interactive games, ranging from solving a crime to saving the planet, make the learning fun.

7 Le Théâtre de L'Oeil
Performances, workshops, and exhibitions are all part of the fun at this puppet theatre. Kids can watch how puppets are made, learn to pull a few strings and watch a show.

8 CinéRobotheque
In the comfort of your own viewing unit, select a film and then watch a robot go through its routines to find and deliver it to you.

9 Labyrinthe du Hanger 16
Each year a tantalizing new theme is created, with which to lure you into an intricate maze of corridors, obstacles, puzzles, surprises and thrills, in this portside hangar. The entire family can solve the mysteries together, or kids can go on their own.

10 Cosmodome, Laval
A fascinating look at space and the universe. Large-scale models of the solar system explain the make-up of every planet, while the rockets exhibition give an insight into space travel.

New England

New England is six states rolled into one amazing, all-season destination of pine-scented mountains, briny ocean villages, sophisticated urban centres and so much more. It's also the birthplace of America – a fact attested by a multitude of historic homes and museums. Icons abound: covered bridges, snowy ski slopes, blazing autumn foliage, lighthouses perched on craggy cliffs, white churches on town greens and tail-flapping lobsters fresh from the sea.

1 Historic Boston

The American past is palpable in New England's largest city, where the cobbled streets seem to echo with the calls of patriots. Restaurants and shops enliven an ancient granite market, and the Freedom Trail unites momentous sites *(left)*.

2 Cape Cod, Massachusetts

The bent arm of Cape Cod is a summer world of untamed dunes, bird-filled marshes and quirky towns *(above)*, where you can savour fresh fish, sticky taffy sweets and the salt tang of sea breezes.

3 Mount Desert Island, Maine

Rugged headlands above a crashing ocean, pine forests crisscrossed with hiking trails and still ponds reflecting the sky's blue bowl express nature in all its unbounded wildness *(below)*.

TOP 10 Colonial and Historic Sites

1 Old Sturbridge Village, MA
Heritage livestock and costumed guides recreate New England's rural life in the early 19th century at this living history museum.

2 Strawbery Banke, NH
Follow the development of Portsmouth, NH, from the 17th to the 20th century through this complex of historic dwellings assembled at Strawbery Banke, the city's original settlement.

3 Billings Farm & Museum, VT
Set up in 1871, Billings Farm was turned into a museum of rural life in 1982. Its rolling green pastures and farm buildings represent the ideal of Vermont dairy farming.

4 Lowell National Historic Park, MA
Lowell launched the Industrial Revolution in the United States, and this urban park preserves the city's network of canals and its 19th-century textile mills.

5 Plimoth Plantation, MA
Step back to 1627 at Plimoth Plantation, where costumed interpreters speaking 17th-century English portray early settlers studiously. Native American interpreters are at the re-created Wampanoag encampment.

6 Canterbury Shaker Village, NH
Founded in 1792, Canterbury was a working Shaker village into the 1960s. Workshops and demonstrations teach you about Shaker skills and ideals, and there are daily tours of Shaker buildings.

7 Weir Farm National Historic Site, CT
The painter J. Alden Weir (1852–1919) made this rustic farm into a retreat for himself and his friends at the end of the 19th century. Two further generations of painters lived here too.

8 Slater Mill, RI
Dating from 1793, water-powered Slater Mill was the first successful cotton-spinning mill in the whole of the United States.

9 Hancock Shaker Village, MA
Learn about the artful skills of the Shakers at this settlement founded in 1790. Note in particular the 1826 Round Stone Barn – both functional and beautiful.

10 Minute Man National Historical Park, MA
This is the site of the opening salvo of the American Revolution, when British troops engaged Colonial rebels in Lexington and Concord on 19 April 1775. Exhibits and annual reenactments commemorate this rout of the British.

4 White Mountains, New Hampshire

ummer hikers and winter kiers relish these rugged ranite mountains cloaked in alpine forest *(right)*. Hike, drive or ride the cog railway up Mount Washington, the northeast's tallest peak.

5 Litchfield Hills, Connecticut

Bistros, bakeries and boutiques often fill the historic white clapboard buildings of hill-country villages in this region, where artists, actors and authors keep their country-home retreats.

6 Berkshires, Massachusetts

Theatre, music and dance flourish in the gentle Berkshire Hills, where lavish estates of a bygone era's millionaires lend a sophisticated air to homespun country villages.

7 Newport, Rhode Island

Opulent mansions on seaside cliffs *(above)* reveal the splendours of the Gilded Age in one of America's most written about yachting harbours.

9 Green Mountains, Vermont

From pre-Revolutionary villages to ridgeline hiking trails, ne Green Mountains form the spine of Vermont. In autumn, s forests blaze with colour *(above)*; in winter, some of the ation's top slopes lure skiers.

8 Lakes Region, New Hampshire

With its shoreline of 386 km (240 miles), Lake Winnipesaukee rules New Hampshire's kingdom of mountain-rimmed lakes *(above)*. Fishing, boating and waterskiing make the region a summer playground.

10 Portland, Maine and Casco Bay

Maine's largest city remains a seafaring centre on a picturesque bay, but the Old Port's handsome brick blocks also host taverns, galleries and boutiques *(left)*.

TOP 10 Ways to See Foliage

1 White River Flyer, VT
Take a jaunt through the southern Vermont woods aboard a vintage train for spectacular views of the Connecticut River and its tributaries' deep gorges.

2 Mohawk Trail, MA
This historic Indian trade route follows the upper ranges of the Deerfield River and climbs through the Charlemont State Forest.

3 K-1 Gondola, VT
After a gondola ride to the highest lift-served terrain in Vermont, a short hike brings you to Killington Peak for a panoramic view of five states and part of Canada.

4 Kancamagus Highway, NH
Few foliage drives in New England match the thrill of hurtling along the "Kanc". Stop along the way to savour the experience by hiking to a waterfall or sunning on mid-stream glacial boulders.

5 Essex Steam Train & Riverboat, CT
Combine a trip through the woods in restored carriages pulled by steam locomotives with a Connecticut River cruise aboard a three-deck Mississippi-style river-boat.

6 Route 100, VT
New England's ultimate road for leaf-peeping, Route 100 passes natural wonders like Moss Glen Falls, follows the Mad River through scenic villages, then rises high into the Green Mountains.

7 Lake Champlain Cruise, VT
Hop aboard the Spirit of Ethan Allen III for a narrated cruise of Lake Champlain. Kids can keep an eye out for Champ, the lake's legendary sea serpent.

8 Deerfield River Rafting, MA
The Deerfield River has some of New England's most exhilarating rapids and scenic gorges.

9 Mount Monadnock, NH
The 965-m (3,165-ft) summit of Mount Monadnock offers incredible views, especially in the autumn, when the trees are a blaze of colour.

10 Boston's Emerald Necklace
Boston is blessed with an almost continuous chain of parks, stretching from downtown sky-scrapers to leafy suburbia. In autumn, this 8-km (5-mile) cycle route is an explosion of colour.

New Orleans

One of the most popular tourist destinations in the United States, New Orleans winds gracefully in a crescent shape around a bend in the Mississippi River. The city has a rich French and Spanish cultural history, evident in its food, architecture and customs. It is known for its historical jazz tradition, colourful festivities and an unmatched *joie de vivre*. Nicknamed "the City that Care Forgot", New Orleans is renowned for its carefree vibe.

1 Aquarium of the Americas

This aquarium *(left)* is one of the finest in the country. A top attraction in New Orleans, the state-of-the-art facility houses 15,000 sea animals and interactive displays on marine life.

2 New Orleans Museum of Art

Founded a century ago by Isaac Delgado, a sugar broker, the New Orleans Museum of Art boasts a collection of more than 40,000 objects in 46 galleries, valued at more than $200 million.

3 Royal Street

The highlight of the French Quarter, Royal Street *(above)* offers the best fine art in the city, as well as antiques and gourmet restaurants.

4 Audubon Zoo

This site *(above)* has sheltered animals since 1884. Considered among the best in the country, it covers 23 ha (58 acres) and houses animals in their natural habitats.

TOP 10 Moments in History

1 Founding of New Orleans (1718)
Jean Baptiste Le Moyne de Bienville of the French Mississippi Company founded a colony on the Lower Mississippi and named it "La Nouvelle Orléans".

2 New Orleans Becomes a Spanish Colony (1763)
New Orleans was ceded to the Spanish in 1763. The Spanish encouraged trade and turned the city into a commercial centre.

3 The Great French Quarter Fire (1788)
Most of New Orleans' buildings were destroyed by a fire on Good Friday, 1788. The city was rebuilt with Spanish-style architecture.

4 Construction of St Louis Cathedral (1794)
The original St Louis Church was destroyed by the fire of 1788. Its replacement was begun the following year and was later elevated to cathedral status.

5 First Mardi Gras Celebrated (1827)
During Spanish rule, pre-Lent festivals were banned. Under US rule, in around 1827, the people were finally permitted to wear masks and celebrate. The first Mardi Gras parade was held 10 years later.

6 World Cotton Exposition (1884)
Up to a third of all cotton produced in the US was handled in New Orleans. The 1884 World Cotton Exposition lasted six months.

7 New Orleans Saints Football Franchise Awarded (1966)
On All Saints Day in 1966, the National Football League awarded New Orleans the league's 16th major team franchise. The aptly named Saints adopted a gold fleur-de-lis as their team symbol, representing the French colonists of Louisiana.

8 Construction of the Louisiana Superdome (1975)
It took four years and $163 million to build the huge Louisiana (now Mercedes-Benz) Superdome. The result is a stunning facility.

9 Louisiana World Exposition (1984)
The centrepiece of this event was a gondola lift that ferried millions of visitors across the Mississippi River. The fair was the precursor to a major redevelopment of the city's riverfront area.

10 Hurricane Katrina (2005)
The largest disaster in the US, Hurricane Katrina hit New Orleans on 29 August 2005. The failing of the city's levees caused massive flooding and destruction.

5 **Jackson Square**
Located in the centre of the French Quarter, Jackson ıuare *(above)* was the main square of old New Orleans. day, it is an attractive park with St Louis Cathedral as a ıckdrop and beautiful architecture all around.

ıew Orleans City Park 9
This park *(right)* is ıew Orleans' version of Central Park in New York. A lush landscaped space with dozens of attractions, it is a ɔpular getaway from the urban bustle.

0 **Mississippi Riverfront**
New Orleans is bordered by the Mississippi. Take streetcar ride alongside it, dine by the river or board a .eamboat *(below)* for a leisurely dinner cruise.

6 **Mardi Gras**
Billed as the world's largest street party, Mardi Gras is an annual spring celebration that culminates on Fat Tuesday (just before Lent). This colourful festival, associated with feasting and parties, marks the last celebration before Lent.

7 **Canal Street**
Ride the streetcar *(above)*, enjoy an outdoor lunch, shop at fine boutiques or try your luck at Harrah's New Orleans Casino on the widest boulevard in the world.

8 **Bourbon Street**
Bourbon Street features some of the French Quarter's main attractions, including beautiful hotels, excellent vintage restaurants and bars, and plenty of live jazz *(above)*. This is a must-see for visitors.

TOP 10 Architectural Highlights

1 Mercedes-Benz Superdome
This stadium is home to the New Orleans Saints football team. The dome covers the world's largest steel-framed room unobstructed by posts.

2 Louisiana Supreme Court
The Louisiana Supreme Court Building (1910) is an imposing example of Beaux Arts architecture.

3 St Patrick's Church
The subtle Gothic exterior of the church belies its ornate interior. Built in the early 19th century, it was later overhauled to create a much grander structure.

4 Napoleon House
This early 19th-century landmark was originally the home of the mayor of New Orleans. In 1821 Mayor Nicholas Girod offered his home as a refuge for Napoleon during the latter's imprisonment at St Helena.

5 The Cabildo
One of five properties comprising the Louisiana State Museum, the Cabildo was the historic site where the Louisiana Purchase was signed in 1803. The present building dates from 1795.

6 Lafitte's Blacksmith Shop
The oldest building in the French Quarter was built in 1772 by alleged slave-traders Pierre and Jean Lafitte. One of the longest bar rooms in the country, it is still candlelit.

7 Pontalba Apartment Buildings
In 1849 the French Baroness Pontalba built these apartments on inherited land. The oldest apartment buildings in the U.S. are three-storey terrace houses that reflect French and American architecture.

8 Hotel Monteleone
This historic hotel underwent a $60-million renovation in 2004, but retained its original grandeur and charm.

9 The Peristyle at City Park
The Neo-Classical Peristyle was built in 1907. It is supported by massive Ionic columns and "guarded" by four cement lions.

10 Whitney Wyndham Hotel
Originally a bank, this stately structure was converted into a hotel in 2000. It retains the old building's ornate columns, chandeliers and bank vault.

New York City

With its towering skyscrapers, world-class museums, top-notch restaurants, vital arts scene and endless opportunities for retail therapy, New York is certainly a city of superlatives, all the way from historic Lower Manhattan through the bright lights of Broadway right up to the streets of Harlem.

1 Empire State Building
This soaring Art Deco skyscraper *(above)* is one of the most widely recognized symbols of the city and a star of countless movies. It offers unforgettable panoramas of New York from its 86th-floor Observatory.

2 Central Park
The vast swathe of green *(above)* provides a 340-ha (843-acre) respite from the concrete of the city. It took 16 years and more than 500,000 trees to complete the park.

Statue of Liberty 3
The symbol of freedom for millions seeking a new life in America, the lady holding the torch of liberty *(right)* is ensconced on her own island.

TOP 10 Historic Landmarks

1 St Paul's Chapel
This church of 1766 has a glorious Georgian interior, lit by Waterford chandeliers. Preserved here is the pew where George Washington prayed after his inauguration as president in 1789.

2 City Hall
A Georgian building of 1803-12 with French Renaissance influences, City Hall is one of New York's finest edifices, its interior featuring a rotunda circled by 10 Corinthian columns.

3 Trinity Church
This lovely, square-towered church has bronze doors designed by Richard Morris Hunt. Built in 1839–46, the spire was once the tallest in Manhattan, but is now dwarfed by Wall Street towers.

4 St Patrick's Cathedral
James Renwick, Jr designed America's largest Catholic cathedral (1879) in French Gothic style. The interior has side altars dedicated to saints and holy figures, chapels and stained-glass windows.

5 Carnegie Hall
Philanthropist Andrew Carnegie financed the city's first great concert hall, built in 1891. Its corridors are lined with memorabilia of great artists who performed here.

6 Cathedral of St John the Divine
The world's largest cathedral was begun in 1892 and is still a work in progress. The part-Romanesque, part-Gothic building is impressive for its stonework, vast nave, altar windows and rose window.

7 New York Stock Exchange
Opened in 1903, the façade of this 17-storey edifice is appropriately monumental for the building at the centre of the US economy.

8 US Custom House
One of the city's best Neo-Classical works, the 1907 Custom House features an elaborate mansard roof and fine sculptures, including four by Daniel Chester French. A nautical mural by Reginald Marsh adorns the rotunda.

9 New York Public Library
This white marble Beaux Arts edifice of 1911 is magnificent inside and out. Imposing stairways, terraces and fountains inspire awe; its reading rooms invite repose.

10 Grand Central Terminal
This public facility of 1913 is remarkable for its beauty. The main concourse is suffused with natural light and the vaulted ceiling is decorated with twinkling constellations.

4 Times Square and the Theater District An explosion of neon illuminates Broadway and Times uare *(above)*, where more than 40 famous theatres play st to a changing parade of hit shows.

5 Metropolitan Museum of Art It would take weeks to see all the treasures of this useum. It houses one of the greatest collections of the estern world and spans 5,000 years of culture.

8 Ellis Island Immigration Museum Carefully restored buildings *(above)* bring to life e experience of the immigrants who have poured to New York over generations, helping to build the ulti-ethnic city of today.

6 Rockefeller Center This urban wonder in the city's centre brings together restaurants, gardens, an underground shopping concourse, office space, a skating rink and more than 100 works of art, from murals to statues.

9 Fifth Avenue A heady mix of fashionable shops *(above)* and world-class architecture makes for an avenue of endless pleasures and some of New York's best-known addresses.

10 Guggenheim Museum
A work of art in itself, this Frank Lloyd Wright building *(left)* is a fitting frame for a major collection of contemporary art.

7 American Museum of Natural History
Long famous for its dinosaurs *(above)*, the museum moved into the space age with the dramatic Rose Center for Earth and Space.

TOP 10 Shopping Locations

1 Macy's
From food to futons, the selection at the world's largest store is vast. And Macy's is a major part of the New York scene, from the spring flower show to Tap-O-Mania, when thousands of tap dancers converge on Herald Square.

2 Bloomingdale's
After Macy's, this is New York's best-known department store, and is renowned for high fashion for men and women.

3 5th Avenue Department Stores
Bergdorf Goodman, Saks Fifth Avenue, and Lord and Taylor have a full range of top-brand clothing for men, women and children, as well as an upmarket selection of home accessories.

4 Barney's New York
Here's the place to find the latest designer labels to please the well-heeled, young and trendy. The sales at Barney's are legendary.

5 Henri Bendel
Set up like a series of boutiques, Bendel's displays innovative, fun women's fashions for glamorous shoppers. Great bags too.

6 Century 21
Savvy uptown shoppers know it's worth making the trek downtown to sift through racks full of designer labels at great prices. The store is also good for cosmetics and ladies' accessories.

7 H&M
This Swedish retailer has proved a smash success in New York. The secret? Kicky, young designs for men, women and children at rock bottom prices.

8 Madison Avenue
Designers such as Giorgio Armani and Yves Saint Laurent have moved to Madison Avenue, and the exclusive shops and boutiques now run from 59th almost to 79th Street.

9 SoHo Boutiques
The 20–30-something crowd does its shopping in trendy SoHo boutiques such as Anna Sui, APC, Miu Miu and Cynthia Rowley.

10 6th Avenue
The cast-iron buildings at around 18th Street form another shopping mecca. Seek out Bed Bath & Beyond for homewares and Old Navy for casual clothes.

USA
Ke'anae Arboretum
on Maui, Hawai'i

Orlando

One word describes Orlando's transformation in the last three decades: stunning. The city and its suburbs have gone through a Cinderella-like metamorphosis, where plain Jane has become a worldly beauty. Millions of tourists are seduced every year by sophisticated resorts, a wide range of theme parks, must-see attractions, happening nightclubs and great restaurants. But if the bright lights get too much, there's also a world of wonderful wildlife within easy reach.

1 Disney Hollywood Studios®
Lights, camera, action! Movies, TV shows and stomach-churning thrill rides come together in a theme park *(left)* that also serves as a working studio.

2 The Magic Kingdom® Park
The park *(above)* that started Disney's Florida empire combines fantasy, adventure and the future in a package of rides and shows that brings the Disney magic to life.

3 Disney's Animal Kingdom® Park
Visitors are brought face-to-face with the wild world of animals, but this kingdom's spacious environmental design doesn't always offer a front-row seat *(above)*.

TOP 10 Parks and Nature Reserves

1 Canaveral National Seashore
This federal preserve borders the Kennedy Space Center. Along with Merritt Island *(see opposite)*, it is home to scores of species, such as sea turtles, manatees, dolphins, alligators, bald eagles and ospreys.

2 Lake Eola Park
Burn a few calories on the 1.4-km (0.9-mile) trail that circles the lake here. Less energetic pursuits include feeding the birds and cruising Lake Eola in a rental boat.

3 Wekiwa Springs State Park
These springs make for a fertile habitat for white-tail deer, gray foxes, bobcats, raccoons and black bears.

4 Lake Louisa State Park
White-tail deer, wild turkeys, marsh rabbits, opossums, and raccoons are common here, and don't be surprised if a polecat or skunk scoots across your path.

5 Lake Kissimmee State Park
This park is one of the best bird-watching areas in the state. You might see bald eagles and snail kites, as well as whooping and sand-hill cranes. On weekends, the park has a re-created 1876 cattle camp.

6 Bill Frederick Park at Turkey Lake
Unlike many state parks with spartan amenities, this city retreat has a pool, picnic grounds, fishing lake, nature and jogging trails, playgrounds and a petting zoo. It also has camping areas if the call of the wild is too strong to leave.

7 Big Tree Park
Senator, the 3,500-year-old bald cypress for which the park is named, is 5 m (17 ft) across, 14 m (47 ft) around and 38 m (125 ft) tall. Board-walk trails run through the cypress swamp.

8 Tosohatchee State Reserve
Swamps dotted with hard-wood "hammocks" (tree islands) and a 30-km (19-mile) stretch of the St John's River combine to make this one of Central Florida's prettiest and most primitive parks. Hawks, eagles, fox squirrels and many types of songbird can be seen from the park's trails.

9 Wheatley Park
This city park is more urban oasis than rustic countryside retreat, with facilities such as basketball, tennis and sand volleyball courts, and barbecue areas with grills.

10 Ralph V Chisholm Park
On the shore of East Lake Tohopekaliga, there's a beach, swimming area, horse trails, softball and baseball fields, and volleyball courts.

Merritt Island 4
Located near the Kennedy Space Center, this wildlife refuge *(right)* is great for learning about local and migrating animals, while also enjoying a bit of fishing or hiking.

5 Kennedy Space Center
The thrill of space exploration makes America's No. 1 space center a stellar attraction complete with live rocket launches and exhibits *(above)*.

6 Universal Studios Florida®
The movie and TV rides and shows here will make your wildest dreams come true and your worst nightmares a (special effects) reality. From *Jaws* to *Shrek*, the silver screen comes to life.

7 Epcot®
Inquiring minds love this Disney park, which features technology in Future World and the culture, architecture and enticing food of 11 nations in World Showcase.

8 SeaWorld® Orlando
Its laid-back pace, educational appeal and aquatic ttractions *(above)* make this a popular alternative to ne queues and crowds at other parks.

9 Islands of Adventure®
Universal's top-of-the-pile theme park is a magnet for nrill jockeys, with some of the fastest, highest and best ides in town. Be warned that 9 of its 13 rides have height r health restrictions, so it's not for the young, weak of tomach or squeamish.

10 Wet 'n Wild®
Some say it's hard to beat Disney's water parks, ut this rival *(above)* has the most thrills money can uy on the city's water scene.

TOP 10 Rockets

1 Jupiter C
This early version of the Mercury Redstone rocket was developed by German scientist Wernher von Braun. It carried the USA's first satellite, Explorer I, which launched on 31 January 1958.

2 X-15
The X-15 rocket plane flew 199 missions from 1959 to 1968, carrying a who's who of astronauts, including the first man on the moon, Neil Armstrong. It reached an altitude of 107,960 m (354,200 ft) and speeds of 7,274 kmph (4,520mph).

3 Mercury Redstone
This rocket carried the first American into space. Alan B Shepard Jr's 15-minute, 22-second ride aboard the Freedom 7 capsule in 1961 was one of six flights in the Mercury programme.

4 Mercury Atlas
When the Mercury programme graduated to orbital flights, the Atlas replaced the Mercury Redstone. This is the rocket that took John Glenn, Scott Carpenter, Wally Schirra and Gordon Cooper into space in 1962–3.

5 Titan II
A larger capsule was needed for two-person crews, and this rocket earned its place in NASA history. It was used for 10 manned Gemini Titan missions in 1965 and 1966.

6 Saturn 1B
The Saturn 1B launched Apollo spacecraft into orbit in the mid-1960s as astronauts trained for manned flights to the moon. Later, it launched missions to the Skylab space station (1973) as well as the American crew for the Apollo/Soyuz Test Project (1975).

7 Saturn V
At 110 m (363 ft), this is the largest launch vehicle ever built. It sent off Apollo 11, the 1969 mission that would land Neil Armstrong and Buzz Aldrin and on the moon.

8 Titan Centaur
The Titan Centaur rocket launched Voyager I and II in 1977 on a mission reaching Jupiter, Saturn, Uranus, Neptune and far beyond.

9 Pegasus
This winged wonder is capable of putting small communications satellites into a low Earth orbit from below a carrier aircraft.

10 X-43A Launch Vehicle
These diminutive rockets may one day boost small, unmanned jets at high speeds and altitudes, improving safety for manned flights.

Peru

For most people, Peru conjures up images of the Inca citadel of Machu Picchu, but there's much more to see as well. Other magnificent examples of ancient civilizations abound, including the mysterious Nazca Lines, while colonial monasteries and churches evoke the Spanish conquest. Unique animals and plants flourish across all the regions, and there are numerous natural wonders, including the world's deepest canyons, the highest navigable lake, Titicaca, and the Amazon jungle, which makes up 60 per cent of this breathtakingly beautiful land.

1 San Francisco, Lima

This religious complex is a masterpiece of Colonial Baroque. The 1656 painting of the *Last Supper (left)* in the Dining Hall shows Jesus and his disciples feasting on the Peruvian delicacy *cuy* (guinea pig).

Top 10 Moments in History

1 Early Peruvians
Evidence of human civilization dates back to around 20,000 BC, to Pikimachay Cave where remnants of the first nomads have been found.

2 Caral: The First City
The most impressive example of monumental architecture during the Formative Period (2700-1000 BC) is Caral, dubbed the oldest city in the New World.

3 The Rise and Fall of Chavín
The Chavín culture flourished around 900 BC in what is known as the First or Early Horizon (1000 BC–AD 200) era. Around 300 BC Chavín's influence began to wane.

4 Regional Development
Regional cultures began to emerge in an epoch known as the Regional Development Period or the Classical Era (200 BC–AD 900). They included tne Moche, Recuay and Cajamarca, Lima, Nazca, Wari and Tiahuanaco. All were strong regional states, each with unique features.

5 Conquering Kingdoms
During the period known as the Conquering Kingdoms (900–1532), two powers emerged on the northern coast: the Sicán in La Leche Valley, and the Chimú (or Chimor) in the Moche Valley.

6 The Incas
The Incas were descended from families based around Cusco. They reached the peak of their power and influence in the 15th century when the Inca Empire covered more than a third of South America.

7 Exploration and Conquest
In 1529 Pizarro was appointed Governor and authorized to conquer Peru. The Spanish invasion was one of the first and the bloodiest clashes between the Old and the New Worlds. The brutally repressed indigenous people rebelled against the Spanish throughout their occupation.

8 Peruvian Independence
Peru gained independence from Spain in 1824, but the following decades were politically volatile, and the country was embroiled in bitter territorial disputes.

9 20th-Century Peru
Peru enjoyed a brief period of stability in the early 20th century, but the Depression hit it hard, and decades of turmoil followed. Guerrilla groups such as Shining Path waged terrorist campaigns in the 1980s and 1990s.

10 Modern Peru
The 21st century began more promisingly with democratic elections and a relatively stable economy.

2 Lima

Lima is a fascinating city, full of contrasts and brimming with activity. Pre-Inca ruins rub shoulders with fine colonial mansions and churches *(above)*, leafy squares become bustling food markets, and music floats above the roar of traffic.

3 Lake Titicaca

According to legend, this is birthplace of the first Incas Manco Cápac and Mama Ocllo. The world's highest navigable lake, it is dotted with inhabited islands, some of which are man-made from *totora* reeds. The people lead a traditional way of life, based around fishing, farming and weaving *(abo*

Nazca Lines 4

It hardly ever rains on the Peruvian coast, which is how these remarkable images, drawn on a grand scale, have survived for centuries to baffle the modern world. A viewing [pl]atform or a light-aircraft trip are [th]e only ways to get a gods'-eye view of the Hummingbird, the Monkey *(right)* and the rest.

5 Reserva Nacional Pacaya-Samiria

Peru's largest reserve covers a huge swathe of original Amazon rainforest. An organized boat trip from Iquitos is the best way to see giant river otters and curious pink freshwater dolphins, and the very lucky and sharp-eyed might even spot a jaguar in the lush jungle on the banks.

9 Machu Picchu

The "lost city" of the Incas *(above)* is the most famous [a]nd iconic archaeological site in South America. The mist-[s]oaked citadel is a huge draw for tourists, due to its [g]randeur, and the sense of mystery that surrounds it.

7 Reserva Nacional de Paracas

The desert meets the sea in dramatic fashion on Peru's longest stretch of protected coastline. The reserve provides a habitat for resident and migratory waterbirds, including flamingoes, pelicans and Humboldt penguins *(above)*, and you may even see condors circling overhead.

6 Cusco

Peru's tourism capital *(above)*, the gateway to the sites of the Sacred Valley, is a picturesque town whose Inca walls are filled with Spanish arches and squares.

8 Chavín de Huántar

The major ceremonial centre for the Chavín people dates back to around 1300 BC. Temple buildings, underground tunnels, carved lintels and monoliths are dwarfed by a great pyramid-like building and a sunken plaza that could hold thousands of pilgrims during important fiestas.

10 Museo Tumbas Reales de Sipán

A stunning modern museum houses the treasures found in "the richest tomb of the New World", the Royal Tombs of Sipán. There are over 1,400 objects in gold, silver, rare stones and ceramics of extraordinary beauty, quality and craftsmanship *(left)*.

TOP 10 The Culture of the Incas

1 Cult of the Sun
The Incas revered Inti, the Sun God, who nourished the earth and controlled the harvests. The Emperor, believed to be the son of the Sun God, made offerings to Inti at religious ceremonies.

2 Inti Raymi
The main Festival of the Sun was celebrated annually on 21 June, the winter solstice in the southern hemisphere. Mummies were brought into Cusco's main plaza to witness the event. It is still held on 24 June at Sacsayhuamán.

3 Ancestors
Ancestors were worshipped with offerings of food and drink. Inca mummies were always lavishly dressed.

4 Sacrifice
The sacrifice of animals was practised daily by the Incas. Human sacrifice was reserved for special occasions, and only the most beautiful children from the most powerful families were chosen to be sacrificed.

5 Divination
Divination played a large part in religious life. Everything, from treating an illness to choosing the correct sacrifice, was done as a result of the high priest consulting the oracles or by his drinking *ayahusca*, a hallucinogenic brew made from the leaves of a giant vine, whose name means "rope of the dead".

6 Record Keeping
No evidence of a formal Incan tradition of writing has been uncovered. However, anthropologists have found many *quipus*, multicoloured wool or cotton strings that were employed as a record-keeping device through a complicated system of knots. Simple or compound knots, and their size and colour, represented details of crops, debts and possibly events.

7 Farming
The Incas carved mountains into vast terraced farmlands, and created complex canal systems to irrigate them. They were the first to use a type of freeze-drying.

8 Keros
Drinking vessels made of ceramic or wood were used to consume *chicha* (corn beer) during ceremonies. They were lavishly decorated with patterns and images.

9 Stonemasonry
The Incas were unrivalled in their stonework, building entire cities without mortar, the blocks fitting so perfectly that not even a piece of paper will slip in between.

10 The Inca World
There were three levels of existence for the Incas: the underworld, represented by the snake; the present, by the puma; and the celestial, in the form of the condor.

Philadelphia

Philadelphia, the City of Brotherly Love, is a living history book, in which the story of the founding of the United States unfolds before your eyes. This compact city has more to offer than just history, however. Philadelphia is a sophisticated city that's awash with art and culture, sports and fun attractions. Many of its most popular sights are to be found in the Old City, in what's called "America's most historic square mile", but there's plenty to see and do elsewhere, with riverside parks and piers, great shopping, fine dining and much more.

1 Penn's Landing This waterfront area on the Delaware is where the city's founder, William Penn, first stepped ashore in 1682. It hosts summer festivals and is home to the city's tall ships, the World War II submarine *Becuna* and the *Olympia (left)*, the only surviving vessel from the 1898 Spanish-American war.

2 Independence Hall An unadorned brick building and clock tower *(above)*, at the heart of Independence National Historical Park, is where the US Constitution and the Declaration of Independence were drafted and signed.

3 Barnes Foundation This museum has one of the best collections of Impressionist, French Modern and Post-Impressionist paintings in the world *(above)*. There are more than 800 works on show, including works by Picasso, Renoir, Cézanne and Matisse.

TOP 10 Moments in History

1 Native Americans
The area was home to the Lenape (Delaware) Indians before the arrival of the first European settlers.

2 First Europeans
Delaware Bay was claimed for Holland in 1609. Trading posts were established along the Delaware and Schuylkill Rivers. In 1643 Swedish Lutheran settlers established a settlement near present-day Philadelphia. In 1664 the English captured the Dutch colonies, calling them New York, after the Duke of York.

3 Foundation
The Charter for Pennsylvania was founded in 1681, when King Charles II granted the land to William Penn. Penn arrived in the capital of his new colony, Philadelphia, in 1682. As a Quaker, Penn espoused nonviolence, and formed treaties with the Native Americans. More settlers followed.

4 Colonial Expansion
By the early 18th century, the port city of Philadelphia was flourishing. After the French and Indian War of 1754–63, the colonists craved independence.

5 A Nation Takes Shape
On 4 July 1776 independence from Britain was declared in Philadelphia. The city was the political heart of the country, and capital from 1790 until 1800 while Washington DC was under construction.

6 Industrialization
The city declined from the 1830s, after Washington DC became the nation's capital. Increasingly industrial, growth brought social clashes, including rebellions against anti-slavery movements.

7 Civil War
During the Civil War (1861–65), the need for weapons, munitions and warships for the Union forces bolstered Philadelphia's economy. After the war, the city held one of the first World's Fairs.

8 World War I and the Great Depression
Economic and industrial activity in Philadelphia remained brisk during World War I, although it suffered during the Great Depression.

9 World War II
World War II revived steel, chemical and petroleum production, but Philadelphia gradually lost most of its manufacturing sector to other regions of the US.

10 Modern Philadelphia
After World War II, the city lost jobs and population to the growing suburbs. Racial tensions mounted in the 1960s before stabilizing in the late 1980s. In 2000 the city hosted the Republican National Convention, which nominated George W Bush for president.

4 Liberty Place
The two steel and sapphire-blue glass towers f Liberty Place were ground-breaking in 1979, when ıey were the first structures to rise higher than the tatue of William Penn atop City Hall *(above)*.

5 National Constitution Center
his museum features ver 100 multimedia and teractive exhibits explaining ıe US Constitution. "We the eople", the opening words of ıe document, are proudly ıscribed on its massive ıdiana limestone façade.

6 Pennsylvania Academy of the Fine Arts
America's oldest fine art school and museum features a superb collection of American art, including works by Mary Cassatt, Winslow Homer and Benjamin West.

Liberty Bell Center 7
Inscribed with the words "Proclaim Liberty throughout all the Land", this huge, cracked bell *(right)* is said to have rung when the Declaration of Independence was adopted.

TOP 10 Pennsylvania Dutch Country Sights

1 Lancaster
Founded in 1730 by John Wright and named after his English birthplace, today Lancaster is the county seat. Its tree-shaded streets are lined with 18th- and 19th-century buildings. A beautiful Beaux Arts building houses the Lancaster Quilt and Textile Museum, which holds a collection of 82 Amish and Mennonite quilts.

2 Landis Valley Museum
This living history village has a village school, a country store, tavern, gun shop and firehouse, plus homes, barns, buggies and lots more from the 18th and 19th centuries. Craftspeople in costume offer classes and demonstrations.

3 Lititz
Named after a town in Bohemia, Lititz was founded by Moravians in 1756 and was a closed community for nearly a century. It has a quaint main street and a lovely spring-fed creek. Its museum is a restored 1792 Moravian stone house.

4 Ephrata
One of America's earliest communal societies was established here in 1732 by a German religious order. They built the medieval-style Ephrata Cloister, parts of which can still be visited.

5 Intercourse
This curiously named village is one of the main centres for Amish business, and pulls in visitors by the busload to buy everything from hand-bottled preserves to baskets to classic Amish furniture.

6 Bird-in-Hand
Taking its name from the inn sign of a 1734 hostelry (in which you can still stay), this pretty village is home to a fine Americana Museum.

7 Paradise
Set along Route 30, the main link in Colonial times between Lancaster and Philadelphia, Paradise grew as the number of inns and taverns increased. It's still a quite lively place.

8 Strasburg Railroad
Established in 1832, the Strasburg Railroad runs trips on historic steam trains, and there's a train museum, a toy train museum and the Choo Choo Barn model railway.

9 Amish Village
North of Strasburg, visitors can explore an 1840s Amish house, smokehouse, blacksmith's forge and working water wheel.

10 National Christmas Center
It's Christmas 365 days a year here, with snowy scenes, Yuletide feasting, nativity displays and Santa Clauses from around the world.

8 Fairmount Park
This extensive greenbelt *(above)* runs along the Schuylkill River and Wissahickon Creek. Its grassy fields and dense woodland areas are dotted with attractive buildings and statues, and feature miles of running and biking paths.

9 Reading Terminal Market
Once the largest arched-roof train shed in the world, this is now a superb farmers' market. It offers a chance to try a wide range of authentic cooking, from Pennyslvania Dutch to soul food.

10 Philadelphia Museum of Art
The city's most important museum is home to over 300,000 objects from Europe, Asia and the Americas, spanning more than 4,000 years. Key exhibits include European paintings from medieval to Post-Impressionist, a reconstructed 12th-century French cloister and one of the largest collections of costumes and textiles in America.

Puerto Rico

Puerto Rico packs tremendous diversity into a relatively small space. From exquisite coral reefs and white-sand beaches to lush rain forests, desert-dry coastal plains and a rugged mountain spine, this isle enraptures with physical beauty. Past and present intertwine, as pre-Columbian sites, castles and charming colonial buildings contrast with hip restaurants, hotels and nightclubs. Spanish-speaking yet unarguably American in style, the people of Puerto Rico are equally diverse, reflecting a potpourri of bloodlines – indigenous, African and European – and a creativity that is expressed colourfully in culture and the arts.

Atlantic Ocean
Parque de las Cavernas del Río Camuy 8
San Juan 2 3 7
Culebra 4
PUERTO RICO
6 El Yunque
San Germán 10
9 Centro Ceremonial Indígena de Tibes
1 Vieques
5 Museo de Arte de Ponce
Caribbean Sea

1 Vieques

This island *(left)*, off the east coast of Puerto Rico's main island, is surrounded by idyllic beaches. It has become a magnet for independent travellers seeking a laid-back lifestyle and trendy boutique hotels.

Condado, San Juan 2

San Juan's lively beachfront *(right)* is lined with cafés and restaurants, fashionable boutiques and high-rise hotels interspersed with parks.

3 Castillo de San Cristóbal, San Juan

This fortress *(above)*, which has been restored to its former grandeur, has bulwarks looming over the shoreline, cannons and other interesting exhibits.

Top 10 Moments in History

1 First Settlers
Puerto Rico's earliest settlers are thought to have arrived from Florida 5,000 years ago. They were later displaced by the Igneris, an Arawak tribe from the Orinoco basin of South America.

2 Taíno Arrival
After a long migration up the Caribbean chain, the Taíno people arrived on the island, which they called Borinquen, in around 500 BC. This peaceful society lived on fishing and farming.

3 Columbus' Arrival
The Genovese explorer set foot on the island in 1493, and christened it San Juan Bautista. By 1521 the island had been renamed Puerto Rico – Rich Port – by conquistador Ponce de León.

4 San Juan Founded
The first Spanish settlement, Caparra, was abandoned in 1521, and Ponce de León established a new town, San Juan, on a peninsula off a huge bay. The town suffered frequent pirate raids.

5 Haitian Rebellion
Fearing a slave rebellion, as had happened in Haiti in 1791, Spain loosened Puerto Rico's trade laws, resulting in an economic boom as US investors poured money into the island's sugar industry.

6 El Grito de Lares
The *criollo* (island born) craved independence, but their aspirations were brutally suppressed. *Independentistas* launched "The Cry of Lares" in September 1869, which resulted in liberal reforms.

7 Fight for Autonomy
A liberal government took over in Spain in the 1890s and Luis Muñoz Rivera petitioned for Puerto Rican autonomy. This resulted in an independent legislature being convened on 17 July 1898.

8 US Take-Over
Covetous of Spain's colonies, the US found a pretext to declare war on the country in 1898. San Juan was attacked and the island invaded. Spain sued for peace and the US took control of Puerto Rico.

9 Citizenship Granted
US investors poured money into Puerto Rico, which was ruled by governors imposed by Washington. Although Puerto Ricans were granted US citizenship in 1917, self-government was denied.

10 Commonwealth Status
On 25 July 1952 the island became the Commonwealth of Puerto Rico, with its own anthem, flag and judiciary. Islanders, however, could still not vote in US elections.

4 Culebra

Boasting the most spectacular beach in Puerto Rico, this small island *(left)* is popular with day-trippers and is easily reached by ferry. It is also a delight for snorkellers and surfers.

5 Museo de Arte de Ponce

This world-class museum displays artworks from the 14th to the 20th centuries, including works by Rossetti, Constable and Reynolds.

7 Old San Juan

This blue-cobbled historic district of restored olonial buildings is the jewel in the capital city's own. Its delightful plazas, centuries-old cathedrals nd dramatic castles *(above)* are well-preserved minders of a bygone era.

8 Parque de las Cavernas del Río Camuy

An hour's drive from the capital, the world's third-rgest known cave system is accessible through guided urs. Floodlights illuminate the dripstone formations.

9 Centro Ceremonial Indígena de Tibes

This pre-Columbian ceremonial site *(above)* splays well-preserved *bateyes* (ball courts) and sacred troglyphs. It is the perfect place to find out about the e of the ancient Taíno culture.

10 San Germán

The best-preserved colonial town outside Old San Juan retains its yesteryear mood. Historic buildings here include Puerto Rico's oldest church, which is packed with an array of interesting religious antiquities *(above)*.

6 El Yunque

The only tropical rain forest within US territory, El Yunque offers great hiking along mountain trails. Waterfalls *(above)* and coquí frogs are among the many lures of this natural paradise.

TOP 10 Outdoor Pursuits

1 Cycling
Heavy traffic makes cycling unsafe in most urban areas, but the countryside is less intimidating and offers spectacular scenery.

2 Sport Fishing
Anglers rave about deep-sea fishing off Puerto Rico, where tuna, wahoo, and white and blue marlin are among the prize catches. Fishing charters are offered from most seafront towns.

3 Scuba Diving
Healthy coral reefs ring the island and the Puerto Rico Trench off the south coast offers fantastic wall dives. Vieques and Culebra are also popular and have sunken wrecks to explore.

4 Golfing
Puerto Rico is a world-class golf destination with more than 23 courses designed by celebrity golfers. Most are associated with resort hotels, although all are also open for public play.

5 Surfing
Surf aficionados proclaim Rincón to be one of the world's finest surf spots, with waves topping 10 m (33 ft) in winter. Aguadilla and Playa de Jobos also offer superb surfing, while Dorado and Luquillo are good for beginners.

6 Swimming
Many of Puerto Rico's beaches are protected from rough waves by coral reefs, but strong undertows are potential dangers. So check the swimming conditions with the locals first.

7 Hiking
Puerto Rico's mountainous interior is ideal for hiking. El Yunque, which boasts a variety of trails, is the most popular location.

8 Parasailing
Popular at the north-coast resorts, parasailing involves being harnessed to a giant kite and towed by a speedboat to experience an exhilarating bird's-eye view.

9 Bird-Watching
With 350 bird species, the island brings bird-watchers flocking to the island's national parks and preserves.

10 Spelunking
The island is riddled with caverns, and spelunking (caving) is popular. Be sure to explore with a reputable adventure company.

Family Attractions

The continent that gave the theme park to the world still naturally excels in doing them to perfection, and anyone who steps inside one almost immediately becomes a kid again. But to spend all your time in one would be a shame when there's such a wonderful world outside to see as well, and so many great places just waiting to introduce you to it.

1 Orlando *USA*

A family trip to the theme parks of Orlando presents almost endless opportunities to interact with world-famous cartoon characters, fairytale figures and movie icons – a life-size Goofy or a masked Spider-Man is always available for a photo opportunity. With its amazing rides, the Magic Kingdom® continues to be the focal point of the region, but there are plenty of other options for great family fun, including Disney's Animal Kingdom®, Blizzard Beach water park and SeaWorld® Orlando. Kennedy Space Center is a magnet for youngsters curious about space exploration, and if you're lucky you may see a rocket launch. Plus, the nearby beaches are a surfer's paradise.

2 Disneyland®, Los Angeles *USA*

Over half a century after it first opened its doors, the landmarks of Disneyland® – the Matterhorn, Sleeping Beauty's Castle and New Orleans Square – have come to seem as familiar and as "real" as the Eiffel Tower or the Empire State Building. A second theme park, Disney's California Adventure™, is adjacent to the original. Downtown Disney®, a further addition, is an outdoor entertainment, restaurant and retail district. Together with the two parks and three Disney hotels, Downtown Disney® forms the enormous complex known as Disneyland® Resort. A one-, two- or, even better, three-day visit is guaranteed to delight, amaze and exhaust the kids.

3 Legoland, San Diego *USA*

Children are fascinated by the 30 million plastic bricks fashioned, in Legoland, into things like famous landmarks, scenes from the Star Wars movies and life-sized African animals and landscapes. In Fun Town, kids are able to get behind the wheel of a real electric car or "pilot" a helicopter, while at the Imagination Zone, they can build race cars and robots. Magicians, ventriloquists and puppeteers all add to the fun.

4 Bronx Zoo, New York *USA*

Now well beyond its 100th birthday, this sprawling zoo – at 107 ha (265 acres) the largest of any American city – gets better all the time. Areas such as the Himalayan Highlands, African Plains and Jungle World ensure that the animals can live and be viewed in authentic natural environments, while Tiger Mountain and the 3-ha (6.5-acre) Congo Gorilla Forest – an African rain-forest habitat – bring you nose to nose with the inhabitants. Madagascar! introduces children to the real-life counterpart of the animated movie stars, including lots of adorable lemurs. All enclosures are easily reached via shuttle trains and elevated rides. The Bug Carousel is a favourite with little ones.

5 Museum of Science and Industry, Chicago *USA*

Though this museum dazzles kids and adults alike with its submarine ship and replica coal mine, it's The Idea Factory that's designed just for Junior. With the pulling of gears and shifting of knobs, kids experiment through play with balance, construction, magnetism and more. A current-fed waterway encourages boat-building. Arrive early at the weekend or be prepared to have to wait for admission.

Bronx Zoo, New York Children visiting the Congo Gorilla Forest *(abo*

Orlando The Kraken roller coaster at SeaWorld® *(below)*

Ipanema beach, Rio de Janeiro Families making the most of sun, sand and sea *(above)*

al Ontario Museum An exterior as amazing as the exhibits inside *(below)*

6 Louisiana Children's Museum *USA*

Although an educational venue for children, this museum also appeals to inquisitive and playful adults. Wonderful interactive displays, such as the Little Port of New Orleans, or the Eye to Eye (where you step inside a giant eyeball), make for a learning experience that just feels like fun. There are monthly special events and visiting exhibits.

7 Xcaret, Riviera Maya *MEXICO*

Created around a natural lagoon, the first and largest of the Mexican Riviera's eco-parks is a vast environment bursting with flora, fauna and sea life. It's a wonderful introduction to the tropical environment of the Yucatán, and a full day's worth of things to do in an easy, family-centred environment. The snorkelling river and dolphin pool are the biggest hits, but children will also enjoy the zoo, butterfly garden and forest paths.

8 Royal Ontario Museum *CANADA*

A truly magical place for kids, Canada's largest museum, with more than six million objects, was created in 1914 to showcase civilization and the natural world. Galleries of art, science, archaeology, world cultures and natural history display everything from Chinese treasures to dinosaur skeletons. The much-loved Dinosaur Gallery and ornate mummy cases are strictly "don't touch", but the Hands-On Biodiversity Gallery enchants as well as educates youngsters as they do things such as excavate for fossils and examine species under a microscope.

9 Planetario Galileo Galilei, Buenos Aires *ARGENTINA*

Housed in a huge sphere poised on three legs and looking like nothing so much as an alien spaceship, this planetarium is not only hugely entertaining and informative, it is also one of the continent's top astronomical research facilities. Daily shows (with narration in Spanish and English) use imagery from satellite missions to take you on a journey through the cosmos, while you sit comfortably beneath the giant domed ceiling. But the star attraction is the three genuine prehistoric meteorites recovered from the northwest provinces.

10 Ipanema and Leblon Beaches, Rio de Janeiro *BRAZIL*

Urban Rio's most beautiful, fashionable and secure beaches – Ipanema and its southern extension Leblon – offer a wealth of different beachside activities for all the family. Most visitors make their base behind the beaches, where chic boutiques and glamorous restaurants line the narrow streets. Although the city centre is 15 km (9 miles) away, Copacabana, as well as the Jardim Botânico, Corcovado and Gávea are easily accessible from here.

Québec City

Poised upon the Cap Diamant escarpment, overlooking both the St Lawrence River and the Laurentides, this city is home to a Francophone population rich in cultural pride, magnificent architecture, well-preserved churches and monuments, fine cuisine and numerous opportunities for outdoor adventure. Québec City is a traveller's dream, sure to charm all those who come here. The annual Carnaval de Québec (late January to mid-February) draws visitors from all over the world.

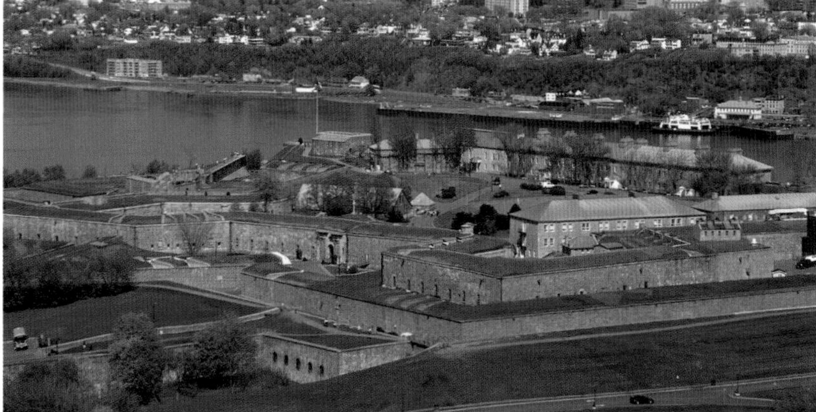

Top 10 Cultural Québécois

1 Gabrielle Roy
Born in Manitoba, the last of 11 children, Roy (1909–83) escaped her family's poverty by moving to Québec in 1939. An award-winning novelist, her first book, *Bonheur d'occasion (The Tin Flute)*, was published in 1945.

2 Émile Nelligan
Nelligan (1879–1941) ushered French-Canadian poetry into a new epoch and is revered by Québécois as their beloved literary spokesman. In later years his mental health deteriorated and he spent his last days in an asylum.

3 Mary Travers
Travers (1894–1941) began her career at family soirées playing jigs on the fiddle and spoons. Known as "La Bolduc," she rose during the Great Depression to become the first popular singer-songwriter from Québec. Today a new generation of Québécois enjoys her music.

4 Paul-Émile Borduas
The painter Borduas (1905–60) is one of Québec's most celebrated artists and also one of its greatest political activists. He was a founding member of the abstract Automatistes school of art.

5 Félix Leclerc
Leclerc (1914–88) is best remembered as a consummate storyteller, singer, and songwriter. There is a statue of him in Parc Lafontaine.

6 Oscar Peterson
Peterson (1925–2007) was given permission by his father to devote his life to jazz on the proviso he worked to be the best jazz pianist in the world. He became one of the greatest of the genre.

7 Mordecai Richler
A novelist, essayist and critic, Richler (1931–2001) was known for his sarcastic wit and opposition to Québec's separatist elements. His most famous novel is *The Apprenticeship of Duddy Kravitz* (1959).

8 Robert Lepage
The first North American to direct a Shakespeare play at England's National Theatre, Lepage (b.1957) is one of the most successful and daring writer/directors in the visual-arts world.

9 Cirque du Soleil
This circus troupe began life as street performers in La Malbaie, east of Québec City. Using their own unique combination of world music, acrobatic brilliance and dazzling costumes, they have conquered the world.

10 Celine Dion
Dion (b.1968), born one of 14 children into a musical family, was a Francophone star from her early teens. Internationally, *My Heart Will Go On*, the theme song from *Titanic*, is her biggest hit.

1 La Citadelle
Three centuries of military presence continue in this working army base *(left)*, which is home to a hospital, officers' mess and the first observatory in Canada.

2 Observatoire de la Capitale
Spectacular views of the entire region can be enjoyed from the 31st floor of the Marie-Guyart Building.

3 Parc de la Chute-Montmorency
The first settlers, sailing up the St Lawrence River, were greeted by the spectacle of these powerful waterfalls *(above)*, which, at 83 m (272 ft), are higher than Niagara. Ride the cable car to the top and visit Manoir Montmorency.

4 Quartier Petit-Champlain
Home to artisans in the 17th century and dockworkers in the 19th century, the houses in this area have now been renovated and adapted into a range of eclectic gift shops, bars and cafés, lining the pretty pedestrianized streets.

5 Musée de la Civilisation le Québec

he MCQ's exhibits include ·tifacts from the First lations, Chinese *objets 'art*, and items relating ɔ everyday life in Québec uring its 400-year history.

6 Ile d'Orleans

Known as the "cradle of French civilization in North America", this island of small farming communities *(left)* continues to preserve the traditions of the original settlers.

7 Porte Saint-Jean-Baptiste

This striking stone gateway is now a tourist draw, from which visitors can access and walk for 4 km (3 miles) along the city's ramparts.

8 Marché du Vieux-Port

The Bassin Louise is home to the Old Town's produce market *(above)*, to which farmers from Ile d'Orléans and other outlying areas bring their harvest to tempt appetites and inspire local chefs.

9 Château Frontenac

The most photographed landmark in the city, this ηposing hotel *(above)* is an architectural jewel designed y Bruce Price as a French-style château. Since it opened ι 1893, the hotel has welcomed the rich, the famous and ne noble through its doors and into its plush salons.

10 Basilique Sainte-Anne-de-Beaupré

This granite basilica *(below)*, completed in 1963, has 240 stained-glass windows and a dazzling mosaic vault.

TOP 10 Carnaval de Québec Attractions

1 Palais de Glace
Over 6,000 frozen blocks of ice are sculpted by an army of artisans into a dreamy castle, complete with turrets, drawbridge and a stage for a sound and light show.

2 Bonhomme Carnaval
A large, jolly snowman, Bonhomme Carnaval, with his red sash and woolly hat, has been the international icon of this frozen extravaganza for the past 50 years.

3 Place de la Famille
This fantasyland of ice and snow is packed with energy-filled games and contests that keep body temperatures high, no matter what the thermometer is reading.

4 International Snow Sculpture Competition
At this famous Carnaval event, competitors from around the globe rough-sculpt blocks of ice with chain-saws, then delicately chisel it away into amazing designs.

5 Ski Competition
Downhill and cross-country skiing competitions are held in the Jacques-Cartier area of Lac Beauport, just a few miles from Québec City.

6 St Hubert's Snow Bath
Teams dressed only in swim-wear compete to see which one can conquer the cold by lying longest in the snow.

7 Hôtel de Glace
Unique in North America and only the second in the world, the Ice Hotel is set in natural parkland only ten minutes from downtown. It offers Carnaval participants a spectacular architectural stay, with themed bedrooms, Absolut Vodka bar, wedding chapel and ice sculptures.

8 La Parade
Every evening of Carnaval two parades mark the end of the day's festivities. The "Little (But Loud) Parade" is for adults; *"La petite fanfare du Bonhomme"*, throughout the Place de la Famille, creates a ceremonial end to the day for children.

9 Caribou
Be prepared for locals to offer you their infamous Caribou, a hot alcoholic drink containing brandy, vodka, sherry, port and, sometimes, maple sugar. Sip with care – it's as potent as it sounds.

10 Les Glissades de la Terrasse Dufferin
The slope beside Château Frontenac is the location for the world's most scenic ice slide. With the St Lawrence River spread out before you, it's an exhilarating ride, and one not to be missed.

Rio de Janeiro

Rio is so beautiful that the locals, known as "Cariocas," claim that after God spent six days making the world, he rested on Sunday in Rio. Not that they ever call it Rio – they simply refer to it as *"a cidade maravilhosa"* or "the wonderful city". And despite its social problems, the city, like its people, is warm, captivating, musical and devoted to enjoying itself. Rio is a city of neighbourhoods, each with its own distinct character and each with a different, unforgettable view of Corcovado, the mountain that is crowned by a magnificent statue of Christ, who watches over Rio with his arms spread out in perpetual welcome.

1 Sugar Loaf Mountain

This boulder-shaped mountain at the southern end of Botafogo beach boasts magnificent views. The summit is best reached by cable car *(left)*.

2 Praia de Copacabana

One of the world's most famous urban beaches *(above)* stretches for 4 km (2.5 miles) from the Morro do Leme, at the northern end, to Arpoador in the south. This tourist hub is renowned for its New Year celebrations.

3 Jardim Botânico

Rio's botanical gardens were founded in 1808 and contain nearly 8,000 species of plants. The orchids are particulary noteworthy *(left)*.

TOP 10 Moments in History

1 The First Brazilians
Brazil's first inhabitants are thought to have crossed from Asia to America at the Bering Straits, then moved south, between 40,000 and 12,000 years ago.

2 Portuguese Arrival
The Portuguese explorer Gaspar de Lemos arrived in Guanabara Bay on 1 January 1502. He built a small fort to claim the bay for Portugal, but hostile confrontations with the indigenous Tamoio forced the Portuguese to go.

3 The French Arrive
In 1555 France sent a fleet to Rio, claiming a tiny island in Guanabara Bay and forging a military alliance with the Tamoio.

4 The Portuguese Defeat the French-Tamoio Alliance
The Portuguese returned to Rio and, with various indigenous groups, fought a series of battles against the French-Tamoio Alliance, eventually defeating it in 1567.

5 The Portuguese Royal Court Moves to Rio
In November 1807 the entire Portuguese royal family fled Napoleon in some 40 ships packed with 15,000 members of the court and government. They reached Brazil in 1808.

6 The French Cultural Mission
In 1816 King Dom João VI of Portugal invited the French to introduce European culture to Rio by bringing their styles of architecture, art and music.

7 Pedro I Declares Independence
King Dom João VI returned to Portugal in 1821, leaving his son Pedro behind as Prince Regent. Pedro declared independence the next year, crowning himself Emperor. He and his son, Pedro II, ruled for the next 67 years.

8 Republican Brazil
The republican movement of 1870 was provoked by discontent over taxes and the movement toward the abolition of slavery. In November 1889 Dom Pedro II was dethroned and a republic was proclaimed by Marechal Deodoro da Fonseca.

9 The Capital Moves from Rio to Brasília
Rio de Janeiro was capital of Brazil until 1960, when it was replaced by Brasília. This was overseen by President Juscelino Kubitschek and three Modernist architects, Lúcio Costa, Oscar Niemeyer, and Roberto Burle Marx.

10 Rio Hosts the World Environmental Summit
In June 1992 Rio hosted the Earth Summit – the first and largest global conference of its kind on the environment. It provided an impetus for Brazil to review its own environmental record.

arque Nacional da Tijuca 4

ne of the world's largest tracts of urban rainforest *ight)*, this lovely park has abundant wildlife, water-alls, and diverse biomes.

Mosteiro de São Bento 5

This Baroque church and Benedictine abbey was founded in 1590, although most of its beautiful gilt interior *(right)* dates from the 17th century.

6 Museu Nacional de Belas Artes

The country's first art gallery displays Brazilian works from colonial times to the late 20th century, as well as works by international masters like Debret and Rodin.

7 Ipanema and Leblon Beachlife

The Atlantic Ocean laps against the shores of Rio's most desirable beaches *(above)*, just south of Copacabana. The beaches front fashionable neighbourhoods that are a magnet for tourists.

8 Corcovado

The Christ statue *(above)* atop this mountain was oted one of the seven wonders of the modern world 2007. Sunset views from here are spectacular.

9 Museu Histórico Nacional

This museum explores Brazilian history om prehistoric times, with replica rock paintings om the Serra da Capivara, through to the early ays of the republic.

10 Praça XV

This square *(left)* was the focal point of Rio in colonial times, with one of largest concentrations of pre-20th-century buildings in the city.

TOP 10 Carnaval Parades and Balls

1 Sunday and Monday at the Sambódromo
The top *samba* schools march through the Sambódromo in *blocos* (parades) until well after dawn.

2 Banda de Ipanema
Flamboyant transvestite and transsexual partygoers dance *samba* with tourists, families, revellers and passers-by.

3 Baile do Copa
The formal "Russian Imperial" black-tie ball is held at the Copacabana Palace hotel.

4 Bloco Santa Teresa
The highlights of this lively street party are its atmosphere and its music. It takes place in the bohemian quarter of Santa Teresa and is popular with a young crowd.

5 Champions' Parade
The winning schools of the spectacular Sambódromo parades dance again on the final Saturday of Carnaval.

6 Bloco Cacique de Ramos
A new *samba* song is written and sung every year at this Avenide Rio Branco parade by one of Rio's famed *sambistas*.

7 Bloco de Segunda
This *bloco* features *Baianas* (Afro-Brazilian women) in enormous flowing dresses who spin as they *samba*.

8 Banda de Carmen Miranda
This *bloco* was created in honour of Carmen Miranda, she of the fruit-covered hats.

9 Baile Vermelho e Preto do Flamengo
Vermelho (red) and *preto* (black) are the colours of the soccer team Flamengo, and are part of the dress code. *Sambas* recount past glories and costumes are skimpy.

10 Gala Gay
One of Rio's most famous and lavish indoor balls takes place at a different location each year on Carnival Tuesday. The star-studded event is heavily televised.

San Antonio and Austin

A colourful history, world-class attractions and lively festivals make San Antonio one of the best destinations in Texas. The city's rich cultural mix of early Spanish mission beginnings, German settlement, cowboy heritage and strong Mexico ties has created a warm and progressive city. It is also home to four of the biggest attractions in the state, including the River Walk, the Alamo, Missions National Historical Park and SeaWorld®. The state capital, Austin, lies 129 km (80 miles) to the northeast.

1 River Walk (El Paseo del Rio)

The vibrant and bustling tree-shaded pathway along the San Antonio river *(left)* is lined with outdoor cafés, popular nightspots and many of the city's best hotels.

2 King William Historic District

One of the most beautiful residential neighbourhoods in Texas is lined with opulent mansions built by merchants in the late 1800s and early 1900s. The elegant Steves Homestead *(above)* is now a museum.

TOP 10 Austin Sights

1 State Capitol
This grand building of 1888 with a red granite dome is one of the country's finest capitol buildings.

2 Capitol Complex Visitors Center
Built in 1857, this is the oldest state office building in Texas and used to house the General Land Office. Today, it is home to exhibits about Texas, the Capitol and the Land Office.

3 Bob Bullock Texas State History Museum
Three floors of exhibits, including dramatic murals, interactive features, a special effects show and Austin's IMAX theatre reveal the history of Texas.

4 Governor's Mansion
This majestic brick mansion has served as official state residence of Texas governors since 1856 and is the most historic home in the state.

5 LBJ Library and Museum
This museum offers insights into the turbulent life and political career of the 36th president, Lyndon Baines Johnson. Do not miss the 7/8 scale replica of his Oval Office, his 1968 presidential limousine and an animatronic version of LBJ telling some of his favourite stories.

6 Lady Bird Johnson Wildflower Center
Dedicated to preserving North America's native plants and wildflowers, this centre was the vision of Lady Bird Johnson, wife of LBJ, who founded it in 1982 with actress Helen Hayes.

7 East 6th Street
Austin's celebrated music scene centres on East 6th Street. On weekends the street is pedestrianized and revellers can choose from more than 70 nightclubs offering an array of live music.

8 Blanton Museum of Art
The Blanton's collection spans the art history of Western civilization. Among the distinguished exhibits are sections on Latin American art and contemporary American art.

9 Zilker Park Barton Springs Pool and Botanical Gardens
With a golf course, athletic fields, hiking trails, the spring-fed Barton Springs Pool and the enchanting Zilker Botanical Garden, this is Austin's most loved park. It also hosts summer concerts and a theatre programme.

10 Congress Avenue Bridge Bat Colony
Crowds gather at sunset from April to October to watch the world's largest urban bat colony soar over Austin skies, as they emerge from the bridge each night to feed on airborne insects.

3 San Antonio Botanical Garden and Lucile Halsell Conservatory

The multiple glass towers at the conservatory *(left)* house a fabulous year-round profusion of flowering plants – all part of a wide spectrum of flora and fauna on display throughout the gardens.

4 The Alamo

One of the most visited historic sites in America, the Alamo *(above)* stands as a symbol of the heroic Texan struggle for independence. The Chapel and Long Barrack are all that remain today.

5 The McNay Art Museum

An exquisite Spanish Colonial mansion houses a comprehensive collection of 19th- to 21st-century paintings and prints by notable artists such as Rodin, Cézanne, Picasso, Gauguin, Matisse, O'Keeffe and Hopper.

6 SeaWorld® San Antonio

The world's largest marine-life adventure park *(right)* presents amazing shows teeming with leaping killer whales, playful dolphins and penguins. There is also an adventure and water park.

7 La Villita National Historic District

This charming historic village of delightful boutiques, craft shops, galleries and restaurants is located above the south bank of the River Walk.

8 Brackenridge Park

San Antonio's idyllic urban park *(left)* along the San Antonio river is home to some of the city's top attractions. The San Antonio Zoo is one of the best in the country and the museums have fascinating displays. A miniature railway line runs through the park too.

9 San Antonio Missions National Historical Park

Four remarkable missions offer a fascinating glimpse into the confluence of Spanish and Native cultures in the 1700s. It offers an opportunity to explore old courtyards and serene churches *(above)*.

10 San Fernando Cathedral

The oldest cathedral in the United States *(right)*, where Mexican General Santa Anna flew the red flag, signalling "no mercy," sits in the centre of the city.

TOP 10 Texas-Style Cuisine

1 Tex-Mex

The cultural blending of southern Texan and northern Mexican foods is known as Tex-Mex. Tex-Mex dishes are mildly spiced and usually contain a combination of meat and hard cheese.

2 Taco

Usually made with fried or soft corn tortillas folded over, tacos contain a beef or chicken filling. Additions may include shredded lettuce, *pico de gallo* (hot salsa), cheese, sour cream and guacamole.

3 Tamale

A tamale is made from a moist corn dough called *masa* wrapped around a seasoned filling – usually shredded pork. This is then wrapped in corn husks and steamed. Remove the husks before eating.

4 Chili

San Antonio claims to be the inventor of the state dish of Texas. Traditionally, chili is a spicy stew with equal amounts of beef and peppers, and is known locally as a "Bowl of Red". Traditional chili has no beans.

5 Enchilada

Corn or flour tortillas are wrapped around a filling of beef, chicken, cheese or shrimp, and are served hot, with a spicy-hot chili or mild gravy sauce. Enchiladas are often served with sour cream or guacamole. When ordered as a platter, they are usually served with beans and rice.

6 Fajita

Fajitas are traditionally made with beef skirt steak, a very flavoursome cut. Grilled strips of steak are served sizzling hot on a platter, with flour tortillas, grilled onions and peppers, and condiments such as *pico de gallo*, sour cream and cheese.

7 Steak

The top choice of steak in San Antonio is the Texan sirloin. An aged steak cooked with salt and pepper and other seasonings is a favourite. Chicken-fried steak is also popular.

8 Barbecue

Often spelled Bar-B-Que, or just B-B-Q, a good barbecue place will have stacks of oak, hickory or mesquite wood to smoke-cook the meat. Sliced beef brisket is the traditional B-B-Q fare, but sausage, pork-ribs and chicken are other popular meats for cooking in this way.

9 German Food

The German influence is evident in the cuisine of San Antonio. Sausage, *sauerkraut* and potato salad are favourites. Sausage, or *wurst*, is as popular as Tex-Mex food at any local festival. New Braunfels holds an annual Wurstfest.

10 Beer and Wine

Breweries were established here in the mid-1800s by German immigrants. Brewed at the nearby Spoetzl Brewery, Shiner is a local favourite with European roots. Several ranches now grow French and German grape varieties, producing fine wines such as Fall Creek and Slaughter-Leftwich.

San Diego

Blessed by a sunny climate that never varies more than 10 degrees from moderate and a splendid setting along the Pacific Ocean, San Diegans could well boast they live the California Dream. Although non-stop outdoor recreation, a vibrant downtown and world-class attractions keep the city's spirit young, its heart lies in its Spanish beginnings as the birthplace of California.

1 Gaslamp Quarter
Old-fashioned wrought-iron gas lamps lead the way to the hottest scene in town. Rocking nightspots and a dazzling selection of restaurants give life to San Diego's original Victorian downtown *(above)*.

2 Balboa Park & San Diego Zoo
San Diegans take pride in having one of the finest urban parks in the world. Its famous zoo, fascinating museums and exquisite gardens offer endless activities.

TOP 10 Moments in History

1 In the Beginning
The Kumeyaay tribe lived in the San Diego area from 12,000 years ago, in small, organized villages. Hunter-gatherers, they subsisted on acorns, berries and small prey.

2 Discovery by Juan Cabrillo (1542)
Cabrillo was the first European to arrive in San Diego Bay. California was to become part of the Spanish Empire for the next 279 years.

3 The Spanish Settlement (1769)
An expedition, led by Gaspar de Portolá and Franciscan friar Junípero Serra, established military posts and missions to Christianize the local tribes.

4 Mexican Independence (1821)
Upon independence, Mexico abolished the missions and distributed their land. The resulting *rancho* system lasted into the 20th century. Without Spanish restrictions, on trade, San Diego became a centre for the hide trade.

5 California Becomes a State (1850)
Mexican rule lasted until 1848. One bloody battle, a payment of $15 million and the treaty of Guadalupe Hidalgo, and California became part of the US and later its 31st state.

6 Alonzo Horton's New City (1867)
Horton siezed an opportunity to buy a parcel of cheap building land closer to the sea than Old Town. Property values there soared, especially after a fire in 1872 in Old Town. "New Town" became today's San Diego.

7 Transcontinental Railroad Arrives (1885)
When the Transcontinental Railroad reached town, real estate speculators poured in. Los Angeles seemed even more promising, however, and San Diego's population, which had risen from 5,000 to 40,000, shrank to 16,000.

8 Panama–California Exposition (1915–16)
To celebrate the opening of the Panama Canal and draw attention to the first US port of call on the West Coast a grand exhibition was held in Balboa Park. Its buildings are now park landmarks.

9 California–Pacific Exposition (1935–6)
Another exposition was held to help alleviate the effects of the Great Depression. Its buildings, also in Balboa Park, featured Aztec, Mayan and Pueblo Indian themes.

10 World War II
The founding of the aircraft industry gave San Diego an enduring industrial base. After Pearl Harbor, the Pacific Fleet moved its headquarters here. The harbour was enlarged and the cityscape transformed.

3 Mission San Diego de Alcalá
Father Junípero Serra established this mission *(above)* in 1769. The first of 21, the mission aimed to Christianize the Native Americans and affirm Spain's presence in California.

4 Coronado
This idyllic community is recognized throughout the world by the fabulous Hotel del Coronado *(above)*. Coronado's white sandy beaches, sidewalk cafés and oceanfront mansions have enticed visitors for over a century

La Jolla 5
Multi-million-dollar seaside villas, boutiques and elegant restaurants line the streets of this exclusive community *(right)*, also known for its prestigious biotech and oceanographic research institute.

6 Point Loma
In 1542 Juan Cabrillo arrived at Ballast Point *(above)*, claiming California for Spain. Once a whaling, fishing and leather processing centre, stunning homes and marinas now grace Point Loma's waterfront.

7 Old Town State Historic Park
The original location and social centre of San Diego until 1872, adobe houses, old wood-frame buildings and artifacts belonging to its pioneer families have been faithfully restored.

8 Embarcadero
With its nautical museums, vintage ships and superb ews across a harbour busy with sailboats, ferries and attleships, the Embarcadero district *(above)* links the ty to its ocean heritage.

SeaWorld® 9
At one of the premier attractions of Southern California, leaping killer whales *(right)*, cavorting dolphins and promenading sea lion divas entertain over four million visitors a year.

10 Tijuana
Only 20 minutes south of San Diego but a whole world way, this famous border town *(below)* offers great shopping nd top-rated restaurants. And yes, striped burros and black elvet Elvis paintings still exist.

TOP 10 Museums and Art Galleries

1 Balboa Park Museums
The buildings, of Spanish-Colonial, Mayan and Aztec design, are treasures in their own right. The exhibitions change constantly.

2 Museum of Contemporary Art
The most important modern art trends are presented at this museum. Tours, lectures and family nights make the art accessible to all.

3 Maritime Museum
This museum pays tribute to the men and ships that so influenced the history and life of San Diego. Several anchored ships can be boarded and explored.

4 Chinese Historical Museum
Artifacts such as ceramics, photographs and an ornate warlord's bed document a fascinating slice of San Diego's history, housed in a former Chinese mission.

5 Tasende Gallery
International contemporary artists are the focus here, including Gaudi-influenced Niki de Saint Phalle, Mexico's José Luis Cuevas, British sculptress Lynn Chadwick and the Chilean Surrealist Roberto Matta.

6 Alcala Gallery
Early Californian Impressionist art is well represented here. The gallery also features pre-Columbian art and Classical and Asian antiquities.

7 David Zapf Gallery
This gallery specializes in San Diego artists. Exhibitions feature paintings, drawings, photography, sculptures and even custom furniture from a wide range of local artists.

8 Michael J. Wolf Fine Arts
The oldest gallery in the Gaslamp Quarter features works by emerging US and international artists.

9 Joseph Bellows Gallery
This intimate gallery show-cases important vintage prints and contemporary photo-graphy of a superb quality, and host a busy programme of themed group exhibitions, as well as solo shows. Both renowned and emerging photographers are exhibited.

10 Spanish Village Art Center
Adobe houses from the 1935–36 California–Pacific Exposition have been transformed into delightful artists' studios, where you can shop or even take a lesson from the artists.

San Francisco

San Franciscans will, rather candidly, admit that they are the most fortunate people on earth, the occasional earthquake notwithstanding; and most visitors, after a few days of taking in the sights and sounds of this magnificent city, will agree. Ask anyone who has been here and they will tell you it's their favourite US city. The geographical setting evokes so much emotional drama, the light seems clearer, the colours more vivid, the cultural diversity of the ethnic neighbourhoods so captivating and inviting, that it's a place almost everyone can fall in love with at first sight.

1 San Francisco Museum of Modern Art
Second only to New York City's MoMA, San Francisco's architectural landmark *(left)* houses 20th-century masterworks of painting, sculpture and photography, and the edgiest digital installations.

2 Cable Cars
San Francisco's little troopers *(above)* have endured technological progress, and are now the only system of the kind in the world that still plays a daily role in urban life.

3 Grace Cathedral
Dominating Nob Hill with its timeless beauty, San Francisco's favourite cathedral *(above)* offers a host of awe-inspiring and historic treasures, including Italian Renaissance masterpieces and beautiful stained-glass windows.

TOP 10 Moments in History

1 Native Americans
There were settlements in the Bay as early as the 11th century BC, made up of hunter-gathers known as the Coast Miwok, the Wintun and the Ohlone.

2 Sir Francis Drake
In 1579 the navigator landed near Point Reyes and claimed Alta California for Queen Elizabeth I. But England didn't follow up its claim to Northern California, leaving it for the Spanish to conquer.

3 Spanish Control
In 1776 an expedition led by Juan Bautista de Anza arrived at San Francisco Bay and established the Presidio (fort). A mission was also founded by Father Junipero Serra.

4 American Takeover
In the 1840s US leaders tried to encourage Bay Area settlers to join the Union. In 1846 the settlers declared independence from Mexico and, soon after, Commodore John Sloat claimed California as US territory.

5 Gold Rush Days
In 1848 landowner John Sutter saw a glitter in the sediment of the American River. It was gold. Word got out, and the subsequent stampede of '49ers turned the city into a boom town.

6 Wells Fargo
Stagecoaches of Wells Fargo & Co began carrying freight and passengers in 1852, taking full advantage of the Gold Rush momentum. It also played a part in the founding of the Pony Express.

7 Panama–Pacific Exposition
Held in 1915 to celebrate the opening of the Panama Canal, the real *raison d'être* for the festivities was that San Francisco had been resurrected in the wake of the 1906 earthquake.

8 Bay and Golden Gate Bridges
The inauguration of the Bay Bridge in 1936 heralded the end of the age of ferryboats by linking the city to the East Bay. The inauguration of the Golden Gate Bridge took place a year later.

9 "Summer of Love"
San Francisco counterculture burst forth in the summer of 1967. Hippies were everywhere, and the poetic music that embodied a new way of thinking filled the air. It was a socio-political shift that affected the whole world.

10 Politics
California has always been a few steps ahead of the rest of the US. In 1992 it became the first state to send two female Senators, Dianne Feinstein and Barbara Boxer, to the US Congress, while Nancy Pelosi was the first female Speaker of the House from 2007 to 2011.

Alcatraz 4
Although it was a federal prison for just under 30 years, the myth of "The Rock" *(right)* continues to capture the imagination of visitors. Even if exploring prison life holds no appeal, the ferry ride makes it well worth a visit.

5 **Fisherman's Wharf**
Despite rampant commercialization, the saltiness and authenticity are still to be found here if you take time to look. The views of the bay are unmatched, and you'll have an opportunity to try great seafood and see barking sea lions.

6 **Wine Country**
The wines from this region have become so internationally recognized that French, Italian and Spanish winemakers have all established vineyards here. A day trip or, even better, a longer stay should not be missed *(see pp142–3)*.

7 **Golden Gate Park**
The city boasts one of the largest public parks in the world *(above)*, with natural beauty and fine museums.

3 **Golden Gate Bridge**
The much-loved symbol of the city and of alifornia's place on the Pacific Rim, the Golden Gate idge *(above)* is the third-largest single span bridge in e world, connecting San Francisco to Marin County.

9 **Mission Dolores**
The city's oldest building is also the only intact apel among the 21 California missions that Father unípero Serra founded in the late 18th century. s founding, just days before the Declaration of dependence, makes San Francisco older than the US.

0 **Chinatown**
The exotic feel of one of the largest Chinese ommunities outside of Asia *(below)* makes this part the city a magnet for locals and visitors alike.

TOP 10 Bay Area Sights

1 Berkeley
The 1960s, when student protesters filled these streets, are a memory now, though Telegraph Avenue still has a funky vibe. Lovely parks, tree-lined streets and unique shops now typify Berkeley.

2 Oakland
Oakland's attractions include the huge Lake Merritt, a beautiful Mormon temple and its Museum of California.

3 Marin County Headlands
A 30-minute drive, by way of the Golden Gate Bridge, this is an unspoiled area of wind-swept ridges, sheltered valleys, deserted beaches and precipitous cliffs.

4 Sausalito
Historically, this has been an artists' town, with an eclectic mix of residents. Boats fill the picturesque marinas, many of them houseboats that locals live in year-round.

5 Mill Valley
The old part of town is flanked by stands of redwoods, lined with old buildings housing restaurants and shops, and centred on a pleasant square.

6 Mount Tamalpais
"Mount Tam" is sacred to the Native Americans who once lived here. The view from the summit takes in practically the entire Bay Area. The area all around is a wilderness nature preserve with over 320 km (200 miles) of trails through redwood groves and alongside creeks.

7 Stinson Beach
Stinson is the preferred swimming beach for the area. Miles of soft sand and the spectacular sunsets are complemented by the quaint village of Seadrift and backed by a wildlife-filled lagoon.

8 Bolinas
Next to Stinson is a hippie village that time forgot. Craftspeople sell their wares in the trendy gallery, and organic produce and 1960s idealism are the rule.

9 Palo Alto and Stanford
Palo Alto experienced a boom as the focal point of Silicon Valley, and is home to prestigious private Stanford University, with its beautiful, well-tended campus.

10 Tiburon
Here, 100-year-old houseboats have been pulled ashore to form "Ark Row", whose shops and sunny cafés enhance the charm of this waterfront village.

USA
Mardi Gras Carnival parade on Canal Street, New Orleans

Santa Fe, Taos and Albuquerque

Contemporary, vibrant "City Different," Santa Fe is the oldest capital city in the united States and a magnet for lovers of art, history, fine cuisine and outdoor activities. Taos offers stunning mountain landscapes that draw numerous working artists, whose studios and galleries are some of the major attractions. Albuquerque, one of the region's fastest growing cities, is well-known for its fascinating museums.

1 Old Town Santa Fe

Adding charm to Santa Fe's world-renowned art galleries, museums and restaurants are the soft-edged adobe buildings *(left)* in which they are housed.

TOP 10 Moments in History

1 Rise of the Pueblos
The ancestors of modern Pueblo peoples first arrived in about 600. More Native Americans from the Southwest were drawn to the drought-resistant Rio Grande Valley in 1000, when the first adobe pueblos were built in the area.

2 First Spanish Expedition: 1540–42
In a quest for gold, Francisco Vásquez de Coronado led 300 Spanish conquistadores and 1,000 Native Americans into the Southwest. He is thought to have wintered near Santa Fe, at Kuaua Pueblo.

3 Spanish Settlement: 1598
In 1595 Juan de Oñate was commissioned by King Philip II of Spain to found a settlement in New Mexico. More than 200 men, some with families in tow, reached San Juan in 1598 and established the first settlement.

4 Santa Fe Capital of New Mexico: 1610
Founded in 1607, La Villa de Santa Fe, "The City of Holy Faith," became capital of New Mexico in 1610.

5 Pueblo Revolt: 1680
After 80 years of Spanish rule, the Pueblos united for the first time under Popé, an able warrior from San Juan Pueblo. The only successful Native American uprising in the US, the Pueblo Revolt drove the Spanish from Santa Fe for 12 years.

6 Santa Fe Recaptured for Spain: 1692
Led by Diego de Vargas, the reconquest of New Mexico lasted two years. The fateful event is celebrated in a popular annual festival.

7 Mexico Gains Independence: 1821
A newly independent Mexico welcomed trade with the US. Loaded wagons poured down the Santa Fe Trail, the first major trade route into the Southwest.

8 New Mexico Becomes a US Territory: 1846
After the US declared war on Mexico, General Stephen Watts Kearney and his forces entered and claimed Santa Fe on 18 August 1846.

9 New Mexico Becomes a State: 1912
By 1912, when New Mexico became a state, it had been discovered by artists, and Santa Fe was already discussing the adoption of a Pueblo Revival architecture.

10 Manhattan Project: 1942–5
This secret government project, headed by J. Robert Oppenheimer, took over a boys' school at Los Alamos to develop the first atomic bombs: "Little Boy" and "Fat Man". The site was chosen for its remoteness.

2 Canyon Road

This mile-long stretch of road up the canyon delivers a unforgettable mix of traditional and contemporary art galleries, sculpture gardens, shops *(above)* and restaurants that attract art buyers and visitors from all around the world.

3 Museum Hill

Four exceptional museums in Santa Fe present Native American art, history and culture, folk art from around the globe and Spanish Colonial artifacts. The museums surround a central plaza *(above)* with stunning mountain vistas.

4 Guadalupe Street/ Historic Railyard District

Warehouses converted into artists' studios, shops and restaurants give an upbeat energy to Santa Fe.

5 Taos Pueblo

Continuously occupied by Pueblo Natives since 1400, these multistorey adobe buildings *(above)* set against a backdrop of towering mountains are a United Nations World Heritage Site.

6 Georgia O'Keeffe Museum

The world's largest permanent collection of paintings by this celebrated New Mexican artist is on display here.

7 Bandelier National Monument

Home to the Ancestral Pueblo people, the towering rock cliffs of Pajarito plateau are puckered with natural and hand-dug cave dwellings *(above)*. The caves overlook the remnants of the streamside village of Tyuonyi.

8 Taos Old Town

Working artists and visitors are drawn to the stunning atural beauty and free spirit of Taos *(above)*. It has great alleries, restaurants, historic buildings and museums.

9 Albuquerque Old Town

Historical buildings and shops encircle a aza in the heart of the Old Town, while nearby useums showcase New Mexico's artists.

10 El Rancho de las Golondrinas

Costumed interpreters and occasional festivals bring ne past alive at this hacienda complex *(above)*, once the st stop before Santa Fe along the Camino Real route.

TOP 10 Aspects of Architecture

1 Traditional Adobe
These are buildings formed with sun-dried bricks of earth and water; the Spanish added straw for greater stability. To maintain the integrity of adobe walls, they are annually recoated with fresh clay.

2 Pueblo Revival
Modelled on the traditional homes of Pueblo people, these box-shaped buildings have flat roofs, adobe or stucco walls, rounded corners and small windows.

3 Territorial Style
This modified Pueblo Revival style has several additional features, such as rows of brick at the roofline, a wide central hallway and an entryway with a broad-roofed portal. The Museum of Spanish Colonial Art in Santa Fe is a classic example.

4 Viga
A viga is a horizontal roof beam made from a large log. It usually extends through the exterior wall and so is visible from the outside.

5 Corbel
An ornately carved wooden bracket, originally placed at the junction of vertical posts and horizontal beams.

6 Blue Doors and Windows
Throughout the region, many doors and windows are painted blue and turquoise. The colours not only accent the earthy tones of adobe, but also are believed to protect the house and its occupants from evil spirits.

7 Portal
A covered walkway or porch designed to offer protection from the sun and rain, a portal is sometimes incorporated into a building with heavy adobe arches.

8 Walled Courtyard
Courtyard walls are usually built with adobe to provide a private outdoor space. A coyote fence of branches wired together is sometimes used instead of adobe.

9 Kiva Fireplace
This rounded adobe fireplace, usually put in the corner of a room, has a practical beauty that has made it a chic addition to modern homes.

10 Horno
A horno is an outdoor domed oven built with adobe. It is used to bake bread and other foods. Such ovens were introduced by Spanish colonists and then later adopted by the Pueblo people.

Seattle

Seattle is a bustling powerhouse of influence, steering the future of high technology as well as popular culture. The population of this vibrant metropolis is fuelled by espresso coffee, the latest developments in software and music, and visual art that's often as far on the leading edge as the city itself. Seattle has emerged as one of the most attractive cities in the United States, with an ever-changing skyline that reflects the pioneering spirit that brought settlers here in the mid-19th century.

Top 10 Moments in History

1 Native American Roots
The Seattle region was first inhabited 11–12,000 years ago by tribes including the Suquamish, Duwamish, Nisqually, Snoqualmie and Muckleshoot.

2 Denny Party
In 1851 Chief Sealth of the Duwamish Tribe greeted Arthur A Denny and his group of European settlers at West Seattle's Alki Point.

3 Northern Pacific Railroad
Seattle's neighbour, Tacoma, was the original terminus of 1873's Northern Pacific Railroad. In 1893 the Great Northern Railway extended into Seattle, which later became the main rail depot.

4 Lumber Mills
Entrepreneurs such as Henry Yesler erected the pioneer town out of lumber from ancient, old-growth forests. In 1900 timber baron Frederick Weyerhaeuser bought nearly a million acres of railroad land and Seattle's logging industry was transformed.

5 Great Fire of 1889
Natural resources created a boomtown pulling in more than 1,000 new residents every month. In 1889 a fire destroyed much of the wood-built downtown area.

6 Klondike Gold Rush
The Alaska Gold Rush kicked off in 1897 after a gold-filled steamship docked at Seattle's waterfront. Seattle was the last refuelling town before the gold fields, and so prospered as never before.

7 Boeing's Beginnings
In 1917, as the United States entered World War I, William E Boeing hired pilot Herb Munter to design a seaplane for the Navy. The rest of the giant Boeing Corporation's success is history.

8 Rise of Microsoft
In 1975 Harvard dropout Bill Gates and his high school friend Paul Allen founded Microsoft. From the suburb of Redmond, they launched a personal computer revolution and have never looked back.

9 Nisqually Earthquake
If Seattle is a boom and bust town, it certainly felt the boom in a magnitude 6.8 earthquake on the morning of 28 February 2001. Roads cracked and masonry fell from buildings. The region suffered more than $1 billion worth of damage.

10 Green River Killer
In the 1980s and '90s the Seattle area lived in the dark shadow of a series of brutal killings, as dozens of women became victims of the Green River Killer. Twenty years of intense investigation led to the arrest of Gary Ridgeway in 2001. He confessed and was imprisoned for life.

1 Seattle Waterfront

Seattle is a major port for both industrial and passenger traffic. Along Puget Sound's Elliott Bay *(left)*, pier shops and restaurants throng with people just blocks from towering industrial cranes loading containers onto freighters.

2 Pike Place Market

An integral part of the Seattle experience, this thriving landmark *(above)* hums with visitors all year round. Explore the invigorating mix of fresh seafood, farmers' produce, flower stalls and ethnic foods.

3 Pioneer Square

A treasure trove of Victorian-era architecture and streets still paved with bricks or cobblestone, Seattle's original commercial centre was established in 1852 when Arthur and David Denny arrived with a handful of fellow pioneers. It is now a protected National Historic District *(above)*.

4 University of Washington

One of the nation's top universities *(right)*, UW has a student body of nearly 40,000 and an attractive campus, and benefits from huge endowments given by local benefactors in the high-tech industry.

5 International District

The ID, as locals call it, is a mélange of Chinese, Korean, Japanese and Southeast Asian cultures. Seattle's Pacific Rim identity makes it a final destination for many immigrants from across the Pacific.

6 Broadway

A summer night along Capitol Hill's main strip *(below)* can resemble midtown Manhattan in terms of lively street scenes. Expect the unexpected, along with outrageous attire and flamboyant behaviour.

7 Discovery Park

Rising above Puget Sound is a gorgeous 216-ha (534-acre) park *(above)*. Densely wooded trails, beaches, historic military homes and wildlife are just some of its appealing features.

8 Lake Washington Ship Canal

Officially completed in 1934, the Canal bisects the city and provides access to the sea for pleasure boaters, research vessels and commercial barges alike.

Seattle Center

The site of the 1962 World's Fair, the Center is now tirely dedicated to arts and entertainment. While many ginal edifices remain – the Space Needle *(above)* being sily the most recognizable – the location also inspires w building designs, such as Frank Gehry's dazzling perience Music Project.

10 Woodland Park Zoo

Seattle's world-class zoo *(left)* affords its animals vast enclosures. Natural habitats surround the viewing areas and pathways snake through its 37 ha (92 acres).

TOP 10 Architectural Highlights

1 Space Needle
Seattle's modern architectural identity began with this iconic tower. The three pairs of beams that support the spire lie buried 8 m (30 ft) underground, and have secured the 185-m (605-ft) Needle during both earthquakes and windstorms.

2 Experience Music Project
Frank Gehry's technicolour facility resembles a smashed guitar, in homage to Jimi Hendrix's incendiary finales. Paul Allen's project reflects Seattle's role as an artistic and musical vanguard.

3 Central Library
Dutch architect Rem Koolhaas designed this 2004 glass and steel structure to replace Seattle's 1960 Central Library. The unusual oblique structure and glass flooring have been controversial.

4 Columbia Center
This 76-storey skyscraper rises higher than any other Seattle structure. Its observation deck has great views of Elliott Bay, the Olympic Peninsula, Mount Rainier and the Cascade Mountains.

5 Seattle Center Monorail
One of the city's favourite attractions, 1.5 million people a year board its original 1962 cars for a two-minute ride on what was then thought to be the mass transit of the future.

6 Rainier Tower
Minoru Yamasaki's 40-storey 1977 structure appears to be an upside-down skyscraper, its tower rising from an inverted pyramid pedestal.

7 Seattle Tower
The brick and granite façade of this 1929 Art Deco gem sets it apart from its steel and glass neighbours. The lobby has a ceiling bas-relief of local flora and fauna.

8 Smith Tower
Typewriter tycoon L C Smith built Seattle's first skyscraper in 1914. Brass hand-operated elevators take visitors to the Chinese Room at the 35th level, with antique carvings, an inlaid porcelain ceiling and an observation deck.

9 Pioneer Building
This striking red brick and terracotta 1892 building boasts National Historic Landmark status. It was the headquarters of a prosperous speakeasy during Prohibition.

10 Downtown Seattle Transit Tunnel (DSTT)
This tunnel runs the length of Downtown, ferrying passengers by light rail and fleets of hybrid buses, easing above-ground congestion.

Festivals and Parties

At every time of year there is a festival going on somewhere in the Americas, be it a religious event, a harvest thanksgiving, a celebration of traditional customs and culture or just a grand excuse for a massive party. With their local music, food and drink, communal dancing and parades, such events are the perfect way for a visitor to really feel a part of local culture.

1 Réveillon, Rio de Janeiro *BRAZIL*

The biggest festival of the Brazilian year is, perhaps surprisingly, not Carnival but the overwhelming spectacle of Réveillon – Rio's New Year's Eve celebrations. As the sun sinks, bands plug in and fill the air with rhythmic beats. Steadily, the beach fills up with millions of partygoers. The fireworks erupt, the crowd roars, the drumbeats rise and suddenly it's midnight. When dawn finally breaks, the beach is left to the Candomblé priestesses. Clad in billowy white robes, they chant to Iemanjá, the goddess of the sea, heralding the first day of the new year.

2 Winterlude, Ottawa *CANADA*

Ottawa has spacious parks, excellent museums and historic sites galore, but it's in February, with the advent of Winterlude, that Canada's capital city truly shines. There are ice-sculpture competitions, the Rideau Canal springs to life with brightly clothed skaters, and the seasonal snow playground across the Ottawa River in Jacques Cartier Park rings from morning to dusk with the cries of children flinging themselves downhill on snow slides. Hockey fans fill pubs across the city, cheering on the Senators in the hope that this will be the year they bring home the coveted Stanley Cup.

3 Carnival *TRINIDAD*

The island of Trinidad comes alive in the days before Lent as thousands of people gather on the streets and beaches to dance to calypso, watch glitzy parades and drink rum. In Port of Spain, the island's capital, traditional contests for the Carnival King and Queen get under way, as endless parades of trucks carrying bands and DJs blast steel bands, calypso music and electric sounds across the city and out to sea. Fantastically costumed partygoers dance and drink long into the night and streets in the historic Savannah district are lined with performers, barbecues and arts and crafts stalls.

4 Calle Ocho Latino Festival, Miami *USA*

Every year in mid-March, Miami's "Little Havana" district is given over to a huge street party celebrating Latino culture, music and dance. Stages on the streets showcase salsa, merengue, reggaeton and jazz, and tempting aromas of *tamales* and *arepas* waft over from sizzling stalls. As well as all this, there are cook-offs, sporting events and even a popular domino tournament.

5 St Patrick's Day, Boston *USA*

Anyone with Irish blood in their veins will enjoy a trip to Boston, whatever the time of year; but in the days surrounding 17 March, New England's largest city rolls out the bright green welcome mat to around half a million visitors as a wide array of events, festivals and parades are held in celebration of St Patrick's Day, Ireland's national holiday. Everything culminates on the Sunday closest to the holiday, when South Boston ("Southie," as locals call it) hosts one of the world's largest St Patrick's Day parades. Revellers in their hundreds of thousands descend upon this working-class neighbourhood to celebrate all things Gaelic. Troupes of step-dancers and pipe-bands come from as far as Ireland to participate.

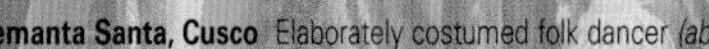

Semanta Santa, Cusco Elaborately costumed folk dancer *(above)*

Winterlude, Ottawa Giant snow sculptures *(below)*

Crop Over, Barbados Dancers in the festival's Grand Kadooment *(above)*

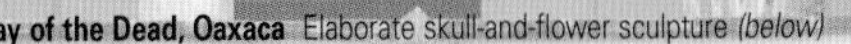

ay of the Dead, Oaxaca Elaborate skull-and-flower sculpture *(below)*

6 Semana Santa, Cusco *PERU*

Holy Week, the seven days before Easter, is celebrated in Cusco with elaborate processions, religious ceremonies and enactments of Biblical scenes. Local food looms large at this time. Stalls dispensing sweet *empanadas* and corn bread invade the Plaza de Armas and, on Holy Thursday, families traditionally gather to share a meal of 12 dishes – representing the apostles – of potatoes, seafood, *tarwi* (Andean lupin) and *llullucha* (algae). Thousands of pilgrims flock to Cusco from remote mountain villages for this moving week of events.

7 Crop Over *BARBADOS*

Barbados Crop Over was originally a celebration of the successful completion of the sugar harvest. Today, for almost two months each summer, Bridgetown, the capital, pulsates with the rhythm of calypso, folk music and dance. It begins with the ceremonial arrival of the last canes, and the crowning of the best male and female cutter as King and Queen of Crop Over. On the spectacular East Coast Road, rival calypso groups compete, against a backdrop of crashing Atlantic surf, while spectators gather on surrounding hillsides with picnics, beer and rum. The festival culminates with the Grand Kadooment, a joyful street parade flaunting magnificent costumes and energetic dances.

8 Montreal Jazz Festival *CANADA*

This musical jamboree lasts 11 days and 11 nights, during which around 750 concerts take place. Over half are outdoors and free, but there are also countless impromptu gigs; soak up the carnival atmosphere of Latin jazz, take in some smouldering salsa or chill to acoustic folk in an underground bar. The summer celebrations and the city's funky mix of cafés, galleries, bistros and green spaces draw crowds of all ages and musical tastes.

9 Cheyenne Frontier Days, Wyoming *USA*

Cheyenne's ten-day rodeo festival each July regards itself as "the daddy of 'em all". A celebration of the Old West, it sees Stetsons fly as young men battle to stay on bucking bulls a full eight seconds, for prize money of over a million dollars. The town's streets bustle with visitors taking in the Grand Parade and nightly musical performances.

10 Day of the Dead, Oaxaca *MEXICO*

In Mexico, on All Souls' Day (2 November) the dead are believed to return to earth to be with their living relatives. In the lovely colonial city of Oaxaca, the celebrations are at their most vivid. Families create altars in their homes, with photos of the deceased, candles, flowers, favourite foods, drinks, even cigarettes, and decorate loved ones' graves – cemeteries glitter with hundreds of candles, and music and dancing accompanies these reunions.

Toronto

Torontonians are justifiably proud of their vibrant and exciting metropolis. Canada's largest city and its financial hub, Toronto has a tremendous amount to offer, including a thriving theatre, music and arts scene, top museums, world-class restaurants and shops, a beautiful lakeside location with lovely beaches and streets that are safe and inviting to walk along. Its cultural diversity – over 90 ethnic groups are represented in Toronto – enhances the urban experience.

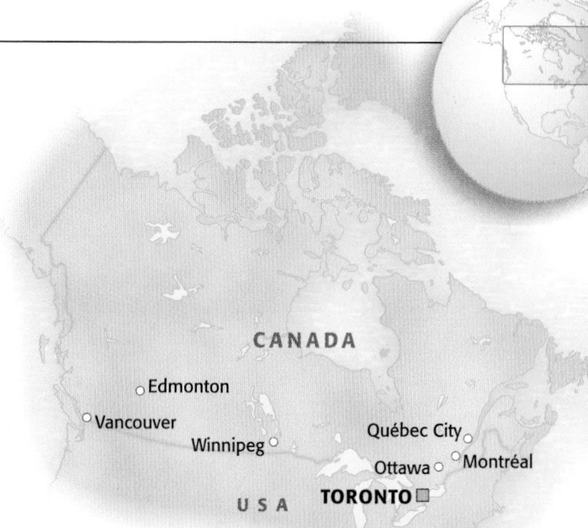

1 Toronto Islands

A short ferry ride from downtown is a chain of small islands, which provide respite from the summer heat and offer beaches, picnic grounds and restaurants *(left)*.

2 Casa Loma

Built by financier Sir Henry Pellatt, this turreted mansion *(above)*, with its 98 grand rooms and beautiful gardens, offers a glimpse of turn-of-the-19th-century luxury.

3 Art Gallery of Ontario

This fabulous museum *(above)* has excellent collection of Canadian art, including that of contemporary artist Michael Snow. There are also galleries for Inuit art, French Impressionist paintings, photography, prints and drawings.

Top 10 Neighbourhoods

1 The Beaches
In this charming enclave east of Woodbine Ave you can browse the eclectic shops or relax in one of the many cosy restaurants or pubs. A popular boardwalk stretches alongside a sandy beach to Ashbridges Bay.

2 Chinatown
With one of the largest ethnic Chinese populations of any North American city, Toronto has several Chinatowns. This, the oldest, originated in the early 1900s. Its hub is at Spadina Ave.

3 Cabbagetown
Settled in the 1840s by Irish immigrants who grew cabbages in their front gardens, this area is now gentrified, with boutiques and gourmet shops.

4 Little Italy
Most of the 500,000 Italians who call Toronto home now live north of the city, but the pizzerias and *trattorias* that remain on this strip of College St west of Bathurst St ensure it retains its Italian flair.

5 Yorkville
Famous in the 1960s as a hippie hangout and now the city's most exclusive retail district, Yorkville is where refined art galleries nestle among chic boutiques, bars and restaurants.

6 The Danforth
This is the social and commercial heart of Greek life in Toronto. At night, lively tavernas are crowded with patrons enjoying *souvlaki* and seafood, accompanied by *retsina* or *ouzo*.

7 The Annex
Tall trees front Edwardian houses here, and busy Bloor St is lined with shops selling books, CDs, and inexpensive clothing and jewellery; there are great value ethnic and vegetarian restaurants too.

8 Roncesvalles
Toronto's Polish community lays claim to this west-end neighbourhood. Its heart, Roncesvalles Ave between Howard Park Ave and Queen St W, is lined with great Polish delis and bakeries.

9 Leslieville
What this district lacks in architectural richness it makes up for in character. Along Queen St E between Carlaw Ave and Leslie St, secondhand furniture, housewares and vintage stores offer 1960s and 1970s bric-a-brac. The cafés are perfect for weekend brunches.

10 Little India
The spirit of the bazaars of the Indian subcontinent is alive and well – even during Toronto's cold winter – on Gerrard St E. Shops sell colourful saris, street vendors cook up tantalizing takeaways, and restaurants serve excellent Indian fare.

4 Ontario Place

Its lakeside location makes this fun-filled playground popular place to spend a summer's day with the family. nildren delight in the many water rides, while the IMAX eatre *(above)* and concert amphitheatre appeal to all ages.

5 Royal Ontario Museum

treasure-trove of cient mummies, xquisitely decorated eriod rooms, huge nosaurs, stuffed birds, unning Chinese art, and nposing Greek and oman sculptures are nong the many warding exhibits.

6 Distillery Historic District

Once the largest distillery in North America, this former industrial complex is one of Toronto's hottest destinations. Victorian buildings and cobblestoned streets provide an unforgettable backdrop to the many unusual stores and galleries, and excellent restaurants and cafés.

TOP 10 Family Events

1 Canadian National Exhibition
The "Ex" is an 18-day extravaganza, with 65 rides, themed pavilions, performers of all kinds, nightly fireworks and a dazzling international airshow starring the Canadian Air Force Snowbirds.

2 Canada Day
This national holiday observes the anniversary of the founding of Canada, in 1867. Festivities include free concerts at Mel Lastman Square and Queen's Park.

3 Luminato
Creativity and cultural diversity are celebrated in this 10-day festival of arts, which features events and performances of dance, theatre, visual arts and film in venues across the city. Most events are free.

4 Royal Agricultural Winter Fair
North America's largest indoor exhibition of agriculture has farm animals, machinery, horticulture and equestrian shows.

5 Caribana
This local celebration of Caribbean culture is now North America's largest street festival, with colourful costumes, steel bands and plenty of dancing.

6 Milk International Children's Festival
Here there's family entertainment galore: dance, music, theatre and puppetry for kids of all ages – and mostly free.

7 Toronto WinterCity Festival
This festival fills two mid-winter weeks with lots of reasons to head outdoors, among them kids' events, circus performances, concerts and fireworks.

8 Sprockets Toronto
The best in contemporary and classic children's film is presented in this satellite of the Toronto International Film Festival. There are movie-making workshops too.

9 Toronto Festival of Storytelling
All ages are invited to listen as storytellers weave tales at venues around the city – a multicultural celebration of the oral tradition.

10 Toronto International Dragon Boat Race
Teams compete in a race at Centre Island in the climax of the two-day Dragon Boat festival – the largest outside Asia. There are also performances, crafts and food.

7 Toronto Eaton Centre

Toronto's pre-eminent downtown mall, named after a now-defunct department store, is conveniently located near several major hotels and attractions. If you are looking for a one-stop shopping destination, this mall, selling everything from batteries to hockey sticks, is it.

8 Niagara Falls

After the 2-hour drive from Toronto, stand on Table Rock for a look at one of the world's wonders, the magnificent Horseshoe Falls *(below)*, where the Niagara river plunges 53 m (176 ft) over a wide precipice. The town of Niagara Falls and its outlying area offer fine dining, entertainment, winery tours, historic museums and more.

9 CN Tower and its Views

High-speed external elevators mounted on this, the world's second-tallest telecommunications tower *(above)*, whisk you up 181 storeys for an unforgettable view of the city.

10 Hockey Hall of Fame

Irrespective of their age, most visitors to Toronto who are ice hockey fans make a pilgrimage to this hall of fame *(left)* to see such revered relics as the original Stanley Cup, to shoot pucks at a video goalie, to walk through the re-creation of a locker room and to watch some of hockey's sterling moments in the Broadcast Zone.

US and British Virgin Islands

Anegada
BRITISH VIRGIN ISLANDS
BVI National Parks 3
Virgin Gorda
Tortola
Coral World 4
5 9 Charlotte Amalie
2 Cruz Bay
6 Virgin Islands National Park
U.S. VIRGIN ISLANDS
Caribbean Sea
St. Croix 1

Mere specks in the Caribbean, the US and British Virgin Islands sit within eyesight of each other. The Stars and Stripes flutter over St Croix, St John and St Thomas; the Union Jack over Tortola, Virgin Gorda and the outer islands. All, though, offer tropical sun, soft sand beaches and turquoise sea. In both territories cars drive on the left and the US dollar is the currency. Each island has its distinct ambience, from bustle in St Thomas to sleepiness in the outer BVIs.

1 Historic St Croix

First settled in 1625 by Holland and England, with other European countries following, this former Danish colony reveals its history at every turn of the road. The Danish influence is especially obvious in the island's two main towns, Christiansted *(left)* and Frederiksted.

2 Cruz Bay, St John

Tucked next to a pretty harbour, this cosy town *(above)* offers eclectic shops, bars, restaurants and people-watching within walking distance of the sea.

3 BVI National Parks and Scenic Spots

History, hiking, diving and lovely sea views greet visitors who seek out these special places *(above)*. Some are off the beaten path, but all are worth the effort.

TOP 10 Moments in History

1 Christopher Columbus Arrives
Sailing through in 1493, Columbus stopped at Salt River, St Croix, to skirmish with the Carib Indians. The many islands he saw prompted him to name the archipelago after St Ursula and the 11,000 Virgins.

2 Slave Rebellion in 1733, St John
In their first attempt to gain freedom, slaves used cane knives to attack the Danish garrison at Coral Bay. They subsequently held the island's planters hostage, the siege ending only with help from French soldiers based in Martinique.

3 Emancipation, BVI
After Great Britain set the stage by outlawing the slave trade in 1807 and then seized a number of slave-carrying ships in BVI waters, this British colony finally freed its slaves on 1 August 1834.

4 Emancipation, USVI
Rioting slaves marched on Frederiksted, St Croix, in 1848, forcing Danish Governor Peter Von Scholten to declare emancipation.

5 Earthquake
In November 1867 an earthquake hit, followed by a huge tsunami that emptied the harbour in Charlotte Amalie, St Thomas, then surged back, killing many.

6 Fireburn, St Croix
Years of poor crops and other calamities pushed agricultural labourers to the brink, leading to the 1878 Fireburn. Frederiksted and other parts of St Croix went up in flames on the only day of the year when labourers could sign new contracts.

7 Transfer of Danish Colonies to the US
After years of negotiations, Denmark sold St Thomas, St John, and St Croix to the US for $25 million. The Stars and Stripes replaced the Danish flag on 31 March 1917.

8 Virgin Islands National Park Opens
Rockefeller bought up land on St John which he donated to the federal government as a nature reserve. The park opened in 1956.

9 Royalty Visits the BVI
Queen Elizabeth and Prince Philip visited Tortola in 1966 and again in 1977, riding in a motorcade through the streets. The late Princess Margaret visited in 1972.

10 Disastrous Hurricanes Hit USVI and BVI
Both territories suffered devastation when Hurricane Hugo hit in September 1989 and Marilyn in September 1995. Other hurricanes in the late 1990s caused further damage, prompting the islands to greatly strengthen their defence infrastructure.

4 Coral World, St Thomas

This marine park *(left)* connects visitors with the undersea life around the islands. Watch colourful fish in tanks or up close on underwater adventures, such as Sea Trekkin' or Snuba.

5 Historic Charlotte Amalie, St Thomas

Settled by Denmark in 1666, this town is the island's historical hub. Streets carry Danish names and many buildings date back several centuries.

6 Virgin Islands National Park, St John

Established in 1956, this park occupies about two-thirds of this 52-sq km (20-sq mile) island. Besides a range of plants and animals, it features gorgeous beaches, hiking trails on its lush hillsides *(above)*, interesting ruins along the hills and coasts, and watersports galore.

7 Sailing in the British Virgin Islands

Year-round balmy weather, gorgeous scenery and pristine anchorages within just a day's sail of each other make these islands one of the world's most desirable locations for sailing.

8 Dive and Snorkel Trips

Reefs teeming with colourful fish and coral provide teresting diving *(above)* no matter where you go, but the est diving is found offshore on a boat trip.

9 Duty-Free Shopping in St Thomas

Good prices, thanks to a duty-free deal from the US government, and the variety of merchandise make this a shopping mecca *(right)*.

10 Beach Resorts

Total calm and laziness by the sea or an abundance f activities – the Virgin Islands' top resorts *(above)* offer verything to make your holiday a dream come true.

Top 10 Local Food and Drink

1 Conch Fritters

Crunchy on the outside and creamy on the inside, these spicy conch and batter morsels are deep fried. While they're traditionally served as a first course or snack, light eaters can make a meal of them.

2 Goatwater

You'll find this tasty stew on the menu at only the most local of West Indian restaurants in the islands. It's cooked with goat, onions, garlic, tomatoes and a range of special spices.

3 Hot Sauce

Conjured up in local kitchens, hot sauce adds extra bite to any dish. It's made of fresh hot peppers, onions, and whatever else strikes the cook's fancy. Every one is different, so try several of them.

4 Kallaloo or Callaloo

The islands' famous spicy soup, *kallaloo* has greens as its base and includes a generous dose of okra, maybe ham or fish, and whatever seasonings the cook likes to use.

5 Lobster

The simplest lobster dish, just drizzled with melted butter and served in the shell, may be the best way to appreciate its sweet flavour, but many here prefer it stuffed with crabmeat.

6 Maubi

A spicy drink, *maubi* is fermented from *maubi* bark with generous helpings of sugar, dried orange peel, cinnamon and cloves added. It's an acquired taste, and folks either love it or hate it. *Maubi* is found on the menu only at local restaurants.

7 Pates

Caribbean pates are turnovers stuffed with a spicy lobster, conch, chicken or beef filling, then deep fried. These make great quick lunches or snacks.

8 Ole Wife

Usually served boiled with onions and spices, ole wife is officially called triggerfish or moonfish. Every cook will conjure up his own version of this tasty catch of the day.

9 Johnnycake

Found on just about all West Indian menus, this staple is simply a deep-fried, flattened biscuit (dumpling).

10 Tarts

Tarts are the Virgin Islands' word for one-crust pies, often filled with coconut, guava or other fruits. They can be extremely sweet.

Vancouver and Victoria

Fringed by the Pacific Ocean's sandy beaches and with a backdrop of the Coast Mountain range, Vancouver is among the most beautifully located metropolises on earth. Also feted as one of the world's best cities to live in, this West Coast gem has a lively cultural scene and superb restaurants and hotels. On Vancouver Island, a short ferry ride away, Victoria offers visitors a peaceful sojourn. The city is an excellent starting-off point for exploring the many natural wonders of the island.

1 UBC Museum of Anthropology

In a stunning building *(left)*, overlooking mountains and sea, is one of North America's finest collections of Northwest Coast native art. The Koerner Ceramics Gallery houses 15th- to 19th-century European ceramics.

2 Canada Place

Built for Expo '86, Canada Place *(above)* is now an outstanding convention and hotel complex, overlooking Vanc Harbour. Cruise ships dock alongside an inviting promenade

3 Capilano Suspension Bridge

Making your way across a wooden bridge high above th Capilano River *(above)* is perhaps the most thrilling experienc at this sight; walking along a boardwalk up into the treetops a close second. Learn about local history, forest ecology anc First Nations culture as you enjoy the beautiful surroundings

TOP 10 Traditional Sculptures

1 'Ksan Mural
Five artists carved this red cedar frieze, in which nine panels tell stories of how the Raven created the elements of the world through his mischievous activities.

2 The Jade Canoe
Haida artist Bill Reid's awe-inspiring bronze creation is the second casting of *The Black Canoe*. Thirteen creatures from Haida mythology paddle an imposing 6-m (20-ft) canoe.

3 Inukshuk
Made by Alvin Kanak for Expo '86, the granite sculpture is an Inuit welcome figure – a traditional traveller's marker – although much larger than those found in the North.

4 Carved Doors
The entrance to the UBC Museum of Anthropology has doors of red cedar made by four Gitxsan master carvers. They convey a narrative from the Skeena river region, and when closed form the shape of a Northwest Coast bent box, used for storage and burials.

5 Kwakwaka'wakw Totem Pole
This pole at Victoria's Royal British Columbia Museum is a modern interpretation of traditional carving by two young Kwakwaka'wakw artists. The pole features a mythical thunderbird.

6 Hetux
International travellers alighting at the Vancouver airport are greeted by *Hetux*, a huge birch-and-aluminum image suspended from the ceiling. It combines animal forms and mythical figures.

7 Thunderbird House Post
This majestic thunderbird standing above a grizzly bear that holds a human being is a replica of two poles carved in the early 1900s. The re-created pole now stands in Stanley Park's Brockton Point Visitor Centre.

8 Chief of the Undersea World
This 5-m- (16-ft-) tall bronze killer whale leaping into the air is a tribute to this West Coast creature.

9 World's Tallest Freestanding Totem Pole
Raised in Beacon Hill Park in 1956, the pole was carved from a cedar nearly 39 m (128 ft) high by Kwakwaka'-wakw chief Mungo Martin, along with David Martin and Henry Hunt.

10 Coast Salish Welcome Figures
Two huge red cedar figures welcome travellers to the airport's Custom Hall in traditional Musqueam style. Both figures were carved from the same log.

4 Granville Island

The popular Granville Island on False Creek *(above)* is a ustling mix of shops, galleries, restaurants and theatres – n both to visit and explore.

6 Vancouver Art Gallery

From the swirling raincoast forests of famed Canadian rtist Emily Carr to radical conceptual installations, the allery features the best of West Coast and international art.

7 Stanley Park

Created in 1886, Stanley Park is North America's hird-largest urban park. It juts into Burrard Inlet, offering n enticing combination of forest, ocean and beaches, nd an encircling sea wall pedestrian loop.

8 Long Beach Area

Spectacular scenery dominates the Long Beach area on Vancouver Island's West Coast *(left)*. Wild Pacific shores and rare old-growth forests make the region perfect for experiencing the rugged essence of British Columbia.

TOP 10 Great Outdoor Places

1 English Bay
This beautiful bay is a popular West End attraction. It's a popular place for walking the sea wall that runs beside the bay into Stanley Park, fuelled with coffee or ice cream from nearby Davie and Denman street cafés.

2 Lighthouse Park
Some 10 km (6 miles) of trails provide day hikes through this entirely natural park, with its native trees and plants, boulder-lined shore and 1912 Point Atkinson Lighthouse.

3 Jericho Beach
Picnics on the beach are a favourite pastime at this family-friendly park. The more active might like to rent a windsurfer.

4 Cypress Provincial Park
Cypress Mountain, one of the park's best peaks, is the biggest alpine ski and snow-boarding area on the North Shore. Summer activities include mountain biking, hiking and wild camping.

5 Grouse Mountain
The gondola ride to the summit provides thrilling city views. Skiing is guaranteed in winter, courtesy of snow-makers, and there are lots of summer activities too.

6 Kitsilano Beach and Park
"Kits" Park is connected by a tree-lined walk to the beach, favoured by volleyball players and sunbathers. Busy Olympic-size Kitsilano Pool overlooks the beach.

7 Wreck Beach
There are spectacular views across the Strait of Georgia to Vancouver Island from this clothing-optional beach. Getting down to the beach is easy, via a steep trail leading from SW Marine Drive on the UBC campus; the hard part is the climb back up.

8 Mount Seymour Provincial Park
On the eastern end of the Coast Mountain range, Mount Seymour Park is popular with skiers and snowboarders in winter and hikers in summer.

9 Beacon Hill Park
Since 1858, Beacon Hill Park has been the queen of Victoria's open-air spaces. Wooden bridges over the stream, a petting zoo and an English-style rose garden add charm to the peaceful setting. Visitors can walk, bird-watch, ride horses and picnic on the beach.

10 Cathedral Grove
The grove, located in MacMillan Provincial Park on Vancouver Island, provides an awe-inspiring look at a virgin coastal forest. Giant ancient Douglas fir trees share the forest with stands of hemlock and Western red cedar. Loop trails are located on either side of Hwy 4.

Whistler 5

Ideal for a day-trip or a longer visit, Whistler *(right)* is an upscale resort a scenic 2-hour drive north from Vancouver. Two mountains tower over alpine-style resort villages. Skiers abound here, but countless other year-round activities ensure Whistler has something for everyone.

9 Royal British Columbia Museum, Victoria

This wonderful museum confidently portrays British Columbia's history and natural assets in its creative galleries.

10 Science World

Science comes alive inside the dome-shaped Science World *(left)*. Hands-on exhibits capture the imaginations of all ages, with fresh approaches to science in all its dimensions.

Washington DC

A symbol of democracy the world over and the seat of American government, Washington DC confronts visitors with stirring icons and monuments at every turn. This sparkling self-styled city on the Potomac river is full of marble and light. Built on former swampland, Washington was set out in quadrants, with the US Capitol at its hub. Its many sights provide unparalleled access to the workings of government, internationally famed museums with priceless exhibits, and the cultural and spiritual foundations of the city and the nation.

1 Mount Vernon
George Washington's estate and mansion *(below)* is a perfect example of the gentleman-farmer roots common to many of America's founders.

2 Library of Congress
The breathtaking interior of the largest library in the world *(left)* does full justice to its 120 million items; the works fill 850 km (530 miles) of shelves.

3 United States Capitol
The Capitol's design combines ancient tradition and New World innovation, perfectly invoking the spirit of US democracy.

4 Washington National Cathedral
Ancient and modern meet in this "nationa house of prayer," from the Gothic architec ture *(above)* to the Space Window.

TOP 10 Moments in History

1 Foundation of the Federal City
The US Constitution, ratified in 1788, provided for: "a District (not exceeding ten Miles square) as may, by Cession of Particular States…, become the Seat of the Government of the United States." Thus Washington DC was born.

2 Layout and Design
In 1790 George Washington selected Pierre Charles L'Enfant, a French engineer, to lay out the city. The plan was influenced by Versailles and the city of Paris.

3 War of 1812
The United States declared war on Britain in 1812, seeking freedom of marine trade. In 1814 British troops entered the capital and burned government buildings, including the White House and the Capitol.

4 Expansion
Thomas Jefferson began western expansion by organizing the Lewis and Clark expedition in 1803. The C&O Canal and the Baltimore and Ohio Railroad provided a route for commerce and a period of prosperity.

5 Civil War
Conflict between the Union and the seceding southern states began in 1861. Union supporters, joined by thousands of blacks escaping slavery in the South, doubled the city's population in four years. The city remained in Union hands throughout the war, which ended in 1865.

6 McMillan Plan
The McMillan Plan of 1901 was the first application of city planning in the United States. It created much of the layout of the Mall and President's Park seen today.

7 New Deal
The Roosevelt era (1933–1945) brought tremendous growth to the city. Efforts to bring the nation out of the Great Depression increased the size and number of government agencies, and provided direct funds for the construction of buildings such as the Supreme Court and National Gallery of Art.

8 World War II
More than 10 per cent of the 115 million US population was in uniform at the peak of the war – the troops being commanded from Washington.

9 March on Washington
On 28 August 1963, African-American leaders led 250,000 people to rally in front of the Lincoln Memorial in support of equal rights. There, Dr Martin Luther King famously expressed his dream for America.

10 Home Rule
The federal government's policy of maintaining full control over the city was modified with the Home Rule Charter in 1973. This gave the city the power to elect its own mayor, city council and school board.

5 National Air and Space Museum

This is reportedly the most visited museum in the world *(left)*. The artifacts of one of mankind's greatest quests – flight above and beyond Earth – are rendered even more impressive by the hangarlike architecture.

National Zoological Park 6

Animals from across the world's varied habitats can be seen and learned about at this internationally recognized leader in animal care, breeding of endangered species and public education *(right)*.

7 The White House

The most elegant and familiar of all the world's political residences, the White House *bove)* has witnessed some of the most consequential decisions of modern history.

9 National Museum of American History

his museum combines the America's attic" approach with ontemporary exhibits. The rtifacts range from political ampaign badges to early ɔcomotives, as well as the Star-pangled Banner *(above)*.

8 National Gallery of Art

The National Gallery's vast collection – one of the greatest in the world – traces Western art from medieval times to the present day.

10 Arlington National Cemetery

Four million people each year visit these rolling lawns studded with the headstones of America's war dead *(above)* – a moving and reflective experience.

TOP 10 Memorials and Monuments

1 Lincoln Memorial
The majestic monument to the president who preserved America's unity and began the long process of ending slavery is built in the form of a Greek temple. The enormous statue of a seated Abraham Lincoln was designed in 1915 by Daniel Chester French.

2 Washington Monument
This spire of 1884 is the dominant feature on the city skyline, gleaming in its marble cladding. It offers stunning views from its observation platform.

3 Jefferson Memorial
Inspired by the Pantheon in Rome, this graceful monument was dedicated in 1943, on the 200th anniversary of Jefferson's birth. It houses a bronze statue of the president.

4 Franklin Delano Roosevelt Memorial
Four outdoor rooms represent Roosevelt's four terms as president. Each is a composition of statues, water, plants and engraved quotations of the president.

5 Vietnam Veterans' Memorial
This simple V-shaped black granite wall, carved with the names of those who died in this divisive war, is a moving tribute. Built in 1982, it is the work of Maya Lin, then an architecture student at Yale.

6 Korean War Veterans Memorial
Nineteen exhausted soldiers plod forward, determined on their goal. These 2-m (7-ft) steel statues are the dominant element in a memorial to the Americans who died in the UN's "police action" in Korea.

7 Iwo Jima Statue (Marine Corps Memorial)
Marines struggling to erect the Stars and Stripes on a ridge at Iwo Jima serves as a memorial to all marines who have fought for their country. The Pacific island saw fierce fighting during World War II, resulting in 7,000 American deaths.

8 World War II Memorial
This memorial built to honour both US veteran soldiers and the civilians of World War II includes commemorative columns, a Freedom Wall, landscaping and fountains.

9 African-American Civil War Memorial
"The Spirit of Freedom," a 1996 sculpture by Ed Hamilton, depicts African-American Union soldiers facing the enemy.

10 US Navy Memorial
The fountains that surround this plaza contain water recirculated from all seven seas. Flagstaffs suggest the rigging of a tall ship.

Best of the Rest: City Sights

Top 10 Historic Buildings

1 Saint Nicholas Russian Orthodox Cathedral, Seattle, USA
The building's ornate turquoise onion domes and spires rise high above the trees and neighbouring homes.

2 Cedar Hill, Washington DC, USA
Frederick Douglass and his family were the first African-Americans in Anacostia when they moved here in 1877. He was America's greatest anti-slavery speaker.

3 Presbytère, New Orleans, USA
This 1791 building houses a fantastic Mardi Gras exhibit, as well as some of the finest costumes from past events.

4 Museo Evita, Buenos Aires, Argentina
On show at this elegant building is a collection of Evita's dresses, plus memorabilia and video clips.

5 Iglesia y Hospital de Jesús Nazareno, Mexico City, Mexico
The tomb of Hernán Cortés lies here. To the rear is the place where Moctezuma II met Cortés in 1519.

6 Todmorden Mills Heritage Museum, Toronto, Canada
Among many exhibits here are two lovingly restored 18th-century houses, and the 1881 Don Train Station.

7 Château Ramezay, Montréal, Canada
An elegant heritage museum sits in an 18th-century former governor's home, with artifacts from indigenous peoples.

8 Place Royale, Quebec, Canada
The site of Nouvelle-France's first settlement in 1608, has always been the hub of the city's cultural activities.

9 Old State House, Boston, USA
Built in 1713, the Boston Massacre occurred outside its doors in 1770, and the Declaration of Independence was first read to Bostonians from its balcony.

10 Grand Central Terminal, New York, USA
One of the world's great rail terminals is an outstanding Beaux Arts building. Look up to see the constellations twinkling on its heaven-blue ceiling.

Top 10 Architectural Gems

1 The Rookery, Chicago, USA
Built in 1888, its stunning skylit lobby was redesigned in 1907 by Frank Lloyd Wright. Its name refers to the rooks that once roosted at the site.

2 Chiat/Day Building, Los Angeles, USA
Frank Gehry's 1991 building has as its centrepiece a three-storey tall pair of binoculars designed by Claes Oldenburg and Coosje van Bruggen.

3 Flatiron Building, New York, USA
When this iconic, 21-storey triangular building was built in 1902, people took bets on whether it would topple over.

4 Transamerica Pyramid, San Francisco, USA
Hated by many at first, the Pyramid is now loved as an icon of the city.

5 Renwick Gallery, Washington DC, USA
This fine gallery of American crafts is housed in a gorgeous 1874 French Renaissance-style building.

6 Museu de Arte Contemporanea de Niterói (MAC), Rio de Janeiro, Brazil
Brazilian art is on show in an iconic concrete spheroid by Oscar Niemeyer, set at the end of a rocky promontory.

7 Floralis Genérica, Buenos Aires, Argentina
Eduardo Catalano's 2002 *Floralis* is an metal flower that "blooms" at 8am, closing its enormous petals at dusk.

8 Louisiana Superdome, New Orleans, USA
Literally a superdome, it covers the world's largest steel-constructed spac[e] unobstructed in any way by posts.

9 Calle Obispo, Havana, Cuba
This pedestrian-only thoroughfare is lined with lovely but faded mansions.

10 Chrysler Building, New York, USA
The gleaming, stainless steel, tiered Art Deco spire, flanked by Chrysler hood ornament eagle gargoyles, adds unique elegance to the skyline day and night.

Top 10 Museums and Galleries

1 Museum of African American History, Boston, USA
The MAAH reveals the daily life of free, pre-Civil War African-Americans in workshops, exhibitions and events.

2 Swedish-American Museum Center, Chicago, USA
This tiny museum displays personal items brought over by early settlers and exhibitions on Swedish culture.

3 Seattle Art Museum, USA
Seattle's largest art museum, its splendid collection includes European, Asian, African, and Northwest Coast Native American works.

4 Wells Fargo History Museum, San Francisco, USA
The Wells Fargo stagecoaches are the stuff of legends, and visitors can get a real feel of the thrills and perils here.

5 Ah-Tah-Thi-Ki Museum, Miami, USA
This excellent museum shows Seminole artifacts, and the important Green Corn Ceremony is explained.

6 National Museum of Women in the Arts, Washington DC, USA
This is the only museum in the world dedicated purely to the work of women artists, from the Renaissance to today.

7 Museu Internacional de Arte Naïf (MIAN), Rio de Janeiro, Brazil
This delightful museum features one of the largest collections of Naive art.

8 Museo Dolores Olmedo, Mexico City, Mexico
With 145 works by Diego Rivera that span his entire career, this stunning 17th-century hacienda also houses some of Frida Kahlo's work.

9 Bata Shoe Museum, Toronto, Canada
Resembling a stylized shoebox, this museum houses over 10,000 shoes, covering 4,500 years of footwear history.

10 MoMa, New York, USA
One of the world's most comprehensive and best collections of modern art, the building itself is also a masterpiece.

Top 10 Religious Buildings

1 Ermita de la Caridad Church, Coconut Grove, Miami, USA
This peculiar conical church draws in Miami's Cuban exiles. The altar is even oriented toward Cuba.

2 Old North Church, Boston, USA
An active Episcopal congregation still worships at Boston's oldest church (1723), officially known as Christ Church.

3 St John Coltrane's African Orthodox Church, San Francisco, USA
Services consist of a performance of the celebrated jazz musician Coltrane's "A Love Supreme".

4 Nossa Senhora da Lapa, Rio de Janeiro, Brazil
The modest church with a lovely interor is a haven of peace in the bustle of central Rio.

5 Templo de Regina Coeli, Mexico City, Mexico
This masterpiece of Churrigueresque style dates from the 17th century.

6 Fourth Presbyterian Church, Chicago, USA
The first Fourth Presbyterian Church celebrated its first sermon just hours before it was incinerated in the Great Fire of 1871. It was rebuilt in 1914.

7 St Patrick's Church, New Orleans, USA
The subtle 19th-century Gothic exterior belies its ornate interior, including 16 stained-glass windows in a half dome.

8 Santuario de Chimayó, Santa Fe, USA
Thousands of pilgrims walk here during the Holy Week. It's a place of Native American legend and Christian visions.

9 Cathedral of Our Lady of the Angels, Los Angeles, USA
The fortress-like exterior opens onto a hall of worship with lovely tapestries.

10 St Patrick's Cathedral, New York, USA
America's largest Catholic cathedral opened in 1879. French Gothic in style, it has twin 100-m (330-ft) towers.

cean Beach, San Diego, USA

Old State House, Boston, USA

Outdoor mural, Pilsen, Chicago, USA

Hollywood Bowl, Los Angeles, USA

TOP 10 Performing Arts Venues

Symphony Hall, Boston, USA
)pened in 1900, Symphony Hall is one f the world's most acoustically perfect enues and a National Landmark.

Buddy Guy's Legends, :hicago, USA
egendary bluesman Buddy Guy runs ne best blues club in the city. Guy imself sometimes headlines.

American Conservatory 'heater, San Francisco, USA
t the heart of ACT is an acclaimed neatre school – former students nclude Denzel Washington, Annette ening and Winona Ryder.

Kennedy Center, Washington C, USA
he many and varied productions at nis landmark arts centre are almost ,ways critically acclaimed.

Mahalia Jackson Theater of he Performing Arts, New)rleans, USA
amed for the Queen of Gospel Music, is theatre is a highlight of Basin Street.

6 Place des Arts, Montréal, Canada
The cultural centrepiece of Montréal. Five modern venues and an outdoor plaza host countless performances.

7 La Jolla Playhouse, San Diego, USA
Gregory Peck, Mel Ferrer, and Dorothy McGuire founded this acclaimed theatre in 1947. All the Hollywood greats once performed here.

8 Hollywood Bowl, Los Angeles, USA
A night out at the world's largest natural amphitheatre is an LA summer tradition.

9 Carver Community Cultural Center, San Antonio, USA
Since 1929 the Center has hosted stars such as Ella Fitzgerald and Dizzy Gillespie and the Soweto Gospel Choir.

10 Lincoln Center for the Performing Arts, New York, USA
A dazzling array of performance venues, covering almost every genre, is housed in this West Side complex.

TOP 10 Beaches and Green Spaces

1 The Esplanade, Boston, USA
Collegiate rowing crews, canoeists, sailboats and the coast guard share the waters here. Relax on a bench and watch their comings and goings.

2 South Bay, Los Angeles, USA
Outdoor pursuits govern the laid-back lifestyle of three picture-perfect beach towns. A paved trail connects them, perfect for bicycling and inline skating.

3 Crandon Park, Miami, USA
Key Biscayne is blessed with some of Miami's top beaches, but this is rated one of the top ten in the country.

4 C&O Canal, Washington, USA
This 295-km (184-mile) waterway dates back to the early 19th century. It's now a haven for walkers, cyclists and for boaters. Catch a mule-drawn boat ride at Georgetown or Great Falls.

5 Praia de Fora, Rio de Janeiro, Brazil
This fabulous beach sweeps majestically between the base of the Morro Cara de Cão and the Sugar Loaf.

6 Jardín Botánico Carlos Thays, Buenos Aires, Argentina
Wild and wonderful, the city's botanical gardens are home to over 5,500 plant species, interspersed with classical statues and fountains.

7 Jardín del Centenario, Coyoacán, Mexico
The atrium of a former convent is today a lovely town park in Coyoacán.

8 Toronto Music Garden, Canada
This playful Bach-themed garden is a collaboration between famed cellist Yo Yo Ma and Toronto landscape architects. Summer concerts are held in its grassy amphitheatre.

9 Pacific Beach, San Diego, USA
A great beach-going spirit fills the air as skaters, joggers and cyclists cruise the promenade parallel to the beach while surfers shoot the curl.

10 Prospect Park, New York, USA
The builders of Central Park considered this green Brooklyn space, with its pools and willows, their masterpiece.

TOP 10 Special Spots

Pilsen, Chicago, USA
1urals and mosaics portray Mexican ulture and history in this lively quarter.

Self-Realization Fellowship ake Shrine, Los Angeles, USA
Vith an aura of beauty and serenity, is hidden sanctuary was created 1950 by Paramahansa Yogananda, ı Indian-born spiritual leader.

Haight-Ashbury, an Francisco, USA
nis anarchic quarter rests firmly n its laurels as ground zero for the ower Power explosion of the 1960s.

Nancy Forrester's Secret arden, Miami, USA
ose – or perhaps find – yourself in this npossibly lush and peaceful garden, ith ravishing flora and friendly parrots.

Plaza Dorrego, uenos Aires, Argentina
nis is one of the city's oldest, most cturesque squares, ringed by old ngo bars and cafés, and famous for s bustling Sunday antiques market.

6 Rumba del Callejón de Hamel, Havana, Cuba
This Afro-Cuban rumba session takes place in an alley whose walls are decked with murals inspired by *Santería*.

7 Museo Frida Kahlo, Mexico City, Mexico
This vibrant blue house where the artist Frida Kahlo was born and worked is filled with her personal belongings.

8 Enid A Haupt Garden, Washington DC, USA
This wonderful public garden in the Smithsonian Institution complex reflects the collections of the museums nearby.

9 The High Line, New York, USA
An abandoned elevated railroad track high over the Chelsea district has been transformed into a leafy public walkway with wonderful vistas.

10 Avenue du Mont-Royal, Montréal, Canada
This street has character and panache, reflected in its bevy of eclectic eateries, curiosity shops and laid-back style.

TOP 10 Shopping

1 Harvard Square Bookstores, Boston, USA
Harvard Square's bookstores are some of the most distinguished in the country.

2 Main Street, Santa Monica, Los Angeles, USA
A laid-back yet sophisticated string of one-of-a-kind boutiques, Main Street makes for fun and eclectic shopping.

3 Darbury Stenderu, Seattle, USA
Stenderu's hand-dyed silk, velvet and light knits for clothes, soft furnishings and accessories are all unique.

4 Art Deco District Welcome Center, Miami, USA
A treasure-trove of Deco kitsch, from cutesy salt-and-pepper sets to really rather nice reproduction lamps.

5 Georgetown, Washington DC, USA
Probably the most famous shopping area in the city, partly because of the hundreds of one-off shops but also for its pervasive sense of style.

6 Bikinis from Lenny, Rio de Janeiro, Brazil
The only place in Rio that has a dress code is the beach. Brazilian swimwear the most fashionable in the world and the best of the best is found at Lenny.

7 Casa López, Buenos Aires, Argentina
Elegant, handmade leather bags are offered in a wide variety of styles, as well as luxurious leather fashions.

8 Fonart, Mexico City, Mexico
One of the best stores to visit for Mexican handicrafts – everything from ceramics to woven baskets.

9 Bucktown Neighborhood, Chicago, USA
This gentrified locale is brimming with edgy music shops, high-style designer boutiques, and antiques importers.

10 Macy's, New York, USA
The world's largest store, and a New York icon, Macy's is a miracle on 34th Street from the Spring Flower Show to the Thanksgiving Parade.

Best of the Rest: Out of Town

Top 10 Towns and Villages

1 St Helena, California, USA
Peaceful St Helena is the archetypal image of small-town America, its old-fashioned Main Street lined with antique stores, restaurants and cafés.

2 Wethersfield, Connecticut, USA
Founded in 1634, Wethersfield has some of the most striking Colonial architecture in the country.

3 Annapolis, Maryland, USA
This enticing city on the Chesapeake Bay is one of the East Coast's great sailing and naval centres.

4 Port Townsend, Washington, USA
This idyllic seaport is known for its Victorian architecture, such as the Jefferson County Historical Society.

5 St Martinville, New Orleans, USA
St Martinville retains a small-town flavour and Southern charm. It hosts La Grande Boucherie des Cajuns, which celebrates Cajun culture.

6 Petrópolis, Brazil
Emperor Dom Pedro II's summer retreat, Petrópolis was founded in 1843 and largely designed by German architect Julius Friedrich Köler.

7 Sancti Spíritus, Cuba
The historic core of Sancti Spíritus (founded in 1522) has brightly coloured colonial homes and a 17th-century church with a spectacular ceiling.

8 Puebla, Mexico City, Mexico
Founded in 1531, Puebla is famous for its beautiful colonial buildings decorated with hand-painted Talavera tiles.

9 San Antonio de Areco, Buenos Aires, Argentina
Just 110 km (68 miles) southwest of Buenos Aires, this cowboy town boasts a historic centre, with wrought-iron lamps lining cobblestone streets.

10 Sucre, Bolivia
Once the country's capital, Sucre is sufficiently small to explore on foot and get a feel for the vibrancy and colour of Bolivian street life.

Top 10 Historic Buildings and Museums

1 The Rhine House, Beringer Winery, California, USA
This extravagant building was built in 1884 to recall German immigrant Frederick Beringer's Rhineland home.

2 Mystic Seaport, CT, USA
Walk the decks of a tall ship, or see carpenters replank a vessel at this "museum of America and the sea."

3 Mark Twain House, Hartford, CT, USA
Tiffany interiors feature in the home of the great storyteller. The adjoining museum revolves around Twain (1835–1910) and his contemporaries.

4 Museum of Indian Arts and Culture, Santa Fe, USA
This museum has the most comprehensive collection of Native American anthropological articles in the country.

5 Ek-Balam, Cancún, Mexico
These ruins contain some of the finest examples of Mayan sculpture, including a temple entrance that's believed to be the tomb of a ruler in around 800.

6 Museo de Antropología, Mérida, Mexico
The grandest of all the Paseo Montejo mansions houses archeological finds from sites all across the Yucatán.

7 Charles Hosmer Morse Museum of American Art, Florida, USA
With work by Tiffany to the fore, this museum represents the high point of America's Arts and Crafts movement.

8 La Chascona, Santiago, Chile
The epitome of a poet's home, La Chascona ("the uncombed") was built by Chilean poet Pablo Neruda.

9 Fallingwater, Pennsylvania, USA
With its terraces jutting out over a waterfall, this Frank Lloyd Wright house appears part of the landscape.

10 Sacsayhuaman, Peru
Just outside the city of Cusco stands this Inca complex, which consists of three tiered walls zigzagging towards a tower, interrupted by great doorways.

Top 10 Religious Buildings

1 Pu'uomahuka Heiau, Oahu, Hawai'i, USA
This *luakini heiau* (sacrificial temple) honours the war god Kū and commands panoramic views of Waimea Bay.

2 Church of San Francisco de Asis, Santa Fe, USA
This simple adobe Mission church built in 1814 became a favourite subject of artist Georgia O'Keeffe.

3 San Bernardino Sisal, Valladolid, Mexico
The Yucatán's oldest church began as part of a Franciscan monastery in 1552.

4 Touro Synagogue, Rhode Island, New England, USA
The oldest synagogue in the country, spare and elegant Touro Synagogue was constructed in 1763 by religious refugees from Spain and Portugal.

5 Canterbury Shaker Village, NH, New England, USA
Founded in 1792, Canterbury was a working Shaker village into the 1960s. Today it is a kind of living museum.

6 Catedral de San Juan Baútista, Puerto Rico
The cathedral was completed in 1852 in a Neo-Classical / Baroque style. It houses the tomb of Ponce de León.

7 Igrejo e Convento de São Francisco, Salvador, Brazil
Built in 1708–50, the convent features beautiful cloisters, blue and white azulejos, and a particularly opulent church interior, gleaming with gold leaf.

8 Catedral de la Immaculada Concepcion, La Plata, Argentina
Argentina's largest church is heavily influenced by European Gothic.

9 Sea Ranch Chapel, Gualala, California, USA
Resembling a huge seashell, the non-denominational Sea Ranch Chapel (1984) is appealing, if slightly kitsch.

10 Church of St Francis, Belo Horizonte, Brazil
Oscar Niemeyer's modernist church with undulating roofline commands a striking position on Pampulha Lake.

Top 10 Islands

1 Nantucket Island, MA, New England, USA
Pristine beaches, museums and upmarket shopping are among Nantucket's many attractions.

2 1000 Islands, Montréal, Canada
There are actually 1,865 islands in this grouping; St Lawrence Islands National Park is the jewel in their crown.

3 Ilha Grande, Brazil
There are no roads on this forested island just south of Rio city, and the beaches and trekking are breathtaking.

4 Culebrita, Puerto Rico
This tiny uninhabited isle just east of Culebra has beautiful beaches shelving into electric-blue waters – perfect for picnicking and snorkelling.

5 Georgian Bay Islands National Park, Toronto, Canada
Thousands of islands dot the Bay; 59 of them make up the park. The largest island, Beausoleil, has hiking trails, sandy beaches and forests to explore.

6 Dry Tortugas, Miami, USA
You can travel to the wonderful island of the Dry Tortugas by seaplane or ferry from Key West. Camping overnight is also possible.

7 Caladesi Island State Park, Orlando, USA
This small island, accessible by ferry from Honeymoon Island, is a lovely retreat, traversed by a nature trail.

8 Moloka'i, Hawai'i, USA
The island offers spectacular scenery, quiet island life and is just a 15-minute flight from Maui.

9 Isla Saona, Dominican Republic
Despite the crowds, the island still looks like a Robinson Crusoe fantasy.

10 Isla Contoy, Cancún, Mexico
This uninhabited island reserve north of Isla Mujeres is home to a huge range of sea birds, including pelicans, boobies and frigate birds, and contains mangroves, turtle-breeding beaches, and superb coral lagoons.

lle de la Luna, Chile

Mississippi Swamps, USA

Church of San Francisco de Asis, Santa Fe, USA

Ilha Grande, Brazil

Top 10 Lakes and Waterways

Lake Sonoma, California, USA
is lake lies at the heart of a park ith extensive trails for hikers, horse ders and mountain bikers.

Snoqualmie Falls, eattle, USA
n observation deck and a steep path the river allow breathtaking views of e 84-m (276-ft) Snoqualmie Falls.

Parc de la Gorge de oaticook, Montréal, Canada
sitors are drawn here to Coaticook ake, a cavernous gorge and the world's ngest pedestrian suspension bridge.

Mississippi Swamps, USA
ours from outside the city limits take sitors through the varied topography a typical Southern swamp.

Long Point Provincial Park, ake Erie, Toronto, Canada
ormed over thousands of years sand washed from Lake Erie's horeline, this sand spit is a world-enowned refuge for migrating birds, specially waterfowl.

6 New York State Canals, USA
The Erie, Oswego, Cayuga-Seneca and Champlain canals can be explored by boat and through their museums.

7 Gocta Falls, Peru
These falls in Peru's Northern Highlands drop an astounding 770 m (2,530 ft) in two tiers. You'll need to complete a 5-hour trek through dense jungle to reach them though.

8 Finger Lakes, New York State, USA
The 11 glacier-carved Finger Lakes are natural marvels, surrounded by gorges with more than 1,000 waterfalls.

9 Rio Grande Gorge, New Mexico, USA
Take in the view of this canyon from the Rio Grande Gorge Bridge on Highway 64 or explore the river by raft.

10 Panama Canal, Panama
Completed in 1914, the canal cuts through the 80-km- (50-mile-) wide Central American isthmus, enabling access from the Atlantic to the Pacific.

Top 10 Mountains and Forests

1 Armstrong Redwoods State Natural Reserve, California, USA
This is simply one of the most majestic groves of coast redwoods in northern California, with many nature trails.

2 Mount Mansfield, Stowe, Vermont, USA
The tallest of the Green Mountains, Mansfield is great for hikers in summer; in winter skiers take over.

3 Diamond Head Crater, Honolulu, Hawai'i, USA
Hawai'i's most-recognized landmark watches over Waikīkī. A 5-km (3-mile) loop walk allows you to see the changeable peak from a full circle.

4 Taos Ski Valley, Santa Fe, USA
With reliable snow each year and one of the nation's steepest slopes, Taos Ski Valley is one of the most popular ski resorts in the country.

5 Mount Rainier, Seattle, USA
This silent, snowcapped sentinel, the centrepiece of Mount Rainier National Park, is an awe-inspiring active volcano.

6 Parque Nacional Iztaccíhuatl-Popocatépetl, Mexico
Some of the highest peaks in Mexico are found in a pine-forested wilderness with excellent hiking and biking trails.

7 Bosque Estatal Toro Negro, Puerto Rico
This forest preserve protects over 28 sq km (10 sq miles) of rain-drenched cloudforest, the waters of which feed tumultuous rivers.

8 Cypress Provincial Park, Vancouver, Canada
Cypress Mountain, one of several peaks, is the biggest ski and snowboarding area on the North Shore.

9 Kodachrome Basin State Park, Utah, USA
The bright hues of the rocks here are outstanding, especially on the chimneys of rock known as "sand pipes".

10 Valle de la Luna, Chile
Wide valleys and steep ridges sculpted by nature cover a spectrum of changing hues on a moonlike landscape.

Top 10 Beaches

Point Reyes National eashore, California, USA
ttractions at this national park include weeping beaches, rocky headlands nd marshes teeming with wildlife.

2 Coast Guard Beach, astham, Massachusetts, USA
long and generous slope of sand eads down to the ocean, so the each here is never crowded.

3 Reid State Park, Georgetown, Maine, USA
wim safely along stretches sheltered om the ocean waves by sand bars, r break out the surf boards for more xposed parts of the beach.

4 Anegada Beaches, Virgin Islands
he reef fringing the island keeps the vaters around the pretty white sand eaches calm and the fish plentiful.

5 Região dos Lago, Brazil
ehind miles of talcum-fine sandy eaches are a series of brackish lakes hat give the region its name.

6 Playa Pilar, Cayo Guillermo, Cuba
Brushed by near constant breezes, the white sands of this beach are swept into dunes overlooking pristine reef-protected ocean waters.

7 Celestún, Cancún, Mexico
Most tourists go to Celestún only to see its flamingoes, but it is also a tranquil village with an endless white-sand beach lined by fishing boats.

8 Ingonish Beach, Canada
The beach here is a temporary bank of sand, swept away by waves in winter and redeposited in spring.

9 Morne Rouge, St George's, Grenada
One of the most secluded beaches in Grenada, Morne Rouge has plenty of natural shade beneath palms.

10 Grayton Beach, Florida, USA
A broad sweep of quartz-white sand lapped by calm, warm Gulf waters, Grayton Beach regularly features high in rankings of the nation's top beaches.

Top 10 Food and Wine Districts

1 Rutherford, California, USA
This AVA is the historical core of the Napa Valley. Cabernet Sauvignon is the grape most widely grown here.

2 Gravenstein Highway, California, USA
The "Gravenstein Highway" (SR-116) passes through a region of apple orchards, with the Gravenstein variety being a speciality of the area.

3 Maricao, Puerto Rico
This pleasant town, surrounded by glossy coffee bushes, holds an annual coffee festival each February.

4 Texas Hill Country, San Antonio, USA
Scattered across the Hill Country are two dozen fine wineries, which produce many award-winning wines.

5 St Jacobs and Elora, Toronto, Canada
These villages boast many food shops and eateries, while the St Jacobs' Farmers' Market includes stalls selling the area's speciality, maple syrup.

6 Cheese Dairies, Vermont, USA
There are world-class farmstead cheeses all across Vermont. Small dairies make everything from fresh goat's milk chèvres to aged, pungent blue-veined cheeses.

7 Blueberries, Maine, USA
The best time for wild blueberries in Maine is from late July to August.

8 Pisco distilleries, Elqui Valley, Chile
Chile's national cocktail, pisco sour, is made from pisco, a brandy produced largely in the Elqui Valley in northern Chile, where distilleries are open for tours followed by tastings.

9 São Paolo State, Brazil
In the town of Santos, the opulent coffee exchange has been turned in to a museum – with an excellent café.

10 Mendoza, Argentina
The bodegas of the Mendoza region grow Torrontes grapes, which produce the most characteristic of Argentina's world-renowned white wines.

Hotels and Restaurants

Top 10 Hotels: City Luxury

1 Alvear Palace Hotel, Buenos Aires, Argentina
The city's most luxurious hotel, its suites boast antique art, Egyptian linen and butler service. *www.alvearpalace.com*

2 Listel Vancouver Hotel, Vancouver, Canada
A boutique hotel whose rooms are filled with art and books by local talents. *www.thelistelhotel.com*

3 Mandarin Oriental, Boston, USA
The large rooms have designer linens, large bathtubs and state-of-the-art electronics. *www.mandarinoriental.com*

4 Four Seasons, New York, USA
For luxury in a modern mode, this dramatic tower by I.M. Pei is the ultimate. The bar and restaurant draw the city's elite. *www.fourseasons.com*

5 Hotel Four Seasons, Mexico City, Mexico
Renowned for service and comfort, the hotel has a breathtaking central atrium garden. *www.fourseasons.com*

6 Ritz-Carlton, Washington DC, USA
Guests luxuriate in feather beds, down duvets and 400-thread-count Egyptian cotton sheets. *www.ritzcarlton.com*

7 The Aubrey, Santiago, Chile
This gorgeously renovated 1927 mansion is Santiago's first boutique hotel. *www.theaubrey.com*

8 Windsor Court Hotel, New Orleans, USA
Some consider this the city's finest contemporary hotel, and it boasts one of the best dining spots, The Grill Room. *www.windsorcourthotel.com*

9 Huntington, San Francisco, USA
This is like staying in the apartment of a rich uncle with impeccable taste. Luxurious rooms, excellent restaurant. *www.huntingtonhotel.com*

10 Fasano, Rio de Janeiro, Brazil
Rooms are beautifully appointed and have private balconies with sea views. *www.fasano.com.br*

Top 10 Hotels: Beside the Seaside

1 Bahia Resort Hotel, San Diego, USA
This venerable Mission Bay Hotel is right next to the bay and Mission Beach. *www.bahiahotel.com*

2 Las Palapas, Playa del Carmen, Mexico
This seductive beach village combines palapas (palm-roofed huts) with luxury fittings. *www.laspalapas.com*

3 Cooper Island Beach Club, British Virgin Islands
This beachfront place has a barefoot ambience. Swim or snorkel steps from your room. *www.cooper-island.com*

4 Sol Cayo Largo, Cayo Largo, Cuba
This classy all-inclusive resort is set on a spectacular stretch of white sand. *http://hotelcayolargo.com*

5 Sands of Kahana, Maui, Hawai'i, USA
Two distinctive condo buildings are set in gardens on a beautiful stretch of beach. *sands-of-kahana.com*

6 Shelborne Resort, South Beach, Miami, USA
An elegant Art Deco hotel, its best feature is the stylish pool with origina diving board. *www.shelborne.com*

7 Hotel Milarepa, Malpaís, Costa Rica
Bungalows sit on the sands, with antique four-poster beds and part ope air bathrooms. *www.milarepahotel.cc*

8 Casa Malibu Inn, Los Angeles, USA
This Mediterranean-style charmer is has its own beach on one of the mos beautiful stretches of the California coast. *310 456 2219*

9 Hilton Hawaiian Village, Honolulu, Hawai'i, USA
On the widest stretch of Waikīkī Beac this huge hotel complex has everything. *www.hiltonhawaiianvillage.com*

10 Villas del Mar Hau, Puerto Ri
Colourful wooden cabins sit under trees on the edge of a perfect beach *www.hauhotelvillas.com*

Top 10 Hotels: Get Away from it All

1 Villa El Saltón, El Saltón, Cuba
This riverside eco-hotel is surrounded by lush forest. Guided hikes and bird-watching are available. *salton@enet.cu*

2 Hotel Cantayo Spa & Resort, Nazca, Peru
A spiritual retreat as well as a spa, it offers yoga and meditation, horse-riding, massages, sand-boarding and 4WD safaris. *www.hotelcantayo.com*

3 Ceiba Country Inn, Puerto Rico
Surrounded by lush countryside, this mountainside B&B is a good option for bird-watchers. *www.ceibacountryinn.com*

4 Playa Nicuesa Rainforest Lodge, Costa Rica
This eco-lodge nestles between ocean and rainforest reserve, near Piedras Blancas. Access is by boat only, from Golfito. *www.nicuesalodge.com*

5 Island Inn, Monhegan, USA
This 1816 inn above the ferry landing has the best views on Monhegan Island. *http://islandinnmonhegan.com*

6 Bromelias Pousada & Spa, Paraty, Brazil
This is an eco-heaven of luxury cabanas set in the heart of the Mata Atlântica rainforest. *http://bromelias.com.br*

7 Calistoga Ranch, California, USA
In a private canyon, guest lodges are hidden in the forest and hot tubs sit over a creek. *www.calistogaranch.com*

8 Hosteria el Faro, Punta Arenas, Chile
All-inclusive packages here include meals, kayaking, trekking and whale-watching. *www.hosteriafarosanisidro.cl*

9 Neptune's Treasure, Anegada, British Virgin Islands
Total beachside relaxation with fishing, snokelling and kayaking as active as it gets. *www.neptunestreasure.com*

10 Wickaninnish Inn, Vancouver Island, Canada
Perched on a crag over a gorgeous beach, this acclaimed inn offers luxury lodgings. *www.wickinn.com*

Top 10 Hotels: Unusual Places

1 Mansión Dandi Royal, Buenos Aires, Argentina
A lovely Art Nouveau mansion houses the tango-themed Dandi Royal. Three salons host tango shows and classes. *www.mansiondandiroyal.com*

2 Triton, San Francisco, USA
Avant-garde touches include evening tarot card readings, feather boa rental, and suites designed by celebrities. *www.hoteltriton.com*

3 Hacienda Uayamón, Campeche, Mexico
An luxury converted hacienda with an astonishing pool in a ruined, roofless building. *www.haciendauayamon.com*

4 Casablanca, New York, USA
A Moroccan theme, and breakfast is served in (where else?) Rick's Café. *www.casablancahotel.com*

5 Dixie Dude Ranch, San Antonio, USA
Campfire sing-alongs and dancing are part of the fun at this laid-back working ranch. *www.dixieduderanch.com*

6 Napa Valley Railway Inn, California, USA
Antique cabooses and rail cars have been converted into luxury rooms and suites. *www.napavalleyrailwayinn.com*

7 The Kendall, Boston, USA
An artist-architect couple transformed this century-old firehouse into a hip boutique hotel. *http://kendallhotel.com*

8 Finca Rosa Blanca Country Inn, Heredia, Costa Rica
On a coffee farm, this is an architectura delight inspired by architect Antoni Gaudí. *www.fincarosablanca.com*

9 Mama Ruisa, Rio de Janeiro, Brazil
In a converted 18th-century mansion, rooms are named after French cultural icons. *www.mamaruisa.com*

10 The Drake Hotel, Toronto, Canada
A former flophouse is now a hip, artsy boutique hotel. Rooms, in a funky mix of vintage and modern, are small but well-designed. *www.thedrakehotel.ca*

…on Hawaiian Village, Honolulu, USA

Alvear Palace Hotel, Buenos Aires, Argentina

Café Pasqual's, Santa Fe, USA

View from St John, Asolare, British Virgin Islands

Top 10 Restaurants: Fine Dining

Four Seasons, New York, USA
…e Grill Room is the prime place for …wer lunches; the Pool Room is perfect … special occasions. ✆ *212 754 9494*

The French Laundry, …untville, USA
…e of the top restaurants in the US, …ers choose one of two nine-course …sting menus; allow four hours and …enty of dollars. ✆ *707 944 2380*

L'Espalier, Boston, USA
…vard-winning cuisine features local, …isanal ingredients in dishes such … butter-poached Maine lobster and …coa-rubbed venison. ✆ *617 262 3023*

Casa Hacienda Moreyra, …n Isidro, Lima, Peru
…ok a balcony table overlooking the …urtyard fountain, or inside, surrounded … 18th-century art. ✆ *01 444 3979*

The Ritz-Carlton Hotel Dining …oom, San Francisco, USA
…ake a reservation here and prepare … be pampered with the very finest …od and wines. ✆ *415 296-7465*

6 L'Ancrage, Montréal, Canada
Chef Jeanine Ouellette cooks fabulous French dishes. Dine on the terrace overlooking Lac Memphrémagog. ✆ *819 843 6521*

7 Nectarine, Buenos Aires, Argentina
This handsome restaurant's open kitchen allows unfettered viewing of masters at work. ✆ *4813 6993*

8 Patina, Los Angeles, USA
Patina takes French-California cuisine to new heights. Try the chef's superb tasting menu. ✆ *213 972 3331*

9 Citronelle, Washington DC, USA
Michel Richard's playful take on new techniques delights diners with its inventiveness and skill. ✆ *202 625 2150*

10 Horned Dorset Primavera, Rincón, Puerto Rico
This restaurant is considered one of the finest in Puerto Rico. Its nightly five-course fusion menu takes local produce to new heights. ✆ *787 823 4030*

Top 10 Restaurants: Cheap and Cheerful

1 E.J.'s Luncheonette, New York, USA
This family-friendly diner serves great breakfasts, brunch, and piles of pancakes all day long. ✆ *212 472 0600*

2 Mercado 28 Restaurants, Cancún, Mexico
The courtyard of the market is packed with canopied tables spilling out from restaurants. ✆ *Av Xel-Ha & Av Tankah*

3 Mystic Pizza, Connecticut, USA
A Julia Roberts movie made this restaurant famous, but diners keep coming back for another taste of the delicious, secret-recipe pizza sauce. ✆ *860 536 3700*

4 Hattie's Hat, Seattle, USA
A great source for huge breakfasts and American rib-sticking dinner standards with a twist, such as Guinness stout meatloaf. ✆ *206 784 0175*

5 Casa Paco, Miami, USA
This family-friendly Spanish-Cuban eatery serves authentic traditional dishes. ✆ *305 554 7633*

6 Saladang Song, Los Angeles, USA
This trendy Thai eatery is a Pasadena favourite. Insiders swear by the rice soup breakfast. Dine on the lovely Post-Modern patio. ✆ *626 793 5200*

7 Parkway Bakery & Tavern, New Orleans, USA
This quaint shop serves some of the city's best fried shrimp po'boys and roast beef sandwiches. ✆ *866 755 9842*

8 Sushi Island, Toronto, Canada
This restaurant draws sushi-lovers from all over the city with perhaps the best sashimi in town. ✆ *416 535 1515*

9 Café la Terraza, Caraz, Peru
A great lunchtime menu that's good value for money. Be sure to try the delicious home-made ice cream. ✆ *Jiron Sucre 1107*

10 Harold's Chicken Shack, Chicago, USA
Enjoy fast soul food, including catfish and fried chicken at this casual, authentic café. ✆ *1 773 752 9260*

Top 10 Restaurants: Regional Cuisine

Arnaud's, New Orleans, USA
…his restaurant has been serving the …ty its classically Creole menu for …ore than 80 years. ✆ *504 523 5433*

Café Pasqual's, Santa Fe, USA
…and-painted murals, and rich South-…estern fare draw a loyal clientele. …egendary breakfasts feature New …lexican favourites. ✆ *505 983 9340*

Los Girasoles, …lexico City, Mexico
…his restaurant serves traditional cuisine …cluding some pre-Hispanic dishes. …heir Aztec Mosaic includes maguey …orms, ants' eggs and grasshoppers. …y a tamarind Margarita. ✆ *5510 0630*

Sabot, Buenos Aires, …rgentina
…abot serves classic Argentinian …uisine, including exquisite *parrilla-*…rilled meats. ✆ *4313 6587*

Pizzeria Uno, Chicago, USA
…no's has been baking deep-dish pizza …nce 1943. Several inches deep, it's a …eal in a slice. ✆ *312 321 1000*

6 Bar Nacional, Santiago, Chile
Among the most traditional restaurants in the country, Bar Nacional has been serving classic Chilean dishes for over 50 years. ✆ *02 6965986*

7 Acenar, Austin, USA
Trendy Acenar adds a Southwest zest to Tex-Mex dishes such as *tinga duck chalupas*. ✆ *210 222 2362*

8 Bayley's Lobster Pound, Pine Point, Maine, USA
Founded in 1915, there are some great specialties here, such as lobster-stuffed mushrooms and excellent crabcakes. ✆ *207 883 4571*

9 Estate, Sonoma, USA
Enjoy a selection of Wine Country dishes, each paired with the perfect glass of wine. ✆ *707 933 3663*

10 Constanza Exquisites Dilenia, Constanza, Dominican Republic
One of the most charming, authentic Dominican restaurants in the country, serving delicious local fare at unbeatable prices. ✆ *809 539 2213*

Top 10 Restaurants: Food with a View

1 Raincity Grill, Vancouver, Canada
With killer views over English Bay and casual yet upscale dining, the menu is organic and seasonal. ✆ *604 685 7337*

2 Pineapple Grill, Maui, USA
Pineapple Grill's delicious upscale menu uses locally grown ingredients. The gorgeous views add to the fine dining experience. ✆ *669 9600*

3 El Rey del Marisco, Villarrica, Chile
The town's lakeshore is the location for this little seafood restaurant. Try the signature eel in garlic, asparagus and white-wine sauce. ✆ *045 412093*

4 Satyricon, Rio de Janeiro, Brazil
Rio's most popular seafood restaurant overlooks the Atlantic; it's great for a romantic meal. ✆ *022 2623 1595*

5 St John, Asolare, British Virgin Islands
The Asian-inspired food alone makes this a must-do; the spectacular sunset views are a bonus. ✆ *340 693 8444*

6 DK Steak House, Honolulu, Hawai'i, USA
The Waikīkī Marriott hosts a steakhouse experience that rivals any in the state. Take a balcony table for breathtaking views of Waikīkī Beach. ✆ *931 6280*

7 California Grill, Orlando, USA
The 15th-floor vista here gets top marks, especially when the lights are dimmed for Magic Kingdom®'s nightly fireworks display. ✆ *407 824 1576*

8 Bertrand at Mr. A's, San Diego, USA
For casually elegant dining with a dazzling city view, this restaurant is hard to beat. ✆ *619 239 1377*

9 Gran Hotel, Camagüey, Cuba
This rooftop restaurant offers a quality buffet dinner. with fine views over the city centre. ✆ *32 29 2093*

10 Atlantic Inn, Block Island, USA
The four-course, fixed-price dinners are the star attraction here. Prized verandah tables have spectacular sunset views. ✆ *401 466 5883*

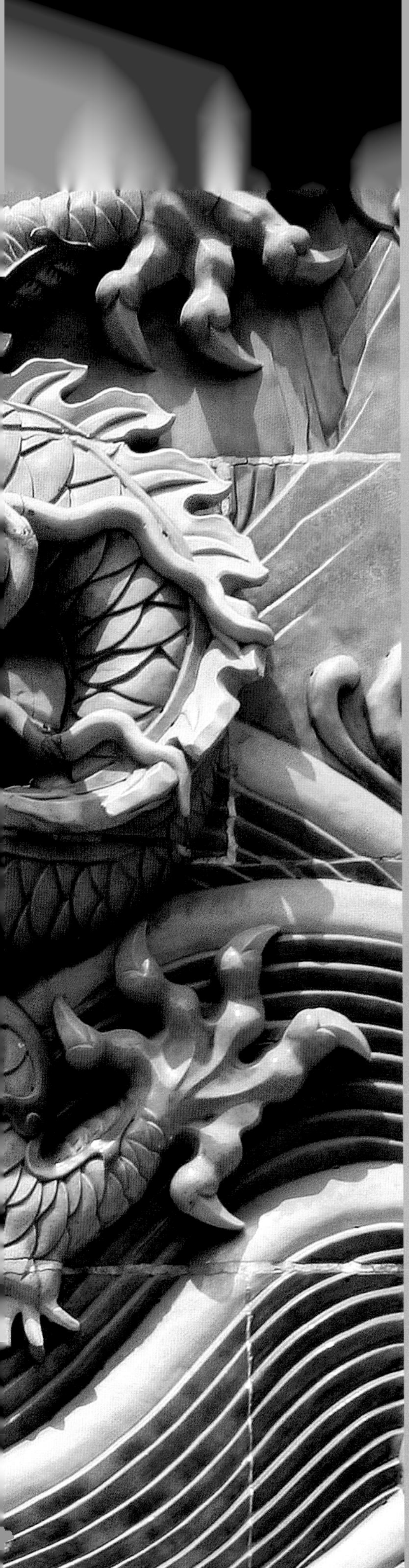

China
A dragon on the Nine Dragon Screen in Bei Hai Park, Beijing

Bali

There is so much to love about Bali that whatever you're looking for in a tropical island, you'll find it here. Ancient volcanoes tower over thick jungle and fertile ricefields, all fringed by seemingly endless beaches. Wildlife abounds in these varied habitats, and the outdoor activities are equally plentiful. These natural splendours are combined with an exotic history, visible in ancient palaces and temples, and a rich cultural heritage of arts, music and crafts. There's plenty of party spirit, too, especially in the lively beach resorts.

1 Bali Bird Park, Batubulan

Huge, walk-in aviaries, filled with lush vegetation and set in beautifully landscaped grounds, are home to over 1,000 birds *(above)* from 250 species, many rare or endangered.

2 Gunung Batur

Bali's largest volcano and the lovely Batur lake are both enclosed in a spectacular caldera, along with several historic temples and shrines, hot springs, small villages and some challenging trekking routes.

Pura Luhur Uluwatu 3

One of Bali's most sacred places occupies a spectacular clifftop setting at the end of the Bukit Peninsula *(right)*. It is particularly breathtaking at sunset.

TOP 10 Moments in History

1 Early Kingdoms
There are few written records of Bali before the 20th century, but ancient artifacts tell of Hindu kingdoms and the influence of Java.

2 Majapahit Bali
Bali maintained independence from East Java until 1284. The Javanese Majapahit empire conquered it in 1343.

3 Bali's Golden Age
By the end of the 15th century Bali had regained its independence. The Balinese kingdom of Gelgel flourished in the 16th century, extending to Java, Lombok and Bima.

4 Rise of New Powers
Over time, warfare and intermarriage created a complex political landscape. The 18th and 19th centuries saw the rise of other kingdoms.

5 Arrival of the Europeans
In 1602 the Dutch founded the United East India Company, succeeded in 1800 by the Dutch East Indies colonial administration. Until the mid-19th century, Dutch colonial attention was concentrated in Java. Bali had little contact with the Dutch, except for trade.

6 19th-Century Bali
The 19th century brought enormous suffering to Bali, as a consequence of volcanic eruption, famine, disease and war. There were military incursions by the Dutch, and wars between the kingdoms. In 1908 Bali was wholly incorporated into the Dutch East Indies.

7 Colonial Rule
The Dutch used compulsory labour to improve irrigation and build roads. New taxes rewarded loyal nobility but impoverished the peasantry. Indonesian nationalism grew.

8 War and Independence
In 1942 Japan occupied the Dutch East Indies. The Dutch returned at the end of World War II, but met with fierce resistance and withdrew from Indonesia in 1949. Bali's highest volcano erupted in 1963.

9 Autocracy and Reform
General Suharto came to power in 1965. The first tourists arrived in the late 1960s and 1970s, sparking a building boom. In the Suharto era, civil liberties were eroded, and in 1998 Suharto was forced to resign.

10 Bali Today
Terrorist bombings in 2002 and 2005 brought tragedy to Bali in the new millennium. However, by 2008, tourist numbers had returned to previous levels.

4 Bali Museum, Denpasar

One of the world's best collections of Balinese art is housed in recreations of a Balinese royal palace and regional pavilions. Theatrical masks *(right)*, musical instruments, textiles, wood carvings and paintings are all on show, along with excavated finds dating from the Bronze Age to the 19th century.

5 Taman Nasional Bali Barat

The far west of Bali is a protected area, the last stretch of natural wilderness, which you can only visit on foot, and with a permit. It is the refuge of the island's one remaining endemic bird species, the pretty Bali Starling.

6 Taman Gili, Klungkung

Built in the early 18th century, this royal compound's name means "moated garden". Badly damaged during the 1908 Dutch conquest, it is still well worth visiting, especially for its superb ceiling paintings *(above)* – the Kerta Gosa building has 267 panels arranged in several tiers.

7 Besakih Temple Complex

This grand complex of 22 temples clings to the slopes of the volcano Gunung Agung, where the spirits of ancestors are believed to dwell. Its terraces, stairways and tiered pagodas create a striking impression.

8 Sanur

Bali's longest-established beach resort *(above)* has a quieter charm than the more famous and lively Kuta, on the other side of the peninsula. The beach is as picture-perfect, the nightlife lively but less raucous, and there are cultural and historic sights for a change of scene.

9 Pura Meduwe Karang, Kubutambahan

This large temple in the north of the island is lavishly decorated with statuary and wall carvings. Visitors are greeted by a parade of 34 carved stone figures, lined up on the terrace. They are characters from the Indian *Ramayana* epic.

10 Pura Taman Ayun, Mengwi

This moated temple *(left)*, set in peaceful gardens (Taman Ayun means "Vast Garden"), symbolizes the Hindu world, set in the cosmic sea.

Top 10 Temple Architecture

1 Temple Layout
The arrangement of Balinese temples generally follows a pattern of individual structures oriented along a mountain-sea axis. The most sacred are closest to the mountain.

2 The *Kori Agung*
The grand gateway entrance to the inner courtyard of a Balinese temple is usually reserved for deities and priests and is kept locked most of the time. Mere mortals must use a more humble side gate.

3 The *Kandi Bentar*
This divided gate is often used as a courtyard entrance. It represents the cosmic mountain, split into the positive and negative forces of the universe.

4 The *Padmasana*
The "Lotus Throne" occupies the most sacred corner of the temple. It has an empty seat at the top, open to the sky, signifying the Supreme God.

5 The *Jeroan*
The inner courtyard of the temple has shrines to its core deities, and often to those of the mountains, lakes and sea. It is usually closed to visitors but can be viewed from outside the walls.

6 The *Bale Kulkul*
This is a watchtower that hold a pair of split drums. When beaten continuously, they are supposed to form a "ladder" by which deities can decend to the temple.

7 *Bales*
As well as the *bale kulkul* there are other structures for specific purposes. The *bale gong* is where ritual music may be played; the *bale agung* is the village council pavilion; and the *bale piasan* is a sacred pavilion in which religious offerings are placed.

8 The *Meru* Shrine
This shrine has 3, 5, 7, 9 or 11 tiers, depending on the importance of its deity. It symbolizes the Hindu holy Mount Meru, but can also represent other sacred peaks.

9 Peliggih
These are the shrines or "seats" of the gods. The dark fibre used for their roofs, which resembles human hair, is a product of the sugar palm.

10 The *Jaba Tengah*
In this, the middle courtyard, are secondary shrines and pavilions used for a variety of practical purposes.

Bangkok

Beguiling and bewildering, subtle and brash, spiritual and sensual, Bangkok is one of Asia's most intriguing cities. Its glittering temples and museums overflow with sumptuous art, and an exploration of the city's canals and markets reveals the locals' hospitable Thai nature. Shopping for bargains, dining out and revelling in the vibrant nightlife should feature high on everyone's itinerary.

MYANMAR (BURMA)
LAOS
Chiang Mai
Udon Thani
THAILAND
BANGKOK
CAMBODIA
Andaman Sea
VIETNAM
Surat Thani
Phuket
Gulf of Thailand
Hat Yai
MALAYSIA

1 National Museum

One of Asia's largest museums, the National Museum displays priceless exhibits, including intricate works of art that clearly document the long and eventful history of Thailand *(left)*.

TOP 10 Moments in History

1 1767: Ayutthaya is Overrun
Ayutthaya was overrun by Burmese troops in 1767. Though they were expelled within a year, Ayutthaya was deemed unsafe as a capital and General Taksin chose Thonburi as the new capital of Siam (now Thailand).

2 1782: Bangkok is Founded
A rebellion against Taksin's autocratic rule led to the succession of General Chao Phraya Chakri. He established the Chakri Dynasty, acquired the title Rama I and set up a new capital, Bangkok.

3 1851: Rama IV is Crowned
After living as a monk for 27 years, King Mongkut acceded to the throne, becoming Rama IV of the Chakri Dynasty. He began to modernize Siam, particularly by opening the country to trade with the West.

4 1868: Rama V's Reign
Rama V ruled for over 40 years and is credited with keeping Siam free from the clutches of colonial powers such as England and France, which were carving up Southeast Asia at the time.

5 1893: First Railway
Stretching just 22 km (14 miles) from Bangkok to Pak Nam, the country's first railway opened in 1893.

6 1932: Constitutional Monarchy
The absolute power of the monarchy was ended by a bloodless coup in 1932. Although it brought the military to power, the monarchy continued to be greatly respected.

7 1946: Rama IX Ascends the Throne
After the death of his brother King Mahidol, who was shot while in bed, King Bhumibol Adulyadej took the throne as Rama IX. He continues to rule as the world's longest-reigning monarch.

8 1992: Military Government Ousted
Following a coup in 1992, the army shot protesting citizens on Bangkok's streets. When Rama IX intervened, General Suchinda Kraprayoon made a hasty exit and democracy was restored.

9 2006: Thaksin Ousted
Thaksin Shinawatra swept to power in 2001 as head of the Thai Rak Thai party, inspiring people with his business acumen. However, he was ousted for corruption in a military coup in 2006.

10 2011: Thailand's First Female Prime Minister
Thaksin Shinawatra's sister Yingluck became Thailand's first female prime minister – as well as the youngest for over 60 years – in a landslide victory in 2011.

2 Grand Palace and Wat Phra Kaeo

This dazzling complex *(above)* is the pinnacle of perfection in Thai religious art and architecture – unmissable.

3 Wat Pho

Bangkok's oldest and biggest temple, and formerly a centre for public education, Wat Pho houses a massive Reclining Buddha *(below)* and a school of Thai massage.

3 Wat Arun
With its five distinctive *prang* (towers), which are often ed as a symbol of the city, this temple *(above)* played an portant historical role in the development of Bangkok and mains one of its most attractive sights.

4 Bangkok's Canals
Boats were once the city's main mode of transport. Tour the canals west of the Chao Phraya river to glimpse a vanishing lifestyle.

5 Jim Thompson's House
Assembled by the man who made Thai silk world-famous, this complex of traditional houses is a fine example of Thai teak architecture. The main house remains as it was during the days of Jim Thompson, and the other buildings display items from his art collection *(below)*.

6 Damnoen Saduak Floating Market
Though designed for tourists, the colourful sights, aromatic smells and cheerful banter of vendors make a visit to this floating market *(above)* a delightful experience.

7 Dusit Park
Seeming a world away from Bangkok's bustle, this tranquil park, studded with royal residences and government offices, is ideal for a peaceful stroll and the opportunity to learn about the Thai monarchy.

Chatuchak Weekend Market 9
Bangkok's biggest narket is a must for ne chance to pick up a unique souvenir nd feel the pulse of Thai culture in the naze of stalls *(right)*.

10 Ayutthaya
The ancient city of Ayutthaya is easily visited in a day. Its huge, crumbling *chedi* (stupas) and blissful Buddha images *(left)* give an idea of the splendour of this former capital.

TOP 10 Places to Shop

1 Nakorn Kasem Market
Still popularly known as "Thieves' Market", the stalls offer little for foreign visitors by way of goods, but a walk through the market's narrow lanes can be great fun.

2 Pratunam Market
Cluttering the pavement and spilling over into the side lanes, this bustling market is a source of cheap clothing; in every shop there seem to be seamstresses bent over sewing machines.

3 Phahurat Market
Shop after shop along this narrow market street sells bolts of cloth, and there are plenty of cut-price travel agents and cheap cafés.

4 Sampeng Lane Market
Phahurat Road leads straight into the Sampeng Lane Market, which is lined with shops selling household goods, fashion accessories, shoes, and clothing.

5 Siam Paragon
The hangout of Bangkok's more fussy shoppers, this mall has six floors full of designer clothes, cosmetics, nail studios, hairdressers, music shops, places to eat and entertainment venues.

6 Mahboonkrong
This mall feels totally Thai. Also known as MBK, it is packed with small stalls selling souvenirs and cheap clothes that include copies of designer brands.

7 Gaysorn Plaza
An upmarket mall, Gaysorn Plaza has designer boutiques, beauty salons, exclusive craft outlets and pricey restaurants. The second floor features "Urban Chic Street," where several Thai fashion designers have outlets.

8 Pantip Plaza
This is an IT mecca, selling all the latest computer software and DVD movies, as well as digital cameras and other electronic equipment. Counterfeit products are rife, however, so be wary when buying.

9 River City
Very much an upmarket shopping centre, River City sells antiques, crafts and Thai silk, and is operated by Mandarin Oriental and the Italthai Group. Located on the banks of the Chao Phraya, it has restaurants with river views too.

10 Narai Phand
If you want to buy gifts to take home, head to Narai Phand, which specializes in Thai handicrafts, including Thai dolls, *khon* theatrical masks, brass statues, lacquerware, wood carvings, silk clothing and silverware.

Beijing

At the heart of Beijing is tradition, given physical form in the mighty Forbidden City, from where successive imperial dynasties have ruled since the 15th century. Neighbouring Tian'an Men Square is the China of recent history, of red-flag socialism and Mao. But this is also a city on the move, as an all-pervading spirit of change makes Beijing the most 21st-century of world capitals.

1 Forbidden City
So called because at one time only members of the imperial court were allowed inside, this is one of the largest and greatest palace complexes ever built *(left)*.

3 Temple of Heaven
Originally the venue for annual winter solstice sacrifices, which were performed by successive emperors to ensure ample harvests, the temple *(above)* remains Beijing's most recognizable icon.

Great Wall 2
"Great" is something of an understatement; the wall *(right)* is nothing less than spectacular. Clamber up the perilously sloping carriageways to one of the crowning watchtowers and the experience is also quite literally breathtaking.

TOP 10 Moments in History

1 500,000 BC: Peking Man Hunts and Gathers
Unearthed in the 1920s in a cave outside Beijing, bones and implements were identified as the remains of Peking Man *(Homo erectus Pekinensis)*, who lived in the vicinity over 500,000 years ago.

2 AD 1215: Genghis Khan Sacks Zhongdu
In 1215 the future Beijing – then known as Zhongdu – was invaded and razed by a Mongol army led by the fearsome Genghis Khan.

3 Late 13th century: Marco Polo Visits
Under Kublai Khan (r. 1260–1294), the city became known as Khanbalik. The Italian traveller Marco Polo was dazzled by its "vast and beautiful" imperial palace.

4 1403–25: Construction of the Forbidden City
The Ming emperor Yongle (r. 1403–24) rebuilt the city, which he renamed Beijing. The Forbidden City and Temple of Heaven began to take shape during his reign.

5 1900: Boxer Rebellion
In 1900, championed by the Empress Cixi, a band of rebels from north China known as the Boxers attacked Beijing's Foreign Legation Quarter. A joint eight-nation army had to be sent to lift the siege.

6 1912: End of Empire
The last emperor, Pu Yi, ascended the throne at the age of three. Just four years later, in February 1912, he was forced to abdicate by general Yuan Shikai's new National Assembly.

7 1949: Founding of the People's Republic of China
In January 1949, Communist forces led by Mao Zedong seized Beijing. On 1 October, Mao proclaimed the foundation of the People's Republic.

8 1965: Launch of the Cultural Revolution
Having socialized industry and agriculture, Mao called for the class system to be eradicated. The revolution peaked in 1967, with the Red Guards spreading fear and havoc.

9 1976: Death of Mao
On 9 September 1976 Mao died. Mao's long-time opponent Deng Xiaoping emerged as leader, implementing reforms that encouraged greater economic freedom.

10 2008: Beijing Hosts the Olympics
In 2008 Beijing hosted the Olympic Games. The city revamped its infrastructures, and some of the most striking and innovative buildings were created to house the various competitions.

4 Bei Hai Park

The most beautiful of Beijing's many city parks is laid out around a central lake, first dug out in the 12th century, with the excavated earth used to create a central island *(left)*. The famed Kublai Khan ruled his empire from a palace here.

5 Tian'an Men Square

The world's largest public square is not pretty, but it is surrounded by august cultural and political institutions, and it is also the final resting place of Chairman Mao Zedong.

6 Lama Temple

The largest and most spectacular of the city's temples *(above)* is a working lamasery, home to monks from Mongolia and Tibet.

7 798 Art District

When former electronic components factory 798 became a venue ›r cutting-edge contemporary art it kick-started a neighbourhood trend ›r converting industrial spaces into galleries and chic cafés and bars.

8 Hou Hai

By day visitors take rickshaw ›urs around the back lanes for a impse of fast-disappearing old eijing *(above)*; by night, attention hifts to the area's lakeside bars nd restaurants.

9 Summer Palace

Beijing summers are unbearably hot, so the imperial court would exchange the Forbidden City for this semi-rural retreat *(below)*, with its ornate pavilions, gardens, and temples ranged around the cool expanse of Kunming Lake.

10 Ming Tombs

Forty-five kilometres (30 niles) northwest of Beijing is the ast burial site of 13 of China's 16 Ming emperors *(above)*. One of ne underground tombs can be 'sited, but most impressive of all s the Sacred Way, with its 12 pairs f stone guardians.

TOP 10 Beijing Opera Facts

1 Acrobatics
Beijing Opera is a form of "total theatre", with singing, speech, mime and acrobatics that combine graceful gymnastics with martial-arts movements. Costumes are designed to make the jumps seem more spectacular by billowing out as they spin.

2 Colours
The colours of the performers' painted faces stand for the individual characters' qualities; red for loyalty and courage; purple for solemnity and a sense of justice; green for bravery and irascibility.

3 Musical instruments
The Chinese say that they go to "listen" to opera, not to see it. Typically six or seven musicians accompany the dramatics. Instruments include the *erhu*, or Chinese two-stringed violin, clappers, gongs and drums.

4 Sheng
There are four main role types in Beijing Opera: *sheng* (male), *dan* (female), *jing* (painted face), and *chou* (clown). *Sheng* are divided into *laosheng* (bearded old men), *xiaosheng* (young men) and *wusheng* (warriors).

5 Dan
Dan roles divide into *laodan* (old ladies), *caidan* (female comedians), *wudan* (martial artists) and *qingyi* (usually elegantly costumed ladies.

6 Jing
With their stylized, patterned, coloured faces, *jing* represent warriors, heroes, statesmen, adventurers and demons. Not only are these characters the most striking-looking but they also usually have the most forceful personalities.

7 Chou
The comic *chou* are denoted by white patches on their noses. Patches of different shape and size mean roles of different character. It is the *chou* who keep the audience laughing.

8 Mei Lanfang
Mei Lanfang was the foremost male interpreter of the female role *(dan)* during Beijing Opera's heyday in the 1920s and 1930s. Traditionally all female roles were played by male actors, although no longer.

9 Repertoire
The traditional repertoire includes more than 1,000 works, mostly based on popular tales. Modern productions aimed at tourists often include English-language displays of the text.

10 Monkey
Clever, resourceful and brave, Monkey is one of the favorite characters in Beijing Opera. He has his origins in classic Chinese literature.

Cambodia

Cambodia is a compact country, flanked by mountains to the north and southeast. The Tonlé Sap Lake dominates the centre and the Mekong river cuts a swathe from north to south. The coast is lined by powder-fine beaches, and the turquoise tropical waters are dotted with thousands of islands. Although the temples of Angkor are the main draw, there is much else to see besides. Phnom Penh and Siem are both lively cities with a Gallic air. National parks shelter rare wildlife, and everywhere you'll meet charming people and eat delicious food.

THAILAND
LAOS
Prasat Preah Vihear 8
7 Ban Lung
9 Angkor
Siem Reap 1
Battambang 2
CAMBODIA
Kratie 4
5 Kompong Cham
Phnom Penh 3
VIETNAM
Sihanoukville and its Islands 10
6 Kbal Chhay Cascades
Gulf of Thailand

1 Siem Reap

Not long ago, this French Indochine town, with its colonial buildings and tree-lined boulevards, was little more than a staging post for visitors on their way to the temples of Angkor, but it's become a destination in its own right, with boutique hotels, fine restaurants and cultural appeal *(left)*.

2 Battambang

The stunningly lovely rural scenery around this attractive colonial city is best viewed from one of its *noris*, or bamboo trains. Powered by a motorbike engine, the sturdy bamboo platform whisks along the single track at a sprightly 40 km/h (25 mph) without the benefit of brakes – it's an experience not to be missed.

TOP 10 Moments in History

1 Early Peoples
The Khmers originated in China and arrived in what is now Cambodia several millennia ago. The first urban civilization in the region had its capital at Angkor Borei.

2 The Rise of the Khmer Empire
Between the 5th and 8th centuries, several city-states thrived in central Cambodia. In the 9th century, Jayavarman II founded the Khmer Empire.

3 Rise of Angkor
Angkor dominated much of Southeast Asia between 802 and 1431. At the end of the 9th century, the capital was moved closer to Siem Reap. Suryavarman II built Angkor Wat from 1130 to 1150.

4 Decline and Fall of Angkor
In the 13th century, Hinduism was largely replaced by Theravada Buddhism In the 14th century, several Theravada kingdoms broke away. The Ayutthaya kingdom sacked Angkor, which was abandoned in 1432. The next centuries were marked by wars with Thailand and the expropriation of land by the Vietnamese.

5 The Colonial Era
In 1863 France offered its protection in exchange for economic privileges. This evolved into complete control after an anti-French rebellion was suppressed in the 1880s.

6 Independence and Revolt
In 1953 King Sihanouk forced the French to grant Cambodia independence. He was deposed in 1970 when a pro-American regime came to power, precipitating the Cambodian Civil War.

7 Pol Pot's Khmer Rouge
Communist forces led by Pol Pot occupied the capital in 1975, and established the government of Democratic Kampuchea (DK). Money and property were abolished, and vast numbers of executions took place.

8 A Democratic State
In 1978 Vietnam invaded DK. When Phnom Penh fell in 1979, more than 1.5 million people had died. The People's Republic of Kampuchea (PRK) was established.

9 Peace at Last
Vietnam withdrew its troops from Cambodia in 1989, and the PRK was renamed the State of Cambodia (SOC). In 1991 a temporary UN protectorate over Cambodia was established to prepare the country for general elections. In 1997 the Khmer Rouge finally collapsed.

10 Vietnam Today
In the new millennium, foreign investment and assistance poured in, as did millions of tourists.

3 Phnom Pehn

Cambodia's capital is a sprawling metropolis abuzz with scooters and tuk-tuks. There are Parisian-style cafés, lively markets and an attractive riverside. Dominating all are the gorgeous, glittering pinnacles of the Royal Palace *(above)* and the Silver Pagoda.

Kratie 4

ımed for its lovely sunsets, Kratie is the place to take a boat trip in search of the endangered Irrawaddy dolphin *(right)*, a colony of which live just upstream in the murky waters of the Mekong river.

5 Kompong Cham

This sleepy little town on the Mekong river s a French feel, with wide boulevards, statue-tted squares and a riverside promenade. Several mples are situated nearby.

6 Kbal Chhay Cascades

Situated on the scenic Toeuk Sap river, not far from Sihanoukville, these lovely waterfalls are a favourite picnicking and swimming spot among locals and visitors alike, especially during the rainy season. Covered platforms with hammocks hang over the water, perfect for a lazy afternoon.

7 Ban Lung

Set in the remote province of Ratanakiri, in the far northeast, Ban Lung awes visitors with its waterfalls, bamboo forests and crater lakes. An emerging hub for ecotourism, it offers exciting activities such as trekking, kayaking and elephant rides.

8 Prasat Preah Vihear

Dramatically located on a clifftop in the Dangkrek Mountains, this temple complex was built by seven different Khmer kings. A majestic stairway ascends through four exquisitely carved *gopuras* (gateway towers) to reach the sanctuary.

9 Angkor

The 12th-century capital of the great Khmer empire, ngkor is without doubt one of the most magnificent onders of the world. Set amid dense jungle, the "lost" mple of Angkor Wat *(above)* was only rediscovered the 1860s.

10 Sihanoukville and its Islands

This bustling town serves as gateway to an archipelago verdant islands with splendid reefs and beaches *(above)*. oat trips, scuba diving, snorkelling, trekking and basic ccommodation are all available.

TOP 10 Wildlife of Cambodia

1 Irawaddy Dolphin
Less than 100 of these snub-nosed, slate-blue creatures live in the waters of the lower Mekong. Pollution, changes in land use and mass fishing techniques all threaten their existence. The river is also home to a range of big fish, including the giant Mekong stingray, measuring up to 4 m (14 ft) across, and the world's largest catfish.

2 Fishing Cat
These reclusive animals depend upon the wetlands for their prey. They mainly eat freshwater fish, but also catch rats and birds. They are often snared and sold by animal traders.

3 Dugong
Also known as the "sea cow", and perhaps the original mermaid, this marine mammal is found off the coast.

4 Hawksbill Turtle
These are common around the Cambodian coast. They have a distinctive beaked mouth and a beautifully patterned shell. Sponges are their main diet. Green turtles are also found in the shallow seagrass beds.

5 Black-Headed Ibis
This exotic wading bird can be seen feeding on the banks of the Tonlé Sap. Its existence is under threat due to drainage and loss of habitat. Other waders include storks, which tend to live in the mangrove forests.

6 Crab-Eating Macaque
Groups of this little primate, also called the long-tailed macaque and "crop raider", can often be seen foraging on beaches for crabs, but their main diet is actually fruits and seeds.

7 Siamese Crocodile
A freshwater reptile, this crocodile lives on the banks of rainforest rivers, and is critically endangered.

8 Loris
These live in the mangrove swamps and are often poached for the Chinese medicine and pet trades.

9 Malasian Porcupine
This is one of the largest rodents in the region. It is a nocturnal resident of the rainforests, emerging to feed on bark, roots and fallen fruits.

10 Clouded Leopard
These beautifully marked big cats are the most agile of their species and superb tree-climbers, as befits their deep jungle habitat. They tend to be active at dawn and dusk, and so are very rarely observed.

History and Culture

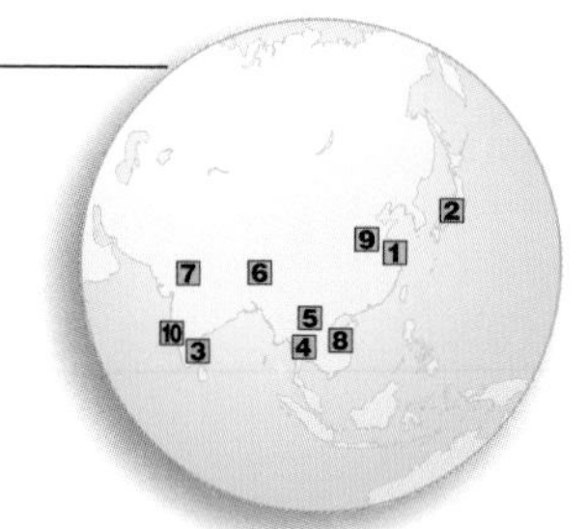

For centuries as shrouded in mystery as its mountains are in cloud, Asia is a continent of ancient gods and legends, and spectacular memorials in their honour. Wars, nature and the ravages of time may have taken its toll on some, but enough of their spectacular beauty remains for western visitors to be dazzled at the dedication of their builders, millennia ago.

1 Huqiu Tower, Suzhou *CHINA*

The "Leaning Tower of China" is an octagonal seven-storey brick tower. While part of its foundations are on a rock base, the rest are soil, which, after more than 1,000 years, has resulted in a noticeable angle of tilt. The tower has no staircase (ladders are used to reach upper levels), so cannot be climbed by the public. Huqiu Tower is set on a hilltop in the ancient gardens of Tiger Hill where, it is said, a pure white tiger guards the tomb of King He Lu, who died in 600 BC.

2 Nara *JAPAN*

The capital of Japan from AD 710 to 794, when it was succeeded by Kyoto, the small city of Nara is at the very centre of the country and is regarded as the birthplace of Japanese culture. It was during Nara's era of prosperity in the 7th and 8th centuries that Buddhism became firmly established in Japan, prompting the construction of a number of superb temples that survive to this day. The greatest are Tōdai-ji, with its spectacular, revered 15-m (49-ft) bronze Buddha, and Hōryū-ji, the country's oldest Buddhist temple. Hōryū-ji also boasts a fine collection of religious statues and ancient artifacts, as well as the world's oldest surviving wooden building.

3 Brihadishwara Temple, Thanjavur *INDIA*

This magnificent temple is the architectural pinnacle of the Tamil Chola Empire, which once dominated southern India. The huge complex, a UNESCO World Heritage Site, is dedicated to the Hindu god Shiva, and is decorated with statues and images representing facets of Hindu cosmology. The pyramidal temple at its heart stands 13 storeys high, and is gloriously decorated with carvings of the gods. The inner sanctum holds a huge stone, which worshippers walk around as part of their dedication to Shiva.

4 Ayutthaya *THAILAND*

The great city of Ayutthaya was founded in 1351 by King Ramathibodi I, who came here from disease-ravaged Lopburi. It served as the Thai capital for over 400 years and boasted three royal palaces, hundreds of temples, 140 km (87 miles) of canals and a cosmopolitan population of a million people, including merchants from Portugal and samurai bodyguards from Japan. The glory days of Ayutthaya ended in 1767, when it was sacked and destroyed by the Burmese, who left the ruins that we see today. These include several needle-sharp stupas, innumerable statues of the Buddha and many crumbling temples, including Wat Phra Mahathat, with its eerie stone Buddha's head smothered with tree roots.

5 Pak Ou Caves, Luang Prabang *LAOS*

Honeycombing limestone cliffs above the confluence of the Mekong and Nam Ou rivers, the caves of Pak Ou are one of Southeast Asia's more unusual historic sights. The caves have been used for centuries as storehouses for damaged or outdated Buddha statues that can no longer be venerated in a working temple. Around 4,000 of them now jostle for elbow room in Pak Ou's two main caves, combining quirky tourist appeal with an enduring religious pull that continues to draw Buddhist pilgrims from across Laos and further afield.

Hue, Vietnam Hien Lam Cac temple gateway in the Imperial Forbidden Purple

Maharaja Palaces, Udaipur Lake Palace (now a hotel), reflected in Lake Pichola *(below)*

Hampi, Karnataka Virupaksha Temple, a centre of pilgrimage for centuries *(above)*

...tthaya Buddha statue outside the Wat Yai Chai Mongkhon temple *(below)*

6 Potala Palace
LHASA

A match for the dramatic mountains that surround it, the great Red Palace sits on top of the great White Palace, which in turn sits atop Red Hill, high above Lhasa. At 3,700 m (12,140 ft) above sea level, the whole complex is way above most of the rest of the world. Potala Palace was the home of the Dalai Lamas from 1649 to 1959, and is a place of immensities, with 200,000 statues, 10,000 shrines and 1,000 rooms. The opening of the Qingzang railway from China in 2006 has brought many visitors, keen for an insight into this remote and spiritual place.

7 Maharaja Palaces, Udaipur *INDIA*

Resplendent with a score of maharajas' palaces, the "City of Lakes" in Rajasthan is one of the most beautiful, tranquil places in the whole subcontinent. City Palace is the largest in Rajasthan and dominates the town. Part museum, part hotel, it's full of artworks and antiques. Lake Palace, made entirely of white marble, has a magical setting on Lake Pichola.

8 Hue *VIETNAM*

Looking at the grand illuminated Ngo Mon Gate at night, it's hard to imagine the battering Hue Citadel received during the Vietnam War. Home of emperors from the mid-18th century until the end of World War I, its jumble of knocked-about monuments is still an impressive sight, utterly tranquil now beside the Song Huong (Perfume River). Better-preserved are the tombs of the emperors, which lie in temples, palaces and lakes to the south of the city.

9 Longmen Caves, Henan Province
CHINA

Construction began on the Longmen caves in AD 495, and spanned four Chinese dynasties and over 400 years. The site consists of over 1,300 grottoes and 400 pagodas, and spreads along both sides of the Yi river. Inside the caves are nearly 100,000 Buddhist statues of all shapes, styles and sizes. The smallest measures less than an inch and the largest, is nearly 18 m (60 ft) high. The caves are considered an icon of Buddhist art, and one of the greatest religious, historical and cultural masterpieces in all of China.

10 Hampi, Karnataka
INDIA

The ruined city of Vijayanagar, more commonly known as Hampi, is all that survives of the capital of what was once the most powerful kingdom in central India. Monuments range from the intricately carved Achyutharaya, Vitthala and Virupaksha temples to the former royal quarters, complete with its famous elephant stables – a lavish stone palace fit for a prince, let alone elephants. Around the city is a surreal, beautiful landscape bisected by the meandering Tungabhadra river and studded with rocky hills and gigantic boulders said to have been tossed down by superhuman armies of the Hindu god Hanuman.

Delhi

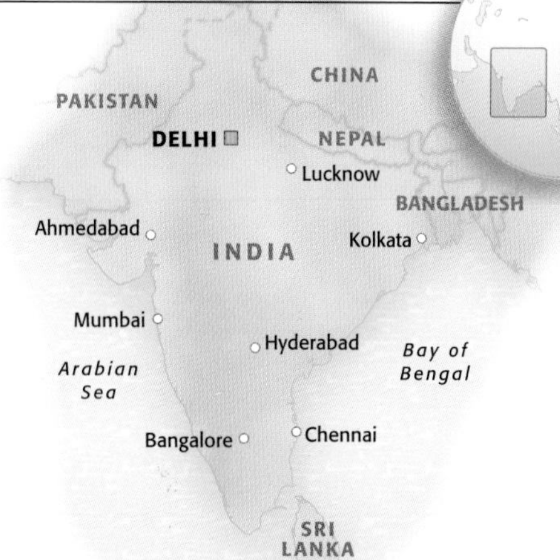

History is writ large in India's capital city, and few other places in the world can rival the city's incredible glut of monuments, spanning 1,000 years of Indian history. These range from the soaring medieval minaret of the Qutb Minar to world-famous Mughal monuments such as the Red Fort, the dramatic Jama Masjid and Humayun's Tomb, as well as some of the most grandiose Imperial landmarks of the British Raj, such as Rajpath, India Gate and Rashtrapati Bhavan.

Red Fort 1
Former residence of the all-powerful Mughal emperors, the enormous Red Fort *(right)* is Old Delhi's showpiece attraction, providing a fascinating glimpse into the opulent and cultured world of the country's most charismatic rulers.

Jama Masjid 2
The largest and most spectacular mosque in India *(right)*, this superb Mughal monument rises dramatically out of the labyrinthine streets of Old Delhi.

3 **Qutb Minar Complex**
Towering over southern Delhi, the Qutb Minar is perhaps the city's single most dramatic sight, surrounded by many monuments dating from the Sultanate and Mughal periods.

4 **Chandni Chowk**
At the heart of Old Delhi, this famous Mughal thoroughfare *(below)* – lined with mosques, temples and myriad shops, and thronged with a constant melee of shoppers and sightseers – offers a colourful slice of quintessentially Indian street life.

Top 10 Moments in History

1 736: Founding of Delhi
Delhi was founded by the Rajput Tomars in the Surajkund area. In 1060 the town was relocated 6 miles (10 km) west and a new fortified citadel called Lal Kot was built there.

2 1192: Founding of the Delhi Sultanate
On his second attempt, Muhammad of Ghori (from Afghanistan) invaded and took control of northern India. He put his general Qutbuddin Aibak in charge, and Aibak became the first sultan of Delhi after Muhammad's death in 1206.

3 1327: To Daulatabad and Back Again
Muhammad bin Tughlaq relocated the capital to Daulatabad, and Delhi's entire population was forcibly moved 932 miles (1,500 km) south. But Tughlaq abandoned Daulatabad within two years and returned to Delhi.

4 1398: Invasion of Timur
A Mongol army led by Timur the Lame, or Tamerlaine as he is known in the West, sacked Delhi and left it in ruins, leading to the fall of the Tughlaq Dynasty.

5 1526: Arrival of the First Mughals
Babur, a Central Asian adventurer defeated the last Delhi sultan, Ibrahim Lodi, at Panipat and ushered in the Mughal Dynasty.

6 1638: Foundation of Shajahanabad
The Mughal emperor Shah Jahan moved the capital from Agra back to the site of Delhi and founded the city of Shahjahanabad, or Old Delhi, as it is known today.

7 1857: Indian Uprising
In 1857 Indian soldiers across north India revolted and seized control of cities under British control, including Delhi, Lucknow and Kanpur. After months of bitter fighting, Delhi was retaken by the British.

8 1911: Foundation of New Delhi
The capital of British India was moved from Calcutta to Delhi and work began on building New Delhi, which was inaugurated in 1931.

9 1947: Independence
India was partitioned and became independent. Delhi lost a large proportion of its former Muslim population, while huge numbers of Hindu and Sikh refugees from Pakistan arrived.

10 1984: Assassination of Indira Gandhi and Anti-Sikh Riots
The assassination of Prime Minister Indira Gandhi by two of her Sikh bodyguards was followed by rioting in which thousands of Sikhs were killed by lynch mobs.

5 Rajpath

This great Raj-era thoroughfare is a fine example of olonial pomp. It stretches more than 3.5 km (2 miles) from ıe stately India Gate to the Rashtrapati Bhavan, where the ecretariat Buildings *(above)* and Presidential Palace sit.

6 Crafts Museum

This engaging museum offers a fascinating snapshot of the myriad local arts-and-crafts traditions of the subcontinent, from arcane religious artifacts to traditionally built village houses.

7 Lodi Gardens

The idyllic Lodi Gardens *(above)* are punctuated with a sequence of atmospheric tombs built in honour of the Delhi sultans. The landscaped grounds make it perfect for a picnic.

8 Humayun's Tomb

The first of the great Mughal garden tombs, Humayun's Tomb *(above)* is one of the most beautiful, and biggest, of all Delhi's ancient monuments.

9 National Museum

The National Museum is India's finest, with an ıormous collection of artifacts and exhibits from different ges and cultures, ranging from the Harappan civilization to ıe 20th century, and covering every aspect of the country's onderfully varied cultural history *(above)*.

10 Taj Mahal

Perhaps the most famous and arguably the most eautiful building in the world, the Taj Mahal *(below)* in gra can be visited in a day trip from Delhi. It never fails ı astonish and amaze, whether seeing it for the first or ıe 50th time.

TOP 10 Cities of Delhi, Old and New

1 Indraprastha
The legendary city of Indraprastha is said to have stood on the site of the Purana Qila. Conclusive evidence is lacking, although archaeological finds have been unearthed here dating back to the 3rd century BC.

2 Lal Kot and Qila Rai Pithora
Lal Kot was established by a Rajput clan, the Tomars, in 1060. Around a century later, Lal Kot was extended and renamed Qila Rai Pithora. Both settlements were largely buried under the Qutb Minar complex.

3 Siri
The second city of Delhi, Siri was built during the reign of Alauddin Khilji in the early 14th century. Little now remains of it except for wall remnants, but what is impressive is the water tank Alauddin built nearby at Hauz Khas to supply water to Siri.

4 Tuqhlaqabad
Built during the reign of Ghiyasuddin Tughlaq (r.1320–24), Tuqhlaqabad was quickly abandoned; according to legend, a sufi saint cursed the place.

5 Jahanpanah
Delhi's fourth city, Jahanpanah, was built by Muhammad bin Tughlaq shortly before the eccentric ruler briefly abandoned Delhi for Daulatabad.

6 Ferozabad
Constructed by Feroz Shah Tughlaq, Ferozabad was the fifth city of Delhi. The principal surviving structure is the walled palace complex known as Feroz Shah Kotla.

7 Purana Qila
The walled citadel of Purana Qila was begun by the second Mughal emperor, Humayun, and completed by his great rival Sher Shah Suri. Following Suri's death, Humayun reclaimed his empire and the Purana Qila, but died within a year after falling down a steep flight of steps within the complex.

8 Shahjahanabad
Begun by Shah Jahan in 1638, Shahjahanabad (now Old Delhi) was the last of the so-called seven cities of Delhi. This was a grand new capital to replace Agra.

9 New Delhi
Designed by Edwin Lutyens and built just a stone's throw from Old Delhi in 1911–31, New Delhi was an attempt by the British to rival the great cities of the Mughals and Delhi sultans.

10 Gurgaon
A few miles south of central Delhi is the satellite city of Gurgaon. A modernistic city of high-rises and shopping malls, Gurgaon is a symbol of the new, affluent, hi-tech India, and is growing rapidly.

India
Rickshaws around Chandni Chowk, Delhi

SIEMENS
MODERN
OPTICALS
Ray-Ban
GENUINE SINCE 1937
Modern Optical Co. (P) Ltd.
SILKEN SOFT CONTACT LENSES
DISPOSABLE LENSES
MODERN OPTICAL CO
G.G.GROUP
She Beauty
जन आहार
दिल्ली
सरकार
501

Hanoi

The oldest and one of the most attractive capital cities in Southeast Asia, Hanoi – the capital of Vietnam – exudes a sense of gracious charm and timelessness. At its core exists a 600-year-old district known as the Old Quarter, or 36 Streets. To the south lie the lovely Hoan Kiem Lake, popular for morning exercise and evening entertainment, and the downtown boulevards and colonial architecture of the French Quarter. In today's Hanoi, the cultural heritage of French, Chinese and Viet traditions come together in perfect harmony.

1 Hoan Kiem Lake

At the northern end of this delightful lake, the Huc bridge *(left)* leads to Den Ngoc Son, one of the most beautiful and revered religious buildings in the city.

2 Bach Ma Temple

The oldest religious building in the Old Quarter, this temple is dedicated to the city's guardian spirit, represented by a magical white horse.

3 Ho Chi Minh Mausoleum

Acclaimed as the driving force behind Vietnam's struggle for independence, Ho Chi Minh died in 1969, six years before his dream became a reality. His wish to be cremated and his ashes scattered could not be further from the grand mausoleum *(right)* in which he lies. It is a site of pilgrimage for many Vietnamese.

4 Hang Ma Street

Typical of the packed, dazzling narrow streets of the Old Quarter, Hang Ma Street's speciality is paper products, such as sparkling, colourful lanterns *(above)* and replicas of material possessions to be burned as votive offerings.

TOP 10 Moments in History

1 Early Settlement
The area has been inhabited for over 10,000 years. Co Loa, the capital of Au Lac, was founded in 258 BC. In 207 BC it was conquered – the start of almost 1,000 years of Chinese occupation.

2 Royal City
In AD 1010 Hanoi became capital of the Dai Vet empire under Emperor Ly Thai To. The city, called Thang Long, would be capital for eight centuries.

3 The Later Le Dynasty
In 1407 the Ming invaded Vietnam but were ousted in 1428 by Le Loi, who founded the Later Le Dynasty (1428–1788). Vietnam went on to become a major power across the Southeast Asian mainland.

4 A Nation Divided
From 1539 power was split between the Trinh and the Nguyen Lords. The nation remained divided for 200 years. The Nguyen built their capital at Hue to rival the Trinh capital at Thang Long.

5 European Interests
In 1545 the Portuguese established factories in Vietnam. The Dutch, then the French, became the principle traders in the 17th century. In 1802 Hue was declared the new capital.

6 French Control
By 1883 France had control of Vietnam. In 1887 it was united with Cambodia and Laos in the Indochinese Union, with its capital at Hanoi.

7 Occupation
After 1940, with Nazi Germany in occupation of France, Hanoi in turn was occupied by the Japanese.

8 Resistance and Independence
In the early 20th century nationalist movements grew. In 1941 Ho Chi Minh formed the Viet Minh to push for an end to the French and Japanese control. The Japanese surrendered in 1945, and Ho Chi Minh declared national independence in Hanoi.

9 War and Independence
French troops returned in 1946, leading to the First Indochina War. In 1954 the Viet Minh prevailed and Hanoi was capital of independent Vietnam. In 1960, war with the USA began.

10 Hanoi Today
At the end of the Vietnamese War in 1976, Hanoi became capital of reunified Vietnam. The city now boasts one of the fastest-growing economies in the world.

5 Temple of Literature

The finest architectural complex in Hanoi *(left)* was established in 1070 in honour of Confucius, and educated future mandarins for more than seven centuries. During the spring festival of Tet, elaborately costumed games of human chess take place here.

6 Memorial House Museum

Once the home of an affluent Chinese family, this is a beautifully restored example of a "tube house", the long, narrow, stacked shop and living units typical of Hanoi. To enter it is to step back in time, into the world of merchants who lived in the Old Quarter centuries ago.

7 Thang Long Water Puppet Theatre

This is the best place in Vietnam to see the ancient art of *roi nuoc*, water puppetry *(above)*. Hidden, waist deep in water, behind the stage, the puppeteers manoeuvre their wooden charges to live music in elaborate performances. Smoke and fireworks add to the excitement of the show.

8 Dong Xuan Market

The oldest and largest covered market in Hanoi s a bustling three-storey structure packed with stalls selling clothes, shoes, fresh produce, household goods and more *(above)*. The night market, complete with street food stalls, is especially worth a visit.

9 Cha Ca La Vong

One of the city's oldest restaurants, Cha Ca La Vong has been serving a single dish – monkfish in a marinade of galangal, saffron, fermented rice and fish sauce – for more than a century.

10 Opera House

Modelled on the Paris Opera, this was the pinnacle of French colonial architecture, not just in Hanoi but for the whole of French Indochina. It fell into disrepair, but is now a showpiece once again *(right)*.

TOP 10 Music and Theatre

1 Quan Ho
These singing contests began in the 13th century and are an important part of spring festivals. This popular folk art features groups of young men and women who take turns to sing in a traditional courtship ritual.

2 Hat Chau Van
This art form originated in the 16th century as an incantation during religious rituals. The rhythmic music and dance induces trance in a person believed to be estranged from the spirits.

3 Nhac Tai Tu
This is a form of chamber music that accompanies *cai luong* theatre. Instruments include a 16-string zither.

4 Ca Tru (Hat A Dao)
Singing for reward is also a form of chamber music. In this geisha-style entertainment, women sign and play a *phach* for well-off men. Out of favour during the Commmunist era, it is being revived as cultural heritage.

5 Nha Nhac
The music of the royal court reached its pinnacle during the Nguyen Dynasty, when performances accompanied special occasions. Forgotten after the fall of the monarchy, it is now classed by UNESCO as a Masterpiece of Oral and Intangible Heritage.

6 Roi Nuoc
This unique art, which uses water as the stage for its puppet cast, enacts tales from folklore, mythology, history and everyday life, accompanied by a musical ensemble, drum rolls and exploding firecrackers.

7 Tuong (Hat Boi)
Influenced by Chinese opera, this uses stylized gestures and symbolism to represent emotion and character. It celebrates Confucian virtues such as courage and loyalty.

8 Cai Luong
"Reformed Theatre" began in South Vietman in the early 20th century. Designed for urban intellectuals it has spoken scenes and covers a range of social issues.

9 Cheo
"Popular Theatre" originated among the rice farmers of the Red River Delta. Performances are usually held outside the community house of the village and combine singing, dancing, poetry and improvisation.

10 Theatrical Symbols
Elaborate make-up, costume and stage settings rely on traditional theatrical convention. For example, in *tuong*, make-up is used to define a character; a face painted red symbolizes bravery, while white stands for villainy.

Hong Kong

"A dream of Manhattan, arising from the South China Sea." For succinctness, modern travel writer Pico Iyer's description of Hong Kong has yet to be bettered. From opium port to Cold War enclave to frenetic financial capital, Hong Kong has never been boring. This is the hedonistic engine room of cultural fusion: East meets West in high style, and the results astonish and delight. Prepare to experience one of the most dramatic urban environments ever conceived.

1 Cheung Chau Island

Of the many islands around Hong Kong, tiny Cheung Chau is arguably the loveliest, with traces of old China in its busy harbourside *(left)*.

2 Star Ferry

Ignore the subterranean road and rail links between Hong Kong Island and Kowloon. The thrilling way to cross the water is on the Star Ferry *(above)*.

3 Big Buddha and Po Lin Monastery

In the middle of hilly Lantau Island, Po Lin Monastery *(above)* is a major destination for devotees and tourists alike. The extraordinary seated Big Buddha image facing the monastery can be seen from miles away.

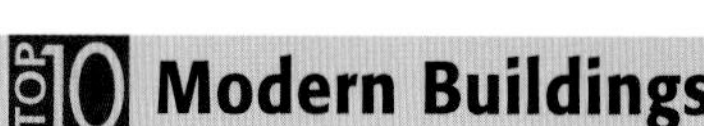

Top 10 Modern Buildings

1 HSBC Building
Sir Norman Foster's Bladerunner-esque edifice cost a whopping HK$5.2bn to build in 1985. The headquarters of the Hong Kong and Shanghai Banking Corporation are reputed to have fantastic feng shui, sitting on five "dragon lines".

2 Bank of China
Also famed in feng shui circles, the glass-skinned tower shoots bad vibes at the old Government House. Its knife-like edges were the inspiration of American-Chinese master architect I. M. Pei. The 70-storey, 368-m (1,207-ft) stack of prisms opened in 1990.

3 Tsing Ma Bridge
The suspension bridge stretches between Tsing Yi and Ma Wan islands and is a striking sight when lit up at night. It opened in May 1997, after five years' building at a cost of HK$7.14bn.

4 Two IFC Tower
The streamlined Two International Finance Centre Tower soars above Victoria Harbour. At 420 m (1,378 ft), it was Hong Kong's tallest building until overtaken in 2010 by the International Commerce Centre in Kowloon.

5 Hong Kong International Airport
Sir Norman Foster strikes again. Landing isn't quite the thrill ride it was at the old airport in Kowloon, but the passenger terminal, which opened in July 1998, is impressive. The airport was constructed on the specially flattened island of Chek Lap Kok.

6 Lippo Towers
These knobbly megaliths look like they have koalas clinging to the sides – a reflection of the original, antipodean owner, jailbird Alan Bond.

7 The Centre
The one with the pretty colours that keep changing all night – fantastic from afar. One of tycoon Li Ka-shing's triumphs.

8 Cheung Kong Centre
Big, boxy and glassy, another one of Li's babies – he lives on the top of this one. Note how it's built parallel to the Bank of China for optimal feng shui.

9 Central Plaza
Confusingly, this is in Wan Chai, not Central. The building has 78 storeys, two fewer than The Centre, but at 374 m (1,227 ft), it's taller.

10 HK Convention and Exhibition Centre
Site of the official Handover ceremony in 1997, the Centre sprawls over a huge area over the harbour and was designed to resemble a bird in flight.

4 Statue Square

Hong Kong Island's northeast is the region's administrative centre. Colonial remnants and exciting modern architecture stand next to each other around Statue Square.

5 Happy Valley Races

Horseracing below the high-rises: Happy Valley *(above)* is where Hong Kongers go to play.

6 The Peak

Take the tram to the lofty heights of Victoria Peak for an amazing view of the city *(above)*.

7 Tai Long Wan Coastline

The remote, rugged Sai Kung Peninsula in the New Territories is the place to find Hong Kong's finest beaches *(left)*.

8 Heritage Museum

Hong Kong's Heritage Museum *(left)* is a must. Splendid high-tech audio-visual displays mix coverage of the region's cultural heritage and its natural history.

9 Stanley

An old barracks steeped in colonial history and eminders of World War II, Stanley on the Southside of ong Kong Island is a quiet diversion from the frenetic city.

10 Temple Street Night Market

Kowloon is at its most atmospheric at night. Head ıp the peninsula to the narrow lanes of Yau Ma Tei for ome serious haggling at the night market *(above)*.

Top 10 Festivals

1 Chinese New Year
Hong Kong's most celebrated festival (late Jan/early Feb) is a riot of neon and noise. Skyscrapers on both sides of the harbour are lit up to varying degrees, depending on the vicissitudes of the economy. Fireworks explode over the harbour, shops shut down and doormen suddenly turn nice, hoping for a handout of *lai see* (lucky money).

2 Spring Lantern (Yuen Siu) Festival
Also known as Chinese Valentine's Day, this festival (end Feb) marks the end of the traditional Lunar New Year celebrations. Canoodling couples take to the parks under the gentle glow of nocturnal lanterns.

3 Tin Hau Festival
This is the big one if you make your living from the sea. Fishermen make floral paper offerings to Tin Hau, the goddess of the sea, hoping for fine weather and full nets. Try the temples at Stanley, Joss House Bay or Tin Hau Temple Road (Apr).

4 Cheung Chau Bun Festival
Young men used to scale 8-m (26-ft) towers covered in buns until, in the 1970s, they started falling off and the practice was banned. Since 2005, it has been revived in a somewhat tamer form (May).

5 Ching Ming
This is when Chinese families visit the graves of ancestors to clear them of weeds and wilted flowers. Many also light incense and burn paper money (first week Apr).

6 Dragon Boat (Tuen Ng) Festival
Drums thunder and paddles churn the waters of Hong Kong as garish craft vie for the top prize. The festival (early Jun) honours Qu Yuan, a 3rd-century poet-statesman who drowned himself to protest against corrupt rulers.

7 Hungry Ghost (Yue Laan) Festival
From the 14th day of the seventh moon (Jul), Chinese believe the gates of hell are thrown open and the undead run riot for a month. "Hell money" goes up in smoke.

8 Mid-Autumn Festival
Families venture out into the country parks to burn candles and feast on yolk-centred moon-cakes (Aug). Traditionally, intricate paper lanterns were lit, though fewer are seen today.

9 Chung Yeung Festival
This outdoor hiking festival (mid- to late Oct) commemorates a Han Dynasty scholar who took his family up a hill and came back to find the rest of his village murdered.

10 Christmas Day
Not a traditional Chinese festival, of course, but Hong Kongers have thoroughly embraced the commercial aspects of Christmas.

Natural Wonders

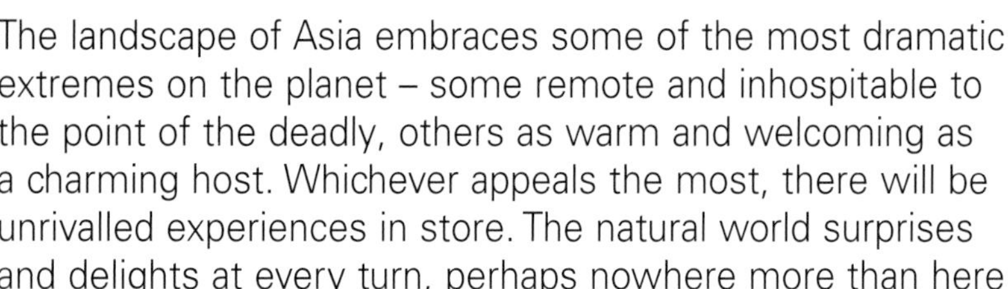

The landscape of Asia embraces some of the most dramatic extremes on the planet – some remote and inhospitable to the point of the deadly, others as warm and welcoming as a charming host. Whichever appeals the most, there will be unrivalled experiences in store. The natural world surprises and delights at every turn, perhaps nowhere more than here.

1 Kerala's Lakes and Backwaters

INDIA

At the southwestern tip of India is a shimmering labyrinth of five lakes and more than 1,000 km (620 miles) of rivers, canals, rivulets and lagoons. Trips aboard houseboats – converted barges once used to transport rice – depart from lakeshore towns. Using long bamboo poles, oarsmen slowly steer you through a maze of silent channels dotted with hamlets and fringed with coconut palms, dazzling green paddy fields and plantations of banana and yam. Plan your trip around Alleppey, known as the "Venice of the East" for its myriad canals.

2 Tiger Leaping Gorge, Yunnan

CHINA

This gorge, said to be the world's deepest, is where the Jinsha-Jiang, the "River of Golden Sand", has sliced apart two 5,000-m (16,400-ft) peaks, Jade Dragon Snow Mountain and Haba Snow Mountain. Yet Tiger Leaping Gorge is so narrow that the sides are almost vertical, and the fast-flowing river is so tightly funnelled that, legend has it, a tiger once escaped from hunters by jumping the 30 m (100 ft) to the other side. Far below, the river rages; high above, the cloud-draped mountain soars.

3 Kyushu Azaleas

JAPAN

In spring, the flush of pink that creeps across the slopes of Japan's most southerly island, Kyushu, is simply shocking. Kyushu azaleas are just one of 300 varieties native to Japan, and they spread like wildfire. It is a joy to see this shrub, so familiar as a garden plant, completely untamed. Locals believe that the sight of them restores the human spirit, and they are surely right.

4 Banda Islands

INDONESIA

The Banda Islands, at the centre of the Spice Islands, were long fought over for their wealth of nutmegs, once worth far more than gold. This small brown nut is still the lifeblood of the islands, but running a close second are its dazzling coral reefs, which have long been protected against marauding fishermen. Slowly descend through the warm, clear water, then swim to the edge of the sheer wall and look down into the abyss. You won't see far; blocking your view will be shoal after shoal of bright coloured fish darting around in ribbon-like waves, like a bizarre three-dimensional screensaver. Indian Ocean triggers occupy the top layer, while pyramid butterflies flutter below and rainbow runners dart about beneath them. Be sure not to miss the fan corals, lower down the wall, which dwarf divers, or the harbour, famed for its assortment of rare bottom-dwelling creatures.

5 Borneo Jungle

The island of Borneo is shared by three countries – Brunei, Indonesia and Malaysia – and has to rank as one of the most out-of-the-way places on earth. This is a truly exotic travel destination – expensive, hot, humid and primitive to the extreme. Yet for the adventurous, it can be a paradise. The rainforests here are still amongst the least explored anywhere, and some of the most biodiverse on the planet. And, despite suffering greatly from deforestation in the 1980s and 1990s, Borneo will still reward you like no other spot on earth.

Tiger Leaping Gorge, Yunnan On the edge of the precipice *(above)*

Borneo Jungle The rainforests of Borneo are still largely unexplored *(below)*

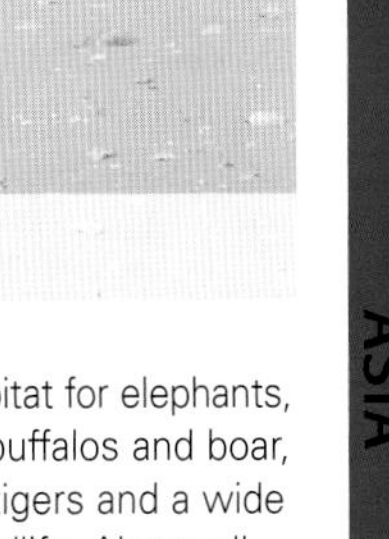

Ha Long Bay Starkly beautiful dramatic jutting limestone crags *(above)*

u Azaleas Vast swathes of Kyushu's shocking pink flowering plants *(below)*

6 Kamchatka, Eastern Siberia

RUSSIA

Skiing in Kamchatka is an almost surreal experience. Many of the peaks your battered Mi-8 helicopter will drop you on have steam issuing from cracks in their flanks; active volcanoes dot the landscape and, at the end of your run, you might find yourself on a black-sand beach pounded by Pacific breakers. You may spot grizzly bears and sea eagles while skiing. And it's not unusual to wind it all up at the end of the day sipping Russian "champagne" in a natural hot spring.

7 Palawan Island

PHILIPPINES

Palawan province comprises a main island and thousands of smaller ones, between Mindoro in the Philippines and Borneo. White beaches slide into turquoise waters, and towering, forested cliffs jut into the ocean. With over 1,600 km (1,000 miles) of coastline, you are bound to find your piece of paradise.

8 Annapurna Sanctuary, The Himalayas

NEPAL

Of the world's highest peaks, none is as rarely climbed as Annapurna I – the deadliest mountain in the world. Just trekking to the Annapurna Sanctuary plateau at 4,100 m (13,450 ft), ringed by eight peaks over 7,000 m (22,965 ft), is excitement enough for most. Here the surrounding mountains rise so sharply and so high that the Sanctuary has only 7 hours of sunlight a day. Sacred to the local villagers, who consider it to be the home of the gods, it was until recently off-limits to Dalits (the "untouchable" caste) and women.

9 Kaziranga National Park, Assam *INDIA*

Along the south bank of the mighty Brahmaputra river, in the remote state of Assam, lies Kaziranga National Park, one of India's most amazing wildlife destinations. Its combination of swamps and grasslands makes it an ideal habitat for elephants, deer, wild buffalos and boar, as well as tigers and a wide range of birdlife. Above all, though, the park is home to the great Indian one-horned rhino – around 1,800 of them, or two-thirds of the world's surviving population, and sightings are guaranteed. The favoured method for rhino-spotting is by elephant, allowing you to approach much closer than you would in a vehicle – a unique and memorable twist on the traditional Indian safari.

10 Ha Long Bay

VIETNAM

You may have an image of Ha Long Bay, with its jutting limestone mountains rising dramatically from the Golf of Tonkin, but nothing can prepare you for its awesome beauty. Around 3,000 islands pierce the sky, reflections shimmering in the emerald waters. Rock arches, pristine lagoons, sheer cliffs, coves and stretches of white-sand beach adorn the dramatic islets, as junks move slowly between them.

Kathmandu

With its colourful Buddhist prayer flags and Hindu temples, the Nepalese capital perfectly encapsulates its country – a tract of land between India and Tibet, offering a mélange of both cultures. A long-term favourite with budget travellers and mountaineers readying to tackle Everest, the city boasts a unique blend of Asian hustle and bustle with a few sparks of Western culture. Delve into ancient temples then dine on a dish of Newari cuisine – often featuring buffalo in various guises – before finishing with a smoothie or a cocktail in one of Thamel's many bars and cafés.

1 Bodhnath Stupa
Brightly coloured prayer flags flutter in the wind all around this enormous *stupa* *(above)* – one of Tibetan Buddhism's holiest sites in Kathmandu. Join the devout as they circle the structure, spinning prayer wheels as they go, or just sit and enjoy tranquil views of the city.

Bhaktapur and Patan 2
A short hop from the capital, Bhaktapur and Patan were once independent kingdoms, and both boast a wealth of historical attractions. The Nyatapola Temple *(right)* offerlooks the cobbled streets of Bhaktapur, while Patan's Durbar Square is architecturally impressive.

TOP 10 Moments in History

1 563 BC: Birth of the Buddha
Prince Siddharta Gautama was born in southern Nepal. His years of meditation led to enlightenment and later went on to have a far-reaching effect on Asian religion.

2 12th Century AD: Malla Dynasty Begins
The Malla kings arrived from India and ruled over the Kathmandu Valley for some 500 years. Many of the finest temples in Kathmandu were constructed during this era.

3 1484: The Three Malla Kingdoms
On the death of Yaksha Malla, the Kathmandu Valley was split into three kingdoms: Kathmandu, Patan and Bhaktapur. A series of wars ensued, weakening all three.

4 1768: Founding of the Nation
Prithvi Narayan Shah, the ruler of the Gorkha Kingdom, took control of the valley. He united scattered tribes and is considered to be the founder of Nepal.

5 1846: The Kot Massacre
After a night of carnage that left dozens of noblemen and soldiers dead, Jung Bahadur pronounced himself prime minister, leaving the Shah kings as mere figureheads.

6 1959: First General Election
With the Shah king returned to the throne, Nepal held its first general election. But a year later, the king tired of mere ceremonial power and fired the entire cabinet.

7 1979: Vote Against Democracy
When a referendum was called on abolishing the "partyless" panchayat system of government in favour of reinstating political parties, the Nepali people voted to stick with panchayat, essentially voting against democracy.

8 1990: Democracy Arrives
After years of protests, the king lifted the ban on political parties. Multi-party elections took place a year later.

9 2001: Royal Massacre
It was a dark day in Nepali history when Crown Prince Dipendra shot nine members of the royal family within the palace walls. The massacre sent Nepal spiralling once more into political instability.

10 2008: Monarchy is Abolished
After a general election that saw the Maoist party seize power, the monarchy was abolished, marking an end to 240 years of turbulent royal rule in Nepal.

3 Swayambhunath
Known colloquially as the "Monkey Temple" for its troop of revered primates that are known to entertain visitors *(left)*, Swayambhunath sits atop a hill to the west of the city. Thought to date back to the 5th century, the temple is shrouded in myth and legend.

4 Durbar Square
Architecture enthusiasts can get their fill of Newari design at the square where kings ere once crowned. Lined with palaces, temples, shrines and market stalls, Durbar Square *bove)* remains the heart of historical Kathmandu and is an essential starting point.

5 Swapna Bagaicha (The Garden of Dreams)
Sitting in the Thamel district and offering relief from all the backpacker bustle, The Garden of Dreams has been restored to its Edwardian glory. Wander the gardens, pause at a Neo-Classical pavilion and take a light lunch at the Kaiser Café.

6 Freak Street
This street off Durbar Square was the centre of traveller action during the hippie years of the 1960s and 70s. It has since been surpassed by Thamel for bustle and vibe, but is a more chilled-out place to have lunch, coffee or to shop.

7 Thamel
Backpackers, trekkers, spiritual avellers – they all meet in Thamel *bove)* to stock up on Nepali trinkets, king gear, bootleg T-shirts and to fill o on Western food. It's also the place r karaoke lounges and cocktail bars.

8 Everest Flight
For those not up to summitting Everest *(right)*, a flight to photograph its snow-capped peak is a good alternative. The small planes guarantee everyone a window seat for the hour-long flight.

Top 10 Religious Sights

1 Pashupitinath
Sitting on the edge of the Bagmati river, Pashupitinath is an important Hindu pilgrimage site that also houses some phallic carvings.

2 Kumari Bahal
Hindus and Nepali Buddhists congregate at this ornate temple hoping to catch a glimpse of the Kumari – a pre-pubescent living goddess who resides within and makes occasional appearances.

3 Kopan Monastery
For those seeking a more in-depth religious encounter, this monastery outside the city offers meditation courses and retreats.

4 Changu Narayan
Often overlooked by tourists, Changu Narayan was built in the 4th century, but destroyed by fire and rebuilt in the early 1700s. It is best-known for its abundant stone sculptures.

5 Budhanikantha
This reclining Vishnu statue is 8 km (5 miles) north of the city. The figure of Vishnu rests in an intricately carved bed of snakes, sitting in the middle of a small pond.

6 Taleju Temple
Dominating Durbar Square, Taleju Temple was built in the 16th century. Non-Hindus cannot enter, but it is worth a visit for the impressive architecture.

7 Kasthamandap
This ornate Hindu temple, which overlooks Durbar Square, is said to have been built using wood from a single tree. The temple gave the city its name.

8 Dakshinkali
This is not an excursion for the squeamish. Built for the goddess Kali, the temple is the site of twice-weekly animal sacrifices that get pretty gruesome.

9 Toothache Tree
One of the city's more unusual religious spots is this offering to the god Vaisya Dev, the Newari god of toothache. Locals nail coins to a gnarled tree stump in a bid to rid themselves of dental pain.

10 Maju Deval
This Shiva temple is known for its erotic carvings, though it's also a great place to just sit and watch the hubbub of Kathmandu.

9 The Rum Doodle
Named after W E Bowden's fictional 40,000½-foot mountain, The Rum Doodle has long been a meeting point for climbers. While getting your Western food fix, seek out Sir Edmund Hillary's signature on the autograph-clad walls.

10 Narayanhiti Palace Museum
Less than a year after the monarchy was abolished in 2008, the royal palace reopened as a museum, allowing visitors to peek inside its lavish rooms for the first time.

Kuala Lumpur

The capital of Malaysia, Kuala Lumpur is a relatively young city, evolving from a humble town of the 1850s into the financial and commercial hub of the country. On the surface a vision of modernity, much of its rich history and culture can still be seen in the buildings of the Colonial District and in neighbouring Chinatown, with its incense-filled temples and chatter-filled coffee shops. Flanked by glitzy shops and trendy bars, the Golden Triangle is the centre of the city's nightlife, while the Lake Gardens are an escape from urban bustle.

1 Thean Hou Temple

Built in the 1980s, this striking three-tiered Chinese temple *(above)* is one of the biggest temples in Malaysia. It is dedicated to Thean Hou, the heavenly mother, patron deity of sailors and fishermen.

2 Lake Gardens

This beautiful expanse of greenery *(right)* on the western edge of the city was laid out in the late 19th century. Within the gardens are the KL Bird Park, said to be the world's largest walk-in aviary, a Butterfly Park, an Orchid Garden and the National Planetarium.

3 Cha See Shu Yuen Temple

Built between 1897 and 1906, this temple is one of the finest examples of southern Chinese architecture in all of Malaysia. Superbly sculpted green- and blue-glazed ceramics depict mythological scenes on the façade. Devotees flock here during Buddhist festivals.

4 Islamic Arts Museum

Set on the eastern edge of Lake Gardens, this striking modern museum *(above)*, topped with turquoise domes, has the largest collection of its kind in Southeast Asia, with over 7,000 artifacts, from Iznik tiles to handwritten Korans.

Top 10 Moments in History

1 The City's Beginnings
Kuala Lumpur was founded in 1857, when a trading post was established for the burgeoning tin industry at the confluence of the Gombak and Klang rivers.

2 Early Growth
Chinese miners and traders constituted a large part of the city's early population. A Kapitan China, or headman, ruled, the most famous of which was Yap Ah Loy (1837–85), who was responsible for the city's early development.

3 Malay Civil War
Civil War broke out over a succession struggle. Kuala Lumpur was dragged into the conflict and burned to the ground. The British were asked to intervene, and took control in the 1880s.

4 British Control
Frank Swettenham was appointed to oversee the city's reconstruction after the destruction of the Civil War. A railway was constructed from Kuala Lumpur to the port of Klang in 1886.

5 Federated Malay States
In 1896 Kuala Lumpur was made the capital of the new Federated Malay States, comprising Pahang, Selangor, Negeri Sembilan and Perak.

6 Early 20th Century
In 1909, under the terms of the Anglo-Siamese Treaty, several former Thai tributaries came under the system of British Residents, as the Unfederated Malay States. British power over Malaya was complete by World War I.

7 World War II
Kuala Lumpur was occupied by the Japanese from 1942 to 1945, in a particularly ruthless regime. At the end of the war, the British took control again, establishing the Malayan Union.

8 State of Emergency
Strongly opposed by the Malay people, the Malayan Union was replaced by the Federation of Malaya, which excluded Singapore and gave special rights to the Malays. In 1948 the Malayan Races Liberation Army (MRLA) began an insurgency against the British which lasted until 1960.

9 Independence
In 1957 the Federation of Malaya won independence. Kuala Lumpur was made capital in 1963, achieving city status in 1972, and became an autonomous Federal Territory in 1974.

10 Kuala Lumpur Today
Kuala Lumpur boomed in the 1990s and the city has grown and thrived since.

5 Merdeka Square

This vast, rectangular, grassy square *(above)* in the Colonial District is ringed with ı eclectic mix of buildings ranging from an English Gothic cathedral to a Mughal-style osque to the Art Deco central market.

6 Menara KL and Bukit Nanas

At the foot of the Menara KL, one of the world's largest telecoms wers, lies Bukit Nanas, one of the oldest stretches of virgin rainforest a city. Although small, it supports a rich variety of wildlife. The tower's ewing platform is higher than the Petronas Towers' Skybridge.

7 Kuala Lumpur Railway Station

ıis ornate station *(below)* a majestic, gleaming white ıilding with Moorish arches, ılustrades, minarets and ıpolas. It was completed 1911 to English railway ecifications, which included iron roof able to withstand metre (3 ft) fall of snow.

8 Petronas Towers

Soaring to a height of 452 m (1,483 ft), these are the symbol of modern Malaysia *(above)*. The Skybridge, linking the towers at the 41st floor, offers dizzying city views.

TOP 10 Malaysian Arts and Crafts

1 Shadow Puppets
Shadow puppet theatre, or *wayang kulit*, is a Malay folk art whose colourful leather puppets are exquisite.

2 Silverware
The very best Malay silverware, with its distinctive filigree embellishments, is crafted in Terngganu and Kelatan. These places are noted especially for belt buckles and tobacco boxes.

3 Kites
While the principal designs of Malay kites are derived from nature, decorations are unique to each craftsman. Kite-making workshops can be found in many villages along the east coast of Peninsular Malaysia.

4 Pottery
Hand-shaped pottery is produced in Selangor and Perak. Ayer Itam, a small town in Peninsular Malaysia, is known for its pottery and porcelain, and the Cameron Highlands for their ceramics.

5 Masks
Malaysian masks represent people, demons and deities. They are cultural icons that help to preserve tradition, religion and history. Malacca is renowned for its masks.

6 Plantware
Items made of bamboo, palm leaf and rattan include finely woven baskets and hats. Some of the best can be found in the bazaars of Sarawak and Sabah.

7 Woodcarvings
Malaysian Borneo boasts some of the best and most varied forms of woodcarving, including spirit and totem figures and good luck charms.

8 *Batik* Fabric
Malay *batik* uses wax and dyes to make designs. Shirts, skirts and sarongs in *batik*-print fabric are typical items.

9 *Songket* Silk
Belonging to the brocade family of textiles, *songket* is handwoven on looms and features elaborate patterns created with a gold and silver weft. *Kain sutera* is a type of *songket* used for formal sarongs, and *kain mastuli* a rich and heavy decorative version.

10 *Ikat* Weaving
Ikat cloth is made using a tie-die technique on the threads before they are woven into elaborate patterns. Often a symbol of status and power, the best *ikat* comes from Sarawak.

9 Sultan Abdul Samad Building

This flamboyant Moorish-style building dates from 1897 and is one of the city's most magnificent colonial structures. Dominating the eastern side of Merdeka Square, it now houses a division of the Malaysian High Court.

10 Jalan Petaling Market

The capital's most lively and famous street market *(below)* is a brash and bustling place where you're expected to haggle hard for fake designer goods. It's best at night, when the food stalls arrive.

Laos

A land of rich social and ethnic diversity, Laos mingles French, Vietnamese, Thai and Chinese influences in its distinct cultural potpourri. The mighty Mekong river runs the length of a land that encompasses steep, verdant mountain ranges, lush forests and high plains where rare wildlife thrives. Beautiful Buddhist art and architecture abounds, especially in the modern capital, Vientiane, and the ancient one, Luang Prabang. All this, combined with its pleasantly agreeable people, make a visit to Laos a memorable experience.

VIETNAM
The Mekong 5
3 Luang Prabang
10 Plain of Jars
Gulf of Tonkin
Vang Vieng 7
Vientiane 2 1 Buddha Park
THAILAND
LAOS
Savannakhet 8
4 Bolaven Plateau
Wat Phu Champasak 9
6 Si Phan Don
CAMBODIA

1 Buddha Park

Also known as Xieng Khuan, this sculpture park in a pleasant meadow by the Mekong south of Vientiane is home to a collection of enigmatic statues *(left)* created by a Lao holy man. Visitors enter the park through the gaping mouth of a giant demon.

2 Vientiane

Asia's smallest capital is no longer the sleepy backwater it once was, but a lively city whose boulevards are lined with colonial buildings and dotted with Buddhist temples *(above)*, as well as chic restaurants and shops.

3 Luang Prabang

Nestled amid green mountains, on the banks of the Mekong, Luang Prabang is as enticing for its natural beauty as for the resplendant golden façades of its many temples. Wat Xieng Thong *(above)* is perhaps the finest of these, and was the coronation venue of Lao kings.

TOP 10 Moments in History

1 Early Settlements
Evidence of human settlement goes as far back as 500 BC. Laos was initially populated by Austro-Asiatic groups such as the Mon-Khmer-speaking people.

2 The Arrival of the Lao
The Lao, who originated in southern China, arrived in the first millennium AD. In the 13th century, as the Khmer Empire weakened, kingdoms sprang up along the Mekong.

3 The Lan Xang Kingdom
In the 14th century the Lan Xang kingdom extended into what is now Thailand. The 16th and 17th centuries were a golden age but, by 1700, it had broken into four semi-independent principalities.

4 Siam and Vietnam
In the late 18th century, Luang Prabang was sacked by the Burmese, and Vientiane by the Siamese. For most of the 19th century, the lowland areas were dependent on Siam, and Vietnam controlled much of the mountainous north.

5 French Rule
From the 1850s France took control of much of the region. In 1907, Laos was formally united for the first time since 1700, under French rule.

6 Early 20th Century
Thailand (as Siam had been renamed) took over part of Laos. The French, fearful of further incursions, proclaimed Laos a unified protectorate in 1941. In 1945 the Japanese forced local rulers throughout Indochina to declare independence, but the French regained control after the end of World War II.

7 Struggle for Independence
The French established the Kingdom of Laos, granting it independence in 1953. Tensions erupted between the Royal Lao Government and the Communist Vietnamese-led resistance movement, and civil war broke out in 1960.

8 The Vietnam War
From 1964 until the ceasefire in 1973, eastern Laos was subjected to intensive aerial bombardment by the US, in order to disrupt North Vietnamese supply lines.

9 Communism and Stability
In 1975 the Lao People's Democratic Republic (LPDR) was established. The Lao People's Revolutionary Party (LPRP) led the new state. The Communists have never been seriously challenged.

10 Laos Today
From the late 1980s tourism picked up and relations with Thailand warmed. Laos joined the Association of Southeast Asian Nations in 1997.

4 Bolaven Plateau

With its temperate climate and rich soil, this area is ıltivated with coffee, rice, cardamom and other crops. Visit ıe of the many ethnic minority communities in the region see how life has been lived here for centuries (*above*).

5 The Mekong

Boat trips on the river are the perfect way soak up the beauty of northern Laos, offering splendid ews of tree-covered mountain slopes, glimpses of veryday pastoral and riverside life and even herds of ild elephants stopping by for a drink. Trips start in ıang Prabang, with an overnight stop at Pat Beng.

TOP 10 Festivals

1 Boun Khun Khao
End Jan/early Feb.
This rural festival celebrates a successful rice harvest. At local temples, unhusked rice is piled into pyramid-shaped mounds and blessed by monks. Feasting follows.

2 Boun Mahka Busaa
Feb full moon.
This festival culminates on the night of the full moon, with candlelit processions of the faithful walking in circles round the temple compound.

3 Boun Pha Vet
End Mar/early Apr.
Performances of Buddhist tales and sermons by the abbot take place in village temples, as well as general merrymaking. It is an auspicious time for Lao men to enter the priesthood.

4 Boun Phi Mai
14–16 Apr.
Lao New Year celebrations last for up to four days, with an abundance of water. Each day has a ritual involving rivers, lakes, water-throwing and ritual cleansing, with both lively parades and sombre processions throughout.

5 Boun Visakha Busaa
May full moon.
This festival commemorates the Buddha's birth, death and enlightenment. It is celebrated at *wats* with sermons and chanting during the day, and candlelit processions during the evening.

6 Boun Bang Fai
Mid-May.
This fertility event occurs at the height of the Hot Season and implores the gods to send the rains by firing off elaborately decorated rockets.

7 Boun Khao Pansa/ Khao Watsa
Early Jul.
This marks the start of the Buddhist Rains Retreat, also known as Buddhist Lent. During this time devout Buddhists strictly observe the practice of their faith.

8 Boun Haw Khao Padap Din
Aug full moon.
During this sombre festival dedicated to the deceased, rice cakes are given to monks, who act as intermediaries, transferring merit to the dead.

9 Boun Ok Pansa/ Ok Watsa
Early Nov.
This marks the end of the monastic Rains Retreat and the start of the Cool Season. Monks are presented with new robes and supplies.

10 Lai Heu Fai/Boun Nam
Oct–Nov, variable.
Candlelit processions are made to a river, where the candles are set on small bamboo boats laden with flowers, and set adrift. In Luang Prabang this takes place with larger boats.

6 Si Phan Don

This inland archipelago *(left)* near the Cambodian border is made up of thousands of islands, islets and sand bars over a distance of 50 km (30 miles). At the southern end, the dramatic Khon Phapeng waterfalls are a spectacular sight in the rainy season.

7 Vang Vien

This town, on the banks of the Nam Song river and surrounded by majestic limestone karst peaks, is the jumping-off point for many adventure sports, ranging from rock-climbing, abseiling and caving to kayaking and – most popular of all – tubing on tractor tyres down the Nam Song.

8 Savannakhet

This charming colonial riverside town *(left)* is linked to Thailand by the Thai-Lao Friendship Bridge. It is the gateway to National Protected Areas, in which small communities live unaffected by the modern world, in harmony with their bountiful natural environment.

9 Wat Phu Champasak

The largest archaeological site in Laos has superb examples of Khmer architecture. A UNESCO World Heritage Site, it is sacred to at least three different cultures.

10 Plain of Jars

From Phonsavan, tuk-tuks take visitors out to this astonishing, mysterious site – a desolate landscape covered in clusters of stone jars *(above)*. There are hundreds of them, ranging in size from 50 cm (18 in) to 3 m (9ft) tall, and they date back about 2,500 years. Their purpose is still debated.

Mumbai

Mumbai (formerly Bombay), capital of the Maharashtra region, is India's most dynamic, cosmopolitan and crowded city. Some 14 million people, from billionaire tycoons to homeless pavement-dwellers, live in this teeming megalopolis. It is a city of striking contrasts. Skyscrapers stand next to stately Victorian and Art Deco buildings; traditional bazaars adjoin glittering shopping malls; and opulent neighbourhoods are surrounded by sprawling slums. The historic Fort area has the best-known sights, hotels and restaurants.

PAKISTAN
CHINA
Delhi
NEPAL
Lucknow
BANGLADESH
Ahmedabad
INDIA
Kolkata
MUMBAI
Hyderabad
Bay of Bengal
Arabian Sea
Bangalore
Chennai
SRI LANKA

1 Kala Ghoda
This attractive, leafy enclave in the Fort district is home to some of Mumbai's finest buildings, including the fortress-like High Court; the historic Kenneseth Eliyaoo Synagogue; the university, with its distinctive Rajabai Clock Tower; the David Sassoon Library *(above)*; and Gothic Elphinstone College.

2 Elephanta Island
Located on an island off Mumbai's eastern shore, the 6th-century Elephanta cave temples *(above)*, chiselled into a rocky cliff and dedicated to Shiva, contain some great masterpieces of Indian sculpture. You can visit this marvellous UNESCO World Heritage Site on a day trip by boat, which departs from the Gateway of India each morning.

3 Prince of Wales Museum
Mumbai's most prestigious museum is renowned for its superb sculptures and miniatures. Its foundation stone was laid by the future George V in 1905. The central hall offers a first taste of the museum's treasures.

TOP 10 Moments in History

1 First Settlers
Archaeological evidence suggests that the seven islands later to become Mumbai were inhabited during the Stone Age.

2 Early Dynasties
The islands came under the control of the Maurya Empire in the 3rd century BC, and became an important hub of Buddhist culture. Over the next millennium they were ruled by a series of dynasties, including the Silhara, which reigned from 810 to 1260.

3 Delhi and Gujarat Sultanates
The Delhi Sultanate annexed the islands in the 14th century, appointing Muslim Gujarat governors to administer them. Control passed to the Gujarat Sultanate in 1407, which fended off attempts by the Bahamani Sultanate to conquer them.

4 Portuguese Rule
In 1535 the Gujarat Sultan ceded the islands to Portugal in return for protection against the Mughal Empire. Roman Catholicism was introduced.

5 British East India Company
In 1668 the Portuguese leased the islands to the British East India Company, which had its headquarters in Bombay. In the 1730s the Marathas seized the last Portuguese enclaves.

6 Expansion
Bombay grew dramatically in the 18th century. Britain took control of Maratha lands in 1782, and an ambitious project to transform the islands into a single land mass was begun in the same year.

7 19th-Century Prosperity
By 1817 Britain had defeated the Marathas and the Bombay region was entirely under its control. Roads and railways were constructed and trade boomed, particularly after the opening of the Suez Canal in 1869. An outbreak of the bubonic plague in 1896 decimated the population.

8 Rise of Nationalism
Resentment against British rule led to the rise of the independence movement during the early 20th century. Bombay became an important centre for nationalism.

9 Independence
India gained independence in 1947. In 1960 Bombay was made capital of the newly created state of Maharashtra.

10 Mumbai Today
In 1996 Bombay was renamed Mumbai, its original Marathi name. The city remains India's commercial and financial hub, but has been plagued by a series of terrorist attacks.

1 Chhatrapati Shivaji Terminus

e most impressive piece Victorian Gothic architec- re in the whole of India, e former Victoria Terminus 1888 is an extravaganza domes, spires and arches. s still very much a working ilding – over 1,000 trains d two million passengers ss through it every day.

5 Film City

The heart of Bollywood, this film studio sprawls over 140 ha (346 acres) in the north of the city, turning out more than 120 feature films a year as well as TV soaps and serials. You can't tour the lots, but star-spotting is an everyday event.

6 General Post Office

Completed in 1913, this fantastic confection of a building combines elements of Indian architecture with classical European traditions. Inside its lofty, three-storeyed rotunda, business is transacted at delightfully old-fashioned wooden counters.

7 Shahid Bhagat Singh Marg

This is the main artery through the Fort area, lined with shops and grand buildings. Highlights include the quirky Kothari Kabutarkhana ("Pigeon House") and the ornate Ruttonsee Mujli drinking fountain *(above)*. At the street's southern end, now called Colaba Causeway, the early morning fish market is worth a visit.

8 Gateway of India

Mumbai's most famous ndmark *(above)* was the first ght to greet travellers to these hores during the days of the Raj, nd the exit point for British troops ter Indian independence in 1947.

9 Malabar Hill

This verdant district is home to Mumbai's rich and famous, but mere mortals can relax in its pleasant Hanging Gardens. It is also home to the Towers of Silence, tall towers on which the Parsi dead are left to be picked clean by vultures. A high wall and belt of trees surround the towers, which are closed to visitors.

Juhu Beach 10

Not a place for a tranquil sunbathe, but an experience not to be missed, at weekends this beach is packed with families and friends picnicking, playing cricket, paddling and having fun on the fairground rides *(right)*.

TOP 10 Bollywood Themes

1 Song and Dance
Probably the most famous and best-loved element of a Bollywood film are the lavish song-and-dance sequences. They range from duets to spectacular set pieces and are often released before the film as music videos. Dreams are a popular setting.

2 The Hero
The hero usually anchors the film, with the plot and other characters revolving around him. The hero cult and Rukh Khan (King Khan) are practically synonymous; Hrithik Roshan is another classic Bollywood hero.

3 The Heroine
Heroines add an essential touch of glamour to the movie. Slender, fashionably dressed, beautiful stars like Katrina Kaif are role models.

4 Romance
Romance underpins almost every plot. The hero wooing the heroine, often in an exotic foreign setting, is always a very popular sequence.

5 Family Values
This is at the core of most films. The home may be a place of great happiness or discord, but in the end everyone comes together.

6 The Meddling Relative
A character that audiences love to hate, there is often a spying, scheming, meddling aunt or uncle to complicate the plot or thwart the lovers.

7 The Villain
Often the strongest role, with some of the best lines, the Bollywood villain is evil incarnate. In *Omkara* (2006), based on Shakespeare's *Othello*, the villain is a loyalist turned traitor who seeks vengeance at the cost of many innocent lives.

8 Violence
This is often of the comic-book variety. Dramatic fights between the hero and the villain at the climax of the film always end with the triumph of good over evil.

9 Youth
The prime focus of any good Bollywood film took a huge leap with *Rang De Basanti* (2006), which made the case for a better society with the help of the young generation.

10 Mumbai Noir
Poles apart from its traditional glitz and glamour, Bollywood is also producing a new wave of darker films dealing with urban social issues.

Festivals and Parties

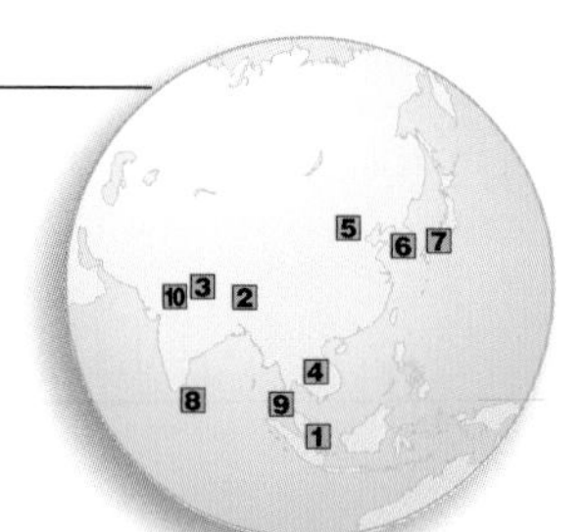

For sheer exuberance, colour, noise and quirkiness, nowhere does a festival better than Asia. Food and fireworks, music and dancing, parades and all-night parties mark everything from change of season to holy rite, a glorious victory to a terrible disaster. Visitors can't expect to view quietly from the sidelines – getting involved is what it's all about here.

1 New Year *SINGAPORE*

The most important event of the Chinese calendar is a breath of fresh air in Singapore. Locals and tourists alike flock to Marina Bay to see in the New Year, which is welcomed with eye-popping fireworks over the water, set spectacularly against the city skyline. In Chinatown, a countdown party kicks off an all-night street rave that throbs with music from international DJs and live bands. All over the city, parties carry on until the wee hours.

2 Punakha Domchoe *BHUTAN*

Featuring war cries and fireworks, silk skirts and resplendent swords, this three-day military festival takes place during the first month of Bhutan's lunar year (Feb–Mar). A recreation of Bhutan's 17th-century victory over Tibet, the final battle is re-enacted with *pazaps* (warriors) wearing traditional military costume, in the courtyard of the majestic *dzong* (fortress).

3 Holi, Barsana *INDIA*

This exuberant "Festival of Colours" heralds the arrival of spring with infectious joy and frivolity. On the night before Holi, large *hola* (bonfires) are lit and an effigy of the demon Holika is burnt. As dawn breaks the next day, the festival erupts. People of all ages swarm onto the streets, splashing and smearing brightly coloured *gulal* on each other, and decorated elephants push through the crowd to the constant beat of *dholaks* (drums). Linked to the lunar cycle and the changing seasons, Holi is presided over by mischievous Lord Krishna, whose roots in Uttar Pradesh give the festivities an increased fervour in the village of Barsana. Here, the festival follows a distinct tradition, in which the women of the village take control, armed with long bamboo sticks, forcing the men to dress up in saris and dance for the rest of the village.

4 Bung Bang Fai, Yasothon *THAILAND*

With a deafening explosion, a rocket 4 m (13 ft) long, packing several kilos of gunpowder, shoots from a bamboo launch into the clear blue sky. The sound is greeted by cheering and murmurs of approval from an appreciative crowd. The "rocket festival", held each May, has its origins in local mythology: this rural community believed that their far-flung offerings would be rewarded by the rain god, who would bless them with plenty of water for the upcoming rice harvest. The celebrations span three days and are accompanied by music, dancing and drinking.

5 Dragon Boat Festival (Duanwu Jie), Beijing *CHINA*

In early June, on the fifth day of the fifth lunar month, drums thunder and paddles churn up the waters of Beijing's lakes and rivers as dragon-headed craft compete for top honours. The festival remembers the honest official, Qu Yuan, who, the story goes, drowned himself 2,500 years ago after banishment from the court of the Duke of Chu. Shocked citizens threw rice cakes into the water to distract the fish from nibbling on his body, hence the wholesale consumption of these delicacies on this date every year.

Gion Matsuri, Kyoto An ornate float being pulled along in the parade *(at*

Holi, Barsana Celebrating the Festival of Colours with lashings of powder paint *(below)*

Dragon Boat Festival (Duanwu Jie), Beijing Dragon-dance performers on stage during the opening ceremony of the festival *(above)*

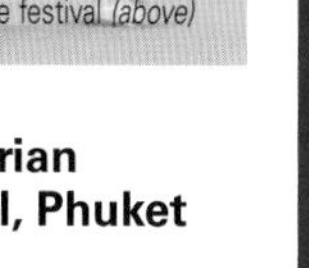

Pushkar Camel Fair, Rajasthan A lavishly decorated camel *(below)*

6 Mud Festival, Boryeong
SOUTH KOREA

Each July, Daecheon Beach and the figures partying along its sands are daubed black with mud. An atmosphere of riotous abandon pervades as tourists hurl themselves gleefully down a mud slide and take each other on in mud-wrestling contests. The festival now attracts well over a million visitors, and has buoyed a local economy traditionally reliant on agriculture.

7 Gion Matsuri, Kyoto *JAPAN*

The highlight of the ancient, month-long Gion festival is Yamahoko-yoko, in which vast floats – some weighing more than 9 tonnes – are paraded through the streets, adorned with 15th-century tapestries. Throughout July the streets throng with festival-goers dressed in traditional summer kimonos and wearing wooden shoes; delicious smells of *yakitori* (skewered chicken) and battered octopus waft from vendors' stalls. The parade dates back to the year 869 when Kyoto fell into the grip of a terrible plague, and a procession was initiated to appease the gods.

8 Esala Perahera, Kandy *SRI LANKA*

One of Asia's great visual spectacles, the Esala Perahera festival at Kandy in Sri Lanka celebrates the Tooth Relic, said to be a tooth from the mouth of the Buddha himself. Once a year, for ten days during the lunar month of Esala (late July/early August), the sacred tooth (in recent years a replica has been used) is taken in a flamboyant 2-hour procession around the streets of Kandy. Visitors can expect cannon shot, drummers, whip-cracking torch-bearers, elaborately costumed dancers and more than 100 elephants accompanied by their flag-waving retainers, plus stilt-walking acrobats and local VIPs dressed up as kings and nobles in 18th-century Kandyan attire.

9 Vegetarian Festival, Phuket
THAILAND

During this festival, held in September–October, you're likely to spot people walking over hot coals or with cheeks pierced by skewers. Such acts, along with abstinence from meat and alcohol, are believed to offer protection from evil. Vegetarian food stalls share the streets with processions and fireworks in this extraordinary event.

10 Pushkar Camel Fair, Rajasthan
INDIA

Pushkar is a sacred place for Hindus who believe that, over the course of this five-day festival the gods pay a visit and bless the devout. Each November, the calm water of its lake is disturbed by thousands of devotees, submerging themselves and filling the air with the sound of their prayers. Their fervour is accompanied by a grand camel fair, at which hundreds of animals are raced, bought and sold, and paraded in fine jewellery, bells and bangles.

Phuket

Phuket's extraordinary tropical setting needs little introduction. The marvellous white-sand beaches, rolling green hills and tranquil emerald-and-turquoise waters of Thailand's most popular island have lured visitors for centuries. But Phuket boasts more than sublime beaches. It and its surrounding areas are also home to pristine national parks, wildlife sanctuaries and scuba diving sites, while cultural highlights include Buddhist temples, museums, shrines and historic architecture.

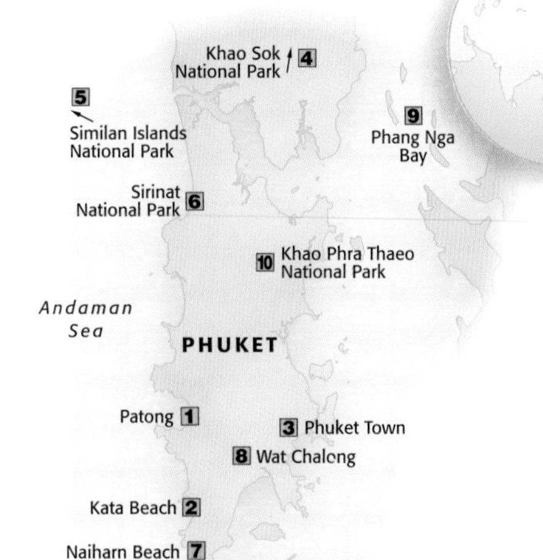

1 Patong

Wild and uninhibited, Patong *(left)* is the island's busiest tourist beach and home to a large number of hotels, restaurants and nightlife venues. This is the ideal spot for people who want to be in the middle of the action.

2 Kata Beach

Once a hippie haven, Kata is today home to upscale resorts and hotels, and is a favourite with couples and families. The gorgeous beach and turquoise waters *(above)* are the area's main draw.

3 Phuket Town

Magnificent architecture, Chinese shrines, bustling outdoor marketplaces and authentic local cuisine are all available at Phuket's cultural heart *(above)*.

Top 10 Moments in History

1 1st Century BC –2nd Century AD: Earliest Records
Phuket was founded by Indian merchants, with trade dating back to the 1st century BC. It was later mentioned by the Greek geographer Ptolemy, who referred to it as "Junk Ceylon," a "cape" en route to the Malaysian peninsula.

2 1500–1700: Tin Seekers
The Dutch established a trading presence in Phuket after vast tin reserves were discovered. The English and French followed shortly after, and the Siamese King Narai (r.1656–88) granted France monopoly in 1685.

3 1688: French Expulsion
After the Siamese revolution of 1688, in which the pro-foreign Siamese King Narai was overthrown, the French were ordered out of Siam.

4 1785: Burmese Invasion Repelled
Led by two sisters – Thao Thep Kasattri and Thao Srisoonthorn – the Siamese defended Phuket against a month-long Burmese attack.

5 Early 19th Century
Thousands of Chinese workers immigrated to Phuket during the early 1800s, establishing communities and customs that define the island to this day. Chinese shrines, architecture and festivals are among the legacies of the era.

6 1876: Tin Worker Rampage
When Chinese tin workers instigated a violent uprising on Phuket, locals had to flee to Wat Chalong for protection.

7 1933: Phuket Province
During the reign of King Rama V (r.1867–1910), Phuket became the administrative centre of the southern provinces. It became a full province in 1933, when the country shifted from an absolute monarchy to a parliamentary government.

8 1970s: Phuket Discovered
As Phuket became popular with Western backpackers in the 1970s, the tourism infrastructure began to develop.

9 2000: *The Beach*
Visitors had been flocking to Thailand's white-sand beaches long before this Hollywood film was made, but after its success large numbers of travellers made their way to Maya Bay.

10 26 December 2004: Indian Ocean Tsunami
The devastation caused by the tsunami was immense, with thousands of lives lost in a matter of minutes. In Thailand, the tsunami represented the worst natural disaster in history.

4 Khao Sok National Park
At the heart of this spectacular national park *(above)* 'e ancient evergreen forests, majestic limestone mountains ıd Cheow Laan Lake, where you can rest in floating ımboo-raft houses.

5 Similan Islands National Park
The clear waters surrounding the Similan Islands are ideal for viewing exotic marine life such as colourful fish, staggering reefs and dramatic underwater rock formations. All this makes it one of the world's favourite scuba diving destinations.

6 Sirinat National Park
Located along Phuket's pristine northwest coast, Sirinat National Park grants protection to a large area of undeveloped beachfront, as well as the island's last mangrove forest. There are upscale hotels as well.

7 Naiharn Beach
This idyllic white-sand beach on Phuket's southern tip is framed by rolling hills and provides one of the island's most picturesque tropical backdrops. Don't miss the fabulous view from the sunset viewpoint at Phromthep Cape.

8 Wat Chalong
Phuket's most important Buddhist temple *(above)* features sacred sculptures and imagery, and the Grand Pagoda reverentially houses a bone fragment of the Buddha.

9 Phang Nga Bay
Staggering limestone cliffs jut up from this bay *(above)*, 'here world-famous sights include James Bond Island and ıe magnificent Ko Phi Phi. You can explore the water ınnels, caves and uninhabited islands by kayak.

10 Khao Phra Thaeo National Park
Home to jungle trekking trails, waterfalls, and exotic animals and plants, this national park *(left)* boasts a wealth of natural attractions. The park also has a Gibbon Rehabilitation Centre.

TOP 10 Chinese Shrines

1 Jui Tui Chinese Temple
This colourful Taoist temple, dedicated to the vegetarian deity Kiu Wong In, plays a central role in the annual Phuket Vegetarian Festival.

2 Shrine of the Serene Light
Built by a local Chinese family more than 100 years ago, this historic shrine, once hidden down a narrow alleyway, can be viewed directly from Thalang Road today. Brightly coloured ornamentation adorns the roof of the shrine's red-pillared entranceway.

3 Boon Kaw Kong Shrine
Drivers often honk their car horns for good luck as they pass by this hilltop shrine between Patong and Kathu. Besides simply hoping for good fortune, the drivers are also acknowledging the ghosts of travellers who have died while passing over the hill in the past. This small but popular shrine frequently shows films on a giant outdoor screen.

4 Bang Niew Shrine
Destroyed twice by fire, this century-old shrine – also known as Tao Bong Keng or Chai Tueng – plays an important role in the annual Vegetarian Festival. Here, one may see devotees with bizarre piercings or walking across red-hot coals.

5 Sam San Shrine
Built in 1853 and dedicated to Mazu, the Chinese goddess of the sea, this shrine frequently hosts ceremonies to consecrate new boats before their maiden sea voyage.

6 Put Jaw Chinese Temple
The island's oldest Chinese temple is dedicated to the goddess of mercy. Those suffering from health afflictions often come here to pray for relief; the monks also hand out prescriptions for herbal medicines.

7 Tha Rua Chinese Shrine
The largest Chinese temple in Phuket, Tha Rua has undergone a series of massive renovations. The new shrine is colourful, with bold dragon motifs, and is brilliantly lit at night.

8 Cherngtalay Shrine
Popular with the local community who seek healing from the shrine's deities, Cherngtalay Shrine dates back more than 100 years to the founding of a settlement of Chinese tin-mine workers.

9 Kathu Shrine
Credited as the first Chinese shrine on Phuket to celebrate the Vegetarian Festival, this temple features a fascinating collection of intricately designed Taoist deity statues in a variety of postures.

10 Kuan Te Kun Shrine
Though less well-known than some of Phuket's other shrines, Kuan Te Kun – also known as Sapam Shrine – served prominently in the Vegetarian Festival in 2010. With brilliantly coloured dragons encircling its four main pillars and others guarding its entrance, the shrine is a visual delight.

Rajasthan

No state in India is as rich in magnificent palaces and forts, colourful festivals and bazaars, as Rajasthan. In western Rajasthan are the Thar desert fortress towns of Jaisalmer, Jodhpur and Bikaner. To the north is Shekhawati, with its painted ancestral homes, while the eastern plains have the bustling state capital, Jaipur. In the wooded, hilly south are the fairytale lakes and forts of Udaipur and spectacular Jain temples. Between them all, little Pushkar explodes into life each winter as host to one of Asia's largest cattle fairs.

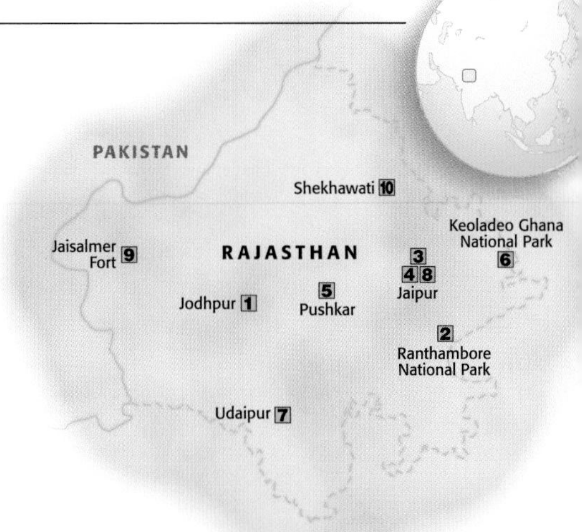

1 Jodhpur

For Rudyard Kipling, Jodhpur *(left)* was "the creation of angels, fairies and giants". And with the majestic Mehrangarh Fort rising out the rock above its blue-washed houses and the sands of the Thar desert, this magnificent city is certainly the very essence of the romance and feudal splendour of Rajasthan.

2 Ranthambore National Park

The razor-sharp ridges, deep gorges, lakes and jungles of this park are home to India's iconic carnivore, the tiger, as well as panthers, sloth bears, crocodiles, pythons and, futher down the food chain, large herds of sambar deer.

3 Jaipur

A labyrinth of bazaars, palaces and historic sights, Jaipur is known as the "Pink City" for the colour washed onto its walls – the rich glow of it at sunset is a sight not to be missed.

4 City Palace, Jaipur

This sprawling complex is a beautiful blend of Rajput and Mughal architecture. Part of it houses a museum packed with treasures. The Pritam Chowk (Court of the Beloved) has four delicately painted doorways representing the seasons *(above)*.

Top 10 Moments in History

1 Indus Valley Civilization
The Indus Valley Civilization (3300–1300 BC) flourished over much of present-day Pakistan, eastern Afghanistan and northeast India, including parts of the Rajasthan region.

2 Early Rulers
The Gupta Empire controlled much of the region from the 2nd to the 5th centuries AD. Their rule was followed by a period of instability, brought about by infighting between local tribes.

3 The Rise of Rajputana
In the 6th century, the first of the Rajput dynasties began. Famed as warriors, they resisted the Arabs in the 7th century but lost territory to the Turks in the 8th century.

4 The Mughal Empire
In the early 13th century, the region was dominated by the Mughal Emperor Akbar, and the Rajputs became reluctant vassals. The Marathas emerged in the 17th century, growing more powerful as the Mughal Empire declined.

5 British Control
The British government took over the East India Company in the 19th century bringing the country under its control. Rajput rulers accepted British sovereignty in return for retaining some autonomy.

6 Rebellion and the Rise of Nationalism
A countrywide rebellion in 1857 was repressed but resentment increased and nationalism, including the non-violent movement led by Mahatma Gandhi, intensified.

7 Decadence and Poverty
The hedonistic Rajput rulers built lavish palaces and forts while their subjects suffered abject poverty. By the 1940s Rajasthan had among the lowest life-expectancy and literacy rates in the region.

8 Indian Independence and Partition
Indian independence finally came in 1947, but the country was partitioned, creating mainly Muslim Pakistan and predominantly Hindu India.

9 Post-War Rajasthan
The nominally independent Rajput states agreed to join India in return for certain privileges, including annual stipends. India was anxious for their co-operation, given the region's strategic location on the border with Pakistan.

10 Rajastan Today
Rajasthan remains one of the poorest regions in India. Many of the opulent former royal palaces have been turned into luxury hotels and tourist attractions.

Pushkar 5

A peaceful town of lakes and 400 temples, Pushkar *(right)* draws devout Hindus on pilgrimage to its holy ghats throughout the year. But it is ten days after Diwali (October/November) that the world comes to Pushkar, for the carnival atmosphere and commerce of the cattle and (especially) camel fair.

8 Amber Fort

Clinging to the contours of a ridge, a few miles north of Jaipur, the assive ramparts of the Amber Fort *(above)* hide some delightful, elegant ildings, decorated with alabaster reliefs, glasswork and, in the Sheesh ahal chamber, tiny mirrors to transform a candle's flame into a starlit sky.

0 Shekhawati

This fascinating region 115 km (72 miles) northwest of Jaipur like a huge open-air museum. It is particularly famous for its *velis* (mansions of wealthy merchants), with their elaborately inted frescoes *(above)*.

9 Jaisalmer Fort

This enormous medieval fortress rises like a fabulous mirage out of the Thar Desert, hewn and carved from its soft, golden sandstone. India's only living fort, it still houses a population of thousands.

6 Keoladeo Ghana National Park

Now a UNESCO World Heritage Site regarded as one of the world's most important bird sanctuaries, this wetland area was created in the 18th century as a hunting reserve. Today over 375 species of bird thrive in safety here, including the rare Siberian crane and the vivid, easily spotted white-throated kingfisher.

7 Udaipur

This is a magical city of marble island palaces reflected in the still waters of Lake Pichola and surrounded by a ring of hills. City Palace *(above)*, on the lake's eastern shore, is the finest of all – its fortress-like façade, crowned with a profusion of graceful balconies, cupolas and turrets has been likened to a plain cake topped with fabulous icing.

Top 10 Jain Temple Marblework

1 Exterior
The white marble exterior of a Jain temple is simple in comparison with the profuse decoration within. This is intended to reflect the fundamental Jain belief in the insignificance of outward form, in contrast to a rich inner life.

2 Pillars
A forest of carved columns leads to the main sanctum of Dilwara's Vimala Vasahi temple. Each one of the 1,444 of them is carved with different patterns of floral motifs – no two are the same. The play of light and shadow is one of the glories of this momument.

3 Image of Adinath
A four-faced Adinath, the first enlightened being in Jain belief, stands in the main sanctum of his temple at Ranakpur. It faces in the four cardinal directions.

4 Corbelled Ceilings
Ceilings are carved into concentric tiers, symbolizing the Jain belief in the universe as a series of cosmic cycles. In places the marble is so fine as to be translucent.

5 Ceiling Supports
Dancers and deities, graceful and yet exuberant, form the struts to support the ceiling.

6 Ceiling Pendants
A magnificent example of Jain temple ceiling pendants is the tiered lotus, carved from a single block of marble, at Luna Vasahi temple.

7 Snake Carvings
The Parsvanatha plaque at Ranakpur shows another of the enlightened ones guarded by a multi-headed cobra.

8 Arches
Known as *torans*, decorative arches are carved from one slab of marble. At Ranakpur there are said to have been 128 of them, of which only three remain today.

9 Windows
The 15th-century temple of Parsvanatha is famed for the exceptional pierced marble work of its windows.

10 Kalpavalli Medallions
These fantastically intricate medallions, with exquisite patterns of foliage, flowers and tendrils, can be seen at both Dilwara and Ranakpur.

Seoul

Though justly regarded as one of the world's most modern and forward-looking cities, there's a tremendous historical depth to the Korean capital. Its two oldest and most splendid palaces – Gyeongbokgung and Changdeokgung – date back to the turn of the 15th century, as does Dongdaemun, Seoul's oldest existing city gate. The neighbourhoods of Insadong, Bukchon and Buamdong offer tantalizing hints of dynastic-era Korean life, while heading to hectic, neon-soaked Hongdae will rapidly speed you into the modern day.

NORTH KOREA
SEOUL
Suwon
East Sea (Sea of Japan)
SOUTH KOREA
Daejeon
Yellow Sea
Daegu
Gwanju
Busan
JAPAN

1 Changdeokgung

This World Heritage-listed palace is exactly what many visitors to Asia are looking for: spectacular wooden architecture *(left)*, perfectly manicured gardens and the timeless air of dynasties long past.

2 Bukchon Hanok Village

Korea's traditional wooden houses – known as *hanok* – are extremely rare nowadays, particularly in high-rise Seoul. But the narrow, hilly lanes of the Bukchon neighbourhood are studded with hundreds of pristine examples.

3 Bukhansan National Park

Bukhansan is the world's most-visited national park – helped, no doubt, by having a city of 25 million people on its border. Temples, hermitages and Confucian academies stud its myriad hiking trails, which lead the way to a series of craggy granite peaks *(above)*.

4 Insadong

Seoul's most popular tourist neighbourhood *(below)* is also one of its most traditional, its charming, zig-zagging lanes crammed with rustic restaurants, superb galleries and delightful handicraft shops.

TOP 10 Moments in History

1 18 BC: Founding of Baekje
King Onjo founded the Baekje dynasty, one of Korea's famed Three Kingdoms. Wiryeseong, Baekje's first capital, is thought to have lain within the boundaries of present-day Seoul.

2 AD 1394: Seoul Becomes a Capital
King Taejo makes Seoul the first capital of Joseon, a dynasty he had founded two years earlier. The palaces of Gyeongbokgung and Changdeokgung were built within a decade.

3 1450: Death of King Sejong
Sejong is still revered as one of Korea's greatest leaders. His main legacy was Hangul, the Korean alphabet – invented to enable the education of the common man, but suppressed by the Confucian aristocracy until the 20th century.

4 1590s: Japanese Invasions
This decade saw two major invasions of Korea by Japanese armies, led by General Hideyoshi. Much of Seoul was also destroyed in the process.

5 1762: Murder at the Palace
At the behest of King Yeongjo, Prince Sado – his son and heir to the Joseon throne – was left to die inside a rice casket.

6 1910: Japanese Annexation
After ramping up its influence over the preceding two decades, Japan formally annexes Korea; Seoul is renamed "Keijo". Eventually, Japan is forced from power at the end of World War II.

7 1950: Korean War
Korea is divided into a Soviet-backed north and a Western-backed south. An inevitable civil war kicks off in 1950, with Seoul changing hands four times before the 1953 armistice.

8 1962: Park Chung-Hee Takes Control
Miliary strongman Park Chung-hee seizes power of South Korea in a coup d'etat, officially becoming president the following year. Though often dictatorial, Park's rule saw Korea develop from war-scarred backwater into an industrial powerhouse.

9 1988: Seoul Olympics
The Summer Games are held in Seoul. Though a great success generally, it is remembered for Ben Johnson's 100m world record then subsequent disqualification.

10 2002: World Cup
Seoul hosts the opening game of football's World Cup, an event co-hosted by Korea and Japan.

5 Dongdaemun
Named after the ancient "Great East Gate" that still tands at its centre today, this earthy district is now more amed for its colossal open-air market – the ideal place to et a handle on Korean food *(above)*, or go shopping for silk.

6 Buamdong
Though just a hop, skip and jump from central Seoul, he neighbourhood of Buamdong exudes the air of a rovincial town, and its galleries, shops, restaurants and afés can easily eat up half a day.

TOP 10 Sights of Modern Seoul

1 Jongno Tower
Uruguayan architect Rafael Viñoly transformed this tower in 1999, endowing the simple block with a "floating platform", supported by three latticed columns.

2 SK Building
Though it caused little fuss when completed in 2000, SK Building has become the city's architectural reference point, and many newer neighbours have aped its wonky-steel-and-glass design.

3 Incheon International Airport
All flowing lines, gentle curves and open space, Incheon International Airport opened in 2001, and has scooped a whole host of international airport awards.

4 Cheonggyecheon
Completed in 2005, the renovation of the Cheonggyecheon stream involved tearing up the elevated highway and market areas that had covered the stream for decades.

5 Samsung D'light
Samsung has revolutionised television and mobile phone design. You can take a peek at the company's designs of the future in D'light, its superb Gangnam showroom.

6 New Districts
Seoul has made a habit of ripping up swathes of the city in an effort to modernize – spectacularly in some cases. Witness the ultra-modern surroundings of Gangnam station and the districts going up in Yongsan and Incheon's Songdo island.

7 City Hall
Completed in 2012, Seoul's new City Hall sits proudly next to its Japanese-designed predecessor. The new building is rather menacing, soaring above the old like a giant wave.

8 Times Square and D Cube City
Created to revitalise the city's moribund south-western corner, these two projects mix office space, shopping malls, parkland, bars and restaurants. Each is topped with a five-star hotel.

9 Hangang Floating Islands
"Floating" in the Hangang river, these three artificial islands opened for business in 2011. Though primarily built for performances, conventions and the like, their park areas are open to the public.

10 Dongdaemun Design Plaza and Culture Park
Designed by Iraqi-born architect Zaha Hadid, this large complex was built on the site of an old baseball stadium – and, evidently, a Joseon-dynasty garrison, remnants from which form part of a museum added to the original designs.

7 Hongdae
Artistic by day, near-hedonistic by night, the student district of Hongdae is filled to bursting with bars, restaurants, galleries and boutique shops. It's the birthplace of most contemporary Korean trends – come to see them taking shape.

8 National Museum
Korea's rich, colourful history is best explored in this gigantic museum, a repository of treasures from the various dynasties that have held power on the peninsula over the last 2,000 years *(below)*.

9 Gyeongbokgung
First completed in 1394, the "Palace of hining Happiness" has been a focal point of he city ever since. Its various halls and avilions *(above)* are superb examples of uddhist decoration, and the on-site nuseums are among the best in the land.

10 Namsan
Rising from Seoul's very centre and topped by the distinctive N Seoul Tower, this 262m- (860-ft) high peak is the ideal place from which to survey the city; its pine-lined trails are great for a gentle hike.

Thailand
Fruit vendor in Damnoen Saduak floating market, Bangkok

Shanghai

This extraordinary city at the mouth of the great Yangzi river has grown from a minor port to become mainland China's economic powerhouse. The Old City is typically Chinese, with alleys, markets, temples and the lovely Yu Gardens. The former concession areas, once under the direct rule of the French, British and Americans, boast The Bund, as well as the city's two main shopping streets, Nanjing Lu and Huaihai Zhong Lu. Shanghai's newest district, Pudong, is a major business and residential zone, with a clutch of museums and some of the world's tallest buildings.

RUSSIA
MONGOLIA
Harbin
Shenyang
Beijing
CHINA
Chengdu
Wuhan
SHANGHAI
Hong Kong

1 The Bund

If Shanghai has a single iconic landmark, it is this imposing riverside avenue lined with grand buildings from the city's colonial past *(below)* – a veritable cornucopia of architectural styles.

2 Yu Gardens and Bazaar

A haven in the bustling heart of Shanghai, the beautiful Ming-dynasty Yu Gardens are divided into six scenic areas separated by "dragon walls". The adjacent bazaar *(left)* peddles everything from tourist souvenirs to traditional medicines.

3 Nanjing Lu

One of the world's busiest shopping streets, Nanjing Lu runs west–east for nearly 10 km (6 miles), from the district of Jing'an to The Bund. By night, the eastern section (Nanjing Dong Lu) resembles a Chinese Las Vegas, its shop fronts illuminated by a multitud of garish neon signs *(above)*.

TOP 10 Collections in the Shanghai Museum

1 Bronzes
China's Bronze Age (18th to 3rd century BC) is represented by an extraordinary collection of wine vessels, three-legged *ding* (cooking vessels) and bells, all cast in bronze using ceramic moulds.

2 Sculpture
The arrival of Buddhism in China and its gradual absorption into the mainstream is reflected in over 120 pieces of bronze, wood, stone and pottery dating from around 475 BC to AD 1644.

3 Painting
Notable treasures in this second-floor gallery include the only surviving original painting by Tang-dynasty artist Sun Wei, showing seven hermits disporting themselves in a bamboo forest.

4 Calligraphy
To the Chinese, calligraphy is one of the highest art forms. Few can understand the classical script of these remarkable scrolls, allowing concentration on the beauty of the shapes alone.

5 Ceramics
Taken together, this magnificent display of 500 pieces from all over China tells the story of 8,000 years of ceramic production. This one gallery alone would make a visit to Shanghai worthwhile.

6 Jade
Jade is the precious substance most commonly associated with China. The museum's collection includes examples of marvellous delicacy, carved into dragons, turtles and tigers.

7 Furniture
On the top floor of the museum, Ming-dynasty constructions of elegant simplicity sit alongside ornately decorated later Qing pieces. Two beautiful brick-floored rooms contain recreations of studies from both eras.

8 Seals
Rightly regarded as the best in China, this collection of 500 seals (or chops, as they are also known) includes miniature works of art in ivory, jade and soapstone. Some are in the form of animals; others are shaped like mythical creatures, or carved with tiny landscapes.

9 Coins
China was one of the first countries to systematically use coins and then notes – a fact amply reflected in this extensive collection.

10 Ethnic Minorities
See pottery, costume, embroidery and lacquerware from some of China's ethnic minority peoples.

4 Shanghai Ocean Aquarium

This vast, multi-million-pound aquarium *(left)* is home to more than 10,000 temperate and tropical fish, as well as turtles and other sea creatures. Clear underwater viewing tunnels – including a submarine escalator – put visitors right in the thick of the aquatic action, from the pretty to the predatory.

5 People's Park and Square

This former racecourse is now occupied by the beautifully landscaped People's Park to the north and People's Square to the south. Locals visit the park to walk, gossip, exercise and fly kites.

6 French Concession

This characterful district of boulevards, shops and cafés once had its own electrical system, judiciary and police force. Today its hub is Huaihai Lu, a vibrant street lined with boutiques, candy stories, hair salons and bars.

7 Jade Buddha Temple (Jufo Si)

Built in 1882, the most famous of Shanghai's temples has several Buddha statues: two of jade (one sitting, the other reclining); one of marble (reclining); and three of gold *(above)*.

8 Oriental Pearl TV Tower

One of the first modern towers to rise on the Pudong side of the Huangpu river *(above)*, the Oriental Pearl – an extraordinary structure of columns and spheres – houses an assortment of entertainments, including viewing platforms, rotating restaurants and the Shanghai History Museum.

9 Song Qingling's Former Residence

This charming example of a mid-20th-century Shanghai villa, complete with wonderful wood panelling and lacquerwork, was the residence of Song Qingling, wife of the revolutionary leader Dr Sun Yat Sen. Her limousines are still parked in the garage.

10 Shanghai Museum

With a collection of over 120,000 pieces, the Shanghai Museum *(above)* displays some of the most impressive cultural relics from 5,000 years of China's past – from the neolithic period to the Qing dynasty.

Top 10 French Concession Sights

1 Old China Hand Reading Room
This quietly idiosyncractic café-cum-bookshop-cum-library specializes in books on the old architecture of Shanghai, produced by the team of American-born but long-time Shanghai resident Tess Johnston and local photographer Deke Erh.

2 Ruijin Er Lu
Look above the modern shop fronts for hints of the city's Art Deco past, and keep an eye peeled for other oddities – such as the particularly Germanic mansion at No. 152.

3 Taikang Lu
Taikang Lu is lined with art shops and tailors happy to make traditional *qipao* dresses. At Zui Zhu Zhai (No. 322), framed calligraphy can be purchased from a living master at a very reasonable price.

4 Wet Market
If you're after live fish, frogs, eels or snakes, this fascinating wet market is definitely the place to come.

5 Tianzifang
Just off Taikang Lu, this labyrinth of lanes is full of cafés, craft shops, galleries and boutiques. Side turnings are lined with fine examples of *shikumen*, Shanghai's equivalent of Beijing's *siheyuan* dwellings.

6 Fuxing Park
In this French-created park, with fountains, flowerbeds and covered pavilions about a central lake, people-watchers will relish the early-morning rituals of dancers, card players, *tai chi* practitioners and others.

7 Russian Orthodox Church of St Nicholas
Built in 1933 at the behest of exiled White Russians and dedicated to the last Tsar, this onion-domed former church has since done service as a warehouse, a laundry and, most recently, a restaurant.

8 Huaihai Zhong Lu
Once the main boulevard of the French Concession, Huaihai Zhong Lu is one one of the city's premier shopping streets, mixing international big-brand names with an appealing array of smaller boutiques.

9 Cathay Theatre
Another piece of 1930s Shanghai, the Cathay Theatre, with its splendid Art Deco exterior, is still in use as a cinema.

10 Ruijin Guesthouse
The main villa of this glorious city-centre estate is now a striking hotel. Satellite buildings, set among beautifully manicured lawns, house a variety of dining and drinking venues.

Singapore

At the crossroads of East and West, Singapore has a complex mix of culture and history. At first glance, the city appears to be wholly modern, with soaring skyscrapers, but a closer look reveals the legacies of its Eastern and European heritage. The grand Neo-Classical buildings of the Colonial District stand alongside the ethnically diverse neighbourhoods of Chinatown, Little India and Kampong Glam, with the Singapore river carving its way between them. It is a multi-faceted city, with both traditional and contemporary appeal.

1 Singapore River
Once the lifeline of the island's early settlers, the Singapore river *(left)* is lined by countless waterside dining and leisure establishments, most in converted warehouses. The river is best experienced from aboard a restored bumboat.

2 Sultan Mosque
With its gold onion domes that rise above Kampong Glam, the city's traditional Muslim quarter, Sultan Mosque *(above)* is a fine blend of Persian, Moorish and Turkish design. It is the heart of the local Muslim community.

3 National Museum of Singapore
The ideal introduction to Singapore and its multitude of cultural influences, the refurbished National Museum *(above)* presents history using interesting multimedia displays.

TOP 10 Moments in History

1 1390: Iskandar Shah
A deposed prince called Iskandar Shah declared himself ruler of the island of Temasek. Legend has it that he saw a lion-like creature and renamed the island *Singapura*, or lion island. The Keramat at Fort Canning is said to be his tomb.

2 1819: Arrival of Sir Stamford Raffles
Convinced that Singapore could be a strategic trade site, Stamford Raffles of the East India Company persuaded its leaders to sign a treaty giving exclusive trading rights to Britain.

3 1824: British East India Company
The East India Company secured undisputed legal rule of the island. The village quickly became a town, and in 1826 was declared capital of the Straits Settlements. By 1867 Singapore was flourishing as a Crown Colony.

4 1869: Suez Canal
The opening of the Suez Canal in Egypt in 1869 opened up new markets to Singapore by reducing the shipping distance between Europe and Asia.

5 1873: Steam Ship Travel
Steam ships brought more reliable shipping schedules. Singapore quickly became a major refuelling port, employing thousands of porters to heave coal.

6 1907: Rubber and Tin
Rubber seedlings grown in the Botanic Gardens were used to create Singapore's first rubber plantation. Meanwhile, tin smelting began at Pulau Brani to satisfy the demands of the US canning industry.

7 1942: World War II
British forces were forced to retreat by the Japanese down the Malay peninsula, and Singapore fell early in 1942. So began Japan's three-year occupation.

8 1959: Singapore's Self-Government
The British finally agreed to hold elections, resulting in a victory for the People's Action Party, which promised unity with Malaya and independence from Britain.

9 1959: Lee Kuan Yew
Lee Kuan Yew became the island's first prime minister in 1959. Revered by many as the father of the nation, Lee stepped down only in 1990. His son Lee Hsien Loong became leader in 2004.

10 1965: Singapore's Independence
Singapore became part of the Federation of Malaysia in 1963. Political and racial tensions led to riots in 1964. A year later the federation ended and the Republic of Singapore was born.

4 Thian Hock Keng Temple

This was Singapore's first Chinese Taoist temple and is undoubtedly one of its finest. It is a good starting point for exploring the many wonders of Chinatown. Since 1839, it has been an important cultural icon for the city's Chinese inhabitants *(left)*.

5 Sri Veeramakaliamman Temple

Statues of Hindu gods crowd this temple's roof *(above)*, where they watch over Little India. Dedicated to the deities Vinayagar, Viswanathan and Kali, the temple is one of Singapore's oldest, having been built in 1881.

TOP 10 Ethnic Groups

1 The Chinese – Hokkiens
The majority (74 per cent) of Singaporeans are ethnic Chinese. Of these, 41 per cent are the Hokkien dialect group from China's southern Fujian province – the earliest Chinese immigrants.

2 The Chinese – Teochews and Other Dialect Groups
Other Chinese groups include the Teochews and Cantonese, from China's Guangdong province, who make up 21 and 15 per cent of the Chinese community. Their cultural contributions include cuisine and opera.

3 The Malays
Though Singapore's native inhabitants, Malays today are a minority comprising 13 per cent of the population. The term "Malay" should not be confused with "Malaysian": Malay is a race; Malaysian is the nationality of Singapore's northern neighbours.

4 The Peranakans
A Peranakan is a person born in colonial Southeast Asia to a Chinese father and non-Chinese mother. Fluency in many languages and cultures made them locally prominent.

5 The Indians – Hindus
Indians came to Singapore in the early 19th century. Many were businessmen who contributed to Singapore's progress. Indians (mostly Hindus) make up 9 per cent of the population.

6 The Indians – Sikhs
Originating from the Indian state of Punjab, the Sikhs are a small yet visible group. Their reputation for bravery inspired the British to employ Sikhs for security work.

7 The South Asians – Muslims
Muslims comprise a quarter of the Indian population. Most are Tamils from southern India and northern Sri Lanka. Tamil is one of the official languages of Singapore, along with Malay, Mandarin and English.

8 The Eurasians
In colonial times, marriages between Europeans and locals created mixed-heritage families who developed their own traditions. Though many locals are Eurasian by race, their heritage is dying out.

9 The Arabs
Singapore's Arab community is small but influential. Most came from Hadramaut in Yemen, heading trading firms and undertaking philanthropic projects, such as building schools.

10 The Expatriates
Almost 20 per cent of the population are non-resident workers. Most are from the Philippines, Indonesia and Bangladesh, but white-collar workers tend to come from China, India and, to a lesser extent, North America, Australia, and Europe.

6 Singapore Botanic Gardens

On sprawling grounds just beyond the city centre, the beautifully maintained botanic gardens *(above)* are especially refreshing in the early mornings, when the air is cool.

7 Singapore Zoo and Night Safari

A perennial tourist favourite, this award-winning zoo is recommended for adults as well as children. The Night Safari is the world's first for viewing nocturnal animals in settings much like their natural habitat.

8 Sentosa

Singapore's popular playground for recreation and relaxation, Sentosa *(left)* is an island of spas and resorts, thrilling water and land sports and other attractions for people of all ages.

9 Singapore Flyer

The largest observation wheel in the world looms high above Marina Bay. It offers incredible views over the Singapore river and from the nearby Colonial District way out to neighbouring islands visible in the far distance.

10 Raffles Hotel

This grand hotel *(below)* represents the unending romance of colonial exploration that helped to build early Singapore, and the drive for absolute luxury that characterizes its success. The hotel has its own museum.

Sri Lanka

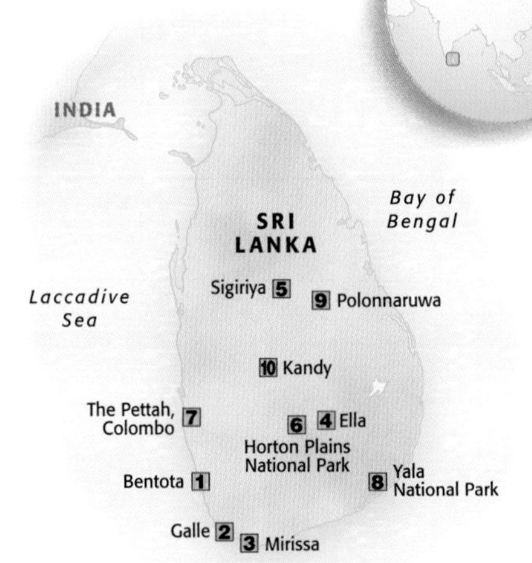

"The finest island of its size in the world," was Marco Polo's verdict, and seven centuries later it's still hard to disagree. Few countries pack so much into such a small and easily explored space, which includes beautiful beaches, amazing wildlife and stunning landscapes, from palm-fringed coastal lagoons and luxuriant rainforest to misty mountains and tea plantations. The island also boasts a spectacular collection of Buddhist monuments, dating back well over 2,000 years, including exquisite palaces, temples and shrines, and gargantuan stupas, bigger than anything in the ancient world save the great pyramids of Egypt.

1 Bentota

Sri Lanka's swankiest resort *(above)* has stylish hotels dotted along a superb stretch of beach. The mangrove-fringed Bentota lagoon provides a beautiful setting for watersports and boat trips, while the idyllic Lunuganga and Brief Garden estates are also close by.

2 Galle

Sri Lanka's most perfectly preserved colonial town is perched on a breezy promontory on the south coast, with a chain of imposing rock-and-coral ramparts enclosing peaceful streets lined with Dutch-era villas, churches and other landmarks.

3 Mirissa

One of Sri Lanka's most enjoyable beach destinations, Mirissa has a fine sweep of sand, an excellent selection of budget guesthouses and rustic seafront cafés, and a lively crowd of independent travellers. It is also a great place for whale-watching.

4 Ella

This lively village is perched on the southern edge of the hill country and has spectacular views through Ella Gap to the plains below. There are fine walks to be had through the surrounding countryside, with beautiful waterfalls, woodland and tea plantations *(above)* en route.

TOP 10 Moments in History

1 543 BC: Arrival of Prince Vijaya
This is the date assigned to the arrival in Sri Lanka of the legendary exiled Indian prince Vijaya. He and his followers are the mythical ancestors of the modern Sinhalese race.

2 246 BC: Arrival of Buddhism
Buddhism came here via Mahinda, son of Indian emperor Ashoka, during an encounter at Mihintale with King Devanampiya Tissa.

3 AD 993: Fall of Anuradhapura
The capital was destroyed by the forces of the invading Chola monarch Rajaraja, from South India. A new capital was established by Rajaraja at Polonnaruwa.

4 1518: Arrival of the Europeans
The Portuguese built a fort in Colombo and subsequently gained control of much of the island's coast, as well as converting large numbers of Sri Lankans to Christianity.

5 1602: Arrival of the Dutch
Dutch envoys arrived in Sri Lanka, attracted by the island's plentiful spices. They met with the king of Kandy, offering assistance to drive out the Portuguese.

6 1794: Arrival of the British
Following France's defeat of the Dutch during the French Revolutionary Wars, the British then gained control of much of the island, taking over Dutch territory.

7 1870s: Tea Time
Tea plantations were established across the island following the collapse of the local coffee industry. Thousands of Tamil immigrants settled in the hill country to work on the new estates.

8 1948: Independence
Sri Lanka achieved independence on 4 February 1948, with D. S. Senanayake becoming prime minister at the head of the United National Party.

9 1983: Black July
Rising ethnic tensions led to anti-Tamil riots in Colombo and the killing of thousands of civilians by local mobs, sparking a civil war between the government and LTTE (Tamil Tigers).

10 2009: End of Civil War
Defeat of the LTTE by the Sri Lankan Army and the death of their notorious leader Prabakharan were followed by mass civilian casualties in the northeast and accusations of war crimes.

5 Sigiriya

Sri Lanka's single most spectacular attraction, this towering rock outcrop *(above)* rises ·amatically from the island's northern plains. It is surrounded by elaborate gardens, ·nbellished with ancient murals of heavenly nymphs and topped with the remains of a ·markable 5th-century palace built by the patricidal King Kassapa.

8 Yala National Park

Tucked away in the southeastern corner of the island, scenic Yala National Park is arguably the best place on the planet to see leopards in the wild. It is also brimful of other wildlife, from elephants, crocodiles and sloth bears to an assortment of rare birdlife.

9 Polonnaruwa

The beautifully tended ruins of the island's second great ·apital *(above)* include some of Sri Lanka's finest art and ·chitecture, with a mixture of chaste Buddhist statues and ·*tupas* alongside more flamboyant Hindu temples and shrines.

Kandy 10

The stately former capital of the kings of Kandy is arranged around a breezy lake *(right)* and dotted with a superb array of temples and museums. Together, it provides an unrivalled showcase of Sri Lankan art, culture and religion – including the revered Temple of the Tooth.

6 Horton Plains National Park

Dotted with stands of misty cloudforest and bounded by the dramatic cliffs of World's End *(above)*, this protected area – one of the highest and wildest sections of the island's hill country – is Sri Lanka at its most scenically spectacular.

7 The Pettah, Colombo

At the heart of the island's capital, the Pettah bazaar district serves up an exhilarating slice of contemporary Sri Lankan commercial life, with narrow streets festooned with colourful signs and packed with tiny shops selling everything from Ayurvedic herbs to mobile phones.

Top 10 Buddhist Sites

1 Adam's Peak
This craggy peak in the hill country is one of the country's major pilgrimage destinations, its summit covered with what is claimed to be an impression of the Buddha's footprint.

2 Aukana Buddha
A monumental 5th-century Buddha looks serenely out over the village of Aukana, its hand raised in blessing, a flame of enlightenment issuing from its head.

3 Dambulla Cave Temples
These five caves are magnificently embellished with a vast array of shrines, statues and the finest murals in the country.

4 Kataragama
This remote southern town is home to the colourful shrine of the god Kataragama and other deities revered by both Buddhists and Hindus.

5 Gal Vihara, Polonnaruwa
At this shrine are four vast Buddha statues carved out of a single rock outcrop – among them a reclining image showing the Buddha entering the state of Nirvana.

6 Mihintale
The place where Buddhism is said to have been introduced to Sri Lanka is marked by a string of *stupas* and other religious monuments scattered across a beautiful wooded hillside.

7 Seema Malaka, Colombo
This iconic modern temple has a pair of blue-tiled pavilions and a small *stupa* set on little platforms amidst the tranquil waters of Beira Lake.

8 Sri Maha Bodhi, Anuradhapura
This venerable tree is said to have been grown from a cutting from the original Indian bo tree beneath which the Buddha gained spiritual enlightment.

9 Temple of the Tooth, Kandy
The revered Tooth Relic is said to have been taken from the mouth of the Buddha himself.

10 Wewurukannala
A gargantuan Buddha statue looks on impassively at this classic modern Sri Lankan Buddhist temple with its entertaining cluster of highly decorated shrines.

Tokyo

The easternmost of the great Asian cities, Tokyo is a place of perpetual change – a city that embraces transformation and fluidity. More interested in the future than the past, the Japanese capital nevertheless carries its history and traditions into the present. This intensely cultural city is one of the world's most energetic and creative. The following ten sights are a must for any first-time visitor; for those who return to Tokyo, there is always something new to discover.

1 Imperial Palace Grounds
Part "Forbidden City," part public park, the palace grounds *(left)* are encircled by moats, stone walls, ancient bridges, keeps and gardens – elements in the history of the original city.

Top 10 Moments in History

1 Founding of Senso-ji Temple
Discovered by fishermen in their nets in 628, the golden image of the goddess Kannon was enshrined at the site of present-day Senso-ji. The temple has been rebuilt several times, and after air raids in 1945 was put up in ferro-concrete.

2 Ota Dokan's Fort
The Musashino Plain was developed into a martial domain with the arrival of Ota Dokan, a minor feudal lord, in 1456. Dokan's fortress was built on a site named Edo, meaning "estuary mouth."

3 Founding of Edo
The development of Edo village into Japan's military capital began when future shogun Tokugawa Ieyasu arrived in 1590. Land was reclaimed, water courses expanded and the massive Edo Castle was erected.

4 The Long-Sleeves Fire
In 1657 priests at Hommyo-ji temple in Hongo tried to burn a kimono worn by a lovelorn girl who died shortly after putting it on. A gust of wind tore it away, starting fresh fires that claimed the lives of over 100,000 people.

5 47 Ronin Incident
In 1701 Lord Asano was ordered to commit ritual suicide for drawing his sword at court. His retainers, 47 *ronin* (masterless samurai), avenged Asano's death by killing his opponent, Lord Kira. The act led the authorities to order the 47 *ronin* to commit suicide.

6 Perry's "Black Ships"
In 1853 Commodore Matthew Calbraith Perry sailed four heavily armed ships into Edo Bay to open Japan to diplomatic and trade relations. The "black ships" were a display of superior Western technology.

7 Great Kanto Earthquake
This 1923 disaster convulsed the city: 100,000 people were killed and nearly half the buildings destroyed.

8 Tokyo Air Raids
US raids on Tokyo during WWII reached a peak on 9 March 1945, when over 300 B-29 bombers swooped over the city and killed between 80,000 and 100,000 civilians.

9 Suicide of Mishima
Having failed in his call for the restoration of the emperor in 1970, author Yukio Mishima committed ritual disembowelment in the samurai tradition.

10 Aum Shinrikyo Subway Attack
On 20 March 1995 members of the death cult Aum Shinrikyo placed sarin gas in carriages on five subway lines, killing 12 and injuring hundreds of passengers.

2 Sumida River
An excursion starting under its famous bridges is a journey through the history and development of the city.

3 Edo-Tokyo Museum
Blending history, art and architecture, this stupendous museum *(above)* traces the history of the city from Edo Castle to the Tokyo Olympics.

4 Ueno Park

A compendium of Japanese cultural history, this extensive park *(right)* contains temples, mausoleums, major museums, a zoo and a splendid lotus pond. With its 1,000 cherry trees, the park serves as a great picnic spot in spring.

5 Koishikawa Korakuen Garden

Tokyo's oldest garden has a heart-shaped pond, lacquered wood and stone bridges, rock arrangements, islands, miniature hills and a lotus pond – all rife with symbolism.

6 Odaiba Island

Featuring high-tech buildings *(above)*, fashion malls, exhibition sites, museums, a giant Ferris wheel and a man-made beach, the artificial island of Odaiba is both entertainment and experiment.

7 Meiji Shrine

At the centre of a forest, the exquisite Shinto architecture of the shrine buildings and a beautiful iris garden embody the theme of nature.

8 Senso-ji Temple

The grounds of this temple *(above)* are packed with attractions, which begin at Kaminari-mon ("Thunder Gate") and the commercial corridor of Nakamise-dori.

9 Tokyo National Museum

The world's largest collection of Japanese art and archaeology, plus Chinese, Korean and Central Asian art treasures, are housed here *(left)*.

10 Yanaka Cemetery

Ghosts of old Edo linger here among the gnarled cherry trees and mouldering tombs *(above)* belonging to shoguns, warriors, writers and Kabuki actors.

TOP 10 Gardens

1 Canadian Embassy Garden
In this garden by Masuno Shunmyo on an upper terrace of the building, stones from Hiroshima represent the rocks of the Canadian Shield, symbolizing the relationship between Japan and Canada.

2 Hibiya Park
With its lawn, rose garden, bandstand and theatre, this was Japan's first Western-style park; it opened in 1903.

3 Imperial Palace East Gardens
This 17th-century garden is resplendent with plum blossoms, spring cherry and azaleas in late winter; irises and lilies in summer; and bush clover, camellias and maple leaves in the fall.

4 Mukojima Hyakka-en Garden
This little-visited Edo-period garden was completed in 1804 close to Sumida river, a district of temples and teahouses, and focal point for a refined cultural life.

5 Kiyosumi-teien Garden
Rare rocks were shipped from all over the country to create this garden. A traditional teahouse overlooks a large pond and islets. Another eye-catching feature of this garden is an artificial hill, shaped into the likeness of Mount Fuji.

6 Nature Study Institute and Park
A carefully preserved section of the Musashino Plain, this park is home to many birds, insects and turtles, as well as more than 8,000 trees.

7 Rikugi-en Garden
Completed in 1702, this garden was named after the six principles of Oriental poetry. The symbolism may be hard to decipher, but the landscape is easy to admire.

8 Shinjuku Gyoen Garden
Though completed in 1772, this garden has evolved. It is now divided into French, English and Japanese sections. The garden is a popular spot for cherry blossom viewing in spring.

9 Hama Rikyu Garden
An original Edo-period garden, Hama Rikyu dates from 1654. Standing near the entrance is a large black pine, planted in 1704 – a miraculous survivor of earthquakes, fires and air raids. A tidal pond brings in saltwater fish.

10 Yoyogi Park
An open area of lawns and recreational facilities popular with cyclists, joggers and skateboarders, Yoyogi Park is a great spot for picnics. A small botanical garden and bird sanctuary add interest, and live music concerts are held here every Sunday.

Best of the Rest: City Sights

Top 10 Historic Buildings

1 Gandhi Smriti, Delhi, India
Formerly known as Birla House, this Neo-Classical mansion is where Gandhi spent his final 144 days.

2 Gokoku-ji Temple, Tokyo, Japan
A rare find in modern Tokyo, this temple was built by the fifth shogun, Tsunayoshi, in 1681.

3 Former Government House, Hong Kong, China
This grand old building served as the British governor's residence from 1855 until 1997, when the last governor handed Hong Kong back to China.

4 Emerald Hill Road, Singapore
Pre-war terrace houses lining this road were some of the earliest private residences to be conserved.

5 Suan Pakkad, Bangkok, Thailand
This compound of traditional Thai houses contains antique paintings, carvings and a stunning display of masks used in *khon* (masked theatre).

6 Great Hall of the People, Beijing, China
This the Chinese parliament building, home of the nation's legislative body, the National People's Congress.

7 Phuket Town Mansions, Thailand
The architecture employed in many of Phuket Town's old mansions and shop houses derives from the British colonial style. Examples include the 19th-century Chinpracha House.

8 Hue Citadel, Hue, Vietnam
The Citadel, established by Emperor Gia Long in 1805, comprises three concentric enclosures – the Civic, Imperial, and Forbidden Purple Cities.

9 Nijo Castle, Kyoto, Japan
Nijo is known for its "nightingale floors", designed to make bird-like squeaking sounds when walked upon.

10 Marble Palace, Kolkata, India
Built in 1835, the Marble Palace offers a wonderful glimpse into the life of a rich 19th-century Bengali household.

Top 10 Architectural Gems

1 Baha'i Temple, Delhi, India
Inspired by the shape of an unfurling lotus flower, this remarkable building was built for the Baha'i faith.

2 Tokyo International Forum, Japan
This majestic building was designed by Rafael Viñoly in 1996, and it functions as a premier culture convention centre.

3 Bank of China, Hong Kong, China
The work of I M Pei, this 70-storey stack of prisms has a viewing platform offering sweeping city views.

4 CHIJMES (Convent of the Holy Infant Jesus), Singapore
This convent was built in 1841 and served its purpose for 131 years. It is now a complex of shops, restaurants and entertainment venues.

5 Bang Pa-In, Bangkok, Thailand
Established by King Prasat Thong in the mid-17th century and later expanded, these exuberant buildings are an eclectic mix of Thai architecture.

6 National Olympic Stadium (Bird's Nest), Beijing, China
Designed by Herzog & de Meuron with Ai Weiwei, the National Olympic Stadium is an architectural icon.

7 Edo-Tokyo Open-Air Architectural Museum, Japan
Buildings of the Edo, Meiji and later periods have been gathered in this fin open-air architectural museum.

8 General Post Office, Ho Chi Minh, Vietnam
Designed by French architect Gustave Eiffel between 1886 and 1891, the building is no less than a temple to the art of communicating by mail.

9 Hawa Mahal, Jaipur, India
The Hawa Mahal, or "Palace of Winds was erected in 1799, and its pink façade has become an icon for Jaipur.

10 Taipei 101, Taipei, China
This 101-storey tower rises high above the city. Its pagoda-like structure combines ultra-modernity with references to traditional Chinese culture.

Top 10 Museums and Galleries

1 National Rail Museum, Delhi, India
Among the highlights are the lavish carriages created for local and foreign aristocrats, from the Maharaja of Mysore to the Prince of Wales.

2 ADMT Advertising Museum, Tokyo, Japan
Exhibits here cover the long history of commercial art in Japan.

3 Museum of History, Hong Kong, China
The Hong Kong Story attempts to chronicle around 400 million years of the island's eventful history.

4 Singapore Art Museum, Singapore
This is the world's largest collection of modern Southeast Asian art.

5 Royal Barge Museum, Bangkok, Thailand
Housed in a dry-dock warehouse, this museum features eight gleaming barges, each nearly 50 m (165 ft) long, which are used for special royal events.

6 Ancient Architecture Museum, Beijing, China
The museum is worth visiting for the building alone, which is the pavilion of a former grand temple complex.

7 Atomic Bomb Museum, Nagasaki, Japan
Displays depict Nagasaki before and after the explosion, and also the reconstruction of the city.

8 Indian Museum, Kolkata, India
The oldest museum in India has an impressive collection of Indus Valley Civilization and Gandhara sculptures.

9 Thavorn Lobby Hotel Museum, Phuket, Thailand
Housed in a wood-panelled hotel lobby is a collection of vintage photographs, Thai movie posters and opium pipes.

10 National Museum, Kuala Lumpur, Malaysia
The National Museum covers ethnography, natural history, colonial times and the battle for independence.

Top 10 Religious Buildings

1 Nizamuddin, Delhi, India
The wonderfully atmospheric religious complex grew up around the revered *dargah* (Muslim shrine) of the Chishti Sufi saint Nizamuddin Aulia.

2 Hie Shrine, Tokyo, Japan
Reconstructed in 1967, the original 1659 building served as the protective shrine of Edo Castle. In gratitude, shoguns donated swords to the shrine.

3 Wong Tai Sin Temple, Hong Kong, China
Worshippers from all three main Chinese religions flock to this temple, making for a noisy, colourful affair.

4 Sakya Muni Buddha Gaya Temple, Singapore
This small Buddhist temple has painted murals depicting episodes from the life of the Buddha.

5 Wat Saket and the Golden Mount, Bangkok, Thailand
The temple has a peaceful atmosphere, but most people come here to climb the 76-m (250-ft) Golden Mount.

6 White Cloud Temple, Beijing, China
Home to the China Daoist Associatior the temple was founded in 739 and is Beijing's largest Daoist shrine.

7 St John's Church, Kolkata, India
The first parish church in Kolkata, St John's (1787) boasts an impressive stained-glass panel of The Last Suppe

8 Wat Phra Sing, Chiang Mai, Thailand
Construction of this temple, the largest in Chiang Mai, began in 1345, though the *bot* dates from 1600.

9 Cao Dai Holy See, Ho Chi Minh City, Vietnam
The main attraction, the Great Divine Temple, is a massive structure that mixes Asian and European architecture

10 Grand Shrine, Ise, Japan
Home of the spirits of past emperors, the Grand Shrine at Ise is the most venerated Shinto site. The inner shrine honours Amaterasu, the sun goddess

awa Mahal, Jaipur, India

East Coast Park, Singapore

Great Hall of the People, Beijing, China

Night Market, Phuket Town, Thailand

TOP 10 Performing Arts Venues

1 Sangeet Natak Akademi,)elhi, India
)pened in 1953, this is one of the ountry's foremost performing arts enues, with a fine open-air theatre.

2 Kanze Noh Theatre, okyo, Japan
pectacular dramas are staged here n the open air by masked actors luminated by burning torches.

3 Cultural Centre, long Kong, China
may be an architectural mishap, but his cultural centre does host some xcellent dance and theatre.

4 The Esplanade – Theatres on he Bay, Singapore
his landmark arts venue houses two ndoor stages and one outdoor space or music, theatre and dance.

5 Joe Louis Puppet Theatre, angkok, Thailand
aptivating puppet shows retelling tories from the Hindu epic *Ramakien* re performed by three puppeteers.

6 Chang'an Grand Theatre, Beijing, China
Beijing Opera is a form of "total theatre" that combines singing, speech, mime and graceful acrobatics.

7 National Theatre, Kuala Lumpur, Malaysia
The striking National Theatre, designed in the shape of a Malay kite, hosts interesting cultural shows as well as national and international theatre.

8 Shanghai Centre, China
The popular Shanghai Centre puts on classical Western music and opera as well as nightly performances of the city's most famous acrobatic group.

9 Gion Corner, Kyoto, Japan
Gion Corner hosts classical Kyoto dance, *koto* music, *Kyogen* comic drama, and even *ikebana* (flower arranging).

10 National Centre for Performing Arts, Mumbai, India
The city's most active venue for music, dance and theatre stages works by international and Indian playwrights.

TOP 10 Beaches and Green Spaces

1 Talkatora Gardens, Delhi, India
These 18th-century gardens are one of central Delhi's most popular parks, and are particularly pretty in spring.

2 Nezu Institute of Fine Arts Garden, Tokyo, Japan
This small but complex garden is a cross between a natural landscape and a tea garden, with Buddhist statuary.

3 Hong Kong Park Aviary, Hong Kong, China
The streams and lush plant life of this improbable mini-rainforest are a shaded home to scores of exotic bird species.

4 East Coast Park, Singapore
The long strip of sandy beach with paths shaded by casuarina trees and coconut palms is popular with cyclists and rollerbladers.

5 Saranrom Park, Bangkok, Thailand
With shady trees and fountains, this park is a great place to take a break after trekking round the Grand Palace.

6 Jing Shan Park, Beijing, China
The park is dotted with pavilions and halls – the highlight is the superb view south from the Wancheng Pavilion.

7 Ko Sirey, Phuket, Thailand
Linked to Phuket Town via a small bridge, Sirey Island features hilly forest trails. Ko Sirey temple enjoys sea views and has a large reclining Buddha.

8 Titiwangsa Lake Gardens, Malaysia
These peaceful, manicured gardens laid out around a vast man-made lake are a visual treat and offer a great view of the Petronas Towers.

9 Marina Promenade and Beach, Chennai, India
One of India's largest urban beaches stretches for 13 km (8 miles) along Chennai's eastern flank.

10 Philosoper's Walk, Kyoto, Japan
One of Kyoto's best-loved spots, Philosopher's Walk follows the course of a cherry-tree-lined canal.

TOP 10 Special Spots

1 Tomb of Razia Sultan,)elhi, India
he tomb of Razia Sultan occupies an tmospheric little roofless enclosure leep in the heart of the old city.

2 Rikugi-en Teahouse, okyo, Japan
et beautifully near Rikugi-en's large ond, this teahouse serves green tea nd tiny Japanese sweets.

3 The Escalator, long Kong, China
he series of escalators in the steep Mid-Levels district of Hong Kong sland was designed for commuters.

4 Kranji War Memorial and emetery, Singapore
his memorial commemorates more han 28,000 Allied servicemen, some ,000 of whom are buried here.

5 Chi, The Spa, Bangkok, hailand
ased on the design of a Tibetan emple, this spa facility is nothing less han a sanctuary of tranquillity.

6 Lai Tai Market, Beijing, China
This covered market, just north of the Third Ring Road, is a mix of garden centre and tropical fish store.

7 Rang Hill, Phuket, Thailand
Wonderful views of Phuket Town can be enjoyed from the summit of Rang Hill, a breezy, tree-shaded park.

8 Horniman Circle, Mumbai, India
The central green here is a delightful spot, frequented by students and office workers. It is also the venue for open-air theatre performances.

9 Huxinting Teahouse, Shanghai, China
Built in 1784, the building only became a teahouse in the late 19th century. The zigzag bridge protects the structure, as evil spirits can't turn corners.

10 Daisen-in Zen Garden at Daitoku-Ji, Kyoto, Japan
Daisen-in's garden is a 3-D version of the Chinese Sung monochrome landscape paintings that inspired it.

TOP 10 Shopping

1 Kinari Bazaar, Delhi, India
The shops of Kinari Bazaar are famous for wedding paraphernalia – garlands of fake flowers and banknotes, bridal veils and sparkly costume jewellery.

2 Takeshita-dori, Tokyo, Japan
This street is packed with garish boutiques, subculture junk, cutesy accessories and fetish costumery.

3 Cat Street Market, Hong Kong, China
Cat Street refers to the Chinese slang for odds and ends. This street and Hollywood Road are chock full of Maoist kitsch curio shops and antiques.

4 Yue Hwa Chinese Emporium, Singapore
This is recommended for the variety of Chinese handicrafts stocked here, from silk clothing to jade jewellery.

5 Komplex Budaya Kraf, Kuala Lumpur, Malaysia
Showcasing a variety of arts and crafts from Malaysia, this complex is one of the best places to buy local handicrafts.

6 Ten Fu's Tea, Beijing, China
Tea from all over China is sold loose or in beautiful presentation boxes. Staff will even brew cups for sampling.

7 Phuket Town Night Market, Thailand
The night market offers "fisherman's pants" and woodcarvings, as well as secondhand clothes and Thai music.

8 Ippodo Chaho, Kyoto, Japan
There are many fine tea shops in town, but Ippodo Chaho, Nakagyo-ku, is the granddaddy of them all.

9 New Market, Kolkata, India
New Market is Kolkata's most famous shopping centre. Established in 1874, this is still a shopper's paradise, where one can find anything from Chinese sausages to gold jewellery.

10 Chinatown, Kuala Lumpur, Malaysia
Kuala Lumpur's little Chinatown is a maze of narrow streets and alleyways lined with old shophouses, medicine stores and family-run coffee shops.

Best of the Rest: Out of Town

Top 10 Towns and Villages

1 Pattaya, Thailand
Pattaya is infamous for its nightlife, yet in recent years it has made an attempt to appeal more to families through theme parks and watersports.

2 Chuandixia, Beijing, China
On a steep mountainside, Chuandixia is a crumbling but picturesque hamlet of courtyard houses *(siheyuan)* dating from the Ming and Qing dynasties.

3 Alwar, India
The traditional northern gateway to Rajasthan, Alwar is home to an imposing fort with ramparts cresting a series of hills above the town.

4 Tai O, Lantau island, Hong Kong, China
Sitting in a tidal estuary, this is one of the last places in Hong Kong where you can see the stilt housing of southern Chinese fishing villages.

5 Guangzho (Canton), China
Cut through the smog and traffic and you'll find Han dynasty tombs, temples and fascinating architecture.

6 Yokohama, Japan
A crucial Meiji-era foreign settlement and port, this waterfront city has plenty to keep you occupied with shopping, gardens and historical sites.

7 Kampot, Cambodia
Kampot's riverside is a delight at sunset, as fishermen cast their nets, while its French colonial buildings are in an appealing state of elegant decay.

8 Singaraja, Bali
With its waterfront mosques, temples, market and well-ordered streets, Singaraja is a pleasure to stroll around.

9 Kanazawa, Japan
Little remains of Kanazawa Castle except a rebuilt gate and walls, but within its grounds lies the exquisite samurai Seisonkaku Villa.

10 Lijiang, China
Lijiang isn't the easiest place to get to, but China's best-preserved ancient town repays the effort. Beneath its rippling roofs, life goes on here much as it has for hundreds of years.

Top 10 Historic Places and Museums

1 Kanchanaburi, Thailand
The main sights are the infamous bridge over the River Kwai and the war cemeteries associated with the thousands of Allied soldiers who died constructing the "Death Railway".

2 Eastern Qing Tombs, China
The splendid Eastern Qing Tombs make up the largest and most complete imperial cemetery in China.

3 Deeg Palace, India
Built in the 18th century, the Deeg Palace blends Hindu and Mughal elements with spacious water gardens dotted with palaces and pavilions.

4 Kamakura, Japan
The shogun's capital from 1192 to 1333, this seaside town has ancient shrines and gardens all within an easy train ride of Tokyo.

5 Kranji War Memorial and Cemetery, Singapore
Overlooking the Strait of Johor, this cemetery is lined by the graves of Allied soldiers of World War II.

6 National Museum, Luang Prabang, Laos
A unique blend of French and Lao architectural styles, this was the home of Lao royalty until 1975.

7 National Museum, Phnom Penh, Cambodia
Housed in four majestic terracotta pavilions, the museum has Cambodia's greatest display of Khmer statuary.

8 Museum Puri Lukisan, Ubud, Bali
The museum displays wooden sculptures and beautifully intricate paintings from the 20th century.

9 Miho Museum, Shigaraki, Japan
A peach-tree-lined path dives into a part-subterranean space full of Western and Asian antiquities.

10 Mountain Resort, Chengde, China
This walled estate is the final flourish of imperial China, built by the emperors of the Qing Dynasty.

Top 10 Religious Buildings

1 Nakhon Pathom Chedi, Bangkok, Thailand
At 120 m (395 ft), this is one of the world's tallest Buddhist monuments and dates to at least the 6th century.

2 Tanzhe Temple, China
This temple dates back to the 3rd century. It has a splendid mountainside setting, its halls rising up the incline.

3 Golden Temple, Amritsar, India
The holiest city of the Sikh faith is home to the Golden Temple, its richly gilded central shrine rising serenely out of the surrounding lake.

4 Ching Chung Koon, Hong Kong, China
The temple's name, "evergreen pine tree", is a symbol of longevity. The Koon, a Taoist sect, began the work in 1961.

5 Wat Prathong, Phuket, Thailand
The half-buried golden Buddha statue is the main attraction here. According to legend, anyone who attempts to uproot the statue will be cursed.

6 Toshogu Shrine, Nikko, Japan
Chosen in 1617 as the burial site of the shogun Ieyasu, Toshogu shrine is a complex of buildings and mausoleums.

7 Lian Shan Shuang Lin Temple, Singapore
Singapore's oldest Buddhist monastery has three main halls, each built in the architectural style of the Fujian province.

8 Itsukushima Shrine, Honshu, Japan
This famous shrine founded in 593 is built on stilts over a cove. Out in the water is the iconic floating *torii*, the shrine's ceremonial gate.

9 Labrang Monastery, Xiahe, China
This monastery is in a beautiful mountain setting by the Daxia river, high on the Tibetan plateau.

10 Pancha Rathas, Mamallapuram, India
The Pancha Rathas are five lovely 7th-century rock temples cut from single pink granite outcrops.

Top 10 Islands

1 Tap Mun, China
To the north of the Sai Kung Peninsula, tiny Tap Mun has striking rock formations, pounding seas, a herd of cattle and relative seclusion.

2 Ko Yao Yai and Noi, Thailand
These picturesque islands in Phang Nga Bay feature charming thatched-roof homes and rubber plantations.

3 Kume Island, Okinawa, Japan
Perhaps the most beautiful island in Okinawa prefecture, volcanic Kume is famous for sugarcane and pineapples.

4 Koh Rong Samloem, Cambodia
A tropical paradise, the island has white-sand beaches, clear turquoise waters and excellent snorkelling.

5 Nusa Penida, Bali
Legendary home of the mythical "King of Magical Powers", this undeveloped island is somewhat feared by many Balinese, and appeals to adventurers who come for the excellent dives and spectacular concentrations of sunfish.

6 Con Dau Islands, Vietnam
A cluster of 16 islands off the coast of southern Vietnam, Con Dau is rich in wildlife and spectacular beaches – an astounding destination.

7 Ha Long Bay by Junk, Vietnam
Around 3,000 islands rise dramatically from the Gulf of Tonkin. Pristine lagoons, sheer cliffs and white-sand beaches adorn the dramatic islets.

8 Don Daeng Island, Laos
On the Mekong, Don Daeng is an enclave of traditional culture, where locals go about their work fishing, farming and weaving.

9 Monkey Bay, Tioman Island, Malaysia
A hike through the rainforest from Salang will lead you to the secluded yellow-sand beach of Monkey Bay.

10 Bangaram Island, Lakshadweep Islands, India
This teardrop of lush green coconut palms is fringed by creamy sand in the warm waters of the Indian Ocean.

ount Fuji, Honshu, Japan

Pattaya, Thailand

Nha Trang, Vietnam

Lake Bratan, Bali

TOP 10 Lakes and Waterways

1 Juma River Walk, hidu, China
hidu offers pleasant walking trails long the riverbank between gorges nd limestone formations.

2 Bride's Pool, Hong Kong, China
he pool is a popular picnic spot. If ou visit midweek, with luck, you will ave this glorious, wooded course of ockpools and cascades all to yourself.

3 Mangroves, Phuket, Thailand
hese fantastic trees, with tangled and xposed roots, can be found along huket's muddy shorelines. Sea canoe ours offer the best way to see them.

4 Sungei Buloh Wetland eserve, Singapore
ingfishers, plovers, sandpipers and erons are some of the bird species ound among these coastal mangrove wamps, mudflats and tidal pools.

5 Lake Towada, Honshu, Japan
n the mountainous Towada-Hachimantai lational Park is Lake Towada, a scenic aldera lake with spa inns to the north.

6 Bonsraa Waterfalls, Cambodia
Cambodia's most dramatic cascade, the double-tiered Bonsraa waterfalls plunge 35 m (115 ft) into dense jungle.

7 Sendangile Waterfalls, Lombok, Indonesia
These falls, which come straight off one of the highest peaks in Southeast Asia, are a 30-minute walk from the trekking base of Senaru.

8 Lake Bratan, Bali
Great for parasailing and waterskiing, the lake is also the starting point for guided treks to nearby peaks.

9 Ba Be National Park, Vietnam
Centred around three linked lakes, this lush park is dominated by dramatic limestone peaks, grottoes and the spectacular Dau Dang Falls.

10 Thale Noi Waterfowl Park, Thailand
The country's largest wetland bird sanctuary serves thousands of exotic migratory birds. Explore the watery reserve by long-tail boat.

TOP 10 Mountains and Forests

1 Ma On Shan, Hong Kong, China
The plateaus and grassy slopes of Ma On Shan ("Saddle Mountain") allow majestic views of mountainous country.

2 Big Buddha Viewpoint, Phuket, Thailand
With sweeping 360-degree views of Phuket, the massive Buddha image sits 400 m (1,300 ft) above sea level.

3 Khao Lak, Thailand
A number of scenic forest paths can be found in and around Khao Lak, starting near Chong Fah Waterfall.

4 The Southern Ridges, Singapore
The coastline on the southwest shore has four parks seamlessly connected by a series of bridges that link hiking trails.

5 Mount Fuji, Honshu, Japan
The graceful, near-perfect cone of Mount Fuji is Japan's highest peak. Beneath it, the Fuji Five Lakes is a playground for Tokyo-ites, with sports facilities and amusement parks.

6 Phnom Santuk, Cambodia
Rising above lush paddy fields, Phnom Santuk is the most sacred mountain in Kompong Thom province.

7 Gunung Agung, Bali
At just over 3000 m (9,900 ft), this active volcano dominates eastern Bali in both a physical and spiritual sense.

8 Doi Inthanon National Park, Thailand
Thailand's highest mountain, Doi Inthanon is surrounded by a park rich in habitats and wildlife. Orchids grow in abundance on its higher slopes.

9 Wolong Nature Reserve, Sichuan, China
The Giant Panda Breeding Centre in the highlands offers an opportunity to watch these gentle creatures.

10 Bako National Park, Sarawak, Malaysia
Bearded pigs, mouse deer, flying lemurs and long-nosed monkeys are some of the fabulous animals you're likely to spot on the jungle trails of Bako Park.

TOP 10 Beaches

1 Koh Samed, Thailand
Just 50 km (31 miles) east of Pattaya and surrounded by clear waters, Koh Samed is easily the best beach escape from Bangkok.

2 Mai Khao Beach, Phuket, Thailand
Phuket's longest beach is a thin, undulating stretch of sand that slopes steeply down into the sea.

3 Koh Kong Island, Cambodia
Just over an hour's speedboat journey from the town of Koh Kong, this island has seven perfect beaches. The one backed by a lovely lagoon is the best.

4 Lovina, Bali
This long stretch of coast encompasses a series of villages and a beach resort area with quiet black-sand coves that are lined with coconut trees.

5 Nha Trang, Vietnam
A bustling city and fishing port, Nha Trang is also Vietnam's primary beach resort. If its beach is too busy, there are many others north along the shore.

6 Yonaha Maehama Beach, Miako Island, Japan
On the main isle of the eight Miyako Islands, Yonaha Maehama Beach offers pristine white sand and great diving.

7 Emerald Bay, Pangkor Laut, Malaysia
On Pangkor Laut's western shore lies Emerald Bay, a super white-sand beach, with bowing palms and green waters.

8 Big Buddha Beach, Ko Samui, Thailand
This beach gets its name from the tall statue that watches over it. The temple is a pilgrimage site, but most visitors come for the sand and sea.

9 White Beach, Boracay, The Philippines
One of the world's best beaches, Boracay and its neighbouring bays offer pristine sand lined with swaying palms.

10 Arambol Beach, Goa, India
The atmosphere at Arambol is distinctly laid back: wake up in a bamboo hut footsteps from the shore.

TOP 10 Food and Crafts

1 Damnoen Saduak Floating Market, Bangkok, Thailand
This market gives an idea of how life here once revolved around the waterways and small boats plying their trade.

2 Jade Market, Guangzhou, China
An extensive jade market surrounds the small Buddhist temple of Hua Lin.

3 Ko Rang Yai, Phuket, Thailand
Home to the Phuket Pearl Farm, this private island cultivates three different types of pearl for export.

4 Mandai Orchid Garden, Singapore
Best visited in conjunction with the Singapore Zoo, this commercial garden grows more than 200 varieties of orchid for local sale and export.

5 Santuk Silk Farm, Cambodia
Here visitors can see the various life stages of the silk worm, from egg to caterpillar to the cocoon, which provides the base for the silk thread, which is woven into attractive scarves.

6 Pringgasela, Lombok, Indonesia
The village of Pringgasela specializes in hand-woven textiles with patterns predominantly in red and black.

7 Bac Ha, Vietnam
A small town high up in the Chay River massif, Bac Ha comes alive on Sunday mornings, when ethnic hill peoples descend on it to trade spices and cloth.

8 Surin, Thailand
Over 700 patterns are used by the silk weavers in Surin province, and the process of silk production can be seen in the villages surrounding Surin town.

9 Patiala, Punjab, India
The lively bazaar in Patiala offers handcrafted shoes (*jutties*), silken braids and brightly embroidered fabric.

10 Pottery, Saga Prefecture, Kyushu, Japan
The Kyushu region is famous for its pottery and the towns of Karatsu, Imari and Arita are great to visit for their kilns and workshops.

Hotels and Restaurants

Top 10 Hotels: City Luxury

1 Imperial Hotel, Tokyo, Japan
With a history dating from the 1890s, the Imperial Hotel enjoys unimpeachable credentials. *www.imperialhotel.co.jp*

2 Raffles Hotel, Beijing, China
A short walk from Tian'an Men Square, find a winning mixture of heritage, luxury and comfort. *www.raffles.com*

3 The Oberoi, Mumbai, India
Offers separate floors for non-smokers and women travellers. There is the option of a butler service. *www.oberoihotels.com*

4 Fairmont Hotel, Singapore
The Fairmont has contemporary rooms and bathrooms feature innovations such as rain forest shower-heads. The hotel also has the largest spa in town. *www.fairmont.com*

5 The Claridges, Delhi, India
Claridges is the epitome of old-world style. The building is characterized by Colonial pillars and high ceilings. This is where The Beatles stayed in 1968. *www.claridges-hotels.com/delhi*

6 Oriental Hotel, Bangkok, Thailand
This historic hotel has superb facilities, exceptional service and great views. *www.mandarinoriental.com/bangkok*

7 Cholon Windsor Plaza, Ho Chi Minh City, Vietnam
The ultra-modern five-star hotel has excellent rooms and services. *www.windsorplazahotel.com*

8 Mystères d'Angkor, Siem Reap, Angkor, Vietnam
This tranquil French-run boutique hotel has tastefully decorated rooms and a lovely pool. *www.mysteres-angkor.com*

9 Royal Garden Hotel, Hong Kong, China
Elegant rooms sit around a bright atrium lobby at the reasonably priced Royal Garden Hotel. *www.rghk.com.hk*

10 Amanjaya Pancam, Phnom Penh, Cambodia
This old-world hotel is right by the river between the Royal Palace and Wat Phnom. *www.amanjaya-pancam-hotel.com*

Top 10 Hotels: Beside the Seaside

1 Jimbaran Puri Bali, Jimbaran, Bali, Indonesia
Set within walled gardens, this group of cottages forms a beachfront boutique hotel. *www.pansea.com*

2 Dusit Thani Laguna Phuket, Phuket, Thailand
Located in the Laguna Phuket Resort complex, this hotel is set on the Bang Tao Beach. *www.dusit.com*

3 The Pulai Desaru Beach, Desaru, Malaysia
Occupying a stretch of pristine beachfront, The Pulai is an award-winning resort. *www.thepulai.com.my*

4 Evason Ana Mandara Spa, Nha Trang, Vietnam
Set amid tropical gardens and with a private beach, Ana Mandara is just wonderful. *www.sixsenses.com*

5 Puri Mas Boutique Hotel, Mangsit, Lombok, Indonesia
Each of the thatched bungalows, rooms and suites here has a different style. *www.purimas-lombok.com*

6 Manathai Resort, Phuket, Thailand
A boutique hotel on Surin Beach, Manathai blends contemporary design with Asian styles. *www.manathai.com*

7 Sihanoukville Villa Hotel, Sihanoukville, Cambodia
A stylish and comfortable place, with original artwork and great attention to detail. *www.sihanoukvillevillahotel.com*

8 Anantara, Seminyak, Bali, Indonesia
This luxurious beachfront hotel is a short walk from the nightlife of Seminyak. *http://bali.anantara.com*

9 Coral Redang Island Resort, Pulau Redang, Malaysia
Set amid dazzling beaches, this basic island resort offers several diving packages. *www.coralredang.com.my*

10 Shangri-La's Rasa Sentosa Resort, Singapore
Sentosa's only beachfront hotel is good for families, with a pool and aquarium next door. *www.shangri-la.com*

Top 10 Hotels: Get Away From It All

1 Sala Kong Lor Lodge, Tham Kong Lo, Laos
Part of a chain of Lao eco-lodges, these riverside bungalows are a great place to relax amid thick forests and lush green surroundings. *www.salalao.com*

2 Red Capital Ranch, Xiaguandi, Beijing, China
Guests looking for a rustic stay will find it at one of Red Capital's 10 stone cottages. *www.redcapitalclub.com.cn*

3 Rohet Garh, Rohet, India
A favourite with authors Bruce Chatwin and William Dalrymple. The delightful owners help guests explore the nearby villages. *www.rohetgarh.com*

4 Paresa, Phuket, Thailand
Perched on a cliff overlooking the Andaman Sea, this boutique resort has spacious villas. *www.paresaresorts.com*

5 Panuba Inn, Pulau Tioman, Malaysia
Located in an isolated bay, Panuba Inn is a peaceful spot that is popular among divers. *www.panubainn.com*

6 Tadlo Lodge Hotel, Bolaven Plateau, Laos
Bungalows are set in a lovely forest close to the Tat Lo and Tat Hang waterfalls. *www.tadlolodge.com*

7 Amanfayun, Hangzhou, Shanghai, China
Tucked away in a picturesque valley, Amanfayun is surrounded by tea fields and temples. *www.amanresorts.com*

8 The Oberoi Lombok, Tanjung, Lombok, Indonesia
A paradise hideaway, set in coconut palm-studded gardens and bordering an exclusive beach. *www.oberoihotels.com*

9 Sea Gypsy Village Resort, Pulau Sibu, Malaysia
It is set in a jungle clearing just off a dazzling beach, with accommodation in wooden chalets. *www.siburesort.com*

10 Pandanus Resort, Mui Ne Beach, Vietnam
This upmarket resort offers a sense of solitude and privacy close to the busy fishing village. *www.pandanusresort.com*

Top 10 Hotels: Unusual Places

1 Ryokan Shigetsu, Tokyo, Japan
This beautiful ryokan is adorned with paper screen windows; the traditional baths are a highlight. *www.shigetsu.com*

2 Red Capital Residence, Beijing, China
Beijing's quirkiest hotel has just five rooms, each with a different theme. *www.redcapitalclub.com.cn*

3 Dead Fish Tower Inn, Siem Reap, Angkor, Cambodia
Much of its charm here comes from quirky touches, such as guests receiving a head massage on arrival. *www.deadfishtower.com*

4 Desa Dunia Beda Beach Resort, Giles Isles, Bali
The traditional wooden houses feature verandas, open shutters and garden bathrooms. *www.desaduniabeda.com*

5 New Majestic Hotel, Singapore
Each room here is decorated by a local artist. *www.newmajestichotel.com*

6 Sawasdee Village Resort & Spa, Phuket, Thailand
A resort resembling a traditional Thai village. *www.phuketsawasdee.com*

7 Rambagh Palace, Jaipur, India
Built in 1835, Rambagh Palace seems to be a place that time forgot, cut off from the world in lavish grounds. *www.tajhotels.com*

8 Taj Lake Palace Hotel, Udaipur, Rajasthan, India
This fairytale island palace is among India's most romantic hotels, with magnificent rooms. *www.tajhotels.com*

9 Bamboo Garden Hotel, Beijing, China
This is the oldest of Beijing's traditional hotels, with large and elaborate courtyards. *www.bbgh.com.cn*

10 Lakeview Restaurant & Hotel, Gunung Batur, Bali, Indonesia
Perched on the rim of a caldera, the hotel has breathtaking views of the active volcano, Gunung Batur, and the crater lake. *http://lakeviewbali.com*

Sirocco, Bangkok, Thailand

Beijing Roast Duck Restaurant, Beijing, China

Ryokan Shigetsu, Tokyo, Japan

The Pulai Desaru Beach, Desaru, Malaysia

TOP 10 Restaurants: Fine Dining

1 Le Nadao, Central Vientiane, Laos
Classy and with a lovely ambience, Le Nadao serves excellent, yet reasonably priced French cuisine. ✆ *021 213 174*

2 Topaz, Central Phnom Penh, Cambodia
Chef Alain presents classic French cuisine with hints of Southeast Asian fusion. ✆ *023 221 622*

3 Maison Boulud, Beijing, China
The cooking is French *haute cuisine* with an Asian twist – expensive but flawless. Smart dress. ✆ *6559 9200*

4 Champa, Mui Ne Beach, Vietnam
Set beside a swimming pool and surrounded by tropical gardens, Champa produces dishes in classic French style. ✆ *062 384 7111*

5 The Dining Room, Tasik Perdana, Malaysia
An unrivalled colonial elegance is backed up by French cuisine, à la carte or as a tasting menu. ✆ *03 2295 0888*

6 The Spice Route, Delhi, India
This gorgeous venue is designed to reflect the art, culture and cuisine along the Spice Route. ✆ *2334 1234*

7 Trishna Bar and Restaurant, Mumbai, India
The decor is a bit dull, the service a bit slow, but the food at one of Mumbai's great seafood restaurants more than makes up for it. ✆ *022 2270 3213*

8 Kisso, Tokyo, Japan
This is the place to sample *kaiseki*, Japan's *haute cuisine* – expensive, but a sublime experience. ✆ *3582 4191*

9 Gado Gado, Seminyak/ Kerobokan, Bali
This lovely upmarket restaurant offers seriously fine dining, with many seafood choices, in a romantic location overlooking the ocean. ✆ *0361 730 955*

10 Silk, Phuket, Thailand
Silk serves local dishes such as white snapper with ginger, celery and pickled plums, as well as *khao soi* (Thai curry with noodles). ✆ *07633 8777*

TOP 10 Restaurants: Cheap and Cheerful

1 Bopha Angkor Restaurant, Siem Reap, Cambodia
Overlooking the river, this traditional Cambodian restaurant serves curries and fragrant teas. ✆ *063 964 928*

2 Old Station, Shanghai, China
Well-executed Shanghai classics are served in the high-ceilinged halls of a former French monastery and disused railway carriages. ✆ *021 6427 2233*

3 Sinario Café, Kota Kinabalu, Malaysia
A simple but spotlessly clean café, Sinario turns out delicious northern Indian and Malay food. ✆ *088 246 286*

4 Namiki Yabu Soba, Tokyo, Japan
This ever-popular *soba* (buckwheat noodle) shop is located near Senso-ji temple. ✆ *3841 1340*

5 Sabar Menanti Restaurant, Singapore
Here you can try meats, seafood and vegetables stewed in spices. Try the rice dish *nasi padang*. ✆ *6396 6919*

6 Saravana Bhavan, Delhi, India
This is an institution when it comes to authentic South Indian food. Try the mini-tiffin. ✆ *2331 6060*

7 Rendezvous Restaurant, Singapore
The 60-year history of this place is evident in its old-world decor. Cuisine is authentic *nasi padang*. ✆ *6339 7508*

8 Papaya, Ko Phi Phi, Thailand
Run by a former *muay thai* boxer, the popular Papaya serves Thai curries, spicy papaya salad and *pad thai*.

9 Tim Ho Wan, Hong Kong, China
Crowds queue up for the Michelin-star rated lotus-leaf rice packets and *cha siu* pastries. ✆ *2332 2896*

10 May Kaidee, Bangkok, Thailand
This restaurant serves some delicious and cheap vegetarian dishes. It has been so successful that it has now opened its own cookery school. ✆ *www.maykaidee.com*

TOP 10 Restaurants: Regional Cuisine

1 Moon The Night, Greater Vientiane, Laos
In a stilted house by the Mekong river, the restaurant serves great Lao food such as sour fish soup. ✆ *021 217 073*

2 Kra Jok See, Phuket, Thailand
Tucked into a small 18th-century Sino-Portuguese shop house, this charming restaurant serves delicious traditional Thai cuisine. ✆ *07621 7903*

3 Karim's, Delhi, India
This Delhi institution has been doling out delicious Mughlai food for over half a century. ✆ *2326 9880*

4 Celadon, Bangkok, Thailand
This award-winning restaurant serves sublime Thai food, and the surrounding lotus pond provides the perfect backdrop. ✆ *02 344 8888*

5 Beijing Roast Duck Restaurant, Beijing, China
There's no finer Beijing duck than that served here – full-flavoured and with just the right balance between tender meat and crispy skin. ✆ *010 5169 0329*

6 Batan Waru, Ubud, Bali
This colonial-style hangout offers a fine selection of authentic Indonesian dishes. ✆ *0361 977 528*

7 Kampung, Genting Highlands, Malaysia
Located in Malaysia's most expensive hill station, this enduringly popular Malay restaurant is famous for its reasonably priced buffet. ✆ *03 2718 1118*

8 Sushi Ouchi, Tokyo, Japan
At this sushi haven, Hisashi Ouchi uses only natural ingredients – even the green tea is organic. ✆ *3407 3543*

9 Pho 24, District 1, Ho Chi Minh City, Vietnam
Vietnam's street food has been taken indoors, cleaned up and served in air-conditioned comfort. ✆ *08 3822 6278*

10 Kampot Ta Ouv, Kampot, Cambodia
This Khmer restaurant is by the river, with tables right next to the water, catching the breeze. Famed for sea-food, particularly crab. ✆ *033 932 422*

TOP 10 Restaurants: Food with a View

1 Joe's Downstairs, Phuket, Thailand
With views of Kalim Bay, this popular spot for sunset cocktails serves Maine lobster and Japanese beef. ✆ *07661 8245*

2 Saigon Restaurant, Phu Quoc Island, Vietnam
On a low hill overlooking the sea, the restaurant cooks up Vietnamese dishes, as well as sushi. ✆ *077 384 6999*

3 Uncle Lim's, Pulau Pangkor, Malaysia
On an outcrop overlooking the Strait of Malacca, Uncle Lim's serves the cuisine of China's Fuzhou province. The seafood is particularly good. ✆ *05 699 1100*

4 Ma Joly, Tuban, Bali
An enchanting beachfront restaurant, Ma Joly serves classy French cuisine and fine wines. ✆ *0361 753 780*

5 Duyong Restaurant, Cherating, Malaysia
At the eastern end of Cherating Beach, Duyong specializes in seafood cooked in spicy central Thai style.

6 Dive Inn, Koh Kong, Cambodia
This bar-restaurant on Koh Kong's riverfront serves a mix of international and Khmer cuisine. ✆ *099 707 434*

7 Sirocco, Bangkok, Thailand
On the rooftop of a skyscraper, Sirocco has stunning city views and serves good international cuisine. ✆ *02 624 9555*

8 The Pearl of The Orient, Mumbai, India
This revolving restaurant offers superb views of the Arabian Sea; the food is a mix of Thai, Chinese and Japanese cuisines. ✆ *022 2204 1131*

9 Jade on 36, Shanghai, China
High on the Shangri-La's tower, Jade on 36 offers a stimulating menu of classic French cuisine with a contemporary twist. ✆ 021 6882 3636

10 The Cliff, Sentosa, Singapore
Occupying a fantastic clifftop location, this restaurant offers fantastic grilled seafood platters along with views of the South China Sea. ✆ *6275 0331*

TOP 10 WORLD

THE REST OF THE WORLD

Egypt
Tomb of Senneferi, Shaykh Abd al-Qurnah necropolis, Thebes

Auckland

To get your bearings in this booming city towards the northern end of New Zealand's North Island, you need to head upwards. Panoramic views of the city, Waitemata Harbour, Hauraki Gulf and its islands can be enjoyed from the observation decks and restaurants of the Sky Tower, Auckland's most distinctive landmark. Most of the inner-city attractions are clustered near the waterfront, a hive of activity day and night. Further inland, the Domain is the city's oldest park, set in an extinct volcano crater. Beyond the city limits there are plenty of things to see and do, including wineries, surfing beaches and Maori sites, and no visit to Auckland is complete without a trip to one of the Gulf Islands.

1 Waterfront

Excellent shops, historic buildings, top restaurants and bars, a superb view – Auckland's waterfront *(left)* has it all. The Maritime Museum runs harbour trips on historic vessels, and at the Ferry Building you can dine and watch the boats go by.

2 Waitemata Harbour

This sparkling harbour, with the green volcanic cone of Rangitoto Island in the background, is one of the city's most cherished sights.

3 Sky Tower

Opened in 1997, this 328-m (1,076-ft) tourist, broadcasting and telecommunications facility receives over a million visitors a year. Its four observation levels offer 80-km (50-mile) views *(above)*.

Top 10 Moments in History

1 Maori Settlers
The Auckland isthmus was settled by Polynesians around 1350. Thanks to the fertility of the land and the proximity of two harbours, it is thought the population grew to 20,000.

2 British Claim New Zealand
Captain James Cook sighted the coast of New Zealand in 1769, and claimed the country for Britain. Europeans trickled rather than flooded into New Zealand, working as whalers, sealers and timber traders.

3 Musket Wars
After firearms were introduced by Europeans, a series of devastating battles, fought between Maori tribes in the 1820s, led to massive depopulation in the Auckland area.

4 The Treaty of Waitangi
Maori chief Te Kawauin signed over the region to the British in 1840. In return, the Maori were granted all the rights and privileges of British subjects. In 1841 Auckland was declared the capital of New Zealand.

5 Early Development
The first settlers came from New South Wales, and the first immigrant ships from Great Britain arrived in 1842. Port Nicholson (Wellington today) replaced Auckland as capital in 1865.

6 New Zealand Wars
Tensions with Maori tribes over land rights led to wars during the 1860s. Ultimately, land was confiscated from the Maori, and the last British troops were withdrawn in 1870.

7 Economic Boom
A gold rush in the Coromandel region and increased agricultural production in the late 19th century fuelled an economic boom. By 1900 Auckland was the largest city in New Zealand.

8 The Expanding City
Auckland expanded rapidly with the construction of tram and railway lines, and the introduction of new ferry services. In 1907 New Zealand became a self-governing Dominion.

9 20th-Century Auckland
Auckland suffered in the worldwide Depression of the 1930s, but continued its expansion from the 1950s, when the Auckland Harbour Bridge was constructed. In 1986 New Zealand became fully independent from the United Kingdom.

10 Auckland Today
Almost a third of New Zealand's population lives in Auckland, which regularly features in lists of the most liveable cities in the world.

6 **Piha Beach**
Little known by tourists but popular [w]ith locals, the wild, rugged, windswept [T]asman Sea beaches of Auckland's west [c]oast are well worth visiting. Piha *(above)* [is] one of the finest, and much prized for [it]s heavy surf.

7 **Devonport**
A 10-minute boat ride from the Ferry Building brings you to this quiet, Victorian suburb, steeped in naval history and still a New Zealand Royal Navy base today. There are fine views from here back to the Auckland skyline.

War Memorial Museum 8
In the tranquil surroundings of the Auckland Domain, this museum and its Cenotaph *(right)* were built to commemorate the end of World War I. As well as displays about the two World Wars there is a superb gallery of Maori artifacts and two Discovery Centres for children.

9 **Auckland Domain and Winter Gardens**
Traces of the volcano that once was here can still be seen in this leafy park. The glasshouses of the Winter Gardens are a striking feature of the Domain, as is a Maori memorial palisade.

10 **Auckland Wineries**
Several vine-growing regions *(left)* lie just outside the city, notably Henderson, Kumeu River and Matua Valley. Tours and tastings are usually on offer, and vineyard restaurants are often very good. Weekend winery safaris are popular with locals and visitors alike.

4 **One Tree Hill**
"Maungakiekie" in the Maori language, this is a dormant volcanic cone *(above)*, once the site of the largest prehistoric Maori settlement in the region.

5 **Hauraki Gulf Islands**
This cluster of 65 islands, of which Rangitoto is the most visible from the mainland, are among the most beautiful in the world. Some are wildlife sanctuaries, others home to commuter or "alternative" communities, and others ideal for weekend leisure activities.

TOP 10 Maori Culture

1 The Haka
Probably the most famous element of Maori culture worldwide, thanks to the All Blacks rugby team, this is a traditional war dance performed by men. Eyes and tongues protrude in a gesture of defiance.

2 *Moko* (Tattoos)
The *moko* involves incising deep patterns, often spirals, into the skin and colouring them with pigment. The tradition has been revived today and some Maori proudly wear *moko*.

3 Song and Dance
Oratory chant, song and dance are the means of passing on ancestral knowledge, and form an essential part of Maori life, key to the rituals of challenge, welcome and farewell.

4 Costume
Cloaks and capes, made of pelts, feathers or flax, are a feature of Maori dress. Skirts are made of flax too, the leaves scraped and dried to form tubes, strips of which hang from a belt.

5 Plaiting and Weaving
Maori women create beautifully patterned and useful household items, such as baskets, rugs and wall hangings, from flax, feathers and reeds.

6 Carving
Wood, bone, stones and shells are all carved into ornaments, jewellery and ceremonial objects such as Tiki pendants.

7 Art
Modern Maori artists are increasingly incorporating traditional techniques and subjects into their work.

8 *Waka* (Canoes)
The Poynesian settlers were skilled boat-builders and navigators. Maori canoes have forward-thrusting prows, carved in intricate patterns, to improve the vessel's performance.

9 *Mau Rakau* (Martial Art)
The traditional weapon is the *taiaha*, a wooden or whalebone staff the height of a person. There has been a revival of the skilled art of its use, known as *Mau Rakau*.

10 Meeting Houses
The buildings are symbolic of a male ancestor – a mask on the gable end represents his head; the wide, sloping bargeboards his open arms.

Cairo

Modern Cairo was founded on the east bank of the River Nile in AD 969, but Egypt boasts a history stretching back to Pharaonic times, as evidenced by the iconic Pyramids of Giza and the Sphinx, which watch over its western outskirts. Often dubbed "the city that never sleeps", Cairo is Africa's largest metropolitan area. Attractions include the mind-boggling riches of the Egyptian Museum, the historic Coptic and Arabic quarters, the Cairo Opera House and the football stadium.

3 Cairo Tower

For the best city views visit this 1962 tower *(left)* on the island of Gezira, where a lift takes you 185 m (610 ft) up to a viewing platform. The best time to go is sunset, when millions of lights twinkle into life and the evening call to prayer sounds out from a thousand or more mosques below.

1 Cairo Opera House Complex

In 1988 Cairo got its new opera house *(above, left)*, a stunning, modernist update on Islamic architecture, designed and funded by the Japanese. It sits in beautifully landscaped grounds, which also house the impressive Museum of Modern Egyptian Art.

2 Egyptian Museum

This is one of the world's greatest museums, not least for the treasures in the Tutankhamun galleries *(right)*, but also for the exhibits from every period of ancient Egyptian history.

4 Mosque of Al-Azhar

Egypt has an unrivalled wealth of historic Islamic architecture stretching back to the 7th century. The Mosque of Al-Azhar *(above)* in Cairo is one of the jewels of this heritage.

Top 10 Moments in Post-Pharaonic History

1 AD 323: Christian Era
After the defeat of Cleopatra in 30 BC Egypt became a province of Rome. Following the conversion of Emperor Constantine, Christianity became the official religion in Egypt, where its followers were known as Copts.

2 640: Arrival of Islam
The armies of Islam entered Egypt and marched on the fortress of Babylon-in-Egypt near Memphis in 640. Beside it, the Arabs founded the city of Fustat, forerunner of Cairo.

3 969: The Fatimids
Egypt was seized by the Fatimids from Tunisia. They built a new walled city called Al-Qahira ("The Victorious"), a name later corrupted by Europeans to "Cairo".

4 1250: The Mamluks
Originally slaves brought from the Caucasus to Egypt, the Mamluks accumulated enough power to seize Egypt in 1250. Fearsome warriors known for great horsemanship, they extended their rule as far north as Turkey.

5 1516: The Ottomans
Ottoman Turks challenged Mamluk power, scoring a decisive victory in 1516. The following year they entered Cairo to take control of Egypt.

6 1798: Napoleon's Invasion
An army led by Napoleon Bonaparte invaded Egypt and scored a victory in the Battle of the Pyramids. It was short-lived, as his fleet was then destroyed in the Battle of the Nile by a British Navy led by Admiral Nelson.

7 1805: Mohammed Ali
Mohammed Ali, an Albanian mercenary, defeated forces of Ottomans and Mamluks to seize control of Egypt in 1805. He promoted industrialization and reform.

8 1882: The British in Egypt
Building railways and the Suez Canal resulted in huge national debt. In 1882 army officers staged a revolt, which was quashed by the British, who subsequently occupied the country.

9 1952: Revolution
In January 1952, on "Black Saturday", European businesses in Cairo were torched by rampaging mobs. On 23 July a group called the Free Officers, led by Gamal Abdel Nasser, seized power in a bloodless coup.

10 1979: Peace with Israel
Battles between Egypt and Israel in 1948, 1967 and 1973 eventually led to peace talks that culminated in the signing of the Camp David peace treaty in 1979.

5 Khan al-Khalili

The covered passageways, stone gates and labyrinthine alleys of Cairo's chaotic and vibrant bazaar area *(left)* still have a wholly medieval feel. Brightly coloured cloth, spices, perfumes, and gold and silver jewellery are traded.

6 Zamalek

The island in the middle of the Nile is known as Gezira, and its northern half is the smart neighbourhood of Zamalek. In its back streets are countless small fashion boutiques, bookshops and galleries.

7 Mosque of Sultan Hassan

After Al-Azhar, the other essential mosque to visit is that of Sultan Hassan *(above)*. Begun in 1356, its size rivals the great cathedrals of Europe. It is entered through a soaring portal with a stalactite hood, which leads to a simple but impressive courtyard with four massive arched recesses.

8 The Pyramids of Giza

The only survivor of the Seven Wonders of the Ancient World, the Great Pyramid and its two companions *(above)* are no less wondrous now than they were when they were built four and a half millennia ago.

9 Al-Azhar Park

This beautiful park *(above)* opened to great acclaim in 2004. It has a tall, grassy hill at one end which slopes down to an artificial lake at the other. It is landscaped in classical Islamic fashion, but also has an amphitheatre, children's play area, a fine restaurant and cafés.

10 Manial Palace

The other island in the Nile is Rhoda, home to the Manial Palace *(above)*, built 1899 –1929. Five pavilions are decorated in various Islamic styles: Moorish, Ottoman, Persian and Syrian.

Top 10 Islamic Monuments

1 Madrassa – Sultan Qalaoun's Mausoleum
Built in just 13 months in 1284–5, this grand complex marries scale with fantastic detailing, particularly in the mausoleum itself.

2 Mosque of al-Nasir Mohammed
This mosque, built during the reign of Al-Nasir Mohammed (1293–1340), a son of Qalaoun, is noteworthy for its minaret, which has fabulously intricate, lace-like decoration.

3 Madrassa of Sultan Barquq
This grand religious school was completed in 1386. It is possible to go up to the roof and ascend the minaret.

4 Sabil-Kuttab of Abdel Rahman Katkhuda
This graceful Ottoman structure was a charitable institution funded by a nobleman. The *sabil* (public fountain) was on the ground floor, the *kuttab* (primary school) upstairs.

5 Mosque of Al-Aqmar
This pretty mosque dates back to 1125. It supposedly gets its name ("the moonlit") from the way its masonry shon in the moonlight.

6 Beit al-Sihaymi
Visit this house to see how a wealthy 18th-century merchant would have lived. It is also the venue for free weekly concerts of Arabic music on Sunday evenings.

7 Mosque of Al-Hakim
The Fatimid caliph Al-Hakim bi-Amr Allah (996–1021) was infamous for his strange laws and random acts of violence. His mosque is noted for its curious pepper-pot minarets.

8 Northern Walls
The northern walls date from 1087 and are the most complete part of the fortifications that once encircled Al-Qahira. They include two gates from which the ramparts can be accessed.

9 Mosque, Madrassa and Mausoleum of Al-Ghouri
The striped twin buildings of this complex were built in 1505 by the last Mamluk sultan, Al-Ghouri.

10 Bab Zuweyla
This is one of the original gates of the city of Al-Qahira. Its two minarets were added later – they can be ascended for marvellous views over Islamic Cairo.

Cape Town and the Cape Peninsula

BOTSWANA
NAMIBIA
Pretoria
Johannesburg
Bloemfontein
LESOTHO
Durban
Atlantic Ocean
SOUTH AFRICA
Indian Ocean
East London
CAPE TOWN
Port Elizabeth

Modern visitors would agree with Sir Francis Drake's testament to South Africa's Cape region: "the fairest Cape in the whole circumference of the earth". Sandwiched between the imperious heights of Table Mountain and the blue depths of the Atlantic, Cape Town has a sensational setting. With its Mediterranean climate, the city and its environs offer hiking opportunities along the spine of the Cape Peninsula, local wildlife to glimpse, lush vineyards to explore and pristine beaches on which to relax. For visitors inclined towards cultural pursuits, Cape Town has a vibrant Afro-fusion cultural scene, a rich sense of history and eye-catching colonial architecture.

1 Kirstenbosch National Botanical Garden

At its best during the spring wild-flower season, this garden *(left)* protects the floral wealth of the Western Cape and is a year-round visitor attraction.

2 Groot Constantia Wine Estate

South Africa's oldest estate, Groot Constantia *(above)* is noted for its old-world Cape Dutch architecture that lies nestled amongst the leafy vineyards.

3 Simon's Town and Boulders Beach

All quaint Victorian façades overlooking the splendid False Bay, this sleepy naval town is famed for the comical penguins *(left)* that waddle around on nearby Boulders Beach.

TOP 10 Moments in History

1 Prehistory
The earliest signs of human habitation along Table Bay are of the Acheulean culture and date back 1.4 million years. San hunter-gatherers arrived around 30,000 years ago and left a legacy of rock art sites.

2 The Portuguese Arrive
In 1488 Portuguese navigator Bartolomeu Dias became the first European to round the Cape. This led to a succession of clashes with the Khoikhoi that culminated in Captain d'Almeida's death in Table Bay in 1510.

3 Cape Town Founded
In 1652 the Dutch East India Company (VOC) founded a station in Table Bay to provide fresh produce to their ships. Within a century, Cape Town was home to settlers from Europe.

4 British Occupation and the Great Trek
British governance of the Cape led to the emancipation of slaves in 1834. This so angered slave-owning Boers that over 12,000 moved north in the Great Trek of 1836–43 to found Boer Republics.

5 South African War and Unionization
This war of 1899–1902 was initiated by English imperialists eager to gain control of the Johannesburg goldfields. It culminated in the formation of the Union of South Africa in 1910, which comprised the Cape, Natal, Transvaal and the Free State.

6 Apartheid
The National Party (NP) won the 1948 election and passed acts that formalized racial inequities into the apartheid ("separateness") ideology.

7 Sharpeville Massacre
The police massacre of 69 civilians at a peaceful protest in Sharpeville in 1960 led to the formation of the armed wing of the ANC under Nelson Mandela. Along with other leaders, Mandela was convicted of treason in the Rivonia Trial of 1962–3.

8 Foundation of UDF
In 1983 15,000 anti-apartheid activists gathered to form the United Democratic Front (UDF), the domestic representative of the ANC in apartheid's dying years.

9 Release of Nelson Mandela
President FW de Klerk lifted the ban on the ANC in February 1990, and Mandela was released from prison after 27 years.

10 Democracy
In May 1994 the ANC swept to victory in South Africa's first fully democratic elections, after securing eight of the nine provinces; the exception was the Western Cape, the last stronghold of the NP. Mandela was inaugurated as president.

The V&A Waterfront 4
Outdoor cafés, a vibrant nightlife and exciting shopping can be enjoyed at this waterfront complex *(right)*. It is also the eparture point for trips to Robben Island.

5 Table Mountain
The thrilling aerial ascent of Table Mountain leads to a succession of stunning views over the Cape Peninsula *(left)* and the Winelands.

6 The Company's Garden
Overshadowed by majestic Table Mountain, this park *(above)* was established by the first Dutch settlers in 1652 and features an eclectic mix of museums and galleries.

7 Castle of Good Hope
Constructed in the 1670s, South Africa's oldest extant building now houses several museums.

8 Cape of Good Hope
Pink-hued protea flowers, grazing antelope and mischievous baboons can be observed at the peninsula's southern tip, where a clifftop lighthouse *(left)* offers spectacular bird's-eye views over Cape Point.

9 Michaelis Collection
This world-renowned collection of paintings by Dutch and Flemish masters of the Golden Age (16th–18th centuries) is housed in the Old Townhouse, which served as the City Hall until 1905.

District Six Museum 10
This stirring Cape Town museum *(right)* documents the apartheid-era evictions of "non-whites" from the central suburb of District Six to the remote Cape Flats.

TOP 10 Cape Peninsula Sights

1 Cape Floral Kingdom
The smallest of the world's six floral kingdoms, the Cape consists of a unique floral community known as fynbos ("fine bush"), a reference to the narrow leaves of many plants.

2 Rondevlei Nature Reserve
Cape Town's best bird sanctuary is home to 230 marine and freshwater species. Grebes, rails, herons and gulls are well represented, and hippos have been introduced to control surface vegetation.

3 Muizenberg
This resort town on False Bay is where you'll find the battlements of the 1795 Anglo-Dutch Battle of Muizenberg. The wide, sheltered beach is a haven for surfers and swimmers.

4 Fish Hoek
The quaint village of Fish Hoek lies at the mouth of the Silvermine River and boasts one of the warmest and safest swimming beaches on the Peninsula.

5 Imizamo Yethu Township
This small township was established on the outskirts of Hout Bay post-apartheid. Its picturesque setting contrasts with the harsh conditions endured here.

6 Noordhoek Beach
An expanse of bone-white sand running from the base of Chapman's Peak to Kommetjie, Noordhoek is the most beautiful beach on the Cape Peninsula.

7 Chapman's Peak Drive
Excavated into a band of soft shale in the almost-vertical cliff face that connects Hout Bay to Noordhoek, the road runs past parking spots from where you can watch the Atlantic batter the coast.

8 Hout Bay Harbour and Seal Island
Hout Bay's busy little harbour is the launching point for boat trips to Seal Island, which supports up to 75,000 Cape fur seals.

9 The Sentinel
This impressive rock outcrop towers at the mouth of Hout Bay.

10 World of Birds
In a leafy suburb of Hout Bay, the World of Birds houses about 400 species, from indigenous birds, such as bulbuls and parrots, to the scarlet ibis and other exotica.

Namibia
Damaraland,
Kunene Region

History and Culture

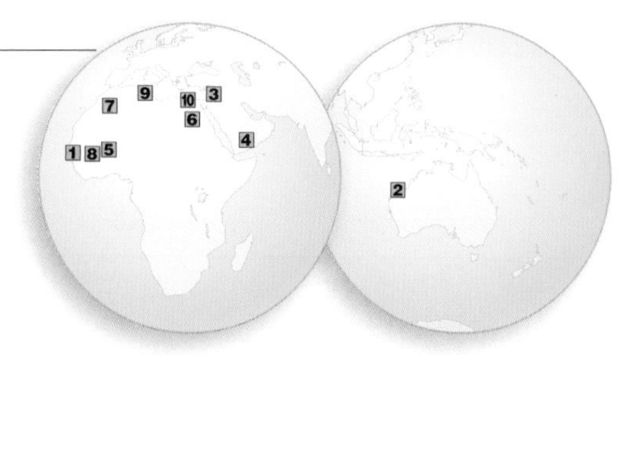

It's clear, from places such as these, that there was never just one "cradle of civilization" – there was a whole nursery-full, scattered across the earliest ancient world. Its charges built, painted, told stories, read and wrote, made instruments and sang. What they have left behind and what still exists, gives us a tantalizing glimpse into our ancestors' early days.

1 Wassu Stone Circles, Janjangbureh *GAMBIA*

At Wassu, ancient stones of similar shape have been arranged in circles, like people getting together for a square dance. This site has 11 such circles, and is one of the largest stone-circle complexes among hundreds spread over 333 km (200 miles) on the Gambia river's north bank. It is said to be the world's greatest concentration of stone circles. Most were made between 1300 BC and AD 750 from a local sandstone, laterite, and the largest weigh up to 10 tons. They formed part of a burial ritual, and superstitions about their powers have kept them from being plundered. A museum explains their mysteries.

2 Murujuga, Pilbara *AUSTRALIA*

The Burrup Peninsula, or Murujuga, in northwestern Australia, is home to what is claimed to be the world's largest array of rock carvings, dating back some 10,000 years or more. According to estimates, there are as many as a million carvings here, with an astonishing range of images including animals (kangaroos, emus, snakes, dogs, turtles and whales) and humans, some depicted carrying objects such as boomerangs and wearing a ceremonial head-dress. The threat of industrial development has become a *cause célèbre* and in 2007 most of the area was added to the National Heritage list. There are ongoing appeals for it to be given UNESCO World Heritage status.

3 Dome of the Rock, Jerusalem *ISRAEL*

This is the earliest Islamic building to have survived in its original form to the present day. Intended as a shrine for pilgrims, it stands near the centre of the Haram al-Sharif ("The Noble Sanctuary"), or Temple Mount, a site of importance to both Muslim and Jewish faiths. Its octagonal form stems from local Christian church architecture, and the interior is decorated with glittering mosaics that reveal Byzantine influence. It has undergone several restorations, notably in the 1540s by Süleyman the Magnificent, who replaced the colourful tiles on the exterior. The central dome was originally covered in pure gold, but this has been replaced by anodized aluminium, coated in gold leaf.

4 Shibam *YEMEN*

Shibam, in the Valley of Hadhramaut, is known as the Manhattan of the Desert for its strangely reminiscent skyline. It has stood here for around 2,000 years, although most of the buildings date from the 16th century. Its narrow streets are lined by six-storey, mud-built houses with finely engraved wooden doors and small, latticed windows. Although it is UNESCO-protected, this is not a museum but a living city, home to around 7,000 people, whose families have been here for generations.

5 Great Mosque of Djenné *MALI*

In the 13th century Djenné was an important centre of Islamic study, and there has been a mosque on this site ever since. The present one was completed only in 1907, replacing the original which fell into disrepair in the 19th century. With a capacity of 3,000, it is the largest adobe building in the world, using local techniques to combat heat and humidity and keep the prayer hall cool. Its *qibla* (prayer wall), is dominated by three minarets.

Hatshepsut's Temple, Deir el-Bahari The mortuary temple of Queen Hatsheps

Ait Benhaddou An ancient walled city, now home to just ten families *(below)*

Great Mosque of Djenné The world's largest adobe building *(above)*

Shibam Yemen's "Manhattan of the Desert" *(below)*

6 Hatshepsut's Temple, Deir el-Bahari *EGYPT*

Called "sublime of sublimes" by the ancient Egyptians, the mortuary temple of Queen Hatshepsut (1479–1458 BC) was the grandest in all of Thebes. The partly rock-hewn building rises theatrically from the valley of Deir el-Bahri in a series of colonnaded terraces, beneath the golden lime-stone curtain of rocks that separates the area from the Valley of the Kings. It contains exquisite decorative reliefs and murals, including scenes portraying the divine birth of the queen.

7 Ait Benhaddou *MOROCCO*

Looking like a page out of a living bible, this beautiful walled collection of ancient fortresses or kasbahs make up the *ksar*, which seems to rise out of the red earth from another era. The town dates from the 16th century and thrived on trade, sited on the caravan route between the Sahara and Marrakech. Today, its earthen houses and decorative crenellated towers are gradually eroding, and it is inhabited by fewer than ten families.

8 National Museum of Mali, Bamako *MALI*

This is one of Africa's finest museums. Among several thousand cultural and art objects, perhaps the most interesting are the vast collections of photographs and musical instruments. Mali is renowned worldwide for its music, and museum field research has produced countless hours of unique and valuable recordings.

9 Roman Amphitheatre, El Djem *TUNISIA*

Rising three storeys high, dominating the town and visible for miles from the surrounding desert, this amphitheatre seems more like a fortress than a place of entertainment – and it has been used as one. The largest amphitheatre outside Italy, it was probably the last to be built, in the late 3rd century AD. Superbly preserved, it shows clearly how the animals, gladiators and actors entered the arena, via passages that slope from outside to the underground galleries. Two lift shafts mark where the stars of the show were carried to their deadly moment of glory.

10 Bibliotheca Alexandrina, Alexandria *EGYPT*

The new Alexandria Library, inaugurated in 2003, has set itself a challenging task: to live up to the example set by its predecessor, the Ancient Library of Alexandria. The building itself, near the site of the original, is breathtaking – a giant glass disc, tilted towards the sea. Outside, carved into its shield-like, curved granite walls, are letters in more than a hundred scripts, to encourage understanding between all cultures and all nations. Inside, over 11 cascading levels, there is enough shelf space to stack eight million tomes.

Dubai and Abu Dhabi

The Arabian emirates of Dubai and Abu Dhabi, the richest and most powerful of the seven city-states that make up the United Arab Emirates, offer the best of East and West – Arab culture, Bedouin heritage and Islamic architecture, alongside excellent shopping, sophisticated dining and luxurious hotels. Dubai is divided by its bustling Creek and skirted with white sand beaches, while Abu Dhabi is situated on a splendid corniche.

1 Dubai Creek
Criss-crossed by *abras* (water taxis) and *dhows* (old wooden boats) each day, this waterway *(left)* is Dubai's lifeblood.

Bastakiya 2
The gypsum and coral courtyard houses in this quarter *(right)* were constructed by Persian merchants who settled here in the last century.

3 Burj Al Arab
This iconic, attention-grabbing hotel *(above)* is certainly a sight you cannot miss. It's the world's tallest, all-suite hotel building.

TOP 10 Cultural Traditions

1 Bedouin Society
The semi-nomadic Bedu tribes spent the harsh summers inland at the cool date-palm oases and their winters fishing by the sea.

2 The Camel
Mainstay of the Bedouin's nomadic life, the camel enabled tribes to move their possessions from coastal villages to inland oases. Camel's milk quenched thirsts and the fur was used to make tents, textiles, rugs, bags and cloaks.

3 The Arabian Horse
Beloved by the Bedouin for its elegance and valued for its strength and sturdiness, the Arabian horse is one of the world's oldest and purest of breeds due to the Bedouin's careful inbreeding, practised for centuries.

4 Falconry
Falcons were used by the Bedu to capture small birds and hares. Today, Emirati men still train their falcons daily. Some desert resorts and safaris display falconry.

5 The Date Palm
Dates were essential for desert survival. They were used to create *tamr*, a preserve, which helped sustain the Bedu over long journeys. There are over 50 date varieties in the UAE.

6 Fishing and the Dhow
Historically, fishing, dhow building and pearl diving were the main occupations along coastal settlements. Today, Emiratis still use the old wooden dhow boats for fishing, trading and tours.

7 Poetry, Dance & Song
Emirati poetry takes many forms, from the romantic *baiti* style to the vernacular *nabati* poetry. Songs and group dances such as the *ayyalah* and *liwa* celebrate bravery in war and at sea.

8 Rifle-Throwing
The Bedu were greatly respected for their ability to handle weapons. These days, young Emirati men imitate the Bedu by throwing their rifles high in the air while dancing and clapping.

9 Traditional Dress
Women wear a black cloak-like *abaya* and *shayla* to cover their hair. Men wear a white *dishdasha* and a white or checked *gutra* (head scarf), held in place by a black *agal*.

10 Henna
Intricate henna patterns were painted on pottery across the Middle East in Neolithic times, around 9000 BC. Today, Emirati women have henna designs painted on their hands and feet for weddings and other celebrations.

4 Madinat Jumeirah (Dubai)

Shop for handicrafts, dine at a waterfront restaurant *(left)*, see theatre or sip a cocktail as you enjoy the sunset at this Arabian-themed souk, entertainment and hotel complex.

5 Dubai Museum

Set in a well-preserved fort, the Dubai museum, with its whimsical dioramas and fascinating displays, provides a comprehensive introduction to the city.

6 Jumeirah Mosque

This is Dubai's most beautiful mosque *(above)*, and it is also the only one open to non-Muslims. A guided visit to learn about Islam and culture is a must.

7 Desert Escapes

A visit to the UAE is ncomplete without a desert experience *(above)*. Stay at enchanting desert resorts Al Maha or Bab Al Shams, or take a fun desert safari.

8 Emirates Palace

The jaw-dropping display of gold lining the walls and Swarovski crystals dripping from the chandeliers at Abu Dhabi's Emirates Palace hotel *(right)* make for an impressive sight.

9 Dubai Souks

Bargain for gold, perfume, spices and textiles, or simply take in the heady atmosphere of Dubai's souks *(left)*.

10 Abu Dhabi Authority for Culture and Heritage

Enjoy the tranquil palm-shaded gardens of Abu Dhabi's elegant white fort palace before taking in the handicraft displays and art shows on Emirati culture at the Authority for Culture and Heritage.

Top 10 Excursions

1 Sharjah
The Sharjah Art Museum, the Heritage Museum and the Archaeological Museum are must-sees. The souks are good for shopping.

2 Al Ain
Known as Garden City, this green emirate is home to the Al Ain Palace Museum. Also here are the Al Ain Livestock Souk and the late 19th-century Jahili Fort.

3 Hatta
Visit the Heritage Village at this serene oasis town. A drive into the Hajar Mountains leads to the clear Hatta Rock Pools, tucked into narrow rocky corridors.

4 Fujairah
Fujairah has a coastline of coral reefs and hillsides with forts and watchtowers. The Fujairah Fort is the oldest in the UAE, dating to 1670. Watch a bit of bloodless bull butting on a Friday here.

5 Khor Kalba
This small fishing village has the oldest mangrove in Arabia and is now a conservation area. Explore its swamps by canoe.

6 Bidiya
This tiny fishing village is home to the oldest mosque in the UAE. Dating to 1446, it is made from mud brick, stone and gypsum.

7 Khor Fakkan
A pretty coastal town that sits on a curving bay, this makes a good draw for divers, thanks to excellent visibility and reef potential.

8 Dibba
A sleepy spot with an open beach. Nearby is Sandy Beach, with one of the best dive centres in the area and close to an ocean outcrop called Snoopy Island – ideal for snorkelling and diving.

9 Musandam Peninsula
This northerly enclave is part of Oman and boasts spectacular mountain cliffs and a coastline of inlets and fjords. Visit to enjoy day-long dhow trips into the fjords.

10 Liwa
Liwa's high golden dunes are almost entirely devoid of vegetation, yet close by are flourishing date-producing farms – a strange and awesome spectacle.

Natural Wonders

Nature is always at its most wonderful when it is far from the things of man, and there are still plenty of places around the world to fit that description. The results are untouched landscapes, creatures unique to one habitat alone and, of course, idyllics spots where the traveller off the beaten track can find his or her own personal paradise.

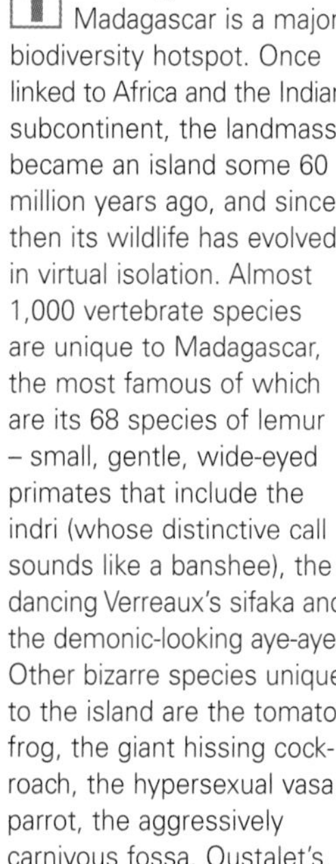

1 Madagascar

Madagascar is a major biodiversity hotspot. Once linked to Africa and the Indian subcontinent, the landmass became an island some 60 million years ago, and since then its wildlife has evolved in virtual isolation. Almost 1,000 vertebrate species are unique to Madagascar, the most famous of which are its 68 species of lemur – small, gentle, wide-eyed primates that include the indri (whose distinctive call sounds like a banshee), the dancing Verreaux's sifaka and the demonic-looking aye-aye. Other bizarre species unique to the island are the tomato frog, the giant hissing cockroach, the hypersexual vasa parrot, the aggressively carnivous fossa, Oustalet's chameleon, the giraffe-necked weevil and the astonishingly camouflaged leaf-tailed gecko.

2 Blue Mountains, New South Wales

AUSTRALIA

Australia's Blue Mountains range, set in arguably the continent's most beautiful region, defies classification. Comprising seven national parks and a UNESCO World Heritage Site, this remarkable area is a mix of everything Australia has to offer. The mountain ranges, referred to as Upper and Lower, are home to Australia's only temperate rainforest and a wealth of flora, including dozens of species found nowhere else on the continent. With many walking trails and out-of-the-way reserves begging to be explored, there is something for everyone, served up against the backdrop of the Blue Mountains.

3 Antarctic Peninsula

ANTARCTICA

A setting of incomparable beauty, Antarctica is an unforgettable destination and one of the few untouched places in the world. Days here will be spent cruising deep-blue waters known for their breaching whales and icebergs the size of ships. The region has fascinating wildlife. Penguins are found in their thousands, along with whales, seals and a large number of birds.

4 Karoo National Park *SOUTH AFRICA*

Where should one go in South Africa to see as much of its famed flora and fauna as possible, up close and personal? Head to Karoo National Park – which has it all, and in abundance. The park is set within the wild and unforgiving area known as the Great Karoo, the country's largest – and most diverse – ecosystem. Much of the park's wildlife is specially adapted to this harsh environment and, thanks to conservation programmes, many species of endangered game have come back to call it home. You can see these from the relative comfort and safety of your 4WD.

5 Aitutaki

COOK ISLANDS

At one corner of a triangular lagoon in the South Pacific sits Aitutaki, the most idyllic of the Cook Islands. The lagoon is dotted with 14 *motu* – small volcanic and coral islets – which offer some great snorkelling and diving opportunities. There's plenty to do away from the beaches, too. Attempt the spectacular climb up Munga Poo, Aitutaki's highest point, enjoying the renowned local hula dancing and local grilled fish at villages along the way. There is affordable accommodation next to pristine beaches on the island, and a boat tour of the lagoon is a must.

Madagascar The demonic-looking aye-aye, one of 68 species of lemur unique to the

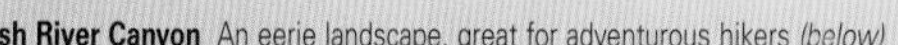

Fish River Canyon An eerie landscape, great for adventurous hikers *(below)*

Antarctic Peninsula Gentoo penguins *(above)*

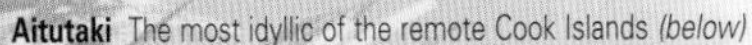

Aitutaki The most idyllic of the remote Cook Islands *(below)*

6 Fish River Canyon

NAMIBIA

This magnificent canyon, one of the largest in the world, was created by the wear and tear of the river and the collapse of the valley bottom through a shift in the earth's crust. The best way to get to know it is on a hiking trail, but you must come prepared, as there are no facilities. In winter (May–September) the river is less torrential than in the summer months.

7 Waitomo Caves, North Island

NEW ZEALAND

Three hours' drive from Auckland are the labyrinthine limestone caves of Waitomo, which drip with the silken, sticky threads of fungus gnat larvae, otherwise known as glow-worms. Each worm hangs up to 70 long, glowing threads from its ceiling nest to attract and trap insects. It's a magical display – like the Milky Way in microcosm. Tours include rides on rubber rafts through underground waterways, black-water raft trips and cave abseiling.

8 Anse Source D'Argent, La Digue

SEYCHELLES

Perhaps the world's most photographed beach, this is the stuff of tropical-island fantasy. A series of small, crescent-shaped, pink-sand beaches are separated by huge, smooth granite boulders worn into weird and wonderful shapes by the waves and the wind. The water is turquoise and shallow and protected by an offshore reef.

9 East Coast of Zanzibar

TANZANIA

The east coast of Zanzibar isn't the place to go for bland, international beach-resort luxury. Although its sandy palm-lined beaches are as idyllic as they come, the east coast offers visitors much more. The seafront is studded with traditional Swahili villages, including Bwejuu, Paje and Jambiani, each one smaller and more rustically somnambulant than the one before, making it a great place to experience rural Africa on its own terms. Accommodation tends to be low rise, low key, low impact and low cost – it's the ideal place to relax after a safari. Look out for the endangered Kirk's red colobus, a fringed monkey endemic to Zanzibar.

10 Mount Augustus, Gascoyne

AUSTRALIA

This spectacular solitary peak, which is known as Burringurrah by the local Aboriginal people, stands above an arid plain of shrub-land dotted with emu bushes, river gums and wattles. Red kangaroos, emus, snakes and small rodents are common in the area. Surrounding the rock are trails and dirt roads that lead to Aboriginal rock engravings, pools and caves, and there is a 12-km (8-mile) round-trip summit trail for fit hikers. The visible part of this sandstone mountain, which stands upon a subterranean granite base, might look like Uluru, but it's more than twice as large as its more famous rival, with a summit ridge of 8 km (5 miles).

Israel

This tiny slice of land is holy to the world's three great monotheistic religions, with a corresponding wealth of history, monuments, ruins and places of worship to discover. Israel also offers extraordinary natural beauty and amazing contrasts, from the forested slopes of the Galilee region to Mediterranean white-sand beaches and the harsh desertscapes of the Negev. Although politics here has long been, and is likely to remain, contentious, travel throughout Israel is remarkably safe and secure, and so pilgrims and travellers continue to visit the Holy Land as they have since antiquity.

1 Church of the Holy Sepulchre
The holiest church in the world *(above)* is built over the site where tradition says Jesus was crucified. Amid the charged and frenzied atmosphere, it is possible to touch the rock of Golgotha and to enter Christ's tomb.

Haram esh-Sharif 2
This huge platform, known as the Haram esh-Sharif ('Noble Sanctuary') or the Temple Mount, is topped by the gold-leaf Dome of the Rock *(right)* – the quintessential image of Jerusalem.

TOP 10 Moments in History

1 c. 1800 BC: Arrival of the Hebrew Tribes
Abraham led early Hebrews to the coastal plain where the Canaanite civilization had been established, so beginning the history of the Jewish people.

2 587 BC: Babylonian Exile
The Babylonians captured Jerusalem. Solomon's Temple was destroyed and the Ark of the Covenant lost forever. The Judean Jews were forced into exile.

3 AD 70: Destruction of the Second Temple
The temple begun by Herod the Great in 22 BC was a remodelling of Solomon's. It was destroyed when Jerusalem was burned by the Romans suppressing a Jewish revolt.

4 638: Islam Arrives
After Prophet Muhammad's death, his successor Caliph Omar became ruler of Palestine. Islam became the dominant religion in the region for the next 1,300 years.

5 1099: Crusaders Capture Jerusalem
The Crusaders took four years and a 100,000-man army to create a Christian-dominated Kingdom of Jerusalem. Saladin retook the city in 1187, however, and the Crusaders were eventually ousted from the Holy Land in 1291.

6 1516: Ottomans Defeat the Mamelukes
The Ottoman victory was the start of a 400-year rule, when Suleyman the Magnificent rebuilt the Old City walls.

7 1922: The Balfour Declaration
British troops took Jerusalem in 1917. The same year British Foreign Secretary Balfour declared that the government "favourably views the creation of a national Jewish home in Palestine".

8 1948: Declaration of the State of Israel
The UN voted to partition the Holy Land and the British pulled out in 1948, just as Ben-Gurion declared the birth of the State of Israel.

9 1967: Six-Day War
The Six-Day War saw the Israelis launch a preemptive strike and capture the Golan Heights, the Sinai, the Gaza Strip and the whole of Jerusalem. The Sinai was returned to Egypt in 1982.

10 1994: Limited Palestinian Autonomy
The Oslo Accords (1993) allowed the Palestinian Authority to govern West Bank towns. In 1994 Jordan and Israel signed a peace treaty that has since stalled.

4 Jaffa

The fortunes of this ancient port have waxed and waned through the ages, but now Old Jaffa boasts a wealth of renovated Ottoman architecture and bursts with art galleries, cultural activities, atmospheric restaurants and diverse shopping options.

3 Citadel (Tower of David)

This Jerusalem landmark greets visitors who enter the Old City through Jaffa Gate. A fortification *(above)* has stood in this place for more than 20 centuries, rebuilt and destroyed by invaders from the Crusaders to the Ottomans.

5 Bethlehem

As the place where Jesus was born, Bethlehem *(above)* has been a major pilgrimage centre since the 4th century. Yet the town retains an authentic air in its central square and the surrounding market streets, and this is equally true of its neighbouring villages.

6 Mount of Olives

Although no longer covered with olive trees, this hill, east of the Old City, presents one of Jerusalem's most beautiful aspects. Adorned with churches, tombs and towers *(right)*, the Mount of Olives holds a crucial place in Jewish and Christian tradition.

7 Israel Museum

The newly renovated Israel Museum houses an encyclopedic collection of archaeology, art and Jewish artifacts, plus the iconic Shrine of the Book displaying the Dead Sea Scrolls. It requires a full day to do the museum justice.

8 Masada

Perched on an isolated mountain plateau *(right)*, Masada has become synonymous with the sentiment "they'll never take us alive". Here in the 1st century, nearly 1,000 Jewish rebels chose death by their own hands rather than surrender to the rule of Rome.

9 Sea of Galilee

Israel's chief source of water, this beautiful lake 212 m (696 ft) below sea level has been famous since biblical times for its abundance of fish. Today it is one of Israel's most popular attractions.

10 Akko

Aside from Jerusalem, Akko (the historic Acre) has the most complete and charming old town *(left)* in all of Israel. Once a Crusader stronghold, today's city is largely an 18th-century Turkish town, built on the site of the medieval one.

Top 10 Churches and Monasteries

1 St James' Cathedral, Jerusalem
Hung with oil lamps, this beautiful church with a blue-and-white-tiled interior is built over the reputed tomb of St James the Apostle.

2 Basilica of the Agony, Jerusalem
The Church of All Nations, as it also known, is suffused with a calming violet light. Sections of the original mosaic floor can be viewed beneath glass panels.

3 St Catherine's Church, Bethelem
This church was built by the Franciscans in 1882 on the site of a 5th-century monastery associated with St Jerome, whose tomb is in the grotto below the church.

4 Church of St Anne's, Jerusalem
This beautiful Crusader church, which retains its Romanesque structure, is believed to mark the birthplace of the Virgin Mary.

5 Monastery of the Flagellation, Jerusalem
This complex includes the Chapel of the Flagellation, where Christ was flogged by the Romans, and the Chapel of the Condemnation, where Pontius Pilate is said to have made his judgment.

6 Monastery of the Cross, Jerusalem
Funded by the Georgian king in the 11th century, the monastery marks the site of the tree used for Jesus's cross. There are exceptional frescoes inside.

7 Church of the Nativity, Bethlehem
Steps here lead down to the Grotto of the Nativity, a series of caves under the guardianship of the Greek Orthodox Church, where pilgrims jostle to touch the Star of Bethlehem.

8 Basilica of the Annunciation, Nazareth
Consecrated in 1969 over remains of older buildings, the church is the traditional site of the Annunciation.

9 Church of the Transfiguration, Galilee
This "high mountain apart" has been identified with Christ's Transfiguration since the 4th century, though the present church is of 1924.

10 Church of the Visitation, Ein Kerem
Designed by Barluzzi, this two-tiered church commemorates Mary's visit to the mother of John the Baptist. The vividly painted upper church rests on Byzantine and Crusader remains.

Kenya

Kenya is quite simply a natural wonder. On the Indian Ocean seaboard, white sandy beaches are backed by dense forests, and intriguing alleyways and mosques in the ancient towns reveal the coast's history. The Southeastern Savannah's burnt grasslands host East Africa's big game. Volcanoes and lakes dot the Rift Valley, and above lie Western Kenya's fertile hills and escarpments. To the south, the Masai Mara, part of Africa's greatest ecosystems, supports a wealth of wildlife. The Central Highlands' dense forest and moorland sit in the shadow of Mount Kenya, while nomads wander the stony deserts of the north. And if all that weren't enough, the capital, Nairobi, is an appealing, lively city.

1 Nairobi

Kenya's capital *(left)* began life as a swampy railway camp, but is now a busy modern city. Packed with a mixture of markets and museums, curio shops and casinos, it offers plenty of attractions for visitors before or after a long safari.

Masai Mara 2

The highlight of Kenya's best-known reserve is the annual migration of the wildebeest *(right)*, which cut across the savannah seeking rainfall and new pastures, with predators in hot pursuit.

3 Mount Kenya

Africa's second tallest mountain *(above)* straddles the Equator, and is set in a vast area of very diverse National Reserve. The ring road that runs around it offers sweeping views of its peaks towering over the forest.

TOP 10 Moments in History

1 The Earliest Peoples
Early hominids lived in what is now Kenya about 4–6 million years ago. By 1.76 million years BC they had stone tools, discovered fire and formed communities. From 2000 BC pastoral nomads arrived.

2 Swahili Civilization
In the 8th century, Arab traders had settlements in Kenya. They traded goods and mixed with the local Bantu people, creating the conditions from which Swahili language and culture developed.

3 Portuguese Conquest
Vasco de Gama landed at Malindi in 1498, and by 1512 most Swahili cities had been taken over by the Portuguese. Malindi became their headquarters in East Africa.

4 Resistance and Omani Rule
The Arabs resisted the Portuguese throughout the 17th century, and in 1698 regained control of the coast. Kenya came under the control of Oman and its Sultan, and a slave trade was developed.

5 End to Slavery
In 1822 Sultan Seyyid Sa'id signed the Moresby Treaty which made it illegal to sell slaves to people from Christian countries, and slavery was banned altogether in 1873.

6 British Control
Britain established a consulate in Zanzibar in 1840. The interior was explored and the land mapped out. European powers carved up Africa at the Berlin Conference of 1884. Kenya was given to Britain, along with Uganda.

7 Crown Colony
In 1920 Kenya was declared a crown colony. White settlers arrived and were granted prime agricultural land, while the Africans were dispossessed of their land.

8 Nationalism and Protest
Resentment at colonial rule led to the rise of nationalist political groups. In 1952 the Mau Mau rebellion broke out and a state of emergency was declared. Thousands died before it ended in 1957.

9 Independence
Kenya finally became an independent state in 1963. Jomo Kenyatta became the first president of the new republic in 1965 and Kenya joined the Commonwealth.

10 Kenya Today
Kenyatta's successor Daniel Arap Moi was president from 1978 until 2002. His regime was criticized for corruption and human rights abuses. Since then, there has been some progress towards social and political reform.

4 Kilimanjaro

On the Tanzanian border, with its upper slopes actually across it, Mount Kilimanjaro *(above)* is an iconic image of Kenya, with Amboseli National Park, home to giant-tusked elephants, the best and most popular vantage point.

5 Samburu-Buffalo Springs-Shaba National Reserves

These reserves of palms and woodland, fed by the Ewaso Nyiro river, offer perhaps the best chance in Kenya of sighting leopard, with lion, elephant *(above)* and buffalo also quite easy to spot.

6 Diani Beach

One of Kenya's best beaches *(left)* stretches for 20 km (12 miles) to the south of Mombasa. It's known for its pristine white sand, palm trees, clear turquoise sea and a coral reef teeming with life.

7 Kakamega Forest National Reserve

At one time, indigenous rainforest spread across most of central Africa, but today this is Kenya's last remaining patch. Pathways wind between a rich canopy full of monkeys, birds and clouds of butterflies.

8 Karen Blixen Museum, Nairobi

Karen Blixen, who wrote under the pseudonym of Isak Dinensen, lived in this farmhouse. Now a museum, it has original features as well as props from the 1985 movie of her famous novel, *Out of Africa*, which was filmed here.

9 Mombasa

Set on a small island, linked by bridge and ferry to the south coast mainland, Mombasa has an appealing Old Town, with historic Fort Jesus *(below)* standing sentinel over its harbour.

10 Lamu

Donkeys wander the maze of narrow alleyways and white-sail dhows drift past the waterfront of this, the main town of the Lamu Archipelago *(above)*. Steeped in Swahili culture, it has remained unchanged for centuries.

TOP 10 Safari Animal Sightings

1 Lion
For most people, the "king of the jungle" is the ultimate safari icon. Prides can easily be viewed resting during the day, but safarigoers need to be around at dawn or dusk to watch them in action.

2 Cheetah
You are most likely to sight this handsome beast trotting purposefully through the grass but they are more likely to be seen hunting in daylight than other big cats.

3 Leopard
The most abundant and yet the most elusive of Africa's large predators, they often rest in the branches of tall trees, where they may be detected by a tail flickering below the canopy.

4 African Bush Elephant
The world's largest land animal is fascinating to observe in the wild for its imposing bulk as well as its complex social behaviour.

5 Rhinoceros
This ancient and endangered creature is very reclusive, and most safarigoers count themselves lucky to see one, the white or especially the rare black, in the wild.

6 Hippopotamus
The most familiar resident of Africa's rivers and fresh-water lakes lives in pods of up to 30. Their communal grunting is a familiar sound at waterside lodges.

7 Giraffe
Hard to miss in any safari reserve, and spectacular to observe running or splaying its long legs to bend and drink, the giraffe is an iconic sight of the savannah.

8 Zebra
The two main types of zebra found in Kenya are the wide-striped plains zebra and the narrow-striped Grevy's, which also has round, bear-like ears. Herds of either are a striking sight on any safari.

9 African Buffalo
Africa's only wild ox has a continent-wide population of over a million, so is not hard to spot, roaming in herds of ten to 50 animals or enjoying a muddy daytime wallow.

10 Antelopes
Encompassing numerous species, from the tiny duiker to the horse-like roan, the extremely photogenic and socially fascinating antelope could be said to define the African safari experience.

Madagascar

For lovers of the strange, the special, the weird and the wonderful, Madagascar is a treasure trove, rich beyond imagining. Left to go its own evolutionary way for millions of years, more than 80 per cent of the island's wildlife is found nowhere else on earth. Most famous for its charismatic lemurs, it's also popular for diving and beach holidays. Combined with a diverse geography, ranging from misty rainforests to dry thickets to tropical islands, and a friendly local population with a language and culture as singular as everything else about the place, Madagascar is quite simply unmissable.

Nosy Be 3
Mozambique Channel
Nosy Mangabe 2 9 Masoala Peninsula
MADAGASCAR
Tsingy de Bemaraha 10
4 6 Andasibe Mantadia
Antananarivo
Avenue of Baobabs 5 8 Isalo
7 Ranomafana
1 Spiny Forests
Indian Ocean

1 Spiny Forests

The dry southern regions of Madagascar have produced some of the island's most varied and unique plant life, including the strange and spectacular octopus tree. This much-threatened habitat is also where you can find the Verreaux's sifakas, better known as dancing lemurs *(below)*.

2 Nosy Mangabe

This small island in Antongil Bay is a tropical rainforest reserve, sanctuary for the shy aye-aye, two species of tenrec and rare tree boas. Visitors reach it by boat from the town of Maraonsetra and can either do day hikes or camp overnight for a chance to see nocturnal aye-ayes.

Nosy Be 3

The largest of several islands on the northwest coast (Nosy Be means "big island"), this is one of Madagascar's most popular tourism destinations *(right)*. With a resort atmosphere, it's an established starting point for boat charters, dive trips and fishing expeditions, and a good base for visiting the surrounding islands.

TOP 10 Moments in History

1 110–80 Million Years BC: Separation
Madagascar drifted away from Gondwanaland, leaving the island's plant and animal life to evolve in isolation for the next 88 million years.

2 200–500 BC: Humans
The first settlers (known as the Vahoaka Ntaolo or Canoe People) reached Madagascar from the Indonesian Archipelago. Waves of settlers from Africa, Asia, Arabia and Europe continued to arrive for 2,000 years.

3 AD 1000–1600: Agriculture
Over a dozen Malagasy ethnic identities developed and communities moved inland, practising *tavy* – slash and burn agriculture. Rice paddies were created.

4 1500: Europeans
Portuguese captain Diogo Dias sighted the island when his ship went off course on its way to India – the first known European contact. The Portuguese named the island São Lourenço (St Lawrence).

5 1680–1725: Pirates
Famous pirates, including Captain Kidd and Henry Every, made Madagascar their stronghold. There is even a legend that they established an independent pirate colony called Libertatia.

6 1780–1883: Kingdom
Merina monarchs in the central highlands region established authority over the whole island and ruled over the Kingdom of Madagascar from their capital, Antananarivo.

7 1896: Colonization
Madagascar lost its monarchy and became a French colony after France took the island in 1893–95. The royal family was exiled to Algeria.

8 1960–2009: Independence
After Madagascar regained independence in 1960, a series of republics followed one another in rapid and unruly succession. The president of the Fourth Republic, Andry Rajoelina, seized power in a 2009 coup.

9 1964: Olympics
Madagascar sent its first competitors to the 1964 Olympic games. They have sent athletes to every games since, except 1976 and 1988, but have never won a medal.

10 1990: Natural Heritage
The Tsingy de Bemaraha Strict Nature Reserve was inscribed in 1990 as the island's first natural World Heritage site. Madagascar's second, the six parks of the Antsinanana Rainforests, was announced in 2007.

4 Antananarivo

Known as "Tana", the City of a Thousand Warriors *(left)* is built on the slopes of a mountain. Jumbled houses, lively markets, narrow alleyways and steep staircases – not to mention the royal palaces at its summit – give it a fairytale flavour and make it one of Africa's most charming capital cities.

5 Avenue of Baobabs

This is a remnant of a once-mighty forest in Western Madagascar. Travellers come to marvel at the columns of a dozen or so 30-m (98-ft) Adansonia grandidieri *(above)*, one of the six baobab species endemic to Madagascar. Baobabs are respected in Madagascar as *renala*, "mothers of the forest", which is why these were preserved.

6 Andasibe Mantadia

This ancient virgin rainforest offers visitors a good chance to see indris and diademed sifakas, the two largest living lemurs. Its towering trees practically crawl with chameleons, lemurs, geckos and frogs, and resound to the calls of indris and rare birds such as mesites, ground rollers and greenbuls.

7 Ranomafana

The National Park here was created to protect the golden bamboo lemur, which was discovered in 1986. The montane rainforest boasts magnificent waterfalls and exceptional birding. A night-feeding station provides an opportunity to see nocturnal species.

8 Isalo

A landscape of bizarrely eroded sandstone formations known as uniforms can be found at this national park in the southwest. Streams flow through forested canyons, while the hot, dry cliff tops are covered in succulents. The scenery and plants (over 500 species) attract hikers here.

9 Masoala Peninsula

The last extensive coastal rainforest in Madagascar is one of the six rainforests accorded World Heritage status in 2007. In this staggeringly beautiful reserve is found the locally endemic red-ruffed lemur. Twitchers flock here for megatick sightings of the helmet vanga *(above)* and the recently rediscovered Madagascar serpent eagle.

10 Tsingy de Bemaraha

Madagascar's first World Heritage Site is famous for its stone forest of jagged limestone pinnacles *(left)* up to 45 m (148 ft) tall, where lemurs leap between razor-sharp peaks. The area is one of strong *fady* (taboo) for locals, who believe a prehistoric pygmy people known as Vazimba lived here.

Top 10 Endemic Species

1 Aye-Aye
Distinctive for its long, thin middle finger, the aye-aye uses this to tap on trees to find and extract grubs. Unfortunately, local superstition says it's a harbinger of death and few survive outside reserves.

2 Indri
This large tree-dwelling lemur looks like a black and white teddy bear but sings like a humpback whale.

3 Tenrec
Sharing a common ancestry with aardvarks and elephants, these remarkable mammals have diversified to take the place of hedgehogs, mice, opposums and even otters in Madgascar.

4 Fossa
Madagascar's largest predator looks like a small cougar with the head of a mongoose. Its powerful jaws, retractile claws and agility on trees spell doom for unwary lemurs.

5 Brookesia Chameleon
Many of these chameleons have been discovered very recently. Brookesia micra – at 16 mm (0.63 in) – is the world's smallest chameleon.

6 Giraffe Weevil
This funny-looking insect is appropriately named for its long neck. Males use their necks to fight for the right to mate, while females employ them to roll leaf-tubes for their eggs.

7 Elephant Bird
The largest bird ever to live has been extinct since the 1600s. About 3 m (10 ft) tall, it was a flightless plant-eater. Its eggs, 160 times the size of chickens' eggs, could have made breakfast for 80 people.

8 Flat-Tailed Gecko
These masters of disguise use colouration and a fringe of skin that eliminates shadows to blend in with decayed leaves or tree bark.

9 Octopus Tree
The splendid succulents that are such a distinctive feature of Madagascar's spiny forests range from 2 to 20 m (7 to 66 ft) tall and are distantly related to cacti.

10 Helmet Vanga
This peculiar-looking bird, with a big blue arched bill and red-brown wings, is found only in small areas of rainforest on the northeast coast of Madagascar.

Marrakech

An oasis in every sense of the word, Marrakech was once a beacon for trading caravans that had driven north through the desert and over the often snow-capped Atlas Mountains. Marrakech may be Morocco's third most important city after Rabat and Casablanca, but its fabulous palaces and lush palm groves exercise a powerful hold over tourists. It has always been the place where sub-Saharan Africa meets Arab North Africa, and, even today, this market town located on the edge of nowhere remains a compellingly exotic port of call.

1 City Walls and Gates

Marrakech's medina, or old city, is encircled by several miles of reddish-pink, dried mud walls, punctuated by nearly 20 gates *(left)*. Having proved ineffective against attackers throughout history, the walls are more ornamental than functional.

The Night Market 2

By night, Jemaa El Fna *(see opposite)* transforms into a circus, theatre and restaurant, with itinerant musicians and entertainers drawing excitable crowds *(right)*.

3 Koutoubia Mosque

Marrakech's landmark monument *(above)* boasts a tower that dominates the skyline for many miles around. Like most mosques in Morocco, the Koutoubia Mosque is closed to non-Muslims but it remains an impressive sight from without.

Top 10 Moments in History

1 Founding of Marrakech
The Almoravids, the most powerful Berber tribe, founded the military outpost of Marra Kouch in 1062, giving them control of the Saharan trade routes.

2 The Almohads Take Marrakech
The Almohads laid siege to Marrakech in 1147 and the city changed hands. The Almohads created such impressive monuments as the Koutoubia Mosque.

3 Decline Under the Merenids
Emerging from eastern Morocco, the Merenids took the city in 1269. However, Fès was their power base, and Marrakech was reduced to a provincial outpost.

4 The Saadians
Prosperity returned to Marrakech under the rule of the Saadians, who overthrew the Merenids in 1549. This first Arab dynasty expanded its territory across the Sahara to Mali and Mauritania.

5 The Alaouite Dynasty
The Saadians were swept aside by the Alaouites in 1668, and their second ruler, Moulay Ismail, was noted for his cruelty. This successful dynasty still rules today.

6 The Sultan of Spliff
Moulay Hassan, a powerful sultan who ruled from 1873 to 1894, legalized cannabis cultivation. Today the Rif region is one of the world's largest cultivators, even though measures have been taken to eradicate this crop.

7 French Rule
The lynching of Europeans in Casablanca gave cause for France to make Morocco its protectorate in 1912. In this period, a whole new city was constructed outside the walls of the medina in Marrakech.

8 The Lord of the Atlas
The French enlisted Thami El Glaoui to govern southern Morocco from 1918 to 1955. The self-styled "Lord of the Atlas" ruled with an iron fist. With French withdrawal in 1955, he fell into disgrace.

9 The Coronation
1955 marked the return of exiled Sultan Mohammed V, who was crowned king. Morocco got independence a year later. The present monarch, Mohammed VI, is his grandson.

10 Global Appeal
When a French TV show in the 1990s claimed a palace in Marrakech could be bought for the price of a Paris flat, the city's popularity grew. Five-star hotels and budget airlines soon followed.

5 Jemaa El Fna

This is a vast plaza at the heart of the medina (the old walled city) and is as old as Marrakech itself. The site of parades and executions in the past, Jemaa El Fna is still right at the centre of modern city life.

4 Medersa Ben Youssef

Behind a typically blank Marrakech façade hides what is arguably the city's finest building. This ancient religious school boasts exquisite decorative detail *(above)*.

6 Badii Palace

The ruins of this once fabled palace provide a picturesque setting for nesting storks *(above)* – and a salutary warning from history against extravagance.

7 Mamounia Hotel

A *grande dame* among hotels worldwide, the Mamounia *(above)* has been providing hospitality to the visiting rich and famous for almost a century.

8 Majorelle Gardens

Jacques Majorelle, a French artist who came to Marrakech to recuperate, created this beautiful garden *(right)*, which was later owned by French couturier Yves Saint-Laurent. It is open to the public.

9 The Souks

Laid out in the narrow streets to the north of central Jemaa El Fna are a dizzying array of souks, or bazaars *(left)*. Different areas specialize in their own specific wares, selling anything from carpets, lanterns and slippers, to ingredients for magic spells.

10 Saadian Tombs

A tranquil garden hidden at the end of the narrowest of meandering passageways shelters the royal tombs of one of Morocco's ruling dynasties. They were shrouded from the world till the 1920s.

Top 10 Architectural Features

1 Horseshoe Arches
Also known as outrepassé arches, these are where the arch curves back inwards after its widest point, to give an effect like a horseshoe or keyhole.

2 Zellij Tiling
One of the most striking features of Moroccan architecture is its use of multicoloured, small tiles laid in complex geometric patterns. This is known as the *zellij* technique.

3 Tadelakt Plaster
Walls are treated with a limestone plaster, which is polished with flat stones, then painted with a glaze of egg whites and polished again with the local black soap. The finished surface looks like soft leather.

4 Stucco Plaster
Fantastic curvilinear and geometric designs can cover entire walls, the work executed by craftsmen cutting into the plaster while it is still damp.

5 Carved Woodwork
Though similar designs are used to decorate both plaster and wood, often wood is deployed as a frieze and carries inscriptions in Arabic, usually of a religious nature, praising Allah.

6 Square Minarets
The design of square Moroccan minarets can be traced to the Umayyad rulers of Islamic Spain, who were of Syrian origin. Syrians are almost unique in the Middle East for their square minarets.

7 Courtyards
A distinctive feature of Islamic architecture is its focus on internal spaces – façades are generally blank window-less walls. Courtyards serve as air-wells into which the cool night air sinks and also act as private outdoor spaces.

8 Fountains
Fountains and basins are required for ritual ablutions before prayers. Also, in an arid climate, the provision of drinking water is seen as a charitable act.

9 Pisé
The basic building material used in Morocco, pisé is wet earth mixed with straw and gravel, then pounded between two boards and strengthened with lime.

10 Pigeonholes
The numerous pigeonholes peppering walls in the city are, in reality, marks left by wooden scaffolding used in the construction process.

Dubai
View of the Emirates Towers
on Sheikh Zayed Road

The Nile

The Nile is synonymous with Egypt. Almost the entire population of the country is crammed onto the narrow fertile plain fringing the river. It was so during the ancient Egyptian era, when the temples and cities of the pharaohs rarely strayed far from the life-sustaining area of the Nile's banks. Today, the best way to experience Egypt is to explore the Nile, from the awe-inspiring pyramids on the outskirts of the capital Cairo *(see pp284–5)*, in the north, to the great temples in the far south of the country.

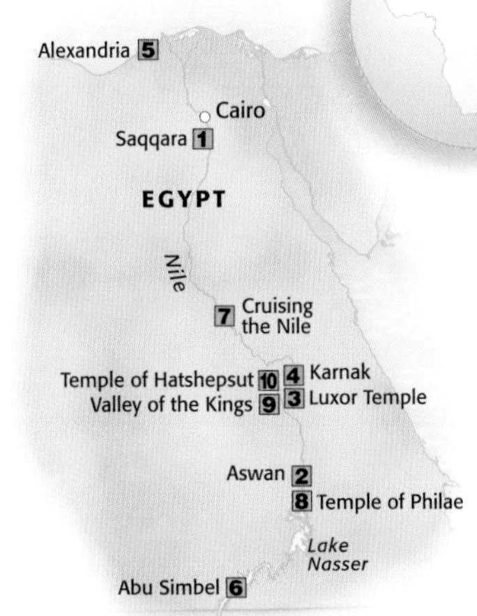

1 Saqqara One of the richest archaeological sites in Egypt, Saqqara *(left)* was the royal burial ground for some of the earliest rulers and their courtiers, and the site of Egypt's prototype pyramid, a stepped structure built for King Djoser.

Aswan 2 Life moves at a languid pace in Egypt's southernmost city *(right)*. The Nile is particularly beautiful here, dotted with islands and with a west bank of sandy, desert slopes that come right down to the water's edge.

3 Luxor Temple Once connected to Karnak by an avenue of sphinxes, Luxor *(above)* is more modest in size than Karnak, but was built by two of the greatest pharaohs, Amenhotep III and Ramses II.

TOP 10 Periods of Ancient Egyptian History

1 3100–2890 BC: Early Dynastic Period
What's regarded as ancient Egypt began in 3100 BC with the unification of Upper and Lower Egypt by King Narmer (also known as Menes), who created a capital at Memphis.

2 2686–2181 BC: Old Kingdom
Successive dynasties raised a chain of pyramids, the greatest of which were at Giza. Poor harvests depleted the royal coffers, evidenced by smaller later pyramids.

3 2181–2055 BC: 1st Intermediate Period
This period saw a weakening of centralized power and the creation of local dynasties, notably at Herakleopolis in the Fayoum Oasis and Thebes in the south.

4 2055–1650 BC: Middle Kingdom
The powerful warlord Montuhotep II conquered the north to reunite the country, with Thebes (modern-day Luxor) as its new capital, which grew into a major metropolis.

5 1650–1550 BC: 2nd Intermediate Period
Migrants from lands north of Egypt, referred to as Hyksos, assumed control and formed an alliance with Nubia to dominate southern Egypt. Intermittent civil wars ensued.

6 1550–1069 BC: New Kingdom
With the reunification of north and south and the expulsion of the Hyksos, Egypt entered a Golden Age, expanding its rule into Asia Minor and as far as the Euphrates.

7 1069–715 BC: 3rd Intermediate Period
Four centuries of disunity and foreign infiltration saw Egypt again divided into north (ruled from Tanis in the Delta) and south (ruled by the priests of Karnak).

8 747–332 BC: Late Period
First came Assyrian invasion and then Persian, in 525 BC. The Persians ruled for 200 years interrupted only by the 30th Dynasty of Egyptian pharaohs (380–343 BC).

9 332–30 BC: Graeco-Roman Period
Alexander the Great took Egypt from the Persians and founded Alexandria. This period ended with the death of the last of the Ptolemies, Cleopatra VII, lover of Julius Caesar and Marc Antony.

10 After the Pharaohs
Egypt became part of the Roman empire then the Eastern Roman empire, with its capital at Constantinople, until the arrival of conquering Arab armies in AD 640.

4 Karnak

The mother of all ancient Egyptian temple complexes, Karnak was the powerbase of successive dynasties of pharaohs and the priesthood at the zenith of ancient Egypt's military and artistic might.

5 Alexandria

Alexander the Great founded his new capital city on the Mediterranean coast in 332 BC, after defeating the Persians. Little of its ancient heritage remains, but there's still plenty to see in modern Alexandria, Egypt's second largest city.

6 Abu Simbel

This is perhaps the temple that best symbolizes the grandeur of ancient Egypt. The Sun Temple is carved out of a mountainside and fronted by four towering colossi *(above)* depicting its builder, Ramses II.

7 Cruising the Nile

When Cleopatra romanced Caesar she did so on a cruise down the Nile. A boat trip on the Nile *(above)* remains the most romantic and enjoyable way to view Egypt.

8 Temple of Philae

A mix of Egyptian and Roman elements characterize this temple complex, which is sited on a picturesque island in the middle of the Nile *(above)*.

9 Valley of the Kings

The treasures are long gone from the tombs of the pharaohs, but it is possible to descend the dimly-lit passageways to underground chambers decorated with vivid scenes from the afterlife.

10 Temple of Hatshepsut

Among the many monuments at Luxor, the temple of Egypt's only female pharaoh, Hatshepsut *(right)*, stands out for its almost modernistic design of ascending terraces.

Top 10 Culture and Myths

1 Religious Life
For the ancient Egyptians, the universe was composed of dualities held in balance by the goddess Maat. To maintain the equilibrium, they built great temples dedicated to the gods.

2 Hieroglyphs
Hieroglyph means "sacred carved letter" and refers to the pictorial script used by the ancient Egyptians.

3 The Cult Temple
At the centre of every settlement was a cult temple, which served as a storehouse of divine power. Maintained by priests, it was also an economic and political centre, as well as medical centre and college.

4 The Mortuary Temple
Each pharaoh would build a mortuary temple to serve as a place where, following his death, offerings could be made for his soul.

5 Burial Traditions
Ancient Egyptians believed in an eternal afterlife and developed a funerary cult. This involved preserving the body through mummification. The tombs were stocked with everything that might be needed in the afterlife.

6 Mummification
Priests would remove the internal organs from the dead body and store them in canopic jars. The heart, though, remained in place to be weighed in the afterlife. The corpse would be dried out and wrapped in linen.

7 Tomb Paintings
Ritual images and texts decorated the tomb. These included scenes from the *Book of the Dead*, which showed how the deceased could pass safely through obstacles in the afterlife.

8 Mythology
Ancient Egyptian religion was a complex belief system involving deities based on aspects of the natural world.

9 The Creation Myth
Out of the sea of chaos, Nun, Atum thought himself into being, sneezing to create Shu and Tefnut, who gave birth to Geb (the earth) and Nut (the sky), who in turn gave birth to the stars.

10 Osiris and Isis
When Osiris's murdered body was scattered all over Egypt, his wife Isis put him back together and Osiris then became lord and judge of the dead.

Oman

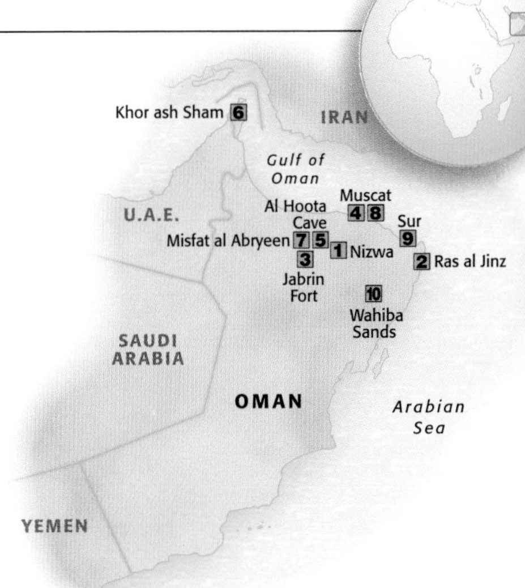

Amidst the frantically modernizing city-states of the Arabian Gulf, Oman offers a throwback to older and more traditional times: a country that has succeeded in embracing the modern world whilst holding fast to its cultural roots. Magnificent old forts, mountain villages and mudbrick towns still dot the landscape, nestled among palm-filled oases or clinging to the mountain heights, patrolled by Omanis in flowing white robes, plus the occasional wandering camel. Scenically, too, the country is magnificent, from the rolling dunes of the Wahiba sands through to the red-rock massif of the great Hajar mountains, scored with precipitous wadis and canyons.

1 Nizwa

Oman's most historic city *(above)* is capital of the interior and former seat of the country's venerated *imams* (religious leaders). Modern Nizwa still boasts plenty of antique character, including a grand mosque, a fascinating sprawl of bazaars and one of Oman's mightiest forts.

2 Ras al Jinz

Close to Oman's most easterly point, the windswept beach at Ras al Jinz is the country's leading wildlife attraction, famous for the thousands of green turtles *(above)* that come here virtually every night of the year to lay their eggs in the sands.

3 Jabrin Fort

Of the hundreds of forts which dot Oman, this is perhaps the finest. The simple exterior, half-hidden amidst the surrounding palms, gives little hint of the extravagance inside, with labyrinthine courtyards, corridors and staircases, and a sequence of lavishly decorated rooms offering a rare glimpse into the lifestyle of Oman's former sultans.

TOP 10 Moments in History

1 c. 2300 BC: Magan
Records from ancient Sumeria show evidence of trade with the kingdom of Magan (modern UAE and Oman), including the import of copper and other minerals.

2 c. 530 BC: Cyrus the Great
Cyrus conquered large areas of Magan, his people settling around the coast and in the hills of the Jebel Akdhar. The Omani population was further bolstered by Arab migrations from Yemen and Arabia.

3 AD 630: Arrival of Islam
The Arab tribes of Oman became some of the first converts to Islam. However, the Persians of Oman rejected the new faith and were driven out of the country.

4 1154: Beginning of the Bani Nabhan Dynasty
This dynasty, which is also known as the Nabhani, ruled Oman from the mid-12th century until around 1500. Their power base was the huge fort at Bahla.

5 1507: Arrival of the Portuguese
A small fleet under Admiral Afonso de Albuquerque arrived in Oman. They attacked Muscat and gained control of the coast, retaining it for over a century.

6 1742: Beginning of Al Bu Said Dynasty
Following another Persian invasion, the ruler of Sohar, Ahmad Bin Said Al Bu Said, seized power and united the country. The Al Bu Said dynasty continues to this day.

7 1806: Accession of Said the Great
Sultan Said bin Sultan (reigned 1806–56) oversaw the country's period of greatest power and prosperity, which included the development of the Omani colony of Zanzibar.

8 1920: Treaty of Seeb
The split between coast and interior was formalized with this treaty. The ruling sultan, Taimur, handed over control of the interior to the imam and his tribal leaders.

9 1962: Dhofar Rebellion
Oil was discovered at the same time that a major rebellion erupted in the southern province of Dhofar, threatening the integrity of the entire Omani state; it lasted almost a decade.

10 1970: Accession of Sultan Qaboos
Oman's current ruler, Sultan Qaboos, came to the throne following a bloodless coup. He instigated a programme of modernization, known as the "Omani Renaissance".

4 Sultan Qaboos Mosque, Muscat

Rising imperiously above western Muscat, the majestic Sultan Qaboos Mosque *(above)* showcases contemporary Islamic architecture at its most memorable. Outside, five huge minarets soar high over the surrounding streets; inside, the prayer hall is expansive and opulent.

8 Muttrah Souk, Muscat

Getting lost is half the fun in what is perhaps the most spectacular *souk* in the Gulf, with a vast and labyrinthine network of tiny alleyways. Inside, the innumerable tiny shops are piled high with exotic merchandise.

9 Sur

South of Muscat, this historic port was formerly one of Oman's great centres of maritime trade and still retains plenty of sleepy charm, with a trio of old castles, a lively bazaar and the only surviving *dhow*-building yard in Oman.

10 Wahiba Sands

This magnificent swathe of pristine desert is criss-crossed with towering ridges of wind-blown dunes *(above)*, sheltering rare desert flora and fauna. The dunes also provide a home to the hardy communities of local Bedouin, who continue to eke out a living from the harsh natural environment.

5 Al Hoota Cave

Deep in the heart of the Hajar mountains, the Al Hoota Cave *(above)* is one of the most dramatic in the Middle East – a huge, underground cavern fringed with stalagmites and stalactites, and concealing a trio of underground lakes populated with their own unique species of blind fish.

6 Khor ash Sham

Best explored by traditional *dhow*, this is the largest and most spectacular of the various *khors* (fjords) which cut through the remote and rugged Musandam peninsula, with sheer red-rock mountains rising either side of the tranquil blue waters.

7 Misfat al Abryeen

Perched high in the Western Hajar mountains, this perfect mountain village has twisting streets of old mud-brick buildings, lush gardens watered by a traditional *falaj* irrigation system and sweeping views across the peaks.

Top 10 Mountains, Wadis and Canyons

1 Al Ayn Tombs
A haunting sight, these Bronze Age beehive tombs form a line atop a craggy ridge in the Hajar mountains, spectacularly backdropped by the huge rocky outline of Jebel Misht.

2 Jebel Harim
At the far northern tip of Oman, the Jebel Harim is one of the country's highest and wildest mountain ranges, studded with prehistoric petroglyphs and incongruous clumps of submarine fossils.

3 Jebel Samhan
This is the most beautiful stretch of the Dhofar mountains, running east along the coast from Salalah. It is particularly beautiful during the annual *khareef* (monsoon), when the craggy uplands turn a lush green.

4 Jebel Shams and Wadi Nakhr
The highest peak in Oman, Jebel Shams rises rather imposingly above the vertiginous Wadi Nakhr – Oman's "Grand Canyon", as it's popularly described.

5 Saiq Plateau
High in the Jebel Akhdar mountains lies this incongruous oasis of greenery, threaded with a string of spectacular mountain villages surrounded by neat gardens and agricultural terraces teetering on the edge of the precipitous Wadi Al Ayn.

6 Salma Plateau
This bleak, high-altitude plateau at the very top of the Eastern Hajar mountains is superbly wild, remote and empty, save for the occasional tiny village and windswept clusters of prehistoric beehive tombs.

7 Wadi Bani Auf
The most spectacular of Oman's innumerable *wadis* cuts precipitously down from the highest point of the Western Hajar to the plains below, via the postcard-perfect mountain village of Bilad Sayt and the dramatic-looking canyon of Wadi Bimah.

8 Wadi Bimah
About halfway down the spectacular Wadi Bani Auf, a side-turning leads into Wadi Bimah, or "Snake Gorge", an incredibly deep and narrow canyon, hemmed in by sheer, smooth sandstone cliffs.

9 Wadi Mistal
This classic inland *wadi* twists between vertiginous cliffs before opening up into the impressive Ghubrah Bowl and the spectacular village of Wekan, a perfect jumping-off point for hikes through the high *jebel*.

10 Wadi Shab
One of the most beautiful *wadis* in Oman has a narrow, boulder-strewn floor that is dotted with rock pools. The scene is framed by palm trees and high sandstone cliffs that run down to the sea.

Festivals and Parties

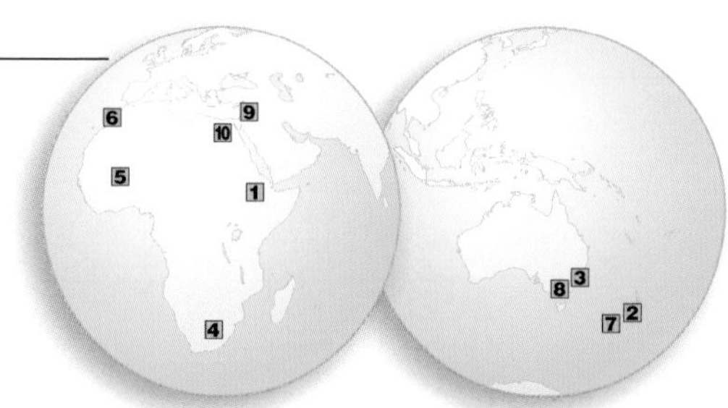

There's not a corner of the world that doesn't need to kick up its heels and party at some point in the year, or to celebrate its pride in its achievements, history, culture or creativity. From big-city razzle-dazzle to places far, far off the beaten track – somewhere, somebody is always planning a new way, or a very ancient way, to bring people together.

1 Leddet, Lalibela *ETHIOPIA*

High in the wild and rugged Lasta Mountains, Lalibela, dubbed "Africa's Petra" for its fabulous and enigmatic rock-hewn churches, ranks among the greatest religious sites on the continent of Africa. At festival time – 6 to 7 January each year – the normal trickle of visitors turns into a torrent, with pilgrims travelling for days and even weeks to reach the little town. The chanting, singing and dancing of processions ring out from all corners, and the town is coloured with the bright and beautiful textiles worn by the participants. To visitors, it feels as though they've travelled six or seven centuries back in time.

2 Golden Shears, Masterton *NEW ZEALAND*

The town of Masterton, host to what it claims is the "world's greatest shearing competition", greets visitors with a giant pair of golden shears. Each February it draws hundreds of entrants from North and South Island to take part in sheep-shearing and wool-handling contests. Dating back to 1961, the competition is fierce and winners are local heroes.

3 Sydney Gay and Lesbian Mardi Gras *AUSTRALIA*

This global gay event held ever year in mid-February began more than 30 years ago when a handful of pioneers took to the streets demanding their rights. Events in Sydney include the Sol y Luna Harbour Party, a family-friendly Fair Day and a pooch parade known as Doggywood. For most people, though, the highlight of the three-week period is the main parade, for which some 10,000 partygoers strap on soaring stilettos, technicolour outfits, diabolical wigs, infinitesimal shorts, quirky codpieces and lashings of leather. Leading the parade is the Dykes on Bikes motorcycle group, which is followed by 150 floats. Some 500,000 cheering onlookers, many waving rainbow flags, line the streets to take in the spectacle, which concludes with an all-night party in Moore Park, with a star-studded line-up of live performers and DJs.

4 Rustler's Valley Festival *SOUTH AFRICA*

Set in the foothills of the Maluti Mountains, amid verdant pasture, this four-day Easter festival is a New Age, holistic experience, run by a long-standing alternative community based in what they describe as the valley of transformation. Here you'll find bands, drumming and world music on the main stage, trance and dance tents, a picturesque campsite, a sweat lodge and some delicious vegetarian food. New Year's Eve also draws the crowds.

5 Fêtes de Masques, Pays Dogon *MALI*

Every April and May, in a vast, arid escarpment in central Mali, six men in dramatic hand-carved masks dance vigorously before an enthusiastic crowd, in memory of their ancestors and to celebrate the new harvest. These enactments are said to represent the story of the origin of the Dogon, and to help ward off evil spirits. Two big festivals, Sigui and Dama, take place every 60 and 12 years respectively, but dances are performed throughout the year.

Winter Festival, Queenstown A competitor in the Cyclocross championships

International Film Festival, Cairo Dancers perform at the opening ceremony *(below)*

Sydney Gay and Lesbian Mardi Gras Joining in the fun at the Mardi Gras parade *(above)*

ëtes de Masques, Pays Dogon A dancer wearing a Kananga mask *(below)*

6 Gnawa and World Music Festival, Assaouira *MOROCCO*

Since 1998, the music of Africa's funkiest, most mystical religious brotherhoods has been celebrated at this annual festival in Essaouira, which lasts for four days at the end of June. The pentatonic (five-note) sounds of Gnawa music have been adopted by many Western rock, blues and jazz musicians including Jimi Hendrix and Cat Stevens, who both stayed here in the 1960s. Crowds of around 450,000 pack out the town's indoor acoustic concert venues and swarm around its large outdoor stages. Mainly Moroccan youths convulse to its late-night *lila* rituals – healing ceremonies in which spirits are invoked and trances entered into.

7 Winter Festival, Queenstown *NEW ZEALAND*

Queenstown greets winter – June to July – with a ten-day jamboree attracting 60,000 party-goers. It combines eccentricities such as the Birdman and Dog Derby with Mardi Gras parades, fireworks, live music and comedy. The party continues on the slopes with snow mountain-biking and night skiing.

8 Melbourne Arts Festival *AUSTRALIA*

Australia's foremost celebration of the arts offers its visitors a multicultural smorgasbord of dance, theatre, opera, music, visual arts, multimedia and outdoor events for 17 days every October. Each year boasts around 60 to 80 events held in a host of inner-city venues. Past events have included performances by the Merce Cunningham Dance Company, a photography exhibition and concert by "Godmother of Punk" Patti Smith, a collaborative event with composer Philip Glass and a performance by the indigenous Australian group, the Black Arm Band. There are workshops, lectures and school and family events.

9 Oud Festival, Jerusalem *ISRAEL*

Named after the short-necked lute traditionally played across the Middle East, Oud, held in November, uses music to reach beyond religious and political divisions to showcase the rich ethnic and social traditions that inspire music, poetry and literature today's Jerusalem. Concerts feature modern and traditional music with Bedouin, Flamenco and Sufi influences.

10 International Film Festival, Cairo *EGYPT*

An often somewhat chaotic and disorganized celebration of local and international film takes place each year in November or December, at various cinemas across Egypt's capital city. The festival is usually attended by a bevy of both Arab world and international film stars. It is hugely popular with local Egyptians because, for the festival screenings, censorship laws are relaxed and international films are shown uncut.

Queensland

Daintree National Park 1
Port Douglas 6
Cairns 4
Great Barrier Reef 3
Whitsunday Islands 10
QUEENSLAND
Coral Sea
Marlborough 2
The Outback 9
Fraser Island 8
Brisbane 5
Surfer's Paradise 7

Australia's second largest state, Queensland, is also its second most popular destination for visitors, after Sydney, for both its balmy tropical climate and its spectacular natural wonders. Brisbane, the state capital, is a modern city, but one with an old-fashioned charm and friendliness. The southern coastline is a haven for surfers, and it's this region that perhaps best typifies the nation's beach culture. The spectacular Great Barrier Reef runs almost the length of the coast, covering 2,000 km (1,250 miles), encompassing the staggeringly beautiful Whitsunday archipelago and, at Cape Tribulation, meeting up with another natural wonder, the Daintree, the oldest tropical rainforest in the world.

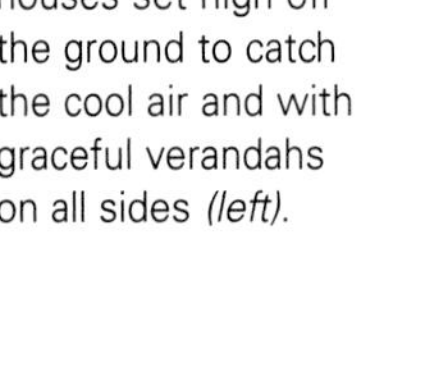

1 Marlborough

On the banks of the Mary river, this Heritage City is known for its many "Queenslanders" – houses set high off the ground to catch the cool air and with graceful verandahs on all sides *(left)*.

2 Daintree National Park

On even the shortest walk through this ancient forest, you are almost sure to spot bandicoots *(right)*, forest dragons, tree frogs and kingfishers, and might even glimpse the region's most reclusive but spectacular bird, the cassowary.

3 Great Barrier Reef

This vast, living structure teems with marine life *(right)*. There are plenty of ways to view its wonders at close range, from glass-bottom boat or semi-submersible trips to snorkelling to scuba diving.

TOP 10 Moments in History

1 Early Peoples
The first Aboriginals arrived about 40–60,000 years ago. Sites in Queensland, once densely populated, date from 15,000 and 30,000 years ago.

2 First Explorers
In 1606 Dutch explorer Willem Janszoon was the first European to document contact with Australian Aboriginals after landing on the western coast of Cape York. The Torres Strait is named for Spaniard Luis Váez de Torres, who passed the coast in 1614.

3 Arrival of the British
In 1770 James Cook claimed the eastern coast of Australia for the British, naming the region New South Wales. Cape Tribulation marks the point where his ship almost foundered on the Reef.

4 Penal Colony
In 1824 the first penal colony was established in Queensland. The isolated colony was infamous for the harshness of its regime. Around 1840 the area was opened up to free settlers.

5 Frontier Wars
Conflict between Aboriginals and Europeans led to a series of skirmishes and battles which lasted for 150 years. The wars were particularly bloody in Queensland, where thousands died.

6 The Colony of Queensland
In 1859 Queensland formally separated from New South Wales and became a self-governing colony. George Ferguson Bowen was made the region's first governor.

7 Gold Rush and Industrialization
The discovery of gold in 1858 led to the first of several gold rushes in Queensland. An influx of immigrants, including thousands of Chinese, began, until laws had to be passed to stem the flow.

8 Early 20th-Century Queensland
In 1901 the Federation of Australia was declared. During World War II the region was heavily militarized due to the fear of Japanese invasion.

9 Post-War Queensland
In 1971 the South African rugby team toured the region: fierce anti-apartheid protests led to a State of Emergency. In 1982 Brisbane hosted the Commonwealth Games. The same year, indigenous Torres Strait islanders were granted their claim to land ownership.

10 Queensland Today
Queensland is now one of most booming regions in Australia. The coast has been hit by cyclones in recent years but always bounces back.

4 Cairns

Queensland's most northerly city is a boarding point for trips to the Great Barrier Reef, but it's also a lively place with plenty to see and do, and an attractive esplanade lined with shops and cafés.

5 Brisbane

In Queensland's capital, glass and steel high-rises sit side-by-side with graceful Victorian landmarks. A riverside city surrounded by misty blue hills, the city is known for its scenic tropical beauty and welcoming air.

6 Port Douglas

This pretty little town has a laid-back, arty vibe and plenty of Victorian buildings to add to its charm. It's also a major tourist draw, as a departure point for boats to the Outer Barrier Reef.

7 Surfer's Paradise

The main city of the Gold Coast *(right)* more than lives up to its name, with everything you need to surf by day and party by night. Nearby Burleigh Heads is a tiny, peaceful national park of dense eucalypt forest.

8 Fraser Island

The world's largest sand island measures 123 km (76 miles) by 25 km (16 miles) and is a mix of hills, rainforest, freshwater lakes, white beaches and spectacular sand structures. Seventy-Five-Mile Beach is marked by the shipwreck of the liner *Maneho*, dating from 1935.

TOP 10 Life on the Reef

1 Hard Coral
The coral that most people think of is formed from the outer skeleton of polyps. The most common species on the Reef is staghorn coral.

2 Soft Coral
This has no outer skeleton, and resembles the fronds of a plant, rippling in the warm currents of water.

3 Manta Rays
These huge fish can measure up to 6 m (20 ft) across. But despite their disconcerting size, they are very gentle creatures that are happy to swim close to divers. They have no sting in their tail.

4 Sharks
Great white sharks are occasional visitors to the reef, but they usually live in the open ocean. Reef sharks are small and timid.

5 Beaked Coralfish
Abundant and beautiful, beaked coralfish usually swim in pairs in shallow water and around coral heads. They use their long, delicate snouts to pick out food from among the coral, unlike another colourful reef-dweller, the parrot fish, which grinds up coral in its "beak".

6 Clown Anemone Fish
This is the fish that everyone knows these days as Nemo. They are immune to the stinging tentacles of the sea anemones in which they live.

7 Giant Clams
These massive bivalves are one of the most spectacular reef sights, with their wavy "jaws". They have suffered from being a delicacy, and are now protected by law.

8 Batfish
Batfish swim in large groups that colonize and graze a patch of reef for a long time before moving on. Scientists think this may help to protect the reef from the worst ravages of weed.

9 Moray Eels
Another giant of the reef, the moray can grow to 2 m (6 ft) long, but is so gentle it can be hand-fed by divers.

10 Crown of Thorns Starfish
Once thought the real villain of the reef, when it burst onto the scene in the 1960s feasting on staghorn coral, it's now thought that it contributes to reef life by destroying old coral and allowing new to generate.

9 The Outback

In stark contrast to the lush greenery of the eastern rainforests, northwest Queensland is made up of dry plains, mining areas and Aboriginal settlements. Those who visit are rewarded with unique wildlife and an insight into Australia's tough outback pioneer way of life.

10 Whitsunday Islands

This archipelago of 74 islands is among the most perfect holiday destinations in Australia, especially if you are able to island-hop by boat. Whitehaven Beach *(left)* is acknowledged as one of the world's best beaches.

South Africa's Winelands

South Africa's Cape Winelands are a scenically enchanting region of lofty mountains, fertile valleys and slopes planted with orchards and vines. Variable soil types and the diversity of conditions created by the cool mountain and sea breezes ensure a wide range of superb wines that make South Africa the world's eighth-largest producer. Nestled in the valleys are graceful Cape Dutch manor houses, like those of Tulbagh and Stellenbosch, and a drive through any of the Wineland towns reveals the rich cultural heritage of the first settlers.

9 Tulbagh
SOUTH AFRICA
4 Paarl
Butterfly World 3
8 Drakenstein Lion Park
Boschendal Wine Estate 5
Cape Town
Stellenbosch 1
7 Franschhoek
Spier Wine Farm 2
6 Jonkershoek Nature Reserve
10 Vergelegen Wine Estate

1 Stellenbosch

Despite its wealth of impressive Cape Dutch architecture *(above)*, South Africa's second-oldest town is better known – and justifiably so – as the most central base for exploring the renowned Cape Winelands.

2 Spier Wine Farm

This estate adopts an unashamedly populist approach to wine, with plenty to keep the whole family amused. It has a pool, spa, playground, craft shop, falcon and raptors centre, horse riding stables and a superb hotel.

3 Butterfly World

South Africa's largest butterfly park supports more than 20 free-flying indigenous species in a landscaped indoor garden *(below)*.

TOP 10 Iconic Wines

1 Kanonkop Paul Sauer
The winner of numerous local and international awards, this Bordeaux-style blend is dominated by Cabernet Sauvignon, with smaller amounts of Cabernet Franc and Merlot. The wine is aged in oak for approximately two years.

2 Meerlust Rubicon
Another iconic Bordeaux-style blend, this is one of South Africa's best-known wines, with several awards to its name and a reputation for benefiting from cellaring.

3 Ernie Els Red Blend
The association with South Africa's top golfer may come across as a gimmick, but the wine, another Cabernet-based Bordeaux blend, is anything but, having drawn many accolades.

4 Beyerskloof Pinotage
This is a good introduction to Pinotage, a uniquely South African cross between Cinsaut and Pinot Noir, pioneered in 1925. It tends to produce soft, dry, medium-bodied wines with hints of banana, plum or tropical fruit.

5 Zonnebloem Shiraz (and Other Reds)
Zonnebloem's flavoursome reds are good for daily consumption. The Shiraz is currently the favourite, but the Pinotage and Cabernet Sauvignon are also drinkable.

6 Vergelegen White Blend
An oak-matured blend of two-thirds Semillon to one-third Sauvignon Blanc, Vergelegen usually improves with cellaring for between two and three years. It can keep well for up to 10 years.

7 Ken Forrester Chenin Blanc Range
South Africa's most heavily planted grape, comprising 18 per cent of the national vineyard, is Chenin Blanc. Ken Forrester's Chenin Blanc and FMC Chenin Blanc, rank with the very best.

8 Boschendal Blanc de Noir
Perfect for fans of rosé and off-dry whites, this refreshing salmon-coloured wine is made from black grapes but fermented as a white wine. It is best drunk chilled.

9 Porcupine Ridge Sauvignon Blanc
You will often come across this zesty favourite on supermarket shelves and restaurant wine lists. It is reliable and affords good value for its price.

10 JC Le Roux Scintilla
This Chardonnay-based wine, with 25% Pinot Noir, is made by South Africa's leading exponent of Cap Classique – a type of sparkling wine that is almost identical to champagne. It is dry, but quite soft on the palate.

4 Paarl

The largest town in the Winelands is rather scruffy compared to Stellenbosch, but Paarl Mountain, a fantastic granite outcrop in a pedestrian-friendly nature reserve, and the Afrikaner Taal (Language) Monument *(left)* are worth a visit.

5 Boschendal Wine Estate

The most popular estate in the Stellenbosch-Franschhoek area, Boschendal includes a manor house dating to 1812 and a cellar built in 1795. There's a classy buffet restaurant and shady café. On sunny days, the French-style "Pique Nique" on the lawns is irresistible.

6 Jonkershoek Nature Reserve

One of the Cape's most overlooked attractions, this mountainous reserve *(above)* on the outskirts of Stellenbosch is traversed by a selection of hiking trails. The plantlife is extremely varied and the reserve is good for bird-watching.

7 Franschhoek

Many wine estates *(above)* lie in the immediate vicinity of Franschhoek, the self-styled culinary capital of South Africa, with its world-class restaurants and boutique shops. The town's distinct French influence dates back to its settlement by Huguenot refugees in the late 17th century.

8 Drakenstein Lion Park

Established in 1998, this park provides lifelong sanctuary to captive lions that cannot be released into the wild. The animals are housed in large enclosures and can be viewed from raised platforms. Kids love it especially for the drama of feeding time.

9 Tulbagh

With its many Cape Dutch buildings, Tulbagh exudes period character. The Groot Winterhoek Mountains form a dramatic backdrop and offer good walking, horse-riding and bird-watching opportunities. There are about two dozen wine estates to visit nearby.

10 Vergelegen Wine Estate

This estate started life as an outpost of the Cape Colony in 1685. In 1700 it was bought by Willem van der Stel, who established the gracious manor house *(above)* and garden, and planted the gnarled camphor trees at its entrance.

TOP 10 Beyond the Winelands

1 Hermanus
Perched on sheer cliffs to the southeast of Cape Town, Hermanus is the world's best place for watching southern right whales from June to November.

2 Gansbaai
This fishing village is known for the sharks and whales that live offshore. Its shark safaris focus on Dyer Island, which supports penguins, black oystercatchers and the Cape fur seal colony.

3 Agulhas National Park
Agulhas is the Portuguese for "needles", and here it alludes to the jagged offshore formations that have caused 250 shipwrecks, despite the presence of South Africa's oldest lighthouse (1849).

4 De Hoop Nature Reserve
The coastline of tall dunes and sheer cliffs can be explored on short walking and mountain biking trails, or along a five-day hiking trail.

5 Swellendam
Founded in 1745, this small town has an old world feel, reinforced by Cape Dutch buildings such as the Old Drostdy (Magistrate's Seat), now a local history museum.

6 Cederberg
This area of wilderness is revered for its stunning sandstone formations, profusion of prehistoric rock art and a rich mix of endemic flora and fauna.

7 West Coast National Park
Extending around the sparkling waters of Langebaan Lagoon, this pristine coastline lies just an hour's drive north of Cape Town.

8 Paternoster and Cape Columbine
This coastal village is renowned for its traditional whitewashed fishermen's cottages, superb crayfish and the adjacent Columbine Nature Reserve which offers excellent kayaking.

9 Lambert's Bay
Though the main attraction here is Bird Island, with its colony of Cape gannets, the pretty harbour is regularly visited by seals, while boat trips offer a chance to spot the local dolphin population.

10 Namaqualand
In August and September, this desert landscape is soaked by light but predictable rains, and transforms into dazzling fields of multi-hued flowers, including some 300 species of daisy.

Sydney

Set on the southeast coast of Australia, Sydney is blessed with stunning ocean beaches, magnificent national parks and a wonderful subtropical climate that makes the great outdoors irresistible to its four million inhabitants. The Aborigines who settled around Sydney Harbour arrived approximately 50,000 years ago, while the earliest white settlers arrived in 1788. Free settlers soon followed in the wake of the First Fleet of transported convicts, and after them several waves of migrants seeking a new life. Over two centuries later, the once far-flung penal colony has matured into a culturally diverse, tolerant and mesmerizing city, as exciting and bustling as it is laid back and relaxing.

1 Sydney Harbour Bridge

This enormous and beautiful structure *(left)* was an economic and engineering triumph. It reshaped Sydney's landscape and lifted the city's spirits during the dark days of the Great Depression in the 1930s.

2 Royal Botanic Gardens and The Domain

This lovely green belt east of the city centre incorporates the Royal Botanic Gardens *(right)* and the Art Gallery of New South Wales *(see opposite)*, and has been one of Sydney's best-loved public spaces for almost 200 years.

3 The Rocks and Circular Quay

Governor Phillip and the First Fleet arrived here in 1788 to lay the foundations for Australia's white settlement. Now it's an engaging historic precinct and a lively transport hub *(above)*.

TOP 10 Moments in History

1 Aborigines at Sydney Harbour
The original settlers, the Aboriginal Eora people, arrived almost 50,000 years ago. At the time of white settlement, 1,500 Eora were estimated to live around the Sydney Harbour area.

2 Captain Cook Lands
Captain James Cook was instructed by the British Admiralty in 1769 to discover and claim the "Great South Continent". He arrived at Botany Bay on 29 April 1770.

3 First Fleet Arrives
Governor Phillip and the First Fleet of 11 ships arrived at Botany Bay in 1788. Searching for fresh water, Phillip sailed north and found one of the world's "finest harbours", which he named after his neighbour, Viscount Sydney.

4 Rum Rebellion
Officers of the NSW "Rum Corps", so named for their use of liquor as currency, "arrested" Governor Bligh in 1808, in a short-lived coup that was put down in 1810.

5 Macquarie Takes Charge
Governor Lachlan Macquarie took charge of the colony in 1810. The ramshackle penal colony began to develop into a proper town and former convicts were encouraged to stay and make a life here.

6 Dunbar Sinks
On a wild night in 1857, the migrant ship *Dunbar*, en route to Sydney from England, struck rocks near the Heads and sunk with only one survivor.

7 Troops Set Sail
The first of Australia's World War I volunteers set sail from Sydney in November 1914. Almost 330,000 troops served and 60,000 died – the highest death rate per head of population of all the warring nations.

8 Builders' Labourers Impose Green Bans
In the 1970s the Builders' Labourers Federation imposed "Green Bans" on projects that threatened environmentally or historically significant buildings and sites.

9 Mardi Gras is Born
Over 1,000 gay activists took to Sydney's streets to demand equal rights in 1978. This started what has turned into an annual celebration.

10 Cathy Freeman Lights the Olympic Flame
Aboriginal runner Cathy Freeman was seen as a symbol of a more socially integrated and cohesive Australia when she lit the flame to signal the start of the first Olympic Games of the new millennium in September 2000.

4 Darling Harbour and Chinatown

Chinatown's authentic bustle and flavour *(above)* is the perfect counterpoint to the ritzy Darling Harbour precinct. An extension of the city centre, Darling Harbour offers numerous museums, bars, cafés and tourist attractions.

5 Taronga Zoo

The zoo's collection *(below)* of Australian and exotic animals, not to mention its gorgeous setting overlooking the harbour, makes it a must-see destination for visitors.

6 Sydney Opera House

Sydney's architectural icon *(above)* and world-renowned performing arts venue enjoys the most spectacular setting of any cultural institution in the world. The work of Danish architect Jørn Utzon, it was completed in 1973 and is the city's most popular tourist attraction.

7 Bondi Beach

Sydney's swimmers, surfers and sybarites all love Australia's most iconic beach *(above)*. Don't leave the city without spending some time here, body surfing, walking along the clifftops or working on your tan.

8 Art Gallery of New South Wales

Boasting one of the country's most extensive collections of Australian and international art, this striking building in The Domain is not to be missed.

9 Powerhouse Museum

A hands-on experience and plenty of fun, Powerhouse's eclectic and sometimes eccentric science and design collection appeals to children and adults alike.

Top 10 Historic Places

1 Aboriginal Rock Art
Aboriginal art can be seen at Ku-ring-gai Chase National Park, the Royal National Park and the Brisbane Water National Park, as well as on the North Bondi Golf Course, where there are rock carvings below the tower on Military Road.

2 Captain Cook's Landing Place
Captain James Cook and the crew of the *Endeavour* came ashore at what is now Botany Bay on 29 April 1770. On 6 May they sailed north, to what is now Sydney Harbour.

3 Tank Stream
The site of white settlement in 1788 was determined by a freshwater stream which, after improvements, became known as the Tank Stream.

4 Collins Beach
In 1790 Governor Phillip was speared through the shoulder by an Aborigine when he landed at Collins Beach. Assuming the man had misunderstood his intentions, Philip made no reprisal – that time.

5 Fort Denison
Here, the body of a criminal, Francis Morgan, executed in 1796, was left to rot on the gallows for three years as a warning to new convicts.

6 Old Government House
Governor Phillip's cottage, constructed in 1790, was rebuilt by Governor Hunter in 1799 and later altered by Governor Macquarie. The oldest public building in Australia, it is now a National Trust museum.

7 "Granny" Smith Memorial Park
A small park on Sydney's North Shore commemorates Maria "Granny" Smith who, in 1868, discovered the variety of cooking apple that now bears her name.

8 Federation Pavilion
This pavilion in Centennial Park marks the site where Australia became a nation. Prior to Federation in 1901, Australia was six unaligned and competing colonies.

9 Manly Beach
Newspaper editor William Gocher challenged the law in 1902 by enjoying a midday swim at Manly. Thanks to Gocher's bold action, daylight bathing was legalized within a year.

10 Sydney Olympic Park
The park for the 2000 Olympics is west of the city. It contains a Tennis Centre, Aquatic Centre and the Sydney Showgrounds, all of which can be visited.

10 Sydney Harbour

From its pristine beaches to its working docklands, this deep-water port *(below)* at the heart of this maritime city is often described as the world's finest natural harbour.

Tanzania

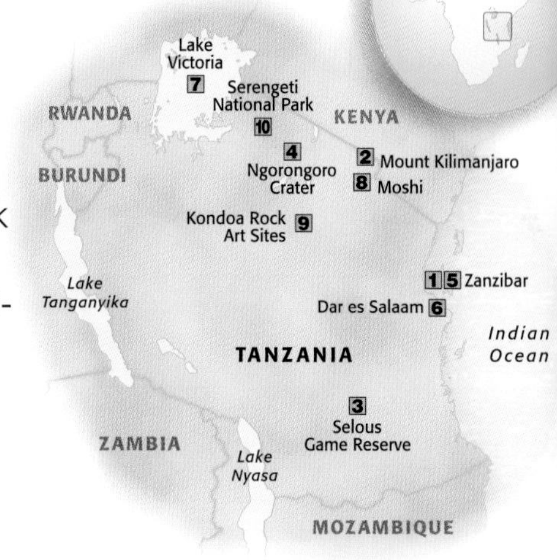

Herds of wildebeest, zebra and elephant sweeping across savannah landscapes, big cats preying on nervy antelope, the snow-capped peak of Kilimanjaro and fiery sunsets that seem to fill the sky – Tanzania harbours many of Africa's most iconic images. Add to that the postcard-perfect beaches of Zanzibar and Pemba, the world's second largest freshwater lake, a history dating back three million years and a cast of animals both well known and quirky, and you have a destination that can satisfy even the most demanding travel junkie.

1 Zanzibar's Beaches

The talcum-powder beaches and turquoise waters *(above)* of Zanzibar's north and east coasts rightly attract a stream of sun-worshippers, snorkellers and scuba divers. Pemba, the smaller island to the north, is a quieter option, with long stretches of often empty sand.

2 Mount Kilimanjaro

Soaring 5 km (3 miles) up from its surrounds, Kilimanjaro is Africa's highest peak and the highest mountain that can be conquered without technical equipment or expertise. If one of the five-day hikes to the snow-capped summit is too much, opt for day-walks on the lower slopes.

3 Selous Game Reserve

The vast Selous Game Reserve in Tanzania's southeastern corner is the country's largest and one of the most expansive on the continent. Take a game drive to spot elephant, buffalo and perhaps a black rhino, or stay at your riverside camp to watch hippos lounging in the river.

4 Ngorongoro Crater

Sitting in the Ngorongoro Conservation Area, this is the world's largest intact volcanic caldera and one of Africa's finest wildlife-watching spots *(right)*. Vast numbers of mammals, large and small, inhabit the caldera's 260-sq-km (100 sq-mile) floor, making for first-rate safaris with guaranteed sightings.

Top 10 Moments in History

1 3 Million BC: Early Man
Archaeologists working around the Olduvai Gorge discovered skeletons, footprints and tools dating back up to 3 million years, making them some of the oldest found to date.

2 8th Century AD: Islamic Settlements
Merchant vessels trading in spices and slaves had been landing here for centuries and by the 8th century there was a solid Islamic presence, largely on the island of Zanzibar.

3 1498: Arrival of the Portuguese
Vasco Da Gama was the first known European to set foot on the East African coast in 1498. His Portuguese compatriots seized Zanzibar in 1505.

4 1699: Departure of the Portuguese
After two centuries in control of Zanzibar, the Portuguese were expelled by Omani Arabs, who even moved their capital to the Spice Island. Their influence is still evident today.

5 1871: Dr Livingstone
It was here, on the shores of Lake Tanganyika, that H M Stanley uttered the immortal phrase, "Dr Livingstone, I presume?", on locating the British explorer who had been missing for six years.

6 1886: Spheres of Influence
In 1886 German and British officials signed an agreement that sliced the country into sections, giving both nations some element of control. It became known as Tanganyika.

7 1905-1907: The Maji Maji Rebellion
After years of discontent in the German-run regions, tribes from southern Tanzania united in an attempt to defy colonial rule. The uprising, called the Maji Maji Rebellion, was brutally quashed.

8 1961: Independence
In December 1961 Tanganyika gained independence from Britain, with Julius Nyerere as the first prime minister and, the following year, as President of a new republic.

9 1964 – Revolution and Union
Zanzibar gained independence in 1963 but remained under control of the Sultan. In 1964 the Sultan and his government were overthrown. Zanzibar united with the mainland as part of a joint republic.

10 1995: Democracy Arrives
Tanzania's first multi-party elections were held in 1995, with Benjamin Mkapa of Nyerere's CCM party emerging victorious.

5 Stone Town, Zanzibar

Zanzibar's main town is a labyrinth of narrow alleys harbouring quaint coffee shops and Arabian architecture. Don't miss the old slave market *(left)* or Beit el-Sahel, a former Sultan's palace-turned-museum. Enjoy evening cocktails with a sunset view and dine on seafood or Zanzibari pizza at the bustling night market.

6 Museums of Dar es Salaam

Before jumping on a ferry to Zanzibar, don't miss a dose of Tanzanian history in Dar's excellent National Museum. The Village Museum, 10 km (6 miles) north of the city, offers a peek into traditional Tanzanian culture with mocked-up huts and occasional dance performances.

7 Lake Victoria

It's Africa's largest lake *(above)*, and over half of its 70,000 sq km (27,000 sq miles) falls within Tanzania's borders – yet many visitors overlook Lake Victoria entirely. Pass by the lakeside towns in favour of its islands – Ukerewe for its pretty and often deserted beaches and Rubondo for its exquisite national park.

8 Coffee in Moshi

Enjoy the quintessential Tanzanian view of Kilimanjaro's peak peeping through the clouds with the country's quintessential beverage – coffee. Moshi is the centre of the coffee industry and boasts some cafés serving a superlative brew.

9 Kondoa Rock Art Sites

For a spot of true off-the-beaten-track exploration, head to the village of Kolo, north of Tanzania's capital, Dodoma. Here, thousands of mysterious rock paintings have been etched onto cave walls, some thought to date back around 20,000 years.

10 Serengeti National Park

For many, the Serengeti represents the ultimate African animal encounter, and you won't leave disappointed, even if you're not around for the migration. As well as safaris on foot, by jeep *(above)* or in a hot air balloon, don't miss the opportunity to delve into Maasai culture.

TOP 10 Animal Encounters

1 The Great Migration, Serengeti National Park
This annual wildebeest migration sees over a million cross the Serengeti. Watch the 40-km (25-mile) moving column of animals from the basket of a hot-air balloon.

2 Chimpanzee Trekking, Gombe Stream National Park
Jane Goodall started her work with chimpanzees at Gombe Stream. Trek with them here or track them on foot further south at Mahale Mountains National Park.

3 Water Safari, Rubondo Island
In Lake Victoria, Rubondo Island National Park is the place to enjoy a boat-safari to spot hippos, crocodiles and the very rare sitatunga, an amphibious antelope.

4 Flamingoes, Lake Manyara
This alkaline lake attracts flamingoes in their thousands when the water level is right. You may also see Manyara's renowned tree-climbing lions.

5 Hippo Skirmishes, Katavi National Park
Katavi is best visited in the dry season (May–October), when hundreds of hippos are confined to small, muddy tracts. Territorial tussles and bloody clashes are frequent.

6 Elephants, Ruaha National Park
With numbers in excess of 10,000, Ruaha has the largest population of elephants in any East African park. Big cats and the rare African wild dog also roam here.

7 Turtles, Zanzibar
Five marine turtle species can be spotted in the waters around Zanzibar, or see them at Nungwi's turtle sanctuary.

8 Red Colobus Monkey, Jozani Forest
Endemic to Zanzibar, this rare creature can be glimpsed in the swamp-like Jozani Forest.

9 Black Rhino, Ngorongoro Crater
Critically endangered and seldom seen, the black rhino is occasionally spotted in the Ngorongoro Crater. Anyway, you're guaranteed great sightings of other mammals.

10 Duiker, Mount Kilimanjaro
The endangered Abbot's duiker lives on the lower slopes along with two other species of the forest-dwelling antelope.

Tunisia

Visitors who arrive in Tunisia expecting only beach resorts may be surprised by the astonishing wealth of other attractions that this relatively small African nation has to offer. The landscape is full of pleasant surprises, with lush date gardens, vast olive groves and forest-covered hills to be found in the fertile north. Shimmering salt lakes, scorching sands and sparkling oases can be enjoyed in the desert regions of central and southern Tunisia. There's an astonishing wealth of ancient remains to be discovered, too, from Roman ruins to medieval Berber fortified *ksars*. The capital, Tunis, still encompasses a 1,000-year-old market and medina, and well as modern, luxury hotels.

1 Carthage
Scattered ruins *(above)* remain of one of the most powerful cities of the ancient world and the home town of Hannibal. A splendid amphitheatre, vaulted baths and Hadrian's theatre can still be seen.

2 Tatouine
Numerous fascinating fortified villages, or *ksars*, surround the town of Tatouine, famous for inspiring the name of Luke Skywalker's home planet in *Star Wars*, which was filmed in the area.

Tunis Medina 3
The medina is centred on an axis formed by the Great Mosque *(right)* and its surrounding souks. Its narrow streets offer countless surprises to the curious explorer, as colourful doorways reveal lovely palaces and leafy courtyards.

TOP 10 Moments in History

1 The Berbers
Little is known about the early history of the original inhabitants, the Berbers, but when the Phoenicians arrived, they encountered a people living in family-based tribal societies.

2 Founding of Carthage
The Phoenicians, a race of expert sailors and traders who had built a maritime empire, founded the city of Carthage in 814 BC. This would go on to become an independent state by the 4th century BC, establishing its own colonies.

3 Roman Rule
The Romans sacked Carthage in 146 BC, founding the province of Africa, the first outside Italy, and extending into Libya. The region was stable and prosperous under Octavian Augustus, becoming an agricultural powerhouse.

4 The Vandals
The Vandals, barbarians of Aryan decent, arrived in AD 429 and seized Carthage in 439. It became capital of a new state covering the territory of modern-day Tunisia.

5 Byzantine Rule
The Emperor of Byzantium, Justinian, sent his general Belisarius to attack the Vandals in Ad Decimum, near modern-day Tunis. He won a quick victory and entered Carthage in September 553.

6 Arab Rule
The Muslim army, which had conquered most of the North African coast, met strong resistance in Tunisia. Muslim general Oqba ibn Nafi defeated the Byzantine army in 647, and in 670 Kairouan was founded.

7 Ottoman Rule
The Ottomans took control of Tunisia from the Arabs with the help of mercenaries, under the Rule of Süleyman the Great (1520–66). Tunisia became an Ottoman province under a Pasha.

8 Colonial Era
In 1881 France sent 80,000 troops across the border from French-controlled Algeria into Tunisia. They quickly took Le Kef and then Tunis. Having quashed a rebellion France established a Protectorate.

9 Independence
Upon independence in March 1956, the new Republic of Tunisia affirmed that Islam was the state religion and Arabic its official language.

10 Ben Ali and the Arab Spring
On 2 October 1987 Zine el-Abidine Ben Ali was elected Prime Minister, a position he held for 24 years. Ben Ali was finally ousted during the Arab Spring, a series of revolutions across the Arab world from late 2010 to 2011.

4 The Sahara

The Sahara, the world's largest desert, occupies a third of the continent of Africa. Only small part of it is controlled by Tunisia; however, no visit to the country is complete without enturing into its shifting sands by camel *(above)* or four-wheel drive on an organized tour.

Tabarka 5

This seaside resort *(right)* is a picturesque place, nestling beneath mountain slopes. It is a favourite spot for divers, who come to explore the offshore rocks and caves.

6 Jerba

The island of Jerba is known for its vonderful sandy beaches, its warm climate nd its picturesque capital of Houmt Souk.)ther attractions include fortified small-oldings *(menzels)* and Ibadite mosques.

7 Bardo Museum, Tunis

This museum *(above)* in Tunis is famous or its magnificent collection of Roman artifacts, mong which are some of the finest mosaics n the world, found in ancient towns such as 3ulla Regia in the north.

8 Sfax

Sfax is renowned for its medina, one of the most beautiful in the country. The 17th-century Dar Jellouli, a handsome 17th-century courtyard house, is a museum that recreates a wealthy family's life in the medina.

9 Chott el-Jerid

An extraordinary phenomenon, this vast seasonal salt lake *(below)* is dry for much of the year, and has salt pans that glitter in a multitude of colours. A trip across it is an unforgettable experience.

10 Sufelta

Close to the modern town of Sbeïtla, Sufelta is a wonderfully well-preserved Roman city. Its buildings, from the Basilica and the Capitol to the market, complete with the remains of stalls, can be explored.

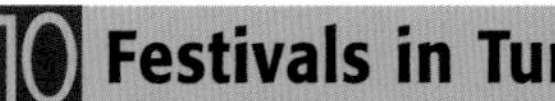

Top 10 Festivals in Tunisia

1 Mouled
This marks the anniversary of the Prophet Mohammed's birth, and is celebrated on the 12th day of the third month of the Muslim calendar. For the majority of the population it is an occasion for family gatherings and festivities.

2 Ramadan
The Muslim holy month is when the faithful renew their covenant by fasting during the hours of daylight. Food may only be eaten after the sun has set, and following communal prayers.

3 Aid el-Firt
"The small festival" marks the end of Ramadan. Custom decrees that, on this day, entirely new clothes must be worn, and money is given to children and the poor.

4 Aid el-Adha
"The day of offering" takes place 68 days after Ramadan, marking the day Abraham prepared to sacrifice his son. Allah provided a ram in place of the child and today rams are sacrificed and much of the meat given to the poor.

5 Al-Hijira
The first day of the Muslim year marks the anniversary of the Prophet's migration from Mecca to Medina.

6 Independence Day
Celebrated on 20 March, the day the French gave Tunisia its independence, this is a national holiday.

7 Festival of the Mountain Oases
In late April, in Midès and Tamezret, a celebration of Berber culture takes place, including a Berber wedding ceremony, body painting with henna, performances of traditional music and displays of horsemanship.

8 Ksour Festival
Held in Tatouine in April, this festival celebrates the life and customs of the *ksar* dwellers, with displays about their everyday life, music and camel races.

9 International Festival of the Sahara
The most famous Tunisian festival of all takes place at Douz in November and offers the chance to see many local traditions and practices in action. Tents are pitched in the desert, and lit at night with torches – a timeless and beautiful sight.

10 Olive Festivals
Many villages celebrate in grand style the end of this important but back-breaking harvest in December.

Best of the Rest: City Sights

Historic Buildings

1 Cairo Marriott, Cairo, Egypt
In 1869 French Empress Eugénie visited Egypt for the opening of the Suez Canal. This magnificent palace was built especially for her stay.

2 Beit as-Sennari, Cairo, Egypt
This centre for applied arts is in an 18th-century townhouse where Napoleon stayed after his invasion of Egypt.

3 Susannah Place Museum, Sydney, Australia
Built in 1844, this row of quaint terrace houses is as much a historic site as it is a museum, evoking life in early Sydney.

4 Hyde Park Barracks, Sydney, Australia
Built in 1819 to house convicts, later a hostel for immigrant women, then a court, the Barracks are now a museum of the site and its varied occupants.

5 Bahia Palace, Marrakech, Morocco
The palace of a wealthy vizier and his four wives is lavishly decorated with *zellij* tiling and carved cedarwood.

6 Heritage Village & Diving Village, Dubai
This complex is a living museum of potters and weavers practising crafts as they have for centuries.

7 Dar ben Abdallah, Tunis, Tunisia
This 18th-century palace has arcaded galleries decorated with ceramic tiles. Displays illustrate the lives of the medina's 19th-century inhabitants.

8 Rippon Lea, Melbourne, Australia
Built in 1868, this high-society house and its formal gardens are a much loved fixture of the city's heritage.

9 Parliament House, Brisbane, Australia
This stained-glass window depicting Queen Victoria is one of many beautiful features of this 19th-century building.

10 National Archives, Nairobi, Kenya
A former Bank of India building holds this excellent collection of tribal and contemporary art.

Architectural Gems

1 Gawhara Palace, Cairo, Egypt
This small palace is decorated in a French style. Its rooms contain displays of 19th-century furniture and dress.

2 Gayer-Anderson Museum, Cairo, Egypt
Two 16th-century houses are filled with antiquities and art. Rooms are decorated in Turkish, Persian and other styles.

3 Biblioteca Alexandrina, Alexandria, Egypt
Visit for its architecture, Antiquities Museum and Manuscripts Museum.

4 Aurora Place, Sydney, Australia
The white glass skin and sails atop this building echo the Opera House's shells but also regulate temperature, making it a marvel of energy efficiency.

5 Rose Seidler House, Sydney, Australia
Harry Seidler was pivotal bringing Bauhaus and European Modernism to Australia. This modest but lovely house was built for his mother in 1950.

6 Musée de Marrakech, Morocco
This 19th-century palace is a museum. Its former *hammam* (bath house) makes an unusual exhibition space.

7 Sheikh Juma Al-Maktoum House, Dubai
Built in 1828, this building is a text-book of Arab structural design, using a wide range of construction materials and windtowers for internal cooling.

8 Parliament Area, Melbourne, Australia
The streets retain the elegance of the Victorian era; the buildings are among the most impressive in the city.

9 Parliament House, Canberra, Australia
Parliament House is the focal point of Canberra. The 1988 building reflects a commitment to open government.

10 Dar Lasram, Tunis, Tunisia
A visit to this spectacular palace offers a unique insight into how the wealthy lived in 19th-century Tunis.

Museums and Galleries

1 Coptic Museum, Cairo, Egypt
Treasures from the 300 years between the end of the worship of pagan gods and the birth of Islam are on show here.

2 Museum of Islamic Art, Cairo, Egypt
This museum of 7th–19th-century arts and crafts has stunning exhibits, many of which came from the mosques and houses of Cairo's medieval quarters.

3 Graeco-Roman Museum, Alexandria, Egypt
Highlights include superb mosaics and a giant basalt bull from the site of Alexandria's main temple.

4 Australian Museum, Sydney, Australia
This is the place to explore the country's natural and cultural history through its huge collection of artifacts.

5 National Maritime Museum, Sydney, Australia
From the watercraft of indigenous Australians to the history of the Royal Australian Navy, the museum has it all.

6 Dar Si Said Museum, Marrakech, Morocco
Exhibits include carved wooden panels and painted Berber doors, as well as jewellery, carpets and metalwork.

7 The Third Line, Dubai
This sleek gallery shows provocative and playful work by artists from around the Gulf in changing exhibitions.

8 South African National Gallery, Cape Town, South Africa
From an initial bequest of 45 paintings in 1871, this gallery is now the sub-Saharan region's leading art museum.

9 Bomas of Kenya, Nairobi, Kenya
Recreations of traditional *bomas* (homesteads) and an amphitheatre are the setting for warrior dances, crafts demonstrations and story-telling.

10 Gallery of Modern Art (GoMA), Brisbane, Australia
Australia's largest gallery of modern art has two galleries devoted to contemporary indigenous Australian art.

Religious Buildings

1 Mosque of Ibn Tulun, Cairo, Egypt
A staircase spirals around the outside of the minaret. It is possible to climb it to admire the splendid view.

2 St Mary's Cathedral, Sydney, Australia
This Gothic Revival building was completed in 2000. The terrazzo floor in the crypt is based on the *Book of Kells*.

3 Sze Yup Buddhist Chinese Temple, Sydney, Austalia
The city's Chinese community, the largest in Australia, built this temple on the site of a market garden in 1898.

4 Kasbah Mosque, Marrakech, Morocco
This mosque was built in 1190. The cut-brick on green-tile background that decorates the minaret is original.

5 St George's Cathedral, Cape Town, South Africa
This Anglican cathedral was a beacon of the anti-apartheid movement during the 1980s, and the site of protests.

6 Bin Zayed Mosque, Dubai
An unusual square mosque without a traditional dome, this mosque was built in 1968. The nearby Al Mulla Mosque is made of mud.

7 Abu al-Abbas Mursi Mosque, Alexandria, Egypt
This mosque is named after a 13th-century Andalusian, the city's patron saint of fishermen.

8 St Paul's Cathedral, Melbourne, Australia
St Paul's is in 1880s Gothic Revival style, with a splendid altar screen and spectacular stained-glass windows.

9 Cathedral of St Stephen, Brisbane, Australia
This Gothic-style cathedral is a Brisbane city centre landmark. Particularly notable are its white twin spires.

10 Jamia Mosque, Nairobi, Kenya
Kenya's leading mosque has a pillared façade, twin minarets and gleaming silver domes.

El Alamein Fountain, Sydney, Australia

Bahia Palace, Marrakech, Morocco

Artscape Theatre Centre, Cape Town, South Africa

City Park, Nairobi, Kenya

Top 10 Performing Arts Venues

1 Al-Sawy Culture Wheel, Cairo, Egypt
The best venue in Cairo to catch live music has local bands and artists at least a couple of nights a week.

2 Cairo Jazz Club, Cairo, Egypt
Bands take the stage four to six nights a week, performing mainly jazz, but also some blues and oriental music.

3 Al-Ghouri Complex, Cairo, Egypt
The most unusual and compelling folkloric performance here is given by the Whirling Dervishes.

4 Artscape Theatre Centre, Cape Town, South Africa
Cape Town's premier performing arts complex hosts ballet, opera and cabaret performances.

5 Baxter Theatre, Cape Town, South Africa
The Baxter has long been at the cutting edge of local theatre, particularly during the 1980s when it openly defied apartheid laws.

6 Madinat Amphitheatre, Dubai
Built around a lagoon, this amphitheatre seats over 1,000 people. It is designed in the style of an old fortress.

7 State Theatre, Sydney, Australia
Originally a cinema with over-the-top Gothic, Baroque and Art Deco elements. The 20,000-piece Koh-i-Nor chandelier dominates the 2,000-seat auditorium.

8 Victorian Arts Centre, Melbourne, Australia
The centre stages the Australian Ballet and the Melbourne Theatre Company. The spire is a Melbourne landmark.

9 Queensland Performing Arts Centre, Brisbane, Australia.
QPAC comprises a main concert hall and three theatres. The Queensland Ballet is also based here.

10 Théâtre Municipal, Tunis, Tunisia
This Art Nouveau classic was built by the French in the early 20th century and is still in use today.

Top 10 Green Spaces

1 Fish Gardens, Cairo, Egypt
This small public park on the island of Zamalek is dotted with grassy hillocks that cover cave-like aquariums.

2 Rietvlei Wetland Reserve, Cape Town, South Africa
Rietvlei is a top bird-watching site and provides protection to the important Diep River floodplain.

3 Camps Bay, Cape Town, South Africa
This wide, sandy beach is overlooked by the spectacular Twelve Apostles crags on the west face of Table Mountain.

4 Nielsen Park, Sydney, Australia
On summer weekends, this sheltered harbourside beach is packed with picnicking families.

5 Arthur McElhone Reserve, Sydney, Australia
This tiny, manicured park is located in Elizabeth Bay. It has a stone bridge over a pond filled with Koi, and fine views of the yachts in Rushcutters Bay.

6 Menara Gardens, Marrakech, Morocco
Laid out in the 12th century, with their orchard, pool and tile-roofed pavilion, these epitomize the Islamic garden.

7 Jumeirah Beach, Dubai
This is a 9-km (6-mile) stretch of golden coastline. Jumeirah Beach Park is a delightful spot to spend a sunny day.

8 City Park, Nairobi, Kenya
Laid out in 1904 as Nairobi's first recreational area, City Park has landscaped gardens, ponds and a canal.

9 Royal Botanic Gardens/Kings Domain, Melbourne, Australia
Two adjoining gardens form the green heart of Melbourne: the magnificent Botanic Gardens, and Kings Domain, a gracious, statue-dotted civic parkland.

10 Lone Pine Koala Sanctuary, Brisbane, Australia
The oldest Koala Sanctuary in Australia has more than 100 koalas, as well as kangaroos, emus, possums, dingoes, wombats, and native reptiles and birds.

Top 10 Special Spots

1 Sharia Al-Qalaa, Cairo, Egypt
At least a dozen shops here sell traditional musical instruments, such as the *oud* (lute).

2 Pastroudis Café, Alexandria, Egypt
Featured in Lawrence Durell's *Alexandria Quartet*, this was a haunt of the city's bohemia and has an old-fashioned air.

3 Greenmarket Square, Cape Town, South Africa
Surrounded by historic buildings, this graceful square is home to a popular pan-African craft market.

4 Signal Hill, Cape Town, South Africa
This picnic site affords a stunning view over the city, especially at sunset with the red western Atlantic sky.

5 Sydney Fish Market, Sydney, Australia
Home to the fishing fleet, wholesale and retail fish markets, delicatessens, oyster bars, sushi bars, restaurants, cafés and the Sydney Seafood School.

6 El Alamein Fountain, Sydney, Australia
This dandelion-shaped fountain in the Fitzroy Gardens is especially pleasant when illuminated at night.

7 Palais Rhoul Hamman, Marrakech, Morocco
The *hammam* attached to an exclusive Palmeraie villa is open to all. Purpose-built, palatial, with a central plunge pool.

8 Assawan Spa, Dubai
The infinity pool of this stunning spa with its lavish ancient Middle Eastern decor is 18 floors above the Arabian Gulf, with long views of sea and sky.

9 Story Bridge, Brisbane, Australia
The Story Bridge Adventure Climb is a spectacular introduction to Brisbane – climb leaders tell its story as you ascend.

10 Brunswick Street, Melbourne, Australia
Brunswick Street has an alternative air and a cosmopolitan street life thanks to its 1960s Bohemian past.

Top 10 Shopping

1 Dr Ragab's Papyrus Institute, Cairo, Egypt
Genuine hand-painted papyrus is sold only at specialist galleries such as this.

2 El-Abd Bakery, Cairo, Egypt
This bakery may be the most popular shop in all of Cairo. Squeeze in and order a quarter kilo of *baklava* or *konafa*.

3 The Cape Gallery, Cape Town, South Africa
Set in a historic building, this is one of the best places to buy works by a selection of local artists.

4 Strand Arcade, Sydney, Australia
This may be Australia's finest Victorian-era glass-roofed shopping arcade. Quiet and elegant, it is home to boutiques, jewellers, tailors and coffee shops.

5 Paddington Markets, Sydney, Australia
Sydney's best loved weekend markets are held every Saturday in the shaded grounds of Paddington Village's St John's Uniting Church.

6 Ibn Battuta Mall, Dubai
There are five themed malls within this super-mall, six shopping zones, food courts and a 21-screen cinema.

7 Queen Victoria Market, Melbourne, Australia
From the 1880s to the 1930s, this complex of decorative, high-vaulted market buildings has grown to occupy 7 ha (17 acres) with over 1,000 stalls. In summer there's a Night Market too.

8 Brisbane Arcade, Brisbane, Australia
With a 1923 marbled interior and polished wood balustrades, this offers quality jewellers and stylish fashion.

9 City Market, Nairobi, Kenya
With a huge range of good quality art, curios and tribal artifacts from all over Africa, it also has a café serving authentic African cuisine.

10 Souk et-Trouk, Tunis, Tunisia
Built in 1630, this is one of the medina's most colourful rows of shops. One has a terrace view of the medina.

Best of the Rest: Out of Town

Top 10 Towns and Villages

1 Taroudant, Morocco
Taroudant resembles a smaller, sleepier Marrakech. It features a grand kasbah, some foul-smelling tanneries and two excellent souks, including an Arab one with a focus on traditional crafts.

2 Kiama, Australia
At Kiama, south of Sydney, a 25-m (82-ft) blowhole in the cliffs erupts whenever a wave hits with enough force, which can be every few minutes.

3 Ismailia, Egypt
Halfway along the the Suez Canal, pretty Ismailia was founded to house the construction workers in the 1860s.

4 Sidi Bou Saïd, Tunisia
Set high on a cliff, the village attracted artists and writers such as Paul Klee and André Gide and was for a time the cradle of modern Tunisian painting.

5 Fremantle, Australia
Fremantle's heyday as a major port was at the end of the 19th century, and many historic buildings remain. Today it is renowned for its crafts markets.

6 Alice Springs, Australia
Alice Springs is a lively city with around 400,000 visitors a year, many of whom use it as a base from which to tour the surrounding spectacular natural sights.

7 Adelaide, Australia
Adelaide is an elegant state capital with many well-preserved colonial buildings, a cosmopolitan atmosphere and a lively arts and entertainment scene.

8 Makindu, Kenya
On the Nairobi–Mombasa Highway, Makindu is home to the most revered and possibly the oldest Sikh temple in the East African interior.

9 Sidi Ifni, Morocco
This former Spanish colonial outpost brought Art Deco to Africa, and the characteristic tiles and ironwork are on display in many places around the city.

10 Addis Ababa, Ethiopia
The city's name means "new flower", a fitting way to describe the rising star of Africa, where ancient monuments and hip bars stand side-by-side.

Top 10 Historic Places and Museums

1 Musée des Arts et Traditions Populaires, Marrakech, Morocco
This small but fascinating ethnographic museum occupies a 19th-century house that was formerly the town hall.

2 Kasbah Telouet, Morocco
Telouet is dominated by a magnificent kasbah, abandoned for nearly half a century. You can still reach the rooftop terrace, which gives stunning views.

3 Elizabeth Farm, Sydney, Australia
This 1793 estate was once a social, political and cultural centre. The cottage is Australia's oldest surviving building.

4 Luxor Museum, Egypt
On the Corniche between Luxor Temple and Karnak, this modern, purpose-built museum exhibits statuary and artifacts, almost all of which were found nearby.

5 Bulla Regia, Tunisia
These Roman ruins include baths, a temple complex and theatre, as well as villas that were built underground to escape the heat.

6 Ksar Haddada, Tunisia
This superbly restored *ksar* (fort) is one of the most striking of the former Berber fortress-granaries in Tunisia. It was a location in the *Star Wars* films.

7 National Gallery of Australia, Canberra, Australia
The 100,000 works of art owned by the National Gallery of Australia reflect the nation's diverse, vibrant spirit.

8 Sovereign Hill, Australia
This former gold mining town is a living museum where visitors can explore a unique period of Australia's history.

9 Gedi Ruins, Kenya
This ruined city is an impressive relic of one of the most important Islamic medieval trade centres along the Swahili coast of Kenya.

10 Museum of Islamic Art, Doha, Qatar
This elegant, understated building is set on an island. With a wonderful domed atrium, it holds treasures from across the Islamic world.

Top 10 Religious Sites

1 Tin Mal, Morocco
An ancient mosque here, though roofless, remains the venue for Friday prayers. It is open at other times.

2 Wadi Natroun Monasteries, Egypt
This remote valley was used by early Christians. Four monasteries that they built remain today.

3 Temple of Seti I, Abydos, Egypt
This is one of the most intact temples in Egypt. Away from the main tourist centres, it is a less visited site.

4 Lalibela Rock Churches, Ethiopia
Extraordinary rock-hewn churches and the passageways linking them date back 900 years, and are still in use today.

5 St Catherine's Monastery, Mount Sinai, Egypt
Dating from the 6th century, this is one of the oldest working monasteries in the world. It contains priceless religious art, icons and manuscripts.

6 Great Mosque of Djenné, Mali
In the 13th century Djenné was a main centre of Islamic study, and there has been a mosque on this site ever since.

7 St John's Anglican Cathedral, Brisbane, Australia
With the foundation stone laid in 1901, St John's Anglican Cathedral is regarded as one of the most splendid churches in the southern hemisphere.

8 Uluru, Australia
An outstanding natural phenomenon, the whole Uluru area is sacred and was returned to the Aborigines in 1985.

9 El-Ghriba Synagogue, Jerba, Tunisia
Claimed as the oldest synagogue site in the world, dating back to 586 BC, this is an important place of pilgrimage for Jews from all over North Africa.

10 The Great Mosque, Sousse, Tunisia
The Great Mosque stands at the edge of the medina, because it formed part of the town's defensive system.

Top 10 Islands

1 Elephantine Island, Egypt
The largest of the islands at Aswan, in ancient times it was the cult centre of the ram-headed god of the Nile flood. Ferries connect it with the Corniche.

2 Pharaoh's Island, Egypt
Surrounded by fabulous reefs in the Gulf of Aqaba, Pharaoh's Island (known as Coral Island by Israelis) has restored ruins of a 12th-century crusader castle.

3 Kerkennah Islands, Tunisia
Off the coast of Sfax, these seven flat islands, where Hannibal was once exiled, have fine white-sand beaches and excellent snorkelling.

4 Rottnest Island, Australia
Rottnest's rugged coastline comprises beaches, coves and reefs – ideal for many water-based activities – salt lakes and several visible shipwrecks.

5 Kangaroo Island, Australia
Kangaroo Island is an unspoiled haven for native wildlife. At Kirkpatrick Point in the southwest lie the Remarkable Rocks, sculpted by wind, rain and sea.

6 Wasini Island, Kenya
A boardwalk here runs through a landscape of coral outcrops, sand flats and mangroves, home to the coconut crab, the world's largest terrestrial crustacean.

7 Fiji
Over 300 islands and islets form a paradise of palm-fringed, deserted beaches and idyllic lagoons.

8 New Caledonia Barrier Reef, Melanesia
This coral formation in the southwest Pacific runs nearly 1,600 km (1,000 miles) through the islands of New Caledonia, encircling a vast lagoon.

9 Bora Bora, French Polynesia
Matira, with its shallow turquoise water protected by an offshore lagoon, is undoubtedly the most scenic of Bora Bora's many perfect beaches.

10 Raratonga, Cook Islands
Surrounded by a lagoon that stretches to an offshore reef, and with forest-clad mountainous ridges, Raratonga is the most dramatic of the Cook Islands.

Kasbah Telouet, Morocco

Bulla Regia, Tunisia

Elephantine Island, Egypt

Uluru, Australia

Top 10 Lakes and Waterways

1 Cascades d'Ouzoud, Morocco
These are the most beautiful waterfalls in Morocco. Trek through wooded groves to reach them. There's a lovely riad at the top of the Cascades.

2 Hawkesbury River, Australia
This broad river passes sandstone escarpments, historic riverside towns, national parks, mangrove islands, fishing villages, creeks and coves.

3 Drâa River, Morocco
The Drâa carves a path between Agdz and Zagora in the Atlas Mountains. The valley is full of date-palm plantations, oases and *ksour*, old fortified towns.

4 Chebika, Tunisia
One of Tunisia's best-known oases, Chebika has a picturesque spring and waterfall, and groves of apricots, pomegranates, citrus and olives.

5 Lake Ichkeul, Tunisia
A nature reserve, the shallow freshwater lake and surrounding marshes are a sanctuary for thousands of waterfowl nesting here in winter.

6 Yellow Water, Kadaku National Park, Australia
A cruise on the wetlands of Yellow Water reveals lotus lilies, crocodiles, kookaburras, magpie geese and jabirus.

7 Blue Lake, Australia
One of four crater lakes on volcanic Mount Gambier, this otherwise grey expanse of water turns an intense blue between November and March.

8 Galana River, Kenya
The main landmark is the Lugard Falls, white-water rapids across a bed of black dolomite and quartzite. Nearby is a pool where hippos and crocodiles relax.

9 Lake Bogoria, Kenya
Boiling geysers erupt on the western shore of Bogoria, a reminder of recent tectonic activity.

10 Victoria Falls, Zambia and Zimbabwe
Victoria Falls is a spectacular sight at any time, but especially when a clear sky, a full moon and the Zambezi's spray produce a nighttime rainbow.

Top 10 Mountains and Forests

1 Jbel Toubkal, Morocco
Take the left fork at Asni to Imlil at the foot of Jbel Toubkal, North Africa's highest peak. Mountain guides can be hired in Imlil at the *bureau des guides*.

2 Wollemi National Park, Australia
This rugged terrain is a maze of canyons and gorges that traverse rainforested mountains, offering riverside beaches, whitewater rafting and camping.

3 Lopé National Park, Gabon
Lopé's rainforests are a refuge for baboon-like mandrills, and home to gorillas, chimpanzees and rich birdlife.

4 Milford Track, New Zealand
Running from Glade Wharf to Milford Sound, this trail crosses swinging bridges over roaring creeks, with views of twinkling fjords and snowy peaks.

5 Chambi National Park, Tunisia
The park includes Tunisia's highest mountain, Jebel Chambi. Its dense Aleppo pine forests contain moufflon (wild sheep) and a variety of birds.

6 Mount Kosciuszko, Australia
Fine views of the Snowy Mountains can be had from the Lookout of Mount Kosciuszko, Australia's highest peak, reached via a walking trail or chairlift.

7 Hell's Gate National Park, Kenya
The most overtly volcanic Kenyan landscape is very popular for the chance to walk or cycle among big game.

8 Kakamega Forest National Reserve, Kenya
This swath of beautiful rainforest lies in the heart of an intensively cultivated agricultural region. It is home to a wide range of fascinating wildlife.

9 Tongariro National Park, New Zealand
Head to this park if you're looking for superb hiking in a volcanic landscape and extensive geothermal features.

10 Drakensberg, South Africa
In this breathtaking mountain wilderness, prehistoric rock art is preserved in 500 shelters and caves.

Top 10 Beaches

1 Essaouira Beach, Morocco
Essaouira's beach, to the south of the medina, is one of the finest in Morocco – a bit windy for some, but great for windsurfing.

2 Pearl Beach, Australia
This National Trust hamlet is cradled by Brisbane Water National Park. The calm waters, curve of beach and rock swimming pool are magical.

3 Hurghada, Egypt
With resorts stretching all along the coast, Hurghada is famous for its dive centres which offer scuba and snorkel trips to explore Red Sea marine life.

4 La Marsa, Tunisia
La Marsa is known for its beaches and is the favourite weekend playground for Tunis's residents. Its chic hotels all have direct access to the sea.

5 90 Mile Beach, Australia
An unbroken stretch of pristine beaches along Australia's southeastern coast is backed by the Gippsland Lakes lagoons and backwaters, rich in bird life.

6 Tiwi Beach, Kenya
One of the most alluring beaches near Mombasa, Tiwi Beach is great for snorkelling. Twiga Lodge has been a famous backpacker's haunt since the 1970s.

7 Wineglass Bay, Tasmania, Australia
A brilliant azure bay on the east coast, Wineglass Bay is scooped in a perfect semi-circle from pink granite mountains.

8 Bosluisbaii, Namibia
Beach meets desert in the north corner of Namibia's Skeleton Coast. This is a beach for fans of raw beauty.

9 Llandudno Beach, Cape Town, South Africa
The shy neighbour of glitzy Clifton and Camps Bay beaches, this picturesque sandy sweep is the perfect spot for a cold beer as the sun sets.

10 Cathedral Cove, New Zealand
North Island's Coromandel Peninsula is an ecological paradise renowned for its marine wildlife and beaches, the loveliest of which is Cathedral Cove.

Top 10 Foods and Crafts

1 Tazenakht, Morocco
In Tazenakht, beneath the Jbel Siroua peak, carpets with an orange weft are woven by the Ouaouzgite tribe.

2 Taliouine, Morocco
Taliouine, a town with a ruined kasbah, is at the heart of the world's largest saffron-growing area.

3 Hunter Valley, Australia
Grapes have been grown here since the 1830s. Now there are more than 60 vineyards and countless providores offering gourmet delicacies. Day and weekend tours are run from Sydney.

4 Siwa Oasis, Egypt
The oasis is renowned for its Berber silver jewellery and handwoven baskets. Siwans are very conservative and visitors should dress modestly.

5 Barossa, Australia
The Barossa wine region takes in the Barossa Valley and Eden Valley. Both are lush areas of rolling hills and home to dozens of famous wineries dating from the 19th century.

6 Mindil Beach Sunset Market, Darwin, Australia
Outdoor stalls set up around dusk on Thursdays and Sundays, selling food and crafts, including local mangoes and aboriginal designs.

7 Guellala, Tunisia
This ancient village on the south coast of the island of Jerba has been producing ceramics for centuries.

8 Nabeul, Tunisia
Brightly blue and green Nabeul pottery can be found in every street of town, with displays laid out in courtyards.

9 Kericho, Kenya
The heart of western Kenya's tea industry, Kericho is surrounded by plantations. The charming Tea Hotel runs tours and serves delicious tea.

10 Marlborough, South Island, New Zealand
Some of the world's best Sauvignon Blanc is made here. Enjoy tours and tastings before heading to the coast to swim with dolphins and watch whales.

Hotels and Restaurants

Top 10 Hotels: City Luxury

1 Mount Nelson Hotel, Cape Town, South Africa
With marshmallow-pink Victorian exteriors and grand views, the "Nellie" is the city's most prestigious hotel. *www.mountnelson.co.za*

2 Grand Hyatt, Cairo, Egypt
On the northern tip of the island of Rhoda. Almost all rooms enjoy stunning Nile views and facilities are first class. *www.cairo.grand.hyatt.com*

3 Old Winter Palace, Luxor, Egypt
The oldest hotel in town is still the finest, with bathrooms the size of tennis courts, and views across the Nile are unbeatable. *www.sofitel.com*

4 Burj Al Arab, Dubai
Dramatically jutting into the sea, this iconic, luxury hotel offers the ultimate in personal attention. *www.jumeirah.com*

5 King David Hotel, Jerusalem, Israel
This stately hotel with a splendid terrace, pool and gardens overlooks the Old City. *www.danhotels.com*

6 Mamounia, Marrakech, Morocco
A multi-million-dollar renovation has turned Mamounia into the best hotel in North Africa. *www.mamounia. com*

7 Tunisia Palace, Tunis, Tunisia
At the gate of the medina, this hotel is in a grand Belle Epoque building. *www.goldenyasmin.com/tunisia-palace*

8 Park Hyatt Sydney, Australia
Many rooms have Opera House views, as does the rooftop swimming pool. *http://sydney.park.hyatt.com*

9 Fairmont The Norfolk Hotel, Nairobi, Kenya
Built in 1904 and frequented by early colonial adventurers, The Norfolk still exudes old world charm. Lovely tropical gardens. *www.fairmont.com/norfolkhotel*

10 Hotel DeBrett, Auckland, New Zealand
Built in 1841, this historic building in the centre of town has bespoke rooms featuring every 21st-century luxury and facility. *www.hoteldebrett.com*

Top 10 Hotels: Beside the Seaside

1 One&Only Royal Mirage, Dubai
This Moroccan-inspired hotel is one of the world's most romantic resorts. The white-sand beach overlooks Palm Island. *www.oneandonlyresorts.com*

2 Hilton Abu Dhabi
Guests love the beautiful swimming pools and private beach, lined with shady palm trees. *www.hilton.com*

3 Résidence Dar Ali, Jerba Island, Tunisia
This villa-like hotel has a tiny private stretch of beach, a lovely rooftop terrace and a swimming pool in the garden. *Tel 75 75 80 45*

4 Les Aiguilles, Tabarka, Tunisia
Les Aiguilles is housed in a charming colonial building and stands close to the beach. Some rooms have sea views. *Tel 78 67 37 89*

5 Ravesi's, Sydney, Australia
This lovely boutique hotel epitomizes the relaxed style of beach life at Bondi. Split-level suites have private terraces with ocean views. *www.ravesis.com.au*

6 Ala Moana, Hamilton Island, Australia
Five opulent guest rooms overlook the eastern Whitsundays, each with wrap-around deck, butler and private yacht. *www.alamoana.com.au*

7 Mombasa Serena Beach Hotel & Spa, Kenya
A superior spa hotel styled on an old Swahili town. *www.serenahotels.com*

8 The Boatshed, Auckland, New Zealand
Set on Oneroa Bay, suites resemble a lighthouse, boatsheds and the bridge of a ship. *www.boatshed.co.nz*

9 Windsor Palace, Alexandria, Egypt
Perched since 1906 on the Corniche facing the sea. Limited facilities but fine views. *www.paradiseinnegypt.com*

10 The Bay Hotel, Cape Town, South Africa
This elegant hotel has direct access to lovely Camps Bay beach and stunning mountain views. *www.thebay.co.za*

Top 10 Hotels: Get Away from it All

1 Kleine Zalze Lodge, Winelands, South Africa
This lodge lies in an oak copse, a short drive from Stellenbosch, at Kleine Zalze Winery. *www.kleinezalze.co.za*

2 Alluvia Guesthouse, Winelands, South Africa
Set on the eponymous boutique wine estate. Wine-tastings, fly-fishing and golf for guests only. *www.alluvia.co.za*

3 Maritim Jolie Ville Kings Island, Luxor, Egypt
Bungalows are set among palm trees on the hotel's own island just south of Luxor. *www.jolieville-hotels.com*

4 Dar Rhizlane, Marrakech, Morocco
Rooms are luxurious, some even have their own walled garden. A retreat in the heart of the city. *www.dar-rhizlane.com*

5 Binna Burra Mountain Lodge, Gold Coast Hinterland, Australia
This ecotourism retreat offers rustic timber cabins set in the rainforest. *www.binnaburralodge.com.au*

6 Daintree Wilderness Lodge, Alexander Bay, Australia
A small lodge in the ancient Daintree rainforest combines luxury and ecology. *www.daintreewildernesslodge.com.au*

7 Basecamp Masai Mara, Kenya
A relaxed, eco-friendly, tented camp in a loop of the Talek river offers game drives and walks with Maasai guides. *www.basecampexplorer.com*

8 Fitzroy House, Auckland, New Zealand
This 1920s cottage is in a quiet cove, with trails through native bush and sea kayaks available. *www.fitzroyhouse.co.nz*

9 Rondo Retreat, Kakamega, Kenya
A Christian-run, tranquil retreat in the heart of a forest. Good wholesome food but no alcohol. *www.rondoretreat.com*

10 Lane Cove River Tourist Park, Sydney, Australia
Close to the city, this eco-campground offers bushwalking, nocturnal animal treks and stargazing. *www.lcrtp.com.au*

Top 10 Hotels: Unusual Places

1 The Grand Daddy Hotel, Winelands, South Africa
This hotel has a penthouse trailer park, featuring seven vintage Airstream caravans. *www.granddaddy.co.za*

2 Al-Moudira, Luxor, Egypt
Al-Moudira is an oasis – a low-rise hotel of traditional mud-bricks, set in lush gardens. *www.moudira.com*

3 Mina A'Salam, Dubai
With Arabian architecture inspired by the ancient towers of Yemen and Saudi Arabia, it overlooks the waterways and palm-lined beach. *www.jumeirah.com*

4 Austrian Hospice, Jerusalem, Israel
Built in 1857 in Viennese style, this hostel has gardens, a café-bar and great rooftop views. *www.austrianhospice.com*

5 Genghis Khan in the Golan, Israel
Stay in Mongolian yurts (large circular tents) at a *moshav* (cooperative settlement) in the Golan hills for a unique experience. *www.gkhan.co.il*

6 Canopy Rainforest Treehouses, Malanda, Australia
Set in rainforest, on a riverbank, the treehouses balance wilderness and luxury. *www.canopytreehouses.com.au*

7 The Giraffe Manor, Langata, Kenya
A lovely ivy-clad stone manor house, is possibly the only place in the world where giraffes can be fed from the breakfast table. *www.giraffemanor.com*

8 Yumbe House, Lamu, Kenya
A typical Swahili house set around a courtyard, in the heart of the old town. No hot water. *042 4633101*

9 Medusa Boutique Hotel, Sydney, Australia
A Victorian row house has been transformed into a brightly coloured miracle of modernism. *www.medusa.com.au*

10 Riad Enija, Marrakech, Morocco
This former palace is set around a wild garden courtyard. Rooms verge on the fantastical. *www.riadenija.com*

White & Blue, Alexandria, Egypt

Mombasa Serena Beach Hotel & Spa, Kenya

Carnivore, Nairobi, Kenya

Burj Al Arab, Dubai

TOP 10 Restaurants: Fine Dining

1 Catit, Tel Aviv, Israel
Chef Meir Adoni's stunning molecular gastronomy is influenced by his North African roots. Very expensive, but there are good lunch deals. ✆ *(03) 510 7001*

2 La Colombe, the Winelands, South Africa
Set among Constantia's vineyards, this restaurant is consistently rated as one of the region's best. ✆ *021 794 2390*

3 Le Quartier Francais, the Winelands, South Africa
The ultimate culinary splash-out is the Tasting Room at Le Quartier Francais in central Franschhoek, one of the world's top restaurants. ✆ *021 876 8442*

4 Aqua at the Four Seasons Nile Plaza, Cairo, Egypt
This superb seafood restaurant has splendid views of the Nile and an excellent sushi bar. ✆ *02 2791 6900*

5 Stylia, Marrakech, Morocco
Dine at a petal-strewn table at this top restaurant housed in a 16th-century palace. ✆ *0524 44 35 87*

6 Tamarind, Nairobi, Kenya
Renowned for its seafood which is flown up from the coast daily. Try the Swahili-style lobster. ✆ *020 2251811*

7 Rockpool, Sydney, Australia
Neil Perry opened this Sydney fine-dining institution in 1989 and invented modern Australian cuisine. ✆ *9252 1888*

8 Q Restaurant, Auckland, New Zealand
One of the best restaurants in the city, it overlooks Viaduct Harbour and serves European cuisine with a New Zealand twist. ✆ *(09) 909 8000*

9 Dar Hammouda Pacha, Tunis, Tunisia
In a beautiful 17th-century mansion in the heart of the medina, delicious food is served in a sumptuous salon or the tiled covered courtyard. ✆ *71 56 17 46*

10 Restaurant Two, Brisbane, Australia
In the heritage-listed Old Mineral House, this restaurant is known for its elegant, imaginative food. ✆ *(07) 3210 0600*

TOP 10 Restaurants: Cheap and Cheerful

1 Maayan Habira, Haifa, Israel
This traditional Jewish pub has been a Haifa institution for over 50 years. East European food, draught beers and a great atmosphere. ✆ *(04) 862 3193*

2 Rooti's Cape Malay Restaurant, Cape Town, South Africa
A great selection of Cape Malay and other dishes make this a popular lunchtime hangout. ✆ *021 425 8810*

3 Felfela, Cairo, Egypt
Delicious Egyptian street food, served in a hip setting with tree-trunk seats and twittering birds. ✆ *02 2392 2751*

4 Chez Chegrouni, Marrakech, Morocco
A ringside view of Jemaa El Fna makes this modest restaurant worthy of a mention. Dishes are traditional, simple and affordable. ✆ *0665 47 46 15*

5 Hapa Hapa, Lamu, Kenya
With a waterfront setting, the seafood platters are excellent, and it serves a great selection of fruit juices but no alcohol. ✆ *042 633 145*

6 Mother Chu's Vegetarian Kitchen, Sydney, Australia
Big helpings of hearty food, blending flavours of Taiwan, China and Japan, are served with warm Buddhist hospitality in a canteen-like setting. ✆ *9283 2828*

7 Zibar, Sydney, Australia
This small café–restaurant serves good food and the arguably the best coffee in the area. ✆ *9268 0222*

8 Coco's Cantina, Auckland, New Zealand
This busy meeting place serves rustic Italian and Mediterranean food and classic desserts, such as lemon curd steamed pudding. ✆ *(09) 300 7582*

9 Abid, Tunis, Tunisia
The great food is typically Tunisian, so expect hot and spicy couscous, *chorba* (soup) and tagine dishes. ✆ *71 25 70 52*

10 Belesis, Cooparoo, Australia
This fabulous Mediterranean café is worth the short drive from Brisbane. All the dishes are lovingly crafted with fresh ingredients. ✆ *07) 3324 2446*

TOP 10 Restaurants: Regional/Local Cuisine

1 Raphael, Tel Aviv, Israel
Raphael is the place to sample New Israeli Cuisine, which uses classic ingredients and flavours in exciting, inventive ways. ✆ *(03) 522 6464*

2 Diana, Nazareth, Israel
This restaurant offers the best local Arabic cooking in "The Arab Capital of Israel", serving dishes handed down through the family. ✆ *(04) 657 2919*

3 Africa Café, Cape Town, South Africa
This eatery is renowned for its evening buffet of pan-African dishes, offering a "flying tour" of flavours. ✆ *021 422 0221*

4 Abu al-Sid, Cairo, Egypt
It is often said that Egyptian cooking is a domestic cuisine, but Abu al-Sid has made dining out on traditional delicacies fashionable. ✆ *02 2735 9640*

5 Bastakiah Nights, Dubai
With its rooftop overlooking historic Bastakiya, this is a must-visit for authentic Arabic and Emirati cuisine. ✆ *04 353 7772*

6 Carnivore, Nairobi, Kenya
Nairobi's best-known restaurant, the speciality is meat roasted on Maasai spears over hot coals and carved until you can eat no more. ✆ *020 6005933*

7 Bowmans, Auckland, New Zealand
This relaxed, welcoming place serves hearty portions of modern Pacific Rim fusion food. Great New Zealand lamb and beef. ✆ *09 638 9676*

8 Chez Abid, Tunis, Tunisia
Traditional Sfaxienne cuisine focuses on fish and seafood dishes. The fish soup and the couscous with fish are highly recommended. ✆ *71 99 63 41*

9 El-Guestile, Jerba, Tunisia
El-Guestile is famous for its excellent Tunisian food, particularly the seafood and the fish dishes. ✆ *75 65 77 24*

10 Julaymba, Daintree, Australia
The menu combines reef fish and other local produce with native and indigenous nuts, berries, flowers, leaves and seeds. ✆ *(07) 4098 6100*

TOP 10 Restaurants: Food with a View

1 Te'enim, Jerusalem, Israel
This charming vegan and veggie restaurant has perhaps the best Old City views of all. ✆ *(02) 625 1967*

2 Baia Seafood Restaurant, Cape Town, South Africa
Top-notch seafood dishes are best enjoyed from the balcony with its fine view of Table Mountain. ✆ *021 421 0935*

3 White & Blue, Alexandria, Egypt
Set above a small beach and overlooking the fishing fleet in the harbour. Choose your fresh fish and wait while it's fried, baked or grilled. ✆ *03 480 2690*

4 Kasbah Tamadot, Tizi-n-Test Pass, Morocco
In the Atlas Mountains, Sir Richard Branson's stunning kasbah hotel has a superb terrace restaurant with breathtaking views. ✆ *0524 36 82 00*

5 Pierchic, Dubai
Be sure to book a terrace table at this seafood restaurant, situated on a wooden pier overlooking the Arabian Gulf. ✆ *04 366 6730*

6 Rangers, Nairobi, Kenya
At the gates of Nairobi National Park, Rangers has fantastic views of the animals in Safari Walk. ✆ *020 235 7470*

7 Aria, Sydney, Australia
Aria has uninterrupted panoramic views of the harbour, the Opera House and the Bridge, with outstanding food to match. ✆ *9252 2555*

8 Hammerheads Restaurant, Auckland, New Zealand
On the waterfront at Okahu Bay, with views of the Auckland harbour skyline, sample seafood dishes with Asian and Mediterranean flavours. ✆ *(09) 521 4400*

9 Les Mimosas, Tabaka, Tunisia
Situated on a hilltop, with panoramic views over the town and the sea. Try wild boar from Aïn Draham. ✆ *78 67 30 28*

10 On the Inlet, Port Douglas, Australia
On the waterfront of Dickson Inlet, this stylish restaurant offers views across the Coral Sea to Mossman and the Daintree. ✆ *(07) 4099 5255*

Index

Numbers in **bold** refer to main entries

A

B

C

D

E

F

G

H

I

J

N

O

P

Q

R

S

T

U

V

W

X

Y

Z

Acknowledgments

PRODUCED BY
Coppermill Books
Editorial Director Chris Barstow
Creative Director Ian Midson
Editors Fay Franklin, Michael Ellis
Additional editorial assistance Anna Streiffert, Marianne Petrou, Mary-Ann Gallagher
Designers Tessa Bindloss, Stephen Bere
Proofreader Antony Mason
Indexer Vanessa Bird
Additional contributions Lucy Corne (Kathmandu, Tanzania), Gavin Thomas (Oman, Sri Lanka), Alison Westwood (Madagascar)

FOR DORLING KINDERSLEY
List Manager Christine Stroyan
Senior Design Manager Mabel Chan
Additional editorial and design assistance Sadie Smith, Georgina Palffy, Diana Jarvis
Senior DTP Designer Jason Little
Senior Executive Cartographic Editor Casper Morris
Cartographers Suresh Kumar, Hassan Mohammad and Uma Bhattacharya
Picture Research Ellen Root, Marta Bescos, Lisa Jacobs, Romaine Werblow
Production Controller Gemma Sharpe
Publisher Vivien Antwi

Jacket design by Greg Whyte

PICTURE CREDITS
Key: a-above; b-below/bottom; c-centre; f-far; l-left; r-right; t-top

DK Photographers
Idris Ahmed, Max Alexander, Olaf Beer, Stephen Bere, Philip Blenkinsop, Maciej Bronarski, Demetrio Carrasco, Terry Carter, Chen Chao, Joe Cornish, John Cooke, Geoff Dann, Alistair Duncan, Mike Dunning, Christopher and Sally Gable, Eddie Gerald, Adam Hajder, Andrew Harris, Paul Harris, Alex Havret, David Henley, John Heseltine, Nigel Hicks, Trevor Hill, Martin Hladik, Robert Holmes, Ed Homonylo, Rupert Horrox, Nick Inman, Stuart Isett, Dorota and Mariusz Jarymowiczowie, Britta Jaschinski, Koes Karnadi, Paul Kenward, Alan Keohane, Dave King, Mariusz Kowalewscy, Andrew Leyerle, Gerald Lopez, Neil Lukas, Brent Madison, Thomas Marent, Gunter Marx, Andrew McKinney, Lynne McPeake, Eric Meacher, Katarzyna and Wojciech Medrzakowie, Ella Milroy, Gary Ombler, Amit Pashricha, David Peart, Peter Peevers, Scott Pitts, Bharath Ramamrutham, Rob Reichenfeld, Magnus Rew, Alex Robinson, Lucio Rossi, Alessandra Santarelli/ Jeoff Davis, Kim Sayer, Mike Severns, Colin Sinclair, Helena Smith, Tony Souter, Jon Spaull, Chris Stowers, Erik Svensson and Jeppe Wikstrom, Stanislav Tereba, Kathryn Tomasetti, Cecile Treal and Jean-Michel Ruiz, James Tye, Robert Vente, Richard Watson, Christine Webb, Stephen Whitehorn, Linda Whitwam, Alan Williams, Peter Wilson, Pawel Wojcik, Francesca Yorke, Bartlomies Zaranek, Leandro Zoppe

Rough Guides Photographers
Dave Abram, Ian Aitken, Dan Bannister, Michelle Bhatia, Victor Paul Borg, Simon Bracken, Anthony Cassidy, Chris Christoforou, Tim Draper, Paul Franklin, Robin Gauldie, Andrew Goldie, Michelle Grant, Matthew Hancock, Nelson Hancock, Chris Hutty, Roger Norum, Roger d'Olivere Mapp, Angus Oborn, Suzanne Porter, Martin Richardson, Greg Roden, Neil Setchfield, Natascha Sturny, Mark Thomas, Enrique Uranga, Greg Ward and James McConnachie, Paul Whitfield, Alex Wilson

The publisher would like to thank the following for their kind permission to photograph at their sights:

Courtesy of The American Museum of Natural History; Courtesy of the Anne Frankhuis, Amsterdam; ARF/ TAP (Archaeological Receipts Fund); Courtesy of the Audubon Zoo/ Audubon Nature Institute, New Orleans; Courtesy of the Bayerische Verwaltung der Staatlichen Schlosser, Garten und Seen; Courtesy of the Catedral Metropolitana; (c) CONACULTA-INAH-MEX. Instituto Nacional de Antropologia e Historia; Courtesy of Coral Gables Venetian Pool, Florida; Courtesy of the National Museum, Bankgok; Courtesy of the Egyptian Museum, Cairo; Courtesy of the Field Museum, Chicago; Courtesy of San Antonio Botanical Gardens; Courtesy of the Hockey Hall of Fame; Courtesy of the Hotel Bellagio, Las Vegas; Courtesy of the Islamic Arts Museum; Courtesy of Kato Pafos Archaeological Park; Courtesy of the Massachusetts State House, Boston; Herge Moulinsart; Courtesy of Museo Chileno de Arte Precolombino; Courtesy of Museo de Arte Latinoamericano de Buenos Aires (MALBA); Courtesy of Museo Nacional de Bellas Artes, Buenos Aires; Courtesy of the Museum of Science and Industry, Chicago; National Trust, Courtesy of Nea Moni; Courtesy of the New England Aquarium, Boston; Courtesy of the Olympiapark, Munchen GmbH, Germany; Courtesy of Quincy Market, Boston; Courtesy of San Francisco Monastery, Lima; Courtesy of The Science Museum, London; Courtesy of SeaWorld San Antonio; Courtesy of Singapore Botanic Gardens; Courtesy of the Tokyo National Museum; Courtesy of Trinity Church, Boston; Courtesy of The Venetian, Las Vegas; Jim Warych;

The publisher would like to thank the following for their kind permission to reproduce their photographs:

ALAMY IMAGES: Bluered 103t.

CORBIS: Paul Almasy 129tr, 319tr; Aurore Belkin 309tr; Nathan Benn 204-5; Walter Bibikow 321tl; Alberto Biscaro 320cl; Tibor Bognar 294br; Maurizio Borgese 125bl; Tim Clayton 310cr; Marco Cristofori 31cl; Richard Cummins 188cl; Yiorgos Depollas 58-59; epa / DIEGO AZUBEL 257tl; Rob Francis 270cr; Jose Fuste Raga 5bl, 110-1, 136-7, 251tl, 304-5, 309tl; Gianni Giorgi 308cl; Philip Gould 143cl; Tom Grill 188cr; Franck Guiziou 237t; Robert Harding 229cla; Blaine Harrington III 82cla, 319bc, 321br; Hemis / Bertrand Gardel 1c; Hemis / Maurizio Borgese 128cr; Jon Hicks 27t; Robert Holmes 247bl; Dave G. Houser 78br, 129tl, 211t; JAI / Demetrio Carrasco 5fbl, 6-7; JAI / Nigel Pavitt 168br; Bob Krist 189tl, 189crb; Frans Lanting 301bl, 319cl; Frank Leather 256cr; Danny Lehman 240-1; Stéphane Lemaire 103bl; Mark Makela 188br; John and Lisa Merrill 211bl; Minden Pictures/ Kevin Schafer 47bl; Momatiuk - Eastcott 295t; Amos Nachoum 152br; Nasser Nouri 310br; Richard T. Nowitz 210br; Ocean 18-9; Steve Parish/ Steve Parish Publishing 313tr; Doug Pearson 47t; Martin Puddy 247t; Radius Images 319tl; Reuters/ TIM WIMBORNE 2-3; Reuters/X01072/ CHOR SOKUNTHEA 235tr; Robert Harding World Imagery/ Marco Simoni 168cr; Joel Santos 46br; Kevin Schafer 169bl, 301c; SOPA/ Maurizio Rellini 313bl; Keren Su 320cr; Sygma/ Bernard Annebicque 60cr; Topic Photo Agency 262cr, 263bl, 263br; Craig Tuttle 295bl; Steven Vidler 188bl, 259cra; Visuals Unlimited/ Dave Watts 312cla; Visuals Unlimited/ Thomas Marent 294cr; Konrad Wothe 301cr; Wang Ye 256br; Jim Zuckerman 193t;

DORLING KINDERSLEY: Dun Bannister 187ca; Peter Cook 90 cr, 260cra, 275ftl; Bethany Dawn 301tl; Rowan Greenwood 114cr; Thomas Marent 153bl; Jamie Marshall 156br, 248cl, 252br, 293cl, 318cl

GETTY IMAGES: A DEMOTES 291bl; AFP/DON EMMERT 192cr; age fotostock / Gonzalo Azumendi 312–3c; altrendo travel 155bl; Jose Manuel Azcona 27bl; Bloomberg 242cla; Buena Vista Images 197cla; Caesda Photography 228cra; Martin Child 236br; By Counteragent 273cla; Lars Dahlstrom 79t; Bruno De Hogues 236cr; De Agostini 26br; DEA/ G. DAGLI ORTI 5fbr; 280–1; Danita Delimont 311bl; Jim Dyson 155t; Flickr RF 144–5/5; Norbert Hohn 237bl; B Holland 257bl; HUGHES HervÃ © 210cr; The Image Bank/ PNC 86cl; LatinContent/ Raphael Alves 154br; LOOK/ Ingolf Pompe 60cl; Barrett & MacKay 193bl; Lisa Maree Williams/ Stringer 311t; Brian Maslyar 154cr; National Geographic/ Albert Moldvay 26cr; Daniel Newcombe 169t; Max Paddler 260cl; Nigel Pavitt 291t; Photographer's Choice/ Marco Brivio 100cla; Andy Sheppard 102b; Dennis Stone 79bl; Nico Tondini 288–9; Hein von Horsten 315tr; Vittorio Zunino Celotto 83bl;

SHUTTERSTOCK: Neale Cousland 239bl; Songquan Deng 180cra; Pichugin Dmitry 249br; fotokik_dot_com 179bl; Frontpage 219cl; Markus Gann 61tl; Jarno Gonzalez Zarraonandia 187cl; Sergio Hayashi 171tr; holbox 147cra; Izmael 232clb; JeniFoto 101tl; jiawangkun 138cl; Vladimir Kondrachov 299cla; krechet 162br; Hugh Lansdown 300cl; Muriel Lasure 301tr; Chee-Onn Leong 139tl; Caitlin Mirra 223tl; Luciano Mortula 235cl; Andrei Nekrassov 112clb; onairda 131tl; Mark Van Overmeire 287cl; Mark Payne 208cl; Ryan Rodrick 296cr; sculpies 285cl; Fedor Selivanov 244cr; Nickolay Stanev 203t; szefei 246br; taboga 252cla; toonman 277tr; Vacclav 203cla; Xufang 232cla; Colin D. Young; 191tr; Andy Z 163cl; 163bl;

Jacket Images
Front and Back: ISTOCKPHOTO.COM: Vaara; Back: DORLING KINDERSLEY: Rough Guides/Tim Draper tc, /Lydia Evans tl, /Suzanne Porter ftr, /Greg Roden tr, /Karen Trist ftl.

NORWAY
SWEDEN
Shetland Islands
Orkney Islands
NORTH SEA
DENMARK
REPUBLIC OF IRELAND
UNITED KINGDOM
NETHERLANDS
GERMANY
BELGIUM
ENGLISH CHANNEL
LUXEMBOURG
CZECH REPUBLIC
ATLANTIC OCEAN
AUSTRIA
SWITZERLAND
FRANCE
SLOVENIA
BAY OF BISCAY
LIGURIAN SEA
ITALY
Corsica
SPAIN
Menorca
Mallorca
Sardinia
TYRRHENIAN SEA
PORTUGAL
Ibiza
Sicily
BAY OF CÁDIZ
Gibraltar (UK)
MALTA
TUNISIA
ALGERIA
MOROCCO
Madeira (Portugal)
LIBYA